OECD ECONOMIC OUTLOOK

89

MAY 2011

The *OECD Economic Outlook* is published on the responsibility of the Secretary-General of the OECD. The assessments given of countries' prospects do not necessarily correspond to those of the national authorities concerned. The OECD is the source of statistical material contained in tables and figures, except where other sources are explicitly cited.

Please cite this publication as:
OECD (2011), *OECD Economic Outlook, Vol. 2011/1*, OECD Publishing.
http://dx.doi.org/10.1787/eco_outlook-v2011-1-en

ISBN 978-92-64-06347-1 (print)
ISBN 978-92-64-09217-4 (PDF)

Series: OECD Economic Outlook
ISSN 0474-5574 (print)
ISSN 1609-7408 (online)

The statistical data for Israel are supplied by and under the responsibility of the relevant Israeli authorities. The use of such data by the OECD is without prejudice to the status of the Golan Heights, East Jerusalem and Israeli settlements in the West Bank under the terms of international law.

Corrigenda to OECD publications may be found on line at: *www.oecd.org/publishing/corrigenda*.

TABLE OF CONTENTS

This book has...

StatLinks

**A service that delivers Excel® files
from the printed page!**

Look for the StatLinks at the bottom right-hand corner of the tables or graphs in this book.
To download the matching Excel® spreadsheet, just type the link into your Internet browser,
starting with the **http://dx.doi.org** prefix.
If you're reading the PDF e-book edition, and your PC is connected to the Internet, simply
click on the link. You'll find StatLinks appearing in more OECD books.

Conventional signs

$	US dollar	.	Decimal point
¥	Japanese yen	I, II	Calendar half-years
£	Pound sterling	Q1, Q4	Calendar quarters
€	Euro	Billion	Thousand million
mb/d	Million barrels per day	Trillion	Thousand billion
..	Data not available	s.a.a.r.	Seasonally adjusted at annual rates
0	Nil or negligible	n.s.a.	Not seasonally adjusted
–	Irrelevant		

Summary of projections

	2010	2011	2012	2010 Q3	2010 Q4	2011 Q1	2011 Q2	2011 Q3	2011 Q4	2012 Q1	2012 Q2	2012 Q3	2012 Q4	2010 Q4/Q4	2011 Q4/Q4	2012 Q4/Q4
													Per cent			
Real GDP growth																
United States	2.9	2.6	3.1	2.6	3.1	1.7	3.1	2.9	3.0	3.1	3.3	3.3	3.4	2.8	2.7	3.3
Euro area	1.7	2.0	2.0	1.5	1.0	3.4	1.3	1.7	1.9	2.1	2.2	2.3	2.4	2.0	2.1	2.2
Japan	4.0	-0.9	2.2	3.8	-3.1	-3.7	-3.7	5.3	3.5	2.3	1.6	1.2	1.2	2.4	0.3	1.5
Total OECD	2.9	2.3	2.8	2.5	2.0	2.2	2.0	2.8	2.7	2.9	3.0	3.1	3.2	2.8	2.4	3.0
Inflation[1]										year-on-year						
United States	1.7	1.9	1.3	1.4	1.1	1.6	2.1	2.1	2.0	1.4	1.2	1.3	1.3			
Euro area	1.6	2.6	1.6	1.7	2.0	2.5	2.8	2.9	2.5	1.9	1.5	1.4	1.4			
Japan	-0.7	0.3	-0.2	-0.8	0.1	0.0	0.4	0.8	0.1	0.0	-0.2	-0.2	-0.2			
Total OECD	1.8	2.3	1.7	1.7	1.8	2.0	2.3	2.4	2.3	1.8	1.6	1.7	1.7			
Unemployment rate[2]																
United States	9.6	8.8	7.9	9.6	9.6	8.9	8.9	8.7	8.5	8.3	8.1	7.8	7.5			
Euro area	9.9	9.7	9.3	9.9	9.9	9.9	9.8	9.7	9.6	9.5	9.4	9.2	9.1			
Japan	5.1	4.8	4.6	5.0	5.0	4.7	4.8	4.8	4.7	4.7	4.7	4.6	4.5			
Total OECD	8.3	7.9	7.4	8.3	8.2	8.0	7.9	7.8	7.7	7.6	7.5	7.3	7.1			
World trade growth	12.5	8.1	8.4	8.7	5.0	9.1	6.0	9.0	8.6	8.4	8.4	8.5	8.5	11.2	8.2	8.5
Current account balance[3]																
United States	-3.2	-3.7	-4.0													
Euro area	0.2	0.3	0.8													
Japan	3.6	2.6	2.5													
Total OECD	-0.6	-0.7	-0.7													
Fiscal balance[3]																
United States	-10.6	-10.1	-9.1													
Euro area	-6.0	-4.2	-3.0													
Japan	-8.1	-8.9	-8.2													
Total OECD	-7.7	-6.7	-5.6													
Short-term interest rate																
United States	0.5	0.8	1.9	0.6	0.4	0.4	0.4	1.0	1.3	1.4	1.6	2.1	2.5			
Euro area	0.8	1.3	2.0	0.9	1.0	1.1	1.4	1.4	1.5	1.6	1.8	2.1	2.3			
Japan	0.2	0.3	0.2	0.1	0.1	0.3	0.3	0.2	0.2	0.2	0.2	0.2	0.2			

Note: Real GDP growth, inflation (measured by the increase in the consumer price index or private consumption deflator for total OECD) and world trade growth (the arithmetic average of world merchandise import and export volumes) are seasonally and working-day (except inflation) adjusted annual rates. The "fourth quarter" columns are expressed in year-on-year growth rates where appropriate and in levels otherwise. Interest rates are for the United States: 3-month eurodollar deposit; Japan: 3-month certificate of deposits; euro area: 3-month interbank rate.

The cut-off date for information used in the compilation of the projections is 19 May 2011.

1. USA; price index for personal consumption expenditure, Japan; consumer price index and the euro area; harmonised index of consumer prices.
2. Per cent of the labour force.
3. Per cent of GDP.
Source: OECD Economic Outlook 89 database.

StatLink http://dx.doi.org/10.1787/888932434105

EDITORIAL
SEEKING A DURABLE RECOVERY FOR ALL

The global recovery is becoming self-sustained and more broad based. The recovery is taking place at different speeds, between advanced and emerging economies, but also within the first group of countries. Unemployment remains high across most of the OECD countries. In most, headline inflation has risen strongly, and expectations are also drifting up; however, underlying inflation seems likely to edge up only slowly. Vibrant domestic demand growth, negative supply shocks and strong capital inflows in non-OECD economies are generating inflationary pressures prompting policy restraint that could slow the recovery.

Such a scenario calls for differentiated policy responses in advanced and emerging economies. In both groups of countries structural reforms should play a key role while taking into account country-specific needs and institutional features. In advanced economies, structural reforms can boost potential growth, thereby facilitating fiscal consolidation and easing the pace of monetary policy normalisation. In emerging economies, monetary policy should tighten more to curb inflation, but this option risks being constrained by inducing stronger capital inflows. In emerging economies, structural reforms could make growth more sustainable and inclusive, while contributing to global rebalancing and enhancing long-term capital flows.

The outlook is surrounded by risks. Some of them are endogenous to the pace of expansion; others are associated with the possibility of specific events. Upside risks include unexpected short-term stimulus from additional structural measures and more buoyant private-sector activity as confidence increases. Some of the risks are two-sided. Oil prices may rise or fall back over the projection period. While the earthquake and tsunami in Japan could have additional negative consequences on activity further reconstruction packages could hasten the rebound. Most risks are on the downside, however, including: further increases in oil and other commodity prices which could feed into core inflation, a deeper slowdown in China, an unsettled fiscal situation in the United States and Japan and renewed weakness in housing markets. Financial vulnerabilities are increasing in the euro area in spite of strong adjustment efforts in peripheral countries. A concern is that, if downside risks interact, their cumulative impact could weaken the recovery significantly, possibly triggering stagflationary developments in some advanced economies.

All this suggests that the global crisis may not be over yet. Policy makers must intensify efforts to deal with medium-term challenges. Four such challenges stand out: dealing with high unemployment and preventing it from becoming entrenched; sustaining growth and avoiding stagnation; making progress in fiscal consolidation; and managing global imbalances while supporting orderly saving reallocation. These challenges are interconnected and require a comprehensive and credible policy approach.

While the recovery is bringing some improvements in labour market conditions in advanced economies, total, and especially long-term, unemployment remains high in many countries. Also drawing on lessons from the crisis, labour market policies have a key role to play in preventing cyclical unemployment from turning structural. Such policies could include more effective placement services with training to match workers and jobs; rebalancing employment protection towards temporary workers;

and temporary reduction in labour taxation through well targeted marginal job subsidies in countries where labour demand is weak. The employment impact of such measures would be boosted by stronger competition in sectors such as retail trade and professional services. Moreover, the crisis has demonstrated the utility of well designed work-sharing arrangements in minimising employment loss during downturns.

Return to work and competition-enhancing measures would also contribute to stronger potential growth, which could otherwise remain weak. Indeed, as experience shows, following financial crises there are risks of stagnation as structural adjustment and financial repair are delayed. Stagnation could also emerge from persistent deterioration of the structural and business environment. Even if such risks do not materialise the impact of the crisis in lowering potential output is becoming clearer. Such permanent output loss could, eventually, lower realised growth rates. The potential for growth-enhancing structural reforms and policies to unleash new sources of growth is substantial. Governments should intensify their efforts in implementing them.

Lower growth would feed back negatively on fiscal consolidation, while evidence shows that, beyond some thresholds, public debt levels have a negative impact on growth. In spite of some improvement in fiscal positions, consolidation requirements to merely stabilise debt are substantial for many countries. The United States and Japan, for which such requirements are among the largest, have yet to produce credible medium-term plans while other countries need to bolster medium-term fiscal targets by specifying the measures that will be implemented to achieve them. For most countries, further action would be needed to bring debt levels back to pre-crisis levels. The overall scenario has changed with respect to the pre-crisis situation when a significant contribution to fiscal sustainability came from the fact that interest rates were well below growth rates. This is unlikely to be the case in the years to come as interest rates will rise and growth could be slower. Structural reforms, while boosting growth, can also help fiscal consolidation by increasing efficiency in the provision of key services such as health and education. Finally, it would be dangerous to believe that higher inflation could address debt sustainability. Higher and persistent inflation could damp real growth by raising price and exchange-rate volatility. It could also risk unhinging inflation expectations, with the result that interest rates would soon increase more than inflation.

Last but not least, imbalances have been widening again as the global economy is recovering. They show, however, a somewhat different configuration as China's current account surplus is well below pre-crisis peaks due to adverse terms–of–trade movements and less buoyant export performance, and high-saving oil-producing economies see mounting surpluses. A desirable rebalancing mechanism should be growth-enhancing and sufficiently symmetric to avoid putting an excessive burden on deficit countries. Such a rebalancing would require more exchange-rate flexibility, which could also help mitigate inflationary pressures in countries where these are strong, while country-specific structural reforms could help to reduce saving and raise investment in surplus countries, and boost saving in deficit countries. In monetary unions, competition-enhancing reforms of labour and product markets could also facilitate adjustments in external positions.

The policy challenge is not to eliminate imbalances but to keep them sustainable, so as to facilitate international reallocation of savings in ways that are supportive of growth. This requires open and long-term-oriented capital markets. Structural policies have an important impact on size and composition of capital movements. At the same time there is a need to reconcile open capital markets with the goal of coping with short-term instability through temporary measures. It is important that, including under the auspices of the G20, advanced and emerging economies agree on a framework that would allow such goals to be reconciled.

The global economy is exiting the recession but is not returning to business as usual. The post-crisis economy will have to deal with old and new challenges, while pursuing new, green and inclusive sources of growth. This requires rethinking the policy paradigm as we draw lessons from the crisis.

In framing the new, post-crisis policy paradigm, some of the existing principles underlying policy should be confirmed, such as those related to supply-side responses to boost growth, while recognising that such policies have additional positive effects on rebalancing and fiscal consolidation. The assignment of monetary policy to achieve price stability and a rule-based fiscal policy to achieve sustainable public finances should be confirmed, while the contribution of fiscal institutions to fiscal discipline could be further explored. But additional lessons should be drawn. The endogenous generation of instability and imbalances out of (apparent) tranquillity, a phenomenon common to several if not all crisis episodes, has been dangerously overlooked. This reinforces the need for financial-sector reform and tighter prudential policies, both at the micro and macro levels.

Finally, as a more complex world than what we believed to be the case requires a broader policy tool kit, we also need to take a closer look at how such tools interact and what can be done to enhance synergies. In this vein another lesson from the crisis is that international cooperation is important both in dealing with emergency situations and in shaping the way forward. This requires agreement on common principles, and, if necessary, common rules, while allowing for country-specific needs. As we slowly leave the crisis behind us, we should be wary of the risk of losing impetus in the search for better global economic governance.

25 May 2011

Pier Carlo Padoan
Deputy Secretary-General and Chief Economist

Chapter 1

GENERAL ASSESSMENT
OF THE MACROECONOMIC SITUATION

The statistical data for Israel are supplied by and under the responsibility of the relevant Israeli authorities. The use of such data by the OECD is without prejudice to the status of the Golan Heights, East Jerusalem and Israeli settlements in the West Bank under the terms of international law.

Overview

The recovery has broadened...

The recovery from the deepest recession in decades is becoming more broadly based. Global growth has picked up since the soft patch in the middle of last year and activity is driven increasingly by strengthening private final demand. However, progress remains uneven across economies. In the near term, the adverse supply-side shocks from high commodity prices and the earthquake in Japan and its aftermath are damping activity somewhat and pushing up headline inflation. Such effects should fade from the latter half of this year, provided commodity prices stabilise and inflation expectations do not become unanchored. Financial conditions continue to improve and monetary policy remains accommodative in the OECD economies, though increasingly less so in emerging market economies where spare capacity has been largely absorbed. This should allow the recovery to strengthen, despite increasingly widespread fiscal consolidation. Global output growth is expected to be close to 4¼ per cent this year and 4½ per cent in 2012 (Table 1.1). On this basis, labour market conditions would continue to improve slowly, though at 7% by the end of 2012, the OECD

Table 1.1. **The global recovery will remain moderate**
OECD area, unless noted otherwise

	Average 1998-2007	2008	2009	2010	2011	2012	2010 Q4/Q4	2011 Q4/Q4	2012 Q4/Q4
				Per cent					
Real GDP growth[1]	2.7	0.3	-3.5	2.9	2.3	2.8	2.8	2.4	3.0
United States	3.0	0.0	-2.6	2.9	2.6	3.1	2.8	2.7	3.3
Euro area	2.3	0.3	-4.1	1.7	2.0	2.0	2.0	2.1	2.2
Japan	1.2	-1.2	-6.3	4.0	-0.9	2.2	2.4	0.3	1.5
Output gap[2]	0.3	0.1	-4.9	-3.7	-3.2	-2.4			
Unemployment rate[3]	6.4	6.0	8.2	8.3	7.9	7.4	8.2	7.7	7.1
Inflation[4]	2.8	3.2	0.5	1.8	2.3	1.7	1.8	2.3	1.7
Fiscal balance[5]	-2.1	-3.3	-8.2	-7.7	-6.7	-5.6			
Memorandum Items									
World real trade growth	6.8	3.1	-10.8	12.5	8.1	8.4	11.2	8.2	8.5
World real GDP growth[6]	3.8	2.6	-1.0	4.9	4.2	4.6	4.8	4.2	4.8

1. Year-on-year increase; last three columns show the increase over a year earlier.
2. Per cent of potential GDP.
3. Per cent of labour force.
4. Private consumption deflator. Year-on-year increase; last 3 columns show the increase over a year earlier.
5. Per cent of GDP.
6. Moving nominal GDP weights, using purchasing power parities.
Source: OECD Economic Outlook 89 database.

StatLink http://dx.doi.org/10.1787/888932434124

unemployment rate would still remain well above the pre-crisis level. Underlying inflation is expected to edge up slowly, as economic slack diminishes, to around 1¾ per cent by end-2012. Outside the OECD area, domestic demand is expected to remain robust, necessitating further policy measures to damp inflationary pressures.

... but risks remain elevated...

The risks around the projection remain elevated, even though earlier concerns about possible widespread weakness in private sector activity and deflation outcomes have receded. Some of the key risks are endogenous to the pace of the expansion, whereas others are associated with the possibility of particular events that could trigger renewed weakness in activity or financial markets, or add to inflationary pressures. A further concern is that some of the downside risks, if they were to interact, could result in a mild stagflation-type outcome in the OECD economies, which would be difficult for conventional macroeconomic policies to tackle.

... on the upside...

● The key upside risk is that private sector final demand could gain more momentum than projected. Household and business confidence could strengthen further as the recovery progresses, amidst favourable financial conditions and improving labour market outcomes, giving rise to strong pent-up demand for durables and capital equipment. There is also a possibility that additional near-term impetus could arise from growth-friendly structural reforms, although relatively little progress has been made in this respect since the recovery began.

... and on the downside

● On the downside, important near-term risks to the pace of the recovery stem from the possibilities of renewed rises in oil prices as a result of political instability, a slow recovery in Japan from the effects of the earthquake and its aftermath, with associated disruptions in global supply chains, and a deeper than projected slowdown in China. Higher oil prices would add to inflationary pressures, damp income growth and widen global imbalances by raising further the already elevated external surpluses of the high-saving oil producing economies. Clear risks also remain from continuing concerns about public debt sustainability in some OECD countries and, to a lesser extent, ongoing weaknesses in property markets. If these were to strengthen, they could provoke significant financial market disruption with adverse effects on confidence.

Structural reforms are essential for a balanced and sustainable recovery

The concerns about high unemployment becoming entrenched and a permanent post-crisis reduction in potential output, together with the need to strengthen confidence in the sustainability of public sector debt dynamics and ensure a sustainable, balanced recovery at the global level, raise the urgency of enacting well-designed, growth-enhancing structural reforms. Such reforms would facilitate the tasks facing the monetary and fiscal authorities, and could help to support the near-term recovery. Against the background of impaired fiscal positions, still-high unemployment and the moderate pace of the recovery, priority should be given to implementing reforms that offer comparatively strong short-term employment gains and facilitate fiscal consolidation. These include measures that help to ensure that job losers and other vulnerable groups remain attached to labour markets and quickly return to employment, reforms that increase productivity in the public sector, and measures to improve product market competition. In conjunction with fiscal consolidation in OECD countries, a well-designed package of structural reforms to reduce product market regulations in sheltered sectors of countries with an external surplus, and deepen financial markets and improve social welfare systems in non-OECD countries, would also help to narrow global imbalances over time.

Macroeconomic and financial policy requirements are:

Against this background, the macroeconomic and financial policy requirements at present and in the longer term are as follows:

... to pursue fiscal consolidation actively...

● Given the precarious state of public finances in many OECD countries, particularly in the United States and Japan, the priority has to be to either establish credible and growth-friendly medium-term consolidation plans if they do not already exist, or to develop existing plans more fully. In some countries this will require unblocking political stalemate that makes fiscal policy unpredictable over both short and long horizons. More generally, the pace of consolidation and the choice of policy instruments will have to reflect the urgency of ensuring sustainable public debt dynamics, the strength of the recovery, the enactment of growth-friendly structural reforms and the scope for monetary policy to offset the adverse effects of fiscal tightening. In countries that have unsustainable fiscal positions, an early consolidation "downpayment" would help to give credibility to medium-term plans.

... normalise policy rates at a pace contingent on the recovery...

● The monetary authorities must judge how to react to higher headline inflation and risks to the anchoring of expectations at a time when sizable, but increasingly uncertain, slack remains in most OECD economies, underlying inflation remains low and fiscal consolidation is underway, albeit at a sometimes uncertain pace. Overall, these factors imply that policy rates should remain accommodative through the projection period. However, the need to keep close-to-zero policy rates for risk management reasons has now faded and an early upward adjustment in policy rates to establish a visibly positive level, as in the euro area, is merited in the United States and the United Kingdom, but not yet in Japan. This would also help to guard against a renewed build-up of financial fragilities and provide a better starting point in event of a need to react to upside inflation surprises. After a pause, and provided the initial rises do not have adverse effects on the recovery, policy rates should be raised steadily in the United States, the euro area and the United Kingdom in the course of 2012, reflecting the gradual, though incomplete, erosion of economic slack and the edging up of underlying inflation. In larger non-OECD economies, and several smaller OECD economies, monetary conditions should be tightened further to contain inflation. It also remains important, both in OECD and non-OECD countries, that exchange rate adjustments consistent with domestic needs and necessary international rebalancing be allowed to occur.

... and maintain momentum towards financial reforms

- In the short term, it is important to ensure that upcoming stress tests of banking systems provide a credible assessment of the capacity of banks to withstand adverse shocks and to deal swiftly with vulnerable institutions. At the same time, the momentum toward financial reform needs to be maintained to strengthen the stability of the global financial system: in this regard, implementing the recent global agreement on capital and liquidity standards should be seen as the first building block of a broader regulatory structure. Beyond this, progress is needed to reduce significant vulnerabilities that could arise from the failures of systemically important financial institutions.

Forces acting on OECD economies

The forces acting on the OECD economies remain supportive

Global economic activity is becoming more self-sustaining, with the recovery driven increasingly by stronger private final demand. In the near term, the supply-side shocks arising both from high food and energy prices, in part due to the political disruptions in the Middle East and North Africa (MENA), and from the earthquake and its aftermath in Japan are damping the momentum of the recovery somewhat. However, such effects seem likely to fade from the latter half of the year. Surveys of business confidence and order levels generally remain robust in most major economies in both manufacturing and service sectors, outside of Japan and several other Asian economies, and point to ongoing improvements in hiring and investment, notwithstanding their recent tendency to overstate the growth of real output. With still-improving financial conditions, still-strong growth in emerging and developing economies, and accommodative monetary policies, the forces acting on OECD economies are favourable on balance, although the pace of the recovery is likely to remain constrained by ongoing adjustments in property markets, still-high unemployment and the gradual withdrawal of crisis-related support. As is often the case following a severe financial crisis (Haugh *et al.*, 2009), the recovery is relatively slow (Figure 1.1), with OECD-wide output expected to surpass the pre-crisis peak level only by the middle of this year.

Global trade growth has rebounded...

Global trade volumes have already risen past their pre-crisis peak, and, with the pace of the recovery picking up, trade growth has bounced back this year; the annualised rate of trade growth in the first quarter of this year is estimated to have been around 9%, compared with growth of 5% in the final quarter of last year. Several monthly trade and global indicators, notably export orders, point to trade growth gaining further momentum, but these are being offset, at least in the second quarter, by the disruption to global supply chains and Japanese export capacity in the aftermath of the earthquake in Japan (Box 1.1). Japanese export volumes

Figure 1.1. **Real GDP in recessions and recoveries**

Pre-recession peak = 100 at time t

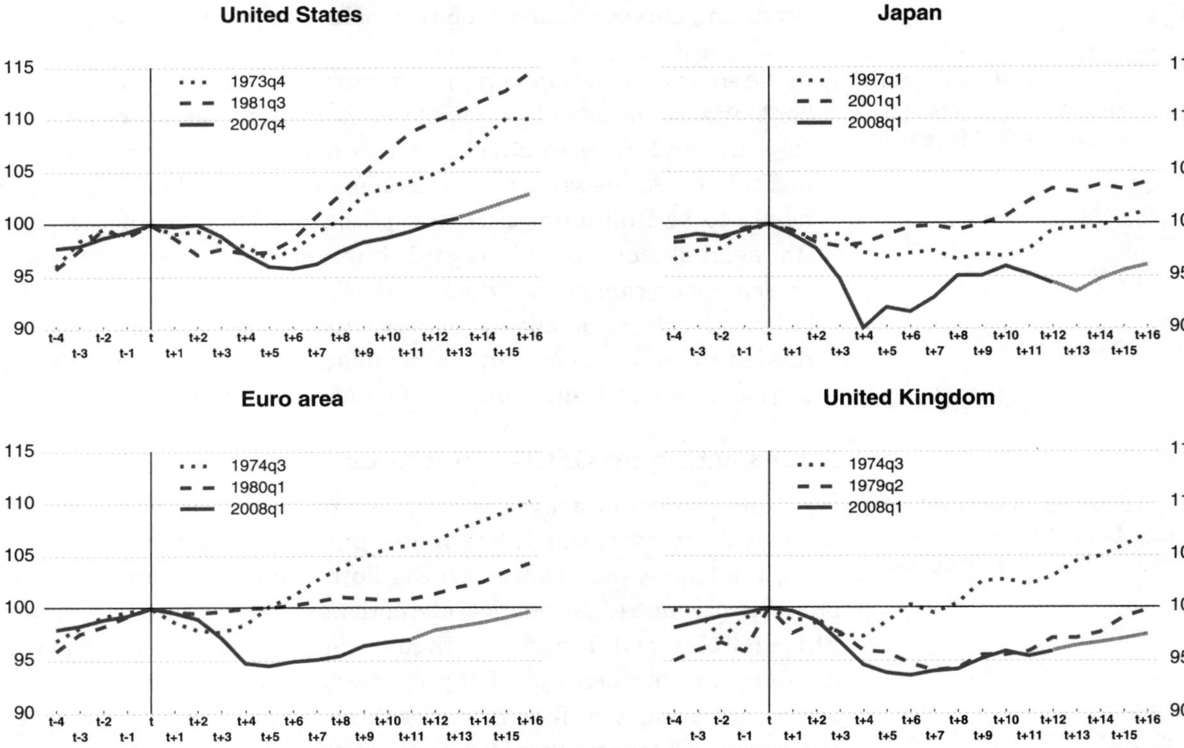

United States

Japan

Euro area

United Kingdom

Note: Horizontal axis represents quarters before and after the peak in GDP (given by the respective dates). Grey lines correspond to forecasts.
Source: OECD Economic Outlook 89 database.

StatLink ⟡ http://dx.doi.org/10.1787/888932433630

Box 1.1. **The Great East Japan Earthquake and global economic effects**

Effects on the Japanese economy

The earthquake and accompanying tsunami which hit Japan on 11 March 2011 left approximately 15 000 people dead and 9900 people missing (as of 9 May 2011). According to the Japanese government's preliminary estimate (Cabinet Office, 2011), the earthquake and tsunami caused some 16-25 trillion yen (3.3% to 5.2% of GDP) of damage to the capital stock in seven prefectures.[1] The impact was focused mainly on three prefectures – Iwate, Miyagi and Fukushima – which account for about 4% of nationwide economic output and 4.5% of Japan's population, with the impact concentrated along the Pacific coast in these prefectures. The figures include damage to buildings (housing and fixed capital of private firms), public utilities (electricity, gas and water), public infrastructure (such as railroads, ports and highways) and public parks.

The experience of past disasters in Japan and other developed countries suggests that any negative short-term impact on economic growth (relative to trend) is likely to be soon followed by a rebound as reconstruction spending picks up (see Cavallo and Noy, 2010). The sizable damage to the capital stock and near-term disruption of supply chains have already resulted in a sizable decline in output. Industrial production plummeted by over 15% in March, the sharpest drop on record. GDP declined at an annualised rate of 3.7% in the first quarter, pushing Japan into recession, and a further decline is likely in the second quarter of 2011. Thereafter, activity should rebound promptly, and grow at above-trend rates in the latter half of 2011, boosted by government reconstruction spending as well as business and residential investment, as was the case in the aftermath of the 1995 Kobe earthquake (see OECD, 2011b for the details).

Box 1.1. **The Great East Japan Earthquake and global economic effects** (*cont.*)

The uncertainty surrounding any projection is particularly acute in these circumstances, not least because the reduced capacity of electricity generation and the disruption to supply chains creates uncertainty about the depth and length of the decline in output. Indeed, the earthquake and tsunami damaged a number of thermal as well as nuclear power plants, which supply around 30% of Japan's electricity. And estimates by the MIT Billion Prices Project suggest that the range of consumer products available on line has declined by approximately by 15% since the natural disasters.

The adverse effects have also begun to be reflected in other hard data, which also show large negative impacts in March. Exports fell by 2.3% (and by 9.7% for the period after the natural disaster) while imports increased by 11.9% (9.5% after the natural disaster) in March (year-on-year). Retail sales in March plunged by 8.5% (year–on–year), likely reflecting a sizeable negative impact on discretionary spending from supply constraints as well as weaker consumer sentiment and voluntary self-restraint (*jishuku*).

Effects on the rest of the world

The Japanese economy accounts for 8.7% of world GDP (using nominal exchange rates), thus the estimated net impact of the natural disaster and associated effects, including reconstruction, should not have a large negative direct impact on global output. Even if a large decline in imports to Japan were to occur, arising, for example, from a decline in domestic demand, it would have only a small direct effect on overall economic activity for most countries. For example, in the United States and the euro area, exports to Japan account for less than 0.5% of GDP (see figure below). The impact would be modest even in neighbouring Asian economies where bilateral trade with Japan is relatively more important, as for instance exports to Japan account for 2% of GDP in China.

However, indirect effects could be more severe in the near-term. Although the direct impacts are likely to be limited, the near-term loss of Japanese exports has marked effects on industrial activity elsewhere, through highly integrated cross-border supply chains and a reliance on just-in-time inventory management. One illustration is provided by the number of car manufacturers in North America and Europe who have stopped or reduced production temporarily because of a shortage of key components sourced from Japan. Japanese manufacturing is an important contributor to a number of industries elsewhere; for example, more than 10% of the total supply of some electronic products in the United States is imported from Japan (Japan Research Institute, 2011). Prices have already risen for some electrical components (for instance, flash memory chips), as a result of the production disruption in Japan, especially in cases where alternative suppliers cannot be found.[2] These negative impacts ultimately depend on the availability and substitutability of other products.

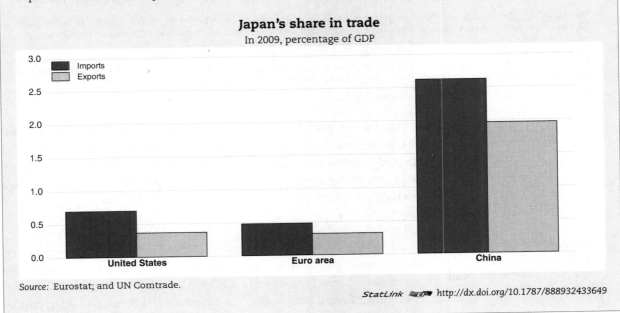

Japan's share in trade
In 2009, percentage of GDP

Source: Eurostat; and UN Comtrade.

StatLink ⬛⬛⬛ http://dx.doi.org/10.1787/888932433649

Box 1.1. **The Great East Japan Earthquake and global economic effects** (cont.)

It is difficult to assess the extent to which certain Japanese products play a key role in cross-border vertical linkages. Japan's outward FDI and export data suggest that these matter mainly for Asian economies. In China, 13% of total imports are from Japan (or 2.6% of GDP). In the United States and the euro area, the share is much lower (6.1% and 3.4% of total imports, or 0.7% and 0.5% of GDP, respectively). According to a recent survey by the Japan External Trade Organisation (JETRO, 2010), Japanese affiliates in Asia and Pacific regions rely relatively heavily on procurement from Japan. In manufacturing, the procurement of raw materials and parts from Japan accounts for a third of total procurement. Local procurement represents just under a half of total procurement. Procurement from Japan tends to be particularly high amongst firms in the electric machinery and precision instrument industries. In the United States, by contrast, Japanese affiliates tend to rely more on local procurement. At least one-half, and in many cases 80% to 100%, of procurement is sourced locally for around two-thirds of Japanese affiliates (JETRO, 2008). Hence the production disruption and its related consequences from events in Japan would be more severe for Japanese affiliates in neighbouring countries in Asia.

Another possible source of global effects could be through capital flows, since foreign insurance companies have incurred some new liabilities in Japan as a result of the natural disasters, and domestic financial institutions could need to repatriate some assets held abroad. However, so far, there does not appear to have been a sizable repatriation of assets by domestic institutions, with those institutions in need of cash having largely raised funds in Japan.

Possible longer-term economic effects

The production disruption and its consequences could have some longer-term global effects. The expansion of cross-border vertical linkages might slow or even be reversed, insofar as producers might revise their just-in-time inventory management in order to have larger buffers and might strive for greater diversification of their suppliers, especially geographically, at the expense of immediate efficiency gains.

In the short run at least, oil and gas demand in Japan is likely to be bolstered as losses in energy production from damage to nuclear power plants need to be offset, and energy-intensive reconstruction work will be in progress. More generally, at a global level, if countries were prompted to revisit their nuclear electricity production policy, it would have to be offset by increasing demand for other traditional energy resources such as oil and gas, improvements in the efficiency of energy use and possibly more intensive exploitation of alternative energy resources.

1. In comparison: the damage from the Great Hanshin-Awaji (Kobe) Earthquake in 1995 – the most costly disaster in Japan's post-war history prior to the Great East Japan Earthquake – and from the Great Kanto Earthquake in 1923 amounted to 2% and 29% of GDP respectively (Shirakawa, 2011).
2. Japan accounts for around one-fifth of global production of semiconductors and around two-fifths of global production of flash memory chips. Thus there is some possibility for firms to switch to suppliers from other countries. This is much harder for high-end raw materials such as BT resin (used for printed circuit board), where Japan accounts for around 90% of global supply.

are projected to decline by over 11% at an annualised rate in the second quarter, before bouncing back in the third quarter. Global trade is expected to generally remain buoyant through the latter half of 2011 and rise by around 8½ per cent in 2012, with trade growth close to the average pre-crisis (2004-2008) rate of 1.7 times world output growth (Figure 1.2 and Table 1.5 below).

... and domestic demand in the non-OECD economies remains solid

Many emerging market economies have continued to experience strong output growth in recent quarters, and capacity constraints have started to become increasingly apparent, with commodity prices and underlying inflation both rising. The expansion has been fuelled in part by

Figure 1.2. **World trade growth remains solid**

Index 2005=100

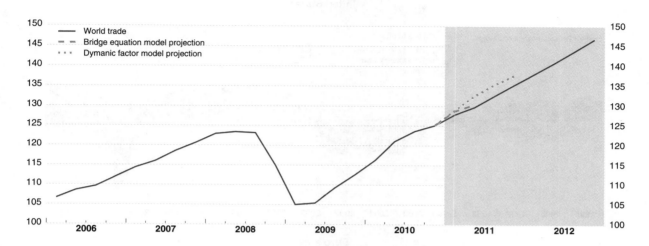

Note: The solid line represents the main projection for world trade. For details on the methodology used for bridge equation and dynamic factor models, see Guichard and Rusticelli (2011).

Source: OECD Economic Outlook 89 database; and OECD calculations.

StatLink ᴍᴀᴘ http://dx.doi.org/10.1787/888932433668

strong domestic credit growth and robust private final demand, which has helped to boost the export markets of OECD economies, but also created new policy challenges for non-OECD economies. Past moves to tighten monetary policies and, in some countries, embark on fiscal consolidation, together with the drag on real incomes from higher commodity prices, are however starting to moderate activity. In China, GDP growth softened to an annualised rate of 8¾ per cent in the first quarter, with retail sales still rising strongly but investment slackening. Ongoing monetary policy tightening and higher inflation have begun to damp income and credit growth, and recent PMI surveys point to some near-term softening in activity. In contrast, PMI surveys have yet to weaken noticeably in India, although private investment is now moderating after strong growth through much of last year. In Brazil, where the output gap closed rapidly in the aftermath of the recession, fiscal consolidation has begun and output growth has started to slow, with strong investment growth being offset by a continued drag on growth from net trade, in part due to the marked appreciation of the exchange rate fuelled by strong capital inflows. In contrast, growth has begun to pick up in Russia and South Africa, with higher international commodity prices helping to stimulate activity.

Overall financial conditions have continued to improve in the major OECD economies...

Financial condition indices (FCIs) summarising growth-relevant information in different areas of the financial system are continuing to improve across all major OECD economies (Figure 1.3). Underlying the broad improvement in financial conditions are several factors which pull in different directions across countries.

Figure 1.3. **Financial conditions indices have improved markedly**

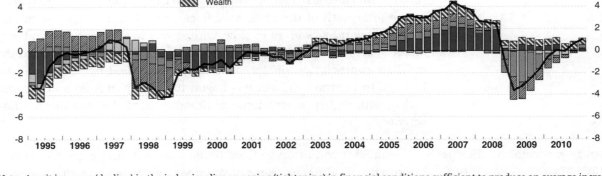

Note: A unit increase (decline) in the index implies an easing (tightening) in financial conditions sufficient to produce an average increase (reduction) in the level of GDP of ½ to 1% after four to six quarters. See details in Guichard et al. (2009).

Source: Datastream; OECD Economic Outlook 89 database; and OECD calculations.

StatLink http://dx.doi.org/10.1787/888932433687

... supported by corporate debt and equity markets...

● Corporate debt funding conditions remain supportive of economic activity. Firms with access to capital markets have benefitted from falling corporate spreads, especially for sub-investment-grade borrowers in the United States, which are now close to pre-crisis levels.[1] In the United States, banks have continued to ease corporate credit standards steadily, but the improvement has been more uneven in the euro area. Although equity markets have become more volatile due to geopolitical risks, rising oil prices and the worries sparked by the earthquake and its aftermath in Japan, they have posted sizeable gains, with share prices significantly above their level half a year ago in the United States and, to a lesser extent, the euro area (Figure 1.4).

... in spite of higher long-term government yields

● The increase in real yields on long-term government bonds is acting as a drag on aggregate financial conditions. In the euro area, renewed sovereign debt concerns during the first quarter of this year have resulted in substantial increases in long-term government borrowing costs in Greece, Ireland and Portugal (see Figure 1.16 below).

Outside the OECD, financial conditions remain favourable but volatile

Financial conditions remain favourable but volatile in emerging markets. Abundant global liquidity has resulted in historically low sovereign spreads in many economies, though stock prices have been volatile, with net equity outflows to developed countries since the beginning of this year. Tighter policy settings in China have led to a slowing in bank lending growth. Underlying credit dynamics are however difficult to assess in China, because the authorities have introduced month-by-month lending quotas in place of the previous annual quota that led banks to make large amounts of loans at the beginning of the year.

Business investment has rebounded...

Business investment has picked up since the start of the recovery but has yet to accelerate significantly in many countries, despite ongoing improvements in corporate profitability and generally healthy corporate balance sheets. This suggests that uncertainty about the pace and durability of the recovery, along with the comparatively modest level of activity in IT sectors in recent months, may have been damping investment growth somewhat. But capital-goods orders have picked up in many major OECD economies and survey-based measures of investment intentions have continued to rise, pointing to solid growth ahead in equipment investment. Reconstruction expenditure in the aftermath of the natural disasters should also lead to a large jump in investment levels in Japan from the second half of this year. With business investment intensity still well below pre-crisis levels (Figure 1.5), and uncertainty

1. Another indication of considerable risk appetite is that in the first quarter of the year US companies issued one and a quarter as much "covenant-light" loans, i.e. loans which offer less protection to the lending party than traditional covenants, than in 2006, the last year prior to the onset of the crisis.

Figure 1.4. **Price-earnings ratios remain below long-run averages**
Last observation: April 2011

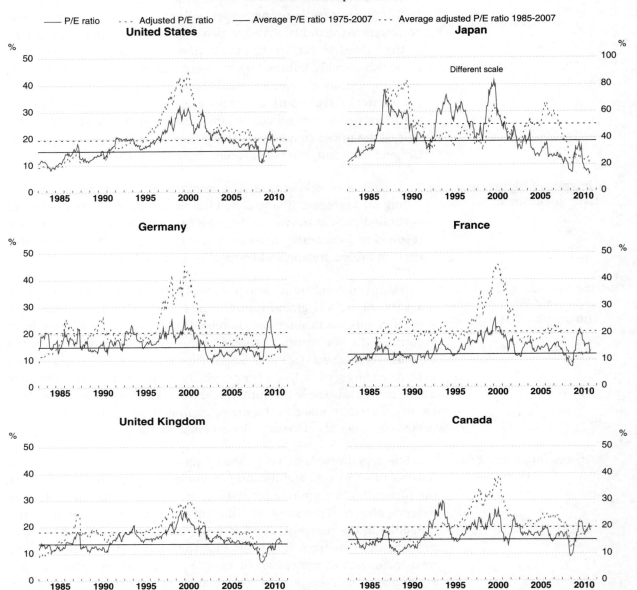

—— P/E ratio   - - - Adjusted P/E ratio   —— Average P/E ratio 1975-2007   - - - Average adjusted P/E ratio 1985-2007

Note: Adjusted P/E ratios are calculated as the ratio of stock prices to the moving average of the previous 10 years' earnings, adjusted for nominal trend growth. Averages shown exclude the period 1998-2000 to remove the asset bubble effects.

Source: Datastream; OECD calculations.

StatLink ⬚⬚ *http://dx.doi.org/10.1787/888932433706*

Figure 1.5. **Changes in business investment intensity in recessions and recoveries**

Change from investment intensity at pre-crisis peak of GDP, at time t, percentage points

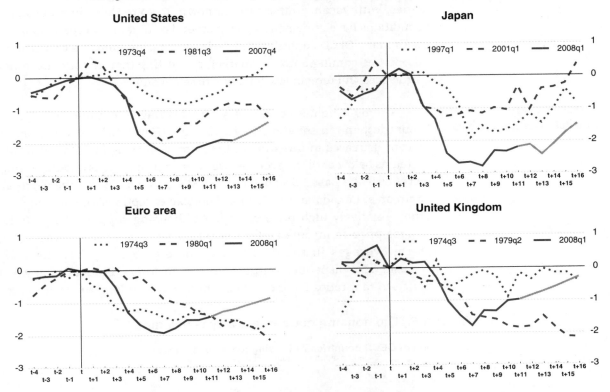

Note: Horizontal axis represents quarters before and after the peak. Grey lines correspond to forecasts.

Source: OECD Economic Outlook 89 database.

StatLink http://dx.doi.org/10.1787/888932433725

about the recovery likely to fade further, normal cyclical forces and healthier financial conditions should encourage strong upward momentum in investment levels over the projection period.[2]

... but the recovery in commercial property markets is more hesitant

However, non-residential construction output and investment remain very weak in many countries, reflecting the hesitant recovery in commercial property markets. Some signs of improvement are now appearing, although prices generally remain well below pre-recession levels. Commercial property values are now rising in the euro area and the United Kingdom, in part reflecting the support provided by low interest rates, but in the United States, where there is considerable excess

2. A simple indicator-type model for business investment in the United States, in which investment growth is related to current and past lags of survey measures of investment intentions and the OECD US financial conditions index, points to solid growth in investment volumes of just over 9% this year, compared with a projected rise of 8¼ per cent. For the euro area, where information on investment intentions is less timely and published less frequently, an indicator-type model using survey measures of production expectations and the euro area financial conditions index is found to track business investment reasonably well. This model points to investment growth of just over 6½ per cent in the euro area in 2011, a little stronger than the projected rise of 5¼ per cent.

capacity, commercial property prices in nominal terms remain low and volatile. Global office rents have also now begun rising, especially in major cities, with vacancy rates turning down. Despite these improvements, conditions have remained fragile in several commercial property markets, with many OECD countries still seeing increasing numbers of distressed properties coming onto the market, suggesting that investment in new structures will remain low for some time to come.

The recovery in housing markets remains mixed...

The housing market recovery remains fragile in a number of OECD countries, and in some it has yet to begin (Figure 1.6). Notwithstanding recent increases in investment, the ratio of housing investment to GDP remains below both the average level seen in past troughs and the average level over the past 3 decades in the OECD as a whole and the aggregate euro area. Canada and Finland are notable exceptions, in part reflecting their relatively high price elasticity of housing supply (OECD, 2011a). House price-to-income and price-to-rent ratios are close to their long-term averages in the OECD as a whole (Table 1.2), but there are considerable disparities across countries. In several economies in which price-to-rent ratios are more than 50% above their long-run average, real

Figure 1.6. **The housing market recovery is hesitant**

Proportion of OECD countries with rising real house prices[1]
Based on quarter-on-quarter change

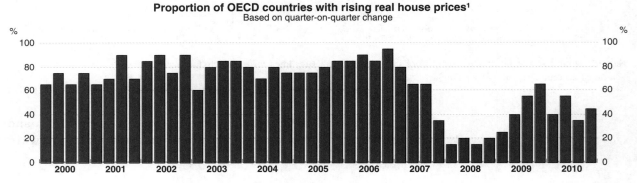

Proportion of OECD countries with rising real housing investment
Based on quarter-on-quarter change

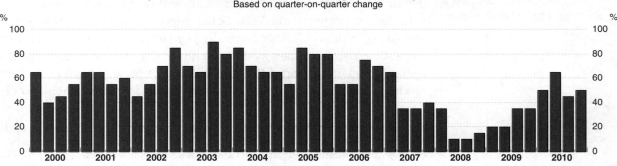

1. House prices deflated by the private consumption deflator. Calculation based on 20 countries (18 available in 2010q4).
Source: OECD Economic Outlook 89 database; and various national sources, see Table A.1 in Girouard *et al.* (2006).

StatLink ⟶ http://dx.doi.org/10.1787/888932433744

Table 1.2. **Real house prices remain fragile in some countries**

	Per cent annual rate of change				Level relative to long-term average[1]		
	2002-2008	2009	2010[2]	Latest quarter[3]	Price-to-rent ratio	Price-to-income ratio	Latest available quarter
United States	2.5	-4.3	-5.0	-2.4	108	93	Q4 2010
Japan	-3.2	-1.7	-2.0	-2.1	64	64	Q3 2010
Germany	-1.8	0.5	0.4	0.5	80	76	Q4 2010
France	8.0	-6.7	5.0	7.7	143	134	Q4 2010
Italy	4.1	-3.7	-3.1	-3.2	107	118	Q3 2010
United Kingdom	5.5	-9.1	3.0	-0.3	140	129	Q4 2010
Canada	6.5	4.0	5.4	0.0	155	132	Q4 2010
Australia	5.7	1.7	10.1	3.2	157	142	Q4 2010
Belgium	6.2	0.1	2.9	2.7	166	149	Q4 2010
Denmark	6.4	-13.2	-0.2	-0.6	127	126	Q4 2010
Finland	4.5	-0.9	7.6	3.6	138	103	Q4 2010
Greece	3.0	-5.3	-8.2	-10.6	98	97	Q4 2010
Ireland	3.0	-9.8	-13.6	-9.7	110	97	Q4 2010
Korea	2.1	-2.3	-0.2	-1.5	109	60	Q4 2010
Netherlands	2.1	-2.7	-3.6	-2.8	136	139	Q4 2010
Norway	5.4	-0.6	6.2	4.1	163	128	Q4 2010
New Zealand	8.9	-3.9	0.5	-4.6	152	116	Q4 2010
Spain	7.5	-7.7	-6.2	-6.5	134	134	Q4 2010
Sweden	6.8	-0.4	6.5	4.2	143	132	Q4 2010
Switzerland	1.1	5.5	4.5	4.2	92	93	Q4 2010
Total of above euro area[4,]	3.6	-3.6	-0.8	-0.3	116	113	Q4 2010
Total of above countries[5]	2.6	-3.5	-1.7	-1.2	111	100	

Note: House prices deflated by the private consumption deflator.
1. Average from 1980 (or earliest available date) to latest quarter available = 100.
2. Average of available quarters where full year is not yet complete.
3. Increase over a year earlier to the latest available quarter.
4. Germany, France, Italy, Belgium, Finland, Grece, Ireland, Netherlands and Spain.
5. Using 2009 GDP weights, calculated using latest country data available.
Source: Girouard *et al.* (2006); and OECD.

StatLink ᘏᔍᖮ http://dx.doi.org/10.1787/888932434143

prices may be close to peaking, despite still-low real interest rates (Box 1.6 below). In contrast, long-standing declines in real house prices are persisting in the United States, Spain and Ireland, and have now begun once more in the United Kingdom. Survey indicators are generally weak in these markets, and an overhang of unsold properties will take time to clear. Unsettled legal disputes around foreclosure proceedings may also prolong adjustment in the United States. This will likely damp new construction for some time, although there is some evidence that real prices may be nearing a trough in these economies (Box 1.6).

... but investment is expected to edge up

Going forward, OECD-wide housing investment is expected to rise gently relative to GDP from the latter half of 2011, but more rapidly in Japan and New Zealand, with reconstruction expenditure generating strong investment growth in these economies from mid-2011 onwards. Nonetheless, given the now-small share of housing investment in OECD GDP, the contribution from the projected recovery in investment will provide only a modest boost to OECD output growth.

Inventory levels are close to longer-term norms...

High-frequency indicators suggest that inventories are now close to normal levels in most major OECD economies, although supply-chain disruptions in the aftermath of the earthquake in Japan are likely to result in some temporary depletion of stocks. The contribution of inventories to quarterly output growth is assumed to be zero from the third quarter of 2011 onwards in the projections.

... and household saving rates have begun to edge down

Household saving rates have recently begun to edge down in many OECD countries, though they still remain elevated relative to pre-crisis norms. Asset price increases, higher saving and associated debt deleveraging have all helped to repair household balance sheets since the recovery began, softening the need for any additional increases in saving rates for balance-sheet purposes. Improving labour market outcomes and credit conditions may also continue to diminish the need for precautionary saving. Wealth-to-income ratios are now above 5-10 year pre-crisis averages in the United Kingdom, and, in the euro area, are close to the peak level since the formation of the euro area. This suggests that the saving ratio might soften further in these economies, provided credit conditions do not deteriorate. In the United States, additional balance sheet adjustment is likely to be required, reflecting ongoing housing market weakness and the consequent implications for household net worth. But with debt on a clearly declining trajectory, a higher saving rate will not be required to ensure adjustment. Indeed, with the rate of job creation gathering pace, the US saving ratio is projected to edge down by around ¾ of a percentage point from the current level of 5¾ per cent over the projection period. In Japan, the uncertainty created by the earthquake and its aftermath may increase household precautionary saving for a while, although this could be offset, at least in part, by the need to finance replacement of lost goods and property.[3] An updated comparison of actual and trend car sales, with the latter derived as in Haugh *et al.* (2010), provides a further indication of the potential for strong growth in consumer demand at present, with sales in the euro area, Japan, the United Kingdom and the United States still remaining below longer-term trends (Figure 1.7).

Global commodity prices have surged...

In the near term, strong commodity price growth is reducing real income growth, and thus damping consumer expenditure somewhat. Brent crude oil prices have increased by around 50% since mid 2010

---

3. Consumption might also be postponed temporarily due to the supply-side disruptions and the related unavailability of products.

Figure 1.7. **Car sales are generally below trend levels**
Actual[1] and trend car sales 1995 – 2012, number of cars in millions

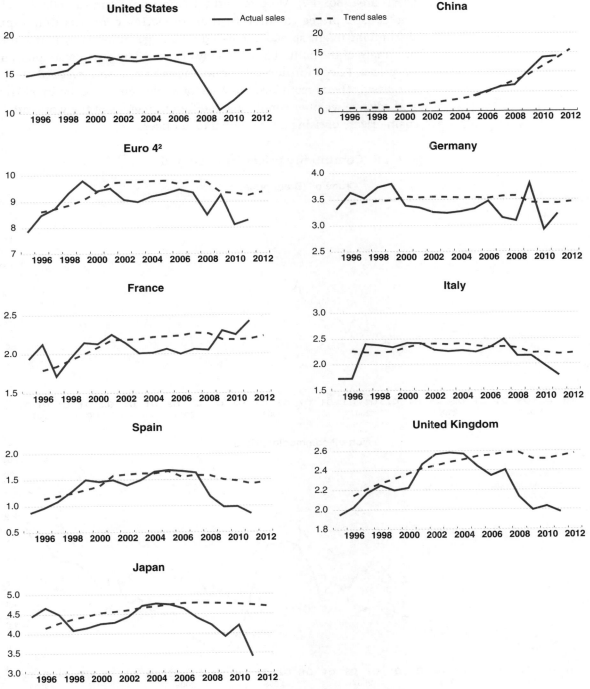

1. Seasonally adjusted. For 2011 based on annualised sales in first four months for the United States, China, Germany, France, Italy, Spain and the United Kingdom and in first three months for Japan.
2. Euro 4 includes Germany, France, Italy and Spain.
Source: Haugh *et al.* (2010); Datastream; China Association of Automobile Manufacturers; Japan Automobile Manufacturers Association; and OECD calculations.

StatLink http://dx.doi.org/10.1787/888932433763

(Figure 1.8), and volatility has been high. Up to the end of 2010, most of the increase in the oil price seemed to relate to strong oil demand outside the OECD area (Box 1.2). More recently, political unrest in the MENA region has caused prices to surge further, reflecting concerns that supply disruptions might spread. Increased oil and gas imports by Japan in the aftermath of the natural disaster may also be adding to upward pressures on prices. Prices for non-oil commodities have also increased steeply, surpassing their record levels of 2008 for many items. The rise in oil prices and adverse weather conditions in different regions of the world are the main drivers of rising international food prices.

Figure 1.8. **Commodity prices have surged**

Crude oil (Brent price)

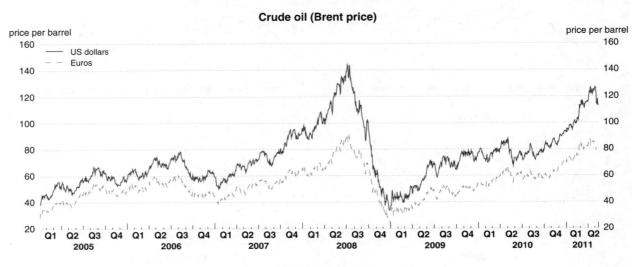

Non-oil commodity prices

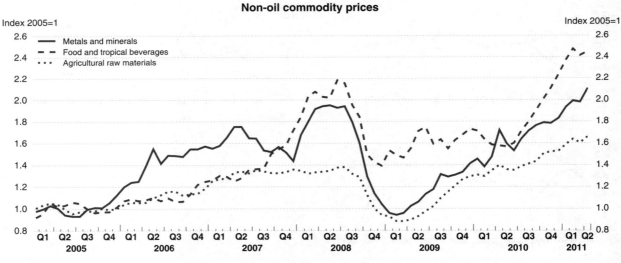

Source: OECD, Main Economic Indicators database; and Datastream.

StatLink ⬛🖳 http://dx.doi.org/10.1787/888932433782

Box 1.2. **What is driving commodity prices?**

Empirical research indicates that strong world oil demand was a major factor behind the run-up in crude oil prices to record levels in summer 2008, driven by buoyant demand from emerging market economies, notably China and the Middle East (see figure below).[1] The recent episode of rising oil prices since 2009 also coincides with a strong upswing in oil demand outside the OECD area. Supply side factors also play a role. Crude oil supply levelled off in the middle of the last decade. Long time lags between investment decisions and new oil production coming on stream, declining oil production from many conventional oil fields outside OPEC and shortages of qualified labour all contributed to this development. Climatic and geopolitical factors, production cuts by OPEC and low levels of spare capacity as well as constraints in the refining system have at times also restrained supply. However, higher prices have been accompanied by renewed growth in OPEC production capacity in 2009 and 2010. In the current episode of rising oil prices, political unrest in North Africa and the Middle East caused prices to surge further, both reflecting direct supply disruptions and concerns that they might spread.

Oil demand and supply
Million barrels per day

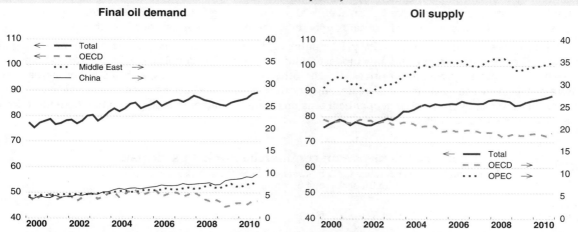

Note: The balancing item between (final) oil demand and supply are changes in stocks.

Source: IEA, Monthly Oil Data service.

StatLink ⋙ http://dx.doi.org/10.1787/888932433801

Other macroeconomic factors, such as movements in exchange rates and interest rates, also play a role. Low real interest rates are likely to have contributed to the upward pressure on oil prices. Lower interest rates make it less profitable for producers to extract oil and invest the proceeds on the financial market, which might reduce the supply of oil, putting upward pressure on the spot price. At the same time, the opportunity costs of holding stocks of oil decline, which can put upward pressure on oil demand. Indeed, estimates from a simple structural vector auto-regression model suggest that a reduction in the US 3-month real interest rate by one percentage point could push up oil prices by about $4 cumulatively by the end of the second year after the shock occurred.[2] While the precise size of the effect is subject to uncertainty, and is likely to depend on the initial level of oil prices, the estimates suggest that the marked reductions in short-term interest rates that occurred in response to the crisis could have contributed substantially to the recent upswing in oil prices.

Buoyant income growth in emerging markets, coupled with deepening world trade integration, was also an important driver for the upswing in non-oil commodity prices. With respect to food, rising underlying demand growth for meat in emerging markets is part of this effect. Adverse supply side factors also played a role. In particular, rising oil prices contributed substantially to rising prices for non-oil commodities, food in particular, whose production is generally energy intensive. For food, this link was reinforced by bio-fuel policies. Between 2000 and 2009, global output of bio-ethanol quadrupled and production of biodiesel increased tenfold, with government support policies having been a major driver behind the upswing.[3]

Box 1.2. **What is driving commodity prices?** *(cont.)*

Increases in the price of oil enhance ethanol's competitiveness relative to petrol and strengthen its demand. With both bio-energy and food utilising the same inputs and the supply elasticity of crops limited in the short run, increases in the production of ethanol reduce the supply of crops for food and raise food prices. Supply disruptions due to extreme weather conditions added to upward pressure on prices, as did export restrictions in some traditional large commodity-export countries.

Moreover, concerns have been expressed that commodity prices may have been pushed up by speculation. Indeed, net long positions (*i.e.* current purchases for future selling) held by non-commercial oil traders have markedly increased on average over recent years as oil prices were trending upwards (see second figure). However, recent commodity price increases have been broad-based, including in particular certain food commodities for which organised futures markets do not exist. This suggests that factors other than financial market speculation are the main drivers for a number of commodity prices, although oil prices could be a channel through which financial factors influence other commodities as well.

Also, information concerning future oil prices is conflicting. On the one hand, record levels of net long positions by non-commercial traders appear to indicate expectations of further rising oil prices. On the other hand, with the futures curve flat until end-2011 and bending downwards thereafter, lower oil prices are expected in the future – though caveats apply to the information content of oil futures.

Overall, forces acting on commodity prices point in different directions. On the one hand, rising oil demand by emerging markets, and only modest additions to world oil supply capacity over the next couple of years, put upward pressure on prices. On the other hand, other factors, such as likely increases in interest rates over the next couple of years, suggest that oil and food prices might well come down from current high levels, the more so if geopolitical tensions were to abate and food production benefitted from less extreme weather conditions.

Long positions by non commercial market participants
Futures and options contracts for light sweet crude oil (New York Mercantile Exchange),
net number of long non commercial contracts

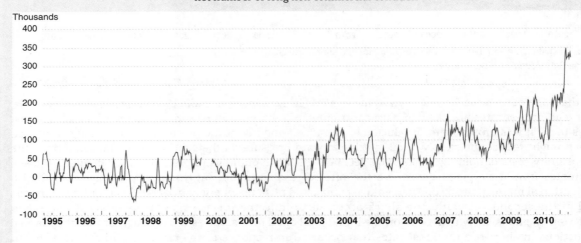

Source: US Commodity Futures Trading Commission and Datastream.

StatLink ⟲⟲⟲⟲ http://dx.doi.org/10.1787/888932433820

1. See in particular Pain *et al.* (2008) and Wurzel *et al.* (2009). Increasing oil demand in Asian and Middle Eastern emerging markets has been reinforced by the relatively high energy intensity in power generation and industry in these economies as well as by the pervasiveness of capped retail prices that insulate consumers from increases in world market prices.
2. The result, evaluated at the sample mean real oil price over 1986-2010, is derived from a structural vector-autoregression, estimated with quarterly data over the period 1986 to 2010 and involving, besides the real price for Brent oil, a measure of real world GDP, US real short-term interest rates and the US real effective exchange rate. The order of variables follows Akram (2009).
3. See OECD (2008a) and Jones and Kwiecinski (2010).

... which will damp the near-term recovery

Food items make up a large share of consumption baskets in lower-income countries but are also significant in OECD economies. For example, the share of food items in domestic private consumption is around 14% in the United States and 19% in Japan. The raw material part of private consumption baskets is much lower though, due to trade margins and various non-commodity inputs into food production. Back-of-the-envelope calculations with these factors taken into consideration, and under the assumption of unchanged exchange rates and nominal incomes, suggest that a sustained increase in food and oil commodity prices of the size seen over the past six months would mechanically reduce, all else being equal, households' real disposable incomes by almost 1½ per cent in the major OECD areas. Economy-wide income effects would be smaller though, with domestic food producers benefitting from price increases and consumption patterns adjusting in favour of goods with smaller relative price increases. Empirical estimates suggest that the short-term impact of a $10 increase in crude oil prices could be two-tenths of a percentage point lower GDP growth in the OECD area over the first two years (Table 1.3).

Growth prospects

Growth is set to gather pace gradually...

Output growth strengthened moderately in the OECD area in the first quarter, notwithstanding the hit to real household incomes from higher energy costs and the large decline in activity in Japan following the earthquake in early March. Growth in the non-OECD economies remained robust. Looking ahead, the recovery is expected to gain further momentum only slowly (Figure 1.9), notwithstanding the support provided by still-accommodative monetary policies throughout the projection period and favourable financial conditions. Necessary fiscal consolidation (Box 1.3), adverse terms-of-trade effects and continued headwinds from the legacies of the recession in labour, housing and credit markets will all check the pace of the upturn in the OECD. As a result, it seems likely that economic slack will still remain in most OECD economies at the end of the projection period.

The key features of the economic outlook for the major economies are as follows:

... in the United States...

● Growth in the United States is expected to pick up modestly from the second quarter of 2011, supported by accommodative monetary policy and favourable financial conditions, and the gradual fading of the adverse effects from high commodity prices and remaining weaknesses in labour and property markets and household balance sheets. Nonetheless, the momentum of the recovery is likely to remain muted, with a modest drag on activity from fiscal consolidation in 2012. Low interest rates, strong corporate profits and normal cyclical forces should support robust growth in equipment investment, but excess supply in property markets will continue to weigh on housing and commercial property investment for some time. Private consumption

Table 1.3. **Effects of an oil price increase on GDP and inflation –
Survey of recent estimates**

Study	Approach	Type of stock	Impact on real GDP	Impact on inflation
Carabenciov *et al.* (2008), IMF	Macro-econometric model	(Permanent) 10% increase	Average deviation of growth rates in the following two years: -0.10% points for the United States -0.03% points for the euro area -0.02% points for Japan	Average deviation of growth rates in the following two years: +0.13% points for the United States +0.08% points for the EA +0.04% points for Japan
Barell and Pomerantz (2004), NIESR	NiGEM Macro-econometric model	(Permanent) $10 increase	Deviation from baseline in the second year: -0.47% points for the United States -0.38% points for the euro area	Deviation from baseline in the second year: +0.51% points for the United States +0.28% points for the euro area
European Commission (2004)	QUEST Macro-econometric model	(Permanent) 25% increase	Deviation from baseline in the second year: -0.38% points for the euro area	Deviation from baseline in terms of CPI level in the second year: +0.28% points for the euro area
European Commission (2008)	QUEST III Dynamic stochastic general equilibrium model (DSGE)	Gradual increase of 100% over a period of three years	Deviation from baseline in the second year: -0.59% points for the euro area	Deviation from baseline in terms of CPI level in the second year: +1.27% points for the euro area
Jimenez-Rodoriguez and Sanchez (2004), ECB	Vector autoregression (VAR)	Impulse response to a 1% oil price shock	Accumulated effects in the growth rate to the 8th quarter: -0.039% points for the United States -0.011% points for the euro area	
OECD Global Model, Hervé *et al.* (2010)	Macro-econometric model	(Permanent) $10 increase	Deviation from baseline in the second year: -0.3% points for the United States -0.3% for Japan -0.2% for the euro area	Deviation of consumer price level from baseline in the second year: +0.4% points for the United States +0.1% for Japan +0.3% points for the euro area

Source: OECD.

StatLink ⬛⬛ http://dx.doi.org/10.1787/888932434162

growth should be helped by further improvements in labour market conditions, but ongoing balance-sheet adjustment is likely to constrain the extent to which the household saving rate can fall. With a continuation of the recent pick-up in employment growth, the unemployment rate is projected to decline to around 7½ per cent by the end of 2012, still well above the pre-crisis level.

Figure 1.9. **Global growth continues be led by the non-OECD economies**

Contribution to annualised quarterly world real GDP growth

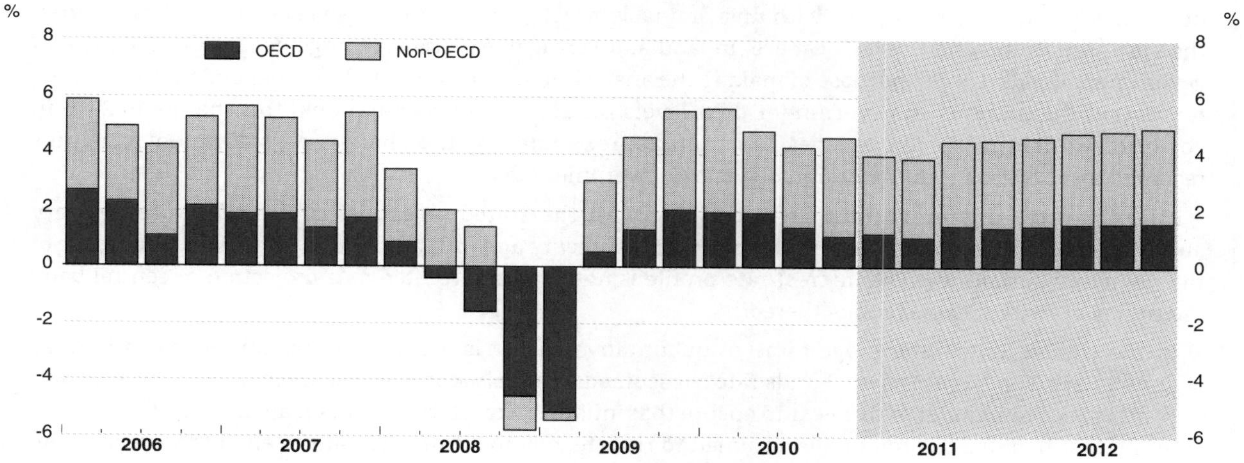

Note: Calculated using moving nominal GDP weights, based on national GDP at purchasing power parities.

Source: OECD Economic Outlook 89 database.

StatLink ⟨⟨⟨ http://dx.doi.org/10.1787/888932433839

Box 1.3. **Policy and other assumptions underlying the projections**

Fiscal policy settings for 2011 are based as closely as possible on legislated tax and spending provisions. Where policy changes have been announced but not legislated, they are incorporated if it is deemed clear that they will be implemented in a shape close to that announced. Where government plans are available for 2012, fiscal projections follow the plans. Otherwise, in countries with impaired public finances, a tightening of the underlying primary balance of 1% of GDP in 2012 has been built into the projections. Where there is insufficient information to determine the allocation of budget cuts, the presumption is that they apply equally to the spending and revenue side, and are spread proportionally across components. These conventions allow for needed consolidation in countries where plans have not been announced at a sufficiently detailed level to be incorporated in the projections. Along this line, the following assumptions were adopted (with additional adjustments if OECD and government projections for economic activity differ):

● For the United States, the assumptions for 2011 are based on legislated measures. Given the legislative uncertainty about budget policy for 2012, the general government underlying primary deficit is assumed to decline by 1% of GDP from the level in 2011.

● For Japan, the projections are based on the Fiscal Management Strategy announced in June 2010, which limits the issuance of new government bonds in FY 2011-12 to the FY 2010 level. This constraint is broadly respected through a combination of spending and revenue measures, notwithstanding the need for earthquake-related reconstruction spending.

● For Germany, the government's medium-term consolidation programme, announced in September 2010, as well as the phasing out of the temporary components of the fiscal stimulus packages have been built into the projections. For France, the projections incorporate the government's medium-term consolidation programme. For Italy, the projections incorporate the measures announced in the 2011 budget legislation and confirmed in the revised Stability Programme. For the United Kingdom, the projections are based on tax measures and spending paths set in the March 2011 budget.

The concept of general government financial liabilities applied in the OECD Economic Outlook is based on national accounting conventions. These require that liabilities are recorded at market prices as opposed to constant nominal prices (as is the case, in particular, for the Maastricht definition of general government

Box 1.3. **Policy and other assumptions underlying the projections** (cont.)

debt). In 2010, euro area countries with unsustainable fiscal positions that have asked for assistance from the European Union and the IMF (Greece, Ireland and Portugal) experienced large declines in the price of government bonds. For the purpose of making the analysis in the *Economic Outlook* independent from strong temporary fluctuations in government debt levels on account of revaluations, the change in 2010 in government debt in these countries has been approximated by the change in government liabilities recorded for the Maastricht definition of general government debt.

Policy-controlled interest rates are set in line with the stated objectives of the relevant monetary authorities, conditional upon the OECD projections of activity and inflation, which may differ from those of the monetary authorities. The interest rate profile is not to be interpreted as a projection of central bank intentions or market expectations thereof.

● In the United States, the programme of quantitative easing is assumed to be completed in June as announced. The target Federal Funds rate is assumed to be raised in a series of small steps by 100 basis points in the remainder of this year to ensure that inflation expectations remain anchored. After a pause in the first half of 2012, the rate is assumed to rise steadily to 2¼ per cent at the end of the year as the recovery progresses.

● In the euro area, after having raised the refinancing rate in April 2011, the European Central Bank is assumed to keep the rate constant for the remainder of this year. A gradual normalisation of the main policy rate would be warranted from early 2012, with an erosion of economic slack and edging up of underlying inflation. Thus, the main refinancing rate is assumed to increase through 2012 to 2¼ per cent by the end of 2012.

● In Japan, the current interest rate policy needs to be continued until inflation is firmly positive. The short-term policy interest rate is assumed to remain at 10 basis points for the entire projection horizon.

● In the United Kingdom, the policy interest rate is assumed to increase by 50 basis by the end of the current year to prevent continued increases in inflation expectations. After a pause, to assess the effects on the recovery, the policy rate is assumed to increase further by an additional 125 basis points in 2012 as the recovery firms.

For the United States, Japan, Germany and other countries outside the euro area, 10-year government bond yields are assumed to converge towards a reference rate, determined as future projected short rates plus a term premium and an additional premium for countries with government gross debt exceeding 75% of GDP, equal to 4 basis points for each percentage point of the debt ratio above 75%. The assumptions regarding long-term sovereign debt spreads in the euro area *vis-à-vis* Germany are as follows:

● For Greece, Portugal and Ireland, spreads are assumed to remain constant until end 2011 at the average observed in April, before halving through 2012 as progress in consolidation and economic adjustment leads to a spontaneous increase in confidence or perceptions increase that additional official financing would be forthcoming, if needed.

● For Spain, spreads are assumed to remain constant until end 2011 at the average value observed in April, before falling by a quarter through 2012.

● For other euro area countries, spreads are assumed to remain constant until end 2012 at the average value observed in April.

The projections assume unchanged exchange rates from those prevailing on 6 May 2011: $1 equals 80.31 JPY, 0.70 EUR (or equivalently, 1 EUR equals $1.43) and CNY 6.49.

The price of a barrel of Brent crude oil is assumed to be constant at $120 from the second quarter of this year onwards. Non-oil commodity prices are assumed to be constant at the average level in March and April 2011 over the projection period.

The cut-off date for information used in the projections is 19 May 2011. Details of assumptions for individual countries are provided in Chapters 2 and 3.

... Japan...

- In Japan, the immediate aftermath of the Great East Japan Earthquake has seen sizable declines in production and consumption, as well as business and consumer confidence. Given the experience of past disasters in Japan and elsewhere, the large negative impact on GDP in the first and second quarters is expected to be reversed quickly as reconstruction efforts get underway. Strong growth in both public and private investment is projected in the latter half of the year and the early months of 2012 to replace housing and fixed capital assets destroyed in the disaster, and export growth should bounce back as supply chains are restored. Private consumption is also projected to pick up from the latter half of this year. However, after a temporary sharp decline in the second quarter, import volume growth is likely to be higher than otherwise, given the need for higher oil imports to replace nuclear power. Over the year to the fourth quarter of 2011 output is projected to be broadly constant, but calendar year growth is likely to be negative this year. By the latter half of 2012, as the level of reconstruction spending falls, growth is expected to soften, with public consumption and fixed investment both contracting as consolidation efforts strengthen. The unemployment rate is expected to decline only gently over the projection period to 4½ per cent, thus remaining above its pre-crisis level.

... the aggregate euro area...

- In the euro area as a whole, the recovery has taken hold and is spreading beyond manufacturing to service sectors. Growth is becoming better balanced, with final private demand expected to strengthen gradually through the projection period, with the effects from still-accommodative monetary policy and favourable financial conditions outweighing the drag exerted by fiscal consolidation and the near-term pressures on real incomes from high energy prices. Labour market conditions are likely to improve, with output growth increasingly accompanied by net job creation, but the unemployment rate is projected to decline only to around 9% by the end of next year, leaving still-sizable economic slack. Labour market improvements should augment the boost to private consumption from low interest rates, strengthening confidence and leading to further reductions in the saving rate. Business investment should also continue to recover from extraordinarily low post-crisis levels, helped by normal cyclical effects and favourable financing conditions. As discussed in Box 1.4, economic prospects are projected to remain uneven within the euro area.

... and the non-OECD area

- In China, output growth is projected to average a little over 9% over 2011-12. The near-term softening in the growth rate of GDP is projected to continue into the latter half of this year, with domestic demand damped by the effects of tighter monetary conditions, rising headline inflation and some near-term adverse effects from weakness in the Japanese economy. As these effects fade, domestic demand is expected to strengthen once more, helped by ongoing public investment in social housing. In India, further fiscal consolidation and continued monetary policy tightening should help GDP growth

Box 1.4. **The euro area programme countries:**
Current situation, outlook and policy options

Within the euro area, economic prospects remain uneven, reflecting the ongoing and necessary rebalancing between the core economies and some of those at the periphery. This adjustment is particularly forceful in countries that have asked for assistance from the European Union and the IMF and are facing intense financial market scrutiny. In these economies, sizable fiscal consolidation is being implemented, area-wide monetary policy is tighter than appropriate on purely domestic grounds, and private sector demand is constrained by still-weak balance sheets and adverse labour market conditions. However, some signs of rebalancing are appearing, with external competitiveness now improving in Ireland and Greece, on the back of falling unit labour costs, which should boost export growth over the projection period. Domestic demand is projected to weaken in Portugal, Greece and Ireland in both 2011 and 2012, but strong export growth could result in modest GDP growth by 2012, except in Portugal.

The necessary budget consolidation in these countries is proceeding. In Greece, budget consolidation in 2010 amounted to around 7½ per cent of GDP, a little less than targeted. On the OECD projection, this effort is set to be followed by additional reductions in the underlying deficit of around 4¼ per cent of GDP in 2011 and 1% in 2012, in line with EU/IMF programme targets. In Ireland, the budget deficit ballooned in 2010 due to bank rescue costs, but the underlying deficit is now projected to be cut by 3½ per cent of potential GDP (5% in terms of the underlying primary balance) from 2010 to 2012, in line with the agreement with the European Union and the IMF. In Portugal, strong consolidation is underway this year and further measures will be introduced in the context of the EU/IMF financial assistance programme; the underlying fiscal deficit is projected to decline by 4¼ and 2¼ per cent of potential GDP in 2011 and 2012, respectively. However, notwithstanding these consolidation efforts, the ratio of gross government debt to GDP will climb to almost 160% in Greece, about 125% in Ireland and around 115% in Portugal by 2012. Governments in all three countries have contingent liabilities related to explicit and implicit guarantees of banks which could raise government gross debt ratios even further.

Some structural reforms have been introduced to facilitate the necessary adjustment. Greece committed to wide-ranging structural reforms as part of the financial assistance package, including easing of restrictions in product markets, strengthening adjustment capacity in labour markets and revamping the pension system. Many of these commitments have already been translated into law, although legislation and implementation has fallen behind schedule in some cases. Similarly, Ireland will implement labour market reforms as part of its agreement with the EU and IMF. Structural reforms also feature prominently in the programme in Portugal, including adjustments to employment protection and benefit systems.

Despite financing support, strong fiscal consolidation efforts, structural reforms and signs of rebalancing, sovereign spreads have continued to widen in Greece, Ireland and Portugal. In mid-May, 10-year government bond yields were around 16% in Greece and 10% in Ireland and Portugal; shorter maturities carried even higher yields. Thus, markets have priced in significant probabilities of sovereign debt restructuring occurring in these countries. For example, in Greece, the market price of insurance against sovereign default corresponds to a 64% probability that the government will default over the next two years (assuming a 45% loss in the event of default). Even if the governments are more or less on track to meet their fiscal targets, their fiscal positions would not be sustainable if market interest rates were to remain for long at their current level.

At the same time, banks in Greece, Ireland and Portugal have been cut off from market finance and are dependent on liquidity provided by the ECB. This has been made possible by the decision of the ECB to relax its standards on the quality of collateral it accepts for repurchase agreements. At the end of February, the three countries accounted for 55% of all liquidity provided by the ECB.

Box 1.4. **The euro area programme countries:
Current situation, outlook and policy options** (cont.)

The ultimate goal for Greece, Ireland and Portugal is to achieve sustainable fiscal positions and restore access to market finance for governments and banks. In the absence of a return of market confidence regarding solvency risks, the unsustainable situation can be tackled in different ways:

● A first option is that foreign official lenders keep funding these governments at interest rates well below current market yields in exchange for additional measures to restore fiscal sustainability. However, if eventually any of these countries were to be unable to repay their debts at the interest rate on offer, such continued assistance would only have postponed the resolution of unsustainable positions. Also, while expectations about continued assistance could calm markets in the short term, it might drive up market yields on government debt if investors judged that official finance reduced the value of their claims, particularly if official loans were seen to have *de facto* senior status. Unless such senior assistance reduces the probability of default significantly, it thus translates into higher risk premia (Gros, 2010, and Chamley and Pinto, 2011).

● A second option is to reschedule the existing stock of debt. However, for heavily indebted countries government debt would have to be rescheduled over a very extended period, and at low interest rates to restore fiscal sustainability.

● At least in theory, a third option is to reduce the size of government liabilities in line with current market expectations. In practice, however, the use of this option is severely circumscribed by the need to find adequate answers to three issues: how to avoid a breakdown of domestic financial sectors, which would have calamitous effects; how to address spillovers to other countries through the financial system; and how to prevent contagion effects from one country to others.

---

moderate to a more sustainable rate of around 8½ per cent per annum over the projection period. Domestic demand will remain a key source of growth, led by private investment underpinned by buoyant corporate sentiment and a need for higher infrastructure spending. In Brazil, domestic demand is also set to remain solid and be driven by large infrastructure and energy development programmes, although ongoing policy normalisation and continued small declines in net exports should help keep growth at trend rates. In Russia, domestic demand is projected to increase strongly, supported by the high level of commodity prices. Despite the drag from strong import growth and tighter monetary conditions, output growth is expected to be around 5% in 2011 and 4½ per cent in 2012.

Headline inflation is being pushed up...

Recent strong rises in commodity prices have helped to push up the annual rate of headline consumer price inflation to around 2¾ per cent in both the United States and the euro area this year (Figure 1.10). In Japan, the headline inflation rate has now stopped declining for the first time in almost two years, although the planned rebasing of the consumer price index in August is expected to reduce the annual inflation rate by around ½ of a percentage point. The increase in headline inflation is even more marked in many emerging market economies, reflecting the greater weight of food and energy in total consumption in these economies and the greater energy intensity of production. There are also clear signs that

Figure 1.10. **Underlying inflation is edging up from low rates**
12-month percentage change

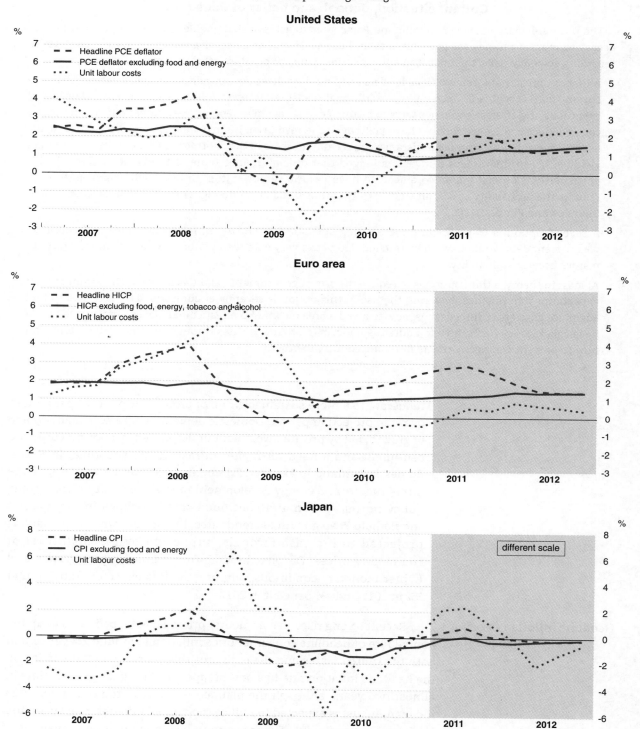

Note: PCE deflator refers to the deflator of personal consumption expenditures, HICP to the harmonised index of consumer prices and CPI to the consumer price index. Unit labour costs are economy-wide measures.

Source: OECD Economic Outlook 89 database.

StatLink ᵃᵍ⟡ http://dx.doi.org/10.1787/888932433858

underlying inflationary pressures are now building up in economies such as China, India, Brazil and Indonesia as a result of domestic capacity constraints.

... and inflation expectations have drifted up

Short and long-term inflation expectations have drifted up in recent months against the backdrop of relatively high global inflation and increasing commodity prices. The rise in long-term inflation expectations (Figure 1.11), notwithstanding some near-term volatility, suggests that part of the recent rise in headline inflation may now be expected to persist for longer than previously thought. Survey-based long-term expectations have risen only slightly in the major OECD countries, but measures of long-term inflation expectations derived from yield differences between nominal and indexed bonds have increased more substantially over the past year. Though part of this rise could reflect the correction of past mis-measurement, stemming from a flight to more liquid nominal bonds during the crisis, these expectation measures have now returned to or surpassed pre-crisis levels, suggesting some market perceptions that inflationary pressures are developing. The recent strength of gold prices, a traditional hedge against inflation, may also point to concerns about future inflation.

Economic slack is becoming harder to gauge...

Core inflation rates, abstracting from the direct effects of food and energy price inflation, are now edging up in OECD economies, but only gently and from a low level. The drift-up in core inflation likely reflects the diminishing drag on inflation from the economic slack that remains in labour and product markets (Moccero *et al.*, 2011). However, the level and rate of change of such slack is becoming harder to judge in some OECD economies, especially those in which unemployment is now falling relatively sharply and those in which survey-based measures of capacity utilisation in the manufacturing sector have moved close to normal levels, despite estimates of still-large negative economy-wide output gaps (Figure 1.12).

... but underlying inflation seems likely to edge up only slowly

Ongoing economic slack is expected to diminish only gradually and should still bear down on inflation through the projection period. Labour-cost pressures are also still modest (Figure 1.10), with wage pressures remaining muted in most major economies, even as labour productivity is strengthening, reflecting continued labour market slack. In the United States, the annual rate of core inflation is projected to drift up from around 1% at present to just above 1½ per cent over the projection period. In the euro area, core inflation is expected to edge up from 1¼ per cent in the latter half of this year to 1½ per cent by the latter half of 2012. Deflation is expected to persist in Japan. These figures include price-level adjustments from indirect tax increases and higher administered prices, which are also pushing up the core inflation rate temporarily in the United Kingdom and several economies in the periphery of the euro area (Box 1.5). Some further progress is likely to be made in reversing past cost inflation patterns within the euro area. If

Figure 1.11. **Long-term inflation expectations have drifted up in some countries**

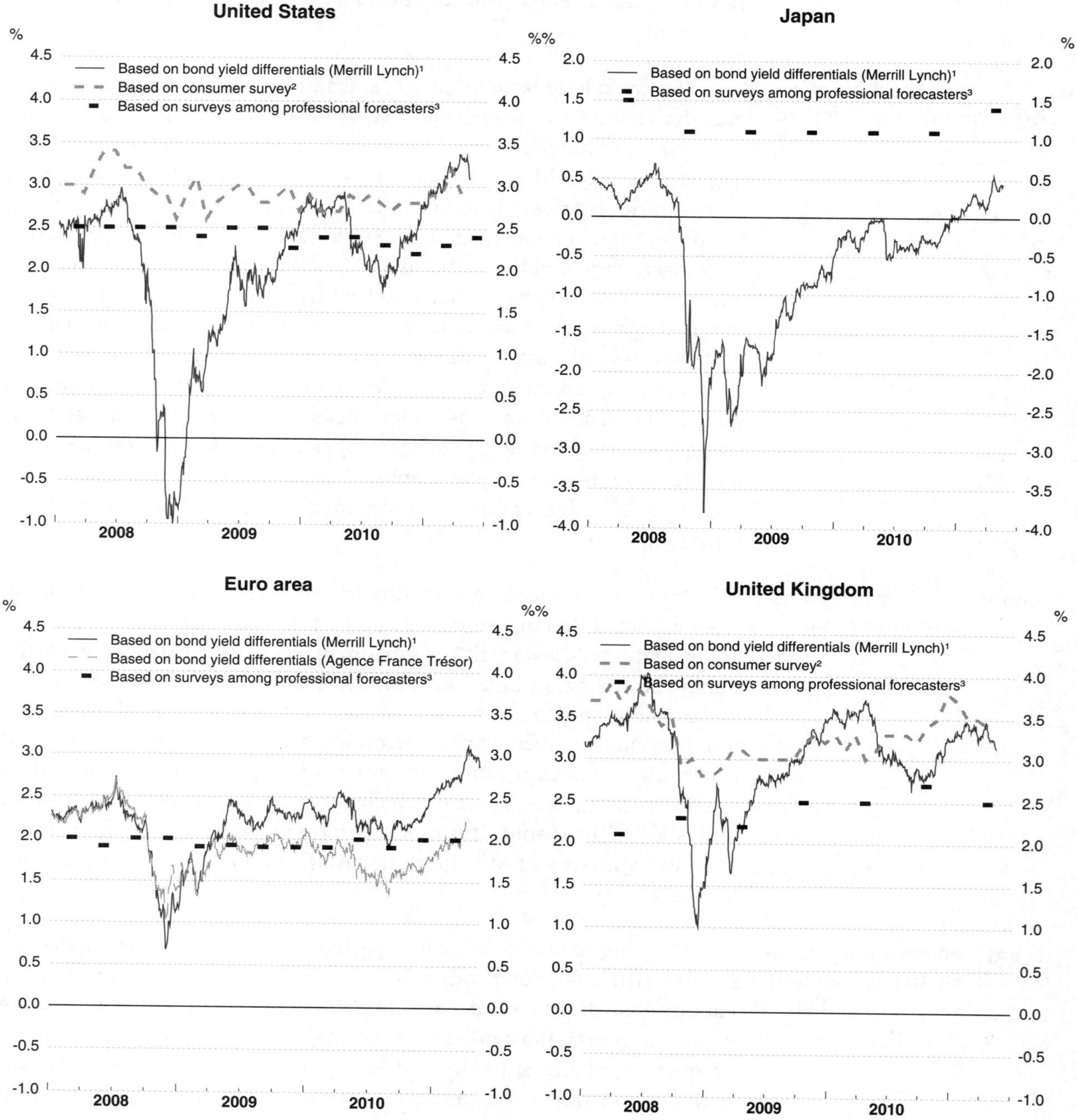

1. Expected inflation implied by the yield differential between 10-year government benchmark and inflation-indexed bonds.
2. Expected inflation over the next five to ten years. Based on the Reuters/University of Michigan Surveys of Consumers for the United States, and on Citigroup/YouGov survey for the United Kingdom.
3. Expected average rate of CPI inflation over the next 10 years for the United States, based on the Survey of Professional Forecasters (SPF) by the Federal Reserve Bank of Philadelphia. Expected HICP inflation rate five years ahead for the euro area, based on the SPF by the ECB. Expected average rate of CPI inflation six to ten years ahead for the United Kingdom based on Consensus Forecasts.

Source: Datastream; Agence France Trésor; University of Michigan Survey of Consumers; Citigroup; Federal Reserve Bank of Philadelphia; ECB; and Consensus Forecasts.

StatLink ᔥᔥᔥ http://dx.doi.org/10.1787/888932433877

Figure 1.12. **The output gap and normalised capacity utilisation are diverging**

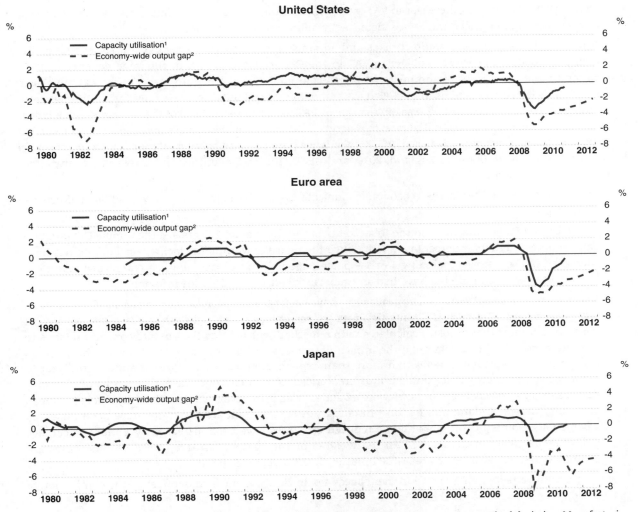

1. Capacity utilisation has been normalised by subtracting the historical average and dividing by the standard deviation. Manufacturing sector for Japan and the euro area; all industries for the United States.
2. The output gap is an economy-wide measure. It has not been adjusted for the effect of extended unemployment benefit duration, which might reduce its absolute magnitude.

Source: OECD, Main Economic Indicators database; OECD Economic Outlook 89 database; and Datastream.

StatLink http://dx.doi.org/10.1787/888932433896

additional structural measures to improve competitive pressures in product and labour markets were to be introduced in Greece, Ireland and Portugal, this might help the necessary price adjustment that needs to take place within the euro area.

Labour market conditions should continue to improve

The pace of the recovery remains dependent on the progress made in tackling slack in labour markets. Labour market conditions are now improving modestly, and for the first time in the post-crisis period unemployment rates are now stable or declining in the majority of OECD economies. Survey measures of hiring intentions are also strengthening (Figure 1.13), and stronger labour demand is now gradually being met

Box 1.5. **Inflation impacts of indirect taxes and administered prices**

In many OECD countries, increases in VAT rates, other indirect taxes and administered prices have raised the level of consumer prices and hence increased headline and core inflation.

The impact of increases in indirect taxes and administered prices can be significant. For example, the weights of goods and services subject to VAT in the CPI are close to 90% in the large advanced OECD economies and the weight of administered prices is around 10% in the euro area.[1] In the extreme case where VAT is levied on all items in the CPI at the standard rate and the increase is fully passed through into prices, a one percentage point increase in the rate of VAT would raise the level of the consumer price index by 0.8 to 1% depending on the initial rate. In practice, producers and distributors may reduce their margins to protect sales. A recent study based on UK experience puts the pass-through of indirect tax increases at 0.5 in the short term (Bank of England, 2010, and OECD, 2011c). By contrast, increases in administered prices have immediate effects.

Recent official estimates in OECD economies indicate that such tax measures have had large effects on consumer prices.

- In the United States, increases in the tobacco tax in the first half of 2009 raised the annual CPI inflation rate by an estimated 0.2 percentage point. Since then, local governments facing fiscal difficulties have increased indirect taxes, including 1 or 1¼ percentage point increases in some state sales taxes, but these moves are too limited to have had any substantial effects on US-wide inflation.

- In the euro area, VAT revenue-raising measures have been taken by periphery countries in 2010 and 2011, with the current 12-month HICP inflation rate 0.4 percentage point higher than the rate measured at constant tax rates that Eurostat calculates with a method which holds the tax rate constant relative to the reference period (Box Figure). If the impact of increases in indirect tax rates has been the same on core inflation, fiscal measures would more than explain the increase in core inflation in the year to January 2011: excluding taxes and administered prices, core inflation in the early months of 2011 may have been close to ½ per cent. If taxes were excluded, core price levels would be broadly stable (Portugal) or falling (Greece, Ireland and Spain).[2] In January 2011, the standard VAT rates have been raised by 2 percentage points in Portugal and two reduced VAT rates have been increased by 1 and 2 percentage points respectively in Greece.[3] Given the weights of Portugal and Greece, these VAT increases are estimated to have raised euro area HICP inflation by 0.1 percentage point.

- In Japan, the effect of an increase in the tobacco tax in 2010 was more than offset by the elimination of tuition fees at public high schools.[4]

- In the United Kingdom, the standard VAT rate has been raised by 2½ percentage points in January this year as well as last year and CPI inflation in March 2011 was 1.7 percentage points higher than when evaluated by consumer prices at constant tax rates.

Administered price inflation is affected everywhere by commodity price increases through regulated energy and transport prices, but the even higher rate of administered price inflation in the EU/IMF programme countries suggests that cost-recovery measures are an additional factor there.

The assessment of underlying inflation needs to take into account that the effects of fiscal measures on annual inflation disappear a year later in most cases. Consequently, the necessity of monetary policy tightening depends on the extent of the second round effects of VAT increases on inflation expectations. In particular, repeated increases in VAT may result in inflation expectations drifting up.

Box 1.5. **Inflation impacts of indirect taxes and administered prices** (cont.)

Inflation in European countries

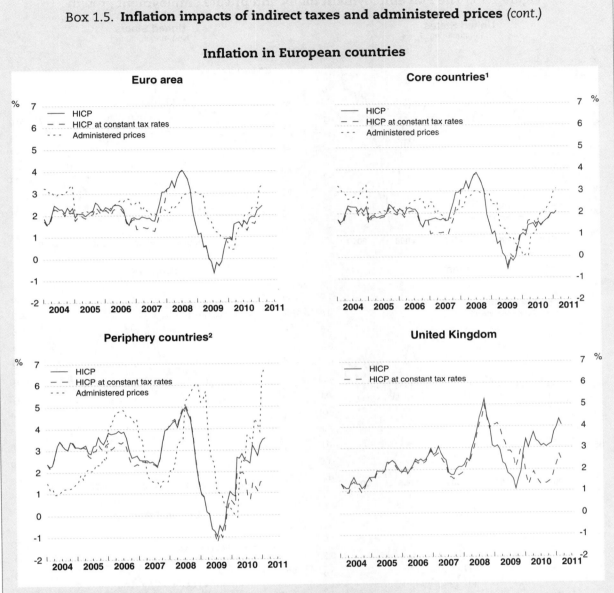

Note: HICP refers to the harmonised index of consumer prices.
1. Core countries include Germany, France and Italy.
2. Periphery countries include Greece, Portugal and Spain and do not include Ireland for which HICP at constant tax rates is not published.
Source: Eurostat; United Kingdom Office for National Statistics.

StatLink http://dx.doi.org/10.1787/888932433915

1. These weights are for goods and services other than standard VAT exemptions. Indirect taxes are levied on some of the standard exemptions and not levied on some items other than the standard exemptions. See OECD (2008b) for more details.
2. In Greece, the annual inflation rate is high, largely reflecting a 4 percentage point increase in the standard VAT rate in 2010, however, the HICP at constant rates indicates that the economy has actually fallen into deflation. In Spain and Portugal, headline HICP inflation rates are about 1 percentage point higher than evaluated at constant rates as a result of 2 and 3 percentage point increases, respectively, in the standard VAT rate since 2010.
3. VAT rates have also been raised in other European countries such as Switzerland, Poland and the Slovak Republic in January 2011.
4. The tax increase, which was accompanied by authorised price increases, raised the price of tobacco by more than 30%.

Figure 1.13. **The PMI employment index and private employment growth**

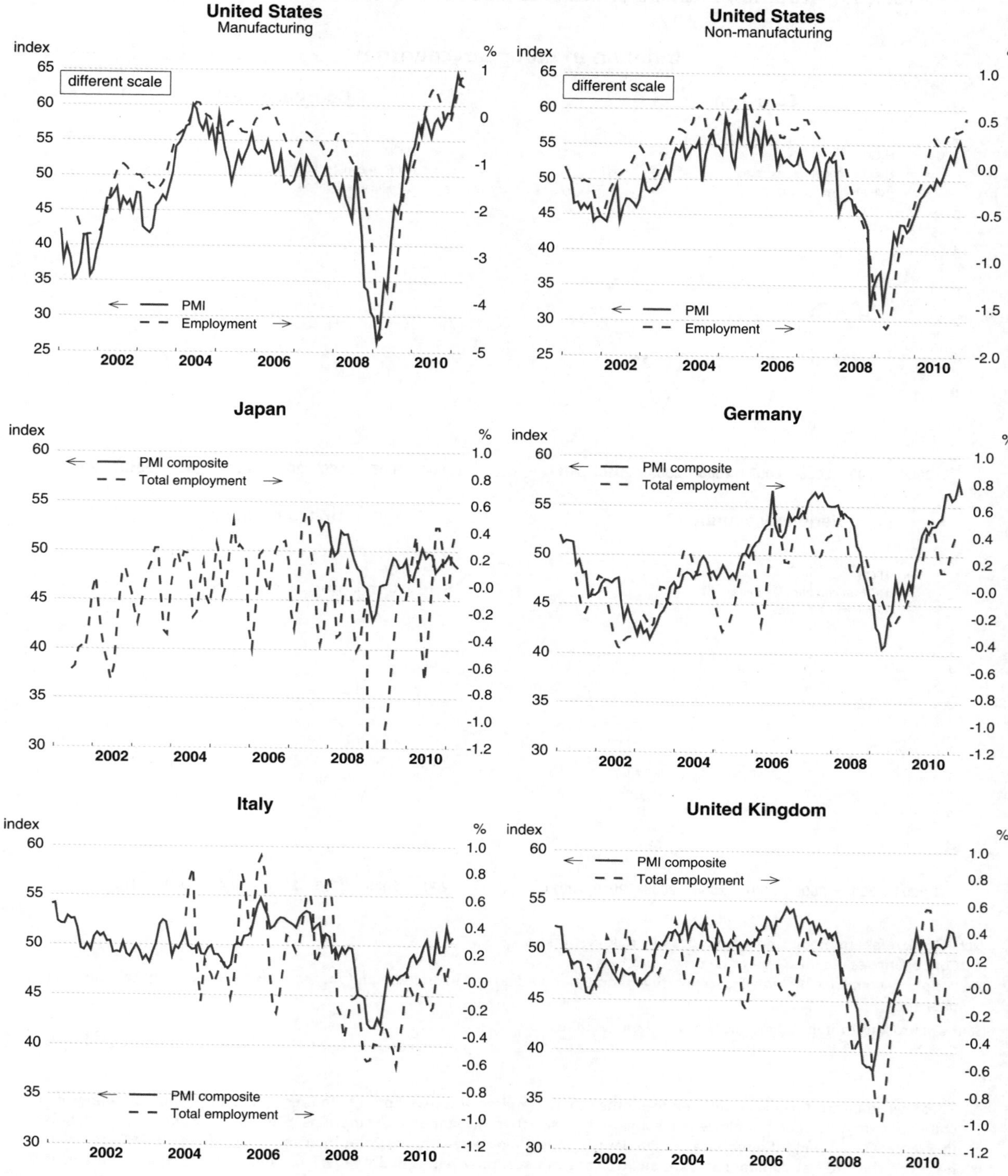

Source: Markit; Bureau of Labour Statistics; BEA; and Datastream.

StatLink http://dx.doi.org/10.1787/888932433934

through new hiring rather than through an increase in hours worked, contrary to the first year of the recovery. Total OECD employment is projected to rise by around 1% this year and 1¼ per cent in 2012 (Table 1.4). With labour force participation rates expected to increase somewhat in most economies, after having held up better in the recent past than in earlier downturns, in part due to structural reforms such as the closing down of early retirement pathways out of the labour market, the OECD-wide unemployment rate is projected to decline to around 7% by the end of 2012 (Figure 1.14). This would still leave a degree of labour market slack in most large OECD economies, helping to keep wage pressures in check, even allowing for the extent to which factors such as higher long-term unemployment and unemployment benefit extensions may have pushed up the natural rate of unemployment in some countries (Guichard and Rusticelli, 2010; Weidner and Williams, 2011). Germany is a striking exception. There, the unemployment rate is already well below pre-crisis levels, helped by earlier labour market reforms and the flexibility provided by short-time working accounts, and is projected to fall by a further percentage point over the projection period. The increasing tightness in German labour markets suggests that wage pressures might strengthen further beyond the projection period. In the United States, the unemployment rate is also projected to decline relatively sharply, reflecting stronger employment growth as well as the impact from the assumed phased reduction in the maximum duration of benefit eligibility through 2012.

Table 1.4. **Labour market conditions will improve slowly**

	2007	2008	2009	2010	2011	2012
	Percentage change from previous period					
Employment						
United States	1.1	-0.5	-3.8	-0.6	0.9	1.9
Euro area	1.8	1.0	-1.8	-0.5	0.3	0.7
Japan	0.5	-0.4	-1.6	-0.4	0.0	-0.2
OECD	1.5	0.6	-1.8	0.3	0.9	1.2
Labour force						
United States	1.1	0.8	-0.1	-0.2	-0.1	0.9
Euro area	0.9	1.0	0.2	0.1	0.1	0.2
Japan	0.2	-0.3	-0.5	-0.4	-0.3	-0.4
OECD	1.0	1.0	0.5	0.5	0.4	0.6
Unemployment rate	Per cent of labour force					
United States	4.6	5.8	9.3	9.6	8.8	7.9
Euro area	7.4	7.4	9.4	9.9	9.7	9.3
Japan	3.8	4.0	5.1	5.1	4.8	4.6
OECD	5.7	6.0	8.2	8.3	7.9	7.4

Source: OECD Economic Outlook 89 database.

StatLink ᴍᴍ🔗 *http://dx.doi.org/10.1787/888932434181*

Structural labour market policies have an important role to play

Structural labour market policies have an important role to play in minimising the potential transformation of cyclical into structural unemployment. In contrast to earlier recessions and recoveries, this issue

Figure 1.14. **Unemployment rates are now declining**
Percentage of labour force

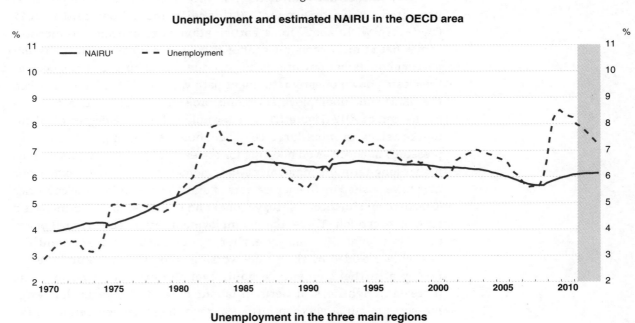

Unemployment and estimated NAIRU in the OECD area

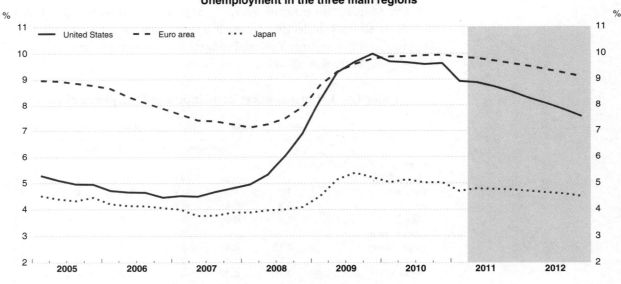

Unemployment in the three main regions

1. NAIRU is based on OECD Secretariat estimates. For the United States, it has not been adjusted for the effect of extended unemployment benefit duration.

Source: OECD Economic Outlook 89 database.

StatLink ⟨ᴍ�S⟩ http://dx.doi.org/10.1787/888932433953

has now also become a concern in the United States, where there has been a long-run downward trend in the outflow rate from unemployment and the mean duration of unemployment remains historically high, with about 44% of the unemployed having been out of work for 27 weeks or more. Reforms that could help to foster near-term employment growth and minimise the employment cost of the recession are discussed in detail in Chapter 5. They include: strengthening public employment services and training programmes to improve the matching of workers and jobs; rebalancing employment protection towards less-strict protection for regular workers, but more protection for temporary workers; and temporary reductions in labour taxation, where feasible through well-targeted marginal job subsidies (for new hires where net jobs are rising) rather than through across-the-board reductions in payroll taxes. Reforms to strengthen competitive pressures in sectors in which there is a strong potential for new job growth, such as retail trade and professional services, could also improve labour market outcomes relatively quickly.

External imbalances remain elevated...

Following substantial narrowing during the crisis, global imbalances are set to remain broadly stable over the projection period (Figure 1.15, Table 1.5). The US external deficit is projected to widen by just over ½ per cent of GDP, and the euro area in aggregate is projected to move into a small external surplus, with ongoing progress in reducing intra-area trade imbalances. The Chinese current account surplus is projected to be around 4½ per cent of GDP, well below earlier peaks, with adverse terms-of-trade effects and a more modest rate of improvement in export performance helping to keep the surplus lower than in the recent past. However, global imbalances will be kept elevated by the large rise projected in the external surpluses of the high-saving non-OECD oil-producing economies, on the back of the elevated level of oil prices. Whilst respending of oil revenues is likely to rise as a result, it will not be sufficient to reduce their surplus significantly. Much of the additional

Figure 1.15. **Global imbalances remain elevated**

Current account balance, in per cent of world GDP

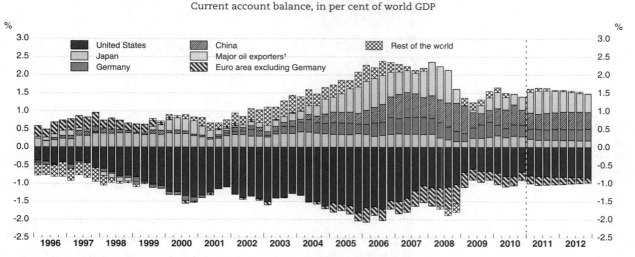

Note: The vertical dotted line separates actual data from forecasts.

1. Include Azerbaijan, Kazakhstan, Turkmenistan, Brunei, Timor-Leste, Bahrain, Iran, Iraq, Kuwait, Libya, Oman, Qatar, Saudi Arabia, United Arab Emirates, Yemen, Ecuador, Trinidad and Tobago, Venezuela, Algeria, Angola, Chad, Rep. of Congo, Equatorial Guinea, Gabon, Nigeria and Sudan.

Source: OECD Economic Outlook 89 database.

StatLink 🔗 http://dx.doi.org/10.1787/888932433972

Table 1.5. **World trade remains robust and imbalances remain elevated**

	2008	2009	2010	2011	2012
Goods and services trade volume	Percentage change from previous period				
World trade[1]	3.1	-10.8	12.5	8.1	8.4
of which: OECD	1.2	-12.2	11.3	6.9	7.5
OECD America	0.8	-12.8	13.1	6.5	8.6
OECD Asia-Pacific	3.3	-12.7	15.3	6.7	9.3
OECD Europe	1.0	-11.8	9.7	7.1	6.6
China	6.5	-4.0	24.8	10.4	12.2
Other industrialised Asia[2]	6.7	-9.7	16.6	9.6	9.4
Russia	7.0	-17.2	14.6	11.8	8.2
Brazil	7.8	-10.9	24.4	15.6	12.7
Other oil producers	8.7	-3.6	1.5	9.8	10.1
Rest of the world	7.3	-10.6	8.5	11.8	7.0
OECD exports	2.0	-11.7	11.3	7.5	7.7
OECD imports	0.5	-12.5	11.1	6.3	7.3
Trade prices[3]					
OECD exports	9.0	-9.1	2.7	10.3	2.2
OECD imports	11.1	-11.2	3.9	11.7	2.2
Non-OECD exports	14.7	-13.7	10.9	15.4	2.7
Non-OECD imports	12.0	-9.8	10.1	11.8	2.4
Current account balances	Per cent of GDP				
United States	-4.7	-2.7	-3.2	-3.7	-4.0
Japan	3.3	2.8	3.6	2.6	2.5
Euro area	-0.7	0.0	0.2	0.3	0.8
OECD	-1.5	-0.5	-0.6	-0.7	-0.7
China	9.1	5.2	5.2	4.5	4.4
	$ billion				
United States	-669	-378	-470	-568	-631
Japan	158	143	195	152	151
Euro area	-97	9	21	42	107
OECD	-660	-197	-252	-347	-365
China	412	261	305	318	362
Other industrialised Asia[2]	89	137	109	120	137
Russia	104	49	71	133	130
Brazil	-28	-24	-48	-47	-58
Other oil producers	484	99	226	429	406
Rest of the world	-194	-86	-106	-186	-195
Non-OECD	867	434	558	765	782
World	207	237	306	419	416

Note: Regional aggregates include intra-regional trade.
1. Growth rates of the arithmetic average of import volumes and export volumes.
2. Chinese Taipei; Hong Kong, China; Malaysia; Philippines; Singapore: Vietnam; Thailand; India and Indonesia.
3. Average unit values in dollars.
Source: OECD Economic Outlook 89 database.

StatLink ᴍᴤ᰷ http://dx.doi.org/10.1787/888932434200

revenue accrued is likely to be saved, as appropriate for countries in which oil reserves are being depleted gradually. This is likely to remain particularly relevant beyond the short term, as oil prices are likely to rise as the resource is depleted.

... but could be narrowed by structural reforms

Further reductions in imbalances will likely require exchange rate flexibility, as well as structural reforms and fiscal adjustments. Structural reforms could help to address the underlying determinants of global and euro area external imbalances over the medium term through their impact on national saving and investment rates (OECD, 2011a). In particular, measures to stimulate investment in external surplus economies by reducing product market regulations in sheltered sectors, in conjunction with measures to improve social welfare systems and liberalise financial markets (while ensuring adequate prudential regulation) in non-OECD economies with an external surplus, could help to narrow global imbalances in the years ahead.[4] Likewise, improvements to product and labour market flexibility in the euro area external deficit countries could moreover facilitate the necessary adjustment of the real exchange rate and the internal allocation of resources in these countries (Barnes, 2010). Fiscal consolidation could also help to bring about sizable reductions in both global and intra-euro area imbalances, with consolidation needs generally larger in external deficit OECD countries than in external surplus ones.

Risks

Risks remain elevated

Significant and numerous risks remain around the projection, even though the downside risks of widespread weakness in private sector activity following the ending of fiscal support measures, and of possible deflation, have now receded. On the upside, the risks are largely economic ones, endogenous to the pace of the expansion. In contrast, on the downside, risks are more diverse, either being endogenous to the pace of the recovery or being associated with the possibility of particular events that could trigger renewed weakness in activity. Finally, some of the risks identified are two-sided. For example, oil prices may rise or fall back during the projection period, and sovereign debt tensions in the euro area may either rise or fade more rapidly than expected. And while the earthquake in Japan and its aftermath represents a negative risk in the short term, further reconstruction packages could hasten the rebound.

On the upside...

At present, key positive risks include:

... the recovery may have more momentum...

● The possibility that the recovery in private sector final demand could gain greater momentum than projected, especially if household and business confidence were to strengthen further as the recovery progresses and lingering uncertainty about the durability of the recovery was to moderate still further. In particular, after a period of restraint, purchases of consumer durables, especially cars, could go above trend as household confidence strengthens. Scope also remains

4. A scenario analysis indicates that the necessary fiscal tightening required to stabilise debt-to-GDP ratios in OECD countries by 2025 could reduce the size of global imbalances – measured as the GDP-weighted sum of countries' ratios of absolute saving-investment gaps to GDP – by almost one-sixth. If, in addition, Japan, Germany and China were to deregulate their product markets, aligning the level of economy-wide product market regulation with OECD best practice, and China were to raise public health spending by 2 percentage points of GDP (in a fiscally neutral way) and liberalise its financial markets, global imbalances could decline by twice as much (OECD, 2011a). Sizable exchange rate change is also incorporated in this scenario.

for business investment to expand more strongly than in the main projection.

... and structural reforms could have short-run benefits

- Although relatively few growth-friendly structural reforms have been undertaken since the recovery began, it remains the case that the enactment of such policies, as recommended in OECD (2011a), could also provide a boost to the recovery in the near term. This could occur if the future beneficial effects of new reforms on activity and government debt ratios were to be incorporated into forward-looking asset prices, helping to strengthen balance sheets and support aggregate demand, or if reforms helped to improve near-term labour market outcomes. Structural reforms to boost product market competition and depeen financial markets would also boost growth prospects in the non-OECD economies.

On the downside, key risks stem from...

There is a broad range of possible downside risks around the projections. Some of these are applicable to all economies, but others are specific to the euro area. At present key downside risks include:

... further increases in oil prices...

- A broadening of political instability in the MENA region could raise oil prices substantially further. As past episodes, such as the first Gulf War in 1990-91, have demonstrated, instability in a major oil producer can quickly lead to a large spike in oil prices, particularly as the short-run price demand and supply elasticities for oil are low and spare capacity can shrink rapidly. This would magnify the adverse effects on incomes and demand of the recent oil price increase (discussed above), whilst intensifying the upward pressures on headline inflation. Heightened geopolitical uncertainty could add to these downside effects and lead to a broader pull-back in risk taking in financial markets. Higher oil prices would also further widen global imbalances, by increasing the already elevated external surpluses of high-saving oil producing economies and possibly place downward pressure on real interest rates by altering the *ex-ante* balance between global saving and investment.

... a delayed recovery in Japan...

- In Japan, there is a possibility that the adverse consequences of the earthquake and its aftermath could prove greater or more prolonged than expected, especially if power shortages and supply-chain disruptions persist. This would be likely to damage household and business confidence further, with adverse effects on domestic demand, and also damp global activity somewhat, especially for producers in other countries that rely on specialised inputs from Japan that cannot be sourced from elsewhere.

... and a deeper slowdown in China

- In China, there are risks that policy actions prompted by rising inflation and rapid asset price growth could result in activity slowing by more than projected. In the near term, activity could moderate sharply if the tightening of monetary conditions over the past year proves to have been more marked than necessary to damp price pressures. Alternatively, if past tightening is insufficient, inflationary pressures are likely to build further, ultimately necessitating strong further policy actions and raising a risk of a much deeper slowdown in the medium term.

Financial vulnerabilities could arise from exposures to sovereign debt in the euro area...

- Significant financial vulnerabilities remain, especially in Europe. The sovereign risk spreads over Germany remain elevated in the EU/IMF programme countries (Greece, Ireland and Portugal; Figure 1.16 and Box 1.4) and also, but to a more limited extent, in some larger countries (Belgium, Italy and Spain). Concern about the value of government bonds is tied closely to fears about banks' solvency, reflecting the large exposures of many European banks to sovereign bonds, *de jure* or *de facto* government commitments to stand behind banks and the lack of a clear EU infrastructure to deal with bank and sovereign default. If disorderly debt restructuring were to occur, contagion to the core of the

Figure 1.16. **Sovereign spreads remain very high for peripheral euro area countries**

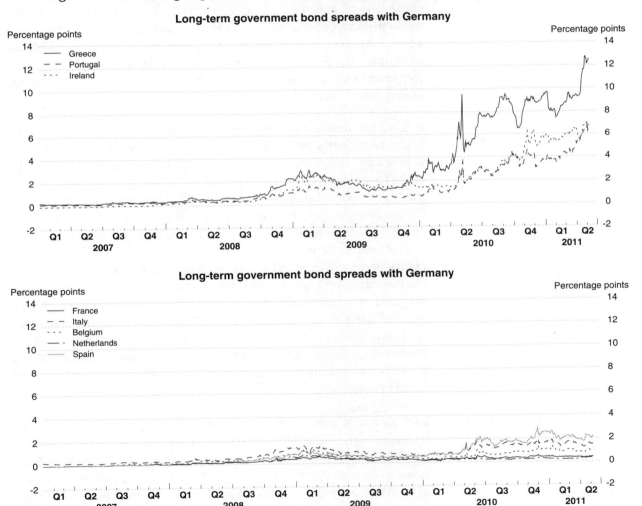

Source: Datastream.

StatLink http://dx.doi.org/10.1787/888932433991

euro area financial system could not be ruled out, with adverse effects on activity and heightened risk aversion globally (Blundell-Wignall and Slovik, 2010). In this event, there could also be adverse fiscal effects in the core countries if further support for the banking system were required, and risks to the credibility of monetary policy, given likely large hits to the ECB balance sheet.

... and the United States and Japan...
- The unsettled fiscal situation in the United States and Japan also remains a cause for concern. Fiscal consolidation is clearly required in both economies given high and rising public debt levels. In the United States, political problems make fiscal policy almost unpredictable. In the near term, should excessively abrupt consolidation be implemented, the recovery could be endangered. In Japan, fiscal policies in the near term are subject to uncertainty about the scale, timing and financing of reconstruction spending; a lack of political consensus on specific measures to employ to attain the goals of the medium-term consolidation plan is a further source of uncertainty. If additional reconstruction packages prove necessary to support the economy, they should be accompanied by clear and detailed communication on the measures to be adopted in the medium-term consolidation plans.

... and renewed weakness in housing markets...
- A lingering downside risk stems from the large exposures of many banks to property markets with ongoing price weakness and excess supply and, at the other extreme, to markets in which prices may be close to peaking.[5] In the United States, the prices of residential mortgage-backed securities have so far held up to the renewed falls in US property prices, but the risk of a strong correction cannot be excluded if this weakness in the US property sector were to become deeper and more entrenched. In other economies, such as Canada, France and Sweden, in which house prices have rebounded rapidly in the context of very low interest rates and house price-to-rent ratios are elevated compared with historical norms, there is some risk of a marked price correction (Box 1.6). While this possibility need not threaten banking sector stability in the short run, especially if prudential policies are being applied effectively, there remains a risk it could lead eventually to large adverse balance sheet effects and banking stress.

... and commercial property markets
- Banking sector exposures to commercial property markets also remain a clear concern, especially in the euro area and the United Kingdom. As noted in the December *Financial Stability Review* by the ECB and the *Financial Stability Report* of the Bank of England, a significant proportion of commercial property mortgages remain in negative equity, with ongoing risks of possible losses for the banking sector.

5. At the onset of the crisis, foreign banks accounted for 29% of total exposure to securitised US non-conforming loans (Beltran *et al.*, 2008).

Box 1.6. **Peaks and troughs in real house prices**

Prior to the financial crisis, OECD work (Box 1.3. in *Economic Outlook* No. 79; van den Noord, 2006) suggested that real prices in several housing markets in the OECD area had become increasingly vulnerable to a change in financial and economic conditions, with the risk of a subsequent downturn becoming increasingly possible, as proved to be the case. With corrections in many, but not all, housing markets having now occurred, and, in some countries, prices having risen rapidly in the low interest rate environment, the issue of whether prices are now close to another turning point is again of considerable policy interest. For countries in which price corrections are still ongoing, it is useful to explore whether the correction will be completed and recovery will begin. For countries where corrections have been completed, or where corrections did not materialise, it is useful to examine when a (next) peak will be reached.

As one means of addressing this issue, separate probit models have been estimated to provide an indication of possible peaks and troughs in real house prices in 2011 or 2012, using data for 20 OECD countries (Rousova and van den Noord, 2011). The definition of peaks and troughs used here is set out in the note of the accompanying table. The explanatory variables used in the models include the estimated gap between actual and trend real house prices, real house price growth in the recent past, the number of peaks in real house prices in other OECD countries, the interest rate, inflation, residential investment and the unemployment gap.

To obtain the predictions, two different scenarios have been assumed. In the first (scenario 1), real house prices are assumed to be constant from the last observed quarter onwards (see main text, Table 1.2). In the second scenario (scenario 2), real house prices are assumed to either fall or increase by 10% over the projection period – depending on whether prices are either falling or rising up to the last observed quarter. The path of the main explanatory variables used in the model is set to be consistent with the projections in this *Economic Outlook*.

The main results from these exercises are summarised below (see also the Table). The range of scenarios applied provides some indication of the underlying robustness of the conclusions drawn, although false alarms can also be prevalent in these forms of models (Crespo Cuaresma, 2010). The main results are:

● The countries in which real house prices peaked prior to the financial crisis and have been in a downturn since are: Denmark, Greece, Ireland, Italy, Korea, the Netherlands, New Zealand, Spain, the United Kingdom and the United States. Of these, Greece, Ireland and Spain are predicted to see troughs in 2011 or 2012 in both scenarios. For the two euro area programme countries, this result partly hinges on the assumed fall in bond yield spreads in the main projection (see Box 1.3). Without this, the likely troughs would be pushed back beyond the projection period. In the United States, a trough in real house prices is predicted only in scenario 2.

● The countries experiencing upswings in real house prices which have not yet been completed are: Australia, Belgium, Canada, Finland, France, Norway, Sweden and Switzerland. In Sweden, a peak in real prices is predicted to occur in 2011 or 2012 in both scenarios. Amongst the other countries in this group, a peak is signaled in Australia, Belgium, Canada, France and Norway only in scenario 2.

● There are two countries, Japan and Germany, where real house prices have been in long-term decline. In the case of Japan, there is a significant likelihood that real house prices may finally trough in scenario 2. For Germany, even though prices have picked up somewhat since 2008, the analysis does not signal a trough in either scenario.

Box 1.6. **Peaks and troughs in real house prices** (*cont.*)

Predicted real house price peaks and troughs in 2011-12
Summary of analytical results

	Consistent signal across scenarios	Signal of trough / peak in one scenario only
Predicted troughs in 2011 and/or 2012	United States Greece Ireland Spain	Denmark Italy Japan Korea New Zealand
Predicted peaks in 2011 and/or 2012	Sweden	Australia Belgium Canada France Norway
Neither peaks nor troughs predicted in 2011 or 2012	Germany Finland Netherlands Switzerland United Kingdom	

Note: Peaks (troughs) as predicted by the probit models.

A peak (trough) is called if real house prices for six quarters prior and after the peak (trough) are below (over) the price at the peak (trough) and when the cumulative price increase (decrease) between the nearest preceding trough (peak) and the peak (trough) is at least 15 (7.5) per cent and the cumulative price decrease (increase) between the peak (trough) and the following though (peak) is at least 7.5 (15) per cent. For the two different scenarios, see text in the box.

Source: OECD Economic Outlook 89 database; Datastream; and various national sources.

StatLink 🔗 http://dx.doi.org/10.1787/888932434238

The interaction of different downside risks could be particularly costly

The downside risks are not fully independent of each other. Indeed, their interaction could trigger a mild stagflation-type outcome in the OECD economies, if further increases in headline inflation from adverse supply-side shocks were to result in inflation expectations becoming unanchored, and damp activity for a prolonged period. For example, further additional increases in oil prices could raise inflation expectations, with the resulting increase in interest rates undermining banking stability and public finances. In such a scenario, output growth would be weaker than projected, and most likely well below trend rates, and inflation would be clearly above the inflation objective of the monetary authorities. It would prove difficult for conventional macroeconomic policies to offer much support in such circumstances.

Policy responses and requirements

Macroeconomic and financial policy normalisation is required...

With the recovery becoming more self-sustained and slowly gaining momentum, key policy priorities are to support the recovery and keep projected inflation close to target whilst implementing growth-friendly medium-term consolidation plans and gradually normalising monetary policies. Policies should also take into account the importance of current uncertainties and remain ready to adjust as necessary. Internationally co-ordinated financial reforms should also be pursued to enhance financial market resilience.

... augmented by structural reforms

As discussed above, the implementation of well-designed structural reforms is also essential if the recovery is to strengthen in a balanced and sustainable manner. In the context of the recovery, priority should be given to reforms that offer the most likely prospects of strengthening near-term growth and which help the unemployed remain in close contact with the labour market. Given the backdrop of impaired public finances, reforms should be consistent with the need to strengthen confidence in the sustainability of public sector debt dynamics. In so doing, they could result in lower long-term interest rates than would otherwise be the case. In the medium term, successful structural reforms also could yield important fiscal benefits, in addition to the benefits they could have on per capita incomes. Growth-enhancing structural reforms are also needed to moderate external imbalances, both at the global level and within the euro area.

Fiscal Policy

Large consolidation is required in most OECD countries

Fiscal deficits remain high in many OECD countries...

The stance of fiscal policy differs markedly across countries in the projections. In 2011, in line with government plans, the underlying budget deficit is projected to remain roughly stable in the United States. In Japan, where fiscal developments are surrounded by uncertainty about the scale, timing and financing of reconstruction spending, the OECD's assumptions imply a modest decline in the underlying balance. By contrast, in the euro area and most other OECD countries sizable consolidation is projected (Table 1.6).[6] In 2012, given the large degree of political uncertainty about fiscal developments in the United States, the OECD has assumed some tightening (see below), leaving a headline deficit of about 9% of GDP. A modest tightening has also been assumed in Japan, leading to a deficit of around 8¼ per cent. In most other OECD countries underlying balances are projected to improve in 2012, on the basis of official plans, with the budget deficit declining to close to 3% of GDP on average for the OECD area excluding the United States and Japan. Nonetheless, for most OECD countries, general government debt is set to continue drifting up as a proportion of GDP over the next couple of years as a result of large underlying deficits, still moderate economic growth and mounting interest payments.

6.   The decomposition of fiscal balances into cyclical and underlying components is subject to heightened uncertainty, however, as the impact of the crisis on potential output remains unclear.

Table 1.6. **Fiscal positions will improve in coming years**
Per cent of GDP / Potential GDP

	2008	2009	2010	2011	2012
United States					
Actual balance	-6.3	-11.3	-10.6	-10.1	-9.1
Underlying balance	-5.9	-8.7	-8.6	-8.7	-8.2
Underlying primary balance	-4.2	-7.3	-7.0	-6.8	-5.8
Gross financial liabilities	71.0	84.3	93.6	101.1	107.0
Euro area					
Actual balance	-2.1	-6.3	-6.0	-4.2	-3.0
Underlying balance	-2.2	-4.2	-3.5	-2.5	-1.9
Underlying primary balance	0.5	-1.8	-1.1	0.0	0.9
Gross financial liabilities	76.5	86.9	92.7	95.6	96.5
Japan					
Actual balance	-2.2	-8.7	-8.1	-8.9	-8.2
Underlying balance	-3.5	-7.2	-6.9	-6.4	-5.9
Underlying primary balance	-2.6	-6.1	-5.5	-4.9	-4.2
Gross financial liabilities	174.1	194.1	199.7	212.7	218.7
OECD[1]					
Actual balance[1]	-3.3	-8.2	-7.7	-6.7	-5.6
Underlying balance[2]	-3.8	-6.4	-6.1	-5.7	-5.0
Underlying primary balance[2]	-2.0	-4.8	-4.4	-3.7	-2.8
Gross financial liabilities[2,3]	79.3	90.9	97.6	102.4	105.4

Note: Actual balances and liabilities are in per cent of nominal GDP. Underlying balances are in per cent of potential GDP and they refer to fiscal balances adjusted for the cycle and for one-offs. Underlying primary balance is the underlying balance excluding net debt interest payments.
1. Excludes Chile and Mexico.
2. Excludes Chile, Mexico and Turkey.
3. See Box 1.3 for the treatment of gross financial liabilities in Greece, Ireland and Portugal.
Source: OECD Economic Outlook 89 database.

StatLink ⧉ http://dx.doi.org/10.1787/888932434219

... requiring significant consolidation to arrest and reverse increases in the debt ratio

For most OECD countries with large underlying deficits, economic growth on its own will not suffice to stabilise debt-to-GDP ratios, let alone to reduce them. Correspondingly, reducing debt ratios to pre-crisis levels or below will require unprecedented consolidation efforts. Subject to the stylised assumptions on growth and interest rates made in the long-term baseline scenario reported in Chapter 4, attaining pre-crisis debt-to-GDP ratios by 2026 would require improvements in underlying primary balances of 6½ per cent of (potential) GDP for the typical (median) OECD country, and 15% or more for *inter alia* the United States, Japan and the United Kingdom. Sales of public sector assets could enable some gross debt to be retired, but careful *ex ante* evaluation would be required (Box 1.7). Historically, high debt levels have often been brought down by high inflation. However, as shown in Box 1.8, high inflation rates would not materially reduce the debt burden given the current maturity structure of public debt.

Public finances are relatively healthy in emerging markets

In emerging market economies, fiscal positions vary considerably, though in most cases they are better than in the majority of OECD countries, not least because high growth rates tend to ease debt dynamics. In China, the deficit and debt of the government sector are low.

Box 1.7. **Government assets and net debt**

The sustainability of general government fiscal positions is usually assessed based on gross debt as opposed to net debt, which is defined as the difference between gross debt and financial assets. This is conceptually dubious as taking government assets into consideration, fiscal positions might actually be better than indicated by gross debt levels alone. In particular, asset sales could help restore fiscal sustainability, depending on the size and composition of assets and associated rates of return.

Government financial assets consist commonly of securities, currency and deposits, loans and other assets. Shares of these categories vary considerably across the OECD countries (see first figure). Total securities are the largest category for most OECD countries, accounting on average for a half of total financial assets. They include mainly shares and other equity (an average 40% of total assets) and securities other than shares, like bills, bonds and certificates of deposit, whose nominal value is determined on issue (on average 10% of total assets). Following the System of National Accounts (SNA) convention, shares are valued at current market prices, and if those are not available they are estimated. Currency and deposits comprise on average 20% of total assets, while loans – mainly long-term – account on average for 10%. Other assets account on average for 20% of total financial assets. They include primarily financial claims that arise from timing differences between accrued transactions and payments made for items such as taxes, wages, interest, etc. In some countries, trade credits and advances as well as monetary gold and special drawing rights (SDRs) held outside the central bank are also important.[1]

Composition of financial assets, 2009 (% of the total)

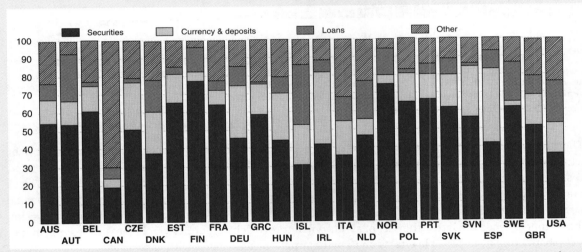

Note: See the text in the box for definitions of the included categories of financial assets. Assets are consolidated across layers of government.

Source: Eurostat, Quarterly financial accounts for general government; and OECD, System of National Accounts.

StatLink ᵃᵍᵉ http://dx.doi.org/10.1787/888932434010

OECD countries differ considerably with respect to the level of general government financial assets, with Finland, Iceland, Japan, Korea, Norway and Sweden recording levels in terms of GDP between 70% (Korea) to 200% (Norway) and the other countries around 40% of GDP (2009; see second figure). Accordingly, in 2009 the (unweighted) OECD average of net debt totalled 22% of GDP, while gross debt stood at 72% of GDP. In ten countries net debt was zero or even negative. In part, sizeable asset levels reflect the response to the financial crisis, as financial assets in the government sector increased substantially due to the recapitalisation or take-over of financial institutions. Indeed, financial assets increased by between 10 and 26% of GDP in Canada, Denmark, Iceland, Ireland, the Netherlands and the United Kingdom between 2007 and 2009.

Box 1.7. **Government assets and net debt** (*cont.*)

General government debt and financial assets in OECD countries, 2009 (% of GDP)

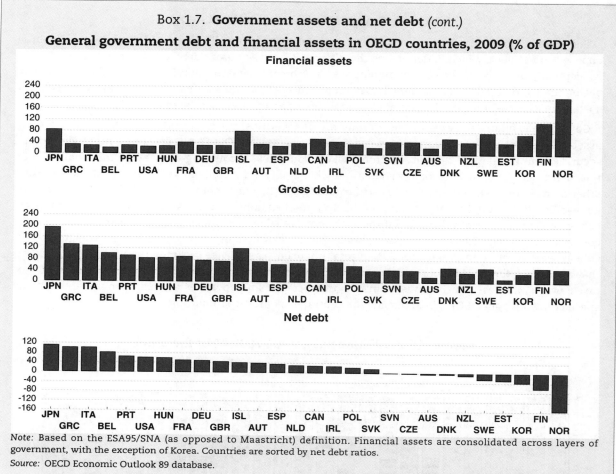

Note: Based on the ESA95/SNA (as opposed to Maastricht) definition. Financial assets are consolidated across layers of government, with the exception of Korea. Countries are sorted by net debt ratios.

Source: OECD Economic Outlook 89 database.

StatLink ⫘ http://dx.doi.org/10.1787/888932434029

The proceeds from selling financial assets can be used to reduce gross debt, while leaving net debt unchanged. This implies a reduction in debt servicing costs, and possibly reductions in government bond rates, if markets perceive the improvement in the fiscal stance as a marked step towards fiscal sustainability. However, the sale of assets also eliminates income earned on them. The net effect depends, *inter alia*, on the difference between the interest rate paid on debt and the rate of return earned on assets. If the former exceeds the latter, the sale of assets will improve debt dynamics via the net interest payments effect (abstracting from possible effects on GDP that might be associated with asset sales).

However, selling financial assets might not be desirable or immediately possible given market conditions, the composition of assets and policy objectives. Privatisation programmes should be based on cost-benefit analysis, taking into account existing market failures in the sectors involved and the potential for absorbing sales without excessive discounts, rather than be driven solely by debt-reduction objectives. In some cases, reserves have been built to cover future implicit liabilities related to pensions and thus should not be liquidated. Also, from a debt management perspective it may be prudent to hold assets as a cushion. In addition, it may take time before long-term loans are paid back. Consequently, it is difficult to assess the scope of asset sales, although in several countries the governments' equity participations in banks are likely to be unwound over time. As a stylised illustration, the table below shows gross debt reductions, for countries with debt exceeding 75% of GDP in 2009 or being fiscally stressed, that would prevail if all securities, or all shares, were sold (Japan is not included due to missing data). For most countries, such sales would not be enough to reduce gross debt to pre-crisis (2007) levels. The situation is even worse when assessed on the basis of 2010 data, with gross debt in many of these countries estimated to have increased by more than assets.

Box 1.7. **Government assets and net debt** *(cont.)*

Stylised gross debt reductions via financial asset sales, 2009

Per cent of GDP

| | Gross debt (A) | Financial assets | | | (A)-(C) | (A)-(D) |
		Total (B)	Total securities (C)	Shares and other equity (D)		
Belgium	100	20	12	10	88	90
Canada	83	55	11	5	73	79
France	89	36	23	21	66	68
Germany	76	28	13	10	64	66
Greece	132	31	17	17	114	115
Hungary	85	26	12	11	73	73
Iceland	120	80	25	25	95	95
Ireland	72	45	19	13	53	59
Italy	128	28	10	9	118	119
Portugal	93	29	19	18	74	75
Spain	62	28	12	9	51	53
United Kingdom	72	30	16	14	57	59
United States	84	25	9	3	75	82

Note: Total securities include securities other than shares and shares and other equity. Financial assets are consolidated across layers of government.
Source: Eurostat, Quarterly financial accounts for general government; and OECD, System of National Accounts.

StatLink http://dx.doi.org/10.1787/888932434257

The scope for reducing gross debt would widen if non-financial assets were taken into consideration as well. They usually include residential and non-residential buildings, machinery and equipment (classified as tangible fixed assets), copyrights, patents, computer software (intangible fixed assets) and land (tangible non-produced assets). Data coverage is however very patchy across countries and across specific asset categories, as many governments do not have an appropriate inventory and the valuation of these assets at market prices is challenging. For those countries which publish complete data on non-financial assets (including Australia, the Czech Republic, France and the United Kingdom), these assets are much larger than financial assets. Clearly, as with financial assets, not all of them could and should be for sale. However, continuing fiscal stress in many OECD countries should be taken as an opportunity to evaluate if such assets should be sold. Greece is an example in this regard. Under the financial aid agreement, the Greek government has committed to compile a fixed-asset inventory and implement a privatisation and real estate development programme worth 50 billion euro (22% of 2010 GDP). Beyond current needs to lower gross debt, a full account of government non-financial assets is desirable also for a comprehensive assessment of government asset holdings and the efficiency of public asset use.

1. While the central bank is outside the general government sector, under some circumstances gold might be held within the government sector. This is the case for the United Kingdom (4% of total financial assets) and the United States (2% of financial assets).

Although off-budget spending by government-backed investment companies expanded sharply during the global slowdown, the government has begun to rein in this form of stimulus. However, the impact on the economy will be offset to some extent by a new subsidised housing programme. Some modest consolidation has taken place in India and continued reductions of high deficits are planned. Consolidation has also been announced in Brazil and the Russian Federation, whereas a broadly neutral fiscal stance is projected for Indonesia and South Africa.

Planned fiscal consolidation in the short and medium term

The state of public finances differs across OECD countries

In the majority of OECD countries, phased consolidation has started either in 2010 or from the beginning of 2011, which appears appropriate given the unprecedented size of fiscal imbalances and the outlook for activity. In a few OECD countries (notably Estonia, Finland, Norway, Sweden and Switzerland) there is no or little need for consolidation.

The situation is serious and consolidation prospects are uncertain...

Notwithstanding high and rising debt in the United States and Japan, the budget outlook is particularly uncertain in these countries:

... in the United States...

- In the United States, after a long period of political discussion, legislation of the budget for fiscal year 2011 (which started in October 2010) passed Congress at the end of April. Based on this legislation, the underlying general government deficit is projected to remain roughly unchanged. However, there is no consensus on fiscal consolidation strategies, which casts doubt on the extent to which the President's budget proposal for next year will be adopted.[7] Therefore, the projection assumes that the consolidation will amount to 1 percentage point of GDP, following standard procedures used in such circumstances (Box 1.3). This would still leave government finances in a highly unsustainable position, risking serious adverse reactions in financial markets. Hence, a larger degree of fiscal tightening than assumed here would be appropriate, taking into consideration that the economy has yet to fully recover from its cyclical trough. A well articulated medium-term consolidation strategy aimed at putting general government finances on a sustainable path also needs to be agreed as a matter of urgency and with sufficiently wide support to give it credibility. Given the scale of the required consolidation, such a plan would have to include all the big categories of expenditure, notably entitlement spending and defence outlays as well as revenue increases. In view of the rapid rise of public debt and the need to make plans credible, any plan should contain up-front measures.

... and Japan

- In Japan, the government's Fiscal Management Strategy (FMS), announced in June 2010, aims to halve the primary deficit of the central and local governments by fiscal year (FY) 2015 and eliminating it by FY 2020. Towards this end, the FMS calls for keeping central government primary spending (i.e. excluding debt repayments and interest) in FY 2011-13 below the initial budget for FY 2010, and limiting bond issuance in FY 2011-12 to that in FY 2010. The initial reconstruction package announced by the government in April 2011 is

---

7. The US Congressional Budget Office estimated in March 2011 that the President's budget proposal would reduce the federal deficit from 9.9% of GDP in 2011 to 7% in 2012 (CBO, 2011). The estimates incorporate the assumption that, as scheduled under current law, the provisions of the 2010 Tax Act terminate in 2012.

Box 1.8. **Inflation and debt dynamics**

In the context of high and rising public debt in many OECD countries, the possibility of eroding debt-to-GDP ratios (debt ratios) through higher inflation has been discussed.[1] Indeed, unsustainable debt positions in the past have often been "solved" by higher inflation. However, this box shows that in current circumstances higher inflation would not make significant inroads into high debt burdens, and could have negative side effects.

Higher inflation lowers the debt level in real terms but it also increases the nominal cost of debt servicing when nominal interest rates are rising with inflation. The latter effect is stronger with a higher debt turnover (*i.e.* shorter maturity). Whether the real cost of debt servicing rises or falls depends on whether nominal interest rates increase by more or less than inflation.

The first table below illustrates how the debt ratio changes with higher inflation given different debt turnover assumptions. This exercise assumes a permanent inflation increase of 1 percentage point which is immediately and fully reflected in all nominal interest rates. The calculations are done for a stylised economy that has initial debt and asset ratios of 100% and 25% respectively, with a real rate of growth and inflation in the baseline of 2%, and the cost of debt at 4% (see notes under the table). These parameters are stylised but correspond to projected characteristics of many OECD countries in the current decade. The assumed different debt repayment profiles attempt to reflect varied maturity structures in the OECD countries (see second table). For the sake of simplicity, the primary balance and the maturity structure do not react to higher inflation.

In this setup, the inflation shock lowers the debt ratio after ten years by between 5 percentage points (with high debt turnover) and 9 percentage points (with low debt turnover). This result is primarily driven by the decline in the real stock of debt and the delayed pass-through of higher nominal interest rates to the actual cost of debt, stemming from the assumed debt turnover parameters. It suggests that a sustained increase in inflation by 2 percentage points would be required over a 10-year period to erode the average crisis-induced increase in the debt ratio in the OECD area, which totalled around 20 percentage points between 2007 and 2010.

Impact of a 1-percentage point increase in inflation on the debt ratio after 10 years with different debt turnover parameters

per cent of GDP

| The annual turnover of initial debt from the 2nd year onwards[2] | The difference between the alternative and baseline scenario in the debt ratio after 10 years[1] | | | |
| | The share of initial debt maturing in the 1st year | | | |
	10%	20%	30%	40%
5 %	-9.2	-8.5	-7.9	-7.2
10 %	-7.8	-7.1	-6.5	-6.0
15 %	-6.7	-6.2	-5.8	-5.4
20 %	-6.2	-5.8	-5.4	-5.1
25 %	-5.8	-5.5	-5.2	-4.9

1. The baseline hypothetical scenario assumes that: *i*) initial debt and assets (*i.e.* in the year prior to the inflation shock – year t_0) are equal to 100% and 25% of GDP, respectively; *ii*) the implied cost of debt in year t_0 is 4.1%; *iii*) during the ten years after year t_0 the primary balance is zero, nominal GDP grows at 4%, GDP deflator increases by 2%, the interest rate earned on assets is 2.3%, and long and short-term interest rates are 5.5% and 4.0%, respectively; *iv*) in the first year of the inflation shock, initial debt turns over in the proportions indicated in the heading row, in subsequent years, it matures annually by a constant share indicated in the first column; *v*) new debt (*i.e.* debt issued after year t_0) matures annually in equal proportions as indicated in the first column; *vi*) interest payments on initial debt are proportional to the implied cost of debt in year t_0 and the share of remaining debt in a given year; *vi*) interest payments on new debt start only after one year and in any given year they are proportional to interest rates in the year of issuance and the share of remaining debt; *viii*) interest rates on new debt depend on maturity – the short-term interest rate is paid on 1-year debt, the long-term interest rate is paid on 10-year debt and the linear combination of short and long-term rates is paid on debt of any other maturity. In the alternative scenario, inflation (in terms of GDP deflator) and all interest rates are increased permanently by 1 percentage point over ten years.
2. For some combinations of maturity parameters, in the last year of debt life, the turnover share may be smaller than indicated.

Source: OECD.

StatLink ⌨ http://dx.doi.org/10.1787/888932434276

Box 1.8. **Inflation and debt dynamics** (cont.)

While there are economic benefits from lower real debt, resorting to higher inflation also involves many potential adverse effects that are not accounted for in the stylised calculations in the first table. High and persistent inflation could affect macroeconomic stability negatively and damp real growth by raising price and exchange rate volatility, reducing real money balances and increasing the dispersion of relative prices. The precise magnitude of these effects is however uncertain. In such an environment, it is also likely that investors would demand more short-term and inflation–indexed instruments. In some OECD countries, current maturities are already relatively short and the share of inflation-indexed bonds is not negligible (see the second table). In addition, there is large uncertainty regarding the authorities' capability to generate higher, but still stable, inflation without de-anchoring inflation expectations. With de-anchored inflation expectations, interest rates paid on debt would likely increase more than inflation. Finally, persistent and high inflation may lead to a more widespread use of indexation contracts that are likely to magnify inflation shocks.

Overall, the benefits of lower real debt due to higher inflation do not appear large relative to the risks. The effect on debt of a one-percentage-point increase in inflation is limited relative to the size of average indebtedness in the OECD area. Reducing debt ratios to below-crisis levels would require substantially higher rates of inflation, which would likely be associated with more adverse effects on economic activity.

Debt structure in selected OECD countries (as of end-2010)

	Average maturity in years	Share of outstanding debt that	
		matures within a year	is indexed to inflation
France	7.2	22.9	11.6
Germany[1]	6.2	21.3	4.0
Greece	7.1	11.9	5.3
Ireland	5.9	12.5	0.0
Italy	7.2	19.1	6.8
Japan	6.7	17.8 [2]	0.8
Portugal	5.8	19.8	0.0
Spain	6.6	25.1	0.0
United Kingdom	13.4	21.6	20.8
United States	4.9	29.7	7.0

Note: Refers generally to marketable debt of the central government.
1. Debt outstanding at 26 April 2011. Proportion maturing within a year covers debt from 26 April 2011 through 25 April 2012.
2. Debt outstanding at end-March 2010 and the amount due during fiscal year 2010 (April 2010- March 2011).
Source: National authorities and OECD calculations.

StatLink http://dx.doi.org/10.1787/888932434295

1. Cottarelli and Viñals (2009) and Aizenman and Marion (2009).

worth 4 trillion yen (0.8% of GDP). Subsequent packages are expected later in FY 2011. If introduced, these could provide a near-term boost to the economy. The measures in the initial reconstruction package are to be financed without additional borrowing, in line with the authorities' intentions of maintaining an unchanged level of bond issuance in FY 2011, largely by using budgetary reserves. Such a strategy is necessary in view of the serious fiscal situation, with gross debt at 200% of GDP in 2010. While Japan's reliance on domestic financial investors, which hold some 95% of government debt, reduces the risk of a run-up in the risk premia on sovereign debt, weakening sovereign bond ratings point to increasing market concerns about the sustainability of the fiscal position. Even without additional borrowing to fund reconstruction expenditure, general government gross debt is projected to reach 219% of GDP in 2012. A more detailed medium-term consolidation plan, identifying the revenue and spending components to be employed to attain the stated targets, therefore needs to be elaborated urgently to put general government finances on a sustainable path. The medium-term consolidation plans should aim at a primary budget surplus that is large enough to stabilise the debt ratio rather than just a primary budget balance. As stated in OECD (2011b), the consumption tax should be the main source of additional revenue, given that it is low and its impact on economic activity is less negative than other taxes. Tax measures should be accompanied by social security reform that limits spending increases, including in health care, and addresses problems in pensions.

In the euro area, a framework has been agreed to make government finances sustainable...

In the euro area, against the background of heightened sovereign debt concerns, all governments have formulated multi-annual consolidation targets aimed at attaining a budget deficit of 3% of GDP or less by 2015 at the latest. In March 2011, heads of state and government in the euro area also agreed that the numerical benchmark for government debt reduction should be roughly equal to one-twentieth of the amount exceeding 60% of GDP per year, although not in a binding form.[8] Furthermore, the Euro Plus Pact agreed at the end of the March calls for *inter alia* enhanced coordination to secure the full implementation of the Stability and Growth Pact, including establishing national fiscal frameworks based on EU fiscal rules.

... though planned consolidation varies across countries...

In the majority of euro area countries, including Germany, France and Italy, fiscal outcomes were better than expected in 2010. Targeted consolidation varies significantly across member countries, depending on their current situation:

- In 2011, particularly strong consolidation of 2½ per cent of GDP or more is necessary and planned in the countries that have asked for assistance from the EFSF and the IMF or are facing intense scrutiny in financial markets, followed by a consolidation of 1% or more of GDP next year (Box 1.4 above).

- By contrast, consolidation of ½ per cent of GDP or less is planned in both 2011 and 2012 in some of the countries with comparatively healthy public finances (Germany and Austria).

8. A debt-to-GDP ratio above 60% would be considered to be sufficiently diminishing if the gap with respect to the reference value had fallen over the previous three years at an annual rate of one-twentieth. A country that would not respect this would not be automatically subject to excessive deficit procedure as other factors would also be taken into account, such as implicit liabilities related to private sector debt and ageing costs.

● The programmed reduction in the underlying structural deficit in France is close to the euro area average in both 2011 and 2012. In Italy, the programmed deficit reduction is smaller than the euro area average in 2011, but close to the average in 2012. In view of the high gross debt levels in these countries and required consolidation to bring the debt ratio to the reference value of 60% of GDP, it is important that the planned fiscal tightening is implemented.

In some of the highly indebted countries, the consolidation may not suffice to satisfy the proposed debt criterion of the Excessive Deficit Procedure discussed above.

Vigorous consolidation is underway in the United Kingdom...

In the United Kingdom, the government's medium-term consolidation strategy aims to eliminate the structural deficit by FY 2014/15, with consolidation scheduled to be front-loaded. The consolidation programme strikes the right balance between addressing fiscal sustainability, thereby reducing tail-risks to fiscal positions and preserving growth (OECD, 2011c). The recent drift in inflation expectations indeed supports the front-loaded fiscal tightening. The automatic stabilisers should be allowed to operate, as envisaged in the government consolidation plan.

... while consolidation needs vary in other OECD countries

In Canada, the federal and regional government should proceed to consolidate budgets as planned to restore the long-term sustainability of public finances. Little or no consolidation is required in countries with low debt and general government budgets close to balance or in surplus (Estonia, Finland, Norway, Sweden and Switzerland).

Structural reforms can facilitate fiscal consolidation

Consolidation efforts can be helped by structural reforms aimed at...

Against the background of impaired fiscal positions and the moderate pace of the recovery, it is particularly important to implement structural reforms that facilitate fiscal consolidation, in addition to strengthening growth in the short and medium term (OECD, 2011a).

... increasing employment...

● Reforms that could help to improve fiscal positions and foster employment growth without having strong negative effects on near-term activity include reforms to pension systems, incentives for early retirement and disability, sickness and unemployment benefits. Particular steps that could be taken include raising the retirement age, gradually tightening the eligibility criteria for sickness and disability benefits to exclude them being granted for labour market purposes and, once unemployment begins to fall, reducing disincentives to work embedded in unemployment benefit systems in some countries (notably many continental European economies). Secretariat estimates suggest that a 1 percentage point improvement in potential employment could improve government balances by between 0.3-0.8% of GDP (OECD, 2010).

... reforming benefit and short-time work schemes...

- In this context, and to the extent that labour market prospects improve sufficiently to prevent the affected individuals from falling into persistent poverty, extension of unemployment benefit duration should be scaled back in the United States[9] and other countries that have used this measure in the crisis. On the other hand, where the coverage of the unemployment benefit system has been extended, the extensions should be made permanent for social reasons and to maintain the labour force attachments of the newly covered. Crisis-related measures to encourage short-time working in Japan and the euro area should also be scaled back. An advantage of the approach in Germany is that it contains built-in incentives to encourage automatic unwinding of crisis-induced short-term work.

... raising productivity in the public sector...

- Reforms to increase productivity in the public sector would improve fiscal positions markedly in many countries. Particular measures include the scope to improve public-sector efficiency by moving to national or international best practice in the provision of health and education services.[10]

... and changing the tax structure

- Other structural fiscal reforms that could help to facilitate growth and improve welfare include reductions in tax expenditure and subsidies, the introduction of pollution-pricing mechanisms such as carbon taxes or the auctioning of emission permits, and the gradual implementation of revenue-neutral changes in the tax structure, away from taxes on corporate and labour income to higher taxes on consumption and, once housing market activity picks up, property (OECD, 2009).

Consolidation measures will affect economic growth

Some of the consolidation measures being implemented may have beneficial effects on growth. For example, on current plans, outlays for welfare, health care and pensions are most frequently scheduled to be cut (Figure 1.17). This may prompt an increase in public sector efficiency and, as discussed above, encourage higher employment levels if designed in a careful way. Cuts in infrastructure investment are also given high priority in consolidation plans, probably reflecting the fact that they are relatively easy to implement. However, there is a risk that the short-term financial gains from cutting infrastructure spending will come at the expense of

9. In the United States, the temporary extension of the duration of unemployment insurance benefits from 26 to 99 weeks, is estimated to have raised the US structural unemployment rate by between 1-1½ percentage points (Fujita, 2011; Mazumder, 2011).
10. The potential gains from improving service delivery in the primary and secondary education sectors are estimated to be between 0.5% to 1% of GDP in Italy, Germany, the United Kingdom, Sweden and the United States (OECD, 2011a). Improvements in healthcare efficiency could potentially offer larger fiscal gains, exceeding 2% of GDP in Belgium, Canada, the Netherlands, the United States, Sweden and the United Kingdom (OECD, 2011a).

Figure 1.17. **Major spending programmes targeted for consolidation**
Frequency across countries

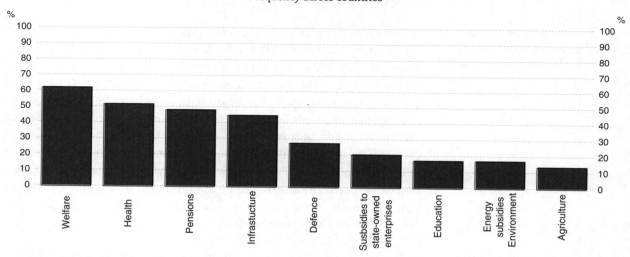

Note: Based on 29 countries.
Source: OECD (2011d).

StatLink 🔗 http://dx.doi.org/10.1787/888932434048

reducing future potential growth. Growth-friendly cuts in agriculture expenditures, subsidies to state-owned enterprises and energy subsidies are among the least prioritised saving areas for OECD countries, despite sizable support for agriculture, and high levels of subsidies more generally, in many countries. On the revenue side, increases in consumption taxes have been announced most frequently, followed by reductions in tax expenditures (Figure 1.18). These are the revenue components that are least likely to have adverse effects on growth.

Figure 1.18. **Revenue measures targeted for consolidation**
Frequency across countries

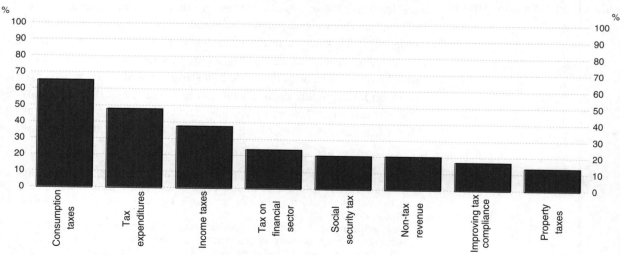

Note: Based on 29 countries.
Source: OECD (2011d).

StatLink 🔗 http://dx.doi.org/10.1787/888932434485

Monetary Policy

Monetary policy settings are increasingly differentiated...

Monetary policy settings have become increasingly differentiated as the recovery has progressed, reflecting cross-country differences in economic conditions and prospects and seemingly also in approaches to policy setting. While the US Federal Reserve has remained in an easing cycle, with the current quantitative easing programme to be completed in June, the European Central Bank has now implemented an initial increase in policy rates, and central banks in many countries, including Australia, Canada, Chile, Israel, Korea, Norway and Sweden, are well into their tightening cycle. This is also the case in many emerging market economies, which exited from the recession much earlier and in which past growth has eliminated most spare capacity and is now generating inflationary pressures. The range of policy measures adopted to manage monetary conditions also remains broad, with many emerging countries using both conventional and unconventional monetary policies, including non-market-based measures, such as reserve requirements and capital controls.

... with striking differences between the United States and the euro area

There are striking differences in both policy settings and communication across the major OECD economies, especially the United States and the euro area, in spite of underlying economic conditions that show many similarities, such as still-low underlying inflation, output gaps of sizable, albeit uncertain, magnitude and conflicting signals on the anchoring of inflation expectations from surveys and break-even rates. Indeed, given the differences in fiscal policies this year, developments in financial conditions and pre-existing levels of policy interest rates, there could even be grounds for suggesting that policy tightening in the United States should precede that in the euro area.

Deflation risks have faded...

Overall, with the surge in commodity prices and economic recovery gaining momentum, the distribution of risks to inflation has become more balanced in the advanced economies, and there is less need to maintain close-to-zero policy rates for risk management purposes. The risk of deflation appears to have receded significantly and, in the present set of economic projections, inflation is expected to drift up gradually closer to implicit or explicit targets as spare capacity becomes eroded. And with near-term inflation expectations and estimates of break-even inflation rates having risen, there could be even a risk that recent increases in headline inflation could feed through into longer-term inflation expectations, making the rise in headline inflation rates more persistent than would otherwise be the case. Core inflation remains low, but uncertainty about the amount of spare capacity still existing in OECD economies has increased as the recovery has progressed, as discussed above.

... implying earlier moves to withdraw some monetary stimulus...

This strengthens the argument for an early move to visibly positive, but still low, policy rates, except in Japan and those countries in which policy rates have already been raised. Upside risks to inflation expectations cannot now be excluded, but may be diminished by an early move that makes it easier for rates to be raised subsequently if such risks were to materialise. Equally, if an adverse shock were to occur, it would be preferable to be able to react by reducing policy rates, with fairly certain effects, rather than by renewed quantitative easing. An early move to still-accommodative interest rates would also continue to support demand whilst helping to guard against excessive risk-taking arising from close-to-zero policy rates, and the attendant risks of capital misallocation or a build-up of financial fragilities. Thereafter, the challenge for the monetary authorities will be to judge the pace at which to raise policy rates so as to maintain support for the recovery whilst keeping projected inflation close to implicit or explicit target levels. The existing stock of assets acquired by central banks via quantitative easing programmes should be maintained until policy interest rates are well above current levels. Otherwise, asset sales would be likely to push up longer-term yields to an uncertain extent, creating considerable communication challenges and possibly also the need for offsetting policy rate responses if long-term interest rates were to jump excessively.

... in the United States...

- In the United States, the asset purchase programme and the commitment of the Federal Reserve to an exceptionally low level of the policy rate for an extended period have contributed to the buoyancy of stock markets and tempered rises in long-term interest rates (Yellen, 2011). The still-elevated rate of unemployment and modest core inflation appear to be consistent with the decision to complete the quantitative easing programme in June. Nevertheless, with some signs that long-term inflation expectations have edged up, there is a strong case for an initial and visibly positive rise in the policy rate from mid-2011, followed later by a gradual reduction in the degree of accommodation as the recovery progresses and the extent of economic slack diminishes. In this set of economic projections, the target Federal Funds rate is assumed to be raised in a series of small steps by 100 basis points in the remainder of this year and, after a pause at this level to assess the impact on the economy, thereafter be increased steadily to reach 2¼ per cent by the end of 2012. Further increases in policy rates towards neutral levels would be likely soon thereafter, with the remaining output gap continuing to be eroded steadily.

... in the euro area...

- In the euro area, against the backdrop of improving economic prospects and a pick-up in some measures of inflation expectations, the European Central Bank raised the main refinancing rate in April 2011. In the immediate future, there is little pressure to make additional moves, since, although headline inflation has risen above the ECB's definition of price stability, core inflation rates are relatively low, especially once indirect tax changes are excluded. Moreover, a visibly positive level of money market interest rates now exists. During 2012, a gradual normalisation of the main policy rate would be warranted. In this set of projections, the main refinancing rate is assumed to be increaseed through 2012 to 2¼ per cent by the end of the year, still providing considerable stimulus in the context of remaining large, but increasingly uncertain, economic slack.

... despite ongoing differences between euro area member countries...

- One difficulty in the euro area is that, under current divergent economic conditions across member countries, the single monetary policy is too accommodative for some large countries that have recovered rapidly from recession and too tight for the EU/IMF programme countries.[11] For the fragile financial systems in the latter countries, one option would be for the ECB to maintain special liquidity supports whilst raising policy rates (Minegishi and Cournède, 2010). At the same time, authorities in the larger countries should consider using macro-prudential tools to deal with excessively strong, country-specific asset-price growth, should it materialise. Over the medium term structural reforms in all euro area countries are necessary to enhance economic integration, thus increasing the benefits of the monetary union.

... the United Kingdom...

- In the United Kingdom, earlier action is warranted, with the CPI inflation target of 2% having been overshot for the past 17 months and with some measures of inflation expectations having started to drift up. If the recent increases in long-term inflation expectations were allowed to become entrenched, the Bank of England could face difficulty in curbing the consumer price inflation rate. The Bank of England should therefore start to raise the policy rate soon, with the subsequent pace of monetary policy normalisation depending on the projected impact of strong fiscal consolidation on the economy and the speed at which economic slack is eroded. In the projections, policy rates are assumed to be raised to 1% by the end of 2011, and to then, after a pause, be raised gradually during 2012 to around 2¼ per cent by the end of the year.

... and a continuation of withdrawal in other OECD economies...

- In OECD countries in which monetary policy tightening started somewhat earlier, the pace of policy rate increases should generally be faster than previously thought in response to the improved prospects for the global economic recovery. In economies that operate at, or close to, full capacity, central banks should stand ready to raise policy rates above neutral levels if the recent strong run-up in commodity prices is

11. This issue is not specific to the euro area. On a conceptual level, the Swiss and US currency unions raise the same question as to whether a single monetary policy can fit all cantons and states. In practice, the difference is considerable because Swiss cantons and US states have a sizeable central government able to manage fiscal transfers and labour, services and financial markets that are much more integrated.

expected to generate second-round effects that create underlying inflationary pressures.

... but not in Japan
- In the wake of the earthquake and related events, the Bank of Japan provided ample funds to money market participants to prevent financial market instability. It also decided to supply longer-tem funds amounting to 1 trillion yen (0.2% of GDP) to financial institutions in disaster areas in order to support reconstruction efforts, and raised the size of the asset purchase programme from 5 to 10 trillion yen. Going forward, the current zero interest rate policy needs to be continued until inflation is firmly positive, especially given the uncertainty about the effect of the earthquake on economic slack. In the absence of signs of a clear trend toward achieving the 1% implicit inflation target, the Bank of Japan should stand ready to undertake further measures, focusing on reducing long-term interest rates through expanded purchases of government bonds. The first policy rate increase can wait until 2013 or later, occurring only when inflation is clearly set to reach about 1%. The potential accumulation of financial imbalances that could result from very low interest rates has to be monitored closely, but the Bank should be patient because of the risk of losing credibility in the event of having to return to zero interest rates soon after a premature policy rate increase.

In large non-OECD economies further tightening is required
- In the large emerging market economies outside the OECD, there is a need to tighten monetary conditions further, including through currency appreciation, to damp growing inflationary pressures. In China, where inflation has become markedly more entrenched in recent months, loan and deposit rates and the reserve requirement ratio have already been raised and the real exchange rate is now appreciating as a result of higher inflation. With output growth easing to below trend rates, and thus closing the positive output gap, only modest further tightening may be needed this year to stabilise underlying inflation, with the priority being given to market-based measures rather than reserve requirements. Allowing an appreciation of the nominal effective exchange rate would also help to reduce inflationary pressures. In India, the annual rate of inflation remains high and is becoming more widespread. Further policy tightening is warranted to help contain demand pressures and reduce the risk of inflation expectations becoming destabilised. In Brazil, with still-strong credit growth, continued capacity constraints and inflation now at the upper bound of the target range, tightening policies are warranted through higher policy rates and adequate micro and macro-prudential measures. Fiscal tightening would reduce the size of any required policy rate increases in both Brazil and India.

Macro-prudential measures would help to damp the effects of strong capital inflows

Many emerging market economies continue to face large capital inflows. These can pose considerable policy challenges for host economies, given the associated risks of excessive currency appreciation, asset price and credit booms and busts, and sudden stops. In the longer term, as discussed in Chapter 6, financial market deepening and other growth-friendly structural reforms can affect net international asset positions and help achieve a better composition of inflows, with more FDI and less debt, providing a defence against the negative effects of strong, speculative capital inflows. They can also ensure that domestic credit is intermediated effectively. But such reforms take time to put in place. In the near term, macroeconomic policies have an important role to play, though the extent to which they can be used will likely vary across countries. As mentioned above, allowing an exchange rate appreciation would help to contain any inflationary pressures arising from inflows and also reduce the incentives for further inflows. If accompanied by fiscal consolidation, there would be greater scope to loosen monetary policy, which would also damp inflows. Micro and macro-prudential policies should also have a key role, both in limiting excessive risk-taking and in tackling risks in particular sectors or asset classes. Other possible policy options in the near-term include reserve accumulation, via foreign exchange intervention, and other measures to damp capital inflows such as taxes on inflows or direct capital controls. As discussed in Chapter 6, reserve accumulation is costly, often inefficient, and should normally not be pursued for prolonged periods. Capital controls could prove effective in the near term in helping to damp potential financial vulnerabilities from large capital inflows, but are best seen as a temporary solution, so as to minimise distortions to longer-term investments, and preferably should be subject to multilateral surveillance within a framework provided by the OECD Code of Liberalisation of Capital Movements.

Financial and macro-prudential policy

Strict and transparent stress tests could improve confidence in EU banks

Given ongoing concerns about the health of the banking system in some countries, especially in the European Union, planned stress tests have an important role to play in providing reliable information on the extent to which banks can withstand adverse shocks. Compared with the 2010 EU-wide stress test, which failed to uncover vulnerabilities in some countries, the planned 2011 stress test will have a more demanding capital threshold based on Core Tier 1 capital instead of Tier 1 capital (which includes hybrid capital) and greater macroeconomic stress (though relative to a stronger baseline scenario). However, the adverse scenario regrettably excludes haircuts on sovereign debt held on banking books, which remains a sizeable risk.[12] Ahead of the publication of the results, euro area governments have committed to prepare specific strategies to restructure vulnerable institutions. Such backstop strategies should increase confidence in the tests. In the longer term, the priority

12. See also Blundell-Wignall and Slovik (2010).

should be to encourage market discipline, for which supervisory stress tests can be only an imperfect substitute. Key measures to progress in the direction of this objective include addressing the "too-big-to-fail" problem, strengthening bank resolution regimes and improving bank information disclosures.

Basel III capital requirements should be implemented rigorously

Looking further ahead, the implementation of the recently agreed Basel III capital requirements will strengthen bank loss-absorption capacity. Estimates in Slovik and Cournède (2011) suggest that in the three main OECD economies, banks may raise their target capital ratios by at least 3.7 percentage points, reducing the annual rate of GDP growth by 0.05 to 0.15 percentage point (Table 1.7). The introduction of countercyclical buffers during the credit cycle could further strengthen the long-term resilience of the banking sector (Basel Committee on Bank Supervision, 2010). However, it is as yet undecided at the global level, if and how, required capital ratios will be increased for systemically important financial institutions to reflect their greater risk-taking on the back of explicit government guarantees (Blundell-Wignall et al., 2010). Some countries have already introduced or are considering specific capital requirements for systemically important banks (e.g. Switzerland and the United Kingdom[13]), not only to address the " too-big-to-fail" problem, but also in recognition of the fact that, especially in small countries such as Switzerland that host very large financial institutions, some may be too big to save. The planned introduction of a binding leverage coverage ratio is particularly important for systemically important institutions, as these tend to be more leveraged than others.

Table 1.7. **Estimated medium-term macroeconomic impact of Basel III**

Five year change in

	Core capital ratio	Bank lending spreads	Annual GDP growth
	percentage points	basis points	percentage points
United States	3.1	12.3 - 46.2	-0.02 - -0.12
Euro area	3.8	18.6 - 56.6	-0.08 - -0.23
Japan	4.2	14.3 - 62.6	-0.04 - -0.09
Average (unweighted)	3.7	15.1 - 55.1	-0.05 - -0.15
Average (GDP weighted)	3.5	15.6 - 52.9	-0.05 - -0.16

Note: The capital requirements result in a widening of lending spreads as banks attempt to maintain the return on equity. Higher lending spreads in turn damp activity. The bound estimates correspond to the impact of meeting the 2015 target while the upper bound estimates correspond to the 2019 target. See Slovik and Cournède (2009) for more details.
Source: Slovik and Cournède (2011).

StatLink ᵍ᷍ᵍ᷍ *http://dx.doi.org/10.1787/888932434314*

13. See the Independent Commission on Banking (2011).

Liquidity regulations should be carefully designed

In principle, very strong capital buffers should reassure debt and money-market investors about a bank's solvency, ensuring its access to funding. In practice, however, even under Basel III and additional national capital regimes, the equity cushion is unlikely to be large enough to secure continued liquidity at all times.[14] Against this background, the Basel III framework will include liquidity requirements aimed at improving individual banks' resilience to liquidity shocks. The Liquidity Coverage Ratio will require banks to hold the minimum level of high-quality liquid assets necessary to withstand an adverse liquidity stress scenario lasting for one month. The Net Stable Funding Ratio is a structural measure that requires banks to rely on stable medium to long-term funding instead of short-term money market financing. Although these requirements reduce the vulnerability of banks to liquidity risk, some concerns remain about their implementation. The liquidity requirements in their current form put a lot of emphasis on government bonds although recent developments have underscored that the safety and liquidity of government bonds cannot be taken for granted. The liquidity and stable funding requirements may also create incentives for regulatory arbitrage between different asset classes, as was the case with risk-weighted regulation in the run-up to the current financial crisis. Moreover, since the banking sector will require large amounts of medium to long-term funding, there is a risk that asset-liability maturity mismatches may emerge and create vulnerabilities elsewhere in the financial system. These caveats suggest that liquidity regulation should: avoid assuming that domestic government bonds are necessarily always fully liquid, especially for members of a currency union; rely on simple rules rather than overly complicated weighting schemes that could open new avenues for regulatory arbitrage; and be accompanied by adequate supervision of other parts of the financial system, including insurance companies, where potentially destabilising asset-liability mismatches could migrate to.

Reform is also needed in other areas

Addressing the challenges raised by the financial crisis will also require reform in a number of other areas. The efforts to move most trading in derivatives to public exchanges or at least central clearing houses should be completed rapidly. Effective cross-border resolution regimes also need to be put in place for large global banks to reduce the moral hazard created by a situation where they cannot be closed without destabilising repercussions. Further international convergence in accounting rules, especially for financial institutions, remains important to facilitate the implementation of global regulatory standards, particularly leverage caps. Furthermore, as mentioned above in the case of liquidity but also more generally, regulation and supervision must effectively cover areas, such as insurance and pensions, where

---

14. Until banks started benefitting from gradually expanding government backing from the middle of the 19th century, they typically maintained capital positions above or close to 50% to convince depositors and lenders that their investments were safe.

vulnerabilities and systemic risk could migrate as a result of tighter banking regulation.

The interaction of monetary and macro-prudential policies

Monetary and macro-prudential policies need close co-ordination...

As discussed in Chapter 7, macro-prudential policy and monetary policy make use of different policy instruments, but there is a need for close co-ordination between monetary and regulatory functions to ensure that systemic risk and macro-financial linkages are monitored effectively and incorporated fully in both monetary and macro-prudential policy decisions. Due account also needs to be taken of the extent to which macro-prudential policies affect monetary policy transmission, especially through the credit channel, and the extent to which monetary policy affects risk-taking and the build-up of leverage.

... but need not always be aligned

In practice, the alignment of monetary and macro-prudential policies will depend on the type of shocks occurring and the ability of each policy to respond. Both types of policy are likely to respond to aggregate demand shocks in a similar manner, but this may not be the case for aggregate supply shocks. And, if macro-prudential policies are impaired for any reason, or not yet fully in place, monetary policy may need to place greater weight on financial stability issues than would otherwise be merited. Equally, if policy interest rates are at the zero bound, macro-prudential policies might have to place greater weight on their macroeconomic effects than would otherwise be the case (Yellen, 2010).

Bibliography

Aizenman, J. and N. Marion (2009), "Using Inflation to Erode the US Public Debt", *NBER Working Papers*, No. 15562.

Akram, Q. F. (2009), "Commodity Prices, Interest Rates and the Dollar", *Energy Economics*, Vol. 31.

Bank of England (2010), *Inflation Report*, November 2010.

Barnes, S. (2010), "Resolving and Avoiding Unsustainable Imbalances in the Euro Area", *OECD Economics Department Working Papers*, No. 827.

Barrell, R. and O. Pomerantz (2004), "Oil Prices and the World Economy", *NIESR Discussion Paper*, No. 242.

Basel Committee on Bank Supervision (2010), *Guidance for National Authorities Operating the Countercyclical Buffer*, Bank for International Settlements, December 2010, Basel.

Beltran, D., L. Pounder and C. Thomas (2008), "Foreign Exposure to Asset-Backed Securities of US Origin,"*Board of Governors of the Federal Reserve System International Finance Discussion Papers*, Number 939.

Blundell-Wignall, A., G. Wehinger and P. Slovik (2010), "The Elephant in the Room: The Need to Deal with What Banks Do", *OECD Financial Market Trends*, Vol. 2009/2.

Blundell-Wignall, A. and P. Slovik (2010) The EU Stress Test and Sovereign Debt Exposures," *OECD Working Papers on Finance, Insurance and Private Pensions*, No. 4.

Cabinet Office (2011), *Monthly Economic Report*, 23 March, Japan.

Carabenciov, I., *et al.* (2008), "A Small Quarterly Multi-Country Projection Model with Financial-Real Linkages and Oil Prices", *IMF Working Papers*, No. 08/280.

Cavallo, E., and I. Noy (2010), "The Economics of Natural Disasters: A Survey", *IDB Working Paper Series*, No. IDB-WP-124.

CBO (2011), *An Analysis of the President's Budgetary Proposals for Fiscal Year 2012*, Washington D.C.

Chamley, C. and B. Pinto (2011), "Why Official Bailouts Tend Not To Work: An Example Motivated by Greece 2010", *The Economist's Voice*, February.

Cottarelli, C. and J. Viñals (2009), "A Strategy for Renormalizing Fiscal and Monetary Policies in Advanced Economies", *IMF Staff Position Note*, SPN/09/22.

Crespo Cuaresma, J.C. (2010), "Can Emerging Asset Price Bubbles be Detected?", *OECD Economics Department Working Papers*, No. 772.

European Commission (2004), "How Vulnerable is the Euro Area Economy to Higher Oil Prices?", *Quarterly Report on the Euro Area*, No. 3.

European Commission (2008), "Recent Economic Developments and Short-Term Prospects", *Quarterly Report on the Euro Area*, No. 7.

Fujita, S. (2011), "Effects of Extended Unemployment Insurance Benefits: Evidence from the Monthly CPS", *Federal Reserve Bank of Philadelphia Working Paper*, No. 10-35/R.

Girouard, N., M. Kennedy, P. van den Noord and C. André (2006), "Recent House Price Developments: the Role of Fundamentals", *OECD Economics Department Working Papers*, No. 475.

Gros, D. (2010), "The Seniority Conundrum: Bail Out Countries But Bail in Private, Short-Term Creditors?", 5 December, *www.voxeu.org*.

Guichard, S., D.Haugh and D.Turner (2009), "Quantifying the Effect of Financial Conditions in the Euro Area, Japan, United Kingdom and United States", *OECD Economics Department Working Papers*, No. 677.

Guichard, S. and E. Rusticelli (2010), "Assessing the Impact of the Financial Crisis on Structural Unemployment in OECD Countries", *OECD Economics Department Working Papers*, No. 767.

Guichard S. and E. Rusticelli (2011) "A Dynamic Factor Model for World Trade Growth", *OECD Economics Department Working Paper*, forthcoming.

Haugh, D., P. Ollivaud and D. Turner (2009), "The Macroeconomic Effects of Banking Crises in OECD Countries", *OECD Economics Department Working Papers*, No. 683.

Haugh, D., A. Mourougane and O. Chantal (2010), "The Automobile Industry In and Beyond the Crisis", *OECD Economics Department Working Papers*, No. 745.

Hervé, K., Pain, N., Richardson, P., Sédillot, F. and P.O. Beffy (2010), "The OECD's New Global Model", *Economic Modelling*, Vol. 28.

Independent Commission on Banking (2011), *Interim Report: Consultation on Reform Options*, April 2011, London.

Japan External Trade Organisation (2008), *Survey on Business Conditions of Japanese Companies in the US and Canada*, October 2008.

Japan External Trade Organisation (2010), *Survey of Japanese-Affiliated Firms in Asia and Oceania*, October 2010.

Japan Research Institute (2011), *Kaigai Keizai Tenbou*, April 2011 (in Japanese).

Jiménez-Rodriguez, R. and M. Sánchez (2004), "Oil Price Shocks and Real GDP Growth: Empirical Evidence for Some OECD Countries", *European Central Bank Working Papers*, No. 362.

Jones, D. and A. Kwiecinski (2010), "Policy Responses in Emerging Economies to International Agricultural Commodity Price Surges", *OECD Food, Agriculture and Fisheries Working Papers*, No. 34.

Mazumder, B. (2011), "How did the Unemployment Insurance Extensions Affect the Unemployment Rate in 2008-2010?", *Chicago Fed Letter*, April.

Minegishi, M. and B. Cournède (2010), "Monetary Policy Responses to the Crisis and Exit Strategies", *OECD Economics Department Working Papers*, No. 753.

Moccero, D., S. Watanabe and B. Cournède (2011), "What Drives Inflation in the Major OECD Economies?", *OECD Economics Department Working Papers*, No. 854.

Mody, A., Saravia, D., (2003). "Catalyzing Capital Fows: Do IMF-supported Programs Work as Commitment Devices?", *IMF Working Paper 03/100*.

van den Noord, P. (2006), "Are House Prices Nearing a Peak? A Probit Analysis for 17 OECD Countries", *OECD Economics Department Working Papers*, No. 488.

OECD (2008a), *Biofuel Support Policies – An Economic Assessment*, OECD, Paris.

OECD (2008b), *Consumption Tax Trends 2008: VAT/GST and Excise Rates, Trends, and Administration Issues*, Paris.

OECD (2009), *Going for Growth: Economic Policy Reforms*, Paris.

OECD (2010) *OECDEconomic Outlook*, No. 88, Vol. 2010/2, Paris.

OECD (2011a), *Going for Growth: Economic Policy Reforms*, Paris.

OECD (2011b), *Economic Survey of Japan*, Paris.

OECD (2011c), *OECD Economic Surveys: United Kingdom*, Paris.

OECD (2011d), *Restoring Public Finances*, Special Issue of the OECD *Journal on Budgeting*, Volume 2011/2, OECD Publishing, Paris.

Pain, N., I. Koske and M. Sollie (2008), "Globalisation and OECD Consumer Price Inflation", *OECD Economic Studies*, No. 44.

Rousova, L, and P. van den Noord (2011), "Predicting Peaks and Troughs in Real House Prices", *OECD Economics Department Working Papers*, forthcoming.

Shirakawa, M. (2011), "Great East Japan Earthquake: Resilience of Society and Determination to Rebuild", remarks at the Council on Foreign Relations, New York, April.

Slovik, P. and B. Cournède (2011), "Macroeconomic Impact of Basel III", *OECD Economics Department Working Papers*, No. 844.

Weidner, J. and J. Williams (2011), "What Is The New Normal Unemployment Rate?", *Federal Reserve Bank of San Francisco Economic Letter*, No. 2011-05.

Wurzel, E., L. Willard and P. Ollivaud (2009), "Recent Oil Price Movements: Forces and Policy Issues", *OECD Economics Department Working Papers*, No. 737.

Yellen, J. (2010), "Macroprudential Supervision and Monetary Policy in the Post-Crisis World", speech at the Annual Meeting of the National Association for Business Economics, Denver, November.

Yellen, J. (2011), "The Federal Reserve's Asset Purchase Program", speech at the Brimmer Policy Forum, Denver, January.

OECD Economic Outlook
Volume 2011/1
© OECD 2011

Chapter 2

DEVELOPMENTS IN INDIVIDUAL OECD COUNTRIES

UNITED STATES

Supported by accommodative monetary policy and financial conditions the economy continues to recover gradually from the recession that ended a year and a half ago. Nevertheless, the adverse effects of the crisis are still being felt, particularly in the form of still-high unemployment. Output growth should gain speed and the unemployment rate should continue to decline through 2012 though the pace of expansion will be limited by household deleveraging and initial steps at fiscal consolidation.

The Federal Reserve should continue to support growth, as the economy lingers below capacity and core inflation remains low, but a modest reduction in monetary stimulus starting in the second half of this year would reduce the likelihood of a potentially destabilising rapid increase in interest rates later. With very large budget deficits and fast-rising federal debt, an agreement on a credible medium-term fiscal consolidation programme will become increasingly urgent as the economy continues to recover.

The economic recovery is continuing...

Economic growth slowed in the first quarter of 2011 owing to a jump in energy prices and a temporary slackening in consumption growth at the turn of the year. Nonetheless, with financial conditions remaining accommodative, economic growth should gradually strengthen over the next couple of years, even as fiscal stimulus gives way to contraction.

... but the economy is working below capacity

Both capacity utilisation and average hours worked for those currently employed have regained about two-thirds of their decline during the recession. Even so, unemployment, currently at 9%, is well above its natural rate.

The unemployment rate will be elevated for some time

Further growth will slowly improve the labour market. The unemployment rate has already fallen in the pastcouple of quarters, although much of the reduction is attributable to falling labour force participation. Substantial employment gains are projected through the

United States

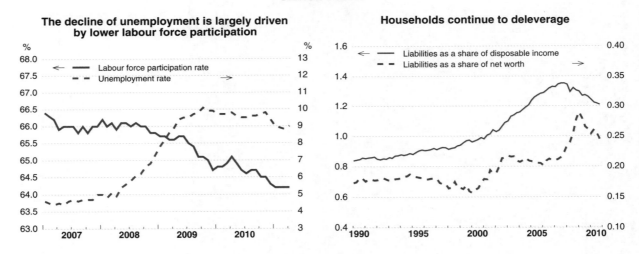

Source: OECD Economic Outlook 89 database; Bureau of Economic Analysis and Federal Reserve.

StatLink http://dx.doi.org/10.1787/888932429108

United States: **Employment, income and inflation**
Percentage changes

	2008	2009	2010	2011	2012
Employment[1]	-0.7	-4.3	-0.7	1.1	2.0
Unemployment rate[2]	5.8	9.3	9.6	8.8	7.9
Employment cost index	2.9	1.4	1.9	1.9	1.6
Compensation per employee[3]	2.9	0.6	3.1	3.0	3.5
Labour productivity	0.7	1.7	3.6	1.5	1.1
Unit labour cost	2.6	-0.6	-0.5	1.5	2.2
GDP deflator	2.2	0.9	1.0	1.4	1.4
Consumer price index	3.8	-0.3	1.6	2.6	1.5
Core PCE deflator[4]	2.3	1.5	1.3	1.1	1.4
PCE deflator[5]	3.3	0.2	1.7	1.9	1.3
Real household disposable income	1.7	0.6	1.4	2.4	2.4

1. Based on the Bureau of Labor Statistics (BLS) Establishment Survey.
2. As a percentage of labour force, based on the BLS Household Survey.
3. In the private sector.
4. Deflator for private consumption excluding food and energy.
5. Private consumption deflator. PCE stands for personal consumption expenditures.
Source: OECD Economic Outlook 89 database.

StatLink http://dx.doi.org/10.1787/888932430115

remainder of 2011 and in 2012, cutting the unemployment rate to 7½ per cent by the end of 2012, still well above pre-recession levels.

Consumption growth will remain moderate

Household consumption growth increased steadily from late 2009 through the end of 2010 before slowing in the first quarter of 2011, as higher energy and food prices crimped budgets. Consumption growth should pick up again in coming months as employment strengthens, though increases are likely to remain moderate as households continue to reduce debts.

United States

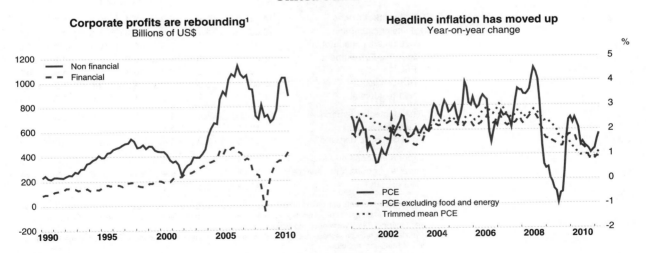

Corporate profits are rebounding[1]
Billions of US$

Headline inflation has moved up
Year-on-year change

1. Corporate profits before tax with inventory valuation adjustment.
Source: OECD Economic Outlook 89 database; Federal Reserve; United States Department of Commerce; Bureau of Economic Analysis and Datastream.

StatLink http://dx.doi.org/10.1787/888932429127

United States: **Financial indicators**

	2008	2009	2010	2011	2012
Household saving ratio[1]	4.1	5.9	5.8	5.5	5.0
General government financial balance[2]	-6.3	-11.3	-10.6	-10.1	-9.1
Current account balance[2]	-4.7	-2.7	-3.2	-3.7	-4.0
Short-term interest rate[3]	3.2	0.9	0.5	0.8	1.9
Long-term interest rate[4]	3.7	3.3	3.2	3.5	4.6

1. As a percentage of disposable income.
2. As a percentage of GDP.
3. 3-month rate on euro-dollar deposits.
4. 10-year government bonds.
Source: OECD Economic Outlook 89 database.

StatLink http://dx.doi.org/10.1787/888932430134

Strong investment growth should continue

Growth in business investment has slowed from the elevated pace of early 2010, but remains strong. Low interest rates and increases in corporate profits, which have nearly recovered the ground lost during the recession, should continue to support strong business investment growth despite capacity utilisation remaining below pre-recession levels.

Real estate markets are still weak

Residential investment increased modestly at the end of 2010, but a robust recovery in the sector remains some time off. The significant backlog of housing with delinquent mortgages or in foreclosure that have yet to be put on the market is diminishing slowly. However, it will

United States: **Demand and output**

	2009	2010	2011	2012	Fourth quarter		
					2010	2011	2012
	Current prices $ billion	Percentage changes from previous year, volume (2005 prices)					
GDP at market prices	14 119.1	2.9	2.6	3.1	2.8	2.7	3.3
Private consumption	10 001.3	1.7	2.9	2.9	2.6	2.8	3.0
Government consumption	2 411.5	0.9	-0.6	0.2	0.7	-0.7	0.5
Gross fixed investment	2 219.8	3.3	4.2	8.0	6.5	4.7	8.0
Public	503.4	1.3	-3.0	0.8	3.2	-4.6	0.9
Residential	352.1	-3.0	-1.9	3.3	-4.6	1.2	3.6
Non-residential	1 364.4	5.7	8.3	11.4	10.6	8.9	11.1
Final domestic demand	14 632.6	1.9	2.5	3.2	2.9	2.5	3.3
Stockbuilding[1]	- 127.2	1.4	-0.1	0.0			
Total domestic demand	14 505.5	3.2	2.4	3.3	3.2	2.8	3.3
Exports of goods and services	1 578.4	11.7	7.5	8.9	8.9	7.8	9.0
Imports of goods and services	1 964.8	12.6	5.4	8.4	10.9	7.6	8.1
Net exports[1]	- 386.4	-0.4	0.1	-0.3			

Note: National accounts are based on official chain-linked data. This introduces a discrepancy in the identity between real demand components and GDP. For further details see *OECD Economic Outlook* Sources and Methods *(http://www.oecd.org/eco/sources-and-methods).*
Detailed quarterly projections are reported for the major seven countries, the euro area and the total OECD in the Statistical Annex.
1. Contributions to changes in real GDP (percentage of real GDP in previous year), actual amount in the first column.
Source: OECD Economic Outlook 89 database.

StatLink http://dx.doi.org/10.1787/888932430153

United States: **External indicators**

	2008	2009	2010	2011	2012
	\$ billion				
Goods and services exports	1 843.4	1 578.4	1 837.6	2 085	2 306
Goods and services imports	2 553.8	1 964.8	2 353.9	2 684	2 943
Foreign balance	- 710.5	- 386.4	- 516.4	- 599	- 637
Invisibles, net	41.6	8.0	46.1	31	7
Current account balance	- 668.9	- 378.4	- 470.2	- 568	- 631
	Percentage changes				
Goods and services export volumes	6.0	- 9.5	11.7	7.5	8.9
Goods and services import volumes	- 2.6	- 13.8	12.6	5.4	8.4
Export performance[1]	2.1	2.4	- 1.9	- 0.5	0.2
Terms of trade	- 5.2	6.0	- 2.0	- 2.4	0.4

1. Ratio between export volume and export market of total goods and services.
Source: OECD Economic Outlook 89 database.

StatLink http://dx.doi.org/10.1787/888932430172

continue to weigh on residential construction, housing prices and financial industry balance sheets over the next couple of years. Similar problems are affecting the commercial real estate market.

Fiscal deficits remain very large

Budget positions are poor at all levels of government, owing to both the effect of the recession and weak positions prior to it. Government support for economic growth is winding down and deficit reduction is likely to begin later this year. The general government deficit is assumed to fall from 10½ per cent of GDP in 2010 to 9 per cent in 2012. This is a much more moderate pace of fiscal consolidation than currently suggested by government plans, but has been assumed given the lack of political consensus on how to cut the deficit. Further progress to unwind fiscal imbalances beyond 2012 would require ambitious reforms of the tax system and entitlement spending, along the lines recommended by the President's Fiscal Commission in late 2010.

A modest reduction of monetary stimulus would be prudent

Substantial slack in the economy, relatively low levels of inflation, subdued bank lending and the prospect that banks will have to meet stricter capital standards under Basel III all imply that, monetary policy should remain accommodative for the foreseeable future. At present, there is little sign that continued extraordinarily loose macroeconomic policy settings have increased inflation expectations more than a small amount or are resulting in another asset price bubble (with the possible exception of oil and other commodities), though such outcomes remain a risk. Even so, a modest reduction in monetary stimulus should get underway in the second half of this year following the ending of the second round of quantitative easing in June. Tightening somewhat now would reduce the need for steeper, and potentially disruptive, increases in interest rates later, smoothing the transition to neutral rates as the recovery matures.

The current account deficit will deteriorate somewhat

Following a considerable reduction from 6% of GDP in 2006 to 2¾ per cent in 2009, the current account deficit has begun widening again slightly as the fiscal deficit, consumption and investment growth have risen. The current account deficit is likely to continue to increase somewhat as consumption and investment rise, but the increase should be attenuated by the fall in the value of the dollar and the overall balance should remain much improved from its pre-recession levels.

The level of uncertainty remains high, with significant downside and upside risks

Macroeconomic policy support remains considerable and the response of the economy to the withdrawal of fiscal stimulus presents a downside risk over the next couple of years. Further increases in fuel and commodity prices would squeeze household and business budgets, presenting an additional downside risk. On the other hand, ample corporate profits and easy financial conditions could trigger a faster recovery of business investment and hiring than projected.

JAPAN

The 11 March 2011 Great East Japan Earthquake triggered the country's worst disaster of the post-war era. The immediate impact has been to reduce output, although this is likely to be reversed by a strong recovery in the second half of 2011 led by reconstruction efforts. However, deflationary pressures are likely to continue through 2012, with unemployment remaining above its pre-2008 crisis level.

Reconstruction spending in areas devastated by the earthquake and tsunami will be significant given the scale of destruction. With public debt exceeding 200% of GDP, it is important to finance reconstruction spending by shifting expenditures and increasing revenues. A detailed and credible fiscal consolidation programme, including tax increases and spending cuts large enough to achieve the government's target of stabilising the public debt ratio by 2020, is a priority. The Bank of Japan should maintain an accommodative stance until underlying inflation is firmly positive.

Japan's expansion was back on track in early 2011...

The earthquake and tsunami hit when Japan's expansion appeared to be back on track, thanks to buoyant exports and improving labour market conditions, following the slowdown in the latter part of 2010. By early 2011, the unemployment rate had fallen to 4½ per cent, down from its record high of 5.4% in mid-2009, and the decline in the core consumer price index had slowed to 0.6% (year-on-year) from 1.5% in mid-2010.

... when it was hit by the powerful earthquake and tsunami in March

The Great East Japan Earthquake claimed around 25 000 lives and caused damage to social infrastructure, housing and private firms' fixed capital that has been initially estimated by the government at between 3.3% and 5.2% of 2010 GDP. Moreover, significant damage to nuclear and thermal power plants reduced the electricity supply and created concern about radiation from the Fukushima plant. The disaster also disrupted

Japan

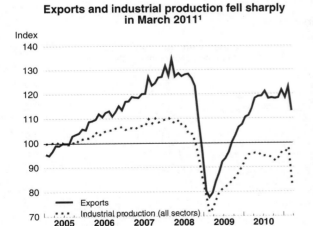

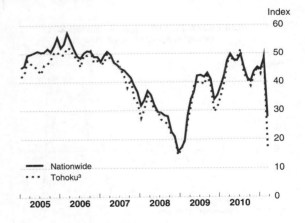

1. Data are seasonally-adjusted volume indices (2005=100).
2. The "Economy Watchers" index, which includes workers such as taxi drivers and shop clerks, whose jobs are sensitive to economic conditions.
3. Tohoku is the region directly hit by the March earthquake and tsunami.
Source: Ministry of Economy, Trade and Industry and Bank of Japan; Cabinet Office.

StatLink http://dx.doi.org/10.1787/888932429146

Japan: **Employment, income and inflation**
Percentage changes

	2008	2009	2010	2011	2012
Employment	-0.4	-1.6	-0.4	0.0	-0.2
Unemployment rate[1]	4.0	5.1	5.1	4.8	4.6
Compensation of employees	0.2	-4.2	0.8	0.6	1.1
Unit labour cost	1.4	2.2	-3.1	1.5	-1.0
Household disposable income	-0.3	-1.2	1.4	-0.3	0.9
GDP deflator[2]	-1.0	-0.4	-2.1	-1.3	-0.5
Consumer price index[2,3]	1.4	-1.3	-0.7	0.3	-0.2
Core consumer price index[2,4]	0.1	-0.6	-1.2	-0.3	-0.3
Private consumption deflator[2]	0.4	-2.1	-1.5	-0.5	-0.2

1. As a percentage of labour force.
2. The outlook for inflation does not include the impact of the change in the base year planned for August 2011, which is likely to cause a downward revision in the rate of increase in prices.
3. Calculated as the sum of the seasonally adjusted quarterly indices for each year.
4. Consumer price index excluding food and energy.
Source: OECD Economic Outlook 89 database.

StatLink ᵃᵍᵖ *http://dx.doi.org/10.1787/888932430191*

supply chains, reducing output in parts of Japan that were not hit by the earthquake and tsunami, contributing to a 15% decline in industrial production (seasonally-adjusted, month-on-month) in March, the largest ever recorded. Consequently, the Bank of Japan's April report downgraded its assessment of seven of Japan's nine regional economies. The disaster also had an immediate impact on business and consumer confidence, which recorded its largest drop on record in March, as did the "Economy Watchers" index, which surveys workers whose jobs are sensitive to changes in the economy, such as taxi drivers and shop clerks. Car sales plummeted by 37% (year-on-year) in March. The disaster caused a large contraction in output in the first quarter of 2011.

Japan

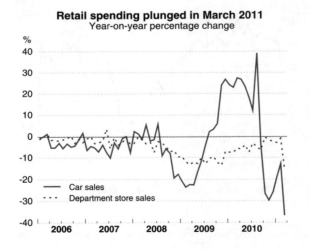

Retail spending plunged in March 2011
Year-on-year percentage change

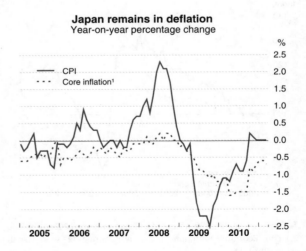

Japan remains in deflation
Year-on-year percentage change

1. Corresponds to the OECD measure of core inflation.
Source: Cabinet Office and Ministry of Economy, Trade and Industry; OECD, Economic Outlook 89 database.

StatLink ᵃᵍᵖ *http://dx.doi.org/10.1787/888932429165*

Japan: **Financial indicators**

	2008	2009	2010	2011	2012
Household saving ratio[1]	2.2	5.0	6.5	7.9	7.5
General government financial balance[2]	-2.2	-8.7	-8.1	-8.9	-8.2
Current account balance[2]	3.3	2.8	3.6	2.6	2.5
Short-term interest rate[3]	0.7	0.3	0.2	0.3	0.2
Long-term interest rate[4]	1.5	1.3	1.1	1.3	1.8

1. As a percentage of disposable income.
2. As a percentage of GDP.
3. 3-month CDs.
4. 10-year government bonds.
Source: OECD Economic Outlook 89 database.

StatLink http://dx.doi.org/10.1787/888932430210

Public reconstruction spending...

The initial reconstruction package approved in May 2011 amounts to 4 trillion yen (0.8%) of GDP. It will be financed without additional borrowing, in line with the government's goal of restricting bond issuance in FY 2011 to its FY 2010 level of 44 trillion yen (9% of GDP). Instead, it will be funded primarily by diverting the central government's 2.5 trillion yen contribution to the basic pension system to reconstruction efforts and by reserves in the FY 2011 budget. The government's budget deficit is projected to remain above 9% of GDP (excluding one-off factors) in 2011.

Japan: **Demand and output**

	2009	2010	2011	2012	Fourth quarter		
					2010	2011	2012
	Current prices ¥ trillion	Percentage changes from previous year, volume (2000 prices)					
GDP at market prices	470.9	4.0	-0.9	2.2	2.4	0.3	1.5
Private consumption	279.9	1.8	-1.3	1.6	0.6	-0.5	1.8
Government consumption	94.5	2.3	2.6	-0.4	1.5	2.2	-1.0
Gross fixed investment	99.6	-0.2	0.0	6.5	1.3	3.2	4.0
Public[1]	20.8	-3.4	-6.5	-3.5	-12.9	1.0	-10.1
Residential	13.7	-6.3	6.8	10.2	6.5	7.4	9.0
Non-residential	65.1	2.1	0.7	8.5	5.1	3.1	6.9
Final domestic demand	474.0	1.5	-0.3	2.2	0.9	0.8	1.7
Stockbuilding[2]	-4.5	0.7	-0.4	0.0			
Total domestic demand	469.5	2.2	-0.6	2.2	2.0	0.4	1.7
Exports of goods and service	59.5	23.9	3.2	8.2	12.9	5.7	6.5
Imports of goods and service	58.1	9.7	5.2	8.7	9.8	6.7	7.4
Net exports[2]	1.4	1.8	-0.2	-0.1			

Note: National accounts are based on official chain-linked data. This introduces a discrepancy in the identity between real demand components and GDP. For further details see *OECD Economic Outlook* Sources and Methods *(http://www.oecd.org/eco/sources-and-methods).*
Detailed quarterly projections are reported for the major seven countries, the euro area and the total OECD in the Statistical Annex.
1. Including public corporations.
2. Contributions to changes in real GDP (percentage of real GDP in previous year), actual amount in the first column.
Source: OECD Economic Outlook 89 database.

StatLink http://dx.doi.org/10.1787/888932430229

Japan: **External indicators**

	2008	2009	2010	2011	2012
	\$ billion				
Goods and services exports	853.8	637.7	832.3	921	999
Goods and services imports	847.6	621.9	769.9	917	1 010
Foreign balance	6.1	15.7	62.4	4	- 11
Invisibles, net	152.1	126.9	132.9	148	161
Current account balance	158.2	142.7	195.3	152	151
	Percentage changes				
Goods and services export volumes	1.6	- 23.9	23.9	3.2	8.2
Goods and services import volumes	0.4	- 15.3	9.7	5.2	8.7
Export performance[1]	- 2.3	- 17.0	7.7	- 5.1	- 1.4
Terms of trade	- 9.8	13.1	- 6.6	- 5.3	- 1.1

1. Ratio between export volume and export market of total goods and services.
Source: OECD Economic Outlook 89 database.

StatLink http://dx.doi.org/10.1787/888932430248

While this financing plan avoids an increase in gross debt, it implies a reduction in government assets, thus boosting net debt. Additional reconstruction spending packages are expected in FY 2011, in line with the experience of the 1995 Kobe earthquake, which was followed by three supplementary budgets within one year. Even without additional reconstruction spending, gross government debt is projected to reach 219% of GDP in 2012, pushing Japan's public finances farther into uncharted territory.

... and measures by the authorities...

The Bank of Japan reacted promptly following the disaster by providing liquidity on a large scale to stabilise financial markets. In addition, the Bank announced that it would double the size of its asset purchase programme to 10 trillion yen (2% of GDP) to prevent a deterioration in business sentiment and an increase in risk aversion. The authorities also intervened in foreign exchange markets in March as part of a multilateral commitment by the G7 countries to curb excess exchange rate volatility. This joint intervention immediately reduced the currency's value relative to the dollar, which had risen to a record high, to around its pre-earthquake level and prompted a recovery in equity prices.

... will help launch a recovery in the second half of 2011

The experience of past disasters in Japan and other developed countries suggests that the large negative impact on economic output in the first half of 2011 will be followed by a rebound as reconstruction spending picks up. In addition to public outlays, business and residential investment will increase as firms and households replace fixed capital and housing damaged in the disaster. In contrast to fixed investment, private consumption is projected to remain relatively subdued during 2011, reflecting weaker household confidence, as occurred following the Kobe earthquake. However, as residential investment gains momentum, private consumption, particularly for consumer durables, is likely to strengthen. These factors imply growth running at an average rate of around 4½ per cent during the second half of 2011. As public and private investment moderate following the completion of the 4 trillion yen initial package, the pace of output growth may slow to close to 1% by the end of 2012, leaving a large negative output gap. Consequently, headline inflation, which is likely to be positive in 2011 as a result of rising oil and commodity prices and the dislocations related to the disaster, may return to negative territory in 2012. The current account surplus is projected to fall from 3.6% of GDP in 2010 to around 2½ per cent in 2011-12, partly reflecting increased imports of oil to temporarily replace nuclear power.

Uncertainty is exceptionally large

The extent of the damage from this unprecedented disaster in Japan and its economic impact will only become fully apparent in the months to come. There is great uncertainty, notably as regards the duration of electricity shortages and the problems at the Fukushima nuclear plant. In addition, the pace of government reconstruction spending, as well as the size and financing of future fiscal packages, will have an important impact on the path of the economy. Consequently, the timing and strength of an economic rebound is exceptionally difficult to project. In addition, there are risks related to developments in the world economy, exchange rates and commodity prices. The delay in fiscal consolidation and continuing rise in the public debt ratio also increase the risk of a run-up in long-term interest rates.

EURO AREA

The recovery in domestic demand is gaining momentum and exports continue to support growth. Confidence is strengthening and financial conditions have improved. The pace of recovery is likely to be dampened by required fiscal consolidation, on-going private sector balance sheet adjustment and higher energy prices. Headline inflation has risen sharply due to energy price increases and higher indirect taxes, but underlying price pressures remain weak, reflecting high unemployment and significant spare capacity. The sovereign debt crisis and persisting imbalances within the euro area are a major risk to the outlook.

Prolonged fiscal consolidation is needed in most countries to stop rising debt-to-GDP ratios and then reduce them to more prudent levels. More credible and detailed multi-year budget plans need to be put in place. Strengthening EU and national fiscal institutions, including through proposed reforms, would help. Monetary policy stimulus should gradually be withdrawn once underlying inflationary pressures begin to emerge. Reforms of labour and product markets are needed to facilitate economic rebalancing and to boost long-term growth. Together with reforms of fiscal and macro-prudential policies, structural reforms would make the euro area more resilient.

Consumption and investment have gained momentum

GDP expanded at an average quarterly rate of 0.3% during the second half of 2010, despite a rundown of inventories and bad weather at the end of the year. Indicators point to strong growth in the near term. Private consumption and business investment have increased gradually, driven by stronger confidence and low interest rates. Exports have contributed strongly to growth, as world trade has continued to recover, boosted by rapidly expanding demand from emerging economies. Employment has expanded only modestly over the past year, however, and the unemployment rate remains close to 10%.

Euro area

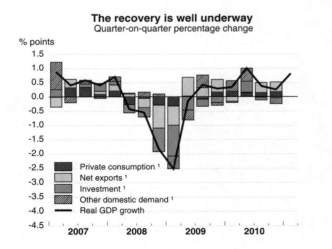

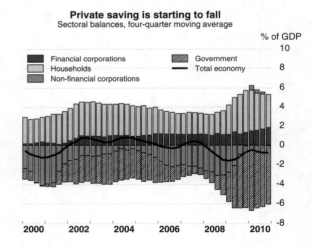

1. Contribution to the quarterly percentage change of the euro area GDP.
Source: OECD Economic Outlook 89 database and European Central Bank.

StatLink ⟨⟩ http://dx.doi.org/10.1787/888932429184

Euro area: **Employment, income and inflation**
Percentage changes

	2008	2009	2010	2011	2012
Employment	1.0	-1.8	-0.5	0.3	0.7
Unemployment rate[1]	7.4	9.4	9.9	9.7	9.3
Compensation per employee[2]	3.2	0.9	1.8	2.3	2.4
Labour productivity	-0.4	-2.3	2.2	1.6	1.3
Unit labour cost	3.9	3.9	-0.6	0.1	0.6
Household disposable income	3.4	-0.2	1.6	2.4	2.7
GDP deflator	2.0	1.0	0.9	1.1	1.3
Harmonised index of consumer prices	3.3	0.3	1.6	2.6	1.6
Core harmonised index of consumer prices[3]	1.8	1.4	1.0	1.2	1.4
Private consumption deflator	2.7	-0.2	1.8	2.4	1.5

Note: Covers the euro area countries that are members of the OECD.
1. As a percentage of labour force.
2. In the private sector.
3. Harmonised index of consumer prices excluding energy, food, drink and tobacco.
Source: OECD Economic Outlook 89 database.

StatLink ᴥᴥᴥ *http://dx.doi.org/10.1787/888932430267*

Some countries have remained in recession

While growth in the euro area as a whole has been picking up, some countries have lagged behind. GDP contracted in Greece, Ireland and Portugal during the second half of 2010 and there was a sharp fall in domestic demand in Spain. Output has remained weak in the early months of 2011. The contractionary short-run effect of rapid fiscal consolidation has added to weak private demand in most of these countries.

Euro area

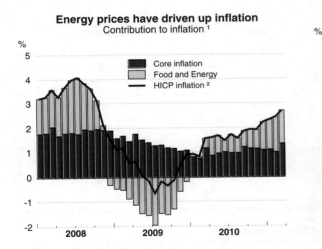

Energy prices have driven up inflation
Contribution to inflation [1]

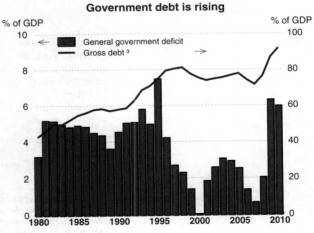

Government debt is rising

1. Represented by the harmonised consumer price index (HICP).
2. Year-on-year percentage change.
3. National accounts basis.
Source: OECD Economic Outlook 89 database.

StatLink ᴥᴥᴥ *http://dx.doi.org/10.1787/888932429203*

Euro area: **Financial indicators**

	2008	2009	2010	2011	2012
Household saving ratio[1]	9.0	10.0	9.2	8.4	8.3
General government financial balance[2]	-2.1	-6.3	-6.0	-4.2	-3.0
Current account balance[2]	-0.7	0.0	0.2	0.3	0.8
Short-term interest rate[3]	4.6	1.2	0.8	1.3	2.0
Long-term interest rate[4]	4.3	3.8	3.6	4.4	4.9

Note: Covers the euro area countries that are members of the OECD.
1. As a percentage of disposable income.
2. As a percentage of GDP.
3. 3-month interbank rate.
4. 10-year government bonds.
Source: OECD Economic Outlook 89 database.

StatLink http://dx.doi.org/10.1787/888932430286

Financial conditions continue to improve overall

Improved overall financial conditions are contributing positively to growth, while non-standard policy measures and government support for the financial sector are being gradually wound down. Credit to non-financial sector corporations and, especially, households is expanding. The publication of the third EU-wide stress tests should be used to address remaining weakness in the banking system to ensure that credit availability does not constrain the recovery. For several countries, sovereign spreads remain at very high levels and the state of the banking system, as well as financial conditions, is still fragile.

Euro area: **Demand and output**

	2009	2010	2011	2012	Fourth quarter		
					2010	2011	2012
	Current prices € billion	Percentage changes from previous year, volume (2009 prices)					
GDP at market prices	8 945.1	1.7	2.0	2.0	2.0	2.1	2.2
Private consumption	5 158.1	0.7	0.8	1.4	0.9	0.8	1.7
Government consumption	1 981.6	0.6	0.0	-0.1	0.4	-0.6	-0.1
Gross fixed investment	1 758.5	-0.8	2.5	3.4	1.5	3.1	3.9
Public	251.8	-7.3	-6.1	-6.0	-8.5	-6.3	-5.4
Residential	473.4	-3.2	0.6	1.8	-0.5	1.7	2.1
Non-residential	975.1	2.0	5.2	6.1	5.1	5.8	6.7
Final domestic demand	8 898.2	0.4	0.9	1.5	0.9	1.0	1.7
Stockbuilding[1]	- 69.1	0.6	0.2	0.0			
Total domestic demand	8 829.1	1.0	1.2	1.4	1.5	1.3	1.7
Net exports[1]	116.0	0.8	0.9	0.7			

Note: Detailed quarterly projections are reported for the major seven countries, the euro area and the total OECD in the Statistical Annex.
Covers the euro area countries that are members of the OECD.
1. Contributions to changes in real GDP (percentage of real GDP in previous year), actual amount in the first column.
Source: OECD Economic Outlook 89 database.

StatLink http://dx.doi.org/10.1787/888932430305

Euro area: **External indicators**

	2008	2009	2010	2011	2012
	$ billion				
Foreign balance	142.1	164.4	158.6	169	251
Invisibles, net	- 239.5	- 155.5	- 137.4	- 126	- 144
Current account balance	- 97.3	8.9	21.2	42	107

Note: Covers the euro area countries that are members of the OECD.
Source: OECD Economic Outlook 89 database.

StatLink http://dx.doi.org/10.1787/888932430324

Inflation has risen sharply

Headline annual inflation rose to 2.8% in April from 1.9% six months previously. The sharp increase was primarily due to a jump in energy prices. Over the past year, unusually large increases in indirect tax rates have contributed strongly to inflation. By contrast, annual inflation excluding food and energy prices, and at constant tax rates, has remained weak, consistent with the large degree of economic slack. Nominal hourly labour costs increased by just 1.6% during 2010 and available information on negiotated wages suggests further moderation in the short term. Inflation is likely to pick up only slowly, and the large degree of remaining slack suggests that the energy price increases will not trigger pronounced second-round effects.

Monetary conditions have remained accommodative

Monetary conditions have tightened slightly, albeit from a highly accommodative stance. The ECB's main refinancing rate was increased by 25 basis points to 1.25% in April, while short-term interbank rates have been on a rising trend as a result of expectations of future rate rises and greater convergence of market rates with the policy rate. Three-month refinancing operations allocated with full allotment will continue, at least for the coming months. The euro effective exchange rate has appreciated modestly over recent months. Provided that the recovery continues and that underlying inflationary pressures remain weak, monetary policy stimulus should be withdrawn only gradually, and further increases in policy rates are not required immediately. Non-standard measures should continue to be wound down as conditions allow.

On-going fiscal consolidation is required

The euro area government debt-to-GDP ratio is rising and passed 90% of GDP during 2010. Structural deficits must be brought down so that the debt burden can be stabilised and then reduced to more prudent levels. Fiscal consolidation is now underway in all countries, with consolidation particularly marked in countries with stabilisation programmes. Prolonged consolidation and tight public finances will be required for many years in numerous countries to meet the 60% ceiling set out in the Stability and Growth Pact. More credible and detailed multi-year plans need to be put in place. The commitment to consolidation would be enhanced by reforms to the Stability and Growth Pact and to national fiscal institutions, including by implementing and going beyond proposed reforms to the Pact. The agreed quantitative standard for debt reduction may help, but its effectiveness risks being undermined by the inclusion of other factors. The creation of the European Stability Mechanism (ESM) has the potential to add to stability both in the near and longer term, although its credibility requires that banking system exposure to governments is well managed.

The recovery will continue to gain strength

The recovery is projected to continue to gain strength during 2011 and 2012. Consumption will accelerate as improving labour market conditions, low interest rates and higher confidence reduce saving, offsetting the headwinds from pressures on real disposable income due to tax increases and energy prices. Private non-residential investment will bounce back as growth prospects improve and spare capacity is gradually absorbed, assisted by more favourable financial conditions. Export growth will remain strong as export markets grow, even if the rate of expansion eases modestly and the effects of the stronger euro are felt. However, the required fiscal consolidation implies only very modest growth in government spending over the forecast horizon. Growth will also be held back by on-going balance sheet adjustment and rebalancing of demand in several countries. The growth rate of potential output, in the absence of further major structural reforms, would be lower than in previous recoveries, continuing past trends in productivity growth and reflecting the impact of demographic ageing.

Uncertainty has increased, but risks are broadly balanced

The euro area is sensitive to uncertainty around future energy prices and world trade following in the wake of the earthquake in Japan. Risks around the pace of the recovery in domestic demand remain substantial but broadly balanced. The recovery in consumption and business investment could be stronger than anticipated, although weakness in countries undergoing difficult adjustment could be greater than foreseen. Remaining imbalances within the euro area and a disorderly unwinding of economic and financial imbalances in the context of the sovereign debt crisis pose major risks to the outlook. Weaknesses in government and bank solvency could lead to wider financial tensions and contagion, which would test the European Financial Stability Fund (EFSF) and the banking system.

GERMANY

The export-led recovery is continuing, with domestic demand, notably business investment and private consumption, increasingly contributing to growth. Employment continues to rise and, coupled with wage increases, should support private consumption growth over the next couple of years. Growth is projected to slow somewhat in 2012 as the output gap closes during that year.

Government finances have benefitted from strong economic growth with the deficit increasing only marginally in 2010, to 3.3% of GDP, by far the lowest among G7 countries. Nevertheless, government debt rose significantly in 2010, for the most part owing to measures to stabilise the banking sector. The consolidation measures that the government has appropriately put forward should be implemented as planned to bring down the budget deficit and meet the fiscal rule.

Real GDP has accelerated sharply...

The economy continues its robust rebound. After weakening at the end of 2010, due to adverse weather, growth bounced back strongly at the start of 2011. The underlying growth momentum accelerated, thanks to solid investment in machinery and equipment and rising export demand. Private consumption also contributed to growth, not least reflecting a reduction in households' saving rates as the unemployment rate fell significantly below its pre-crisis lows.

... and growth momentum is expected to remain strong

Recent indicators suggest that growth will continue to be strong in the near term, though less buoyant than at the start of the year. Manufacturing orders increased further, with those coming from countries outside the euro area already reaching their pre-crisis levels. Business confidence remains at historically high levels, suggesting that any adverse growth effects from the earthquake in Japan – notably through supply chains – will be limited. As spare capacity is being reduced with the output gap closing fast, firms are increasingly undertaking

Germany

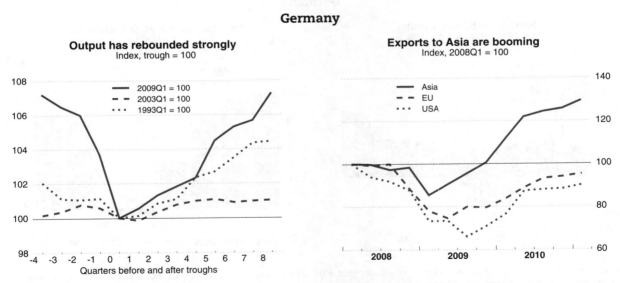

Note: Growth refers to that of real GDP. Exports are of goods and for 2011Q1 refer to January and February 2011.
Source: Deutsche Bundesbank; OECD, National Accounts database.

StatLink ᵐˢᵖ http://dx.doi.org/10.1787/888932429222

Germany: **Employment, income and inflation**
Percentage changes

	2008	2009	2010	2011	2012
Employment	1.4	0.0	0.5	1.0	0.6
Unemployment rate[1]	7.3	7.4	6.8	6.0	5.4
Compensation of employees	3.6	0.3	2.8	3.4	3.2
Unit labour cost	2.8	5.2	-0.7	-0.1	0.6
Household disposable income	3.2	-1.0	2.7	3.0	3.1
GDP deflator	1.0	1.4	0.6	0.7	1.2
Harmonised index of consumer prices	2.8	0.2	1.2	2.6	1.7
Core harmonised index of consumer prices[2]	1.3	1.3	0.6	1.1	1.5
Private consumption deflator	1.7	0.0	2.0	2.2	1.6

1. As a percentage of labour force, based on national accounts.
2. Harmonised index of consumer prices excluding food, energy, alcohol and tobacco.
Source: OECD Economic Outlook 89 database.

StatLink http://dx.doi.org/10.1787/888932430343

capital-widening investment. While the currently high inflation rates, boosted by high energy and food prices, may hamper private consumption, higher but still moderate wage settlements and continued employment gains are likely to foster spending by households.

The labour market is tightening

Even though firms both hoarded labour and substantially reduced hours worked during the downturn, employment grew faster than in most other major OECD economies in 2010 and had already reached its pre-crisis level by the middle of the year. This suggests that past labour market reforms that raised employment incentives continue to enhance labour market performance. Indeed, the structural unemployment rate is

Germany

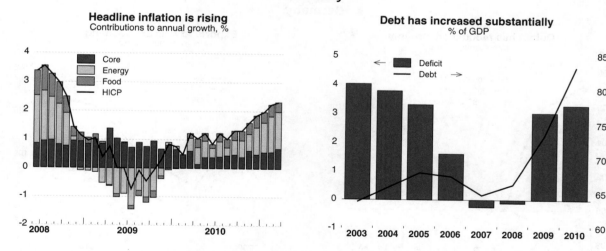

Headline inflation is rising
Contributions to annual growth, %

Debt has increased substantially
% of GDP

Note: Core refers to the harmonised index of consumer prices (HICP) excluding food, energy, alcohol and tobacco. Deficit and debt (Maastricht definition) refer to general government.
Source: Eurostat; OECD, Economic Outlook 89 database.

StatLink http://dx.doi.org/10.1787/888932429241

Germany: **Financial indicators**

	2008	2009	2010	2011	2012
Household saving ratio[1]	11.7	11.1	11.4	10.9	10.9
General government financial balance[2]	0.1	-3.0	-3.3	-2.1	-1.2
Current account balance[2]	6.3	5.6	5.6	5.5	6.0
Short-term interest rate[3]	4.6	1.2	0.8	1.3	2.0
Long-term interest rate[4]	4.0	3.2	2.7	3.3	4.0

1. As a percentage of disposable income.
2. As a percentage of GDP.
3. 3-month interbank rate.
4. 10-year government bonds.
Source: OECD Economic Outlook 89 database.

StatLink ⟨≡⟩ http://dx.doi.org/10.1787/888932430362

estimated to have kept falling throughout the crisis. However, with unemployment continuing to fall, the labour market is getting tighter and labour shortages are beginning to emerge in some sectors. This will lead to wage pressure and compensation per employee is projected to rise by around 3% in 2012, the highest rate since the mid-1990s. As a

Germany: **Demand and output**

	2009	2010	2011	2012	Fourth quarter		
					2010	2011	2012
	Current prices € billion	Percentage changes from previous year, volume (2000 prices)					
GDP at market prices	2 395.0	3.5	3.4	2.5	4.0	3.1	2.7
Private consumption	1 411.4	0.4	1.3	1.4	1.4	1.2	1.6
Government consumption	472.1	2.3	1.5	1.0	2.9	1.0	1.0
Gross fixed investment	421.7	5.7	6.3	4.0	7.5	6.2	4.6
Public	39.3	-0.6	0.7	-6.6	-7.5	-2.1	-4.0
Residential	134.2	4.0	2.3	2.2	2.8	4.3	2.6
Non-residential	248.2	7.6	9.3	6.3	12.7	8.4	6.7
Final domestic demand	2 305.2	1.7	2.3	1.8	2.8	2.1	2.1
Stockbuilding[1]	- 27.8	0.6	-0.2	0.0			
Total domestic demand	2 277.4	2.4	2.1	1.8	3.6	2.4	2.1
Exports of goods and services	976.7	13.8	10.4	7.7	15.7	8.1	7.6
Imports of goods and services	859.2	12.4	8.0	6.7	16.5	7.1	7.0
Net exports[1]	117.6	1.2	1.5	0.8			
Memorandum items							
GDP without working day adjustments	2 397.2	3.6	3.4	2.3			
Investment in machinery and equipment	182.2	9.8	11.0	6.0	16.0	7.9	6.2
Construction investment	239.6	2.6	2.5	2.3	1.1	4.8	3.2

Note: National accounts are based on official chain-linked data. This introduces a discrepancy in the identity between real demand components and GDP. For further details see *OECD Economic Outlook* Sources and Methods *(http://www.oecd.org/eco/sources-and-methods).*
Detailed quarterly projections are reported for the major seven countries, the euro area and the total OECD in the Statistical Annex.
1. Contributions to changes in real GDP (percentage of real GDP in previous year), actual amount in the first column.
Source: OECD Economic Outlook 89 database.

StatLink ⟨≡⟩ http://dx.doi.org/10.1787/888932430381

consequence, core inflation is likely to increase even as headline inflation falls back as the impact of energy and food price increases fades out.

The budget deficit is falling rapidly

In 2010, the fiscal deficit was little changed as cyclical improvements, helped by one-off measures (such as the proceeds from a mobile phone frequency auction) almost fully offset expenditure increasing measures worth around 1% of GDP. At 3.3% of GDP, general government net lending in 2010 was by far the lowest among G7 countries. With continued above-trend growth and consolidation measures worth about 0.5% of GDP a year through 2014, the deficit is set to fall further. This consolidation is appropriate and well-timed given the cyclical position of the economy and is needed to meet the constitutional fiscal rule. Some of the announced measures, however, still need to be further specified. Despite the relatively good deficit position, public debt increased sharply in 2010 to over 80% of GDP, mostly reflecting the government's assumption of risk assets and liabilities in connection with the setting up of resolution agencies for some banks. Financing this additional debt burden coupled with the rise in government bond yields will raise interest expenditures by around 0.3% of GDP. These developments, and the prospect of higher ageing-related spending, underline the necessity to keep public finances on a prudent track.

Above potential growth is projected for 2012

The economy is projected to continue growing significantly above its potential growth rate (estimated at around 1½ per cent) in both 2011 and 2012. Growth will be boosted by the ECB monetary conditions, which are too loose given the rise in Germany's nominal GDP. In particular investment spending, including residential investment, benefits from the current situation that is expected to prevail over the projection horizon. Even though quarterly growth in the remainder of 2011 will slow somewhat from the buoyant level in the first quarter, annual average growth is projected to reach around 3½ per cent. The main contributions will come from both investment spending, as firms expand capacity in view of the closing output gap, and exports, due to continued strong growth in the main export partners. Private consumption growth is also projected to accelerate, in particular once headline inflation rates decrease. In 2012, domestic demand is projected to contribute two-thirds to overall GDP growth of 2½ per cent on a working-day adjusted basis (annual growth in non-adjusted terms will be 2¼ per cent).

Risks go in both directions

There are upside as well as downside risks to this forecast. On the negative side, export growth could be weaker, possibly related to a further rise in commodity and energy prices hampering world trade. Higher inflation would further dent real disposable income of households and, thus, consumption growth. A deterioration of financial conditions or the situation in the banking sector, potentially related to a government debt restructuring in the euro area periphery, would hurt investment. On the positive side, private consumption could grow more rapidly if household income grew more rapidly than projected or if consumers became more confident and lower their saving rate.

FRANCE

A modest recovery is underway, but the recession will leave lasting traces. Real GDP is projected to grow by over 2% in both 2011 and 2012, led by business investment and exports. The unemployment rate is set to decline slightly towards 9% by the end of 2012. Substantial spare capacity is expected to limit any second-round effects of rising import prices, and underlying and headline inflation should converge to about 1½ per cent in 2012.

The government's fiscal consolidation trajectory is appropriate, but more efforts will be required down the road. The focus should be on curbing spending through bolstering public-sector efficiency and limiting health-care costs. Revenue increases could be achieved by broadening tax bases and raising environmental and property tax rates. Fiscal credibility needs to be reinforced through a meaningful institutional reform. Boosting potential output by addressing labour market weaknesses and continuing to enhance the supply side of the economy would help ease fiscal imbalances.

Growth has been robust recently...

Real GDP growth rose sharply and job creation moved up in the first quarter, and indicators point to prolonged strength, though at a slower pace. Part of the recent strength is due to temporary factors: weather conditions, which were a drag on activity at the end of last year, have been particularly favourable, while car orders related to the end of the 2010 "cash-for-clunkers" scheme translated into robust consumption in the first quarter (due to lags in deliveries). So far private consumption and exports have been the main engines of the recovery, but business investment is now picking up speed after a moderate recovery in 2010.

... but the labour market remains deeply affected

The unemployment rate has been decreasing only slowly. However, even this modest decline disappears when the definition of unemployment is broadened to include registered jobseekers who are currently employed

France

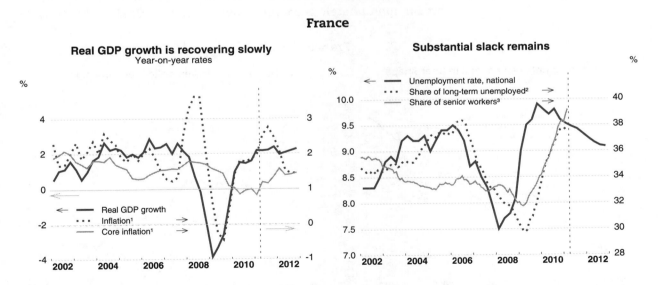

Real GDP growth is recovering slowly
Year-on-year rates

Real GDP growth
Inflation[1]
Core inflation[1]

Substantial slack remains

Unemployment rate, national
Share of long-term unemployed[2]
Share of senior workers[3]

1. Harmonised consumer prices.
2. Workers registered at Pole emploi for more than 1 year (categories A, B and C).
3. Workers aged 50 or more registered in Pole emploi's A category, multiplied by 2.

Source: Dares; OECD, Economic Outlook 89 database.

StatLink http://dx.doi.org/10.1787/888932429260

France: **Employment, income and inflation**
Percentage changes

	2008	2009	2010	2011	2012
Employment	1.4	-0.9	0.2	0.6	1.0
Unemployment rate[1]	7.4	9.1	9.3	9.1	8.8
Compensation of employees	3.1	0.1	2.3	3.3	3.5
Unit labour cost	3.0	2.8	0.9	1.0	1.4
Household disposable income	3.0	1.1	2.4	2.8	3.2
GDP deflator	2.6	0.7	0.8	1.5	1.3
Harmonised index of consumer prices	3.2	0.1	1.7	2.4	1.6
Core harmonised index of consumer prices[2]	1.8	1.4	1.0	1.1	1.5
Private consumption deflator	2.9	-0.4	1.2	2.1	1.4
Memorandum item					
Unemployment rate[3]	7.8	9.5	9.7	9.5	9.3

1. As a percentage of labour force, metropolitan France.
2. Harmonised index of consumer prices excluding food, energy, alcohol and tobacco.
3. As a percentage of labour force, national unemployment rate, includes overseas departments and territories.
Source: OECD Economic Outlook 89 database.

StatLink http://dx.doi.org/10.1787/888932430400

part-time (and still have to actively make job-search efforts). Also, long-term unemployment is still increasing. Combined with the rising share of older workers among the unemployed, the risk that structural unemployment will rise is significant. Recent labour-market and pension reforms will tend to increase participation and eventually employment, even though recorded unemployment could rise in the short run.

Monetary policy is still stimulative...

Despite the recent modest tightening of the monetary stance and the increase in long-term interest rates since last fall, credit conditions remain appropriately accommodative for France. Credit to the private

France

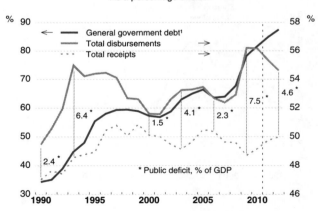

Public finances are still in poor shape
As a percentage of GDP

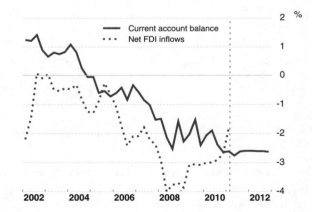

The current account deficit remains high
As a percentage of GDP

1. Maastricht definition.
Source: OECD, Economic Outlook 89 database; Banque de France.

StatLink http://dx.doi.org/10.1787/888932429279

France: **Financial indicators**

	2008	2009	2010	2011	2012
Household saving ratio[1]	15.4	16.2	16.0	15.4	15.3
General government financial balance[2]	-3.3	-7.5	-7.0	-5.6	-4.6
Current account balance[2]	-1.9	-2.1	-2.2	-2.6	-2.6
Short-term interest rate[3]	4.6	1.2	0.8	1.3	2.0
Long-term interest rate[4]	4.2	3.6	3.1	3.7	4.4

1. As a percentage of disposable income (gross saving).
2. As a percentage of GDP.
3. 3-month interbank rate.
4. 10-year benchmark government bonds.
Source: OECD Economic Outlook 89 database.

StatLink http://dx.doi.org/10.1787/888932430419

sector continues to recover steadily, though credit to non-financial businesses remains weak. Housing-related credit is growing at a fast pace, fuelling demand for housing and contributing to rapidly rising house prices in some areas. The question arises whether a prolonged period of easy finance may be resulting in a price bubble.

... while the terms of trade weigh on income

Sharply increasing commodity prices, although moderated by the euro's recent strengthening, pushed up headline inflation, which reached 2.1% in April and will keep rising for a few more months. However, given

France: **Demand and output**

	2009	2010	2011	2012	Fourth quarter		
					2010	2011	2012
	Current prices € billion	Percentage changes from previous year, volume (2000 prices)					
GDP at market prices	1 907.2	1.4	2.2	2.1	1.6	2.4	2.3
Private consumption	1 112.6	1.3	1.5	1.9	1.1	1.5	2.2
Government consumption	469.7	1.2	0.5	0.1	0.4	0.3	0.2
Gross fixed investment	392.1	-1.1	4.0	4.6	1.9	4.3	4.8
Public	63.9	-11.3	-1.2	1.0	-8.9	1.7	1.0
Residential	110.2	-1.4	2.2	2.0	2.3	1.4	2.0
Non-residential	218.0	2.0	6.1	6.6	4.5	6.3	7.0
Final domestic demand	1 974.4	0.8	1.8	2.0	1.1	1.7	2.3
Stockbuilding[1]	- 30.1	0.4	0.9	0.0			
Total domestic demand	1 944.4	1.2	2.6	2.0	1.4	2.6	2.3
Exports of goods and services	439.6	9.5	6.6	7.7	11.5	6.9	7.8
Imports of goods and services	476.7	8.2	7.7	6.8	9.8	7.4	7.2
Net exports[1]	- 37.1	0.1	-0.5	0.0			

Note: National accounts are based on official chain-linked data. This introduces a discrepancy in the identity between real demand components and GDP. For further details see *OECD Economic Outlook* Sources and Methods *(http://www.oecd.org/eco/sources-and-methods)*.
Detailed quarterly projections are reported for the major seven countries, the euro area and the total OECD in the Statistical Annex.
1. Contributions to changes in real GDP (percentage of real GDP in previous year), actual amount in the first column.
Source: OECD Economic Outlook 89 database.

StatLink http://dx.doi.org/10.1787/888932430438

the slack in the economy, second-round effects on core inflation should be limited.

The fiscal stance is being appropriately tightened

Against the background of a better-than-expected fiscal deficit in 2010, at 7% of GDP, the government maintained its commitment to reduce the deficit to 4.6% in 2012 and to 2% in 2014. Significant and decisive consolidation is warranted both to move the public finances back towards sustainability and to protect against jittery financial markets. Beyond 2014, the more ambitious objective of eliminating the deficit entirely is called for in order to bring down debt at an appropriate pace.

Discipline should be maintained throughout the pre-election period and beyond

For 2011, the structural balance is expected to improve by almost 1% of GDP thanks to the disappearance of self-reversing policies included in the anti-crisis package, as well as cuts in tax expenditures and current spending. Other actions include a public sector pay freeze, the non-replacement of half of all retiring workers in central government, an increase in capital gains taxation and a new tax on banks. Broadly in line with government objectives, the projection assumes a further reduction in the total deficit from 5.6% in 2011 to 4.6% of GDP in 2012; however, the precise steps that will bring it about should be spelt out quickly. As France is entering a pre-election period, uncertainty as to the achievement of planned consolidation is increasing.

Fiscal efforts should focus mainly on curbing spending

Most of the consolidation effort in France must come from restraining spending. Extending the General Public Policy Review to all levels of public administration and shrinking programmes that are not cost effective will be key. Consolidation of small municipalities and elimination of departments could generate substantial economies of scale. Considerable savings could be made without impairing the quality of the health-care system by reducing the frequency and length of stays in hospitals, lowering administrative costs and expanding the use of generic drugs and capitation-based physician compensation. To the extent increased revenues are needed, tax expenditures should be cut further, including on saving schemes. Also, raising taxes on environmental externalities, such as carbon emissions, as well as others that are the least distortive – in particular, taxes on property and the VAT – should be considered.

Other structural reforms would promote consolidation

The need for a clean break with the past management of fiscal policy is increasingly recognised, but institutional reform, currently under discussion, is needed. A stronger fiscal framework – consisting of a structural deficit rule, detailed multi-year budgeting and an independent fiscal council through a constitutional reform – could lock in the political commitment and anchor long-term credibility. Structural reforms that boost employment and bolster growth would also greatly contribute to restoring public finances. Efforts should focus on overcoming job-market weaknesses and continue to put the accent on the supply of output.

Activity will pick up slowly

Real GDP growth is projected to increase from 1.4% in 2010 to 2.2% in 2011 and 2.1% in 2012, notwithstanding ongoing fiscal consolidation. Private investment and exports should be buoyant, helped by accommodative credit conditions and robust global activity, including stronger German domestic demand. Unfortunately, the unemployment rate is likely to decline only moderately, while price pressures will remain subdued, with underlying inflation remaining well below 2%. With indebted owner-occupier households in a healthy solvency position, there is no need for major deleveraging. Private consumption should thus continue to be supportive, with the saving rate easing to its pre-crisis level as lower joblessness and a shrinking public deficit work to restore household confidence. Given the waning terms-of-trade deterioration, the current account deficit should plateau at around 2.6% of GDP.

Risks remain high

Considerable uncertainty surrounds both economic activity abroad and interest- and exchange-rate developments. The underlying growth momentum could be more robust than anticipated. On the other hand, debt restructuring in EU peripheral countries could prolong turmoil on sovereign bond markets, harming French banks, which are highly exposed to these countries. A correction of the French housing market might also weaken the banking sector. A large degree of uncertainty surrounds the impacts of such factors.

ITALY

Italy's slow recovery is projected to continue with growth strengthening somewhat to around 1½ per cent in 2012. Buoyant world demand will stimulate the export sector and investment growth should re-accelerate too. Unemployment will fall only slowly, partly because the initial improvement in labour demand will be absorbed by reduced use of short-time working. After picking up quite sharply recently, headline inflation is expected to fall back as the impact of increases in energy and food prices diminishes.

After achieving a lower budget deficit than planned in 2010, the government is maintaining its previous fiscal targets for 2011 and 2012. This requires, as assumed in the present projections, continued tight control of expenditure and further improvements in tax collection. Such vigilance is necessary because of the high debt-to-GDP ratio, even though this is set to decline in 2012, and the likely increase in the cost of debt service as long-term interest rates climb in the medium term. The government's National Reform Programme contains an impressive list of priorities for reform; this must be effectively implemented to enhance the economy's potential to reduce the debt burden through growth.

The recovery has slowed, as industrial production is sluggish

The Italian economy continued to recover during 2010, though at an uneven pace and with some slackening at the end of the year. The strong growth in industrial production of the first half of 2010 gave way to a period of sluggish performance through the winter months, as investment demand may have been damped by the ending of fiscal incentives in mid-2010 and production in important partner countries was cut by severe weather. Even so, imports and exports grew much faster than overall domestic activity. In the year to February 2011, growth in goods export volumes considerably outpaced that of imports, though falling terms of trade, as oil and other commodity prices rose substantially, kept the balance of trade in deficit.

Italy

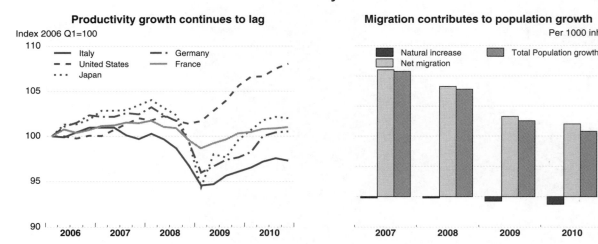

Source: Institute National of Statistics (INSTAT) and OECD Economic Outlook 89 database.

StatLink ⟨⟨⟩⟩ http://dx.doi.org/10.1787/888932429298

Italy: **Employment, income and inflation**
Percentage changes

	2008	2009	2010	2011	2012
Employment[1]	0.3	-1.6	-0.7	0.7	0.8
Unemployment rate[1,2]	6.8	7.8	8.4	8.4	8.1
Compensation of employees	3.9	-1.2	0.7	2.3	2.2
Unit labour cost	5.3	4.3	-0.5	1.2	0.6
Household disposable income	2.2	-3.0	1.4	3.4	2.7
GDP deflator	2.8	2.3	0.6	1.3	1.6
Harmonised index of consumer prices	3.5	0.8	1.6	2.4	1.7
Core harmonised index of consumer prices[3]	2.2	1.6	1.7	1.3	1.6
Private consumption deflator	3.2	0.0	1.5	2.6	1.7

1. Data for whole economy employment are from the national accounts. These data include an estimate made by Istat for employment in the underground economy. Total employment according to the national accounts is higher than labour force survey data indicate, by approximately 2 million or about 10%. The unemployment rate is calculated relative to labour force survey data.
2. As a percentage of labour force.
3. Harmonised index of consumer prices excluding food, energy, alcohol and tobacco.
Source: OECD Economic Outlook 89 database.

StatLink http://dx.doi.org/10.1787/888932430457

Producers are more confident than consumers

Despite weaker output during the winter, confidence in manufacturing companies has continued to improve and is not far below the levels reached before the crisis, although these were not particularly high. By contrast, indicators of consumer confidence have been broadly stable or tending to decline since the high levels reached in early 2010. Bank lending continues to accelerate, while there has been no change in overall credit conditions; a number of banking groups successfully raised equity capital in early 2011.

Italy

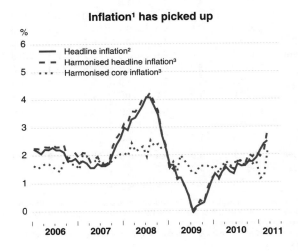

Inflation[1] has picked up

— Headline inflation[2]
-- Harmonised headline inflation[3]
··· Harmonised core inflation[3]

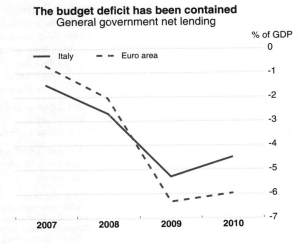

The budget deficit has been contained
General government net lending

— Italy   -- Euro area

1. Year-on year growth rates.
2. National definition.
3. Not seasonally adjusted.
Source: OECD Economic Outlook 89 database.

StatLink http://dx.doi.org/10.1787/888932429317

Italy: **Financial indicators**

	2008	2009	2010	2011	2012
Household saving ratio[1]	8.2	7.1	6.1	6.0	5.7
General government financial balance[2]	-2.7	-5.3	-4.5	-3.9	-2.6
Current account balance[2]	-2.9	-2.1	-3.5	-4.1	-3.6
Short-term interest rate[3]	4.6	1.2	0.8	1.3	2.0
Long-term interest rate[4]	4.7	4.3	4.0	4.8	5.4

1. Net saving as a percentage of net disposable income. Includes "famiglie produttrici".
2. As a percentage of GDP. These figures are national accounts basis; they differ by 0.1% from the frequently quoted Excessive Deficit Procedure figures.
3. 3-month interbank rate.
4. 10-year government bonds.
Source: OECD Economic Outlook 89 database.

StatLink http://dx.doi.org/10.1787/888932430476

Productivity growth has remained low and migration inflows have been strong

As in some other European countries, labour productivity fell substantially during the recession and Italy's slow recovery has done little to raise productivity growth subsequently. The impact of low productivity growth, and the low or negative rate of natural increase in population, have been offset to some extent by high levels of immigration of people of working age. Net immigration has been running at around 400 000 people a year in the past 3 years, while longer term projections by Eurostat are for average flows over the period 2005-60 of about 220 000 people per year.

Italy: **Demand and output**

	2009	2010	2011	2012	Fourth quarter		
					2010	2011	2012
	Current prices € billion	Percentage changes from previous year, volume (2000 prices)					
GDP at market prices	1 519.2	1.2	1.1	1.6	1.5	1.3	1.6
Private consumption	912.4	1.0	0.9	1.2	1.0	0.9	1.3
Government consumption	326.2	-0.6	-0.1	-0.1	-1.1	0.6	-0.5
Gross fixed investment	289.4	2.3	1.2	2.5	2.7	1.9	2.6
Machinery and equipment	134.2	9.4	2.6	3.3	7.7	2.7	3.3
Construction	155.2	-3.7	-0.1	1.8	-1.8	1.1	1.9
Residential	73.2	-2.4	0.6	1.8	0.3	1.1	1.9
Non-residential	82.0	-4.9	-0.8	1.8	-3.6	1.1	1.9
Final domestic demand	1 528.1	0.9	0.8	1.2	0.9	1.0	1.2
Stockbuilding[1]	- 2.7	0.7	0.6	0.0			
Total domestic demand	1 525.4	1.6	1.3	1.2	2.3	0.6	1.2
Exports of goods and services	361.9	8.9	6.9	6.9	10.1	6.9	7.3
Imports of goods and services	368.1	10.3	7.2	4.9	13.3	3.6	5.5
Net exports[1]	- 6.2	-0.4	-0.2	0.4			

Note: National accounts are based on official chain-linked data. This introduces a discrepancy in the identity between real demand components and GDP. For further details see *OECD Economic Outlook* Sources and Methods *(http://www.oecd.org/eco/sources-and-methods).*
Detailed quarterly projections are reported for the major seven countries, the euro area and the total OECD in the Statistical Annex.
1. Contributions to changes in real GDP (percentage of real GDP in previous year), actual amount in the first column.
Source: OECD Economic Outlook 89 database.

StatLink http://dx.doi.org/10.1787/888932430495

Unemployment has stabilised and wage growth has drifted down a little

Labour market slack may have begun to shrink as unemployment began to fall from its peak in October 2010. Use of the short-time working compensation scheme, the *Cassa Integrazione*, has been diminishing as well. However, labour participation has also resumed its decline after showing signs of beginning to recover in the autumn of 2010. Growth in contractual wages has gradually fallen, to around 2% by March 2011. This is similar to wage growth in Germany despite Italy's weaker competitive situation and lower productivity growth.

Inflation has accelerated, largely due to food and energy

Headline price inflation has been rising, as elsewhere, under the influence of energy and commodity prices. It reached 2.5% in March, while core inflation, though it has increased slightly, remained more subdued, at 1.7%. A Bank of Italy survey of companies in December 2010 showed that their expectations of inflation have also been increasing, though inflation was still expected to be only just over 2% over the next one to two years.

Fiscal consolidation has helped to contain interest rate spreads

There was a significant improvement in the budget deficit in 2010, as it fell from 5.3% of GDP in 2009 to 4.5% in 2010, lower than the government's target of 5%. This good performance has helped to contain interest rate spreads against Germany, although there has been some volatility. A sharp fall in public investment was an important contributor to improved government finances, while public consumption also declined and interest payments were lower than planned.

Fiscal consolidation will continue

The government's new Stability Programme confirms the deficit targets of the previous programme for 2011 (3.9% of GDP) and 2012 (2.7%). These should now be easier to achieve given the improvement already seen in 2010. It is notable that fiscal projections are based on lower, more prudent, growth expectations than previous Programmes. The Stability Programme also confirms that the government will seek to bring the budget into approximate balance by 2014. This is an important objective if the debt-GDP ratio is to be brought down in the medium term, especially as rising long-term interest rates are likely to generate an increase in the cost of debt service as existing debt is rolled over.

Growth is picking up, helped by world trade

In the short term, growth is projected to pick up after a weak start to 2011. Strong growth in world trade should support exports; the investment cycle, though rather weak, will also support demand. Private consumption is likely to grow in line with incomes, as little change in the saving ratio is expected, while public consumption and investment will remain very subdued.

Wage and price inflation should stabilise

With labour market conditions improving only slowly, wage growth is projected to remain stable and price inflation will fall back provided that energy and commodity prices stabilise, as assumed in these projections.

The outlook is uncertain but the risks are balanced   Investment has been weaker than expected earlier and, with the possibility of a partial reversal of the strong stockbuilding in 2010, the first half of 2011 could be quite weak. Thereafter Italy should benefit eventually from world trade growth and the investment cycle could then turn out to be even stronger than projected. In contrast, continuation of recent strong increases in commodity prices could weaken prospects for growth. Prolonged turmoil in the euro area periphery might also affect investment prospects negatively.

UNITED KINGDOM

The recovery paused in end-2010 and growth is projected to remain weak in 2011, despite rising exports and business investment, but to pick up in 2012. Above-target inflation, driven by tax increases and commodity prices, and needed fiscal consolidation, will hold back private consumption and public spending during 2011-12. Inflation will remain above the 2% target through 2011 and most of 2012, but is set to fall when the effects of the tax increases and rising import prices wane. As inflation falls, private consumption should start to recover. Unemployment is likely to increase in the short term, reflecting the slow recovery and rising labour force participation.

The current fiscal consolidation strikes the right balance and should continue in line with the government's medium-term plan to eliminate the deficit, while allowing the automatic stabilisers to work. An upward harmonisation of VAT rates combined with higher infrastructure spending would lower the short-term negative growth effects of consolidation without affecting its pace. Further reforms to improve public sector efficiency and increasing the effective retirement age would mitigate fiscal pressures. Monetary policy should remain expansionary over the forecast period to support activity in view of the tightening fiscal stance. However, normalisation of interest rates will need to start during 2011 to stave off significant increases in inflation expectations.

Growth has paused due to strong headwinds

The recovery started in 2009, but output fell in late 2010, hit by severe weather in December and growing headwinds from rising inflation and fiscal consolidation. Growth resumed in early 2011, but at a moderate pace, as government spending was stagnant and household real incomes fell due to above target inflation. Notwithstanding fiscal consolidation, domestic demand will pick up, though only slowly, as business investment rises and, once inflation subsides, household consumption strengthens. Exports have risen significantly but continue to underperform relative to other OECD countries despite a significant

United Kingdom

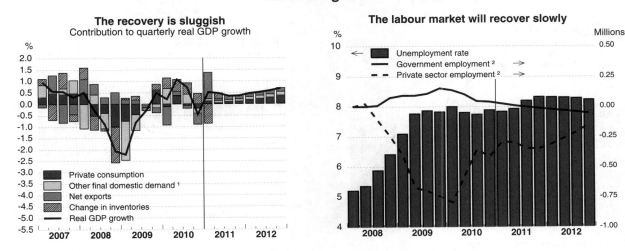

1. Consists of gross fixed capital investment, government consumption and statistical discrepancy.
2. Changes compared to 2008Q1.

Source: OECD Economic Outlook 89 database.

StatLink http://dx.doi.org/10.1787/888932429336

United Kingdom: **Employment, income and inflation**
Percentage changes

	2008	2009	2010	2011	2012
Employment	0.7	-1.6	0.2	0.5	0.2
Unemployment rate[1]	5.7	7.6	7.9	8.1	8.3
Compensation of employees	2.3	0.7	2.8	2.8	2.8
Unit labour cost	2.3	5.9	1.6	1.4	0.9
Household disposable income	5.4	2.8	3.3	3.2	3.3
GDP deflator	3.0	1.4	2.9	3.4	2.1
Harmonised index of consumer prices[2]	3.6	2.2	3.3	4.2	2.1
Core harmonised index of consumer prices[3]	1.6	1.7	2.7	3.2	2.1
Private consumption deflator	3.1	1.3	4.3	4.5	2.2

1. As a percentage of labour force.
2. The HICP is known as the Consumer Price Index in the United Kingdom.
3. Harmonised index of consumer prices excluding food, energy, alcohol and tobacco.
Source: OECD Economic Outlook 89 database.

StatLink http://dx.doi.org/10.1787/888932430514

depreciation of the pound, reflecting limited improvements in relative export prices and still falling financial service exports. Employment started to rise during 2010, but rising labour force participation due to demographic factors has left the unemployment rate virtually unchanged since mid-2009 at slightly below 8%.

Financial conditions continue to improve

Financial conditions remain highly expansionary and access to credit for firms and households continues to improve. Credit growth continues to be subdued, however, mirroring weak demand from households and

United Kingdom

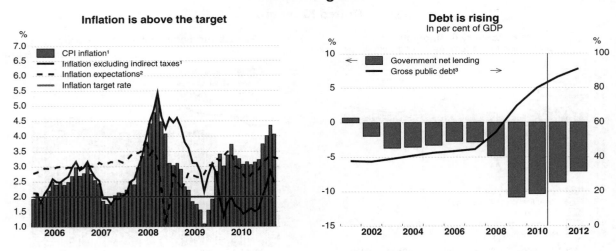

1. Year-on-year percentage change.
2. Implied by yield differentials between 10-year government benchmark bonds and inflation-indexed bonds.
3. Maastricht definition.
Source: OECD Economic Outlook 89 database, Bank of England and Office for National Statistics.

StatLink http://dx.doi.org/10.1787/888932429355

United Kingdom: **Financial indicators**

	2008	2009	2010	2011	2012
Household saving ratio[1]	2.0	6.0	5.4	4.6	4.6
General government financial balance[2]	-4.8	-10.8	-10.3	-8.7	-7.1
Current account balance[2]	-1.6	-1.7	-2.5	-1.5	-0.9
Short-term interest rate[3]	5.5	1.2	0.7	0.9	1.6
Long-term interest rate[4]	4.6	3.6	3.6	3.8	4.5

1. As a percentage of disposable income.
2. As a percentage of GDP.
3. 3-month interbank rate.
4. 10-year government bonds.
Source: OECD Economic Outlook 89 database.

StatLink http://dx.doi.org/10.1787/888932430533

firms. CPI inflation is still above 4%, reflecting lingering effects of the depreciation of the pound, VAT increases in 2010-11 and rising oil and food prices. Inflation expectations remain elevated, illustrating concerns about the Bank of England's willingness to tolerate significant and persistent deviations from the 2% target.

Fiscal consolidation continues

The fiscal deficit peaked at almost 11% of GDP in 2009, but has started to shrink as a consequence of consolidation. The government intends to achieve a cyclically adjusted current balance (that is, excluding net public investment) by the end of the 2015/16 budget year. The planned annual

United Kingdom: **Demand and output**

	2009	2010	2011	2012	Fourth quarter 2010	2011	2012
	Current prices £ billion	Percentage changes from previous year, volume (2006 prices)					
GDP at market prices	1 395.0	1.3	1.4	1.8	1.5	1.7	2.2
Private consumption	910.6	0.6	0.2	1.1	-0.1	0.6	1.6
Government consumption	326.9	0.8	0.2	-0.7	0.6	0.0	-1.0
Gross fixed investment	203.6	3.0	1.7	4.2	5.8	2.4	5.2
Public[1]	41.1	1.6	-11.9	-9.4	-8.0	-12.2	-7.6
Residential	41.3	5.5	1.0	4.2	3.3	2.2	4.6
Non-residential	121.3	2.6	6.7	8.0	12.2	7.2	8.8
Final domestic demand	1 441.2	1.0	0.4	1.1	0.9	0.7	1.6
Stockbuilding[2]	- 16.5	1.4	0.0	0.1			
Total domestic demand	1 424.7	2.4	0.4	1.2	2.8	0.1	1.5
Exports of goods and services	390.9	5.3	8.0	6.1	5.4	7.0	6.6
Imports of goods and services	420.6	8.5	4.0	3.7	9.4	1.2	4.2
Net exports[2]	- 29.7	-1.0	0.9	0.6			

Note: Detailed quarterly projections are reported for the major seven countries, the euro area and the total OECD in the Statistical Annex.
1. Including nationalised industries and public corporations.
2. Contributions to changes in real GDP (percentage of real GDP in previous year), actual amount in the first column.
Source: OECD Economic Outlook 89 database.

StatLink http://dx.doi.org/10.1787/888932430552

United Kingdom: **External indicators**

	2008	2009	2010	2011	2012
	\$ billion				
Goods and services exports	781.8	611.4	661.9	782	847
Goods and services imports	853.2	657.9	736.8	848	900
Foreign balance	- 71.3	- 46.4	- 75.0	- 66	- 52
Invisibles, net	28.3	9.3	18.9	29	30
Current account balance	- 43.1	- 37.1	- 56.1	- 37	- 22
	Percentage changes				
Goods and services export volumes	1.0	- 10.1	5.3	8.0	6.1
Goods and services import volumes	- 1.2	- 11.9	8.5	4.0	3.7
Export performance[1]	- 1.3	1.2	- 4.6	0.3	- 1.7
Terms of trade	0.0	- 0.9	- 0.3	- 1.1	- 0.2

1. Ratio between export volume and export market of total goods and services.
Source: OECD Economic Outlook 89 database.

StatLink ㎙ http://dx.doi.org/10.1787/888932430571

fiscal contraction between 2010 and 2012, which is built into these projections, amounts to roughly 1.6% of GDP. The fiscal deficit is projected by the OECD to fall to 7.1% of GDP in 2012, while gross public debt is expected to reach 93% of GDP.

Consolidation could be more supportive of growth and efficiency

Fiscal adjustment is necessary to rein in the deficit, slow the build-up of debt and ensure market credibility. Consolidation is set out in terms of reaching a cyclically-adjusted current balance, thus allowing the automatic stabilisers to operate. Nevertheless, consolidation measures should be implemented in a way that minimises the detrimental impact on short-term growth. Ending exemptions and increasing lower rates in the VAT system would increase efficiency and raise revenues that could be used to lessen cuts in infrastructure investment. Structural reforms to improve public sector efficiency and further increasing the effective retirement age, on top of the planned increase in the state pension age, would also ease long-term fiscal pressures.

The recovery will gain strength in 2012

Growth is projected to remain slow during 2011. Public consumption and investment are set to fall significantly, while household consumption is expected to stay subdued, reflecting falling real incomes and stagnant asset prices. Further increases in exports, supported by rising global demand, the low exchange rate and a fading drag from financial service exports will eventually underpin a somewhat stronger recovery in 2012. Business investment has fallen to low levels and will gather further pace in 2012, partly in response to rising exports. With weak domestic demand, imports will grow slowly and the current account deficit is expected to narrow through 2012.

The labour market will worsen in 2011

The sluggish growth is likely to temporarily halt the recovery in employment. As labour supply continues to grow, unemployment is therefore set to edge up. As activity picks up during 2012, employment growth should resume and unemployment should start to fall. The labour market recovery will be weak, however, owing to subdued GDP growth, declines in public employment and remaining scope for increases in working hours and productivity gains. Wage settlements and wage growth remain restrained, reflecting significant economic slack.

Inflation will remain above 4% in 2011

Inflation is set to remain above 4% all through 2011, due to the low exchange rate, VAT increases and significant price increases for oil and food. The impact from these factors should wane in 2012. A significant output gap and slow-growing unit labour costs are then expected to generate a slowdown in inflation to below the 2% target during the latter part of 2012.

Monetary policy should remain expansionary

With the Bank of England's policy rate close to zero and quantitative easing amounting to £200 billion (14% of GDP), monetary policy remains highly expansionary. This is appropriate as inflation is expected to fall in 2012. Nevertheless, a modest increase in interest rates should be taken during 2011 to stave off increases in inflation expectations, which are already elevated. As the recovery gathers momentum in 2012, the pace of normalisation of interest rates should be stepped up. A winding-down of quantitative easing should commence once policy rates have increased measurably, probably later than 2012.

Financial sector reforms should continue

The interim report from the Independent Commission on Banking gives useful suggestions on how to deal with banks that are "too big to fail" through ring-fencing retail banking within wider banking groups. A full break-up of banks and further increases in capital requirements should also remain options, however. Moving swiftly and decisively on bank reforms would, in combination with the setting up of the proposed macro-prudential framework, support financial stability.

Risks and uncertainties are significant

Substantial risks and uncertainty surround these projections. The extent to which the economic developments in late 2010 and early 2011 can be attributed to extreme weather conditions, volatility in measured activity in construction, the increase in the VAT rate and international developments remains unclear. The fall in household disposable incomes may bear down more on consumption than projected. Risks to the export sector are significant on both sides of the baseline projection. Whilst a further weakening in financial service exports remains a downside risk, exports, and therefore investment, may recover more quickly than projected in response to the weak pound.

CANADA

Economic activity rebounded vigorously through the winter, supported by strengthening external demand and a healthy rate of business investment. Growth is projected to moderate somewhat over the near term, as international supply chains suffer from the effects of the Japanese disaster, highly indebted households pare back spending and housing markets soften, but then gather speed again as unemployment recedes and the global recovery gains traction. Rising corporate profits and improving credit conditions should buttress robust business capital spending as a key driver of growth.

Fiscal stimulus is slowly being withdrawn this year as growth shifts more durably towards private demand. Federal and provincial governments should implement consolidation plans, largely through expenditure restraint, to reduce structural deficits and restore public-debt sustainability. Monetary policy is currently very accommodative, and short-term inflation expectations appear to be inching upwards. The Bank of Canada should soon resume tightening at a moderate pace.

The recovery has regained momentum

The economic recovery has gained firmer traction as real GDP accelerated in the final quarter of 2010 and into early 2011. Manufacturing activity has begun to expand rapidly following a sharp inventory drawdown at the end of 2010, and industrial capacity utilisation has been gradually increasing for several quarters. Strengthening business-sector confidence, credit growth and profitability are progressively returning private non-residential investment towards pre-recession levels. While the unemployment rate and average hours worked have yet to fully recover, employment has risen substantially, particularly in full-time and private-sector work. This, along with terms-of-trade gains, has bolstered household income and underpinned consumption spending. Government consumption and investment under the fiscal stimulus programme also continued to contribute significantly to growth in the final half of 2010.

Canada

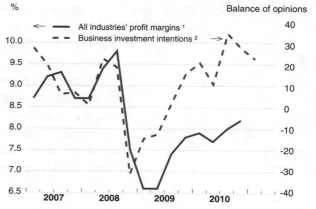

1. All industries operating profit as a share of operating revenue.
2. Spending on machinery and equipment over the next 12 months.
Source: Thomson Datastream; OECD Economic Outlook 89 database.

StatLink http://dx.doi.org/10.1787/888932429374

Canada: **Employment, income and inflation**
Percentage changes

	2008	2009	2010	2011	2012
Employment	1.7	-1.6	1.4	1.7	1.6
Unemployment rate[1]	6.1	8.3	8.0	7.5	7.0
Compensation of employees	4.3	0.1	4.0	4.8	4.9
Unit labour cost	3.8	2.6	0.9	1.7	2.0
Household disposable income	5.3	1.7	4.6	4.2	4.0
GDP deflator	4.0	-2.1	3.0	2.4	1.6
Consumer price index	2.4	0.3	1.8	2.9	1.6
Core consumer price index[2]	1.7	1.8	1.7	1.3	1.5
Private consumption deflator	1.6	0.5	1.3	1.7	1.4

1. As a percentage of labour force.
2. Consumer price index excluding the eight more volatile items.
Source: OECD Economic Outlook 89 database.

StatLink http://dx.doi.org/10.1787/888932430590

Export volumes rebounded vigorously at end-2010, buoyed by a firming global appetite for Canadian commodities and some temporary factors, but have moderated in early-2011.

Growth will be driven increasingly by business investment and exports

Robust growth in emerging market economies combined with a number of supply shocks have driven up the world price of commodities, boosting the terms of trade and demand for exports. A recovering US economy is expected to reinforce the profile of exports, although the high value of the Canadian dollar should continue to depress profitability and international competitiveness in the export-oriented manufacturing sector. Given relatively sluggish labour productivity, the languid performance of non-commodity exports in world markets is likely to

Canada

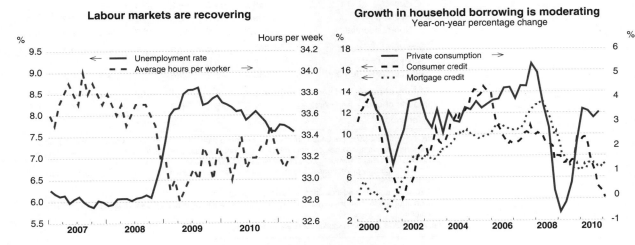

Labour markets are recovering

Growth in household borrowing is moderating
Year-on-year percentage change

Source: Thomson Datastream; OECD Economic Outlook 89 database.

StatLink http://dx.doi.org/10.1787/888932429393

Canada: **Financial indicators**

	2008	2009	2010	2011	2012
Household saving ratio[1]	3.6	4.6	4.4	4.3	4.2
General government financial balance[2]	0.0	-5.5	-5.5	-4.9	-3.5
Current account balance[2]	0.4	-2.8	-3.1	-2.6	-2.3
Short-term interest rate[3]	3.5	0.8	0.8	1.6	3.1
Long-term interest rate[4]	3.6	3.2	3.2	3.4	4.2

1. As a percentage of disposable income.
2. As a percentage of GDP.
3. 3-month deposit rate.
4. 10-year government bonds.
Source: OECD Economic Outlook 89 database.

StatLink http://dx.doi.org/10.1787/888932430609

persist. Providing some offset, the strong exchange rate should nevertheless lower the cost of imported machinery and equipment and encourage capital spending. With firms benefiting from improving credit conditions, sound financial health and lower tax rates, business investment should remain an important driver of growth. Investment intentions appear especially strong in the energy sector, which is enjoying high world prices.

Canada: **Demand and output**

	2009	2010	2011	2012	Fourth quarter 2010	Fourth quarter 2011	Fourth quarter 2012
	Current prices CAD billion	Percentage changes from previous year, volume (2002 prices)					
GDP at market prices	**1 527.3**	**3.1**	**3.0**	**2.8**	**3.2**	**3.0**	**3.0**
Private consumption	898.7	3.4	2.6	2.7	3.4	2.1	3.0
Government consumption	333.9	3.4	1.6	-0.4	2.1	0.6	-0.5
Gross fixed investment	328.5	8.3	6.8	5.4	9.6	6.5	4.4
Public[1]	58.2	14.0	4.2	-3.1	7.9	1.5	-5.0
Residential	99.0	10.3	-0.9	1.3	3.5	-0.3	2.2
Non-residential	171.2	5.2	12.7	10.7	14.2	12.5	8.7
Final domestic demand	1 561.1	4.4	3.3	2.6	4.4	2.7	2.6
Stockbuilding[2]	- 7.7	0.8	-0.7	0.0			
Total domestic demand	1 553.4	5.2	2.6	2.6	4.2	2.9	2.6
Exports of goods and services	438.6	6.4	8.4	7.9	7.2	8.0	7.8
Imports of goods and services	464.7	13.4	6.8	7.1	10.1	7.4	6.5
Net exports[2]	- 26.2	-2.2	0.3	0.2			

Note: National accounts are based on official chain-linked data. This introduces a discrepancy in the identity between real demand components and GDP. For further details see *OECD Economic Outlook* Sources and Methods *(http://www.oecd.org/eco/sources-and-methods).*
Detailed quarterly projections are reported for the major seven countries, the euro area and the total OECD in the Statistical Annex.
1. Excluding nationalised industries and public corporations.
2. Contributions to changes in real GDP (percentage of real GDP in previous year), actual amount in the first column.
Source: OECD Economic Outlook 89 database.

StatLink http://dx.doi.org/10.1787/888932430628

Canada: **External indicators**

	2008	2009	2010	2011	2012
			$ billion		
Goods and services exports	532.2	385.7	462.7	557	616
Goods and services imports	507.4	408.8	492.6	573	628
Foreign balance	24.8	- 23.1	- 29.9	- 16	- 12
Invisibles, net	- 16.8	- 15.5	- 18.6	- 30	- 30
Current account balance	8.0	- 38.6	- 48.5	- 45	- 42
			Percentage changes		
Goods and services export volumes	- 4.6	- 14.2	6.4	8.4	7.9
Goods and services import volumes	1.2	- 13.9	13.4	6.8	7.1
Export performance[1]	- 3.4	- 1.3	- 5.6	2.2	- 0.6
Terms of trade	4.8	- 9.5	6.1	2.0	0.2

1. Ratio between export volume and export market of total goods and services.
Source: OECD Economic Outlook 89 database.

StatLink http://dx.doi.org/10.1787/888932430647

Household spending will moderate

The shift to fiscal contraction, and in particular the trimming of public-sector compensation, will weigh on household income. Household debt inched up to a record 149% of disposable income in the last half of 2010, continuing its longer-term upward trend. Although deleveraging needs are not as severe as in some other OECD countries that experienced housing booms, substantial debt burdens should nonetheless damp consumer spending in the near term. Indeed, growth in consumer and mortgage credit has already eased substantially since mid-2010. The higher purchasing power afforded by the strong exchange rate is not expected to affect consumption growth significantly, given that households are simultaneously facing higher food and energy bills as a result of soaring world commodity prices. Consumers are unlikely to be able to rely on further significant increases in house prices to improve their balance sheets. House prices are already high relative to incomes and rents, and the market appears to have stabilised and may cool. In particular, in mid-March a new set of changes tightening mortgage insurance regulations came into effect (the third since October 2008), including a shortening in the maximum amortisation period by an additional five years.

Fiscal consolidation should be implemented as planned

Fiscal stimulus is gradually being withdrawn in 2011, although plans announced in late 2010 extended the deadline for completion of some infrastructure projects. The draft 2011-12 pre-election federal budget included some new spending measures, funded by greater-than-expected revenues in 2010 and a stronger growth outlook. The projection assumes that consolidation is implemented as planned, and that the total government deficit will fall from 5.5% of GDP in 2010 to 3.5% in 2012. However, achieving these plans will require significant expenditure restraint compared to the previous decade, which will entail curbing public-sector compensation and defence spending. At the provincial level, priorities should include achieving operational efficiencies in health care and providing details on other planned measures based on strategic reviews, which are underway.

Monetary tightening should resume soon

Surging food and energy prices have driven up headline inflation to 3.3% year-on-year in March. While year-on-year core inflation rose to 1.7% in the same month, continued, if narrowing, economic slack suggests it will remain subdued. Nonetheless, monetary policy remains highly stimulative despite indications that short-term inflation expectations have begun creeping upwards in recent quarters. The Bank of Canada should therefore resume the normalisation of policy rates soon in order to pre-empt a broadening of inflationary pressures, although tightening should proceed at a moderate pace in light of the simultaneous fiscal contraction.

Output should continue to expand at a healthy clip

The brisk pace of growth in early 2011 is expected to moderate over the near term before regaining speed in 2012. The natural disaster in Japan should temporarily curb production and trade this spring, particularly in the automotive sector, although this should be offset by a catch-up in activity later in the year. Consumption growth is projected to slow over the remainder of the year as the housing market cools and households rebuild their stretched balance sheets. As firming labour markets support wage growth, consumption should pick up again in 2012. Business investment should remain robust, and exports are projected to contribute more solidly to growth especially as the US recovery strengthens. The output gap should thus narrow significantly over the projection but remain large enough to hold underlying inflation to about 1½ per cent per year.

Uncertainties around the outlook remain wide

Risks surrounding the outlook are considerable, though broadly balanced. The widespread fiscal contraction across many advanced economies, and especially in the United States, may weaken external demand more than projected. Persistent geopolitical instability may meanwhile lead to unsustainable commodity price increases, which would help Canadian exporters but may also raise inflation expectations, forcing a more rapid tightening of monetary policy than assumed. Such a scenario could trigger a more marked house price correction that significantly strains household and bank balance sheets. An unexpected decline in commodity prices would have the opposite effects.

AUSTRALIA

The Australian economy is set to rebound after the disruptions caused by major natural disasters in early 2011. Growth, driven by historically high terms-of-trade, should accelerate from 3% in 2011 to 4½ per cent in 2012. Unemployment is projected to fall, although the remaining slack in the economy will mute the risk of inflation pressures.

The continued fiscal consolidation, despite the cost of the rains and flooding to public accounts, is welcome, including from a cyclical point of view. The current stance of monetary policy seems appropriate, in absence of potential second-round effects on inflation of weather disruption and of oil price hikes. The authorities must take advantage of the favourable economic situation to pursue long-term structural reforms, including those that favour output involving less CO_2 emissions.

The recovery has weakened somewhat

Growth in the Australian economy slowed in the second half of 2010 to 2½ per cent year-on-year. The economic impact of tighter monetary policy in 2010, the appreciation of the exchange rate, and the gradual withdrawal of the budgetary stimulus was only partially offset by the rebound in private demand buoyed by higher terms-of-trade. In early 2011, the country was hit by major flooding and a cyclone and the economic impact of earthquakes in Japan and New Zealand. These shocks reduced output and demand, particularly exports, cutting GDP by up to 1% in the first quarter.

Despite these disruptions, the business climate remains positive. Mining commodity prices are at historical highs and firms have again revised their investment plans upwards. In contrast, households, whose confidence was declining in early 2011, have continued to rein in consumption and reduce their debts. By April 2011, employment had recovered to pre-disaster levels in the regions most affected by the rains

Australia

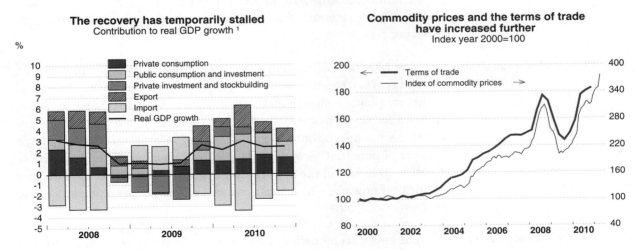

The recovery has temporarily stalled
Contribution to real GDP growth [1]

Commodity prices and the terms of trade have increased further
Index year 2000=100

1. Year-on-year percentage change.
Source: OECD, Economic Outlook 89 database and Reserve Bank of Australia.

StatLink http://dx.doi.org/10.1787/888932429412

Australia: **Demand, output and prices**

	2007	2008	2009	2010	2011	2012
	Current prices AUD billion	Percentage changes, volume (2007/2008 prices)				
GDP at market prices	1 138.3	2.4	1.4	2.6	2.9	4.5
Private consumption	635.2	2.0	1.0	2.7	2.7	3.6
Government consumption	193.9	3.2	1.5	3.5	2.6	1.7
Gross fixed capital formation	326.8	7.2	-2.4	4.9	4.3	9.5
Final domestic demand	1 156.0	3.7	0.1	3.5	3.1	5.0
Stockbuilding[1]	4.1	-0.2	-0.5	0.2	0.3	0.0
Total domestic demand	1 160.1	3.4	-0.4	3.7	3.4	5.0
Exports of goods and services	217.1	4.7	2.8	5.2	6.1	7.5
Imports of goods and services	238.8	11.3	-9.1	13.4	8.4	9.2
Net exports[1]	- 21.8	-1.4	2.8	-1.7	-0.5	-0.5
Memorandum items						
GDP deflator	_	6.4	-0.9	5.1	4.7	2.8
Consumer price index	_	4.4	1.8	2.8	3.4	2.5
Private consumption deflator	_	2.7	1.6	1.9	2.8	2.6
Unemployment rate	_	4.2	5.6	5.2	5.0	4.9
Household saving ratio[2]	_	5.4	9.7	9.3	9.5	9.2
General government financial balance[3]	_	-0.2	-4.9	-5.9	-2.8	-1.4
Current account balance[3]	_	-4.5	-4.3	-2.6	-1.1	-1.3

1. Contributions to changes in real GDP (percentage of real GDP in previous year), actual amount in the first column.
2. As a percentage of disposable income.
3. As a percentage of GDP.
Source: OECD Economic Outlook 89 database.

StatLink ⟐ http://dx.doi.org/10.1787/888932430666

and flooding, and the unemployment rate had fallen to 4.9%. Underlying inflation remained moderate, however, at 2¼ per cent in the first quarter of 2011 because of the easing of demand and the exchange rate appreciation. Headline inflation, pushed by strong rises in fruit and vegetable prices stemming from the recent adverse weather events, rose to 3¼ per cent.

Monetary policy is slightly restrictive

The RBA raised its cash rate in 2010, bringing it up to 4.75% in November. This, together with the exchange rate appreciation, has given monetary policy a slightly restrictive stance. Against this background, demand for credit has remained weak. The current stance of monetary policy seems appropriate. However, inflation pressure might emerge because of potential second-round effects of weather disruptions and of oil price hikes and of the acceleration in growth from the second quarter of this year onward, which could induce bottlenecks in some parts of the economy.

Fiscal consolidation remains on course

The public sector deficit, which rose to almost 6% of GDP in 2010, was a little worse than expected due to the weakening of growth in the second half of last year. The flooding has generated additional budgetary costs of around ½ per cent of GDP, which will be financed by a temporary increase in direct taxes on middle and high-income households and the cancellation or deferment of some government spending. The 2011/12 Budget confirms the authorities' commitment to pursue a restrictive fiscal policy to return to surplus by as early as 2013. To this end, budgetary savings amounting 1½ per cent of GDP have been identified over the next 4 years, with the removal of some tax expenditures and a better targeting of family benefits. The budget also includes several measures to promote labour participation and training, which should have beneficial effects on growth over the medium term.

Activity should rebound after the first quarter

The weaker growth resulting from the natural disasters should be offset by a rebound in activity from the second quarter of 2011 onwards, driven by the rebuilding of destroyed infrastructure. GDP growth, supported by exports and investment, should exceed 4% in 2012. High terms-of-trade continue to favour the mining sector, which has a knock-on effect on the economy. Lower unemployment and higher employment and labour incomes should result in a gradual firming of private consumption. Notwithstanding strong growth, the output gap is estimated to remain through 2012, which will hold down inflationary pressures.

Risks are broadly balanced

A worsening of international financial conditions, or greater than expected tightening of monetary policy in Asia in response to inflation risks, would have a negative impact on the economy. On the domestic front, the rebound in activity after the flooding might be more modest than expected. On the other hand, household confidence might also recover and favour stronger domestic consumption and demand. Should the inflationary pressures described above materialise, central bank might have to tighten its stance to slow the economy.

AUSTRIA

Investment growth picked up strongly in the second half of 2010 and will continue to support the export-led recovery. The labour market continues to improve but large increases in inflation will weigh on consumption. After a strong first quarter of 2011, growth is projected to slow down to its trend rate.

A consolidation package is in place but the government should consider further spending restraint to reverse debt dynamics. By strengthening competition in the service sector, Austria could contain the risk of inflationary pressures as well as re-balance the economy towards stronger domestic growth.

The recovery has broadened

Economic growth remained strong in the first quarter of 2011. With capacity utilisation close to long-term averages, the export-led recovery spilled over to investment. In particular, investment in the metals and machinery sector expanded strongly, more than offsetting further declines in construction. Consumption grew steadily but at a subdued rate. Recent high-frequency business and consumer confidence indicators suggest that a slowdown is expected for the near future.

The labour market has improved and inflation has picked up strongly

The labour market recovered quickly from the crisis with employment growing robustly and the unemployment rate falling to 4.2% in the fourth quarter of 2010, compared with a crisis peak of 5.1%. Wage growth remained subdued, however, supporting Austria's competitiveness. Harmonised consumer price inflation increased sharply at the beginning of 2011 reaching 3% (year-on-year) in the first quarter, mainly due to global energy and food prices, and to excise tax hikes on tobacco and mineral oil products. Core inflation also rose somewhat, to 1.8% in the first quarter.

Austria

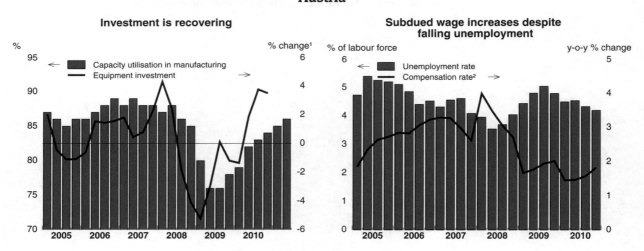

Investment is recovering

Subdued wage increases despite falling unemployment

1. Quarter-on-quarter percentage change.
2. Total economy measure.

Source: OECD Economic Outlook 89 database; OECD, Main Economic Indicators database.

StatLink http://dx.doi.org/10.1787/888932429431

Austria: **Demand, output and prices**

	2007	2008	2009	2010	2011	2012
	Current prices € billion	Percentage changes, volume (2005 prices)				
GDP at market prices	271.5	2.2	-3.9	2.1	2.9	2.1
Private consumption	143.7	0.7	1.2	1.0	0.9	1.2
Government consumption	49.1	3.9	0.4	-2.4	0.3	0.4
Gross fixed capital formation	58.3	2.8	-7.9	-1.2	3.0	2.5
Final domestic demand	251.1	1.8	-1.1	-0.2	1.2	1.3
Stockbuilding[1]	4.1	-0.6	-0.8	0.9	0.6	0.0
Total domestic demand	255.2	1.1	-1.5	0.7	1.6	1.3
Exports of goods and services	161.4	0.5	-15.6	10.6	9.6	6.8
Imports of goods and services	145.1	-1.7	-12.5	7.5	7.7	6.0
Net exports[1]	16.3	1.2	-2.6	1.9	1.5	0.8
Memorandum items						
GDP without working day adjustments	272.0	2.2	-3.9	2.0	2.9	2.1
GDP deflator	_	1.5	1.0	1.6	1.7	1.6
Harmonised index of consumer prices	_	3.2	0.4	1.7	3.1	1.8
Private consumption deflator	_	2.5	-0.7	1.5	2.8	1.9
Unemployment rate[2]	_	3.8	4.8	4.4	4.2	4.0
Household saving ratio[3]	_	11.8	11.1	9.1	9.0	8.9
General government financial balance[4]	_	-1.0	-4.2	-4.6	-3.7	-3.2
Current account balance[4]	_	4.6	2.9	2.6	3.1	3.8

Note: National accounts are based on official chain-linked data. This introduces a discrepancy in the identity between real demand components and GDP. For further details see *OECD Economic Outlook* Sources and Methods *(http://www.oecd.org/eco/sources-and-methods)*.

1. Contributions to changes in real GDP (percentage of real GDP in previous year), actual amount in the first column.
2. Based on Labour Force Survey data.
3. As a percentage of disposable income.
4. As a percentage of GDP.

Source: OECD Economic Outlook 89 database.

StatLink http://dx.doi.org/10.1787/888932430685

Foreign demand and investment are driving growth...

Through its strong trade linkages with Germany, Austria is expected to continue to benefit from robust external demand. The full opening of the labour market to the new EU member countries on 1 May 2011 is likely to ease skill shortages, reducing the scope for more than moderate wage increases. With further increases in labour productivity towards trend, this will support future competitiveness gains. Despite an expected gradual tightening of monetary policy in the euro area, real interest rates are set to remain low in 2011 and will support investment in the near term.

... while consumption remains subdued

Employment growth is expected to remain robust in 2011 before moderating somewhat in 2012, keeping the unemployment rate below the structural level of 4¼ per cent. However, high consumer price inflation will weigh on real disposable income and private consumption growth in 2011. Inflation is expected to decline in 2012, supporting a moderate pick-up in consumption.

Moderate consolidation is underway

Fiscal vulnerabilities have risen following increases in the deficit and the debt during the recession. The situation has become more apparent after comprehensive revisions by Eurostat forced parts of the hitherto off-budget deficit and debt items of the railway company and hospitals back onto public balance sheets. The federal government is implementing a consolidation package to reduce the deficit to below 3% of GDP by 2013, with savings of about ⅓ on the revenue side (mainly increases in excise taxes and a bank levy) and ⅔ on the spending side (mainly social expenditure cuts). In this projection, which builds in fiscal consolidation in line with government plans, the deficit falls to 3.7% of GDP by 2011 and 3.2% of GDP by 2012. However, in view of diminishing slack in the economy, a greater front-loading of consolidation would be warranted.

External risks remain

Further turbulence associated with sovereign debt problems in euro area countries would be likely to affect Austria negatively through trade and bank exposure. Further increases in commodity prices would put additional pressure on private consumption. The liberalisation of labour inflows from central Europe could have a stronger effect on labour supply and potential growth than currently projected.

BELGIUM

The recovery will become more balanced as private consumption and investment strengthen, although growth will be moderated by a more restrictive fiscal policy stance and the gradual withdrawal of monetary policy support. Automatic wage indexation may prolong the period of relatively high consumer price inflation as high global commodity prices are passed through to wage costs.

Fiscal sustainability should be pursued through fiscal consolidation on the spending side at all levels of government. To prevent high levels of unemployment translating into higher structural unemployment, labour market reforms should focus on securing a more flexible wage formation process and stronger job search incentives.

The recovery is set to gather pace

Strong growth at the beginning of 2011 softened due to higher oil prices and some disruption to the supply chains in the automotive industry. Nonetheless, the slowdown is expected to be short-lived. The economy continues to benefit from supportive monetary policies and robust world trade growth. Industrial production continues to grow sufficiently fast to markedly reduce excess production capacity. The savings rate remains high, suggesting there is still room for renewed consumption growth. The improving labour market should also support consumption. Employment growth has averaged around 1% per quarter (seasonally adjusted annual rate) since the beginning of 2010, reflecting mostly higher labour demand. Unemployment peaked in mid-2010 at a harmonised rate of 8½ per cent, before coming down by about ¾ percentage point by spring 2011.

Inflation will remain relatively high

Inflation rose to 3½ per cent in early 2011 as the impact of higher energy prices came through faster and stronger (reflecting relatively high energy use) than in other European countries. Unlike in many other

Belgium

The improvement in confidence is flattening out

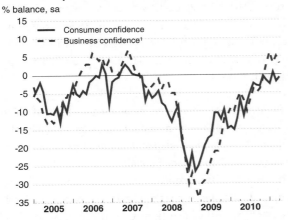

Inflation has increased more than in the euro area[2]

1. Manufacturing.
2. Year-on-year percentage change of headline inflation, harmonised and not seasonnally adjusted.
Source: OECD, Main Economic Indicators and OECD Economic Outlook 89 databases.

StatLink ㎙㎚ http://dx.doi.org/10.1787/888932429450

Belgium: **Demand, output and prices**

	2007	2008	2009	2010	2011	2012
	Current prices € billion	Percentage changes, volume (2008 prices)				
GDP at market prices	335.1	0.8	-2.7	2.1	2.4	2.0
Private consumption	170.9	1.4	-0.2	1.6	2.0	1.9
Government consumption	74.8	2.5	0.4	1.1	1.4	0.5
Gross fixed capital formation	72.7	2.2	-5.0	-1.5	2.2	3.2
Final domestic demand	318.5	1.8	-1.1	0.8	1.9	1.8
Stockbuilding[1]	3.6	0.0	-0.2	0.1	0.0	0.0
Total domestic demand	322.1	1.8	-1.3	0.9	1.9	1.8
Exports of goods and services	279.4	1.4	-11.4	10.6	6.9	6.2
Imports of goods and services	266.5	2.8	-10.9	8.4	6.9	6.1
Net exports[1]	13.0	-1.0	-0.5	1.8	0.3	0.2
Memorandum items						
GDP deflator	_	1.9	1.1	1.9	2.1	2.0
Harmonised index of consumer prices	_	4.5	0.0	2.3	3.6	2.4
Private consumption deflator	_	3.2	-0.5	2.4	3.4	2.3
Unemployment rate	_	7.0	7.9	8.3	7.6	7.3
Household saving ratio[2]	_	11.9	13.4	12.2	11.2	11.0
General government financial balance[3]	_	-1.3	-6.0	-4.2	-3.6	-2.8
Current account balance[3]	_	-1.8	0.3	1.3	1.0	1.2

Note: National accounts are based on official chain-linked data. This introduces a discrepancy in the identity between real demand components and GDP. For further details see *OECD Economic Outlook* Sources and Methods *(http://www.oecd.org/eco/sources-and-methods).*
1. Contributions to changes in real GDP (percentage of real GDP in previous year), actual amount in the first column.
2. As a percentage of disposable income.
3. As a percentage of GDP.
Source: OECD Economic Outlook 89 database.

StatLink ⟨⟨⟨⟨ http://dx.doi.org/10.1787/888932430704

countries, however, there has also been a pick-up in underlying inflation, which increased from 1% in spring 2010 to nearly 2% a year later. To a large extent, this reflected the triggering of the automatic wage indexation in the autumn of 2010. The 2011-12 wage agreement yielded zero *ex ante* real wages increases for 2011 and 0.3% in 2012. However, automatic wage indexation will translate relatively high Belgian inflation into higher nominal wages, intensifying inflationary pressures and eroding external cost competitiveness.

Substantial fiscal consolidation is required to secure sustainability

The 2010 general government deficit of just above 4 per cent of GDP was more than ½ percentage point better than expected, reflecting mostly a positive growth surprise. The 2011 budget stipulates fiscal tightening of about ½ per cent of GDP, reflecting a number of small measures. For 2012, these projections build in the Stability Programme's planned 1% fiscal consolidation, with an even split between revenue raising measures and spending cuts. Against the background of stronger economic growth, this should secure a budget deficit of about 3½ per cent of GDP in 2011 and below 3% the following year. If, as planned, similar consolidation efforts are implemented in the following years, then the medium-term objective of achieving a small budget surplus in 2015 is within reach. Such an

126

achievement would be an important step towards securing fiscal sustainability, but will require a concerted effort by all governments in the federation. Moreover, further consolidation will be needed beyond that to ensure a reduction of the high debt-to-GDP ratio.

Growth is set to resume, but considerable risks remain

Growth should gather pace later in 2011, supported by stronger private demand, particularly for investment goods. Employment will continue to expand, but only in 2012 will the unemployment rate fall significantly further. The main downside risk is that still higher global commodity prices would widen the inflation and labour-cost wedge *vis-à-vis* other European countries. On the upside, successful fiscal consolidation could boost consumer and investor confidence.

CHILE

The Chilean economy is growing strongly, driven by dynamic domestic demand with support from high copper prices. GDP growth is expected to reach 6½ per cent in 2011 and gradually slow towards 5% in 2012, as monetary and fiscal policies tighten.

In the near term, the main challenge for macroeconomic policy will be to avoid overheating. As there are signs of rising inflationary pressures, monetary policy should continue moving toward a neutral stance during 2011 to keep inflation expectations well anchored. The government announced spending reductions recently to counter the strong appreciation of the exchange rate related to exceptionally high copper prices. At the same time, its objective of reducing the structural budget deficit to 1% of GDP by 2014 is rather modest, even taking reconstruction spending needs into account. Letting the exchange rate float and achieving a more ambitious fiscal target should cool internal demand and avoid inflationary pressures.

Demand is expanding vigorously while inflation is picking up

Historically high copper prices and increasingly strong domestic demand are supporting swift growth of the Chilean economy, after a partly reconstruction-led rebound following last year's earthquake and tsunami. Private consumption has been particularly dynamic on the back of favourable consumer confidence, normalised financial conditions and falling unemployment. Investment has expanded strongly as a result of reconstruction efforts and strong mining investment. The current account surplus has declined, as imports grew fast along with domestic demand, but thanks to high copper prices it has remained in positive territory in 2010. The strong growth in output and rapid pace of employment creation has quickly diminished excess capacity contributing to strong nominal wage growth. High international food and

Chile

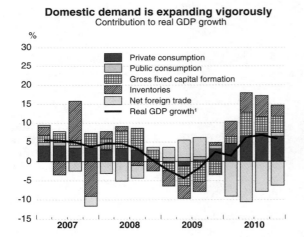

Domestic demand is expanding vigorously
Contribution to real GDP growth

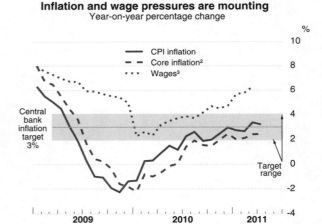

Inflation and wage pressures are mounting
Year-on-year percentage change

1. Year-on-year percentage change.
2. Consumer price index excluding fuels and fresh fruits and vegetables.
3. Nominal wage index, average hourly wage weighted by average hours worked.

Source: Instituto Nacional de Estadísticas (INE); Central Bank of Chile.

StatLink http://dx.doi.org/10.1787/888932429469

Chile: Demand, output and prices

	2007	2008	2009	2010	2011	2012
	Current prices CLP billion	Percentage changes, volume (2003 prices)				
GDP at market prices	85 849.8	3.2	-1.5	5.1	6.5	5.1
Private consumption	46 870.2	4.5	0.9	10.4	7.7	5.7
Government consumption	9 371.7	0.5	7.5	3.3	5.3	2.0
Gross fixed capital formation	16 983.4	19.4	-15.9	18.8	13.4	12.3
Final domestic demand	73 225.3	7.6	-2.9	11.5	8.8	7.0
Stockbuilding[1]	602.7	-0.3	-3.2	4.9	0.4	0.0
Total domestic demand	73 828.0	7.3	-5.8	16.4	9.0	6.9
Exports of goods and services	40 561.3	3.2	-6.4	1.9	7.8	7.3
Imports of goods and services	28 539.5	12.6	-14.6	29.5	12.7	10.1
Net exports[1]	12 021.8	-2.7	3.2	-8.5	-1.1	-0.4
Memorandum items						
GDP deflator	_	0.7	2.7	9.5	5.1	4.5
Consumer price index	_	8.7	0.4	1.4	3.9	3.9
Private consumption deflator	_	7.9	0.9	0.2	2.9	3.9
Unemployment rate	_	7.8	10.8	8.1	7.3	7.2
Central government financial balance[2]	_	4.8	-4.5	-0.4	0.4	0.6
Current account balance[2]	_	-2.2	1.5	2.4	0.7	-0.1

1. Contributions to changes in real GDP (percentage of real GDP in previous year), actual amount in the first column.
2. As a percentage of GDP.
Source: OECD Economic Outlook 89 database.

StatLink http://dx.doi.org/10.1787/888932430723

oil prices are adding to inflationary pressures. Inflation expectations for one year ahead have risen above the mid-point of the central bank's inflation tolerance range of 3% (+/- 1%) according to the central bank financial experts' survey, even though the peso appreciated 23% above its long-term average against the dollar in the second half of 2010.

The central bank should continue the monetary tightening

The central bank has raised the monetary policy rate by 225 basis points since October, to 5.0% in May 2011. To smooth the peso appreciation, and accumulate international reserves, the central bank is implementing the largest foreign currency purchase programme in Chilean history. The central bank plans to continue raising its policy rate to reach a neutral level by the end of 2011. The monetary authorities should closely monitor inflation developments and consider tightening even faster if needed.

Faster fiscal tightening could also help to rein in inflation

Thanks to a strong recovery and high copper prices the headline budget deficit decreased rapidly from 4½ per cent of GDP in 2009 to ½ per cent of GDP in 2010. The government plans to increase spending by 5.4% in real terms in 2011 relative to 2010, to continue reconstruction and expand a number of social programmes. Spending growth is expected to slow in 2012 as reconstruction tapers off. Over the longer term, the government aims to reduce the structural fiscal deficit to 1% of GDP by 2014. This fiscal tightening is modest in a context of strong economic growth and rising inflationary pressures. Reconstruction permitting, Chile should consider tightening the fiscal stance faster to reduce the risk of overheating and ensure fiscal sustainability.

Sustained growth prospects, but inflation is edging up

GDP growth should reach 6½ per cent in 2011 and moderate in 2012 towards its long-term potential of roughly 5% as macroeconomic stimulus is withdrawn. Inflation is projected to continue rising during 2011 and to overshoot the upper bound of the central bank's target range towards end 2011. Inflation should then moderate as the stimulus from reconstruction spending is withdrawn and the central bank increases monetary policy rates rapidly.

An overheating economy is the main risk

The key risk to the projections is higher inflationary pressures due to stronger than projected domestic demand and larger and more persistent food and oil price shocks. In the context of tightening labour market conditions, this may feed through into wage costs and become entrenched.

CZECH REPUBLIC

Despite ongoing fiscal tightening real GDP growth is expected to reach 2.4% this year, driven primarily by strong foreign demand. Growth will broaden and rise further to 3.5% in 2012, as consumption picks up. Headline inflation will spike temporarily due to scheduled indirect tax increases in 2012, but core inflation will remain low given the remaining output gap.

The authorities should continue with fiscal tightening to achieve medium-term targets and use the upswing of the economy as an opportunity to secure the long-term sustainability of pension and healthcare systems. Monetary policy should normalise gradually as the recovery takes stronger hold.

External demand is driving the recovery

GDP expanded by 2.2% in 2010, reflecting strong export performance and restocking as the Czech economy, which is well integrated in international supply chains, benefited from the upswing in world trade. In contrast, private consumption remained weak and investment declined despite a temporary solar panel investment boom ahead of cuts in subsidies. However, capacity utilisation increased to over 80%, setting the stage for stronger investment in the coming quarters.

Indicators point to a broadening of the recovery

Both industrial production and new orders continue to grow at a double digit pace and exports are also growing rapidly. Confidence indicators give a more mixed picture, but retail sales have slowly started to recover. The unemployment rate has been gradually decreasing and stood at 6.9% in March 2011.

Headline inflation has edged up

Inflation rose during 2010 mainly due to increases in indirect taxes, regulated prices and commodity prices. Headline inflation stood at 1.6% in April and core inflation remained close to zero. The central bank has

Czech Republic

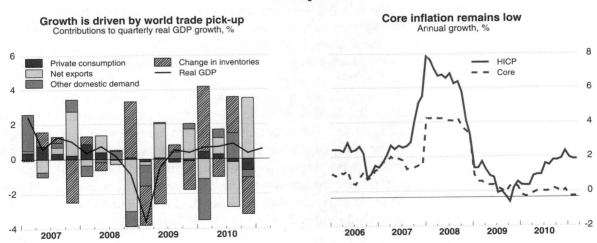

Note: Core refers to the harmonised index of consumer prices (HICP) excluding food, energy, alcohol and tobacco.

Source: Eurostat; OECD, National Accounts database.

StatLink http://dx.doi.org/10.1787/888932429488

Czech Republic: **Demand, output and prices**

	2007	2008	2009	2010	2011	2012
	Current prices CZK billion	Percentage changes, volume (2000 prices)				
GDP at market prices	3 539.1	2.3	-4.0	2.2	2.4	3.5
Private consumption	1 688.7	3.5	-0.1	0.4	0.5	2.6
Government consumption	717.0	1.1	2.6	0.3	-1.2	1.3
Gross fixed capital formation	890.3	-1.5	-7.9	-4.6	3.9	4.8
Final domestic demand	3 296.0	1.6	-1.5	-0.8	0.9	2.8
Stockbuilding[1]	67.4	-0.5	-2.0	1.9	-0.5	0.0
Total domestic demand	3 363.4	1.1	-3.6	1.2	0.3	2.8
Exports of goods and services	2 836.0	5.7	-10.5	17.6	9.4	9.5
Imports of goods and services	2 660.3	4.3	-10.4	17.6	7.2	9.2
Net exports[1]	175.7	1.3	-0.6	1.0	2.0	0.8
Memorandum items						
GDP deflator	_	1.8	2.5	-1.1	0.1	1.5
Consumer price index	_	6.3	1.0	1.5	2.2	3.1
Private consumption deflator	_	4.9	0.3	1.3	2.9	3.0
Unemployment rate	_	4.4	6.7	7.3	6.6	6.3
General government financial balance[2]	_	-2.7	-5.8	-4.7	-3.8	-2.8
Current account balance[2]	_	-0.6	-3.2	-3.8	-3.0	-3.4

Note: National accounts are based on official chain-linked data. This introduces a discrepancy in the identity between real demand components and GDP. For further details see *OECD Economic Outlook* Sources and Methods *(http://www.oecd.org/eco/sources-and-methods)*.
1. Contributions to changes in real GDP (percentage of real GDP in previous year), actual amount in the first column.
2. As a percentage of GDP.
Source: OECD Economic Outlook 89 database.

StatLink http://dx.doi.org/10.1787/888932430742

maintained the policy interest rate at a historically low level of 0.75%, which is currently a half percentage point below the main ECB rate.

Fiscal consolidation continues

The 2010 general government deficit of 4.7% of GDP turned out better than originally budgeted due to lower debt servicing costs and savings in operational costs of the administration. This year, the authorities are pursuing budgetary tightening with an emphasis on expenditure restraint. In particular, cuts in the central-government wage bill are underway. Backed by recently approved medium–term expenditure ceilings, the fiscal deficit is to fall to 3.5% of GDP, and debt is to be held close to 40% of GDP in 2012. With government receipts picking up as a result of renewed growth and additional revenues from a planned VAT increase, these targets are likely to be undershot again. A number of structural reforms are planned for 2012, notably in pensions, healthcare and the tax structure. However, only the tax-structure changes are likely to have a substantial fiscal impact over the projection period.

The recovery will broaden and accelerate further

Output is expected to grow by 2.4% in 2011 and pick up speed to 3.5% in 2012. Exports are expected to perform well and investment is projected to recover strongly. In contrast, private consumption will pick up only in 2012, as this year's fiscal consolidation will have a restraining effect.

Inflation will accelerate temporarily in 2012, due to the scheduled hike in the lower VAT rate and ongoing rent deregulation, but underlying inflationary pressures will remain moderate.

Risks remain broadly balanced

Given its significant export orientation, the Czech economy is dependent on the continued recovery of world trade and an orderly resolution of the debt crisis in the euro area. On the positive side, the fiscal tightening may have less of an impact on domestic demand so that growth could pick up more strongly than projected.

DENMARK

The recovery is expected to gain strength gradually as world trade expands, and to become more broad-based as private domestic demand improves. Given the remaining economic slack, core inflation is projected to be subdued.

The continued implementation of the fiscal consolidation plan would allow the fiscal position to be brought back to a path consistent with long-term targets. This calls for further slowing public consumption and for enhancing the fiscal framework. Structural reforms to improve competitiveness and productivity growth would raise growth prospects.

The recovery is uneven but continues

Notwithstanding a temporary slowdown in the fourth quarter of 2010, the gradual recovery has continued. Boosted by the effects of past strong stimulus, private consumption was the main driver of activity in late 2010 while public consumption started to contract as part of the fiscal consolidation plan. While export growth picked up, Denmark continued to lose market share, reflecting an ongoing deterioration in competitiveness. Private non-residential investment fell further in the second half of 2010. Consumer confidence has recently weakened but remains close to its long-term average. Short-term supply-side indicators point to an expansion of activity and employment in the first quarter of 2011.

The labour market remains weak

Employment fell in the fourth quarter of 2010, driven mainly by public-sector fiscal consolidation; employment in the private sector appears to have stabilised. The unemployment rate was unchanged at 7.9% on the harmonised definition in March 2011, though the registered unemployment rate inched down in the first quarter of 2011, to 5.9%. Real wages fell somewhat in both the private and public sectors in 2010 following several years of rapid increases. Past wage inflation partly explains why labour market recovery is slow.

Denmark

The unemployment rate has reached high levels
Harmonised definition, seasonally-adjusted

Public consumption has declined somewhat
Percentage of GDP

Source: OECD, Economic Outlook 89 database.

StatLink ᵃᵉˢᵖ http://dx.doi.org/10.1787/888932429507

Denmark: **Demand, output and prices**

	2007	2008	2009	2010	2011	2012
	Current prices DKK billion	Percentage changes, volume (2000 prices)				
GDP at market prices	1 695.3	-1.1	-5.2	2.1	1.9	2.1
Private consumption	820.4	-0.6	-4.5	2.2	1.9	2.0
Government consumption	440.0	1.6	3.1	1.0	-0.3	0.3
Gross fixed capital formation	368.7	-3.3	-14.3	-4.0	3.6	5.1
Final domestic demand	1 629.1	-0.6	-4.5	0.7	1.5	2.0
Stockbuilding[1]	27.5	-0.6	-2.0	0.9	-0.1	0.0
Total domestic demand	1 656.5	-1.2	-6.5	1.7	1.3	2.0
Exports of goods and services	885.2	2.8	-9.7	3.6	5.2	4.9
Imports of goods and services	846.5	2.7	-12.5	2.9	4.6	5.1
Net exports[1]	38.7	0.1	1.1	0.5	0.6	0.2
Memorandum items						
GDP deflator	_	3.9	0.4	3.3	2.1	1.7
Consumer price index	_	3.4	1.3	2.3	2.6	1.7
Private consumption deflator	_	3.1	1.3	2.6	2.5	1.7
Unemployment rate[2]	_	3.2	5.9	7.2	7.2	6.4
Household saving ratio[3]	_	-3.3	-0.5	-1.2	-1.4	-1.4
General government financial balance[4]	_	3.3	-2.8	-2.9	-3.8	-3.0
Current account balance[4]	_	2.7	3.6	5.5	5.8	5.6

Note: National accounts are based on official chain-linked data. This introduces a discrepancy in the identity between real demand components and GDP. For further details see *OECD Economic Outlook* Sources and Methods (http://www.oecd.org/eco/sources-and-methods).
1. Contributions to changes in real GDP (percentage of real GDP in previous year), actual amount in the first column.
2. The unemployment rate is based on the Labour Force Survey and differs from the registered unemployment rate.
3. As a percentage of disposable income, net of household consumption of fixed capital.
4. As a percentage of GDP.
Source: OECD Economic Outlook 89 database.

StatLink http://dx.doi.org/10.1787/888932430761

Financial conditions are starting to normalise

According to lending surveys, financial institutions have eased credit standards for firms and households. While bank lending to households and companies fell in the first quarter of 2011, this may merely reflect weaker demand. House prices have stabilised, the number of housing starts has increased and residential investment has picked up in 2010.

Policies will be less supportive

The decline in public consumption in late 2010 reflects the successful initiation of the Fiscal Consolidation Agreement adopted in May 2010. In 2010, the general government deficit turned out to be smaller than expected by the government, and just below the 3% of GDP EU threshold. However, this was largely attributable to exceptional revenues from taxes on pension funds returns (which contributed around 1% of GDP). Going forward, the OECD projection assumes that the government will continue to consolidate general government finances in line with the Agreement. Monetary conditions are expected to remain supportive in 2011, before becoming somewhat tighter in 2012.

The recovery will be driven by both external and private demand

The recovery is expected to regain strength gradually. Public demand is set to contribute less to growth while private demand takes the lead. Exports will benefit from expanding world trade and business investment is projected to gather momentum. Private consumption growth is expected to slow somewhat in 2011 owing to the impact of higher taxes and lower social transfers, before picking up in 2012 on the back of improving labour market conditions. With growth mainly driven by private demand, imports are also projected to grow strongly. Headline inflation will pick up in 2011 on the back of higher commodity prices but core inflation is set to remain subdued as the output gap remains negative at the end of the projection period.

Risks relate mainly to the labour market and export competitiveness

The recovery could be weaker if unemployment becomes entrenched and weighs on household consumption. Exports might benefit less from the buoyancy in world trade should competitiveness deteriorate more than expected. However, the recovery could be stronger if uncertainties surrounding the global environment fade and the rebound in business investment comes earlier and stronger than foreseen.

ESTONIA

The strong export-driven recovery is projected to continue in 2011, reflecting the positive external outlook and improved competitiveness achieved through flexible wage adjustment and restructuring measures. Private consumption will gain momentum in 2012, as unemployment continues to fall, the real wage bill increases, and more bad debt cases are resolved. Despite high headline inflation due to energy and commodity price shocks, no second round effects are projected and core inflation is expected to remain below historical averages.

Estonia adopted the euro on 1 January 2011, consolidating past policy achievements. Fiscal policy remains under tight control, and the general government deficit is expected to stay below the 3% of GDP threshold despite the reversal of large one-off measures. Nevertheless, multi-year expenditure ceilings that take into account the cyclical position of the economy should be introduced in order to prevent fiscal policy becoming pro-cyclical in the upswing. The government should intensify its use of active labour market policies to prevent still high unemployment from becoming structural.

The recovery is driven by booming exports

The economic recovery accelerated in the last two quarters to annualised rates of growth above 8%, the highest in the euro area. Growth was led by a surge in net exports and manufacturing driven by strong external demand and competitiveness gains achieved in the adjustment to the severe recession. Investment bottomed out in mid-2010 and then surged in the fourth quarter, reflecting increasing capacity utilisation in manufacturing. In contrast, deleveraging of households, the relatively high burden of non-performing loans and high unemployment continued to weigh on private consumption, which contracted in the fourth quarter. Construction and consumer confidence indicators remain weak.

Unemployment is falling

Employment growth and nominal wage growth resumed in the second half of 2010, as companies restored profitability through earlier

Estonia

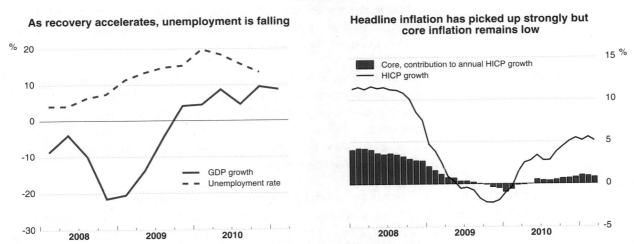

As recovery accelerates, unemployment is falling

Headline inflation has picked up strongly but core inflation remains low

Note: GDP growth is quarterly, annualised. Core refers to the harmonised index of consumer prices (HICP) excluding food, energy, alcohol and tobacco.
Source: Eurostat; OECD, National Accounts database.

StatLink http://dx.doi.org/10.1787/888932429526

Estonia: **Demand, output and prices**

	2007	2008	2009	2010	2011	2012
	Current prices € billion	Percentage changes, volume (2000 prices)				
GDP at market prices	15.8	-5.1	-13.9	3.1	5.9	4.7
Private consumption	8.7	-5.4	-18.4	-1.9	2.3	4.5
Government consumption	2.6	3.8	0.0	-2.1	0.3	1.1
Gross fixed capital formation	5.5	-15.0	-32.9	-9.2	14.8	10.3
Final domestic demand	16.7	-7.1	-19.0	-3.6	4.4	5.1
Stockbuilding[1]	0.7	-4.1	-3.4	4.5	-0.8	0.0
Total domestic demand	17.5	-10.5	-22.1	1.1	3.4	4.9
Exports of goods and services	10.7	0.4	-18.7	21.7	20.0	8.6
Imports of goods and services	12.4	-7.0	-32.6	21.0	15.2	9.2
Net exports[1]	- 1.7	5.7	11.3	1.7	4.7	0.1
Memorandum items						
GDP deflator	_	7.2	-0.1	1.5	2.7	2.2
Harmonised index of consumer prices	_	10.6	0.2	2.7	4.6	3.0
Private consumption deflator	_	8.7	-0.9	2.1	5.6	3.0
Unemployment rate	_	5.6	13.9	16.8	14.2	13.0
General government financial balance[2]	_	-2.9	-1.8	0.1	-0.5	-1.7
Current account balance[2]	_	-9.7	4.5	3.6	3.2	0.7

Note: National accounts are based on official chain-linked data. This introduces a discrepancy in the identity between real demand components and GDP. For further details see *OECD Economic Outlook* Sources and Methods *(http://www.oecd.org/eco/sources-and-methods).*
1. Contributions to changes in real GDP (percentage of real GDP in previous year), actual amount in the first column.
2. As a percentage of GDP.
Source: OECD Economic Outlook 89 database.

StatLink ⟨⟩ *http://dx.doi.org/10.1787/888932430780*

restructuring, downsizing and wage cuts. The unemployment rate continued to fall rapidly from 18.6% in the first quarter of 2010 to 14.5% in the fourth quarter. Notwithstanding employment opportunities in Finland, there is still the risk of an increase in structural unemployment due to the depressed outlook for employment in construction. In this context, it will be important to evaluate and, if needed, improve the effectiveness of active labour market policies.

Inflation is rising

Inflation rose to 5.4% in April (year-on-year) due to energy, fuel, food and administrative price hikes, but also because of weak competition and increasing mark-ups, particularly in food distribution. Headline inflation is projected to fall, as commodity price pressures gradually fade, while core inflation is likely to stay well below its high pre-crisis rates due to remaining slack in the economy.

One-off operations contributed to the balancing of the budget

Estonia successfully undertook a remarkable consolidation effort to meet the conditions for euro entry, and gross public debt (Maastricht definition) was reduced to 6.6% of GDP in 2010. Fiscal balance was achieved in 2010, due to a combination of continued consolidation measures, stronger economic growth, better outcomes at the local level and substantial one-off operations, including a temporary suspension of contributions to the second pension pillar and sales of CO_2 Kyoto emission allowances. The headline fiscal position will deteriorate temporarily during the forecasting period as one-off measures will be phased out, but the underlying fiscal position will remain close to balance.

Exports will lead growth in 2011 and consumption will pick up in 2012

Real GDP is projected to expand strongly. Growth in 2011 will continue to be primarily driven by exports, reflecting the positive external outlook and improved competitiveness. Investment in machinery and equipment should also make a contribution, given increased capacity utilisation in the manufacturing sector, restored profitability and overall accommodating monetary conditions of the euro area, despite relatively high risk premia on corporate loans. Growth in 2012 is expected to be broader based, with a recovery in private consumption gaining momentum as unemployment continues to fall, the real wage bill increases, bad debt problems are resolved, and the saving rate falls gradually from its post crisis peak.

Risks are balanced

The overall risks to the projection are balanced. The main risks in the short term relate to the strength of external demand and the evolution of commodity prices. In the medium term, the main challenge will be to prevent high structural unemployment among the low-skilled and to overcome skill shortages.

FINLAND

The recovery is gathering further strength, boosted by strong exports, private consumption and residential investment. Although external demand in traditional markets is likely to remain robust, growth is projected to slow somewhat as private consumption and residential investment soften as higher commodity prices, taxes and interest rates bite into real incomes. Unemployment will continue to decline as employment grows and the labour force shrinks with ageing.

A strong fiscal position before the recession kept the deficit below 3% of GDP during the crisis. Strong growth and some fiscal consolidation support progress towards budget balance in 2013. Nevertheless, as ageing weighs on public finances, structural reforms to contain public spending and promote labour force participation, together with further reforms of the pension system, remain essential to support medium-term growth and fiscal sustainability.

The economy is growing strongly

The economy has gathered momentum and is now on a solid growth path, while unemployment has fallen significantly over the year. Exports are leading the recovery, benefitting in particular from strong growth in Germany, Sweden and Russia. Private consumption is supported by income growth, improvements in employment, increasing housing wealth, high household confidence and low interest rates. However, rising oil and commodity prices and hikes in indirect taxes have pushed up headline inflation, eroding households' purchasing power.

Strong residential investment is set to slow, but business investment will pick up

Residential investment soared at a rate of over 20% last year, spurred by very low interest rates on mortgages and real house prices that now surpass their pre-crisis level. But the housing boom now seems to be losing momentum. In contrast, business investment, which continued to decline in 2010 as spare capacity remained, is slowly turning around as the economy expands and utilisation rates increase.

Finland

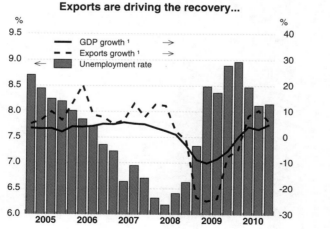

Exports are driving the recovery...

...lifting confidence across the economy

1. In volume, year-on-year percentage change.
2. The series are normalised at the average for the period starting in 1993 and are presented in units of standard deviation.
Source: OECD Economic Outlook 89 database, and OECD, Main Economic database.

StatLink ᔖ http://dx.doi.org/10.1787/888932429545

Finland: **Demand, output and prices**

	2007	2008	2009	2010	2011	2012
	Current prices € billion	Percentage changes, volume (2000 prices)				
GDP at market prices	179.7	1.0	-8.3	3.1	3.8	2.8
Private consumption	90.7	1.6	-2.1	2.7	2.4	2.1
Government consumption	38.6	2.5	0.9	0.4	0.9	0.6
Gross fixed capital formation	38.2	0.0	-14.5	0.1	5.7	5.8
Final domestic demand	167.5	1.4	-4.2	1.6	2.7	2.5
Stockbuilding[1,2]	3.1	-0.7	-1.7	0.8	-0.3	0.0
Total domestic demand	170.6	0.6	-5.9	2.4	2.3	2.5
Exports of goods and services	82.2	6.5	-20.3	5.0	8.2	6.0
Imports of goods and services	73.2	6.5	-17.6	2.6	4.7	5.5
Net exports[1]	9.1	0.3	-2.0	0.9	1.5	0.4
Memorandum items						
GDP without working day adjustments	_	0.9	-8.2	3.1	..	..
GDP deflator	_	1.8	1.1	2.0	1.7	2.0
Harmonised index of consumer prices	_	3.9	1.6	1.7	3.2	1.6
Private consumption deflator	_	3.5	0.6	1.0	3.7	2.1
Unemployment rate	_	6.4	8.3	8.4	7.9	7.1
General government financial balance[3]	_	4.2	-2.9	-2.8	-1.4	-0.6
Current account balance[3]	_	2.9	2.7	2.9	3.0	3.2

Note: National accounts are based on official chain-linked data. This introduces a discrepancy in the identity between real demand components and GDP. For further details see *OECD Economic Outlook* Sources and Methods (http://www.oecd.org/eco/sources-and-methods).
1. Contributions to changes in real GDP (percentage of real GDP in previous year), actual amount in the first column.
2. Including statistical discrepancy.
3. As a percentage of GDP.
Source: OECD Economic Outlook 89 database.

StatLink http://dx.doi.org/10.1787/888932430799

Monetary and fiscal policy will become less supportive

As the European Central Bank has started to move towards normalising interest rates, monetary policy will gradually become less supportive. Households with variable rate mortgages will see their debt burden increase and the user cost of capital for firms will rise, albeit moderately. Fiscal policy, which supported the economy during the downturn, is becoming mildly restrictive.

Growth will continue on the back of strong foreign and domestic demand

Growth is expected to average above 3% over the projection horizon. Exports, which fell sharply during the recession, will remain the main driver of the recovery. Demand from Finland's main trading partners is vigorous and competitiveness is improving as the real effective exchange rate has weakened and pay settlements result in moderate wage growth. Consumer confidence is high and the household sector balance sheet is in good shape. Hence private consumption should remain healthy, though it is expected to weaken somewhat as inflation erodes real incomes. Business investment is set to rebound as firms rebuild capacity in a climate of high business confidence and strong export order books. Residential investment, however, will be soft as house price rises slow and interest rates rise. Unemployment will continue to decrease as a result of modest employment growth and continuing contraction in the labour force due to ageing. Once the effects of higher oil and commodity prices and indirect tax hikes dissipate, inflation is projected to fall back below 2% due to a still substantial output gap.

The fiscal outlook is improving

Finland is one of the few euro area countries that succeeded in maintaining a fiscal deficit below 3% of GDP through the recent downturn. The fiscal position has started to improve thanks to the recovery in activity and increases in indirect taxes. Based on the previous government's tax plans and technical spending assumptions, further progress is expected, bringing the deficit to half a per cent of GDP in 2012. Despite this relatively bright picture, further measures will be needed to preserve fiscal sustainability as ageing increasingly weighs on public finances. Structural reforms to raise labour force participation, improve sustainability of the pension system and enhance public sector efficiency would reinforce medium-term growth prospects and the fiscal outlook.

The international environment could present risks or opportunities

The main risks are linked to the international environment. Strong investment in foreign countries could boost capital goods exports, which have so far remained subdued. However, a slowdown in the global economy would hit an economy which is highly dependent on exports. Economic instability within the euro area linked to financial difficulties in some member countries could also prove disruptive.

GREECE

The economy is suffering a serious recession in the context of the sizeable, but vital, fiscal retrenchment. A return to sustained positive growth is projected for 2012 as external demand strengthens, competitiveness improves and the far-reaching structural reforms implemented in response to the fiscal crisis start to take hold. Substantial economic slack and rising unemployment will keep inflation pressures subdued. The outlook is subject to important, mostly downside risks.

Adherence to the fiscal and structural adjustment programme, agreed in May 2010 with the European Union (EU) and the International Monetary Fund (IMF), is indispensible for restoring credibility and market confidence, long-term public debt sustainability and competitiveness. Success depends crucially on rigorous expenditure control and further progress in fighting tax evasion, combined with comprehensive reforms to address chronic rigidities in fiscal management, and in labour and product markets.

Economic activity contracted sharply

Output declined by 4.5% in 2010 as domestic demand plunged, but rose in the first quarter of 2011 at an annualised rate of 3½ per cent. Private consumption fell sharply in 2010, due to worsening labour markets, falling incomes and a decline in consumer credit. Investment also continued its downward trend since the beginning of the crisis. Exports, by contrast, increased strongly at the end of last year and in the first quarter of 2011. The unemployment rate had climbed to around 16% at the beginning of 2011. Industrial production, retail trade and consumer credit all suggest weak activity in the months ahead, although new export orders in industry remain a bright spot. Headline inflation reached 4.7% in 2010, reflecting indirect tax increases under the current adjustment programme; excluding tax effects, inflation has been well below the euro area average since the second half of the year. Inflationary pressures

Greece

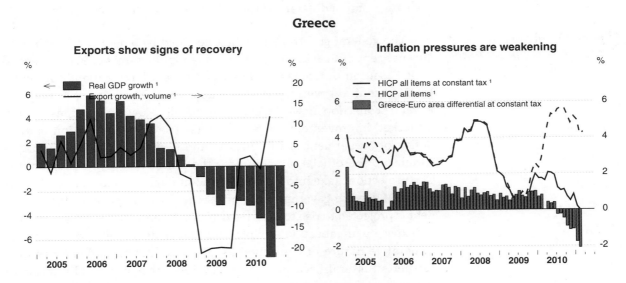

1. Year-on-year percentage change.

Source: OECD Economic Outlook 89 database and Eurostat.

StatLink ⟶ http://dx.doi.org/10.1787/888932429564

Greece: **Demand, output and prices**

	2007	2008	2009	2010	2011	2012
	Current prices € billion	Percentage changes, volume (2000 prices)				
GDP at market prices	227.1	1.0	-2.0	-4.5	-2.9	0.6
Private consumption	162.7	3.2	-2.2	-4.5	-5.4	-0.2
Government consumption	41.8	1.5	10.3	-6.5	-7.1	-4.3
Gross fixed capital formation	47.5	-7.5	-11.2	-16.5	-10.4	0.3
Final domestic demand	252.1	0.8	-1.9	-6.9	-6.5	-0.9
Stockbuilding[1,2]	2.1	0.5	-2.5	0.9	-0.4	0.0
Total domestic demand	254.2	1.2	-4.0	-6.1	-6.9	-0.9
Exports of goods and services	51.4	4.0	-20.1	3.8	9.4	9.4
Imports of goods and services	78.6	4.0	-18.6	-4.9	-8.7	2.7
Net exports[1]	- 27.1	-0.5	2.2	2.3	4.8	1.5
Memorandum items						
GDP deflator	_	3.3	1.3	2.5	0.3	0.7
Harmonised index of consumer prices	_	4.2	1.3	4.7	2.9	0.7
Private consumption deflator	_	4.0	1.1	4.7	2.6	0.7
Unemployment rate	_	7.7	9.5	12.5	16.0	16.4
General government financial balance[3]	_	-9.8	-15.6	-10.4	-7.5	-6.5
Current account balance[4]	_	-14.7	-11.0	-10.4	-8.6	-7.2

1. Contributions to changes in real GDP (percentage of real GDP in previous year), actual amount in the first column.
2. Including statistical discrepancy.
3. National Accounts basis, as a percentage of GDP.
4. On settlement basis, as a percentage of GDP.
Source: OECD Economic Outlook 89 database.

StatLink ᴀᴿ🔗 http://dx.doi.org/10.1787/888932430818

eased further in early 2011 as domestic demand weakened further, and the core inflation differential *vis-à-vis* the euro area has been eliminated.

Rigorous implementation of the austerity programme remains a top priority

The general government deficit declined by 5 percentage points to 10½ per cent of GDP in 2010, missing slightly the target of 9½ per cent of GDP. Based on outcomes so far, which reflect large expenditure cuts, the 2011 central government deficit appears to be in line with targets . Revenue collection, however, continues to fall below expectations despite a marked improvement in VAT receipts. The OECD projection is for a deficit of 7½ per cent of GDP in 2011 and 6½ per cent of GDP by 2012 – similar to the official targets under the EU/IMF economic programme. The projections take into account the additional measures announced in April 2011 by the government to offset the fiscal slippage in 2010. Public debt is projected to rise to over 150% of GDP by end-2012, even accounting for expected privatisation receipts. Such a high debt level underscores the imperative nature of continued fiscal consolidation and the need for further structural fiscal reforms. Comprehensive structural reforms to dynamise labour and product markets are also indispensible to raise employment and incomes, and to improve debt dynamics.

The projections involve some decline in spreads over time

Reflecting heightened concerns about the possible restructuring of public debt, the 10-year government bond differential *vis-à-vis* Germany rose to almost 10% points on average in April. In the projections this spread is assumed to remain constant for the remainder of 2011 and then to fall in 2012 as the fiscal and structural programmes bear fruit, raising confidence, or perceptions increase that additional official financing would be forthcoming, if needed.

Activity should gradually rebound

Output is projected to continue declining in 2011 but at a slower pace of around 3%, as the impact of the frontloaded fiscal adjustment on the economy wears off. GDP is projected to rise in 2012, as investment and exports rebound on the back of competitiveness-enhancing structural reforms and strengthening external demand. Faster absorption of the European Union structural funds should also act as a stimulus. Inflation is set to fall over the projection period as the unemployment rate edges up to over 16% in 2012 and substantial economic slack persists. The current account deficit is likely to narrow to around somewhat over 7% of GDP in 2012, reflecting the positive outlook for exports, especially in tourism and shipping, improvements in competiveness and still-weak domestic demand.

Projections are subject to important risks, mostly on the downside

The path to sustainable public finances and renewed economic growth is clearly fraught with risks. Many things could go wrong in the international sphere, including further loss of confidence or a marked weakening in export markets. The government can do little to influence these factors. It can, however, continue to implement the programme of fiscal adjustment and structural reform. Indeed, a slowdown in these areas would damage credibility, thereby aggravating the already difficult situation. At the same time, exports could surprise on the upside, and clear signs that the benefits of reform were materialising would boost confidence.

HUNGARY

The recovery in economic activity continues, driven mainly by inventory accumulation and external demand. Growth is projected to pick up, supported by vigorous exports and gradually improving domestic demand. Headline inflation is expected to moderate towards the medium-term target of the central bank once the effects of higher global commodity prices fade.

Dissolving the second pillar of the pension system will lead to a dramatic, but one-off, improvement of the general government balance in 2011, despite a fiscal relaxation induced by tax cuts and spending overruns. The publication of a programme outlining the main goals for structural reforms is a step in the right direction. Implementing credible structural measures to consolidate public finances is the next necessary step to foster market confidence and pave the way to sound growth.

The economy is on a slow recovery path

Economic activity has slowly gathered pace, but the weakness in final domestic demand has been a drag on activity. Industrial production has been growing vigorously, due to a strong performance of export-oriented enterprises and business confidence indicators suggest that output expansion should strengthen. However, consumer sentiment has weakened since late 2010 and construction activity is depressed.

The labour market is weak

The increase in the unemployment rate has not yet been contained, as employment losses have recently been stronger than withdrawals from the labour force. A large public works programme targeted at the long-term unemployed has been replaced by a new programme with tighter eligibility criteria, but total enrolment has not yet reached previous levels.

The underlying fiscal position remains weak

The fiscal position so far in 2011 appears to be weakening. By the end of the first quarter, the cumulated cash budget deficit (excluding local governments) already exceeded the full-year official target of 2.4% of GDP,

Hungary

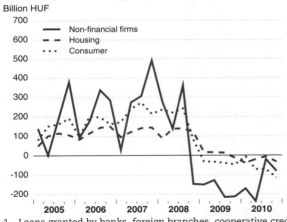

The private sector is deleveraging
Quarterly net increase in loans[1]

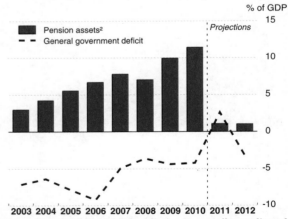

Pension asset transfers will swing the budget balance

1. Loans granted by banks, foreign branches, cooperative credit institutions and other financial intermediaries. Seasonally unadjusted change in outstanding amounts, with rolling exchange rate adjustment.
2. Market value of mandatory pension funds at end of year. OECD estimates for 2011 and 2012.
Source: OECD Economic Outlook 89 database, Magyar Nemzeti Bank and Hungarian Financial Supervisory Authority.

StatLink ᘳᘴᓒ http://dx.doi.org/10.1787/888932429583

Hungary: **Demand, output and prices**

	2007	2008	2009	2010	2011	2012
	Current prices HUF billion	Percentage changes, volume (2000 prices)				
GDP at market prices	25 548.3	0.6	-6.5	1.0	2.7	3.1
Private consumption	13 695.3	0.4	-7.9	-2.1	1.6	2.1
Government consumption	5 390.1	1.0	-0.1	-1.7	-2.6	-0.2
Gross fixed capital formation	5 408.3	2.9	-8.0	-5.6	0.6	2.9
Final domestic demand	24 493.7	1.1	-6.2	-2.7	0.4	1.8
Stockbuilding[1]	765.5	-0.2	-4.7	1.6	1.0	0.0
Total domestic demand	25 259.2	0.8	-10.8	-1.1	0.8	1.7
Exports of goods and services	20 459.6	5.7	-9.6	14.1	9.1	10.5
Imports of goods and services	20 170.5	5.8	-14.6	12.0	8.0	9.8
Net exports[1]	289.1	0.0	4.0	2.2	1.6	1.5
Memorandum items						
GDP deflator	_	4.3	4.7	2.8	3.9	3.2
Consumer price index	_	6.0	4.2	4.9	4.0	3.3
Private consumption deflator	_	5.4	4.1	5.0	4.6	3.2
Unemployment rate	_	7.9	10.1	11.2	11.5	11.0
General government financial balance[2]	_	-3.6	-4.4	-4.2	2.6	-3.3
Current account balance[2]	_	-7.2	0.5	2.1	2.7	1.8

Note: National accounts are based on official chain-linked data. This introduces a discrepancy in the identity between real demand components and GDP. For further details see *OECD Economic Outlook* Sources and Methods *(http://www.oecd.org/eco/sources-and-methods).*
1. Contributions to changes in real GDP (percentage of real GDP in previous year), actual amount in the first column.
2. As a percentage of GDP.
Source: OECD Economic Outlook 89 database.

StatLink 🔗 *http://dx.doi.org/10.1787/888932430837*

although temporary taxes levied on specific sectors should mitigate the extent of the deficit. Furthermore, the dismantling of the second pillar of the pension system will provide sizeable one-off revenues of around 9% of GDP and shift the general government balance to surplus on an accruals basis in 2011. However, since part of the second-pillar pension assets will be used to finance current expenditure while pension liabilities have been transferred to the government, long-term fiscal sustainability has deteriorated. The assumption of the debt of public transport companies by the government and the buyout of public-private projects will, also on a one-off basis, lower the surplus this year.

Fiscal consolidation is planned...

The fiscal balance should swing back to a deficit in 2012 as the one-offs disappear and the switch to a flat-rate personal income tax further reduces revenue. More recently, the authorities have undertaken welcome steps to shore up the fiscal position. A stability fund financed by restraints on current expenditure should reduce the risk of breaching the cash deficit target for 2011. In addition, a programme of structural reforms with expected savings of 2.9% of GDP in 2012 and 2013 has been released, although detailed policy measures and draft legislation have yet to be elaborated. A credible implementation of both steps is critical for improving fiscal sustainability.

... which will ease pressure on monetary policy

Monetary policy has faced large risk premiums, currency volatility and sovereign rating downgrades. Credible fiscal consolidation would ease such financial market concerns. The policy rate has been raised by 75 basis points to 6%. A large degree of slack is projected to reduce inflation to the central bank's target of 3%.

Activity should gradually strengthen

Growth is projected to pick up to around 3% in 2012, mainly driven by exports and gradually strengthening domestic demand. Fiscal consolidation, tight credit conditions, an ongoing deleveraging of the private sector and increases in households' precautionary savings will restrain the pace of expansion, though these effects should be offset to some extent by declining risk premiums.

Risks are balanced, but mainly depend on policy implementation

The main threat to currency stability and net capital inflows would be a failure to follow through on implementation of fiscal consolidation and structural reform. However, should the government stick to its fiscal commitments in full, phase out the temporary taxes earlier than planned and refrain from weakening independent institutions, then better than expected outcomes could follow owing to higher confidence of both domestic and foreign investors.

ICELAND

After a period of severe adjustment to eliminate imbalances and restructure the banking system, the Icelandic economy is projected to begin to grow again in 2011. The recovery is expected to be led by private investment in large energy-intensive projects and strengthening private consumption expenditure. There is considerable uncertainty about the impact of the rejection of the Icesave Agreement on the normalisation of international financial relations and on the attractiveness of Iceland for investment.

The government should continue to implement its multi-year fiscal consolidation programme. For this purpose, adopting explicit debt reduction targets and a new fiscal rule would strengthen the visibility of fiscal commitments and help to rebuild credibility. The modified monetary policy framework, which gives greater weight to exchange rate stability, should be adopted and capital controls should be removed when conditions permit.

Output has stabilised

Compared with a year earlier, the Icelandic economy stopped shrinking in the fourth quarter of 2010. Private consumption grew, supported by rising disposable incomes, domestic debt relief measures, and the authorisation to withdraw third-pillar pension savings. Residential investment also rose as an improving real estate outlook spurred work on incomplete projects. However, business investment continued to decline, albeit more slowly, owing to the ending of large energy-intensive projects, corporate deleveraging and high levels of spare capacity. Employment continued to fall in the year to the first quarter of 2011, increasing the unemployment rate to 7.5% (seasonally adjusted). Compared with a year earlier, real wage increases in the private sector picked up to 3.5% in the fourth quarter of 2010, eroding earlier falls. The annual inflation rate rose to 2.8% in the year to April owing to a decline in

Iceland

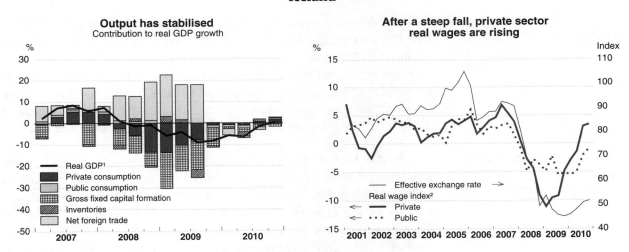

1. Year-on-year percentage change.
2. Deflated by the consumer price index, year-on-year percentage change.
Source: Central Bank of Iceland.

StatLink http://dx.doi.org/10.1787/888932429602

Iceland: **Demand, output and prices**

	2007	2008	2009	2010	2011	2012
	Current prices ISK billion	Percentage changes, volume (2000 prices)				
GDP at market prices	1 308.5	1.4	-6.9	-3.5	2.2	2.9
Private consumption	751.6	-7.9	-15.6	-0.2	2.9	2.7
Government consumption	316.8	4.6	-1.7	-3.2	-4.0	-1.8
Gross fixed capital formation	373.0	-19.7	-50.9	-8.1	14.7	12.4
Final domestic demand	1 441.5	-8.2	-20.7	-2.3	2.6	3.0
Stockbuilding[1]	6.6	-0.4	0.0	-0.2	-0.1	0.0
Total domestic demand	1 448.1	-8.5	-20.7	-2.5	2.7	3.0
Exports of goods and services	453.3	7.0	7.0	1.1	2.7	3.3
Imports of goods and services	592.9	-18.4	-24.0	3.9	3.8	3.5
Net exports[1]	- 139.6	10.8	14.4	-1.2	-0.2	0.2
Memorandum items						
GDP deflator	_	11.8	8.3	6.7	1.9	2.8
Consumer price index	_	12.7	12.0	5.4	2.7	2.6
Private consumption deflator	_	14.0	13.8	3.5	1.2	2.4
Unemployment rate	_	3.0	7.2	7.5	7.0	5.8
General government financial balance[2]	_	-13.5	-10.0	-7.8	-2.7	-1.4
Current account balance[2]	_	-24.8	-10.7	-8.0	-6.2	-3.6

Note: National accounts are based on official chain-linked data. This introduces a discrepancy in the identity between real demand components and GDP. For further details see *OECD Economic Outlook* Sources and Methods *(http://www.oecd.org/eco/sources-and-methods).*
1. Contributions to changes in real GDP (percentage of real GDP in previous year), actual amount in the first column.
2. As a percentage of GDP.
Source: OECD Economic Outlook 89 database.

StatLink http://dx.doi.org/10.1787/888932430856

the exchange rate and a rise in commodity prices. The underlying current account balance (which excludes net income payments of credit institutions in winding-up proceedings) remains in small surplus.

The government is implementing a demanding fiscal consolidation programme

The general government budget deficit fell by 2.2% of GDP to 7.8% of GDP (6.5% excluding called loan guarantees) in 2010. A larger decline is planned in 2011 and the budget is to be balanced by 2013. Spending restraint accounts for about one half of the consolidation. On the basis of these plans, general government gross debt (including civil service pension liabilities, which amount to around 20% of GDP) should peak at 121% of GDP in 2011; net government debt should peak at 44% of GDP.

Monetary policy is accommodative and capital controls remain in place

For the time being, monetary policy continues to be guided by the objective of maintaining currency stability, and the Central Bank of Iceland's (CBI) policy rates were around 4% in April, below the neutral rate. For the period after the IMF programme ends (August 2011), the CBI favours adopting a revised inflation targeting framework that gives greater weight to exchange rate stability, and coordinated monetary, macro-prudential and fiscal policy. Capital controls are unlikely to be removed by 2012. In preparation for their removal, the CBI recently announced proposals to discourage non-residents from converting their holdings of króna-denominated assets (about 30% of GDP) into foreign exchange.

Rejection of the Icesave Agreement may weigh on the economic recovery

The electorate recently rejected the Icesave Agreement, which would have resolved disputes with the British and Dutch governments and had been expected to add about 2% of GDP to government debt. This dispute is now likely to be settled in court. Credit ratings on Iceland sovereign debt remained unchanged, but the vote and the subsequent legal process could delay the removal of capital controls, reduce investment, and delay Iceland's EU accession negotiations.

Economic recovery should get underway in 2011

A domestic-demand led recovery is projected to get underway during the course of 2011, lifting growth to 3% by 2012. Private consumption expenditure should continue to rise, notably in 2011, and investment in energy-related projects and residential construction should expand this year and next. The unemployment rate is projected to begin to fall in 2011, reaching 5½ per cent by the end of 2012. With the stabilisation of commodity prices and the exchange rate, inflation should ease back to around 2½ per cent by 2012. The main risks to the economic outlook concern the effects of the recent vote against the Icesave agreement and the timing of large energy-intensive investment projects, which could differ significantly from what has been assumed in these projections.

IRELAND

Ireland is continuing to undertake a comprehensive and vital adjustment programme to reduce its macroeconomic imbalances and restore its banking system to health. Despite robust export growth, weak domestic demand and ongoing fiscal consolidation have prevented an economic recovery from unfolding so far. As domestic demand stabilises, a modest upturn of output is expected in the course of 2011, with some acceleration in 2012. The unemployment rate is likely to stay high, and core deflation to continue.

The fiscal position remains characterised by high deficits, reflecting negative cyclical effects, the collapse of housing-related tax revenues and the large cost of bank recapitalisation. In line with the EU and IMF programme, the general government deficit needs to be reduced to below 3% of GDP by 2015, in order to arrest the accumulation of public debt and restore fiscal sustainability. The government plans to cover the recapitalisation needs of the banking system revealed by the recent stress tests so as to restore normal bank credit flows and support the economic recovery. This should be done as planned without delay. Improving competitiveness through wage restraint and structural reforms should remain a priority.

Domestic demand remains anaemic

In the three years of recession that began at the end of 2007, GDP has fallen by 14.5%. Output continued to contract sharply in the fourth quarter of 2010 and recent indicators of consumption and construction suggest that weakness in private domestic demand will continue into 2011. The contractionary effects of fiscal consolidation are evident in falls in both public consumption and, particularly, investment. In contrast, a pick-up in global growth and improvement in cost competitiveness have contributed to strong export growth.

Labour market conditions are depressed and underlying deflation is evident

The official unemployment rate rose to 14.7% towards the end of 2010 and registered unemployment numbers suggest that it remained around this level in early 2011. Employment continues to decline but outward migration flows and falls in the participation rate have contributed to

Ireland

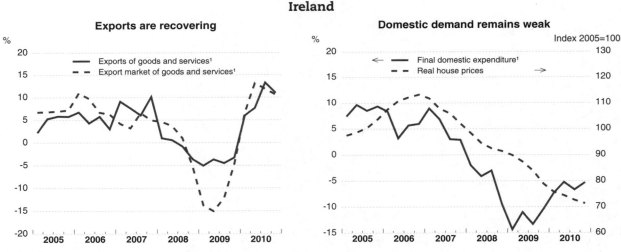

1. In volume, year-on-year percentage change.
Source: OECD Economic Outlook 89 database and Central Statistics Office Ireland.

StatLink ᔕᔕᔕ http://dx.doi.org/10.1787/888932429621

Ireland: **Demand, output and prices**

	2007	2008	2009	2010	2011	2012
	Current prices € billion	Percentage changes, volume (2008 prices)				
GDP at market prices	189.3	-3.6	-7.6	-1.0	0.0	2.3
Private consumption	90.1	-1.8	-7.2	-1.2	-2.1	0.3
Government consumption	30.6	2.8	-4.2	-2.1	-1.9	-2.0
Gross fixed capital formation	50.1	-14.4	-30.9	-27.7	-11.0	0.8
Final domestic demand	170.7	-4.7	-12.4	-6.2	-3.3	-0.2
Stockbuilding[1]	1.4	-0.8	-1.3	0.7	-0.5	0.0
Total domestic demand	172.2	-5.5	-13.8	-5.4	-4.0	-0.2
Exports of goods and services	152.5	-0.8	-4.2	9.4	5.3	6.6
Imports of goods and services	135.3	-2.9	-9.8	6.5	4.0	5.3
Net exports[1]	17.2	1.4	3.8	3.6	2.2	2.5
Memorandum items						
GDP deflator	_	-1.4	-4.0	-2.5	-1.3	1.1
Harmonised index of consumer prices	_	4.1	-4.5	-0.9	1.7	0.5
Private consumption deflator	_	3.0	-4.3	-2.2	0.8	0.5
Unemployment rate	_	6.0	11.7	13.5	14.7	14.6
General government financial balance[2,3]	_	-7.3	-14.3	-32.4	-10.1	-8.2
Current account balance[2]	_	-5.6	-3.0	-0.7	3.7	5.3

Note: National accounts are based on official chain-linked data. This introduces a discrepancy in the identity between real demand components and GDP. For further details see *OECD Economic Outlook* Sources and Methods *(http://www.oecd.org/eco/sources-and-methods).*
1. Contributions to changes in real GDP (percentage of real GDP in previous year), actual amount in the first column.
2. As a percentage of GDP.
3. Includes the one-off impact of recapitalisations in the banking sector.
Source: OECD Economic Outlook 89 database.

StatLink http://dx.doi.org/10.1787/888932430875

stem the rise in unemployment. Wages in both the public and private sectors fell during 2010. Price deflation is illustrated by the decline of domestic output prices, as measured by the GDP deflator, which has fallen 12% from its peak in mid 2007. Excluding the effects of global commodity price increases consumer prices continued to decline mildly in early 2011.

Exports are expected to spur a recovery

Exports are projected to continue growing at a rapid pace, supported by robust import demand from trading partners and recent gains in cost-competitiveness. Weighed down by fiscal consolidation, high indebtedness, tax increases and falling real wages, private domestic demand is expected to continue contracting in 2011, albeit at a slower rate. The recovery is set to gather some speed 2012 thanks to a revival of domestic demand. Significant spare capacity, especially in the labour market, will ensure that wages and inflation remain subdued.

Unemployment will remain elevated

Export-led as opposed to domestic demand-led growth tends to be relatively job poor and employment is expected to continue shrinking in 2011. Nevertheless, stronger growth should lead to an end to employment declines in 2012, a small fall in the unemployment rate and the beginnings of a self-sustaining recovery.

Fiscal consolidation must be fully implemented

The government has announced a detailed multi-year programme, agreed with the EU and IMF, to reduce the fiscal deficit to below 3% of GDP by 2015. It should fully implement the measures necessary to achieve the programme's target and, in doing so, seek to minimise the harmful effects of fiscal consolidation on longer-term growth. This projection assumes that discretionary measures of 3.5% of GDP in 2011 and 2% in 2012 are fully implemented. With public interest payments rising fast, this would result in the fiscal deficit declining from 12.1% of GDP in 2010 (excluding bank support measures) to 10.1% in 2011 and 8.2% in 2012. Further measures will be necessary to reach the target of a deficit of 3% of GDP in 2015.

Banking recapitalisation should proceed quickly

The March 2011 bank stress tests were perceived as credible by financial markets as evidenced by a fall in the spread of Irish over German sovereign bond yields. It is important for the return to growth that the recapitalisation and associated restructuring of the banking system occurs without delay. In line with government and EU-IMF programme partner projections, it is assumed that the government will provide, EUR 19 billion (13% of GDP) of the EUR 24 billion in capital needs identified by the stress tests and that the government will receive equivalent assets in return (thus leaving the headline fiscal deficit unchanged). It is possible that some of this transaction will eventually be classified by Eurostat as a capital transfer. If so, these amounts would be added to the headline deficit, but they would have no implications for the consolidation plan to 2015. Either way, combined with the ongoing borrowing needs of the government, this would result in gross public debt measured on a Maastricht basis increasing from 96% of GDP in 2010 to 119% of GDP in 2012. It is assumed that the government will finance the full fiscal deficit and repayment of maturing debt in 2011 and 2012 using funds disbursed under the EU/IMF programme. These funds are sufficient to cover financing needs in both years. On this basis, net government interest payments are projected to increase from 2.4% of GDP in 2010 to 3.9% of GDP in 2012.

Households face severe headwinds but export potential is strong

A return to healthy GDP growth is essential for the government to eventually return to market financing. The yield differential on long-term bonds vis-à-vis Germany is assumed to remain constant at its level in April throughout 2011 and then to halve in the course of 2012 as progress in consolidation and economic adjustment leads to a spontaneous increase in confidence or perceptions increase that additional official financing would be forthcoming, if needed. Risks to this projection are balanced. Private consumption may be hit harder than projected by declining household incomes and the weak labour market. In addition, although there have been important forward steps, the banking system has yet to be returned to health, constraining its capability to deliver credit for investment. On the upside, ongoing gains in cost-competiveness may see faster export growth with Ireland gaining market share.

ISRAEL*

Growth in real GDP this year should exceed that of 2010, but rising labour-supply constraints and further interest rate hikes will temper activity in 2012. Annual inflation will remain above the 1-3% target band until the beginning of next year.

Recent policy rate increases mark a welcome shift towards normalisation of the monetary stance, but the continued efforts to curb currency appreciation reflect a strategy that is less single-mindedly focused on hitting the inflation target. Fiscal goals will probably be achieved, in spite of budgetary measures countering consumer price increases.

Growth was very rapid at the end of 2010

Real GDP expanded by 7.7% (seasonally adjusted annualised rate) in the fourth quarter of 2010, bringing growth to 4.7% for the year as a whole. Much of the fourth-quarter strength was due to a rebound in private consumption (8.3% compared with 1% in the previous quarter). Growth in the first quarter of 2011 eased to 4.7%. The room for increases in labour utilisation is diminishing. While labour force participation could rise further, the unemployment rate is already historically low (6.6% in the final quarter of 2010).

Inflation is well above the target band

Annual inflation reached 4.3% in March, and bond market measures suggest expectations of 3.1% for the year ahead. Unlike in other countries, inflation has not been pushed up by its food and energy components.

Israel

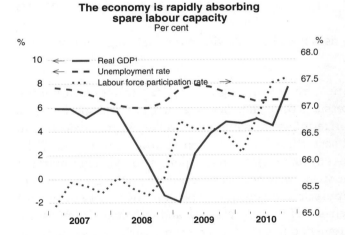

The economy is rapidly absorbing spare labour capacity
Per cent

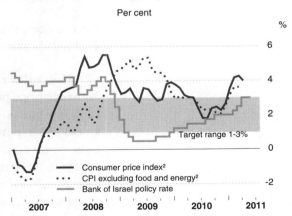

Normalisation of the policy rate continues
Per cent

1. Change from previous quarter at annual rate.
2. Year-on-year change.
Source: Bank of Israel; CBS; OECD Economic Outlook 89 database.

StatLink 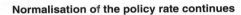 http://dx.doi.org/10.1787/888932429640

* The statistical data for Israel are supplied by and under the responsibility of the relevant Israeli authorities. The use of such data by the OECD is without prejudice to the status of the Golan Heights, East Jerusalem and Israeli settlements in the West Bank under the terms of international law.

Israel: **Demand, output and prices**

	2007	2008	2009	2010	2011	2012
	Current prices NIS billion	Percentage changes, volume (2005 prices)				
GDP at market prices	690.1	4.2	0.8	4.7	5.4	4.7
Private consumption	389.6	3.0	1.7	5.1	4.9	4.5
Government consumption	171.3	2.4	1.9	2.1	3.3	1.5
Gross fixed capital formation	130.5	4.1	-6.5	12.6	13.3	7.2
Final domestic demand	691.4	3.0	0.3	5.7	6.0	4.3
Stockbuilding[1]	7.7	-0.4	-0.6	-1.1	-0.7	0.0
Total domestic demand	699.0	2.6	-0.4	4.5	5.4	4.5
Exports of goods and services	292.9	5.9	-11.7	13.6	7.1	8.7
Imports of goods and services	301.8	2.3	-14.1	12.6	8.1	8.1
Net exports[1]	- 8.9	1.5	1.1	0.6	-0.2	0.2
Memorandum items						
GDP deflator	_	0.9	5.0	1.1	1.4	2.5
Consumer price index	_	4.6	3.3	2.7	3.7	3.4
Private consumption deflator	_	4.8	2.4	2.9	3.6	3.4
Unemployment rate	_	6.1	7.6	6.6	6.2	5.7
General government financial balance[2,3]	_	-3.7	-6.4	-5.0	-3.7	-2.9
Current account balance[2]	_	0.9	3.6	3.1	1.2	1.0

Note: National accounts are based on official chain-linked data. This introduces a discrepancy in the identity between real demand components and GDP. For further details see *OECD Economic Outlook* Sources and Methods *(http://www.oecd.org/eco/sources-and-methods)*.
1. Contributions to changes in real GDP (percentage of real GDP in previous year), actual amount in the first column.
2. As a percentage of GDP.
3. Excluding Bank of Israel profits and the implicit costs of CPI-indexed government bonds.
Source: OECD Economic Outlook 89 database.

StatLink ⬚ᵍᴸ *http://dx.doi.org/10.1787/888932430894*

Also, house-price rises have been slowing but remain high (14% year-on-year in February).

Monetary policy tightening has been stepped up

The authorities are continuing a complex strategy of quelling domestic price pressures through policy-rate increases and specific steps to damp house-price inflation, while also implementing measures to shield the export sector from currency appreciation. Since January the policy rate has been hiked by 100 basis points to 3%. This marks a welcome acceleration in policy normalisation. At the same time, efforts to restrain shekel appreciation continue. The Bank of Israel still makes discretionary purchases of foreign currency, and in January it imposed a 10% reserve requirement on banks' foreign-exchange derivative contracts with non-residents. Furthermore, a bill removing non-residents' exemption from a 15% withholding tax on income from short-term bonds has been passed by the Knesset. These efforts to protect the tradeables sector by restraining the exchange rate are increasingly at odds with the pace of economic recovery. Non-diamond goods exports in the second half of 2010 were rather weak; however, monthly data on the dollar value of exports thus far in 2011 indicate a return to rapid growth. If export growth looks set to be strong, then the authorities should return to straightforward single-instrument monetary policy.

Fiscal balances remain on track to meet targets

Strong revenue growth in 2010 combined with adherence to a spending ceiling rule brought a reduction in the general-government deficit from 6.4% of GDP in 2009 to 5.0% in 2010, according to a standardised OECD definition. The broad fiscal strategy for 2011-12 (Israel has adopted a two-year budget system) continues to give priority to income-tax cuts and deficit reduction through a tight lid on spending increases and selective increases in indirect taxation. In early 2011 there was some softening of this strategy. An increase in excise on vehicle fuel was reversed and commitments have been made to reduce increases in water prices, cut public-transport fares and bring forward minimum–wage increases. To offset the fiscal impact of these moves, scheduled cuts in some income-tax rates may be postponed.

Growth will peak in 2011

Output is expected to grow by 5.4% in 2011 and by 4.7% in 2012, somewhat above estimated potential rates. The most robust components should be exports and investment. Unemployment should fall below 6% in 2012. Underlying consumer price inflation is projected to edge up, reaching 2.7% by the end of 2012. To stem inflationary pressure the policy rate should be boosted to 4.75% by year-end and a further 75 basis points in 2012. These increases may be smaller if the shekel appreciates further, which in turn partly depends on whether currency intervention continues. The fiscal projection embodies deficit reductions of 1.3 percentage points of GDP in 2011 and 0.8 points in 2012, broadly reflecting government targets.

Geopolitical risks have increased

Recent political developments in the region have brought additional risk to the economy; for instance, natural-gas imports via pipeline from Egypt have been interrupted. However, further news on domestic hydrocarbon deposits is likely over the projection period, which may boost confidence among investors and households alike. Should external market growth falter, the existing tensions in monetary policy would be accentuated, especially if inflation pressures persist and house-price increases are sustained.

KOREA

After slowing during 2010, growth picked up in early 2011, driven by the acceleration in world trade. Inflation also increased significantly, due in part to higher oil and commodity prices. Output growth is projected to moderate during 2011 and 2012, resulting in annual growth rates of around 4½ per cent and helping to bring inflation back into the central bank's target range of 2 to 4%.

Fiscal policy should continue to focus on the deficit reduction targets in the medium-term fiscal plan. The central bank will need to raise its policy interest rate from its current level of 3% to contain inflationary pressures; an appreciation of the won would also help. Sustaining high growth over the medium term requires structural reforms to enhance productivity, particularly in services, where productivity is 40% less than in manufacturing.

With the economy regaining momentum...

The pace of growth decelerated from 8.6% (seasonally-adjusted annual rate) to 2.0% between the first and final quarters of 2010. However, the economy regained momentum in the first quarter of 2011, with output growth of 5.6%, driven by strong world trade. The effective exchange rate has remained relatively stable over the past year at about 21% below its early 2008 level, boosting Korea's export competitiveness. Despite the slowdown during 2010, the economy faces capacity constraints, with the unemployment rate falling to around 3½ per cent and the capacity utilisation rate in manufacturing at a historic high.

... inflation has become an important concern...

Consumer price inflation accelerated from 2.6% (year-on-year) in the second quarter of 2010 to 4.5% in the first quarter of 2011, breaching the upper bound of the central bank's target zone. Rising food and commodity prices played a role, pushing up producer price inflation to 6.7% in the first quarter. However, core inflation also picked up from 1.6% to 3.0% over the

Korea

Exports and production have regained momentum
Volume indices 2005=100[1]

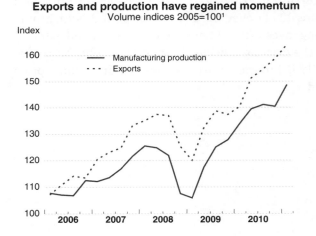

Inflation is above the central bank's target zone
Year-on-year percentage change

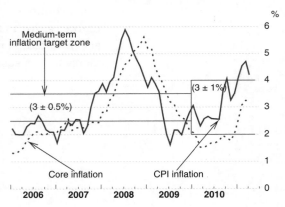

1. Seasonally-adjusted for production and national accounts data for exports.

Source: Korea National Statistical Office, OECD Economic Outlook 89 Database and Bank of Korea.

StatLink ⟨⟩ http://dx.doi.org/10.1787/888932429659

Korea: **Demand, output and prices**

	2007	2008	2009	2010	2011	2012
	Current prices KRW trillion	Percentage changes, volume (2005 prices)				
GDP at market prices	975.0	2.3	0.3	6.2	4.6	4.5
Private consumption	530.3	1.3	0.0	4.1	3.5	3.6
Government consumption	143.3	4.3	5.6	3.0	4.0	4.0
Gross fixed capital formation	278.2	-1.9	-1.0	7.0	-0.4	5.9
Final domestic demand	951.7	0.8	0.6	4.8	2.4	4.3
Stockbuilding[1]	8.6	0.6	-3.9	2.0	0.5	0.0
Total domestic demand	960.3	1.4	-3.3	7.0	2.9	4.3
Exports of goods and services	408.8	6.6	-1.2	14.5	11.7	11.2
Imports of goods and services	394.0	4.4	-8.0	16.9	8.5	10.9
Net exports[1]	14.7	1.0	3.7	-0.6	1.9	0.3
Memorandum items						
GDP deflator	_	2.9	3.4	3.7	1.0	2.6
Consumer price index	_	4.7	2.8	3.0	4.2	3.5
Private consumption deflator	_	4.5	2.6	2.6	4.3	3.6
Unemployment rate	_	3.2	3.6	3.7	3.5	3.4
Household saving ratio[2]	_	2.9	4.6	4.3	3.5	3.5
General government financial balance[3]	_	3.0	-1.1	0.0	0.5	1.3
Current account balance[3]	_	0.5	3.9	2.8	1.9	1.6

Note: National accounts are based on official chain-linked data. This introduces a discrepancy in the identity between real demand components and GDP. For further details see *OECD Economic Outlook* Sources and Methods *(http://www.oecd.org/eco/sources-and-methods)*.
1. Contributions to changes in real GDP (percentage of real GDP in previous year), actual amount in the first column.
2. As a percentage of disposable income.
3. As a percentage of GDP.
Source: OECD Economic Outlook 89 database.

StatLink ᴍᴐ⧏ http://dx.doi.org/10.1787/888932430913

same period. One exception to inflation pressures is a mild decline in housing prices, reflecting the large stock of unsold homes.

... leading to a tightening of monetary policy

Although the Bank of Korea has increased the policy interest rate by 100 basis points from a record-low 2% in July 2010, monetary conditions are still quite relaxed at this stage of the business cycle. Meanwhile, significant fiscal consolidation is under way in line with the National Fiscal Management Plan for 2010-14. Growth in nominal central government spending is to be limited to around 5% per year, helping to reduce the consolidated central government deficit (excluding the social security surplus) from 4.1% of GDP in 2009 to 1.1% in 2012, despite cuts in personal and corporate income tax rates.

The expansion is projected to remain on track...

Despite some drag from tightening monetary and fiscal policy, the expansion is projected to remain on track, with annual output growth rates of around 4½ per cent in 2011 and 2012. The household sector, which had debt amounting to 124% of household income in 2010, will be negatively impacted by higher borrowing costs, as well as the terms-of-trade loss from increased oil and commodity prices, limiting the growth of private consumption. The 11 March disaster in Japan, which supplies about a quarter of Korea's imports of parts and capital equipment, is currently expected to reduce exports only temporarily. A return to double-digit gains in exports, which account for one-half of GDP, will be an important source of growth through 2012. Business and consumer confidence remains high, despite some decline in recent months. Slowing output growth should help bring headline inflation back into the central bank's target zone from the second half of 2011, while the unemployment rate stabilises at around 3½ per cent. The current account surplus in projected to recede from 2.8% of GDP in 2010 to less than 2% in 2011-12, reflecting the impact of higher oil prices.

... depending on developments in the world economy

The major risks for Korea, the world's eighth-largest exporter, are mainly tied to the strength of the recovery in world trade and the exchange rate. The outlook is particularly sensitive to demand from China, which accounts for one-third of Korean exports. In addition, there is a risk that the impact of disruptions to the supply chain related to imports from Japan following the March earthquake may be larger or more prolonged than expected. On the domestic side, rising interest rates may restrain private consumption more than foreseen, in so far as heavily-indebted households use income gains to repay their loans, which are mostly at floating interest rates.

LUXEMBOURG

Strong exports and a robust expansion of domestic demand are driving the continuing recovery. Consumption and investment are anticipated to continue to pick up during 2011, while financial and business services exports will remain strong. Although growth is likely to be higher than in neighbouring countries, uncertainties remain around the post-crisis development of the key financial sector.

Fiscal consolidation plans need to be implemented with a focus on restraining current expenditure and could be more ambitious. Far-reaching and comprehensive pension reforms need to be implemented to achieve long-run sustainability. The high rate of unemployment among residents would be reduced by reforms to labour market institutions and by improving work incentives.

Export growth has led the recovery

The recovery is continuing with GDP rising by 4.6% in the year to the fourth quarter of 2010. Export growth was strong as the result of recovery in financial market activity and demand for industrial goods. Domestic demand expanded at a robust pace, reflecting improvements in confidence, employment gains and low interest rates. The running down of inventories, which dragged down growth during 2010, is likely to have been largely completed.

Employment is expanding

Employment is recovering, with year-on-year growth of 2.4% in February. Both domestic and cross-border employment have been increasing but unemployment among residents has remained high.

Inflation has increased sharply

Annual headline inflation picked up sharply to 4% in March on a harmonised basis, up from 2.6% six months earlier. Although mainly driven by a surge in commodity prices, core inflation has also risen to reach 2.3% in March, up from 1.7% six months earlier. The rise in core

Luxembourg

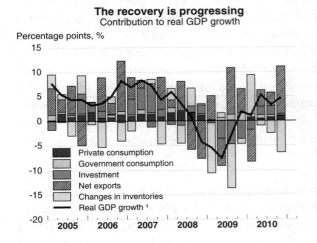

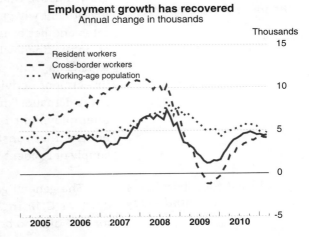

1. Year-on-year percentage change.

Source: OECD, OECD Economic Outlook, No. 89 database and Statec.

StatLink ᴴᴵ http://dx.doi.org/10.1787/888932429678

Luxembourg: **Demand, output and prices**

	2007	2008	2009	2010	2011	2012
	Current prices € billion	Percentage changes, volume (2000 prices)				
GDP at market prices	37.5	1.4	-3.6	3.5	3.2	3.9
Private consumption	12.0	4.7	0.2	2.0	1.8	2.8
Government consumption	5.5	2.7	4.6	2.9	0.4	3.1
Gross fixed capital formation	7.8	1.4	-19.2	2.6	8.0	4.0
Final domestic demand	25.3	3.3	-4.7	2.4	3.0	3.2
Stockbuilding[1]	0.1	-0.1	-0.8	0.4	-0.1	0.0
Total domestic demand	25.4	3.1	-5.9	3.0	2.8	3.4
Exports of goods and services	66.0	6.6	-8.2	6.3	6.3	6.1
Imports of goods and services	53.8	8.5	-10.2	6.7	6.9	6.5
Net exports[1]	12.1	-0.6	0.3	1.5	1.3	1.8
Memorandum items						
GDP deflator	_	4.2	-0.3	5.5	2.6	1.6
Harmonised index of consumer prices	_	3.4	0.4	2.3	3.4	2.3
Private consumption deflator	_	2.0	0.8	1.8	2.8	2.1
Unemployment rate	_	4.4	5.7	6.0	5.4	4.8
General government financial balance[2]	_	3.0	-0.9	-1.7	-0.9	0.0
Current account balance[2]	_	5.3	6.9	7.8	5.5	4.7

Note: National accounts are based on official chain-linked data. This introduces a discrepancy in the identity between real demand components and GDP. For further details see *OECD Economic Outlook* Sources and Methods (*http://www.oecd.org/eco/sources-and-methods*).
1. Contributions to changes in real GDP (percentage of real GDP in previous year), actual amount in the first column.
2. As a percentage of GDP.
Source: OECD Economic Outlook 89 database.

StatLink ⬛⬛⬛ http://dx.doi.org/10.1787/888932430932

inflation partly reflects an increase in administered prices, although strengthening demand will create price pressures in the future.

The financial sector and domestic demand will be the main drivers of growth

The recovery is expected to continue over the coming quarters with growth above that of neighbouring countries. Private consumption and investment will gain momentum from improved confidence, low interest rates and better labour market conditions. Exports are likely to remain strong as financial and business services play a major role in driving the expansion, while demand for goods increases with stronger demand and investment activity elsewhere. Fiscal consolidation should modestly damp demand. Employment will continue to grow at a robust pace but the unemployment rate will fall only gradually, held back by structural policies that constrain labour demand and reduce the effective labour supply of resident workers.

Fiscal consolidation is underway

The general government balance has deteriorated from a deficit of 0.9% of GDP in 2009 to an estimated 1.7% in 2010. The budget for 2011 aims to bring the deficit to 1% of GDP. In addition to the cyclical recovery, the plan includes restraint on expenditures, notably public investment, as well as tax increases, including a hike in the top income tax rate. Some further measures may be needed to meet the objective of balancing the budget by 2014. More ambitious consolidation and major reforms to the pension system are needed to be meet the challenge from large future pension costs,. Implementation of a comprehensive and far-reaching pension reform is needed to achieve sustainability.

The main risks relate to developments in the financial sector

The main short-term risks are uncertainty about international financial conditions and the improvement in trade as the world economy recovers. Further ahead, there is great uncertainty around the medium-term potential of the economy given the specialisation in specific financial activities and prospective changes to the international regulatory environment.

MEXICO

The Mexican economy has embarked on a strong recovery from the recession of 2008-09. Initially driven by exports, activity is expected to be increasingly supported by domestic demand. After a strong rise in 2010 to 5½ per cent, GDP growth will ease in 2011 (4½ per cent) and 2012 (3.8%), as the expansion of exports will normalise.

The government started fiscal consolidation in 2010 with tax increases and a partial withdrawal of stimulus measures. The projection assumes that the government will implement its plans to return to a balanced budget, based on the national definition of the deficit, by 2012. Oil production has stabilised for now, but the government should reduce its dependence on this volatile source of revenue by implementing further tax reform and withdrawing energy subsidies more quickly. Meanwhile, the central bank can wait to raise interest rates, as slack in production capacity remains large, core inflation has fallen throughout 2010 and inflation expectations remain well anchored. Thus recent food price increases are not expected to lead to important second round effects.

The recovery is now supported by stronger domestic demand

The recovery was initially led by a strong rebound in exports, as world trade and industrial production in the United States, Mexico's main trading partner, recovered. Improving business confidence and normalised financial conditions have boosted private investment, while strong employment growth and recovering confidence are supporting private consumption. Thus, activity is increasingly supported by domestic demand, while trade growth has normalised. The trade and current account deficits remain moderate. Employment is now well above pre-crisis levels, although with Mexicans returning to the labour force employment growth has not been strong enough to bring down unemployment significantly.

Mexico

Stronger US industrial production supports growth
Year-on-year percentage change

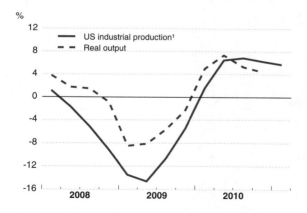

Following exports, domestic demand is now recovering

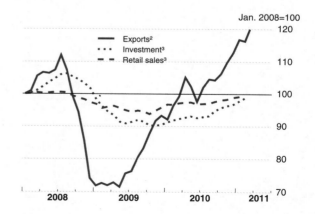

1. Excluding construction.
2. Export data are expressed in USD.
3. 3-month moving average.
Source: OECD Economic Outlook 89 database; Bank of Mexico; INEGI.

StatLink http://dx.doi.org/10.1787/888932429697

Mexico: **Demand, output and prices**

	2007	2008	2009	2010	2011	2012
	Current prices MXN billion	Percentage changes, volume (2003 prices)				
GDP at market prices	11 313.3	1.5	-6.1	5.5	4.4	3.8
Private consumption	7 317.8	1.8	-7.1	5.0	4.7	4.1
Government consumption	1 182.1	1.1	3.5	2.8	0.6	1.5
Gross fixed capital formation	2 391.7	5.9	-11.2	2.3	8.6	8.3
Final domestic demand	10 891.6	2.6	-7.0	4.2	5.1	4.7
Stockbuilding[1]	598.7	-0.3	-1.1	1.0	-0.4	0.0
Total domestic demand	11 490.3	2.3	-8.0	5.2	4.7	4.7
Exports of goods and services	3 159.7	0.7	-14.0	24.5	4.9	8.6
Imports of goods and services	3 336.7	3.2	-19.0	22.3	5.6	11.1
Net exports[1]	- 177.0	-0.9	2.2	0.2	-0.3	-1.0
Memorandum items						
GDP deflator	_	6.2	4.1	4.4	4.0	4.1
Consumer price index	_	5.1	5.3	4.2	4.3	3.7
Private consumption deflator	_	5.5	7.2	3.0	3.0	3.7
Unemployment rate[2]	_	4.0	5.5	5.3	4.6	3.9
Public sector borrowing requirement[3,4]	_	-1.1	-5.2	-4.3	-2.9	-2.6
Current account balance[4]	_	-1.5	-0.7	-0.5	-1.3	-2.1

1. Contributions to changes in real GDP (percentage of real GDP in previous year), actual amount in the first column.
2. Based on National Employment Survey.
3. Central government and public enterprises.
4. As a percentage of GDP.
Source: OECD Economic Outlook 89 database.

StatLink ᐧᐧᐧ *http://dx.doi.org/10.1787/888932430951*

Inflation has declined

Core inflation declined throughout 2010, while headline inflation has been a bit more volatile, reflecting rises in food prices and some administered prices, including energy. Since its post-crisis low of March 2009, the peso has appreciated, restraining price increases.

Fiscal policy has tightened...

Fiscal consolidation began in 2010 with tax increases and expenditure cuts to compensate for decreased revenues due to declining oil production, which has now stabilised, although at a lower level than previously. The projection assumes that the government will implement some further expenditure restraint in 2011 and 2012, as foreseen in the budget. The public sector borrowing requirement is expected to fall from 5½ per cent in 2009 to 2½ per cent in 2012. This would translate into a closing of the combined deficit of the central government and its public enterprises, on the national definition. This excludes PEMEX's investment spending, but – unlike in the standard national accounts definition – includes a number of pure financing operations. This deficit reduction is needed to maintain the sustainability of Mexico's public finances. In the longer term, the government should aim for more independence from oil-related tax revenues, for example through broadening the tax base and removing energy subsidies faster than currently planned. Any extra revenues from higher than expected oil prices should be saved in the oil stabilisation fund.

... but monetary policy remains supportive

The central bank has left the policy rate at 4.5% since July 2009, which is well below its neutral level. Supportive financial conditions have thus contributed to the recovery of domestic demand, as have stronger employment growth and increasing remittances sent by Mexican workers abroad. Mexico can afford to keep policy rates low for some time in view of declining inflation, still considerable unused capacities and moderate wage increases. Medium-term inflation expectations are reasonably well-anchored according to the central bank's survey, with experts expecting inflation to remain within the upper half of the central bank's target range.

Growth is expected to ease

The recovery is expected to continue with increasing support from domestic demand. However, strong internal demand will not fully compensate for the normalisation of export growth, which is tapering off after an exceptionally strong rebound. Growth is thus expected to ease throughout the projection period, from 5½ per cent in 2010 to 4½ per cent in 2011 and a bit below 4% in 2012. Employment is expected to continue its recovery, driving unemployment down to pre-crisis levels in 2012. The current account balance is projected to widen mildly, as imports strengthen along with domestic demand. The recent uptick in headline inflation owing to food price increases is not expected to lead to second-round effects given the still large unused production capacity and continuing slack in labour markets. Both headline and core inflation are expected to remain within the target range in 2012.

Risks from food price inflation and higher-than-expected US growth

Higher-than-expected food price inflation could weigh on consumers' real incomes. If second-round effects appeared, the result could be lower growth combined with higher inflation. In contrast, a stronger US recovery would strengthen Mexico's exports.

NETHERLANDS

The post-crisis recovery has been led by world trade and the rebuilding of stocks, but is set to become increasingly dependent on final domestic demand. Industrial production and capacity utilisation are close to pre-crisis levels, reviving business investment. On the other hand, private consumption is likely to remain subdued due to low wage growth and fiscal and monetary tightening.

The minority government is pursuing a path towards fiscal sustainability by implementing a medium-term consolidation plan of over 3% of GDP, of which 1 percentage point is to occur in 2011-12. As the labour market tightens, the combination of a low unemployment rate and high vacancy rates points to a need for a better allocation of labour, which would benefit from measures to increase housing market flexibility and reduce congestion.

Growth is benefiting from strong external demand

Strong world trade has spurred export growth leading to a recovery in production and supporting a revival in business investment, which is likely to accelerate given the low base level and buoyant orders. Restocking is also making a positive, though less persistent, contribution. On the other hand, public demand, strong throughout the crisis, is now being curtailed by consolidation. Household consumption is picking up only slowly due to slow real household disposable income growth. Consumer confidence, on an upward trend since two years, remains below pre-crisis levels. Headline inflation kept rising in early 2011, on the back of energy and food price hikes, while core inflation dropped to below 1½ per cent in early 2011, reflecting slow wage growth.

Unemployment is falling

Unemployment has been falling slowly since mid-2010, but remains above 4% as widespread labour hoarding during the downturn has slowed hiring. The increase in employment throughout 2010 was accompanied by a pick-up in vacancies, particularly in the private sector. However,

Netherlands

Business sentiment is rebounding as capacity utilisation is approaching pre-crisis levels

The housing market remains weak

1. Manufacturing.

Source: OECD, Main Economic Indicators database and CBS, Statistics Netherlands.

StatLink http://dx.doi.org/10.1787/888932429716

Netherlands: **Demand, output and prices**

	2007	2008	2009	2010	2011	2012
	Current prices € billion	Percentage changes, volume (2000 prices)				
GDP at market prices	571.8	1.9	-3.9	1.8	2.3	1.9
Private consumption	264.1	1.1	-2.5	0.4	0.7	1.3
Government consumption	143.9	2.5	3.7	1.5	-0.2	-0.4
Gross fixed capital formation	114.3	5.1	-12.7	-4.8	5.4	5.0
Final domestic demand	522.3	2.4	-3.0	-0.4	1.3	1.5
Stockbuilding[1]	2.5	-0.1	-0.9	1.1	0.1	0.0
Total domestic demand	524.8	2.2	-4.0	0.9	1.4	1.5
Exports of goods and services	424.2	2.8	-7.9	10.9	6.7	6.7
Imports of goods and services	377.2	3.4	-8.5	10.5	5.4	6.7
Net exports[1]	47.0	-0.2	-0.2	1.0	1.5	0.5
Memorandum items						
GDP deflator	_	2.4	-0.2	1.6	-0.1	1.6
Harmonised index of consumer prices	_	2.2	1.0	0.9	2.2	1.9
Private consumption deflator	_	1.4	-0.6	1.7	2.0	1.9
Unemployment rate	_	3.0	3.7	4.3	4.2	4.0
Household saving ratio[2]	_	5.7	6.8	6.6	6.0	5.7
General government financial balance[3]	_	0.5	-5.5	-5.3	-3.7	-2.1
Current account balance[3]	_	4.4	4.9	7.7	7.2	7.4

Note: National accounts are based on official chain-linked data. This introduces a discrepancy in the identity between real demand components and GDP. For further details see *OECD Economic Outlook* Sources and Methods *(http://www.oecd.org/eco/sources-and-methods)*.
1. Contributions to changes in real GDP (percentage of real GDP in previous year), actual amount in the first column.
2. As a percentage of disposable income, including savings in life insurance and pension schemes.
3. As a percentage of GDP.
Source: OECD Economic Outlook 89 database.

StatLink http://dx.doi.org/10.1787/888932430970

employment has not been increasing fast enough to prevent slowing wage growth, as visible in wage settlements.

Significant fiscal consolidation is underway

At below 5½ per cent of GDP, the 2010 budget deficit was almost 1 percentage point lower than initially planned, mainly due to cyclical developments. Fiscal consolidation, already underway, is set to exceed 1% of GDP over the projection period and be slightly back-loaded. The budget deficit should be below 4% in 2011 and just above 2% the following year. Most measures are on the spending side, particularly in public administration costs, subsidies and social transfers. Small additional budget improvements are to come from the expiration of fiscal stimulus measures and higher natural gas revenues.

Pension funds are recovering slowly

The crisis-related solvency problems of the occupational pension funds seem to be gradually receding. As part of their recovery plans, most pension funds either hiked contributions or decreased payouts, reducing private income. Rising interest rates should markedly improve solvency rates, limiting the need for additional measures and thus no further negative effects on income are projected.

Private domestic demand will pick up

Over the projection period the recovery will depend increasingly on private domestic demand, but will be held back by fiscal and monetary tightening. GDP should return to pre-crisis levels at the turn of 2011. A pick-up in business investment from a low level is projected, reflecting tightening capacity constraints and buoyant orders, though its effect on growth will be contained by the high import content of investment. Private consumption is likely to remain in check due to the slow wage growth and the effects of contractionary policies. Employment should continue to rise, leading a gradual fall in the unemployment rate to below 4% by the end of 2012, but a rapid pick-up in wages is not expected. As a consequence, inflation (both headline and core) should stabilise at below 2%. A spike in headline inflation is expected mid-2011 due to the periodic adjustment of Dutch energy contracts.

Risks are balanced

The main risks concern the recovery in household income and hence private consumption. On the downside, unexpected inflation hikes would reduce real household disposable income while, on the upside, a faster-than-expected recovery in employment would boost incomes and support consumption.

NEW ZEALAND

A devastating second earthquake has derailed a recovery already weakened by exchange-rate appreciation and private-sector efforts to reduce high levels of mortgage debt. Reconstruction and other one-offs will set the stage for a strong rebound in the second half of this year and into 2012.

Macroeconomic policies have accommodated the natural disaster. However, monetary policy should begin to renormalise as rebuilding puts pressure on costs. Fiscal policy should shift to a progressively tighter stance and structural reforms be accelerated in order to raise national savings and thereby reduce the high external debt.

Growth had slackened...

The recovery lost momentum in the second half of 2010. The recovery in global risk appetite led to renewed NZD appreciation, and tradables sectors consequently underperformed. Lingering uncertainty and a high cost of capital, notwithstanding lower interest rates, left business investment at historically low levels, with little new hiring as well. Efforts by households and farms to reduce debt in the wake of property price declines, persisting high unemployment and an early summer drought implied little household spending growth, despite record dairy prices and terms-of-trade gains. The housing market slowed in reaction to monetary tightening and tax changes on property investment.

... when a devastating new earthquake hit

In February 2011, just as indicators were improving and reconstruction from the September earthquake was imminent, a second and far deadlier earthquake struck Christchurch. Besides significant loss of life, injury and disruption to activity, the financial cost of the damage to homes, business structures and local infrastructure from the two earthquakes combined is estimated at 8% of national GDP, equivalent to

New Zealand

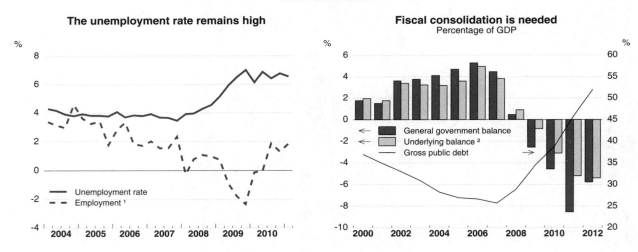

1. Year-on-year percentage change.
2. Percentage of potential GDP.
Source: Statistics New Zealand and OECD Economic Outlook 89 database.

StatLink http://dx.doi.org/10.1787/888932429735

New Zealand: **Demand, output and prices**

	2007	2008	2009	2010	2011	2012
	Current prices NZD billion	Percentage changes, volume (1995/1996 prices)				
GDP at market prices	178.6	-0.7	0.0	2.5	0.8	4.1
Private consumption	104.8	-0.3	-0.7	2.0	0.9	2.2
Government consumption	33.4	5.0	0.6	2.3	1.5	-0.6
Gross fixed capital formation	41.5	-4.4	-10.6	2.4	6.0	17.5
Final domestic demand	179.7	-0.3	-2.6	2.1	2.0	4.8
Stockbuilding[1]	0.9	0.4	-1.9	1.4	1.1	0.0
Total domestic demand	180.7	0.4	-5.0	4.2	2.6	4.7
Exports of goods and services	49.8	-1.7	1.7	3.0	3.1	5.8
Imports of goods and services	51.9	2.1	-14.6	10.2	8.5	8.0
Net exports[1]	- 2.1	-1.1	5.3	-1.9	-1.4	-0.6
Memorandum items						
GDP (production)	_	-0.2	-2.1	1.5	0.6	4.1
GDP deflator	_	4.0	0.7	2.2	4.3	3.2
Consumer price index	_	4.0	2.1	2.3	4.6	2.8
Core consumer price index[2]	_	2.0	2.2	1.9	3.2	2.8
Private consumption deflator	_	3.6	2.3	1.4	3.6	2.6
Unemployment rate	_	4.2	6.1	6.5	6.9	6.0
General government financial balance[3]	_	0.4	-2.6	-4.6	-8.5	-5.8
Current account balance[3]	_	-8.7	-2.9	-2.2	-1.6	-6.3

Note: National accounts are based on official chain-linked data. This introduces a discrepancy in the identity between real demand components and GDP. For further details see *OECD Economic Outlook* Sources and Methods *(http://www.oecd.org/eco/sources-and-methods)*.

1. Contributions to changes in real GDP (percentage of real GDP in previous year), actual amount in the first column.
2. Consumer price index excluding food and energy.
3. As a percentage of GDP.

Source: OECD Economic Outlook 89 database.

StatLink ᴀ᳘ᵴ▰ http://dx.doi.org/10.1787/888932430989

around 2.5% of the national capital stock. Households bore around two-thirds of the property losses, nearly all being covered by a mix of public and private insurance. The government's Earthquake Commission will fund the public insurance payouts (at some 3½ per cent of GDP) by means of both own asset drawdowns and international reinsurance.

Monetary policy has been eased...

Headline inflation is picking up strongly on the back of domestic consumption tax increases and global commodity price inflation, as well as higher insurance premia consequent to the earthquake. However, underlying inflation remains subdued, given the weakness of demand. In March, the Reserve Bank reduced its policy rate by 50 basis points to 2.5% as "insurance" to limit the risk of a widespread fall in confidence following the earthquake. It also noted that the earthquake rebuild in a context of reduced capacity would put pressure on resources. With core inflation expected to remain above the 2% mid-point of the target band throughout the projection horizon, interest rates will need to start to rise around year-end and return to neutral levels by end-2012.

... as has fiscal policy

The earthquakes' medium-term fiscal costs are estimated at 6% of GDP, over two-thirds of which represents higher spending and the remainder lost tax revenues due to weaker economic activity. The major spending items are the public earthquake insurance payments to households and repair of local infrastructure, each estimated at 1.5% of GDP. Exceptional public expenses will also arise for health care, disability, employment income losses, temporary lodging and other assistance programmes. The general government deficit is projected to reach 8½ per cent of GDP in 2011, when many of these costs are incurred. Despite this, the government has signalled that it plans to meet its medium-term consolidation objectives by imposing a freeze on overall nominal discretionary spending in the May budget; that is, spending increases in some areas will be offset by reductions elsewhere. The projections assume spending restraint apart from earthquake expenses.

The recovery will be gradual and uneven

Growth in the first quarter of 2011 is expected to be significantly negative. Though aftershocks are continuing, the second quarter may benefit from a technical rebound. The Rugby World Cup, expected to provide a growth boost of ¼–½ percentage point in the September-October period, and the early stages of earthquake reconstruction imply a step-up in growth around mid-year. Rebuilding is projected to get more fully underway in 2012 and continue to add to demand for several years. Record-high commodity prices will also provide support. Private investment and consumption should start to recover more surely, though needed fiscal consolidation will start to bite and private debt reduction will probably be sustained.

Risks are large, but broadly balanced

The domestic and global situation implies large uncertainties ahead. Renewed carry trade may push up the value of the currency, the large external debt position poses risks in a still volatile global financial market, persistently high house prices are vulnerable to correction and reconstruction may experience delays. However, successful household deleveraging (for example, due to asset price or further terms-of-trade gains) may provide room for more consumption growth than projected.

NORWAY

Norway has fully recovered from the global economic crisis. Growth is projected to rise through 2012 on the back of increasing private consumption and investment, despite stagnating oil and gas exports. Inflation has remained low so far, partly due to moderate wage rises, but the acceleration of output and increasing pressures on production capacity will lift it somewhat through the projection period.

The central bank envisages reducing the monetary stimulus substantially through the projection period to guard against potential disturbances of activity and inflation somewhat further ahead. This policy response appears necessary, despite below-target inflation and the strength of the krone. While the overall budget surplus will benefit from high oil prices, fiscal policy should nonetheless aim to progressively reduce the non-oil budget deficit, keeping it in line with the fiscal guidelines of a structural non-oil budget deficit of 4% of the value of the Government Pension Fund Global (GPFG). Structural reforms in a number of important areas, notably disability insurance and early retirement, would stimulate labour supply and improve the fiscal position.

Most economic indicators point to strong growth ahead

Norway's mainland economy (excluding oil-related activity) has resumed a solid pace of output growth in recent quarters, and the latest indicators suggest continued strengthening. On the domestic side, consumer confidence and investment expectations have returned to their very high pre-crisis levels. Credit demand and housing investment have been rising, with house prices reaching record levels. On the external side, rising oil prices have boosted public revenues and petroleum-sector investment. Recent figures on unemployment indicate the beginning of a recovery in the labour market. Despite the strength of the economy, wage increases were moderate in 2010. This and the appreciation of the krone

Norway

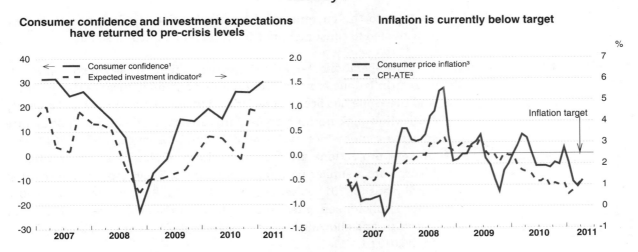

1. Average balance of positive over negative responses to a series of questions.
2. On a scale from –5 (sharp fall) to +5 (strong growth).
3. Seasonally adjusted; CPI-ATE is consumer price inflation adjusted for tax changes and excluding energy products.

Source: Norges Bank, Statistics Norway and TNS Gallup (for consumer confidence).

StatLink ᵐˢᵖ http://dx.doi.org/10.1787/888932429754

Norway: **Demand, output and prices**

	2007	2008	2009	2010	2011	2012
	Current prices NOK billion	Percentage changes, volume (2007 prices)				
GDP at market prices	2 271.6	0.8	-1.4	0.4	2.5	3.0
Private consumption	940.1	1.6	0.2	3.6	3.9	4.1
Government consumption	446.5	4.1	4.7	2.2	2.1	1.9
Gross fixed capital formation	503.9	2.0	-7.4	-8.9	6.4	7.1
Final domestic demand	1 890.5	2.3	-0.8	0.1	4.0	4.2
Stockbuilding[1]	32.8	-0.3	-2.4	3.5	0.2	0.0
Total domestic demand	1 923.3	1.9	-3.7	4.2	4.3	4.2
Exports of goods and services	1 039.7	1.0	-4.0	-1.3	0.7	3.1
Imports of goods and services	691.4	4.3	-11.4	8.7	4.5	6.8
Net exports[1]	348.3	-0.8	1.4	-2.9	-1.0	-0.5
Memorandum items						
Mainland GDP at market prices[2]	_	1.8	-1.3	2.2	3.3	4.0
GDP deflator	_	10.0	-4.0	4.7	8.6	2.8
Consumer price index	_	3.8	2.2	2.4	1.7	2.0
Private consumption deflator	_	3.6	2.5	1.9	1.4	2.0
Unemployment rate	_	2.6	3.2	3.6	3.4	3.2
Household saving ratio[3]	_	3.7	7.3	7.2	7.1	6.7
General government financial balance[4]	_	19.1	10.5	10.5	12.5	11.9
Current account balance[4]	_	17.9	13.1	12.9	15.6	14.9

Note: National accounts are based on official chain-linked data. This introduces a discrepancy in the identity between real demand components and GDP. For further details see *OECD Economic Outlook* Sources and Methods *(http://www.oecd.org/eco/sources-and-methods)*.
1. Contributions to changes in real GDP (percentage of real GDP in previous year), actual amount in the first column.
2. GDP excluding oil and shipping.
3. As a percentage of disposable income.
4. As a percentage of GDP.
Source: OECD Economic Outlook 89 database.

StatLink ᔕᓰᔆᐴ http://dx.doi.org/10.1787/888932431008

relative to the currencies of Norway's major trading partners have contributed to consumer price inflation remaining low so far.

Monetary policy is set to tighten

The operational target of Norges Bank, the central bank of Norway, is to keep inflation near 2.5% over time. Current inflation is well below target and the krone has been appreciating, but with house prices and capacity utilisation picking up Norges Bank envisages raising its policy rate towards a more "normal" level of around 4% by the end of 2012. The present projections are similar to those of Norges Bank, and hence incorporate a similar path for interest rates. They also assume that the fiscal plans for 2011 as set out in the National Budget from October 2010 will be fully implemented, keeping taxes at the same level over the next two years and allowing for a modest increase in the non-oil budget deficit from 2010 to 2011.

Private consumption and investment will drive GDP growth...

Economic growth is projected to rise through the projection period on the back of strong increases in private consumption and private investment, notably in the oil and construction industries. The mainland economy is estimated to expand by 3.3% in 2011 and 4% in 2012. Higher domestic demand will exert favourable effects on the labour market, and will slowly push up wage growth. This will contribute to a gradual increase in consumer price inflation. Partly as a result of high immigration, the unemployment rate will only decline slowly however.

... while public consumption and net exports will exert damping effects

In line with the fiscal plans of the government, increases in public consumption are assumed to slow over the projection period. Strong growth in the GPFG, the repository of net petroleum revenues, should bring the structural non-oil budget deficit down to or below 4% of assets in the GPFG in 2011. The continuing increase in world trade will lead to a modest rise in non-petroleum export growth over the projection period. Nonetheless, owing to high consumer confidence as well as the continued strength of the krone, imports are expected to outpace exports, leading to a moderate reduction of the current account surplus.

Commodity prices are a key uncertainty factor

On the external side, the main risk is oil prices which are assumed constant through the projection period. Changes may have large impacts on GDP growth for the offshore and hence total economy. On the domestic side, by contrast, the risks are mainly contained: The high household debt may weigh on private consumption, and labour market developments will be sensitive to immigration flows and the impact of new rules for flexible retirement.

POLAND

The Polish economy is projected to expand by close to 4% in 2011 and 2012 thanks to strong public investment in 2011, partly related to EU-financed infrastructure projects and the 2012 football championships, a recovery in business investment in 2012 and robust private consumption.

The budget deficit is projected to decrease from 7.9% of GDP in 2010 to 5.8% in 2011 and 3.7% in 2012. Inflation jumped in early 2011 due to booming food and energy prices. Monetary tightening should be continued towards a neutral stance both to tame inflation expectations and forestall second-round effects from the commodity price increases, and also because strong growth will soon result in pressure on productive capacity.

The economy continues to advance

Economic growth reached a robust 3.8% in 2010 on the back of public and private consumption and a turnaround in stockbuilding, even though private consumption decelerated somewhat late in the year. But industrial production has accelerated, and business confidence indicators suggest continued expansion. Fixed investment fell, especially in machinery and equipment and residential construction, but inward direct investment accounted for 2% of GDP and may reach 4% of GDP in 2011. Growth in non-residential construction is still subdued. Credit to the domestic economy seems to be recovering only slowly. The standardised unemployment rate has stabilised at about 9.5% since early 2010.

A number of measures will reduce the fiscal deficit in 2011 and 2012

Despite robust growth, the budget deficit rose to 7.9% of GDP in 2010, a percentage point higher than foreseen in Poland's EU convergence programme. It is projected to fall to 5.8% in 2011 and 3.7% in 2012, in part due to strong economic growth. Also, the decision to divert, as of May 2011, some social security contributions from the mandatory second

Poland

Government deficit and debt rose again in 2010
As a percentage of GDP

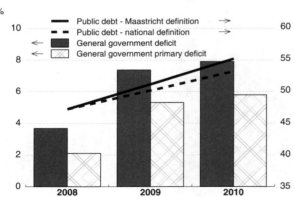

Inflation is above target and rising

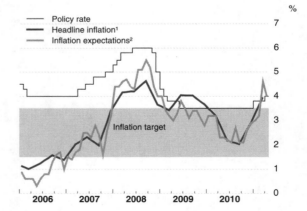

1. Year-on-year growth rates.
2. One year ahead.

Source: NBP; OECD, Economic Outlook 89 database.

StatLink http://dx.doi.org/10.1787/888932429773

Poland: **Demand, output and prices**

	2007	2008	2009	2010	2011	2012
	Current prices PLN billion	Percentage changes, volume (2000 prices)				
GDP at market prices	1 176.7	5.0	1.7	3.8	3.9	3.8
Private consumption	713.2	5.2	2.4	3.0	3.0	3.3
Government consumption	210.3	6.6	2.6	3.8	3.2	0.8
Gross fixed capital formation	251.6	9.6	-0.8	-2.2	9.7	9.7
Final domestic demand	1 175.1	6.4	1.7	2.1	4.3	4.1
Stockbuilding[1]	33.9	-1.0	-2.5	2.1	0.4	0.0
Total domestic demand	1 209.0	5.2	-0.7	4.2	4.7	4.1
Exports of goods and services	481.9	5.9	-6.0	10.1	5.4	6.7
Imports of goods and services	514.3	6.2	-13.2	11.4	7.7	7.2
Net exports[1]	- 32.3	-0.3	3.4	-0.5	-1.0	-0.4
Memorandum items						
GDP deflator	_	3.1	3.5	1.5	2.9	2.9
Consumer price index	_	4.2	3.8	2.6	4.2	3.1
Private consumption deflator	_	4.6	2.1	2.9	3.8	2.9
Unemployment rate	_	7.1	8.2	9.6	9.4	8.5
General government financial balance[2,3]	_	-3.7	-7.4	-7.9	-5.8	-3.7
Current account balance[2]	_	-4.8	-2.2	-3.4	-4.5	-4.8

Note: National accounts are based on official chain-linked data. This introduces a discrepancy in the identity between real demand components and GDP. For further details see *OECD Economic Outlook* Sources and Methods *(http://www.oecd.org/eco/sources-and-methods).*
1. Contributions to changes in real GDP (percentage of real GDP in previous year), actual amount in the first column.
2. As a percentage of GDP.
3. With private pension funds (OFE) classified outside the general government sector.
Source: OECD Economic Outlook 89 database.

StatLink http://dx.doi.org/10.1787/888932431027

pension pillar (which is outside the government sector) to the first pillar (which is in the government sector) will reduce the deficit by around 0.6% of GDP in 2011 and 1.1% in 2012. Other consolidation measures include an increase in VAT and the introduction of spending norms in central government. Public investment spending is projected to slow in 2012, as infrastructure projects come to a halt.

Additional efforts are needed to reach the government's 2012 budget target

The budget deficit is projected to decrease to 3.7% of GDP in 2012 as the diversion of social security contributions takes full effect. Thus, further measures are needed if the government is to achieve its deficit goal of 2.9% of GDP in 2012. The government's proposal to introduce deficit and debt limits for local authorities would be a step in the right direction. Further spending reductions could be achieved by reforming the first pension pillar to eliminate privileges of uniformed services and judges and increase the effective retirement age, by enhancing efficiency in public administration, education and healthcare, and by improving the targeting of selected social spending. There is also room to cut tax expenditures and increase green and property taxes.

Public debt will remain below 60% of GDP in 2012

The government seeks to maintain public debt (national definition) below the intermediate threshold of 55% of GDP in 2011 and 2012 by relying on a number of measures in addition to reducing the deficit: *a*) shifting public infrastructure spending to the National Road Fund (excluded from the domestic definition) and the State-owned National Economy Bank (BGK); *b*) decreasing interest payments on public debt by borrowing from cheaper sources, such as the European Investment Bank, to finance large infrastructure projects; *c*) privatising mostly minority stakes in state-owned companies (around 1% of GDP in 2011); *d*) transferring assets managed by the demographic reserve fund to the budget; *e*) improving the public sector's liquidity management; and *f*) transferring central bank profits to the budget (worth 0.4% of GDP in 2011).

Monetary tightening should be continued

Headline inflation rose sharply in early 2011, chiefly because of food and energy price increases. These may translate into wage increases, especially as inflation expectations have already edged up, economic slack is rapidly diminishing and minimum wages will rise by 8% in 2012. This calls for monetary tightening.

Stable growth and declining unemployment are in prospect

Growth is expected to remain strong, initially on the back of fixed investment fuelled by EU funds and related to the preparations for the 2012 football championship, a revival of business investment in 2012, and robust private consumption. Unemployment is projected to decline gradually and the current account to worsen due to strong import growth.

Risks are policy-related

There is a risk that if structural fiscal tightening measures are not undertaken, given the context of parliamentary elections in late 2011, the general government deficit will be higher than projected, which could jeopardise macroeconomic stability. Any delay in monetary tightening would result in stronger domestic demand and higher inflation.

PORTUGAL

The economy is expected to continue contracting in 2011 and most of 2012, as fiscal consolidation and deleveraging gather pace. Persistent domestic demand weakness will lead to lower inflation once the effects of more expensive oil and hikes in indirect taxes have dissipated. Exports should remain dynamic, underpinning the end of output losses towards the end of 2012 and a gradual reduction of the current account deficit. Unemployment is set to rise further.

Budget deficit reduction is underway and will proceed in the context of a financial assistance programme agreed with the EU and IMF. Despite the short-run costs, strictly implementing consolidation measures is essential to rebalance the economy. To support consolidation, further steps should be taken to reform the budgetary framework. Sustainable public finances also require stronger potential growth and improved competitiveness, which should be fostered by structural reforms in labour and product markets and in the tax system.

Domestic demand is contracting strongly

Real GDP fell in the fourth quarter of 2010, amid private demand weakness and plummeting confidence. Household consumption was nonetheless cushioned by booming purchases of durable goods, in anticipation of the 2011 increase in VAT. With this effect being reversed, consumption has weakened significantly, resulting in a further contraction of output in early 2011. Against this background, the recent acceleration in core inflation has largely reflected increases in the VAT and in regulated prices, and the rise in global oil prices has further fuelled headline inflation. Labour market conditions have remained depressed. Despite strong export growth, the current account deficit narrowed only marginally in 2010, as imports were boosted by the temporary consumption boom and sizeable military equipment purchases.

Portugal

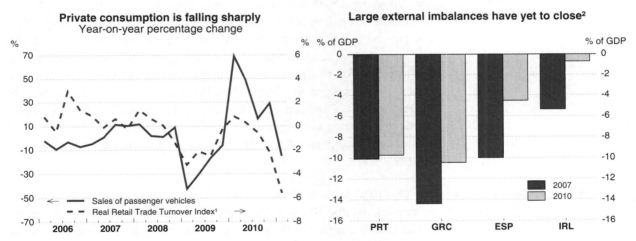

1. Based on index 2005=100, seasonally and working-day adjusted.
2. Current account as a percentage of GDP.
Source: Instituto Nacional de Estatística (INE), Associação Automóvel de Portugal (ACAP) and OECD Economic Outlook 89 database.
StatLink http://dx.doi.org/10.1787/888932429792

Portugal: **Demand, output and prices**

	2007	2008	2009	2010	2011	2012
	Current prices € billion	Percentage changes, volume (2006 prices)				
GDP at market prices	169.3	0.0	-2.5	1.3	-2.1	-1.5
Private consumption	110.6	1.3	-1.1	2.2	-4.1	-3.7
Government consumption	33.6	0.4	3.7	1.8	-7.2	-5.6
Gross fixed capital formation	37.6	-0.3	-11.2	-5.0	-10.0	-6.7
Final domestic demand	181.8	0.8	-2.3	0.8	-5.8	-4.6
Stockbuilding[1]	1.0	0.1	-0.6	-0.1	0.2	0.0
Total domestic demand	182.9	0.9	-2.9	0.7	-5.6	-4.6
Exports of goods and services	54.5	-0.1	-11.6	8.8	6.4	7.4
Imports of goods and services	68.0	2.3	-10.6	5.2	-4.8	-1.8
Net exports[1]	- 13.5	-1.0	0.7	0.6	3.9	3.2
Memorandum items						
GDP deflator	_	1.6	0.5	1.0	1.0	1.0
Harmonised index of consumer prices	_	2.7	-0.9	1.4	3.3	1.3
Private consumption deflator	_	2.6	-2.5	1.6	3.3	1.3
Unemployment rate	_	7.6	9.5	10.8	11.7	12.7
Household saving ratio[2]	_	7.1	10.9	9.8	9.9	12.5
General government financial balance[3,4]	_	-3.6	-10.1	-9.2	-5.9	-4.5
Current account balance[3]	_	-12.6	-10.2	-9.7	-7.8	-5.5

1. Contributions to changes in real GDP (percentage of real GDP in previous year), actual amount in the first column.
2. As a percentage of disposable income.
3. As a percentage of GDP.
4. Based on national accounts definition.
Source: OECD Economic Outlook 89 database.

StatLink ⬛⬛⬛ http://dx.doi.org/10.1787/888932431046

Mounting market pressure culminated in request for external help

After two months of mounting pressure from financial markets, with yields and spreads soaring, the current caretaker government decided in April to request external financial assistance from the European Union and the IMF. Tensions were exacerbated by the government's resignation (announced in late March) in the wake of the parliamentary rejection of a new austerity package. The political crisis triggered a wave of credit rating downgrades for the state and enterprises. Banks continue to have virtually no access to wholesale debt markets and are therefore heavily dependent on ECB financing, amounting to €48 billion in April 2011. Credit growth has slowed, and consumer credit outstanding has even fallen slightly. This trend will likely be aggravated as banks shrink their balance sheets.

Fiscal consolidation is gathering pace

The 2010 budget deficit fell to 9.2% of GDP (national accounts definition), against 10.1% in 2009, with the reduction essentially achieved in the fourth quarter. Several one-offs and exceptional events – mainly receipts from a pension fund, outlays due to banking losses, major military equipment purchases and the reclassification of three public-private partnership projects as part of public investment – partly cancelled each other out, with an overall negative impact on the deficit of around 0.6% of GDP. For 2011, the OECD projections incorporate the consolidation measures legislated in the 2011 Budget, as well as additional restraint in a number of areas, such as subsidies and public investment, as claimed by the authorities. For 2012, the measures envisaged under the EU/IMF financial assistance programme are taken on board. The 10-year government bond yield differential *vis-à-vis* Germany is projected to remain at its average level in April (5.8 percentage points) for the remainder of 2011 and then to halve in 2012 as progress in consolidation and economic adjustment leads to a spontaneous increase in confidence or perceptions increase that additional official financing would be forthcoming, if needed. Further, it is assumed that only a minor part of the government financing needs in 2011 and 2012 will be funded in the markets. Strictly implementing the fiscal and structural policy reforms foreseen in the financial assistance programme is essential both to ensure fiscal sustainability and to enhance the growth potential of the economy.

Unwinding of imbalances weighs on domestic demand and GDP

GDP is set to contract until late 2012, with annual decreases of 2.1% in 2011 and 1.5% in 2012. All components of domestic demand are expected to fall, though export growth is projected to remain strong as the global economy continues to recover. The unemployment rate is expected to rise further. With subdued demand and growing spare capacity, inflation should decrease markedly once the impact of rising oil prices and indirect taxation vanishes. The current account is projected to improve significantly, though the gain from trade volumes is partly undone by trade prices (especially in 2011, largely due to more expensive oil) and a worsening income balance.

Risks are broadly balanced

The risks surrounding the forecast are broadly balanced. Private consumption and investment could be weaker than projected due to scarcer and more expensive credit, in the wake of faster deleveraging or further interest rate increases. Conversely, improvements in competitiveness through lower wage and non-wage labour costs have the potential to yield gains in export market shares.

SLOVAK REPUBLIC

The economy rebounded strongly in 2010, and is expected to continue to do so in 2011, driven by strong external demand and business investment. Household consumption, however, will be damped by fiscal consolidation and persistent high unemployment. Growth should be more balanced in 2012, not least due to more favourable labour market developments.

The fiscal deficit is projected to fall to around 4% of GDP in 2012 owing to planned consolidation measures. Efforts will be appropriately concentrated on the expenditure side. Recently announced reforms of the pension system, in particular the introduction of stabilisation mechanisms in the first pillar, are welcome as they will reduce future increases in ageing-related spending.

Economic activity has recovered strongly...

Economic growth in 2010 was the fastest among euro area countries and real GDP has returned to its pre-crisis level. This mostly reflects buoyant world trade, in particular strong growth in Germany. Business investment also rebounded, reflecting an improvement in business climate and an increase in capacity utilisation, which is converging to its long-term average. By contrast, household consumption growth remained subdued on the back of continued weakness in employment growth and public expenditures began to decline in the last quarter of 2010, reflecting the start of consolidation measures.

... but is expected to slow down in the short run

Recent indicators suggest that the recovery will continue, but at a slower pace over the coming months. Business confidence in the main trading partners has recently weakened, suggesting that external demand will slow somewhat. In addition, consumer confidence has continued to worsen and retail sales have increased only slightly. Employment remained weak and inflation rose significantly mainly due to increases in

Slovak Republic

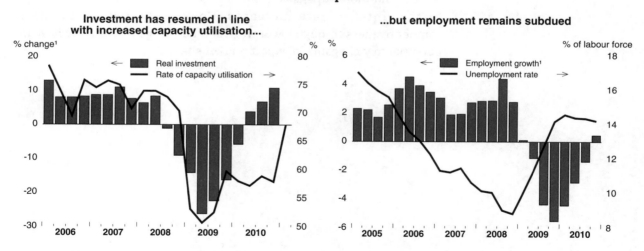

1. Year-on-year percentage change.

Source: OECD Economic Outlook 89 database; OECD, Main Economic Indicators database.

StatLink http://dx.doi.org/10.1787/888932429811

Slovak Republic: **Demand, output and prices**

	2007	2008	2009	2010	2011	2012
	Current prices € billion	Percentage changes, volume (2000 prices)				
GDP at market prices	61.6	5.8	-4.8	4.0	3.6	4.4
Private consumption	34.5	6.2	0.3	-0.3	0.4	3.0
Government consumption	10.6	6.1	5.6	0.1	-3.6	0.3
Gross fixed capital formation	16.1	1.0	-19.9	3.6	6.7	7.1
Final domestic demand	61.2	4.8	-3.8	0.6	0.9	3.4
Stockbuilding[1]	1.0	1.1	-3.6	1.8	0.3	0.0
Total domestic demand	62.2	5.8	-7.3	2.4	1.2	3.3
Exports of goods and services	53.4	3.1	-15.9	16.4	10.4	7.8
Imports of goods and services	54.1	3.1	-18.6	14.9	7.4	6.5
Net exports[1]	- 0.7	0.0	2.6	1.0	2.4	1.1
Memorandum items						
GDP deflator	_	2.9	-1.2	0.5	1.9	2.6
Harmonised index of consumer prices	_	3.9	0.9	0.7	3.9	2.9
Private consumption deflator	_	4.5	0.1	0.9	3.9	2.9
Unemployment rate	_	9.5	12.1	14.4	13.8	12.8
General government financial balance[2]	_	-2.1	-8.0	-7.9	-5.1	-4.0
Current account balance[2]	_	-6.6	-3.2	-3.5	-2.4	-1.3

Note: National accounts are based on official chain-linked data. This introduces a discrepancy in the identity between real demand components and GDP. For further details see *OECD Economic Outlook* Sources and Methods *(http://www.oecd.org/eco/sources-and-methods).*
1. Contributions to changes in real GDP (percentage of real GDP in previous year), actual amount in the first column.
2. As a percentage of GDP.
Source: OECD Economic Outlook 89 database.

StatLink ⫼ http://dx.doi.org/10.1787/888932431065

food and energy prices and a hike in VAT and excise duties. This has weighed on households' purchasing power.

Fiscal consolidation and unemployment will weigh on consumption

The main feature of the projection is the weakness in private consumption in 2011, which reflects fiscal consolidation measures and a slow recovery of employment. The government plans ambitious cuts in the budget deficit in 2011 and 2012 to reach its target of 2.9% of GDP in 2013. In 2011, the consolidation package should amount to around 2.5% of GDP, 60% coming from public expenditure cuts, which will weaken domestic demand. In particular, the planned 10% cut in public wage costs, to be achieved both through layoffs and cuts in remuneration, already has had a negative impact on the labour market. Unemployment rose somewhat further at the beginning of the year, suggesting that layoffs in the public sector exceeded employment gains in the private sector. Together with the increase in hours worked per employee, this will damp the overall employment response during the recovery. As a result, unemployment is expected to decline only slowly in 2011 overall and is likely to induce a certain level of wage moderation and a stagnation in real household disposal income.

Investment will add to the export-driven recovery

Annual GDP growth is projected to slow from 4% in 2010 to 3.6% in 2011. Growth will continue to be mainly driven by exports, as foreign demand is expected to remain strong. In addition, low increases in worker compensation will maintain cost competitiveness of exporting firms. While the partial cancellation of public-private-partnership projects for motorway construction may lower public investment expenditure, announced private investments, in particular in the automotive sector, should boost gross capital formation. Favourable monetary conditions will also sustain investment growth. In 2012, growth is expected to bounce back and reach 4.4% as less fiscal tightening is budgeted and a more progressive employment recovery will trigger a rebound in domestic consumption. While headline inflation will be pushed up in the short run by increases in commodity prices, underlying inflationary pressures are expected to be limited as the output gap remains negative.

Substantial risks remain

As the economy is highly sensitive to the external environment, the main risks relate to growth of its trading partners. A further rise in commodity prices could lead to a weaker-than-projected GDP growth outcome over the projection horizon. Regarding internal risks, employment could accelerate more than expected, which would stimulate consumption.

SLOVENIA

The recovery continues to be mainly supported by external demand and restocking. Growth should gradually strengthen as private investment and consumption gain momentum. The unemployment rate is projected to peak by mid-2011 as activity picks up. Inflationary pressures stemming from a surge in global food and energy prices should peter out, and persistent economic slack will contain underlying inflation pressures.

The 2010 budgetary outturn was in line with the envisaged consolidation path. The pension reform, which has been adopted by parliament but is now being challenged in a referendum to be held in June 2011, is a critical step in ensuring long-term fiscal sustainability. Reforms to enhance labour market flexibility and to align wage growth with labour productivity over the medium-term should be undertaken to foster competitiveness.

The recovery so far has been weak

The recovery in activity has resumed but final domestic demand has remained depressed. Short-term indicators paint a mixed picture, with marginally improving business confidence in manufacturing, retail trade, and services, and still very weak consumer confidence and business confidence in construction. The capacity utilisation rate in manufacturing reached its highest level since the onset of the economic downturn, but substantial slack remains. Headline inflation fell in the second half of 2010 owing to declines in the prices of some subsidised services, but picked up with the acceleration of world food and energy prices in early 2011. Core prices have been falling since the second half of 2010, reflecting the slack in the economy.

The unemployment rate has been increasing

The unemployment rate has reached its highest level since end-2005. In part, this reflects limited wage adjustment, largely due to the

Slovenia

Export performance has not recovered[1]

2007 = 100

— Export performance
- - Relative unit labour cost

Investment continues to shrink[2]

%

■ Residential construction
□ Non-residential construction
▨ Machinery and equipement
— Total

1. Export performance is the ratio between export volumes and export markets for total goods and services. Relative unit labour cost for the manufacturing sector.
2. Contributions to quarterly growth of gross fixed capital formation (volume). The line represents total investment growth.
Source: OECD Economic Outlook 89 database.

StatLink ⟶ http://dx.doi.org/10.1787/888932429830

Slovenia: **Demand, output and prices**

	2007	2008	2009	2010	2011	2012
	Current prices € billion	Percentage changes, volume (2000 prices)				
GDP at market prices	34.6	3.7	-8.1	1.2	1.8	2.6
Private consumption	18.2	2.9	-0.8	0.5	0.9	2.0
Government consumption	6.0	6.2	3.0	0.8	0.6	0.8
Gross fixed capital formation	9.6	8.5	-21.6	-6.7	0.4	4.3
Final domestic demand	33.8	5.1	-6.1	-1.2	0.7	2.3
Stockbuilding[1]	1.4	-0.8	-4.0	1.6	0.9	0.0
Total domestic demand	35.2	4.2	-9.8	0.4	1.1	2.3
Exports of goods and services	24.0	3.3	-17.7	7.8	5.6	6.8
Imports of goods and services	24.6	3.8	-19.7	6.6	5.3	6.3
Net exports[1]	- 0.6	-0.4	2.0	0.8	0.2	0.4
Memorandum items						
GDP deflator	_	4.0	3.2	0.7	1.0	2.1
Harmonised index of consumer prices	_	5.5	0.9	2.1	2.5	2.2
Private consumption deflator	_	5.4	0.0	2.9	2.9	2.0
Unemployment rate	_	4.4	5.8	7.2	7.7	7.5
General government financial balance[2]	_	-1.8	-6.0	-5.6	-5.6	-4.1
Current account balance[2]	_	-6.7	-1.5	-1.1	-1.3	-1.3

Note: National accounts are based on official chain-linked data. This introduces a discrepancy in the identity between real demand components and GDP. For further details see *OECD Economic Outlook* Sources and Methods *(http://www.oecd.org/eco/sources-and-methods)*.
1. Contributions to changes in real GDP (percentage of real GDP in previous year), actual amount in the first column.
2. As a percentage of GDP.
Source: OECD Economic Outlook 89 database.

StatLink ᔑᓯᔆᔗ *http://dx.doi.org/10.1787/888932431084*

sizeable 2010 minimum wage hike. Employment ticked up somewhat in late 2010, however, as public employment in education and health rose. An act to regulate student work and further increase the flexibility of temporary contracts, commonly referred to as the Mini Jobs Act, was voted down decisively in a referendum in April 2011, raising concerns over the viability of additional structural policy initiatives to raise employment.

Fiscal consolidation is underway, but will remain a key policy challenge

The government has embarked on fiscal consolidation to reduce the budget deficit to below 3% of GDP by 2013, primarily through containing the public-sector wage bill and transfers, and cutting capital spending. The plan to reduce public employment by 1% a year through 2013 should be strictly implemented, notwithstanding slippage in 2010. However, a number of factors may jeopardise the fiscal consolidation. The 2010 pension reform will be voted on in a referendum set for 5 June 2011 amid a politically challenging environment. If it is rejected, long-term fiscal sustainability will be undermined and the macroeconomic outlook could deteriorate considerably, given current volatility in international financial markets. The recapitalisation of systemic banks is already underway and will contribute significantly to the 2011 budget deficit. Further capital injections could exert additional pressure on public finances. While banks have to adapt to new regulatory requirements, credit flows to the business sector have been reduced. To encourage credit activity, the authorities plan to introduce a tax applying to banks with a relatively low exposure to the business sector. However, such a measure interferes with the risk management of banks, which is a particular concern at a time when banks need to repair their balance sheets and the corporate sector is overleveraged.

The modest recovery should slowly gain further momentum

The recovery is projected to pick up gradually over the next two years. Growth will depend on domestic demand progressively gathering pace as the unemployment rate declines, if modestly, from the second half of 2011 and as the business environment improves in 2012. Exports are projected to be sustained as the global recovery continues. As economic slack is set to linger, inflation is projected to moderate to close to 2% in 2012.

Downside risks are more prominent

Overall, risks to the projections are skewed towards the downside. Headwinds in the financial sector, an overleveraged corporate sector and a weak housing market will all weigh on growth. Stronger-than-expected external demand would, however, boost activity.

SPAIN

Economic growth is projected to strengthen gradually, reaching 1% in 2011 and 1½ per cent in 2012, as the damping impact of downsizing in residential construction diminishes and the international environment improves. As growth picks up, the unemployment rate will fall slowly to around 19% by end-2012. Consumer price inflation will tend to fall, once the effect of rising energy and food prices and the increase in the VAT rates drop out.

The fiscal deficit is projected to decline from 9.2% of GDP in 2010 to 6.3% in 2011 and to 4.4% in 2012, mostly reflecting measures to lower spending. Some planned spending reductions in 2012 still need to be specified and the government should stand ready to introduce further measures if needed. To boost job creation, legal requirements on firms to apply collective bargaining outcomes negotiated at sectoral levels should be eased. The cost of dismissing workers on permanent contracts should be reduced further, moving closer to a unified contract.

The fragile recovery has gained some momentum

Real GDP grew by 0.3% in the first quarter of 2011 as exports expanded strongly, boosted by recovery in the euro area as well as booming sales to South America and other emerging economies. Industrial production strengthened and strong tourism receipts have raised services revenues. External demand has boosted business equipment investment. Household consumption growth slowed as real disposable incomes were hit by rising oil prices, which pushed consumer price inflation to 3.5% in April. Employment losses continued while the unemployment rate steadied at above 20%. House prices have fallen by around 20% from their peak in real terms and continued to fall in the first quarter of 2011, in part owing to the withdrawal of tax subsidies for owner-occupiers at the end of 2010. While the downsizing of residential

Spain

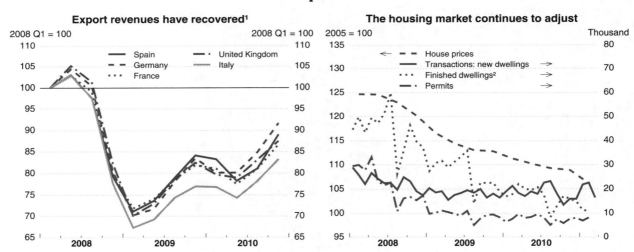

1. Exports of goods and services, value in US dollars, national accounts basis.
2. Finished housing approved by the Surveyors College. Excludes housing promoted by co-operatives, physical persons and owners' communities.
Source: OECD Economic Outlook 89 database, Instituto Nacional de Estadística, Banco de España and Ministerio de Fomento.

StatLink http://dx.doi.org/10.1787/888932429849

Spain: **Demand, output and prices**

	2007	2008	2009	2010	2011	2012
	Current prices € billion	Percentage changes, volume (2000 prices)				
GDP at market prices	1 053.5	0.9	-3.7	-0.1	0.9	1.6
Private consumption	604.4	-0.6	-4.2	1.2	0.4	1.6
Government consumption	193.5	5.8	3.2	-0.7	-1.7	-1.3
Gross fixed capital formation	323.2	-4.8	-16.0	-7.6	-3.4	2.0
Final domestic demand	1 121.1	-0.7	-6.0	-1.2	-0.8	1.1
Stockbuilding[1]	3.2	0.1	0.0	0.1	-0.1	-0.1
Total domestic demand	1 124.3	-0.6	-6.0	-1.1	-0.9	1.0
Exports of goods and services	283.3	-1.1	-11.6	10.3	9.9	8.7
Imports of goods and services	354.1	-5.3	-17.8	5.4	2.9	6.6
Net exports[1]	- 70.8	1.5	2.7	1.0	1.8	0.6
Memorandum items						
GDP deflator	_	2.4	0.6	1.0	1.2	0.9
Harmonised index of consumer prices	_	4.1	-0.2	2.0	2.9	0.9
Private consumption deflator	_	3.5	0.1	2.8	3.0	0.9
Unemployment rate	_	11.3	18.0	20.1	20.3	19.3
Household saving ratio[2]	_	6.6	11.9	6.3	4.0	3.7
General government financial balance[3]	_	-4.2	-11.1	-9.2	-6.3	-4.4
Current account balance[3]	_	-9.6	-5.2	-4.5	-2.9	-2.3

Note: National accounts are based on official chain-linked data. This introduces a discrepancy in the identity between real demand components and GDP. For further details see *OECD Economic Outlook* Sources and Methods (*http://www.oecd.org/eco/sources-and-methods*).
1. Contributions to changes in real GDP (percentage of real GDP in previous year), actual amount in the first column.
2. As a percentage of disposable income.
3. As a percentage of GDP.
Source: OECD Economic Outlook 89 database.

StatLink 📈 http://dx.doi.org/10.1787/888932431103

construction is well-advanced, activity is set to remain depressed for some time, given the overhang of unsold dwellings.

Needed budgetary consolidation is weakening activity

Higher VAT rates, introduced in 2010 and higher tobacco and fuel taxes are expected to boost tax revenues by ½ per cent of GDP in 2011. Regional and local governments also raised personal income and real estate tax rates. Spending cuts are projected to amount to about 2½ per cent of GDP in 2011. Spending restraint measures include continued cutbacks in public investment, as well as in public sector pay and employment at all levels of government and the removal of child benefits. Most pension payments are frozen in nominal terms. In 2012 cuts in public sector employment will continue and the central government has announced further reductions of consumption and transfer spending, although these have yet to be specified. Finally, the government has announced it will lower public investment spending, which remains high in international comparison, by as much as necessary to reach its target. The projections assume that the deficit target of 4.4% of GDP will be reached.

Risk spreads on government bond interest rates remain high

Up to April 2011 risk spreads on government debt stabilised at levels below the peaks reached in 2010, notwithstanding continued turmoil in euro area government debt markets. The authorities have taken several measures to reduce investors' risk perceptions. Banks have been required to publish detailed information on real estate exposures. Capital requirements have been raised. Savings banks, which have undergone restructuring but face substantial exposure to the housing developers, will need injections worth 1.4% of GDP, partly from the government, to meet these new requirements. Exposure of Spanish financial intermediaries to Portuguese debtors is concentrated on the non-financial private sector, which is less affected by the debt crisis. A reform of the public pension system expected to be approved by parliament will damp the expected long-term increase in pension spending and improve work incentives. Higher short-term interest rates will raise households' debt servicing costs with a lag of about one year.

Slow growth will leave unemployment very high

GDP growth is expected to strengthen only gradually, driven by external demand and modest expansion of private consumption. Collective bargaining outcomes indicate that wage growth will be low in 2011, strengthening competitiveness, helping to narrow the current account deficit further. The unemployment rate is expected to fall to around 19% by the end of 2012.

Risks are broadly balanced

As for downside risks, sovereign debt spreads could remain large, in particular if sovereign risk perception increases in the event of a debt-restructuring in the euro area. A persistent interest rate spread on government debt could result in a deterioration of funding conditions in the private sector. Regarding upside risks, strong exports could boost investment further. Far-reaching reforms of the collective bargaining system, which are being discussed by the social partners, would spur job creation.

SWEDEN

GDP has fully recovered its pre-crisis level. Vigorous growth is expected to continue as external demand remains solid, though at a more moderate pace than in recent quarters. Employment growth will also be robust, and accordingly the unemployment rate will continue to decline. However, as some spare capacity remains in the economy, core inflation should remain moderate.

Policy interest rates will need to continue to be gradually raised as the expansion unfolds. With continuing fiscal discipline, the medium-term surplus target is likely to be achieved. Improving the prudential framework would help to limit the risk that rapid growth in household debt and housing prices threaten future growth and stability.

The economy continues to grow strongly

Real GDP continued to grow strongly in the fourth quarter of 2010, exceeding its pre-recession peak. The recovery is broad-based, with private consumption and investment both contributing significantly. Business investment is benefiting from higher bank lending and increasing capacity utilisation. Housing investment, which has been supported by a tax credit for repairs, renovation and improvements and by hitherto low interest rates, continues to grow, albeit more moderately as interest rates begin to rise. Industrial production is growing very strongly and consumer and business confidence are high.

Unemployment is declining

The vigorous recovery has produced significant employment growth, a marked decline in the unemployment rate, shrinking spare capacity and some signs of emerging labour shortages in the construction sector. Changes in the sickness and disability benefit schemes, together with the improvement in labour market conditions, will encourage labour force participation and thereby mitigate potential bottlenecks.

Sweden

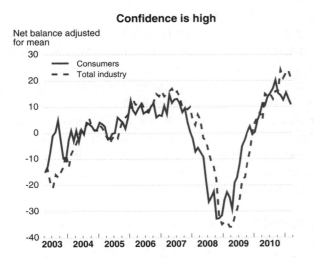

Confidence is high

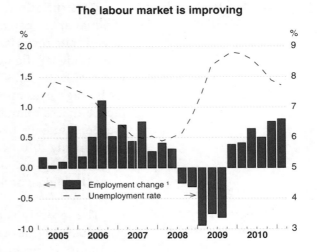

The labour market is improving

1. Percentage change compared to last quarter.

Source: The Riksbank, OECD Economic Outlook 89 database.

StatLink http://dx.doi.org/10.1787/888932429868

Sweden: Demand, output and prices

	2007	2008	2009	2010	2011	2012
	Current prices SEK billion	Percentage changes, volume (2009 prices)				
GDP at market prices	3 126.0	-0.8	-5.3	5.3	4.5	3.1
Private consumption	1 460.2	-0.1	-0.5	3.5	3.4	2.8
Government consumption	797.4	0.7	1.8	2.3	1.7	0.8
Gross fixed capital formation	612.0	1.0	-16.2	5.9	7.8	6.1
Final domestic demand	2 869.5	0.3	-3.2	3.6	3.7	2.8
Stockbuilding[1]	23.2	-0.4	-1.6	2.1	0.1	0.0
Total domestic demand	2 892.8	-0.1	-4.9	5.9	3.8	2.8
Exports of goods and services	1 621.5	1.3	-13.3	10.4	7.9	6.5
Imports of goods and services	1 388.2	3.0	-13.4	12.0	8.0	6.3
Net exports[1]	233.2	-0.6	-0.9	0.0	0.4	0.5
Memorandum items						
GDP deflator	–	3.3	1.8	1.5	1.3	1.5
Consumer price index[2]	–	3.4	-0.5	1.2	2.9	2.4
Private consumption deflator	–	3.2	1.9	1.3	1.3	1.6
Unemployment rate[3]	–	6.2	8.3	8.4	7.5	7.0
Household saving ratio[4]	–	11.2	12.9	10.8	10.0	8.9
General government financial balance[5]	–	2.2	-0.9	-0.3	0.3	1.4
Current account balance[5]	–	8.8	7.0	6.3	5.5	5.5

Note: National accounts are based on official chain-linked data. This introduces a discrepancy in the identity between real demand components and GDP. For further details see *OECD Economic Outlook* Sources and Methods *(http://www.oecd.org/eco/sources-and-methods)*.
1. Contributions to changes in real GDP (percentage of real GDP in previous year), actual amount in the first column.
2. The consumer price index includes mortgage interest costs.
3. Historical data and projections are based on the definition of unemployment which covers 15 to 74 year olds and classifies job-seeking full-time students as unemployed.
4. As a percentage of disposable income.
5. As a percentage of GDP.
Source: OECD Economic Outlook 89 database.

StatLink ⬛🔗 *http://dx.doi.org/10.1787/888932431122*

Monetary and fiscal policies will become less stimulatory

Core inflation is expected to remain moderate, owing to some residual spare capacity. Headline inflation (which includes mortgage interest rate costs) is expected to be around the official target of 2%, which is a bit higher than core inflation reflecting increases in interest rates. However, with some signs that inflation expectations may be rising and with wage pressures likely to pick up if labour force participation increases less than expected, the central bank needs to remain vigilant. Indeed, it intends to continue the hikes in the policy interest rate which began in July 2010. The fiscal stance is set to tighten, starting in 2012. The economic expansion and the government's fiscal framework will help move the budget back into surplus from 2011.

The recovery should continue at a more moderate pace

The recovery is expected to continue, though its pace will ease as stimulus is withdrawn, before regaining some momentum into 2012. Declining unemployment, low (though rising) interest rates and high levels of confidence should support consumer spending. Exports, although expected to be hurt somewhat by the appreciation of the krona in 2010, will pick up during 2012 as export markets strengthen. This, together with a moderation in import growth as domestic demand eases, will help to stabilise the current account surplus and lead to a slight pick-up in GDP growth. The recovery in investment will continue, though it will be moderated somewhat by rising interest rates.

There are potential risks to exports and inflation

Downside risks to export growth include weaker global demand stemming from financial stress or further appreciation of the krona. However, there is also a risk that an unexpectedly rapid decline in the unemployment rate combined with still-low interest rates and possibly higher inflation expectations, might fuel inflationary pressures. Also, continuing growth in lending to households and rising house prices could point to the build-up of imbalances which might pose a risk to price stability and economic activity.

SWITZERLAND

Economic growth is expected to remain firm in 2011 and 2012, driven by strong domestic demand. Growth will slow toward the end of 2012, progressively returning to its potential rate, as the output gap closes. Unemployment is projected to decline further while inflation will rise to slightly above 1% in 2012.

Monetary policy rates will have to rise gradually from 2011 onwards to damp inflationary pressures from domestic demand growth but, most importantly, to avoid overheating in the housing market. Implementing the recent government plans to address the too-big-to-fail problem would reduce the risks stemming from a potential failure of the two big banks.

Economic growth continues to be strong

Real GDP growth continued to be robust in the first half of 2011, mainly driven by strong domestic demand, linked to low short and long-term interest rates which have been stimulating marked growth of bank lending, especially mortgages. Labour market performance remains favourable, further stimulating consumption growth. Despite the strong recovery, consumer price inflation remains low in international comparison, reflecting in part the damping effect due to the exchange rate appreciation, although some measures of core inflation suggest an increase in underlying inflation. Although the Swiss franc has appreciated to a record high, export growth remained positive until the first quarter of 2011. Forward looking business confidence indicators suggest ongoing robust GDP growth for the coming months. Employment growth should also remain positive as suggested by steadily increasing job vacancies.

Monetary policy remains expansionary

Monetary policy remains expansionary, with the 3-month Swiss Franc LIBOR at around 0.25%, in the lower range of the SNB current operational target band for the LIBOR. This policy stance is appropriate for

Switzerland

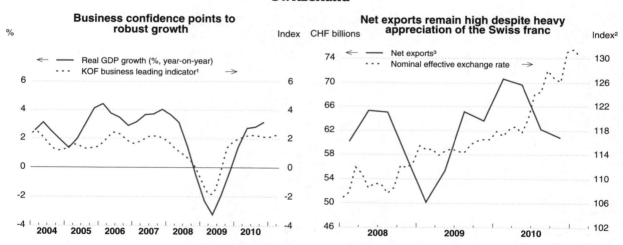

1. Composite leading indicator of business cycle trends in manufacturing, private consumption, financial services, construction and EU export markets.
2. January 1999 = 100.
3. Current prices.

Source: KOF institute; OECD, Economic Outlook 89 database; SNB.

StatLink ⟐ http://dx.doi.org/10.1787/888932429887

Switzerland: **Demand, output and prices**

	2007	2008	2009	2010	2011	2012
	Current prices CHF billion	Percentage changes, volume (2000 prices)				
GDP at market prices	521.1	1.9	-1.9	2.6	2.7	2.5
Private consumption	296.8	1.3	1.0	1.7	1.7	2.3
Government consumption	56.4	1.7	1.6	-1.6	1.1	0.5
Gross fixed capital formation	112.2	0.5	-4.9	4.6	6.5	3.5
Final domestic demand	465.4	1.2	-0.3	2.0	2.7	2.4
Stockbuilding[1]	2.2	-0.9	0.9	-1.3	0.7	0.0
Total domestic demand	467.6	0.2	0.6	0.5	3.6	2.4
Exports of goods and services	293.1	3.3	-8.7	9.3	3.3	5.7
Imports of goods and services	239.5	0.3	-5.4	6.7	5.3	6.3
Net exports[1]	53.5	1.7	-2.5	2.1	-0.4	0.4
Memorandum items						
GDP deflator	_	2.5	0.3	-0.5	0.4	0.7
Consumer price index	_	2.4	-0.5	0.7	0.7	1.1
Private consumption deflator	_	2.6	-0.4	0.2	0.3	0.8
Unemployment rate	_	3.4	4.3	4.5	4.1	3.9
General government financial balance[2]	_	2.3	1.2	0.5	0.6	0.9
Current account balance[2]	_	1.9	11.5	14.7	13.6	13.9

Note: National accounts are based on official chain-linked data. This introduces a discrepancy in the identity between real demand components and GDP. For further details see *OECD Economic Outlook* Sources and Methods *(http://www.oecd.org/eco/sources-and-methods).*
1. Contributions to changes in real GDP (percentage of real GDP in previous year), actual amount in the first column.
2. As a percentage of GDP.
Source: OECD Economic Outlook 89 database.

StatLink ⟨⟩ *http://dx.doi.org/10.1787/888932431141*

the time being, given remaining uncertainties around the global recovery and the appreciation of the Swiss franc. However, it has spurred growth in mortgage lending and some indicators point to a risk of overheating in some sectors. To avoid overheating and consequent inflationary pressures, the policy rate is assumed to rise gradually through the projection period.

Fiscal policy will be slightly restrictive

As a result of a set of recently introduced fiscal policy measures, fiscal policy will be slightly restrictive in 2011 and 2012. Planned consolidation measures, which are assumed to be implemented, will amount to less than 0.3% of GDP, while somewhat higher unemployment insurance contributions and a modest increase of value added tax rates will help reduce the deficits in the unemployment and invalidity insurance.

After a slight increase, GDP growth will slow somewhat

Real GDP growth is projected to accelerate slightly to 2.7% in 2011 as relatively low interest rates continue to stimulate domestic demand. It will slow somewhat in 2012 as macroeconomic policy stimulus is withdrawn. The unemployment rate will continue to decline gradually, stimulating further domestic consumption. Both the policy rate and the inflation rate are forecast to rise gradually reaching 1.2% and 1.1% in 2012, respectively. The general government budget surplus is projected to increase slightly over the projection period.

Risks relate mainly to the exchange rate

Upside and downside risks for growth in Switzerland relate mainly to exchange rate fluctuations. Further flight to the Swiss Franc as a safety currency, especially linked to the developments of the debt crisis in the euro area, could hurt Swiss exports.

TURKEY

After approaching 9% in 2010, growth is projected to slow to 6.5% in 2011 and 5.3% in 2012, as credit conditions, broadly defined, become tighter. The current account deficit is projected to rise further, to 8.9% of GDP by 2012.

The authorities should closely watch if the new policy of raising bank reserve requirements without increasing policy interest rates delivers the intended slowdown in credit and economic activity, and be ready to turn to other measures if needed. Fiscal policy should remain tight, possibly with the help of an explicit spending path. Structural reforms, such as introducing regional minimum wages, continue to be necessary for better balanced growth.

Growth remains strong

Growth reached 8.9% in 2010, far exceeding most projections, including those that underpinned last year's budget. Private investment and consumption were the key drivers. Government demand remained subdued and exports proved weak. With private domestic demand driving the recovery, and against the backdrop of significant real exchange rate appreciation, imports accelerated. Strong business and consumer confidence, as well as rising industrial production and capital good imports, point to continued buoyancy in 2011.

Inflation has come down but upward risks persist

CPI inflation fell from 9.6% in the first quarter of 2010 to just under 4% in March 2011 – a historical low which resulted from favourable base effects and service price moderation. Headline inflation is heavily affected by volatile food prices, which have been subdued recently but are expected to increase. Higher food prices, together with higher prices for other commodities, are expected to put upward pressure on inflation in the rest of the year. Core inflation fell through most of 2010 but has moved back up since November. Producer prices are running ahead of consumer

Turkey

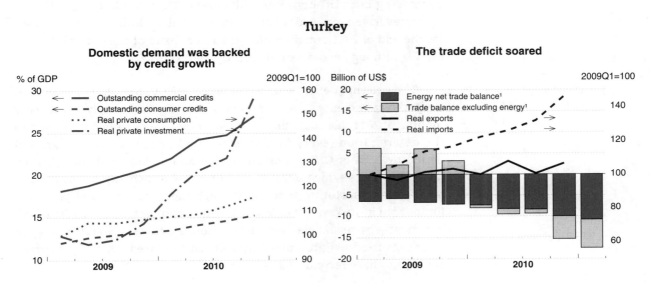

1. Estimates for 2011Q1.
Source: Central Bank of the Republic of Turkey; Turkstat; OECD Economic Outlook 89 database.

StatLink http://dx.doi.org/10.1787/888932429906

Turkey: **Demand, output and prices**

	2007	2008	2009	2010	2011	2012
	Current prices TRY billion	Percentage changes, volume (1998 prices)				
GDP at market prices	843.2	0.7	-4.8	8.9	6.5	5.3
Private consumption	601.2	-0.3	-2.3	6.6	6.6	5.3
Government consumption	107.8	1.7	7.8	2.0	5.3	4.4
Gross fixed capital formation	180.6	-6.2	-19.0	29.9	16.4	9.2
Final domestic demand	889.7	-1.3	-4.3	9.7	8.2	5.9
Stockbuilding[1]	- 3.0	0.3	-2.5	2.0	0.2	0.0
Total domestic demand	886.7	-1.0	-6.5	12.0	8.3	5.8
Exports of goods and services	188.2	2.7	-5.0	3.4	9.1	9.8
Imports of goods and services	231.7	-4.1	-14.3	20.7	17.9	10.6
Net exports[1]	- 43.5	1.7	2.8	-4.3	-2.8	-1.0
Memorandum items						
GDP deflator	_	12.0	5.3	6.5	6.3	6.1
Consumer price index	_	10.4	6.3	8.6	5.7	6.1
Private consumption deflator	_	10.8	4.9	8.3	5.7	6.2
Unemployment rate	_	10.7	13.7	11.7	10.6	10.4
General government financial balance[2]	_	-2.2	-6.7	-4.6	-3.3	-3.0
Current account balance[2]	_	-5.6	-2.2	-6.6	-8.7	-8.9

Note: National accounts are based on official chain-linked data. This introduces a discrepancy in the identity between real demand components and GDP. For further details see *OECD Economic Outlook* Sources and Methods *(http://www.oecd.org/eco/sources-and-methods)*.

1. Contributions to changes in real GDP (percentage of real GDP in previous year), actual amount in the first column.
2. As a percentage of GDP.

Source: OECD Economic Outlook 89 database.

StatLink http://dx.doi.org/10.1787/888932431160

prices. However, economic slack persists, with capacity utilisation at below pre-crisis levels (due to very strong investment growth) and decreasing but still high unemployment. Thus, underlying inflation pressures have remained relatively muted to date. Inflation expectations for the end of 2011 remain within the target band of the Central Bank of 5.5±2%, although above its mid-point.

The current account deficit has reached historical heights

The external deficit widened sharply in 2010, reaching 6.6% of GDP. Despite recent competitiveness gains, imports grew strongly in the early months of 2011, far outpacing exports. Oil price increases contributed to the deterioration (every $10 increase in oil prices raises the external deficit by 0.5% of GDP). Tensions in the Middle East and North Africa (MENA) region – which absorbs 25% of total Turkish exports of goods – damped manufacturing exports, although they also improved prospects for tourism in Turkey. The external deficit continues to be easily financed, but mostly by reversible short-term capital inflows. Capital inflows of undetermined origin – possibly related to unrest in neighbouring countries – have recently accelerated.

A new monetary policy is being pursued

Since December 2010, a new monetary policy has been implemented, combining low policy interest rates (to stem capital inflows) with sizeable increases in banks' required reserves (to slow credit growth). So far, this policy mix has helped to restrain currency appreciation. Credit growth has slowed in certain areas, but exhibits considerable inertia overall. In April 2011, total credit outstanding was still 35% above its level a year ago. Policymakers assert that the targeted credit containment will be secured, if necessary with additional regulatory measures. It is indeed essential that domestic demand starts to slow down already from the second quarter of 2011. OECD projections are predicated on the achievement of this goal. Credit conditions are then expected to normalise in 2012, and policy interest rates are projected to rise.

Fiscal policy should remain tight

Fiscal policy was kept tight through 2010. The bulk of central government windfall revenues from stronger-than-expected growth in 2010 appears to have been saved. No significant fiscal drift has been observed in the run-up to legislative elections in June 2011, although there are signs that agricultural transfers and public investment have significantly accelerated. Indeed, total primary government spending has recently been rising much less than GDP and tax revenues. OECD projections assume that this fiscal stance will be maintained through the projection period, although additional tightening may become necessary through the year. After the postponement of the previously planned fiscal rule, a simpler explicit public expenditure ceiling at the general government level would help anchor fiscal policy.

Structural reforms are needed to improve competitiveness

The external deficit increases rapidly every time the economy accelerates. As Turkey's very high energy dependence cannot be reduced in the short term, it is crucial to strengthen external competitiveness and rebalance the sources of growth. Structural reforms would help reduce the cost of doing business in the formal sector. A regional differentiation of minimum wages, taking into account differences in productivity levels and living costs, would support not only price competitiveness, but also non-price competitiveness by facilitating the development of formal firms, which have higher productivity than informal ones for a number of reasons.

There are risks on both sides

GDP is likely to grow by about 6½ per cent for the year as a whole in 2011, reflecting a policy-induced deceleration through the year. Growth is then projected to pick up strongly in the course of 2012 after the normalisation of credit conditions, with annual growth of about 5½ per cent for the year as a whole. If capital markets were to become uncomfortable with the high and rising current account deficit, some abrupt exchange rate adjustment might ensue, creating financial strains. Any new civic tensions in the MENA region may also depress external demand. On the other hand, if policy-driven restraints prove less effective than intended, growth may be too strong and put excessive pressure on resources. Stronger growth in Europe would lift exports and growth.

Chapter 3

DEVELOPMENTS IN SELECTED NON-MEMBER ECONOMIES

BRAZIL

Strong growth in the course of 2010 removed all slack from the Brazilian economy. Massive infrastructure spending will support strong domestic demand in the coming years. Inflationary pressures are therefore a threat, as labour markets will remain tight and the effects of the significant currency appreciation will dissipate.

Accordingly, the central bank has resumed monetary tightening, including introducing numerous macro-prudential measures to restrain credit expansion. However, additional interest rate increases are necessary to prevent inflation expectations from becoming unanchored. The announcement of public spending cuts that will leave social and infrastructure programmes untouched is welcome, but credibility would be enhanced by the formulation and implementation of a medium-term growth-enhancing fiscal consolidation plan. Over the medium term, fostering the development of long-term financial markets would augment the country's capacity to absorb capital inflows and raise potential growth.

Domestic demand remains strong

The Brazilian economy slowed in the second half of 2010 from the solid growth rates seen earlier in the year, reflecting the withdrawal of some policy stimulus. While the manufacturing sector continued to suffer from the currency appreciation, household confidence points to very strong activity in the first quarter of 2011. Domestic demand has been the main engine of growth, outstripping supply and resulting in markedly increased imports. Private consumption has been supported by credit expansion and increasing labour incomes. Investment has been robust, as infrastructure projects from the Growth and Acceleration Programme have got underway. By contrast, exports have been damped by the steady appreciation of the *real*. The terms of trade have kept improving, though at a slower pace.

Brazil

Domestic demand has sustained growth
Contribution to annualised growth rate, seasonally adjusted

The real has appreciated

1. Includes stockbuilding and statistical discrepancy.
Source: Central Bank of Brazil, IBGE and OECD Economic Outlook 89 database.

StatLink ⟶ http://dx.doi.org/10.1787/888932429925

Brazil: **Macroeconomic indicators**

	2008	2009	2010	2011	2012
Real GDP growth	5.2	-0.7	7.5	4.1	4.5
Inflation (CPI)[1]	5.9	4.3	5.9	6.6	5.1
Fiscal balance (per cent of GDP)[2]	-2.0	-3.3	-2.5	-2.6	-2.6
Primary fiscal balance (per cent of GDP)[2]	3.4	2.0	2.8	2.8	3.0
Current account balance (per cent of GDP)	-1.7	-1.4	-2.3	-1.8	-2.0

Note: Real GDP growth and inflation are defined in percentage change from the previous period.
1. End-year.
2. Takes into account a capital injection (0.5% of GDP) in the Brazilian Sovereign Wealth Fund in 2008, which was treated as expenditure, and excludes Petrobras from the government accounts.
Source: OECD Economic Outlook 89 database.

StatLink http://dx.doi.org/10.1787/888932431179

The real has continued to appreciate

Abundant global liquidity and attractive returns in Brazil have led to capital inflows and currency appreciation. Overall, the real effective exchange rate has kept strengthening, after a 9% appreciation during 2010. Although expected and actual growth in oil production may have pushed up the equilibrium exchange rate somewhat, the central bank has actively intervened and international reserves are now close to USD 300 billion. Past successive increases in the *Imposto sobre Operações Financeiras* (IOF) tax on foreign-income investment did not restrain capital inflows on a sustained basis. The tax may have shifted them towards securities with longer maturities, but it remains to be seen whether this compositional effect will persist. Since March, the authorities have closed a number of loopholes and changed rules on taxes paid on foreign loans several times. They increased the tax applied on repatriated funds and applied the IOF tax rate to renewed, renegotiated or transferred loans.

Brazil

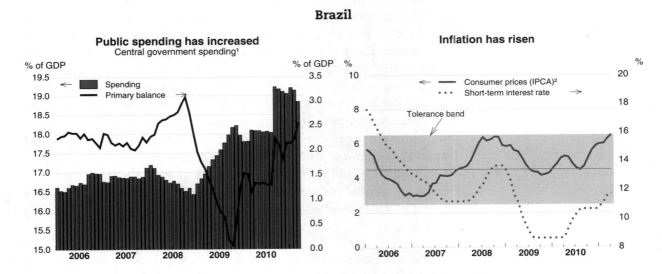

1. Cumulated 12-month flows.
2. Year-on-year growth.
Source: Central Bank of Brazil, IBGE, National Treasury.

StatLink http://dx.doi.org/10.1787/888932429944

Brazil: **External indicators**

	2008	2009	2010	2011	2012
	$ billion				
Goods and services exports	227.1	178.2	233.3	299	346
Goods and services imports	224.1	179.9	254.0	316	370
Foreign balance	3.1	- 1.7	- 20.7	- 17	- 24
Invisibles, net	- 31.3	- 22.7	- 26.8	- 31	- 34
Current account balance	- 28.2	- 24.3	- 47.5	- 47	- 58
	Percentage changes				
Goods and services export volumes	0.5	- 10.2	11.5	12.5	11.2
Goods and services import volumes	15.3	- 11.5	36.2	17.9	13.8
Terms of trade	3.1	- 3.3	12.7	8.1	1.1

Source: OECD Economic Outlook 89 database.

StatLink http://dx.doi.org/10.1787/888932431198

Inflation expectations have moved up

Inflation expectations have edged above the central bank's target range mid-point. The rise in CPI inflation since late 2010 reflects a surge in food and beverage prices and, to a lesser extent, housing prices, while the currency appreciation has been tempering price increases since mid-2009. Rising inflation expectations threaten to pass through into costs, adding to price pressures. The positive output gap has also exerted pressure but to a much lesser extent. Inflationary tensions are expected to persist, even as commodity prices stabilise, as the effects of the currency appreciation dissipate and demand remains strong. The unemployment rate has fallen to a record-low level, and labour markets are tight.

Monetary policy has been tightened

Against this background the Central Bank has taken both conventional and unconventional measures. It tightened reserve and capital requirements in December, increased the tax on consumer credit and lifted its policy rate by a total of 125 basis points, to 12%, since the beginning of the year. Acknowledging that the costs of bringing inflation down to 4.5% in 2011 may be too high, the Central Bank has shifted its focus and aims to guarantee inflation convergence to the target by 2012. It has also signalled it would adopt a gradualist approach and rely heavily on macro-prudential measures. In the current environment, this strategy is not without danger. Core inflation might rise further, and entrenched expectations of higher inflation would be detrimental to the Bank's long-term credibility and make subsequent disinflation more costly. While macro-prudential measures may help to restrain credit growth, they should be considered only as a complement to conventional monetary tightening.

Fiscal consolidation has started

Fiscal policy was strongly expansionary during the recovery, fuelling an unsustainable path of rising domestic demand and contributing to a rapid deterioration of the current account. The authorities have announced a BRL 50 billion spending cut in the 2011 federal budget, corresponding to about 0.5 percentage point of GDP compared with 2010 (after correcting from the capitalisation of the state-owned oil enterprise *Petrobras* which artificially boosted spending in September 2010). To achieve this goal, the government plans to target discretionary spending while safeguarding social and infrastructure programmes. Early signs are promising, as public revenues expanded at a much faster pace than spending in the first quarter of the year. Following some moderation this year, the minimum wage is set to rise by 13% in 2012, with ripple effects on the growth of social security benefits, which are linked to it. Nevertheless, the primary balance target is expected to be reached both in 2011 and 2012, but only with the use of contingency measures, such as the exclusion of some infrastructure spending. The announced spending cuts are a welcome first step toward fiscal consolidation. However, the government needs to persevere with efforts in this direction, to ease both inflationary pressures and capital inflows. The credibility of the fiscal consolidation would be enhanced by committing to a multi-year budgetary programme, which would reassure markets that measures will not be reversed in the coming years.

Activity is expected to grow at near potential rates

Domestic demand should continue to sustain economic growth, although it should gradually slow down in response to policy tightening. A recovery in investment would be supported by a solid economic backdrop and large infrastructure and energy-development programmes. Inflation may gradually diminish, but would remain in the upper part of the target range. The current account deficit is expected to stay at around 2% of GDP in 2011 and 2012.

Risks are broadly balanced

A key risk is higher inflation, which would endanger the Central Bank's credibility. Capital inflows could exacerbate this risk, although a shift in sentiment that reversed such flows could cut growth. On the positive side, spending on infrastructure projects could be faster than envisaged.

CHINA

Tighter monetary conditions have reined in growth, which is projected to average around 9% in 2011-12. Inflation has continued to veer up, with the price of all demand components combined up by 6¾ per cent in the year to the first quarter of 2011. As excess demand in the economy is gradually eliminated and import prices stop rising, inflation should ease back in 2012. The current account surplus is set to fall to 4½ per cent of GDP (from over 10% in 2007), as result of slower export growth and higher commodity prices.

Monetary tightening started late in the cycle and needs to continue to bring inflation down below 4%. Allowing the effective exchange rate to appreciate gradually would also ease inflationary pressures. Fiscal policy should continue to be oriented to increasing social expenditure and take-home pay. As the locus of economic activity is shifting to fast-expanding inland cities, easing urban registration requirements would facilitate migration to the new workplaces and help keep wage inflation in check. To increase competition in sectors dominated by state-owned companies, the government should press ahead firmly with measures to reduce entry barriers.

Growth has started to slow...

In the first quarter of 2011, growth slackened to 8.7% (seasonally-adjusted annual rate), the lowest since late 2008. The deceleration was particularly marked in the primary and secondary sectors of the economy. Domestic demand slowed, as investment by state-owned companies was held back by credit constraints and a wind-down in the stimulus programme. Against this, housing completions have been picking up, boosted by the plan to build 10 million low-cost units in 2011. Retail sales continued to grow rapidly. Even though auto sales fell in the first four months of 2011, they were still running at an annualised rate of 14.5 million in April, double the rate two years ago.

... but inflation remains high

Inflation has continued to rise. Annual CPI inflation exceeded 5% in recent months, with double-digit increases in food and gasoline prices.

China

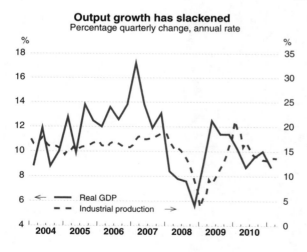

Output growth has slackened
Percentage quarterly change, annual rate

All measures of inflation have risen markedly
Year-on-year percentage change

Source: OECD estimates and CEIC.

StatLink http://dx.doi.org/10.1787/888932429963

China: **Macroeconomic indicators**

	2008	2009	2010	2011	2012
Real GDP growth	9.6	9.2	10.3	9.0	9.2
GDP deflator (per cent change)	7.8	-0.6	5.8	6.0	5.3
Consumer price index (per cent change)	5.9	-0.7	3.2	4.6	3.4
Fiscal balance (per cent of GDP)[1]	0.9	-1.2	-0.7	0.4	0.4
Current account balance (per cent of GDP)	9.1	5.2	5.2	4.5	4.4

Note: The figures given for GDP are percentage changes from the previous year.
1. Consolidated budget, social security and extra-budgetary accounts on a national accounts basis.
Source: OECD Economic Outlook 89 database.

StatLink http://dx.doi.org/10.1787/888932431217

The rise in global crude oil prices has been fully passed on to consumers. However, private consumption represents only slightly more than a quarter of total demand. Prices for consumption, investment and exports combined rose faster than the CPI, and were up by 6.7% in the year to the first quarter. Cost inflation is also on the rise. In the past two years, the minimum wage rate in the southern city of Shenzhen was raised by 32%, though this partly reflected catch-up from a standstill in 2009. Similarly large hikes occurred elsewhere in the country. In addition, by the first quarter of 2011, import prices were up 16% on a year earlier. Against this, prices of electricity are controlled, resulting in local shortages.

The current account surplus has declined markedly

The trade surplus was on a declining trend until the spring. It had fallen to 2.5% of GDP by the first quarter of 2011, although it rebounded in April, in part because imports from Japan dropped by 5% due to supply-chain problems. The oil import bill is estimated to have risen by almost 1½ percentage points of GDP in the year to the second quarter of 2011, given

China

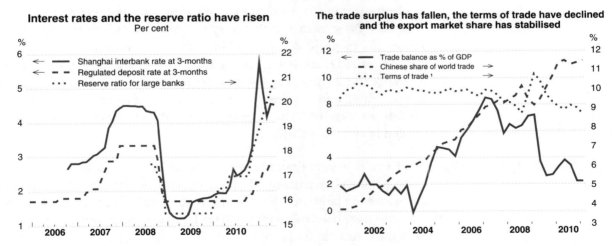

1. Terms of trade is measured as the ratio of export to import unit values multiplied by 10.
Source: CEIC, Peoples' Bank of China and OECD estimates.

StatLink http://dx.doi.org/10.1787/888932429982

China: **External indicators**

	2008	2009	2010	2011	2012
	\$ billion				
Goods and services exports	1 581.7	1 333.3	1 752.6	2 130	2 468
Goods and services imports	1 232.8	1 113.2	1 520.5	1 925	2 238
Foreign balance	348.9	220.1	232.1	205	230
Net investment income and transfers	63.5	41.0	73.3	112	132
Current account balance	412.4	261.1	305.4	318	362
	Percentage changes				
Goods and services export volumes	8.5	- 10.2	28.3	10.5	11.0
Goods and services import volumes	3.9	4.5	20.6	10.2	13.7
Export performance[1]	5.1	2.2	14.2	2.4	2.3
Terms of trade	- 5.3	8.6	- 9.5	- 4.3	2.0

1. Ratio between export volume and export market of total goods and services.
Source: OECD Economic Outlook 89 database.

StatLink 🔗 *http://dx.doi.org/10.1787/888932431236*

the rise in world prices. Other commodity prices have also increased substantially. China's share of world trade ceased to expand over the past year due to higher labour costs and export prices. The continued rapid accumulation of foreign exchange reserves, which by March 2011 exceeded \$3 trillion, has pushed up investment income, helping generate a current account surplus of around 4.6% of GDP in the first quarter of 2011.

Monetary policy has been tightened

Monetary policy has been tightened gradually since October 2010. Official interest rates have been raised, in steps, by a cumulative 114 basis points for three-month deposits. The required reserve ratio has been lifted by 3½ percentage points in total, reaching 21% in May for large banks. Tighter liquidity has pushed the interbank rate well above regulated saving deposit rates. In addition, the central bank introduced lending quotas for each bank. These measures have successfully restrained the growth of both money and credit to just under 16% over the 12 months to April, which is in line with the central bank's monetary targets for 2011. However, the depreciation of the nominal effective exchange rate during this period has tended to offset the impact of higher interest rates and required reserves. Given continued high inflation, a further increase of 50 basis points in regulated interest rates may be needed to stabilise inflation.

Fiscal policy is broadly neutral

Fiscal policy continues to be run in a conservative fashion at the level of the national government. The fiscal deficit was reduced in 2010 and the government plans on a further reduction in 2011 of 0.5% of GDP. Tax revenues have been rising rapidly. This has given the government room to raise the threshold for income taxation substantially, so that, once again, no person earning less than the average wage will pay income tax and the bulk of taxpayers will face a marginal rate of 10%. Taking into account the continuing social security surplus, the general government may run a slight deficit in 2011 and a surplus in 2012. Local authority off-budget borrowing is being restrained this year and must be used to finance social housing.

The outlook is for some weakening in growth in the short term

Tighter monetary policy will restrain growth in 2011. Investment growth is likely to remain weaker than in 2010, as lending is restricted. Further planned increases in minimum wages will push up average wages and unit labour costs, and fuel inflationary pressures. In addition, the higher cost of crude oil will push up consumer prices directly and, as importantly, raise the price of all transported goods with a lag. As a result, CPI inflation is projected to exceed the government's target of 4% for 2011 as a whole. In 2012, more subdued import price increases should clip 1½ percentage points from the inflation rate, boosting real incomes. There should be no further need for monetary tightening in 2012 and growth is projected to edge back up again. The government's target to raise wages by 15% annually for the next five years may result in a slight increase in the growth of unit labour costs, to around 5% per year. Higher domestic costs will erode competitiveness and, along with deteriorating terms of trade, will contribute to holding down the current account surplus to around 4½ per cent of GDP. Structural reforms, such as increasing competition in state-dominated sectors and services, would boost productivity and real incomes, strengthening domestic demand.

The economy faces a number of risks

With the economy slowing, there is a risk that the authorities might not raise interest rates as much as needed and instead attempt to lower inflation rapidly, through further price controls. This would reverse progress in lessening state control of the economy and risk undermining longer-term growth. The increasing movement of activity to the inland regions of the country could boost output and real incomes there more than expected, as new capacity is added to take advantage of lower labour costs. In coastal areas, manufacturers may be able to adapt more rapidly than foreseen to higher labour costs, thus enabling them to achieve greater gains in market shares than projected.

INDIA

Following a strong post-crisis rebound driven by a surge in private investment, growth slowed to a more sustainable pace towards the end of 2010. Going forward, growth will pick up somewhat, underpinned by buoyant corporate sentiment and demand for infrastructure spending. Tighter monetary policy and a modest reduction in the deficit will help cool demand somewhat. After moderating towards the end of 2010, inflation has veered up again and remains high. Moreover, inflationary pressures have become more generalised, with non-food prices accelerating.

The recent increase in world oil prices has been passed through into domestic petroleum product prices only to a limited extent and higher energy subsidy outlays are likely in 2011. A renewed commitment to reducing subsidies is needed to lower the burden on public finances. Efforts to better target subsidies on the needy ought to be stepped up. Further liberalisation of foreign direct investment in the retail sector would promote competition and help modernise supply chains, thereby reducing food inflation pressures.

Activity has moderated to a more sustainable pace

After recording double-digit rates earlier in the year, growth slowed to a more sustainable, but still strong, pace in the fourth quarter of 2010. Much of the slowing reflected an unwinding of a strong post-crisis bounce in investment. Activity in the non-agricultural sector eased somewhat towards the end of the year and recent industrial production figures indicate this slowing has continued into 2011. In contrast, agricultural production has continued to expand at a brisk pace, consolidating its recovery from an earlier drought. Trade also rebounded strongly in 2010, with both import and export volumes rising above pre-crisis highs. The current account deficit has been large by Indian standards, but it narrowed in the fourth quarter, as imports moderated. Inflows of portfolio capital have also slowed to a more normal pace, following a strong rise earlier in the year. At the same time, equity prices have eased.

India

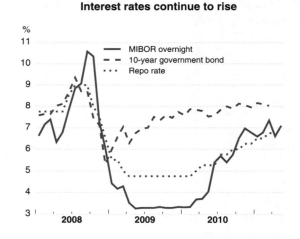

Interest rates continue to rise

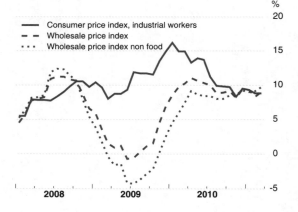

Inflation remains high

Source: CEIC.

StatLink http://dx.doi.org/10.1787/888932430001

India: **Macroeconomic indicators**

	2008	2009	2010	2011	2012
Real GDP growth[1]	4.9	9.1	9.6	8.5	8.6
Inflation[2]	6.7	7.5	10.2	8.4	6.2
Consumer price index[3]	9.1	12.4	10.3	8.9	6.6
Wholesale price index (WPI)[4]	8.0	3.6	9.4	8.8	6.2
Short-term interest rate[5]	7.4	4.8	6.0	7.6	8.3
Long-term interest rate[6]	7.6	7.3	7.9	8.3	8.3
Fiscal balance (per cent of GDP)[7]	-8.5	-9.5	-7.3	-6.8	-6.3
Current account balance (per cent of GDP)	-2.4	-2.7	-2.7	-2.9	-3.0
Memorandum: calendar year basis					
Real GDP growth	6.2	7.2	10.4	8.5	8.5
Fiscal balance (per cent of GDP)[7]	-7.3	-9.7	-7.7	-6.8	-6.4

Note: Data refer to fiscal years starting in April.
1. GDP measured at market prices.
2. Percentage change in GDP deflator.
3. Percentage change in the industrial workers index.
4. Percentage change in the all commodities index.
5. RBI repo rate.
6. 10-year government bond.
7. Gross fiscal balance for central and state governments.
Source: OECD Economic Outlook 89 database.

StatLink 🔗 http://dx.doi.org/10.1787/888932431255

Inflation remains stubbornly high and has become generalised

Although headline inflation moderated from double-digit rates in the second half of 2010, prices have begun accelerating again. Moreover, inflation has become generalised. Higher oil prices have led to sharp increases in fuel and energy prices. A re-emergence of food inflation reflects in part localised supply constraints, but also rising incomes. Wholesale prices for manufactured goods have also accelerated, likely reflecting the emergence of capacity constraints in the wake of very rapid

India

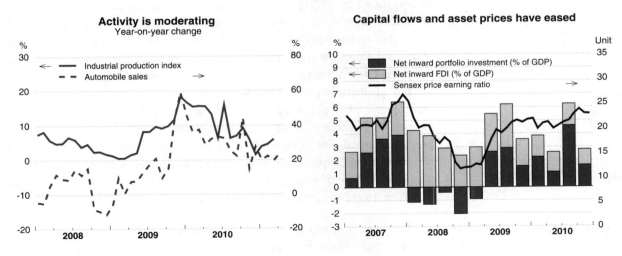

Activity is moderating
Year-on-year change

Capital flows and asset prices have eased

Source: CEIC.

StatLink 🔗 http://dx.doi.org/10.1787/888932430020

India: **External indicators**

	2008	2009	2010	2011	2012
	\$ billion				
Goods and services exports	292.0	274.7	353.9	438	522
Goods and services imports	353.7	346.8	436.7	518	613
Foreign balance	- 61.7	- 72.1	- 82.8	- 80	- 90
Net investment income and transfers	33.8	33.7	35.7	20	32
Current account balance	- 27.9	- 38.4	- 47.1	- 59	- 72
	Percentage changes				
Goods and services export volumes	14.4	- 5.5	12.5	12.9	13.0
Goods and services import volumes	22.7	- 1.8	9.1	9.1	12.6
Export performance[1]	14.9	- 2.2	1.1	3.8	3.0

Note: Data refer to fiscal years starting in April.
1. Ratio between export volume and export market of total goods and services.
Source: OECD Economic Outlook 89 database.

StatLink http://dx.doi.org/10.1787/888932431274

growth. In order to reduce food inflation pressures the government has announced several initiatives aimed at improving the food supply chain, including the upgrading of food storage facilities. These efforts could be complemented by further liberalising restrictions on foreign direct investment in the retail sector.

Progress with fiscal consolidation will be held back by higher spending on subsidies

Incoming budget data confirm that fiscal consolidation commenced in FY 2010, with the central government deficit estimated to have declined by over 1% of GDP, to around 5%. Consolidation has also resumed at the state level, ensuring an even larger improvement in general government finances. The reduction in the central government deficit was, however, significantly aided by one-off revenue windfalls, notably from the auction of 3G and broadband wireless licences. The central government budget plans for a further reduction in the deficit in FY 2011, underpinned by strong revenue growth and a sharp slowing in spending. In addition it commits to improve the delivery of some subsidies through direct cash transfers in 2012. However, in the meantime, the government raised subsidies on fertilisers. With crude oil prices remaining at a high level, the government is projected to split the costs of higher prices for oil-related products equally between consumers, oil companies and itself, leading to higher public spending. Altogether this additional spending is expected to amount to just over ½ per cent of GDP in FY 2011. Further pressure for higher spending could come from wage hikes under the National Rural Employment Guarantee Scheme and increased outlays on an expanded food subsidy programme. Eventually, the government may also have to recapitalise public-sector oil marketing companies.

Monetary policy continues to be tightened incrementally

The Reserve Bank of India continues to tighten monetary policy incrementally. Since the exit from emergency policy settings in early 2010 the main repo rate had been raised by a total of 250 basis points, to 7.25% by May 2011. However, credit-market pressures, reflecting temporary imbalances between deposits and the demand for loans, have led to considerably larger increases in commercial borrowing costs. In the first quarter of 2011 the 3-month interbank rate averaged around 9½ per cent, around 170 basis points higher than in the fourth quarter of 2010. The renewed acceleration in prices and the generalisation of inflationary pressures increase the risk of inflation expectations becoming unanchored. It is therefore important that the Reserve Bank continues to tighten incrementally.

Solid growth is expected to continue

Growth in the non-agriculture sector is expected to remain solid, with a pick-up later in the year due to a cyclical strengthening in investment underpinned by robust sentiment and a strong outlook for infrastructure spending. This will be aided by a small acceleration in consumption due to moderating inflation. Overall, however, growth will be constrained by recent increases in oil prices and tighter monetary policy, including the additional burden associated with recent tightness in credit markets. The general moderation in growth, along with the assumed levelling off in oil and other international commodity prices, will help to damp inflationary pressures.

The current account deficit will remain relatively large

Trade growth is expected to remain strong, supported by robust domestic and external conditions. In the near term, some deterioration in the terms of trade is expected as a result of higher oil prices. The current account deficit is expected to remain around 3% of GDP over the projection horizon. Over the past few years deficits of this order have been financed smoothly, even with the recent slowing in portfolio inflows. Going forward, portfolio and foreign direct investment inflows underpinned by relatively high interest rates and a strong medium-term outlook for growth, will help ensure continued smooth financing. Recently-announced increases in limits for foreign institutional investment in Indian corporate debt will provide a further avenue for capital inflows.

Inflation remains a key risk to the outlook

The main risk to the outlook is the possibility of continued high inflation, which would necessitate a forceful policy response. One source of demand pressure would be a further overshooting in government spending. In contrast, a moderation in relatively high international oil prices would ease inflationary and fiscal pressures.

INDONESIA

Economic growth is expected to accelerate above its potential rate in 2011, buttressed by low interest rates, and then to slow marginally in 2012. External demand will remain strong, and investment is projected to gain momentum. Underlying inflationary pressures are building.

Given the recent monetary ease, meeting the end-2011 inflation target will be challenging. Interest rates should be raised without further delay. Priority areas for fiscal policy, including infrastructure, secondary education and social policy, have suffered from slow budgetary disbursements, a worsening problem that will need to be tackled. Infrastructure investment could also be raised by improving the regulatory environment. In the face of high oil prices, the planned removal of fossil-fuel subsidies should not be delayed.

The economy is expanding fast

Activity has expanded rapidly, driven by widespread growth across most sectors. Investment continued to grow fast, supported by massive direct investment inflows. Exports are rebounding after a dip in the first two months of 2011 related to licensing problems in the coal sector. Private consumption, which accounts for two thirds of demand, has been outpacing overall GDP growth recently.

Inflationary pressures call for raising interest rates now

Inflationary pressures are mounting, not least due to infrastructure bottlenecks and rising commodity prices. Headline inflation has been lower than expected in early 2011 due to easing food prices, but the year-on-year rate is still over 6% and core inflation is accelerating. Business surveys point to further inflationary pressures in the near future, thanks to favourable economic prospects and significant capital inflows. Bank Indonesia (BI) raised the policy rate once by 25 basis points in February, following cumulative cuts of 300 basis points during the downturn. Besides rate increases, BI announced that it will rely on exchange-rate appreciation and macroprudential measures in order to control inflation

Indonesia

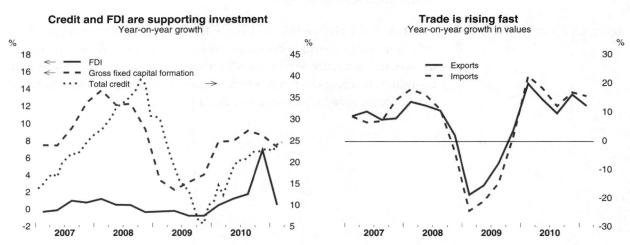

Source: OECD Main Economic Indicators, Statistics Indonesia (BPS), Bank Indonesia.

StatLink ▤▤▥ http://dx.doi.org/10.1787/888932430077

Indonesia: **Macroeconomic indicators**

	2008	2009	2010	2011	2012
Real GDP growth	6.0	4.6	6.1	6.6	6.4
Inflation	10.2	4.4	5.1	6.8	5.5
Fiscal balance (per cent of GDP)	-0.1	-1.6	-0.6	-1.4	-1.6
Current account balance ($ billion)	0.1	10.6	5.7	0.7	0.7
Current account balance (per cent of GDP)	0.0	1.9	0.8	0.1	0.1

Note: Real GDP growth and inflation are defined in percentage change from the previous period.
Source: OECD Economic Outlook 89 database.

StatLink http://dx.doi.org/10.1787/888932431331

without making Indonesia still more attractive as a destination for capital inflows. Though welcome instruments, they will not be able to replace urgently needed interest rate increases. Unless rates are raised immediately the end-2011 inflation target is at considerable risk. Further upgrades in credit ratings, which are now one notch below investment grade, will likely depend on successfully reining in inflation.

Disbursement problems should be addressed and oil subsidies phased out

Public finances are sound and the debt-to-GDP ratio is continuing to fall. Despite some reform efforts, government agencies continue to underspend and to skew spending towards the end of the year. Indeed, spending has again started very slowly in 2011 after having increased strongly in late 2010. To reduce underspending, especially on infrastructure investment and health insurance coverage, disbursement procedures should be simplified even further. Government revenues will increase due to strong growth, higher oil and gas revenues and export taxes. In the light of rising oil prices, the government has postponed the schedule for phasing out fossil fuel subsidies. This will make it more challenging to meet its earlier commitment of eliminating them by 2014, but will leave households with more disposable income in the short term. However, as energy subsidies are not an efficient way to combat poverty, and distort expenditure in undesirable ways, the original phase-out schedule should be maintained.

Investment and exports will drive the economy forward

Activity is projected to accelerate in 2011, buoyed by investment and exports and accommodative monetary policy. The pace of expansion is likely to ease somewhat in 2012 as the effects of interest rate hikes feed through. Strong investment increases are underpinned by solid credit growth, buoyant FDI inflows and new tax incentives for house purchases. Following free trade agreements in 2010, China and India are becoming increasingly important markets for Indonesia. Commodity exports, for which external demand conditions are positive, are likely to be robust, but manufacturing exports will also grow quickly. Reflecting strong domestic demand and rupiah appreciation, imports are expected to grow more rapidly than exports, almost eliminating the current account surplus. Unemployment should keep declining. Inflation is expected to gradually slow, but would at best remain in the upper half of the target range.

The main risk is higher inflation

A reluctance by BI to increase the policy rate could result in inflation expectations becoming unanchored. The increased role of both currency appreciation and macroprudential measures, while helpful, may prove less effective than expected. Further oil price increases or excessive delays in phasing out subsidies would undermine public finances. Implementation bottlenecks with public capital spending may slow investment growth.

RUSSIAN FEDERATION

Growth has picked up, supported by surging commodity prices, and domestic demand is expected to strengthen in the near term. Output is projected to grow by nearly 5% in 2011 and by 4½ per cent in 2012. As the effect of last year's food price shock dissipates, disinflation should resume. The budget is projected to return to surplus this year, as revenues will exceed projections by a large margin due to higher-than-expected oil prices, but the non-oil deficit will remain large.

The budgeted reduction of the non-oil fiscal deficit over 2011-13 is sensible. Pressure to spend the oil price windfalls should be resisted, not because fiscal sustainability is in immediate danger, but to avoid fiscal policy becoming procyclical and, more generally, to reduce the budget's dependence on fluctuations in commodity prices. Restoring a fiscal rule would be helpful in this regard. Even in the absence of financing needs, the government should pursue its privatisation agenda, while also undertaking other structural reforms to reduce entry barriers and improve the business climate.

Growth momentum has returned

Supported by rising prices for oil and other export commodities, real GDP increased by 4% in 2010, with a strong pickup in the fourth quarter to more than 11% (annualised rate). Gross capital formation in 2010 advanced particularly strongly, mostly on account of inventories. Notwithstanding very strong imports, the current account surplus widened as the terms of trade improved. The preliminary GDP estimate for the first quarter of 2011 indicates a slowdown to 2½ per cent annualised. Pronounced weakness in fixed investment appears to have undercut demand growth in the first quarter, although most high-frequency indicators pointed to continued strong expansion.

Inflation appears to have peaked

Having hit a post-Soviet era low of 5.5% in July 2010, inflation picked up to 9.7% year-on-year in January before stabilising. The upsurge was largely driven by food price increases resulting from the heat and drought

Russian Federation

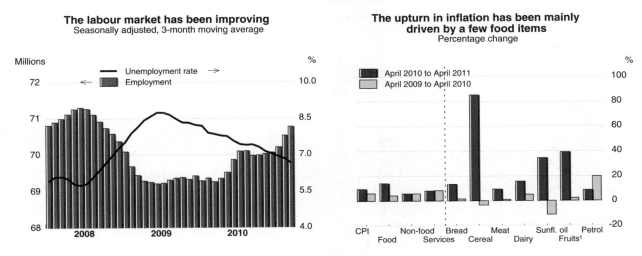

The labour market has been improving
Seasonally adjusted, 3-month moving average

The upturn in inflation has been mainly driven by a few food items
Percentage change

1. Fruits and vegetables.

Source: OECD calculations based Russian Federal Service for State Statistics and Central Bank of Russia.

StatLink http://dx.doi.org/10.1787/888932430039

Russian Federation: **Macroeconomic indicators**

	2008	2009	2010	2011	2012
Real GDP growth	5.2	-7.8	4.0	4.9	4.5
Inflation (CPI), period average	14.1	11.7	6.9	9.4	6.4
Fiscal balance (per cent of GDP)[1]	7.2	-6.8	-4.3	0.2	0.3
Current account balance (per cent of GDP)	6.1	3.9	4.8	6.8	5.8

1. Consolidated budget.
Source: OECD Economic Outlook 89 database.

StatLink http://dx.doi.org/10.1787/888932431293

during last summer. The crop losses and the panic which set in pushed the price of cereals up by 85% in the year to April 2011, an increase that was then passed on to a number of other food items, such as meat and sunflower oil. Monetary factors also played a role, as a significant amount of liquidity was injected into the economy via only partially sterilised foreign exchange interventions and the running down of government deposits at the central bank to finance the budget deficit. Although underlying inflation pressures appear to be contained, given the negative output gap and broadly unchanged core inflation, the government has resorted to a number of interventions to bring the headline rate down, such as curtailing petrol exports, selling grain from reserves and holding down tariff increases for natural monopolies.

Labour market conditions are improving

Employment losses were limited during the crisis due to the adjustment in working hours and real wages, but the labour market recovery has lagged the rebound in output. Recent labour market developments show gradual improvement, with the unemployment rate

Russian Federation

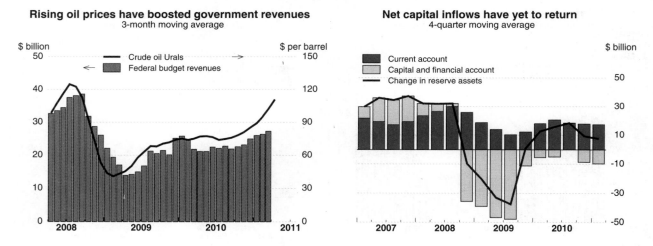

Rising oil prices have boosted government revenues
3-month moving average

Net capital inflows have yet to return
4-quarter moving average

Source: OECD calculations based on Datastream, Russian Federal Service for State Statistics, Central Bank of Russia and Economic Expert Group.

StatLink http://dx.doi.org/10.1787/888932430058

Russian Federation: **External indicators**

	2008	2009	2010	2011	2012
	\$ billion				
Goods and services exports	522.9	345.4	444.5	620	676
Goods and services imports	367.7	251.0	320.9	429	487
Foreign balance	155.2	94.4	123.6	190	190
Invisibles, net	- 51.7	- 45.7	- 52.5	- 57	- 60
Current account balance	103.5	48.6	71.1	133	130
	Percentage changes				
Goods and services export volumes	0.6	- 4.7	7.1	4.1	5.8
Goods and services import volumes	14.8	- 30.4	25.6	21.3	10.9
Terms of trade	15.6	- 29.5	18.5	21.4	1.0

Source: OECD Economic Outlook 89 database.

StatLink ᴍ⬛ᴾ http://dx.doi.org/10.1787/888932431312

continuing its downward trend and employment picking up in the first part of 2011.

The budget is likely to return to surplus this year

The federal budget deficit narrowed to 4% of GDP in 2010, down from 5.9% in 2009, and the 2011-13 budget foresees a further moderate fiscal tightening, with the large non-oil deficit gradually decreasing from its 2010 level of around 13% of GDP. Rising oil prices have boosted revenues and have improved the fiscal position faster than envisaged by the government, however. Based on current oil prices and spending plans, the headline budget deficit should be eliminated this year; the budget was already in surplus in the first four months of the year. Before the surge in oil prices, the government intended to divest its stakes in a number of large companies and banks. These privatisation plans should be pursued, even in the absence of financing needs, as this is one of the measures needed to reduce state control over economic activity.

The central bank has allowed greater exchange rate flexibility

The central bank continues to balance the objectives of disinflation and limiting excessively rapid appreciation of the rouble. It has at times intervened in the foreign exchange markets to mitigate rouble appreciation in the wake of strong current account inflows linked to rising oil prices. At the same time, it has also been allowing more exchange rate fluctuation than in the past and is trying to use its constellation of policy rates and reserve requirements to smooth market interest rates and bring inflation down to low and stable levels. This more flexible exchange rate policy has, however, not yet been tested by large-scale foreign currency inflows through the financial account as, contrary to the pre-crisis period, rising oil prices have not been accompanied by increasing net capital inflows. Instead, Russian corporations and banks have so far chosen to improve their net foreign asset positions.

Positive growth momentum is expected to be sustained

Notwithstanding the growth slowdown in the first quarter indicated by the preliminary estimate, domestic demand is expected to be strong in the near term, given the surge in oil prices which will feed through to higher incomes and faster credit growth. Bank lending has already been boosted by abundant liquidity and the improved creditworthiness of large resource-based companies. Given a high income elasticity of imports, faster growth in absorption should translate into import volume growth which will significantly outpace growth in export volumes this year and next. The current account surplus will nonetheless widen this year to about 7% of GDP due to higher oil prices before narrowing slightly next year. Output growth is projected to approach 5% in 2011, before moderating to 4.5% in 2012. Annual average inflation will exceed 9% in 2011, but then fall to 6.4% in 2012 as the impact of the food price shock fades away.

The key risk factors relate to commodity prices and capital flows

The prices of export commodities, in particular oil and gas, remain the key risk factor. Higher-than-projected commodity prices would give a stronger impetus to domestic demand and further improve the fiscal and external positions. Private capital inflows may resume, fuelling demand but also complicating the conduct of monetary policy. In the context of the 2011 parliamentary and 2012 presidential elections, some fiscal loosening is likely, which would be unhelpfully procyclical. Growth prospects would be robust to a small fall in oil prices from the levels assumed in this projection, but a large decline would pose a significant downside risk.

SOUTH AFRICA

The recovery is expected to gain momentum this year, as strong external conditions and a resumption of employment growth support demand. Notwithstanding upward pressure from food and energy prices, the strong rand and the negative output gap should keep inflation within the Reserve Bank's target range. Buoyant revenues are projected to shrink the budget deficit.

The government should use the opportunity of stronger growth to accelerate the pace of fiscal consolidation. This would not only safeguard fiscal sustainability but also put downward pressure on interest rates and the exchange rate, thereby supporting private-sector-led growth and helping to limit the widening of the current account deficit. Structural measures targeted at employment growth are also a priority, given the massive scale of unemployment, particularly among the young, where the unemployment rate is close to 50%. Entrepreneurship needs to be encouraged, notably by reducing administrative burdens.

Output growth has quickened but has yet to generate many new jobs

After losing momentum in mid-2010, growth reaccelerated to 4.4% (seasonally adjusted annual rate) in the fourth quarter and appears to have remained solid in early 2011. Growth was led by private consumption, despite employment losses that continued for most of 2010. Employment appears now to be rising again, but as of the first quarter of 2011 remained some 6% below its pre-crisis peak.

Inflation has risen somewhat, but does not look worrisome

The strong currency appreciation in 2009 and 2010, combined with the negative output gap (estimated to be still around 3% of GDP), helped drive inflation down almost to the bottom of the Reserve Bank's 3-6% target range by September 2010. Since then, higher food and oil prices have pushed headline inflation up, and it reached 4.1% (year-on-year) in

South Africa

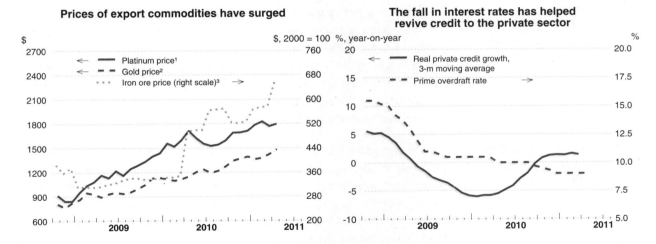

Prices of export commodities have surged

The fall in interest rates has helped revive credit to the private sector

1. London Platinum Free Market USD/Troy oz.
2. Gold Bullion London Bullion Market USD/Troy Ounce.
3. Hamburg Institute for Economic Research, world market price, iron ore, scrap.

Source: Datastream, HWWA, South Africa Reserve Bank and Statistics South Africa.

StatLink http://dx.doi.org/10.1787/888932430096

South Africa: **Macroeconomic indicators**

	2008	2009	2010	2011	2012
Real GDP growth	3.6	-1.7	2.8	3.9	4.2
Inflation	11.0	7.1	4.3	4.8	5.4
Fiscal balance (per cent of GDP)	-0.6	-5.3	-4.5	-4.0	-3.4
Current account balance ($ billion)	-20.1	-11.2	-10.0	-14.1	-20.0
Current account balance (per cent of GDP)	-7.1	-4.1	-2.8	-3.2	-4.2

Source: OECD Economic Outlook 89 database.

StatLink ᴍᴤᴘ http://dx.doi.org/10.1787/888932431350

March 2010. Core inflation remains moderate, however, and survey measures of inflation expectations have continued to move downward.

The time is right to accelerate fiscal consolidation

The government's existing three-year budget plans imply no deficit reduction in the current fiscal year and only a gradual improvement thereafter. The underlying assumptions regarding revenues are probably too cautious, and the outcome may therefore be somewhat better than budgeted. Nonetheless, given the favourable external environment and a cyclical recovery that is picking up steam, a more ambitious profile of fiscal consolidation should be implemented. This would not only safeguard fiscal sustainability but also contribute to raising national savings, reducing upward pressure on the exchange rate and crowding in private investment. Restraint in public sector wage increases would be one measure that would both contribute to fiscal consolidation and help establish a norm of wage moderation which would encourage private sector employment growth. This would complement other government measures to boost employment, which rightly remain a very high priority.

Monetary conditions should be tightened as growth strengthens

Monetary policy was eased last year as the recovery lost momentum and the currency strengthened. When it becomes clearer that the output gap is closing, an upward move in interest rates will be called for, probably in the second half of 2011. In the meantime, unless the rise of international food and energy prices feeds through into higher inflation expectations and wage pressures, which has not so far been the case, the Reserve Bank should accommodate the implied one-off price increase.

The output gap will close gradually, with inflation remaining contained

Output growth is projected to pick up to near 4% in 2011 and to be a bit faster in 2012, driven by strong increases in consumption and rising investment growth but with net exports exerting a drag as South Africa's high propensity to import is reinforced by the strong real appreciation of the rand in the past two years. The output gap is projected to narrow only gradually, remaining negative throughout 2011-12, and the unemployment rate is expected to be still above 20% at end-2012. Headline inflation will trend downwards on a quarterly basis through the projection period as the effects of the food and energy price surge dissipate.

Risks to the baseline scenario are broadly balanced

Growth could well be significantly stronger than projected. For example, higher-than-projected commodity prices or capital inflows would provide further impetus to domestic demand. Prominent downside risks include the possibility that recent weakness in house prices continues, undermining household wealth and consumption growth. Another uncertainty relates to electricity supply – the crisis provided an interlude of lower demand, but now capacity margins are shrinking again and significant new capacity remains some way off, creating a significant risk of power supply constraining growth within the next two years.

OECD Economic Outlook
Volume 2011/1
© OECD 2011

Chapter 4

MEDIUM AND LONG-TERM DEVELOPMENTS: CHALLENGES AND RISKS

The statistical data for Israel are supplied by and under the responsibility of the relevant Israeli authorities. The use of such data by the OECD is without prejudice to the status of the Golan Heights, East Jerusalem and Israeli settlements in the West Bank under the terms of international law.

Introduction and summary

This chapter considers long-term macroeconomic prospects and risks for the OECD

The recovery is projected to strengthen in the near term, but there are concerns about the longer-term legacy of the crisis, particularly because of the emergence of unsustainable fiscal imbalances as well as the possible damage to long-term growth prospects. Based on a technical exercise, this chapter considers macroeconomic prospects for OECD economies to the middle of the next decade and the challenges and the associated risks. The projections described in Chapters 1 and 2 suggest that nearly all OECD economies are expected to improve their fiscal balances over the course of this year and next. However, for many this will still leave fiscal balances too weak to stabilise government debt and for others, where debt is stable, it will be at levels which remain too high. Moreover, this chapter also discusses whether the crisis could have a long-lasting adverse effect on the growth rate of output, particularly as a consequence of large fiscal imbalances or continuing financial fragilities, and so lead to a prolonged period of stagnation. An alternative risk of "stagflation" – stagnation combined with inflation – might arise as a consequence of continuing upward pressure on oil and other commodity prices. These risks are examined in the context of previous historical episodes of stagnation and the implications for policy are considered.

Main conclusions are:

The main conclusions are:

Consolidation needs to stabilise debt are substantial for many countries

- Fiscal consolidation requirements for many countries are substantial. In Japan and the United States, stabilising the debt-to-GDP ratio would require an overall improvement in the underlying primary balance of 10 to 11 percentage points of GDP from the 2010 position, implying a protracted period of fiscal tightening. Other countries for which consolidation requirements are large include Greece, Ireland, Poland, Portugal, the Slovak Republic and the United Kingdom, which all require consolidation of about 6 to 8½ percentage points of GDP from the 2010 position. In addition, for a typical OECD country, additional offsets of 3% of GDP will have to be found over the coming 15 years to meet spending pressures due to increasing pension and health care costs.

On this basis there are large differences in the adequacy of official current plans

- The United States and Japan also stand out because there is, as yet, a lack of any detailed official medium-term fiscal plans that would be sufficient to stabilise debt. In the case of Japan there is a medium-term plan, but it is not sufficiently ambitious. In the United States, there are a number of fiscal plans, but political disagreement makes the extent, pace and instruments of future consolidation very uncertain. For most other countries where consolidation needs are most severe, official medium-term consolidation plans more than match the requirements to stabilise debt, so that the achievement of such plans would put the debt ratio on a downward path. Nevertheless, in some of these cases the credibility of such plans needs to be enhanced by clearly specifying which spending and revenue instruments will be adjusted.

To reduce debt levels would require much greater consolidation

- Consolidation requirements would be much more demanding if the aim were to return debt-to-GDP ratios to their pre-crisis levels. For the OECD area as a whole the improvement in the underlying primary balance from the 2010 position that would be required to reduce the debt ratio to pre-crisis levels by 2026 would be more than 13 percentage points of GDP, compared to 7 percentage points to simply stabilise debt.

Stagnation risks can arise from not dealing with outstanding banking problems

- The baseline scenario embodies a permanent reduction in the level of potential output as a consequence of the financial crisis, but no long-lasting effect on the growth rate. In contrast, a previous banking crisis in Japan in the 1990s ushered in a prolonged period of stagnation, characterised by low productivity growth, which was partly due to a failure to deal promptly with non-performing bank loans. In the current conjuncture this underlines the importance of resolving outstanding banking problems, especially in Europe where financial weakness and a lack of transparency about exposures represent a risk of stagnation.

Stagnation could both exacerbate and be a symptom of fiscal imbalances

- Stagnation and a deteriorating fiscal position have been associated in the past, with causality possibly operating in both directions. Previous episodes of stagnation have led to an acceleration in debt accumulation, but there is also a risk that deteriorating debt positions may adversely affect trend growth. This underlines the importance of fiscal consolidation to reduce debt levels below thresholds where there might be risks to trend growth as well as to create fiscal space for dealing with future shocks.

Consolidation measures should minimise adverse effects on growth

- Many countries will be undertaking fiscal consolidation over a prolonged period and there is a risk that the sustained adverse effect on demand could delay the recovery and even risk stagnation. In this respect, countries face a difficult choice between front-loaded fast consolidation and more gradual consolidation. Fast consolidation has the advantage that it may reduce the overall scale of required consolidation and reassure financial markets, but it also increases the risk of adversely affecting the recovery particularly if monetary policy is constrained. To improve the terms of this trade-off, countries should put greater weight on measures which will improve long-term fiscal sustainability – for example raising retirement ages or containing future increases in health costs – but which have relatively limited immediate negative effects on demand. To reassure financial markets, it is also important to have a clear medium-term fiscal plan specifying objectives and the instruments that will be used. Consolidation should also avoid measures, such as reducing public investment or support for R&D, which weaken the supply side and instead target measures which strengthen it.

Structural reforms can bolster resilience, boost growth and help fiscal consolidation

● Other experiences of stagnation – including recent episodes in Japan, Italy and Portugal – suggest that weak structural policy settings may reduce the resilience of economies in dealing with shocks. Structural reforms are thus paramount, not only to bolster resilience against stagnation, but also to promote growth as well as strengthen public finances.

The impact of the crisis on potential output

The crisis has reduced the level of potential output

The downturn has permanently reduced the level of potential output. For the OECD as a whole, potential output is estimated to be around 2½ per cent lower in 2012 when compared with projections made prior to the crisis. This represents a loss of more than a year's growth for the region as a whole. Underlying the loss are reductions in capital endowment as firms have adjusted to the end of cheap financing and increases in long-duration unemployment resulting in hysteresis-type effects leading to higher structural unemployment.

The impact is becoming clearer as more data become available

With the start of the crisis now further in the past, estimates of the magnitude of its impact have become clearer with more data. Changes in trend participation rates and capital can now be estimated from recent data and projections to 2012. They indicate that the impacts of the crisis on participation and capital inputs are sizeable but somewhat less dramatic than initially expected.

The largest hits are in some of the smaller economies

For the median OECD country, the impact on potential output is around 3¼ per cent in 2012. The difference *vis-à-vis* the OECD as a whole is attributable to the variability of the impact of the crisis, as well as a disproportionate negative effect on some of the smaller countries, including Greece and Ireland, which are experiencing losses as large as 13% of potential output by 2012, relative to earlier projections.

Key features of a stylised long-term scenario

The scenario is underpinned by potential output estimates

A long-term baseline scenario has been constructed by extending the short-term projections described in Chapter 1 under a set of stylised assumptions. For OECD countries, the long-term growth path is underpinned by projections of potential output (Box 4.1). Most of the assumptions underlying the scenario tend to be relatively optimistic – beginning with the proposition that the crisis itself only reduces the level of potential output and has no permanent adverse effect on its growth rate and by the assumption that fiscal consolidation does not affect growth. Output gaps are also generally assumed to close by 2015 as a result of sustained above-trend growth with output growing in line with potential thereafter. In a few countries where the output gap in 2012 is exceptionally large, such as Greece, Ireland, Portugal and Spain, the

Box 4.1. **Assumptions underlying the baseline scenario**

The baseline represents a stylised scenario that is conditional on the following assumptions for the period beyond the short-term projection horizon that ends in 2012:

- The gap between actual and potential output is eliminated by 2015 in all OECD countries, except those where the output gap remains very large in 2012. In the case of the latter, for every 2 percentage points by which the output gap exceeds 6% at the end of 2012 it is assumed to take an additional year to close the gap. This means that for Greece the output gap closes in 2018 and for Ireland, Portugal and Spain in 2016. Once the output gap is closed, GDP grows in line with potential output.

- Participation rates evolve from 2013 to 2026 in a manner consistent with a dynamic cohort effect (Burniaux, Duval and Jaumotte, 2004). The effects on participation of pension reforms legislated up to 2009 have been incorporated.

- Unemployment returns to its estimated structural rate in all OECD countries by 2015. For most countries historical estimates of the structural unemployment rate are based on a Kalman filter method described in Gianella et al. (2008). Since then the structural unemployment rate for Poland has also been estimated using the same Kalman filter method. For a few countries, Chile, the Czech Republic, Estonia, Hungary, Israel, Mexico, the Slovak Republic and Slovenia, the structural unemployment estimates are based on a Hodrick-Prescott filter of unemployment. Over the post-crisis period a hysteresis effect is imposed on the structural unemployment rate which is then assumed to eventually return to pre-crisis levels but at a speed which differs across countries based on previous historical experience (Guichard and Rusticelli, 2010); for those countries with more flexible labour markets structural unemployment returns to pre-crisis levels by 2018 and for other countries by 2026.

- Non-oil commodity prices remain unchanged in real terms, while oil prices rise by 1% per annum in real terms after 2012.

- Exchange rates remain unchanged in real terms in OECD countries; real exchange rates for non-OECD countries appreciate in line with growth differentials (through the so-called Balassa-Samuelson effect) from 2012.

- The adverse effects on the level of potential output resulting from the crisis have reached their peak by about 2013.

- After 2012, non-OECD economies show a slow convergence to US growth rates in per capita income (measured in purchasing power parities).

- For the period 2015 to 2026, OECD countries experience a slow convergence to annual labour productivity growth of 1¾ per cent.

Assumptions regarding fiscal and monetary policy are as follows:

- Policy interest rates continue to normalise as output gaps close and beyond that are directed to bring inflation into line with medium-term objectives.

- From 2013 onwards for those countries where the debt-to-GDP ratio is rising, there is a gradual increase in the underlying fiscal primary balance of ½ percentage point of GDP per year through a combination of reduced government spending and higher taxes until the ratio of government debt to GDP is stable given long-term trend growth and long-term interest rates (see Box 4.4 of *OECD Economic Outlook* No.88 for further details). The rule is asymmetric so that countries for which the debt ratio is falling are not assumed to undertake fiscal expansion. It should be noted that in many cases this assumption implies a degree of fiscal consolidation which is less ambitious than incorporated in current government plans. In addition, the stylised fiscal rule applied here is not necessarily consistent with national or supra-national fiscal objectives, targets or rules.

- There are no further losses to government balance sheets as a result of asset purchases or guarantees made in dealing with the financial crisis. No contribution to deficit or debt reduction is assumed from government asset sales.

- Effects on public budgets from population ageing and continued upward pressures on health spending (Box 4.2) are not explicitly included, or, put differently, implicitly assumed to be offset by other budgetary measures. However, the impact of pension reforms up to 2009 on future participation are incorporated and will have an effect on calculations of fiscal sustainability to the extent they impact on trend participation and potential growth.

output gap takes longer to close (Box 4.1). Also, with the exception of Japan, countries do not experience deflation, despite continued, and in many cases large, negative output gaps over this period, and eventually return to targeted inflation once output gaps close.[1]

Long-term trend growth is lower because of demographic effects

From 2013 onwards, the growth rate of OECD-wide potential output recovers to average about 2% per annum (Table 4.1), below the average potential growth rate of 2¼ per cent per annum achieved over the seven years preceding the crisis. Most of the difference is due to slower growth both in participation rates and in the working-age population, mainly reflecting demographic trends rather than additional effects from the crisis.

Output is assumed to return to potential by 2015 for most countries

Given the assumption that negative output gaps close by 2015 in most countries, and despite slower potential growth, area-wide GDP growth averages almost 3% per annum over the period 2010-15 (Table 4.2), compared to 2½ per cent per annum over the period 2000-07. Unemployment is falling in all countries, with the area-wide unemployment rate down from 8¼ per cent in 2010 to a rate of just over 6¼ per cent by 2015 and just under 6% in 2026, reflecting both the recovery and, perhaps also optimistically, the reversal of post-crisis hysteresis effects.

Most non-OECD countries continue to have strong growth...

Non-OECD countries are included in the baseline using a growth convergence assumption where eventually all countries have productivity growth that is roughly equal to a historical OECD average (1¾ per cent per annum). Since convergence is very slow, this leads to continued strong growth in all the emerging economies – particularly China, India, Russia and Brazil. Strong growth in these regions continues to be a major source of export demand in some OECD economies such as Germany and Japan.

... and imbalances remain to be addressed by structural reforms

Global imbalances, measured in terms of the absolute sum of current account balances divided by world GDP, are projected to increase while not reaching the levels that were attained prior to the crisis. Policy changes to encourage domestic demand in surplus countries and policies to encourage saving in deficit countries can do much to alleviate global imbalances. OECD work on structural policy reform provides guidance in removing distortions that contribute to imbalances. For surplus countries – such as China – this includes removing the incentive for precautionary savings that come from weak government social safety nets – including medical services and retirement pensions, as well as establishing a legal framework facilitating the development of the domestic financial system. In OECD countries, this includes removing incentives for greater consumption in deficit countries (*e.g.* in the United States) and to stimulate investment and capital inflows by implementing product market reforms in surplus countries (*e.g.* in Japan and some European economies). In addition, fiscal consolidation in deficit countries would also be helpful.

---

1. This is consistent with inflation expectations remaining fairly well anchored (both upwards and downwards) and with the operation of "speed-limit" effects.

Table 4.1. **Growth in total economy potential output and its components**

Annual averages, percentage change

| | Output Gap | Potential GDP growth | | | Potential labour productivity growth (output per employee) | | Potential employment growth | | Components of potential employment[1] | | | | | |
| | | | | | | | | | Trend participation rate | | Working age population | | Structural Unemployment | |
	2012	2001-2007	2010-2015	2016-2026	2010-2015	2016-2026	2010-2015	2016-2026	2010-2015	2016-2026	2010-2015	2016-2026	2010-2015	2016-2026
Australia	-1.8	3.3	3.2	2.8	1.4	1.4	1.8	1.5	0.4	0.2	1.4	1.2	0.0	0.0
Austria	-1.6	2.2	1.8	1.5	1.2	1.7	0.6	-0.1	0.4	-0.1	0.3	-0.1	0.0	0.0
Belgium	-1.4	2.0	1.3	1.4	0.5	1.3	0.8	0.2	0.3	0.1	0.5	0.0	0.0	0.0
Canada	-2.2	2.8	2.0	1.8	1.1	1.5	0.9	0.3	0.2	0.2	0.7	0.1	0.0	0.0
Chile	0.7	3.9	4.1	3.0	1.6	1.9	2.5	1.1	1.2	0.8	1.1	0.3	0.2	0.0
Czech Republic	-1.7	4.0	2.7	2.2	2.8	2.5	-0.1	-0.3	0.3	0.0	-0.5	-0.4	-0.1	0.0
Denmark	-4.0	1.6	1.1	1.2	0.9	1.3	0.2	0.0	0.2	0.0	0.0	-0.1	0.0	0.1
Estonia	-2.3	5.9	2.4	2.2	3.0	2.5	-0.5	-0.3	0.6	0.2	-0.7	-0.6	-0.1	0.1
Finland	-3.9	3.1	1.6	1.9	1.8	2.1	-0.2	-0.2	0.2	0.2	-0.4	-0.4	0.0	0.0
France	-2.9	2.0	1.5	1.7	1.1	1.5	0.4	0.1	0.2	0.1	0.3	0.0	0.0	0.1
Germany	0.3	1.2	1.5	1.0	1.4	1.7	0.1	-0.7	0.2	0.0	-0.3	-0.7	0.1	0.0
Greece	-11.2	3.7	1.0	1.8	0.9	1.8	0.1	0.0	0.4	0.1	0.0	-0.3	-0.4	0.2
Hungary	-2.7	3.2	1.2	1.5	1.2	1.8	0.0	-0.3	0.6	0.4	-0.3	-0.6	-0.1	0.1
Iceland	-4.6	4.1	1.4	2.3	1.4	1.7	0.0	0.6	0.1	0.1	-0.1	0.4	-0.1	0.1
Ireland	-8.2	5.4	1.1	3.3	1.5	1.8	-0.4	1.5	0.0	0.1	0.0	0.9	-0.4	0.4
Israel	0.3	3.6	4.1	3.4	1.4	1.6	2.7	1.8	0.6	0.3	1.7	1.3	0.2	0.0
Italy	-1.5	0.9	0.5	1.2	0.4	1.4	0.1	-0.1	0.1	-0.1	0.1	-0.1	-0.1	0.1
Japan	-4.4	1.0	1.0	1.4	1.5	1.8	-0.4	-0.4	0.6	0.3	-1.0	-0.7	0.0	0.0
Korea	0.4	4.4	3.8	2.4	2.8	2.2	1.0	0.2	0.4	0.6	0.4	-0.7	0.0	0.0
Mexico	-1.7	2.6	2.9	3.0	1.1	1.5	1.8	1.4	0.3	0.2	1.6	1.2	0.0	0.0
Netherlands	-0.8	2.0	1.2	1.2	0.7	1.2	0.5	-0.1	0.3	0.1	0.1	-0.3	0.0	0.0
New Zealand	-1.3	3.2	2.1	2.3	0.9	1.6	1.2	0.6	0.0	-0.2	1.2	0.9	0.0	0.0
Norway[2]	-0.3	3.2	3.0	2.7	1.8	2.3	1.1	0.4	0.1	0.1	1.0	0.3	0.0	0.0
Poland	1.3	4.2	2.9	1.7	2.7	2.3	0.2	-0.6	0.4	0.3	-0.2	-0.9	0.0	0.0
Portugal	-7.5	1.5	1.2	2.3	1.2	1.9	0.1	0.3	0.1	0.2	0.1	0.0	-0.1	0.2
Slovak Republic	-2.2	5.2	3.4	1.8	3.5	2.6	-0.1	-0.8	0.0	-0.1	-0.2	-0.7	0.1	0.0
Slovenia	-1.7	3.5	1.7	1.1	1.7	1.7	0.0	-0.7	0.1	0.0	0.0	-0.7	-0.1	0.1
Spain	-7.0	3.7	1.5	2.4	1.3	1.5	0.1	1.0	0.7	0.2	-0.1	0.3	-0.4	0.5
Sweden	-0.8	2.6	2.0	1.9	1.6	1.9	0.4	0.0	0.0	-0.1	0.4	0.1	0.0	0.0
Switzerland	-0.3	1.9	1.9	1.8	0.8	1.4	1.1	0.4	0.2	0.1	0.7	0.1	0.0	0.0
United Kingdom	-2.7	2.3	1.5	1.9	0.9	1.6	0.6	0.3	0.2	0.0	0.4	0.3	0.0	0.0
United States	-2.4	2.5	2.3	2.2	1.5	1.7	0.7	0.5	-0.1	-0.4	1.0	0.9	0.0	0.0
Euro area	-2.3	1.9	1.3	1.5	1.1	1.6	0.2	0.0	0.3	0.0	0.0	-0.2	-0.1	0.1
OECD	-2.4	2.2	1.8	1.9	1.2	1.6	0.6	0.3	0.1	-0.1	0.5	0.4	0.0	0.1

1. Percentage point contributions to potential employment growth. In some cases, components do not sum to the total because of an adjustment to a national accounts concept of labour input or because of rounding.
2. As a % of mainland potential GDP.
Source: OECD Economic Outlook 89 database.

StatLink http://dx.doi.org/10.1787/888932434333

Public finances

Consolidation requirements

Fiscal consolidation is essential to contain debt ratios in many countries

Fiscal deficits are projected to remain large in 2012, with a substantial component which is not explained by the cycle (Table 4.3), even with an assumption that announced fiscal consolidation plans are implemented in full up to 2012 (see Chapter 1 for an outline of those plans). As a result, debt in many countries will remain on an increasing trajectory in the

Table 4.2. **Macroeconomic trends: summary**

	Real GDP growth		Inflation rate[1]		Unemployment rate		
	2010-15	2016-26	2010	2015-26	2010	2015Q4	2026
Australia	3.5	2.9	1.9	2.5	5.2	5.1	5.1
Austria	2.3	1.6	1.5	2.0	4.4	4.3	4.3
Belgium	2.0	1.4	2.4	2.1	8.3	8.4	8.0
Canada	2.9	1.8	1.3	2.1	8.0	6.6	6.5
Chile	4.8	3.0	0.2	3.0	8.1	7.3	7.2
Czech Republic	3.2	2.2	1.3	2.0	7.3	6.2	5.8
Denmark	2.2	1.3	2.6	2.0	7.2	4.9	4.4
Estonia	4.1	2.2	2.1	2.0	16.8	11.6	10.3
Finland	3.1	1.9	1.0	2.0	8.4	7.7	7.4
France	2.2	1.7	1.2	2.0	9.3	8.7	8.2
Germany	2.3	1.0	2.0	2.0	6.8	7.2	7.2
Greece	0.5	2.4	4.7	2.0	12.5	13.3	8.9
Hungary	2.3	1.5	5.0	3.1	11.2	8.0	6.6
Iceland	2.1	2.3	3.5	2.5	7.5	3.4	2.8
Ireland	2.3	3.5	-2.2	2.0	13.5	10.0	4.7
Israel	4.4	3.4	2.9	2.0	6.6	6.1	6.1
Italy	1.3	1.2	1.5	2.0	8.4	7.1	6.3
Japan	2.1	1.4	-1.5	1.0	5.1	4.1	4.1
Korea	4.3	2.4	2.6	3.1	3.7	3.5	3.5
Mexico	4.0	3.0	3.0	3.0	5.3	3.2	3.2
Netherlands	1.7	1.2	1.7	2.0	4.3	3.7	3.7
New Zealand	3.0	2.3	1.4	2.0	6.5	4.3	4.0
Norway[2]	3.4	2.7	1.9	2.5	3.6	3.4	3.3
Poland	3.1	1.6	2.9	2.6	9.6	9.5	9.5
Portugal	1.4	2.5	1.6	2.0	10.8	9.5	6.9
Slovak Republic	3.9	1.8	0.9	2.0	14.4	11.3	11.3
Slovenia	2.0	1.1	2.9	2.0	7.2	6.8	6.3
Spain	2.3	2.7	2.8	2.1	20.1	14.5	8.9
Sweden	3.3	1.9	1.3	2.2	8.4	6.9	6.9
Switzerland	2.3	1.8	0.2	2.0	4.5	3.8	3.7
United Kingdom	2.2	1.9	4.3	2.0	7.9	5.7	5.3
United States	3.1	2.2	1.7	2.0	9.6	5.3	4.9
Euro Area	2.0	1.6	1.8	2.0	9.9	8.7	7.3
OECD	2.8	2.1	1.8	2.3	8.3	6.2	5.6

1. For OECD countries, percentage change from the previous period in the private consumption deflator.
2. As a % of mainland GDP.
Source: OECD Economic Outlook 89 database.

StatLink 📊 http://dx.doi.org/10.1787/888932434352

absence of further action.[2] In these circumstances, additional fiscal consolidation is inevitable for many countries and is here assumed to follow a stylised rule.

2. Government debt in this chapter refers to debt as defined by the System of National Accounts. This definition differs from the Maastricht definition used in the Stability and Growth Pact of the European Union. For euro area countries with unsustainable fiscal positions that have asked for assistance from the European Union and the IMF (Greece, Ireland and Portugal) the change in 2010 in government debt has been approximated by the change in government liabilities recorded for the Maastricht definition of general government debt (see Box 1.3 on policy and other assumptions in Chapter 1).

Table 4.3. **Fiscal trends in the baseline assuming a stylised unambitious consolidation path**

As percentage of nominal GDP (unless otherwise specified)

	Underlying fiscal balance	Number of years of consoli-dation[1]	Financial balances[2]			Net financial liabilities[3]			Gross financial liabilities[4]			Long term interest rate[5] (%)		
	2012		2007	2010	2026	2007	2010	2026	2007	2010	2026	2007	2010	2026
Australia	-1.2	1	1.4	-5.9	-0.3	-7	2	9	14	25	32	6.0	5.4	6.1
Austria	-2.4	2	-1.0	-4.6	-1.8	31	44	48	63	79	82	4.3	3.2	5.0
Belgium	-2.6	1	-0.4	-4.2	-3.7	73	81	85	88	101	105	4.3	3.3	6.0
Canada	-2.7	3	1.4	-5.5	-1.4	23	30	38	67	84	90	4.3	3.2	4.6
Czech Republic	-0.7	1	-0.7	-4.7	-0.3	-14	4	7	34	47	48	4.3	3.9	4.5
Denmark	-0.2	0	4.8	-2.9	-0.7	-4	-1	12	34	55	67	4.3	2.9	5.3
Finland	1.0	2	5.2	-2.8	0.7	-73	-64	-43	41	57	79	4.3	3.0	4.4
France	-3.2	5	-2.7	-7.0	-2.7	35	57	65	72	94	103	4.3	3.1	5.6
Germany	-1.6	1	0.3	-3.3	-1.9	42	50	50	65	87	87	4.2	2.7	4.7
Greece	-1.4	3	-6.7	-10.4	-4.4	80	114	117	113	147	146	4.5	9.1	7.9
Hungary	-2.3	0	-5.0	-4.2	-2.6	52	61	57	72	86	84	6.7	7.3	5.0
Iceland	-1.0	3	5.4	-7.8	-2.5	-1	43	41	53	120	118	9.8	5.0	6.6
Ireland	-4.0	7	0.1	-32.4	-4.0	0	59	81	29	102	131	4.3	6.0	6.9
Italy	-1.3	0	-1.5	-4.5	-3.1	87	99	93	113	127	122	4.5	4.0	6.5
Japan[6]	-5.9	18	-2.4	-8.1	-5.0	81	116	162	167	200	248	1.7	1.1	4.9
Korea	1.2	1	4.7	0.0	2.9	-40	-37	-41	28	34	31	5.4	4.8	5.0
Luxembourg	1.8	0	3.7	-1.7	2.1	-44	-40	-37	12	20	20	4.5	3.2	4.5
Netherlands	-1.7	1	0.2	-5.3	-2.0	28	35	44	52	71	81	4.3	3.0	4.5
New Zealand	-5.4	10	4.5	-4.6	-1.7	-13	-5	37	26	39	78	6.3	5.6	4.9
Poland	-4.1	6	-1.9	-7.9	-1.3	17	29	38	52	62	70	5.5	5.8	4.6
Portugal	-0.9	0	-3.2	-9.2	-1.1	50	69	59	75	103	95	4.4	5.4	5.9
Slovak Republic	-2.8	4	-1.8	-7.9	-1.3	7	20	29	33	45	54	4.5	3.9	5.0
Spain	-1.2	0	1.9	-9.2	-2.4	19	40	52	42	66	78	4.3	4.2	4.7
Sweden	1.6	0	3.6	-0.3	2.2	-23	-26	-36	49	49	30	4.2	2.9	4.1
Switzerland	0.9	0	1.7	0.5	1.2	1	1	-13	47	40	25	2.9	1.6	3.0
United Kingdom	-5.7	9	-2.8	-10.3	-3.7	28	56	83	47	82	109	5.0	3.6	5.6
United States[6]	-8.2	20	-2.9	-10.6	-6.0	43	67	122	62	94	148	4.6	3.2	7.2
Euro Area	-1.9		-0.7	-6.0	-2.4	42	58	61	72	93	96	4.3	3.6	5.4
OECD	-5.0		-1.3	-7.6	-3.5	38	58	83	73	98	122	4.8	3.5	6.2

Note: **These fiscal projections are the consequence of applying a stylised fiscal consolidation path and should not be interpreted as a forecast.**

1. The number of years of fiscal consolidation beyond 2012 is determined so as to stabilise the ratio of government debt to GDP, assuming that each year of consolidation amounts to ½ percent of GDP.
2. General government fiscal surplus (+) or deficit (-) as a percentage of GDP.
3. Includes all financial liabilities minus financial assets as defined by the system of national accounts (where data availability permits) and covers the general government sector, which is a consolidation of central, state and local governments and the social security sector.
4. Includes all financial liabilities as defined by the system of national accounts (where data availability permits) and covers the general government sector, which is a consolidation of central, state and local governments and the social security sector. The definition of gross debt differs from the Maastricht definition used to assess EU fiscal positions.
5. Interest rate on 10-year government bonds.
6. Japan and the United States are the only countries for which the required consolidation to stabilise debt is so large in 2012 that it is not achieved in the baseline scenario by 2026 given the assumed pace of consolidation. The number of years of consolidation reported for these countries is an estimate of when debt would be stabilised assuming consolidation continues at the assumed pace.

Source: OECD Economic Outlook 89 database.

StatLink 🔗 http://dx.doi.org/10.1787/888932434371

Beyond 2012 consolidation is assumed to follow a stylised rule

As a stylised assumption for the baseline, against which alternative fiscal policy scenarios are evaluated, future fiscal consolidation sufficient to stabilise the ratio of government debt to GDP before 2026 has been incorporated (Box 4.1) (Table 4.3). This relatively modest pace of consolidation – assumed to be ½ per cent of GDP per annum reduction in the underlying primary balance from 2013 maintained for as long as it takes to stabilise debt – means that in many cases there is a further build-up in the ratio of government debt to GDP before it levels off. This makes the requirements for consolidation more challenging still, since debt build-up requires more servicing and thus a higher primary balance to stabilise debt. Moreover, as discussed below, an important factor tending to further increase consolidation requirements is that the differential between interest rates and growth rises over the projection. On the other hand, the effects on fiscal balances from population ageing and continued upward pressures on health costs are not explicitly included in the projection, but these will also add to consolidation pressures (Box 4.2).

Most OECD countries require some consolidation beyond 2012 to stabilise debt ratios

The scale of consolidation required to stabilise debt-to-GDP ratios both in relation to 2010 and, following the projected consolidation, from 2012 is summarised in Table 4.4. For less than one-third of OECD countries shown in the table, the efforts announced already for the short term are sufficient to require no further consolidation to stabilise debt beyond 2012. This category includes Italy, for which the debt ratio is initially very high, but is already on a declining path, and Spain, for which the required consolidation of 4 percentage points of GDP is projected to have already taken place by 2012.

Box 4.2. **Health-care and pension spending pressures**

On the spending side of general government budgets, additional pressures arise from ageing populations and increases in longevity as well as rising health care costs. On the basis of unchanged policies, and generally conservative assumptions, increases in public spending on health care, long-term care and pensions over the next 15 years are estimated to amount to between 1% and 6% of GDP in the OECD area, largely as a result of ageing (see Table). In the typical OECD country, about two-thirds of that change is coming from health and long-term care expenditures.

Public expenditure on pensions has been growing faster than national income for the past 20 years and is expected to continue to do so over coming decades. Ageing populations are putting pressure on public pensions which are increasing in all but four OECD countries where data are available, amounting to 1% of GDP by 2025 on average. Nevertheless, as a consequence of past pension reforms, which lower benefits and increase the age of retirement, the rate of growth of pension expenditure will be much slower than demographic change alone would have implied. There is, however, scope for further reform. In particular, although half of all OECD countries have, or will be, increasing statutory pension ages, in all but a handful the projected gains in life expectancy over the next four decades are expected to exceed the prospective increase in pension ages (OECD, 2011).

For the average country the increase in public health and long-term care spending over the next 15 years of about 2 percentage points of GDP is about double that for pensions. This is on the basis of a so called "cost-pressure" scenario in which, on top of demographic effects, expenditures are assumed to grow 1% per annum faster than income, which would be broadly consistent with observed trends over the past two decades. This reflects rapidly rising health-care prices and developments of new and costly treatment which put upward pressure on health-care budgets. Spending on health care is already one of the largest public spending items, accounting for more than 15% of general government spending on average in the OECD in 2007 (equal to more than 6% of GDP), up from 12% in 1995. OECD analysis, comparing the efficiency of health systems across different countries, suggests that there is considerable potential for efficiency gains; estimates suggest that public spending reduction could amount to 2% of GDP on average for the OECD area and over 3% of GDP for Greece, Ireland and the United Kingdom (Joumard *et al.*, 2010).

Box 4.2. **Health-care and pension spending pressures** (cont.)

Changes in ageing-related public spending for selected OECD countries

Change 2010-25, as percentage points of GDP

	Health care	Long-term care	Pensions	Total
Austria	1.2	0.4	0.7	2.3
Australia	1.4	0.5	0.3	2.2
Belgium	1.0	0.5	2.7	4.2
Canada	1.5	0.5	1.3	3.3
Czech Republic	1.4	0.6	-0.1	1.8
Denmark	1.2	0.3	1.1	2.6
Finland	1.4	0.6	2.7	4.8
France	1.2	0.3	0.4	1.9
Germany	1.2	0.6	0.8	2.6
Greece	1.3	1.0	0.0	2.3
Hungary	1.2	0.6	-0.4	1.4
Iceland	1.4	0.2	1.8	3.4
Ireland	1.3	1.2	0.9	3.4
Italy	1.3	1.0	0.3	2.6
Japan	1.5	0.9	0.2	2.6
Korea	1.7	0.9	1.1	3.7
Luxembourg	1.1	1.0	3.5	5.7
Mexico	1.4	1.0	1.1	3.4
Netherlands	1.4	0.6	1.9	3.8
New Zealand	1.4	0.5	1.2	3.1
Norway	1.1	0.2	2.4	3.8
Poland	1.4	0.9	-1.1	1.2
Portugal	1.3	0.5	0.7	2.5
Slovak Republic	1.5	0.6	0.3	2.4
Spain	1.3	0.9	1.2	3.4
Sweden	1.1	0.2	-0.2	1.2
Switzerland	1.3	0.3	1.2	2.8
Turkey	1.3	0.3	1.7	3.3
United Kingdom	1.1	0.5	0.5	2.1
United States	1.2	0.3	0.3	1.8
Average	**1.3**	**0.6**	**1.0**	**2.9**

Note: OECD projections for increases in the costs of health and long-term care have been derived assuming unchanged policies and structural trends as of end 2009. The corresponding hypotheses are detailed in OECD (2006) under the heading "cost-pressure scenario". Projections of pension expenditures are taken from OECD (2011), which itself draws on European Commission Sustainability Report (2009) for EU country projections and various national sources for non-EU countries. An exception is Greece where the pension expenditure estimates incorporate OECD estimates of the effects of very recent pension reforms.

Sources: See note above and OECD calculations.

StatLink ᔖᓭ http://dx.doi.org/10.1787/888932434390

Substantial consolidation is needed in a number of countries

Among those countries requiring the most consolidation, the United States and Japan are the only countries in which the stylised unambitious consolidation path does not stabilise debt by 2026. For both countries the required improvement in the underlying primary balance in 2010 is about 10 percentage points of GDP, with little improvement in this situation by 2012. Other countries for which consolidation requirements are large just to stabilise debt before the middle of the next decade include Greece, Ireland, Poland, Portugal, the Slovak Republic and the United Kingdom, which all require consolidation of about 6 to 8½ percentage points of GDP

Table 4.4. **Consolidation requirements to stabilise debt over the long term**

As per cent of potential GDP

	Underlying primary balance in 2010	Underlying primary balance required to stablise debt[1]	Required change in underlying primary balance	Projected change in underlying primary balance in 2010-12	Requirement beyond 2012
	(A)	(B)	(C) = (B) - (A)	(D)	(C) - (D)
Australia	-2.9	1.1	4.0	3.5	0.5
Austria	-1.0	1.1	2.2	1.1	1.0
Belgium	0.5	1.4	0.8	0.3	0.5
Canada	-3.1	-0.3	2.8	1.3	1.5
Czech Republic	-2.4	0.8	3.2	2.7	0.5
Denmark	1.3	0.2	-1.1	-0.5	-0.6
Finland	0.1	1.8	1.7	0.7	1.0
France	-2.5	1.9	4.4	1.9	2.5
Germany	-0.2	1.1	1.3	0.8	0.5
Greece	-1.7	5.0	6.7	5.2	1.5
Hungary	0.7	0.3	-0.4	0.4	-0.8
Iceland	-1.2	4.1	5.3	3.8	1.5
Ireland	-5.3	3.1	8.4	4.9	3.5
Italy	1.4	3.1	1.7	1.9	-0.2
Japan	-5.5	4.3	9.8	1.3	8.5
Korea	-0.4	1.0	1.4	1.0	0.5
Luxembourg	0.8	0.0	-0.8	1.2	-2.0
Netherlands	-2.0	0.5	2.5	2.0	0.5
New Zealand	-2.5	1.0	3.5	-1.6	5.0
Poland	-5.5	1.5	7.0	4.0	3.0
Portugal	-4.9	1.0	5.9	8.4	-2.5
Slovak Republic	-5.7	0.3	6.0	4.0	2.0
Spain	-3.5	0.3	3.8	4.1	-0.2
Sweden	2.0	-0.1	-2.1	0.5	-2.7
Switzerland	1.3	0.1	-1.2	-0.2	-1.1
United Kingdom	-5.7	1.5	7.2	2.8	4.5
United States	-7.0	3.9	10.9	1.2	9.7
Euro Area	-1.1	1.7	2.8	2.0	0.8
OECD	-4.4	2.5	6.9	1.6	5.3

1. Underlying primary balance required in 2026, based on gradual but steady consolidation paths, to stabilise debt-to-GDP ratios in the long-term baseline scenario. Debt stabilisation may take place at undesirably high levels.
Source: OECD calculations.

StatLink 🔗 http://dx.doi.org/10.1787/888932434409

from the 2010 position. Given the large improvement in the underlying primary balance which is projected to occur between 2010 and 2012, no further consolidation beyond 2012 is required for Portugal, and consolidation of only 1½ to 2 additional percentage points of GDP is required for Greece and the Slovak Republic beyond 2012. For the other countries – Ireland, Poland and the United Kingdom – a further consolidation of 3 to 4½ percentage points of GDP beyond 2012 is required to stabilise debt.

Faster consolidation might reduce the required adjustment

These estimates of total consolidation requirements are, however, dependent on the speed at which consolidation is undertaken. In general, faster consolidation implies that debt stabilises at a lower level, causing lower debt service and requiring less overall consolidation. As an illustrative example, Ireland requires seven years of consolidation beyond 2012 to stabilise debt in the baseline scenario in which 0.5% of GDP consolidation per year is assumed, implying total consolidation of 3½ percentage points of GDP. Alternatively, in a variant scenario in which there is more rapid consolidation of 1.5% of GDP per year, only two years of consolidation are needed to stabilise debt, implying total consolidation of only 3 percentage points of GDP. However, this result needs to be qualified, because rapid consolidation runs the risk of having a larger cumulative adverse effect on GDP than gradual consolidation, particularly over a period when any offsetting response from monetary policy may be constrained, and this in turn would reduce any difference in the total consolidation required.

Debt dynamics are influenced by the interest rate-growth differential...

Together with the level of the primary balance, debt dynamics are also strongly influenced by the differential between growth and interest rates; higher nominal GDP growth reduces the debt-to-GDP ratio (simply by virtue of increasing the denominator), while higher interest rates raise it by increasing debt service. During the years prior to the crisis, this differential between interest rates and growth was unusually favourable to restraining the build-up of debt; the differential between long-term interest rates on government bonds and nominal potential growth was negative for many OECD economies, compared to an average positive differential of over 200 basis points over the 1980s and 1990s (Figure 4.1). The pre-crisis differential was low mainly because interest rates across the maturity spectrum were unusually low, partly the result of global factors including lower inflation pressures (Bernanke, 2005). Policy rates were also very low for much of this period.

Figure 4.1. **The differential between long-term interest rates and nominal potential growth for 20 OECD countries**

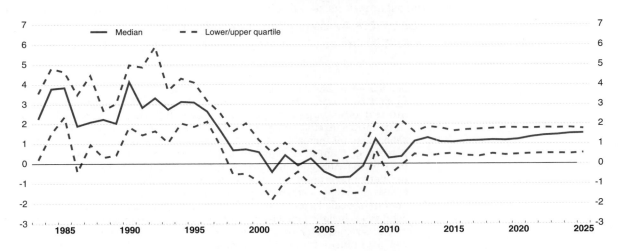

Note: The 20 OECD countries have been chosen on the basis of having consistent time series estimates for potential output and long-term interest rates on 10-year government bonds from 1983. Using nominal potential growth instead of actual GDP growth abstracts from the cycle and so gives a better impression of trend movements in the differential.

Source: OECD calculations.

StatLink ⬛⬛⬛ http://dx.doi.org/10.1787/888932434067

... which is likely to be much less favourable than prior to the crisis

Over the course of the crisis the interest rate-growth differential has been very volatile, particularly when output fell steeply. However, as output gaps close and financial conditions and policy rates begin to normalise and quantitative easing is unwound, the interest rate-growth differential is expected to increase thereby adding to the pressures on debt accumulation. This partly reflects a reversion to historical norms. In addition, the differential might rise because high and rising government debt adds upward pressure on long-term government bond yields. There is a large and controversial empirical literature that examines the impact of public deficits and debt on long-term government bond yields.[3] Drawing on this literature, for the purpose of the current exercise it is assumed that when gross government indebtedness passes a threshold of 75% of GDP then long-term interest rates increase by 4 basis points for every additional percentage point increase in the government debt-to-GDP ratio – an assumption consistent with, for example, the findings of Égert (2010) and Laubach (2009).[4]

Except for Japan, other country-specific influences on long-term interest rates are ignored

For the sake of simplicity, the possible role for a range of country-specific factors, other than debt, in determining government bond yields, is ignored in the stylised projections presented here.[5] The only exception that is made is for Japan, which has seen a substantial increase in indebtedness over the past two decades with little effect so far on interest rates, probably because of the high proportion of debt which is financed domestically, given the large pool of domestic savings and the stable domestic institutional investor base. To take this into account, and again erring on the optimistic side, the responsiveness of interest rates to debt in Japan is assumed to be only one-quarter that for other countries.[6]

Slow fiscal consolidation implies a further increase in debt

OECD general government gross debt is projected to increase by about 32 percentage points of GDP by 2012 relative to pre-crisis levels and, under the assumptions set out above, by about a further 17 percentage points of GDP by 2026. By assumption, the change in net debt levels, as a percentage of GDP, is similar to that for gross debt, although the level of net debt is

3. See Box 4.5 in OECD (2010b) for a selective survey.
4. Égert (2010) finds that the difference between short-term and long-term interest rates appear to be a non-linear function of public debt for the G7 countries (excluding Japan) in recent years. The estimation results indicate a 4 basis point increase in long-term rates relative to short-term rates for each percentage point of GDP in public debt above 76%. Laubach (2009) focuses on the United States and finds that long-term yields increase about 25 basis points per percentage point increase in the projected deficit-to-GDP ratio, and 3 to 4 basis points per percentage point increase in the debt-to-GDP ratio.
5. Country-specific factors that are found in recent studies to influence government bond yields include financial-sector soundness, price competitiveness, fiscal track record, tax-to-GDP ratios, short-term refinancing needs, bond market liquidity as well as a range of other institutional and structural factors (see, for example, Haugh *et al.*, 2009; Hagen *et al.*, 2010; Sgherri and Zoli, 2009; Caceres *et al.*, 2010; and Dötz and Fisher, 2010).
6. The consequence of assuming that interest rates in Japan become as sensitive to the debt-to-GDP ratio as for other OECD countries would be to put debt on an explosive path, implying that gradual consolidation of ½ percentage point of GDP per annum would be inadequate even if sustained over several decades.

lower, particularly for Japan, Canada and the Nordic countries.[7] The magnitude of the area-wide increase in debt is a reflection not least of the magnitude of the increase in some of the largest countries; in particular, the increase in debt by 2026 compared to pre-crisis levels for the United States and Japan is over 80 percentage points of GDP, whereas the median increase across all OECD countries is 21 percentage points of GDP.

Reducing debt levels would require much greater consolidation

The slow pace of consolidation and the high levels of debt reached are in practice unlikely to be sustainable in some countries. The extent of fiscal consolidation needs to be much larger if the aim is to significantly reduce debt-to-GDP ratios, rather than merely stabilise them. Such a reduction would avoid high debt levels and associated high interest rates undermining economic growth and provide a safety margin for public finances to tackle future shocks. Calculations of the cumulative improvement in the primary balance that would be required from 2010 to reduce debt either to pre-crisis (2007) levels or to 60% of GDP by 2026 imply a much greater consolidation effort than to merely stabilise the debt ratio; for the OECD as a whole, on top of the 7 percentage points of GDP to stabilise debt, they imply additional consolidation of 5¼ and 7 percentage points of GDP, respectively (Figure 4.2).

Figure 4.2. **Total consolidation required from 2010 to achieve alternative debt targets**

Total increase in the underlying primary balance, as a percentage of GDP

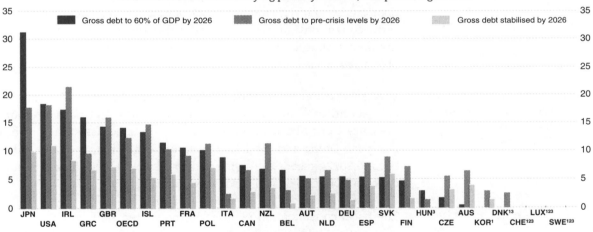

1. No consolidation is needed to achieve the 60% debt-to-GDP ratio by 2026.
2. No consolidation is needed to achieve the pre-crisis debt-to-GDP ratio.
3. No consolidation is needed to stabilise the debt-to-GDP ratio.

Note: The chart shows the total consolidation required to achieve a gross general government debt-to-GDP ratio equal to 60% of GDP and the pre-crisis (2007) ratio by 2026, assuming the projected improvement in the underlying primary balance between 2010-12 is as shown in column (D) of Table 4.4 with an additional constant improvement in the underlying primary balance each year between 2013 and 2026 calculated so as to achieve the debt target in 2026. These consolidation requirements are then compared with that required to stabilise the debt-to-GDP ratio by 2026, as described in the baseline scenario summarised in Tables 4.3 and 4.4. These calculations are mechanical and will not necessarily ensure that the debt ratio is stable once the target is reached. The definition of gross debt used for the purpose of these calculations is as defined in the system of national accounts and differs from the Maastricht definition used to assess EU fiscal positions.

Source: OECD calculations.

 *StatLink* http://dx.doi.org/10.1787/888932434086

7. Net debt is in many respects the superior concept, however, gross debt is more comparable across countries and represents what has to be rolled over and financed through government debt issuance. Moreover, valuation of government assets may in many cases be subject to considerable uncertainty, see Box 1.7 in Chapter 1.

Current consolidation plans

Among countries requiring substantial consolidation...

Most governments recognise the need for further consolidation and have objectives that imply moving back towards more sustainable fiscal positions. Among a group of 12 OECD countries where consolidation needs are greatest (Table 4.5), there are, however, considerable differences in the extent to which such objectives are clearly articulated in terms of credible medium-term fiscal plans.

... US medium-term fiscal plans are unclear...

● In the United States, there are a number of fiscal plans, but political disagreement makes the extent, pace and tools of future consolidation uncertain, as discussed in Chapter 1. Given the scale of the needed consolidation, such plans would need to include the major spending categories, notably entitlement spending and defence outlays, as well as tax increases.

... and those of Japan appear inadequate

● In Japan, the government's medium-term fiscal objectives, announced in June 2010, aimed at halving the primary deficit of the central and local governments by fiscal year (FY) 2015 and eliminating it by FY 2020. This objective is broadly consistant with the stylised baseline scenario to 2020 described above. This in turn implies that, unless there were to be a significant increase in the pace of consolidation thereafter, the debt ratio might not stabilise by 2026. In any case, a detailed medium-term consolidation plan that identifies the revenue and spending measures that will be implemented to achieve these long-term objectives is a priority.

Planned consolidation would put debt on a downward trend in Greece, Ireland and Portugal...

● Very substantial front-loaded consolidation is planned in those euro area countries – Greece, Ireland and Portugal – that have been under pressure from financial markets and requested assistance from the European Union and the IMF. The extent of the planned consolidation beyond 2012 exceeds the stylised rule and would be sufficient to put the debt-to-GDP ratio on a clear downward trajectory.

... and in the United Kingdom

● The fiscal consolidation planned in the United Kingdom is both more substantial and more rapid. If achieved it would put the debt ratio on a downward trend from 2015. The relative speed with which the consolidation is to be achieved implies that the debt ratio would remain below the level projected in the stylised scenario.

There is a need for specific measures to be identified in many countries

● Other EU countries requiring substantial consolidation to stabilise debt – France, Poland, the Slovak Republic and Spain – have targeted a reduction in the overall fiscal deficit to 3% of GDP or below, over the next two to four years. In Belgium and Italy, the deficit targets are closer to balance, but this is warranted to ensure that the debt ratio is put on a clear downward trajectory given the higher initial level of debt.

Table 4.5. **Medium-term fiscal plans in OECD countries requiring substantial consolidation**

	Fiscal balance in 2010	Required consolidation to stabilise the debt ratio[1] by 2026	Required consolidation to achieve pre-crisis debt ratio[2] by 2026	Gross debt in 2010	Summary of latest official medium-term fiscal plans
	Fiscal situation (% of GDP)				
Belgium	-4.2	0.8	3.0	101	Reduce the fiscal deficit to 0.8% of GDP by 2014, with measures not specified yet.
France	-7.0	4.4	9.1	94	Reduce to 5.7% of GDP in 2011 and to 3% by 2013.
Greece	-10.4	6.7	9.5	147	Specific measures, including an ambitious privatisation programme, strict expenditure control, improvements in tax compliance and higher tax rates, to reduce the fiscal deficit to 1% of GDP by 2015 and to maintain a primary surplus of 6%.
Ireland[3]	-32.4	8.4	21.4	102	Front-loaded consolidation based primarily on permanent expenditure cuts (reducing public administration and wages) to improve the underlying primary balance by 7.1% of GDP between 2010 and 2014, and a further 0.8% in 2015.
Italy	-4.5	1.7	2.4	127	Reduce the fiscal deficit to 1.5% of GDP by 2013 and 0.3% in 2014. Measures to achieve this are not yet legislated.
Japan	-8.1	9.8	17.7	200	Halve the central and local government deficit from 6½% GDP by fiscal year 2015, and achieve a gradual reduction in the debt ratio from 2021.
Poland	-7.9	7.0	11.2	62	Reduce the fiscal deficit to 5.6% in 2011 and 2.9% of GDP in 2012.
Portugal	-9.2	5.9	10.2	103	Reduce the fiscal deficit below 3% of GDP by 2013 with slightly more than half of the deficit reduction taking place in 2011. Expenditure restraint accounts for over half of the adjustment.
Slovak Republic	-7.9	6.0	8.9	45	Reduce the fiscal deficit below 3% of GDP by 2013, with most consolidation front-loaded in 2011.
Spain	-9.2	3.8	7.8	66	Front-loaded consolidation with about half of the adjustment in 2011 to reduce the fiscal deficit to 3% of GDP by 2013 and to 2.1% in 2014.
United Kingdom	-10.3	7.2	15.9	82	Front-loaded consolidation with largest adjustment on spending, aiming to achieve a cyclically adjusted current balance (that is, excluding net public investment) by fiscal year 2015/16. Addresses entitlement programmes, notably pensions. On the revenue side, raises value added tax rates.
United States	-10.6	10.9	18.1	94	No specific medium-term plan has yet been adopted. The administration objective is to stabilise the federal debt ratio by 2015.

Note: This table summarises official medium-term fiscal plans for those countries where consolidation requirements are judged to be substantial, based on two criteria, either (a) the required increase in the underlying primary balance to stabilise the debt-to-GDP ratio in 2010 is at least 4% points of GDP or (b) gross government debt as a share of GDP exceeds 90% in 2010.

1. Improvement in the underlying primary balance required to stabilise the debt-to-GDP ratio by 2026, assuming that fiscal consolidation in 2010-12 is as projected in Chapters 1 and 2 and thereafter the primary balance follows the stylised path described in Box 4.1.
2. Improvement in the underlying primary balance required to achieve a debt-to-GDP equal to pre-crisis (2007) level by 2026, assuming that fiscal consolidation in 2010-12 is as projected in Chapters 1 and 2 and thereafter there is a constant improvement in the primary balance each year which is just sufficient to achieve the target.
3. Fiscal balance in 2010 includes the one-off impact of recapitalisation in the banking sector - about 20% of GDP.

Sources: Most recent budget documentation or, for EU countries, the latest Stability Programme.

StatLink http://dx.doi.org/10.1787/888932434428

However, for all of the aforementioned countries, detailed consolidation measures to achieve these targets need to be specified to enhance the credibility of the consolidation plan.

The risks of stagnation

Stagnation is a risk

The weakness of the recovery so far in many OECD countries and the still-large downside risks discussed in Chapter 1 motivate a review of recent stagnation episodes among OECD countries with a view to drawing possible lessons that would help avoid stagnation in the current conjuncture.

Historical experiences of stagnation

Three recent episodes of stagnation are identified among OECD countries

There is no commonly accepted definition of stagnation, but it is here taken to be a period of six or more years during which potential output per capita growth is less than 1% per year.[8] Using potential output eliminates cyclical fluctuations and, although the 1% treshold and the minimum length of spells are arbitrary, the criterion is stringent enough to ensure that the stagnation episodes identified will be both protracted and severe. Applying this criterion to all OECD countries over the period 1995 to 2009 identifies three different episodes: Japan from 1997 to 2002; Portugal from 2003 to 2009; and Italy from 2004 to 2009.

Stagnation followed the 1990s banking crisis in Japan...

The catalyst for the banking crisis in Japan was the collapse of share and land price bubbles at the end of the 1980s, which led to a rise in non-performing loans as construction and real estate companies stopped repaying their loans. Although the problem of bad loans was already obvious by 1992-93 when the non-bank housing loan companies (*jusen*) became insolvent, the authorities chose to adopt a wait-and-see approach because of the large scale of under-capitalisation and insolvency problems in the banking sector. The start of the stagnation episode in 1997 coincides with a sharp escalation of the crisis as a large bank and two large securities firms failed. Share prices of weaker institutions fell, mild bank runs occurred and interbank lending seized up. The resulting credit crunch led to a fall in investment and a cutback in consumption, which in turn fed into weaker growth and further cuts in credit, with the resulting downturn being given further impetus by the Asian crisis in 1997/98.

... which explains the subsequent poor productivity performance...

Large government bailout packages followed to try to recapitalise solvent banks, protect depositors in failed banks and nationalise two major banks. However, recovery of the sector was slow. Competition was distorted by extensive deposit insurance, regulatory forbearance in

---

8. Alternatively, Reddy and Minoiu (2009) define the onset of a stagnation spell as a year in which a country's per capita real income is lower than at any time in the previous two years and higher than at any time in the subsequent four years. The stagnation spells ends in the first year in which that country's real income is at least 1% higher than it was in the previous year and at least 1% lower than in the subsequent year. The authors found that real income stagnation has affected a large number of countries: 103 out of 168 in their sample during the period 1960 to 2001. Recent stagnation spells in OECD countries include Greece (1981-87), Iceland (1990-94), New Zealand (1988-92) and Switzerland (1992-96).

enforcing capital adequacy rules and lending growth requirements to the SME sector. This allowed even the worst banks to continue raising funds and meant lending standards were not rigorously applied (Hoshi and Kashyap, 2004). The poor performance of the banking sector and the poor discrimination between competing demands for funding by firms may explain some of the decline in the growth of total factor productivity over the stagnation period compared to the previous decade (Table 4.6).

Table 4.6. **A decomposition of growth over stagnation episodes**

Contributions to growth in potential output per capita

		Portugal 2003-09	Italy 2004-09	Japan 1997-02
		Period averages in percentage points		
Capital-labour ratio	Stagnation episode	0.4	0.6	1.0
	Previous decade	1.3	0.9	1.2
	Difference	-1.0	-0.3	-0.3
Trend employment rate	Stagnation episode	0.0	0.3	-0.6
	Previous decade	0.5	0.4	-0.5
	Difference	-0.5	-0.1	0.0
Demographic support ratio	Stagnation episode	-0.1	-0.4	-0.5
	Previous decade	0.1	-0.2	0.1
	Difference	-0.2	-0.2	-0.6
Trend productivity	Stagnation episode	0.3	-0.5	0.9
	Previous decade	0.5	0.1	1.7
	Difference	-0.1	-0.7	-0.8
Total	Stagnation episode	0.7	0.0	0.8
	Previous decade	2.4	1.2	2.5
	Difference	-1.8	-1.3	-1.7

Memorandum: macroeconomic and fiscal variables

Average annual change in net public debt as share of GDP (Percentage points)	Stagnation episode	3.4	1.2	7.2
	Previous decade	1.3	-0.8	-0.4
	Difference	2.2	2.0	7.6
Average unemployment rate (Percent)	Stagnation episode	7.6	7.2	4.6
	Previous decade	5.2	10.3	2.6
	Difference	2.4	-3.1	2.0

Source: OECD Economic Outlook 88 database.

StatLink ⟐ *http://dx.doi.org/10.1787/888932434447*

... although other factors may have played a role

The effects of the banking crisis on growth may have been compounded by other factors, including some weak structural policy settings (such as a high degree of state involvement in business operations and burdensome regulations in some sectors) and macroeconomic policy mistakes. The latter include allowing the economy to slip into a period of deflation, from which it has subsequently been very difficult to escape. An additional contributory factor depressing growth over this period is a decline in the ratio of the working-age to total population (the "demographic support ratio" in Table 4.6) as a result of ageing, which subtracted more than ½ per cent per annum from GDP per capita growth over the stagnation episode.

Portugal's stagnation episode was preceded by a credit boom...

Portugal experienced a credit boom prior to its stagnation episode, which began in 2003. During the five years leading up to monetary union, the nominal long-term interest fell by more than 5 percentage points in Portugal (as well as in Italy and Spain), compared with an average of around 3 percentage points for the euro area as a whole. From 1995 to 2000, the current account deficit rose from virtually zero to more than 10% of GDP as households borrowed massively to finance both consumption and housing (household indebtedness reached 103% of disposable income in 2002 from 39% in 1995). This borrowing fuelled domestic demand, and economic growth in Portugal averaged 4% during the five years to 2000, exceeding the euro area average by 1½ percentage points. When it became clear in the early 2000s that the expectations of continued rapid growth and catch-up on which the spending boom had been premised were not going to be realised, both personal and corporate saving went up and consumption and investment fell sharply, triggering a slowdown, which, combined with a tightening of the fiscal stance, morphed into stagnation. The contribution of growth in capital per worker to growth in potential output per capita fell sharply over the stagnation episode: from 1.3 percentage points on average in the decade to 2003 to only 0.4 percentage points per year over the stagnation episode (Table 4.6).

... and weak structural policy settings have made it difficult to end it

Portugal may have had difficulty shaking off this low-growth period due to weak structural policy settings (OECD, 2010a). Relative to its OECD peers, in 2003 Portugal had low educational attainment, low upper-secondary graduation rates, high public ownership and state control of business operations, restrictive barriers to entry in numerous industries, restrictive regulation in some sectors (such as transport, gas and retail), a relatively high cost of labour, an onerous marginal tax wedge on labour for high earners, strict employment protection legislation and low public support to R&D. The resulting rigidities and the absence of reforms have meant losses in competitiveness as new big players like China increasingly competed with traditional Portuguese exports and businesses were not able to move up the quality chain. This lack of competitiveness has contributed to the economy remaining depressed for many years and is reflected in slower growth in the capital-labour ratio after the credit boom ended.

Italy slipped into stagnation as a consequence of structural weakness

There is no obvious trigger event, such as a banking crisis or the ending of a credit boom, coinciding with the start of Italy's period of stagnation from 2004. Rather, the slowdown in potential growth was long in the making and involved a long-term decline in investment and in trend productivity growth that started in the early 1990s (OECD, 2009a). Such trends are most easily ascribed to weak structural policy settings, which may also have made Italy more vulnerable to shocks or to significant economic changes and thus more likely to experience stagnation. Italy compares poorly against other OECD countries in respect of educational attainment, public ownership and state involvement in business operations, administrative burdens on entrepreneurship, legal barriers to entry in industries, barriers to foreign direct investment, the restrictiveness of regulations in certain sectors (road, post, professional services), marginal tax wedges on labour and protection for collective dismissals. Such weaknesses have contributed to a persistent and pronounced trend deterioration in measures of competitiveness based on relative unit labour costs. They have also been reflected in a deterioration in the contribution of total factor productivity growth to potential output per capita growth during the stagnation years as well as weaker growth in the capital-labour ratio.

Current stagnation risks

Lingering banking problems represent an adverse risk to growth

A central assumption underlying the baseline projections described in this chapter is that the financial crisis has had an adverse effect on the level of potential output, but will have no lasting effect on its growth rate. This is in line with the average experience following past banking crises (Cerra and Saxena, 2008; Furceri and Mourougane, 2009; Reinhart and Rogoff, 2009; Abiad *et al.*, 2009). There is, however, considerable heterogeneity among individual country episodes, including some where there have been longer-lasting adverse effects on growth rates as illustrated by the Japanese stagnation episode referred to above. Analysing the consequences of six severe OECD banking crises, Haugh, Ollivaud and Turner (2009) find that only in the case of Japan is there evidence of a reduction in the potential growth rate which they attribute to the protracted nature of the banking problems and the resulting misallocation of capital. In the context of the current crisis, this highlights the importance of resolving outstanding banking problems, especially in Europe where a combination of financial weakness and lack of transparency about exposures by some financial institutions represent a downside risk to the outlook (Box 4.3).

Box 4.3. **Non-performing loans and financial crises: a historical perspective**

Historical experience shows that financial crises (often related to bursting asset bubbles) are usually accompanied by a significant rise in non-performing loans (NPLs). Although the circumstances of the current financial crisis are unique and often country-specific, they share several important parallels with the Nordic (Sweden, Finland and Norway) and the Japanese financial crises of the early 1990s. In both cases, bursting financial asset and property bubbles led to financial turmoil and to recessions. However, the policy responses to the crises were very different:

● In Japan, the authorities injected capital into banks without dealing with the asset side. This approach has often been described as "forbearance and time"; *i.e.* regulators ignore banks' solvency problems and allow them to make up for unrecognised losses through time (Blundell-Wignall and Slovik, 2011). Consequently, the Japanese crisis dragged on unresolved for the entire 1990s, often referred to in Japan as the "lost decade". NPLs reached a peak of 9% of total loans only in 2003 and the banking sector recovered only by 2005.

Box 4.3. **Non-performing loans and financial crises: a historical perspective** (cont.)

● In contrast, in Nordic, governments requested insolvent banks to recognise losses promptly and to transfer bad assets to state-owned asset management companies at book value (OECD, 2009b). Existing shareholders were wiped out and the government took direct ownership of the banks. NPLs in the Nordic countries peaked at around 9% already between 1992 and 1993. The crisis was resolved by 1994, after which business and consumer confidence retuned and the economy recovered.

Thus, the historical experience suggests that a prompt recognition of NPLs and an early resolution of banking sector problems is the preferred policy option.

NPLs in most OECD countries increased rapidly during the recent crisis (Table). It has been particularly apparent in countries that had property bubbles (Ireland, Spain and the United States), in Greece since the start of the sovereign debt crisis, and in Iceland, which faced a massive banking crisis. NPLs increased as well in other major OECD countries that were not directly affected by domestic property or sovereign debt crises (France, Germany, Italy and the United Kingdom), while banking systems outside of the United States and Europe Japan and Canada) appear to have been affected to a much lesser extent.

Bank non-performing loans in selected OECD countries

	2005	2006	2007	2008	2009	2010
			% of total loans			
Australia	0.6	0.6	0.6	1.3	2.0	2.2
Canada	0.5	0.4	0.7	0.8	1.3	1.2
France	3.5	3.0	2.7	2.8	3.6	4.2
Germany	4.1	3.4	2.7	2.9	3.3	…
Greece	6.3	5.4	4.5	5.0	7.7	10.0
Iceland	1.1	0.8	…	…	61.2	60.5
Ireland	0.7	0.7	0.8	2.6	9.0	8.6
Italy	5.3	4.9	4.6	4.9	7.0	7.6
Japan	1.8	1.5	1.4	1.6	1.7	1.8
Portugal	1.5	1.3	1.4	1.8	2.8	3.3
Spain	0.8	0.7	0.9	2.8	4.1	4.3
United Kingdom	1.0	0.9	0.9	1.6	3.5	4.0
United States	0.7	0.8	1.4	3.0	5.4	4.9

Source: IMF Financial Soundness Indicators

StatLink 🔗 http://dx.doi.org/10.1787/888932434466

After a brief period of forbearance in Ireland – also evident by the failure of the 2010 EU-wide stress test to uncover solvency problems – the banking sector had to recognise very large losses in late 2010. The Irish Financial Measures Programme conducted in early 2011 recognised a further capital shortage of € 24 billion on top of the measures already taken last year (Central Bank of Ireland, 2011). Recapitalisation efforts are also underway in Spain, where in early 2011 the Banco de España required the banking sector to increase its capital base by at least a further € 15 billion (Banco de España, 2011).

Rising government debt poses a risk to the growth outlook…

A second source of concern about growth prospects is the build-up of government indebtedness in the aftermath of the crisis. Results from a relatively small literature suggest a negative impact on growth once government debt passes a certain threshold, typically around 75% or 90% of GDP. In Reinhart and Rogoff (2010), the median real per capita GDP growth rate in advanced economies falls by one percentage point when gross public debt reaches 90% of GDP and average growth falls even more. In Kumar and Woo (2010), each 10 percentage point increase in the gross debt-to-GDP ratio is associated with a slowdown in annual real per-capita GDP growth of about 0.15-0.2 percentage points per year for advanced economies, the effect being larger when debt goes above 90% of GDP. Applying these results in a ready reckoner fashion to compute the effect of the recent and projected build-up of government debt can lead to rather alarming conclusions: if applied to the baseline projections described above for the OECD area as whole, the estimates imply a loss in the trend GDP growth rate of ½-¾ percentage point. Moreover, many OECD countries would appear vulnerable with the gross debt-to-GDP ratio in more than half of all OECD countries projected to rise above 75% and in nearly one-third of OECD countries above 90%. The transmission mechanism by which this occurs is likely to involve higher interest rates and a crowding out of private investment and R&D, with adverse consequences for trend productivity growth.

... although causation also runs from slower growth to debt accumulation

At the same time some caution needs to be used in interpreting the findings of this literature, not least because it is difficult to isolate a one-way causal relationship between variables such as trend growth rates and public debt that both move slowly and affect each other. For example, the three episodes of stagnation analysed above, all resulted in a much faster accumulation of government debt (Table 4.6) – but in each case the direction of causation seems to suggest more strongly that stagnation was a cause of the more rapid build-up in government debt rather than a consequence.

Consolidation should minimise adverse effects on growth...

There is unfortunately a trade-off between slowing the accumulation of government debt to stave off its possible negative effect on growth, and the risks that fiscal consolidation itself may create sustained headwinds on the recovery and lead to stagnation. The size of the adverse demand effects will vary by country and depend on the size of the initial fiscal imbalance, the credibility of fiscal consolidation plans, the scope to cut policy interest rates, the fiscal instruments used and the speed of consolidation. Countries face particularly difficult choices regarding the speed of consolidation and the instruments to use, but both provide opportunities to minimise the negative demand effects from consolidation. Fiscal consolidation should be more rapid if there is scope for monetary policy to offset some of the negative demand effects. If the recovery proceeds at the projected pace, the constraints on monetary policy should be less of a concern from 2012 onwards for most countries and the pace of normalisation of interest rates could be then adjusted to partially offset any economic weakness resulting from budget improvements. The contractionary effects of fiscal consolidation could also be partially offset to the extent that credible programmes reduce the risk of sovereign debt defaults, reducing risk premia on government securities which in turn reduce interest rates more generally. Lower long-term interest rates can in turn help boost output in the long-run by raising investment and productivity. These positive expectational effects that work through financial markets are greater the more clear and credible medium-term fiscal plans are regarding the objectives and the instruments that will be used.

... including by a judicious choice of measures

The terms of the growth trade-off between fiscal consolidation and debt accumulation can be further improved by placing more weight on measures that improve long-term fiscal positions but which have relatively limited immediate negative effects on demand. For instance, raising the retirement age can at the same time reduce long-term fiscal pressures and have a positive impact on potential output from higher labour force participation of older people. It may even raise aggregate demand in the short run as people need to save less for shorter retirement periods. Consolidation should also avoid measures, such as reducing public investment or support for R&D, which weaken the supply side and instead target measures which strengthen it. OECD (2010b) has a detailed discussion of the pros and cons of different fiscal consolidation instruments on both the revenue and spending sides.

Higher oil prices may contribute to stagnation but are unlikely to be a main cause

A third factor that may hinder economic growth over the medium term is high and rising oil prices. Sharp rises in oil and commodity prices combined with macroeconomic policy mistakes led to stagflation in the 1970s. By draining away funds that consumers would otherwise spend on other things, high oil prices reduce consumption and demand in the short run (see Chapter 1). But high oil prices can affect the economy's supply side as well. They signify greater intensity in the use of other inputs (labour and capital) which are available only in inelastic or limited elastic supply, implying a fall in productive potential. Previous OECD estimates based on a four-factor Cobb-Douglas production approach (OECD, 2008) suggest that a doubling of real oil prices would reduce the steady-state *level* of output by about 1¾ per cent in the United States and about 1¼ per cent in other (less energy-intensive) OECD economies.[9] Assuming the shock was in the form of a trend increase in the growth rate of real oil prices, so for example real oil prices doubled over the course of a decade, the medium-term effects of rising real oil prices could reduce the growth rate by 0.1-0.2 percentage points per annum. Still, it seems more likely that rising real oil prices would be a contributory factor to stagnation rather than a principal cause, especially if attendant revenues accruing to oil-producing countries are recycled into safe government securities in major OECD countries, so lowering long-term interest rates.

Demographic change will pull down growth across the OECD

Though not a risk of stagnation because it is already included in the baseline scenario presented above, population ageing and accelerating retirements will provide a negative backdrop to growth prospects across

9.   These estimates are likely to exaggerate the long-run costs of higher energy prices because they assume fixed factor shares and do not allow for changes in technology in response to changing relative factor prices.

the OECD. No OECD country is expected to have such a large demographic drag on the growth of potential output per capita as Japan has been experiencing over the past decade, but in nearly all OECD countries a falling demographic support ratio is expected to start pulling per capita growth down within the next ten years. Looking at the 2020-25 period where the demographic effect will be most significant, the drag on annual growth in potential output per capita will be ¼ percentage point per annum or more for several countries. On the other hand, policy changes, especially in public pension provision, and economic necessity may push up the old-age participation rate and increase the average retirement age, offsetting some of the projected impact, which effectively assumes that the maximum age of the working population is fixed at 65.

Structural reforms can help avoid stagnation...

Tentative conclusions from the episodes of stagnation are that weak structural policies make an economy more vulnerable to stagnation and that policy mistakes as seen in Japan can aggravate and prolong it. In the case of Italy it can be argued that this was the underlying cause of stagnation as manifest in the trend deterioration in competitiveness. In the case of Portugal, it may have made it more difficult for the economy to recover from the consequences of a severe shock (in this case the ending of a credit boom). A combination of structural and fiscal reforms thus constitutes the best strategy to reduce the risks that the weak growth observed in many OECD countries in the post-crisis period will turn into stagnation.

... and boost long-term growth, thus facilitating fiscal consolidation

Not only can structural reforms reduce stagnation risks, they can also boost medium- and long-term growth. OECD research has shown that a gradual alignment to OECD best practices of product market regulations, job protection legislation, unemployment benefit systems, activation policies, labour taxes and pension systems could boost aggregate labour productivity levels by several per cent over the next decade in many OECD countries, with large continental European countries such as Italy having the largest benefits to reap from reforms (Bouis and Duval, 2011). By raising potential growth, such reforms would at the same time facilitate fiscal consolidation and help tackle some of the specific legacies of the recession, not least weakness in labour markets that could otherwise turn out to be more persistent and cause higher structural unemployment than assumed in the baseline (see Chapter 1).

Bibliography

Abiad, A., R. Balakrishnan, P. K. Brooks, D. Leigh and I. Tytell (2009), "What's the Damage? Medium-Term Output Dynamics After Banking Crises", *IMF Working Papers*, No. 09/245.

Banco de España (2011), "The Banco de España informs 12 banks they must increase their capital to comply with the Royal Decree-Law", Press Release, March.

Bernanke, B. (2005), "The Global Saving Glut and the US Current Account Deficit", Sandridge Lecture, Virginia Association of Economics, Richmond, Virginia, March.

Bouis, R. and R. Duval (2011), "Raising Potential Growth After the Crisis: A Quantitative Assessment of the Potential Gains from Various Structural Reforms in the OECD Area and Beyond", *OECD Economics Department Working Papers*, No. 835.

Blundell-Wignall, A. and P. Slovik (2011), "A Market Perspective on the European Sovereign Debt and Banking Crisis", *OECD Journal: Financial Market Trends*, Vol. 2010/2.

Burniaux, J., R. Duval and F. Jaumotte (2004), "Coping with Ageing: A Dynamic Approach to Quantify the Impact of Alternative Policy Options on Future Labour Supply in OECD Countries", *OECD Economics Department Working Papers*, No. 371.

Caceres, C., V. Guzzo and M. Segoviano (2010), "Sovereign Spreads: Global Risk Aversion, Contagion or Fundamentals?", *IMF Working Papers*, No. 10/120.

Central Bank of Ireland (2011), *The Financial Measures Programme Report*, March.

Cerra, V. and W. C. Saxena (2008), "Growth Dynamics: The Myth of Economic Recovery", *American Economic Review*, Vol. 98.

Dötz, N. and C. Fischer (2010), "What Can EMU Countries' Sovereign Bond Spreads Tell Us About Market Perceptions of Default Probabilities During the Recent Financial Crisis?", Deutsche Bundesbank, *Discussion Paper, Series 1: Economic Studies No. 11/2010*.

Égert, B. (2010), "Fiscal Policy Reaction to the Cycle in the OECD: Pro- or Counter-Cyclical?", *OECD Economics Department Working Papers*, No. 763.

European Commission (2009), "Sustainability Report 2009", *European Economy*, No 9.

Furceri, D. and A. Mourougane (2009), "How Do Institutions Affect Structural Unemployment in Times of Crises", *OECD Economics Department Working Papers*, No. 730.

Gianella, C., I. Koske, E. Rusticelli and O. Chatal (2008), "What Drives the NAIRU? Evidence from a Panel of OECD Countries", *OECD Economics Department Working Papers*, No. 649.

Guichard, S. and E. Rusticelli (2010), "Assessing the Impact of the Financial Crisis on Structural Unemployment in OECD Countries", *OECD Economics Department Working Papers*, No. 767.

Hagen, J. von, L. Schuknecht and G. Wolswijk (2010), "Government Bond Risk Premiums in the EU Revisited: The Impact of the Financial Crisis", *European Journal of Political Economy*, Vol. 27.

Haugh, D., P. Ollivaud and D. Turner (2009), "What Drives Sovereign Risk Premiums? An Analysis of Recent Evidence from the Euro Area", *OECD Economics Department Working Papers*, No. 718.

Hoshi, T. and A. Kashyap (2004), "Japan's Financial Crisis and Economic Stagnation", *Journal of Economic Perspectives*, Vol. 18.

IMSS (2010), "Informe al Ejecutivo Federal y al Congreso de la Unión sobre la Situación Financiera y los Riesgos del Instituto mexicano del Seguro Social 2009-2010", Instituto Mexicano del Seguo Social, Mexico.

ISSSTE (2009), "Reporte de Actividades Actuariales al 31 de diciembre 2009", Instituto de Seguridad y Servicios para los Trabajadores del Estado.

Joumard, I., C. André and C. Nicq (2010), "Health Care Systems: Efficiency and Institutions", *OECD Economics Department Working Papers*, No. 769.

Kroszner, R. (2002), "Non-Performing Loans, Monetary Policy and Deflation", Economic and Social Institute of the Government of Japan – Workshop on Japanese Monetary Issues, March.

Kumar, M. S. and J. Woo (2010), "Public Debt and Growth", *IMF Working Papers*, No. 10/174.

Laubach, T. (2009), "New Evidence on the Interest Rate Effects of Budget Deficits and Debt", *Journal of the European Economic Association*, Vol. 7.

OECD (2006), "Projecting OECD Health and Long-Term Care Expenditures: What Are the Main Drivers?", *OECD Economics Department Working Papers*, No. 477.

OECD (2008), "Chapter 3 – The Implications of Supply-Side Uncertainties for Economic Policy", *OECD Economic Outlook*, Vol. 2008/1, Paris.

OECD (2009a), "Chapter 3 – Supporting Regulatory Reform", *OECD Economic Surveys: Italy*, Paris.

OECD (2009b), "Dealing with the Financial Crisis: the Swedish and Japanese Precedents", *OECD Economic Outlook*, Vol. 2009/1, Paris.

OECD (2010a), "Chapter 3 – Policy Priorities to Restore Productivity Growth", *OECD Economic Surveys: Portugal*, Paris.

OECD (2010b), "Chapter 4 – Fiscal Consolidation: Requirements, Timing, Instruments and Institutional Arrangements", *OECD Economic Outlook*, Vol. 2010/2, Paris.

OECD (2011), *Pensions at a Glance*, Paris.

Reddy, S. and C. Minoiu (2009), "Real Income Stagnation of Countries 1960-2001", *Journal of Development Studies*, Vol. 45.

Reinhart, C. M. and K. S. Rogoff (2009), *This Time is Different: Eight Centuries of Financial Folly*, Princeton University Press.

Reinhart, C. M. and K. S. Rogoff (2010), "Growth in a Time of Debt", *American Economic Review*, Vol. 100.

OECD Economic Outlook
Volume 2011/1
© OECD 2011

Chapter 5

PERSISTENCE OF HIGH UNEMPLOYMENT: WHAT RISKS? WHAT POLICIES?

Introduction and main findings

The labour market has yet to recover from the crisis

Nearly two years after production began to recover from the worst recession to have hit OECD countries since the 1930s, the labour market situation remains a major preoccupation. At the end of 2010, the average OECD unemployment rate was still close to the historical peak reached during the crisis. In 12 OECD countries it remained two percentage points or more above the pre-crisis level, and even where the rise in joblessness was less severe, the recovery has been generally too weak so far to allow for a significant fall in unemployment (Figure 5.1). A main concern in countries most severely hit is that persistently high levels of unemployment – and a rising share of unemployed workers facing long spells without a job – will eventually result in widespread deterioration of human capital, discouragement and labour market withdrawal. The risk is strongest for youth and less skilled workers who have been disproportionately affected by the rise in unemployment.

Figure 5.1. **The increase in unemployment rates following the crisis**
2007Q3-2010Q4, change in percentage points[1]

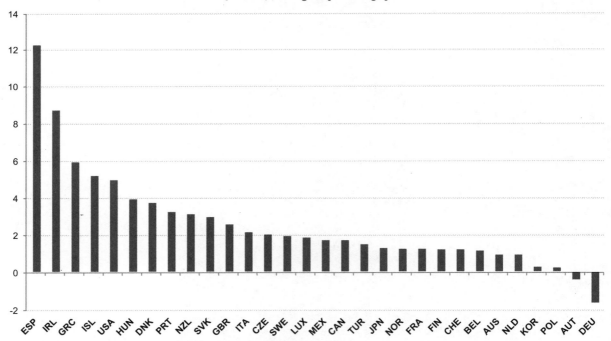

1. Except Ireland, Italy, Mexico, Switzerland and Turkey: 2007Q3-2010Q3.

Source: OECD, *Economic Outlook 88 database.*

StatLink http://dx.doi.org/10.1787/888932401976

The main short-term policy challenge is to accelerate the return to work

The main purpose of this chapter is to assess the role of policies in facilitating a swift return to work so as to minimise these risks. Given the slack remaining in economic activity and labour utilisation, together with still-anchored inflation expectations, aggregate demand policies have a role to play in supporting the economic recovery and stimulate jobs. Indeed, monetary policy remains strongly expansionary in most OECD countries whereas unsustainable public debt path in several of them has necessitated a turn towards fiscal consolidation. Recommendations in the area of macro policies are discussed at length in Chapter 1. This chapter focuses on the role of structural policies even if the budgetary implications of specific options are taken into account in the discussion regarding the appropriate policy mix.

The issues vary across countries

The risk of persistently high unemployment rates is less of a concern in countries where the fall in GDP triggered by the financial crisis was largely absorbed by labour hoarding or some form of time sharing among workers (*e.g.* Austria, Belgium, Finland, Germany, Japan, Korea, Luxembourg and the Netherlands). The ability of these countries to cushion the employment impact of the crisis may offer lessons that could help improve labour market resilience to future shocks. Concerns that average hours worked and productivity remain below pre-crisis levels well after the recovery are not addressed in this chapter and concerns that labour hoarding and time-sharing arrangements hamper the reallocation of resources across businesses and sectors (if maintained for too long) are also not extensively addressed, though the role of time-sharing policies is discussed.

The main risks and policy options are examined

The chapter briefly reviews how OECD labour markets have evolved during the recession and the early phase of the recovery, looks at how vulnerable countries are to risks of strong unemployment persistence and labour force withdrawal and examines policy settings that can facilitate the return to work. The main findings as regards the risks and the policy implications can be summarised as follows:

Some countries are more exposed to risks of unemployment persistence

● Countries with high unemployment levels and a high share of long-term unemployment face a higher risk of unemployment persistence during the recovery:

❖ Before the crisis, relatively weak flows into and out of unemployment as well as high long-term unemployment continued to be observed in large continental EU countries, while pre-crisis turnover was stronger and long-term unemployment lower in North America, Australia and New Zealand.

❖ However, a striking feature of the current situation is an unusually high share of long-term unemployment in the United States, occurring against the backdrop of a sharp rise in unemployment and a trend decline in outflows from unemployment. While the US outflow rate remains significantly higher than in continental EU countries, and although the US unemployment rate has begun to decline, such developments raise concerns about future persistence of unemployment.

Labour force withdrawal has generally been limited overall

- At this stage there has been little evidence of widespread labour force withdrawals, but protracted slack in labour utilisation raises the risk that unemployed workers drift out of the labour force. Past evidence suggests that the peak effect of downturns on labour force participation could display a lag of up to 3 or 4 years.

Boosting labour demand remains a short-term priority in some countries

- Where job prospects remain bleak, the policy focus in the short term should be to continue to boost labour demand so as to increase unemployment outflows. Among the policies that can stimulate labour demand, measures to reduce labour costs through temporary and targeted tax wedge reductions are likely to be most effective. Indeed, such measures have already been put in place in several countries, though not always in a cost-efficient way.

Job-search assistance could be strengthened and access to training expanded

- In parallel to boosting labour demand, and to offset the risks that unemployed workers see their skills eroding to the point of losing attachment to the labour market (through so-called unemployment duration dependence or hysteresis effects), more could be done to improve the matching of workers and jobs, including through measures to strengthen public employment services and training programmes. As the risk of missing a job opportunity by suspending job search to enrol in training is lower in periods of labour market slack, there is a case for strengthening vocational training given the high rate of unemployment among youth and low skilled. Such training could also provide a surrogate test for participants' willingness to work. However, in countries where the financial space for manoeuvre is limited by severe budget constraints (*e.g.* Greece, Ireland, Portugal and Spain), stepping up training programmes may be difficult, and this could also be the case in countries that do not have the sufficient training infrastructure in place (*e.g.* the United States).

Some extensions of unemployment insurance should be permanent while others can lapse

- In the United States, Canada and other countries where unemployment benefit duration has been extended, the case can be made for maintaining the extension until labour market prospects have sufficiently improved to prevent individuals from falling into persistent poverty. Continued extension may also help avoid that the unemployed enter other benefit systems (such as disability pensions) from which exit may be less likely later on. In the meantime, benefits should be made conditional on recipients satisfying job-search requirements and, where benefits are relatively high, they could be made declining with duration. On the other hand, where the scope of unemployment insurance has been extended to workers previously not covered, as for instance in Finland, Japan and the Slovak Republic, the extensions should be made permanent both for social reasons and to maintain the labour force attachments of groups newly covered, provided again that job-search requirement can be enforced on these new beneficiaries.

Short-time working schemes can be useful but subsidies should be phased out

- A large number of countries have encouraged short-time working during the crisis. The significant role played by these programmes in cushioning the crisis – especially in Belgium, Finland, Germany, Japan and Luxembourg – suggests that having such options in place and being able to activate them in severe downturns, can be useful. Such short-time working arrangements should include, as for instance in Germany and the Netherlands, built-in incentives for workers and firms to withdraw from them once they have outlived their conjunctural purpose. And, insofar as the schemes do not have sufficient auto-corrective incentives, a timeframe should be set for the phasing-out of public subsidies so as to avoid negative long-term effects on productivity and labour utilisation.

The gap in job protection between permanent and temporary contracts should be reduced

- In some countries, the impact of the crisis on unemployment has also been cushioned by restrictions on the dismissals of workers on permanent contracts. However, given that tight employment protection provisions – whose costs are often high and unpredictable for employers – reduce outflows from unemployment, there is now a case for streamlining such provisions, especially where substantial risks of unemployment persistence prevail. In particular, "two-tier" systems entailing large differences in protection across different types of contracts – which have contributed to labour market duality in countries like France, Italy and Spain – may have generated unemployment turnover for certain categories of workers (*e.g.* youth and women) with no permanent effects on the unemployment rate. Narrowing, or eliminating, differences in contract provisions across workers, for instance so that protection rises with seniority, could boost hiring during the recovery while at the same time improving labour market resilience to future shocks and lowering the unemployment rate in the longer term.

Labour market outcomes and the concerns moving forward

Labour markets adjusted differently across countries...

The crisis has had different impacts on labour market outcomes across countries. To some extent this reflected differences in the degree of exposure to specific features of the crisis, such as the aftermath of financial and housing market bubbles and the associated contractions in the construction and finance industries. However, the variations in outcomes also reflected differences in policy settings, resulting from both policies in place before the crisis and measures implemented in response to the crisis (see Box 5.1). These differences notwithstanding, considering the magnitude of the recession, the labour market fallout from the crisis has been relatively benign in the majority of countries, and this is due in large measure to past reforms.

Box 5.1. **Pre-crisis reforms and the policy response to the crisis**

In most countries, the crisis took place in a context of low or falling trend unemployment rates, especially relative to the levels prevailing in the mid-1990s. To some extent, this broad improvement in unemployment resulted from labour market reforms implemented in the late 1990s and early 2000s. A number of areas where governments have been particularly active during that period include:[1]

- In labour taxation, many countries have reduced the non-wage cost of labour, in particular for low-wage earners, mainly through a reduction in social security contributions.

- In income support for the unemployed, only a few countries have significantly reduced the overall level or duration of unemployment benefits. By contrast, a vast majority of them have tightened access to the system through more stringent eligibility or work availability conditions. In many countries, measures have been taken to reduce the disincentives to take up work, for instance by allowing the possibility to temporarily combine benefits and earnings and by lowering the benefit withdrawal rates.

- A majority of countries have also strengthened their "activation" programmes, in particular through increased job-search monitoring and individual action plans and profiling. In most cases this has been done without raising average active labour market policy expenditures per person unemployed.

- Several countries have eased employment protection legislation, but reform in this area since the early 1990s has generally focused on the conditions of temporary contracts or taken the form of new types of contracts with different characteristics and restrictions. In a few cases, this has made the labour market more adaptable to macroeconomic conditions, but these reforms have also added to segmentation between permanent employees enjoying stronger job protection, and a growing share of temporary workers bearing the brunt of workforce adjustment (OECD, 2006; Saint-Paul, 1996; Boeri, 2010).

- Reform activity has been more limited in the area of collective bargaining and wage setting, at least as far as legislative changes are concerned. While there were virtually no changes in provisions to extend administratively bargaining outcomes to non-covered parties, some countries have implemented reforms aimed at changing workers' representation mechanisms and allow firms to opt out of collective agreements in certain cases. As a result of this and, especially, of an increasingly competitive global and domestic environment, some movement towards decentralisation of wage bargaining has taken place in many countries. Indeed, the period of wage moderation observed in Germany during the 2000s is to some extent an illustration of the greater flexibility firms have had in adjusting collective wage agreements so as to better reflect local conditions.

Given the unusual severity of the crisis, a number of specific actions were taken to limit its impact. Hence, in addition to macroeconomic measures, all governments introduced different labour market measures aiming at three broad objectives: smooth the employment impact of the output shock (perceived as temporary) by subsidising jobs, encouraging the adjustment to occur in hours worked, and stimulating labour demand; facilitate the re-employment of unemployed workers (or those at strong risk of losing their job) *via* training and other re-deployment measures; and cushion the impact of the shock on the income of the unemployed through extended income-support measures:[2]

- Among the measures to limit the effect of the crisis on employment, the most widely used was the subsidisation of short-time working which took place in two-thirds of OECD countries. In several cases pre-existing schemes just expanded, while in others new schemes were established. In some countries these measures complemented spontaneous private-sector adjustment in average hours worked and their implementation was facilitated by collective bargaining arrangements (*e.g.* Germany). Overall, this led to an increase in the average stock of employees participating in such schemes by more than 2% of all employees in 5 countries (Belgium, Germany, Italy, Japan and Luxembourg). Other measures such as public-sector job creation or private-sector job subsidies and reductions in non-wage labour costs were implemented in at least half of OECD countries.

Box 5.1. **Pre-crisis reforms and the policy response to the crisis** *(cont.)*

● In order to facilitate re-employment and re-deployment, more than two-thirds of OECD countries raised resources for job-search assistance and training programmes. One-third of OECD countries provided additional resources to apprenticeship schemes.

● Measures to improve the access, level or duration of unemployment benefits, to raise other payments or in-kind support for the unemployed and to provide fiscal relief for low earners were implemented in half of OECD countries.

For the most part, governments avoided measures such as direct or indirect job support targeted to specific sectors that could have hampered a necessary restructuring and created international trade tensions (with the main exception of car manufacturing which benefited from demand support). But some of the policy interventions may nevertheless unduly contribute to delay adjustments in the workforce if maintained for too long. Indeed, many of the measures introduced in 2009 were meant to be temporary and a few countries have partially or fully withdrawn some of them, notably the reductions in non-wage labour costs and the subsidies for short-time work. However, the vast majority of countries kept the measures in place in 2010 and in some new ones were brought in, such as for instance a payroll tax cut implemented for 2011 in the United States.

1. A comprehensive review of labour market reforms over that period can be found in Chapter 3 of OECD (2006).
2. See OECD (2009, 2010a) for a review of measures taken in response to the crisis.

How have labour markets adjusted to the decline in output?

... in terms of productivity, average hours worked and employment

The profiles of hours worked, employment and labour productivity since the start of the crisis point to large cross-country differences in the way labour markets responded to the decline in output. In the majority of countries, total hours worked declined less than GDP as the output shock was partly absorbed through labour hoarding (Figure 5.2). In a few countries (Iceland, Spain and the United States), however, hourly productivity gains were substantial as a consequence of a decline in total hours.[1] These gains reflect to some extent composition effects since job losses were largely concentrated in low-productivity sectors such as construction (OECD, 2009). At the same time, those countries that recorded the largest decline in total hours have generally done so primarily *via* lower head-count employment (Denmark, Ireland, Iceland, Spain and the United States) (Figure 5.3). At the other end of the spectrum, the reduction in total hours has been almost entirely absorbed through adjustments in average hours per worker in Austria, Belgium, Germany, Korea and Luxembourg. A substantial contribution of average hours worked to total labour input adjustment has been a recurrent feature of past recessions in several countries (including Belgium and Germany), but the widespread use of short-time work arrangements on a scale as large as that observed during the recent crisis was unprecedented.

1. In both Spain and the United States, productivity growth over the period exceeded trend estimates. Even though hourly productivity gains have been frequently observed during previous recessions in the United States the extent of the increase in 2008-09 has been surprisingly strong (Wilson, 2010).

Figure 5.2. **GDP has generally fallen by more than hours worked during the crisis**

% decline in GDP and total hours worked from peak to trough[1]

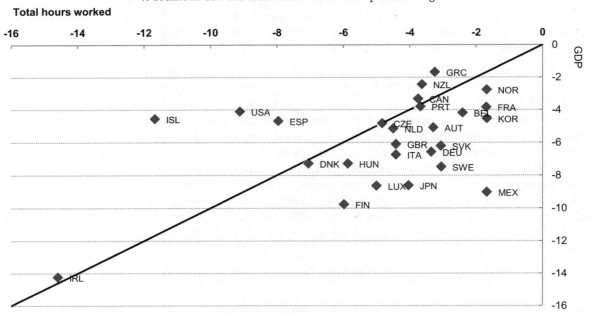

1. The vertical axis shows the percentage decline in the GDP. In the case of countries where GDP has continued to decline, the trough corresponds to the latest data point available.

Source: OECD, *Economic Outlook 88 database.*

StatLink 🔗 http://dx.doi.org/10.1787/888932401995

Figure 5.3. **The decline in total hours worked has been absorbed differently across countries**

Decomposition of the % change in total hours from peak to trough

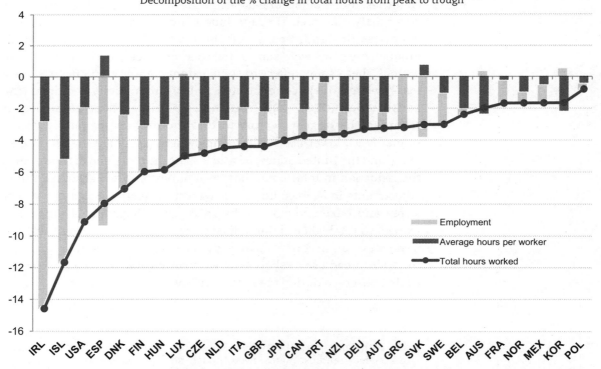

Source: OECD (2011), *Quarterly Labour Market Indicators Database*; Directorate for Employment, Labour and Social Affairs; May, unpublished.

StatLink 🔗 http://dx.doi.org/10.1787/888932402014

In many countries,
unemployment persistence
remains the most pressing
near-term concern...

Differences across countries in the size and nature of the labour market fallout from the crisis imply different policy challenges moving forward. Concerns about unemployment persistence are particularly pronounced in countries that have experienced large increases in long-term unemployment. The longer individuals remain unemployed, the more difficult it becomes for them to find a job and the less they may try, a phenomenon referred to as unemployment duration dependence or hysteresis.[2] In at least ten countries (*e.g.* Canada, Denmark, Hungary, Ireland, New Zealand, Norway, Portugal, Spain, the United Kingdom and the United States) the share of long-term unemployment has risen significantly during the crisis, pointing to a significant risk of hysteresis (Figure 5.4).

... reflecting in some cases
persisting demand gaps

One reason for concern is that even though a recovery has been underway for some time in the majority of OECD countries, growth in aggregate demand has generally been too weak to begin making serious inroads into unemployment. Indeed, the substantial slack in labour productivity and average hours worked that has built up in the wake of the crisis has provided ample room in the majority of countries for accommodating GDP growth through more intense use of currently employed workers. Furthermore, even though GDP is generally expected to grow in 2011 and 2012 faster than productivity and the labour force combined, in several cases the slack may be absorbed too slowly to allow for a significant decline in unemployment over this horizon. Only when growth garners sufficient momentum, unemployment will begin to recede more rapidly and eventually returns to its longer-term or structural level.[3]

Wages have adjusted to
help stem employment
losses

Another factor that could influence the pace of decline in unemployment is the evolution of labour costs. In most countries, wages decelerated sharply, with the adjustment taking place one or two quarters after the recession began. Arguably, that wages reacted moderately to the severity of the output contraction was helpful to limit the risks of deflation at the trough of the recession, as this would have further complicated the task of demand policies. Still, the slowdown in wages in late 2009 and early 2010, combined with a rebound in productivity, was sufficient to bring about a deceleration in unit labour costs (and even a decline in several countries) which helped stem employment losses (Figure 5.5). In addition, measures were taken in several countries to reduce the non-wage component of labour costs, notably through targeted cuts in payroll taxes.

---

2. This phenomenon may be due to a variety of more or less related factors such as the erosion of skills (Pissarides, 1992), discrimination by employers (Lockwood, 1991) and the ranking of job applicants by employers on the basis of their time spent in unemployment (Blanchard and Diamond, 1994). Another factor potentially reinforcing these effects is the reluctance of unemployed workers to adjust downward their reservation wage even as their spells lengthen, which to some extent can reflect a rise in social tolerance *vis-à-vis* the status of long-term unemployment (Lindbeck, 1995).

3. Employment usually lags activity during recoveries as businesses tend to delay investment and hiring decisions until growth prospects look sufficiently robust and labour hoarding has been eliminated.

Figure 5.4. **The share of long-term unemployment (LTU) has risen sharply in some countries**

Share of people unemployed for more than 12 months in total unemployment[1]

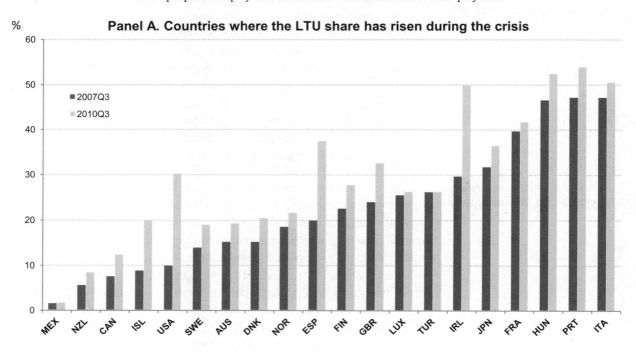

Panel A. Countries where the LTU share has risen during the crisis

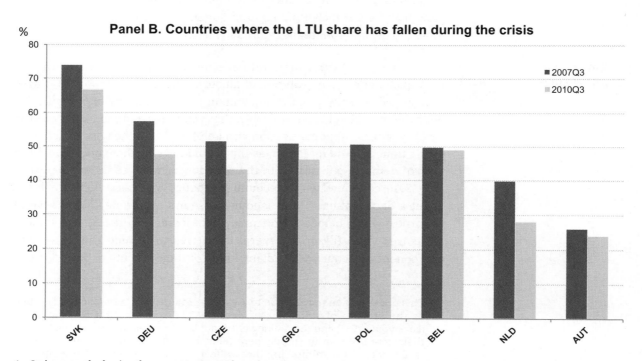

Panel B. Countries where the LTU share has fallen during the crisis

1. Series smoothed using three-quarter centred moving average.

Source: OECD (2011).

StatLink http://dx.doi.org/10.1787/888932402033

Figure 5.5. **Nominal wages and unit labour costs have decelerated**

Annualised average percentage changes before and after the crisis

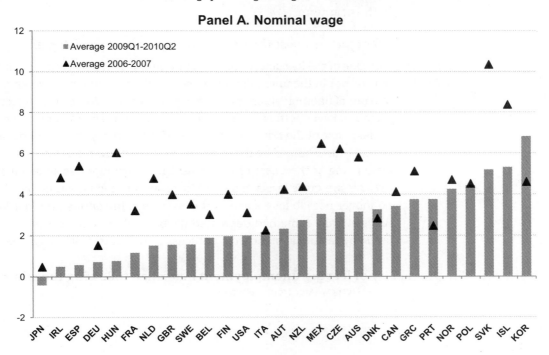

Panel A. Nominal wage

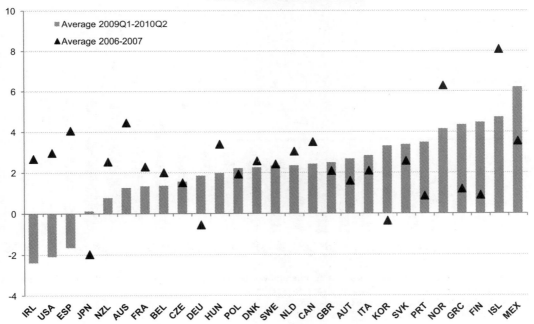

Panel B. Unit labour cost

Source: OECD, *Economic Outlook 88 database*.

StatLink http://dx.doi.org/10.1787/888932402052

It remains unclear whether or not the resulting overall adjustment in labour costs has been sufficient to support sustained employment growth in the near term.

What factors boost the risks of unemployment persistence?

The persistence of unemployment is strongly linked to the outflow rate...

One of the key determinants of unemployment persistence is the degree of turnover in the unemployment pool, *i.e.* the pace at which workers flow in and out of unemployment over a given time period. While both higher inflow rates and lower outflow rates contributed to the rise in unemployment in the initial phase of the crisis, at this stage of the recovery the risk of persistence is largely determined by the evolution of the outflow rate. One reason is that after rising at the onset of the crisis, the inflow rate has since fallen back towards pre-crisis levels in a majority of countries (suggesting that there are no longer net job losses across the economy). In contrast, the outflow rate has generally remained depressed (Figure 5.6), in some cases at very low levels by historical standards, not least in the United States (see Box 5.2).[4]

Figure 5.6. **The probability of leaving unemployment has fallen following the crisis**

Outflow rates from unemployment[1]

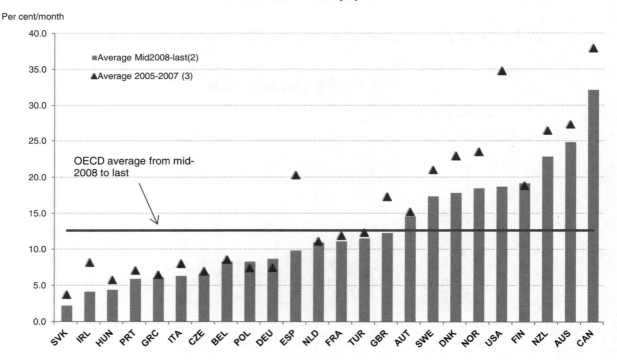

1. Outflow rates are defined as the probabilities that an unemployed worker exits unemployment within the following month. The measured outflow rate includes both outflows to job and to inactivity.
2. Average from mid-2008 to the latest available observation.
3. Except Ireland and Turkey 2006-2007.

Source: OECD calculations based on Eurostat, New Cronos; US Current Population Survey; Australian Bureau of Statistics; Statistics Canada; Labour Force Survey.

StatLink ⟨⟩ http://dx.doi.org/10.1787/888932402071

4. The measured outflow rates shown in Figure 5.6 do not distinguish between exits into jobs and withdrawals from the labour force.

Box 5.2. **The trend decline in the US unemployment outflow rate**

In the United States, the outflow rate from unemployment – defined as the probability that a worker exits unemployment within the following month – has fallen during the recent crisis to levels well below those observed during the previous major recession episodes even though it remains, at around 15%, above the level that has been the norm in many European countries. Since inflows into unemployment have also been falling in parallel, the trend decline in outflow rates had not led to an increase in the aggregate unemployment rate. Nevertheless, the fact that the US outflow rate had already been fluctuating around a clear downward trend over the past three decades suggests that an eventual return to pre-crisis levels may be hampered by structural forces working in the opposite direction.

A recent analysis of the long-term increase in the average duration of unemployment spells in the United States found that shifts in the age structure of the pool of the unemployed, as well as an increase in the unemployment duration spells of women both played major roles, while other factors such as changes in the industrial structure have had little impact (Aaronson *et al.*, 2010). The demographic factor largely reflects a falling share of youth (who tend to have shorter unemployment spells) in the unemployment pool. The rise in the share of long-term unemployment among women need not be worrying insofar as it results from a stronger participation to the labour force and that it has coincided with a trend decline in their overall unemployment rate (Abraham and Shimmer, 2002). However, these factors together only explain about half of the particularly large increase in average duration in the recent episode. The unexplained part could raise policy concerns.

Long-term evolution of the outflow rate in the United States[1]

1. Outflow rates are defined as the probabilities that an unemployed worker exits unemployment within the following month.
Source: OECD calculations based on US Current Population Survey.

StatLink http://dx.doi.org/10.1787/888932402204

This has resulted in a steady lengthening of average unemployment duration. Workers exit unemployment either for a job, or because they withdraw from the labour force, which is a far less desirable outcome.

... which in turn depends on job creation and matching efficiency

Aside from the strength of aggregate demand and the responsiveness of wages to economic conditions, which affect the pace of job creation, one of the key structural determinants of outflows into jobs is the efficiency with which jobseekers (be they unemployed or already in a job) are matched with job openings (matching efficiency). Factors having an influence on matching efficiency include the degree of mismatch across regions or industrial sectors between job openings and workers looking for a job, as well as the overall intensity and effectiveness of the individual's job search, which may diminish as the average unemployment spell lengthens.

Has the matching of jobs and unemployed workers deteriorated?

Clear evidence on the efficiency of the matching process is hard to come by...

The efficiency of matching between job openings and unemployed workers is not directly observable, which makes it hard to say whether it has deteriorated as a result of the crisis. An oft-used gauge of matching efficiency is the relationship between open vacancies and unemployment (the so-called Beveridge curve) but it does not provide clear evidence concerning a shift during the crisis.[5]

... though possible sources of declines include occupational or geographical mismatch

One possible source of a decline in matching efficiency would be an increase in the mismatch between vacancies and jobseekers across types of occupations and geographical areas. This is a recurrent concern during cyclical downturns as they usually hit specific industries and regions harder than others. For instance, while the shock severely depressed manufacturing production across OECD countries, some have in addition been exposed to a large and potentially far more protracted collapse in specific non-manufacturing industries.

Manufacturing has broadly rebounded but not construction

Indeed, in a number of countries the losses in specific sectors have been particularly strong, even taking into account the historical business-cycle sensitivity of these sectors. As shown in Table 5.1 (bolded figures), for a large number of countries this has been the case in construction, which accounts on average for 7% of total employment in OECD area. Important losses have also been recorded for many countries in wholesale and retail trade and financial intermediation. Manufacturing has since largely rebounded but construction has remained depressed in most countries where the sector enjoyed a boom before the crisis. And countries where the latter sector has been hardest hit (*e.g.* Denmark, Ireland, Spain, the United Kingdom, the United States and, to a lesser extent, Portugal) are also the ones where the incidence of long-term

5. For instance, a recent analysis looking beyond the Beveridge curve has found that the outflow rate in the United States is significantly lower than what would be expected even taking into account the low availability of jobs relative to the number of unemployed, a development which could be interpreted as a decline in matching efficiency (Elsby *et al.*, 2010). However, such an interpretation is premature considering that it is not unusual for a pick-up in job openings following a period of steady decline to be fully reflected in lower unemployment only a few quarters later (Yellen, 2010).

Table 5.1. **Sectoral employment changes**

Employment growth between average in 2008 and 2010Q2

	Manufacturing	Construction	Wholesale and retail trade	Financial intermediation	Other services[1]	Total
Austria	-3.9	-7.3	-4.9	5.6	1.3	-2.4
Belgium	-10.1	0.9	4.8	-6.0	-1.7	-2.4
Canada	-10.2	3.9	2.4	6.2	3.0	2.3
Czech Republic	-12.0	-0.4	-4.1	-1.8	2.2	-5.0
Denmark	-12.7	-24.9	-7.9	3.7	0.5	-7.8
Finland	-11.2	-7.5	-0.5	-0.5	1.3	-3.1
France	-8.4	0.9	1.3	3.6	-0.6	-0.8
Germany	-5.4	-1.6	0.2	-0.7	2.7	-1.1
Greece	-10.4	-16.5	-3.3	-2.7	-3.3	-4.6
Hungary	-8.1	-11.0	-7.0	-5.6	1.1	-4.5
Ireland	-16.8	-47.3	-11.7	0.6	-7.4	-16.9
Italy	-8.6	-0.6	-4.9	-2.9	0.8	-3.1
Netherlands	-9.6	-11.7	-5.7	-4.1	-6.2	-7.0
Norway	-8.3	-4.1	-2.6	0.6	1.9	-1.3
Poland	-8.7	5.3	1.5	13.3	10.7	-0.3
Portugal	-5.8	-13.9	-3.2	-11.5	-2.3	-6.0
Slovak Republic	-17.3	-1.4	4.4	-12.2	-1.6	-7.5
Spain	-19.4	-30.7	-10.3	-5.7	-5.6	-13.3
Sweden	-11.5	0.8	-0.4	6.0	1.5	-1.4
United Kingdom	-14.2	-16.1	-6.7	-8.5	3.0	-5.6
United States	-10.2	-13.4	-4.2	-8.4	-3.5	-6.0

Note: The numbers in bold correspond to cases where the decline in employment exceeds what would be the expected drop based on average business-cycle sensitivity of employment in that sector, as reported in Figure 1.4, Chapter 1 of OECD Employment Outlook 2010.
1. Hotels and restaurants, Transport & communication, Real estate and business services.
Source: Eurostat, US Bureau of Labor Statistics and Statistics Canada.

StatLink ⟨⟩ http://dx.doi.org/10.1787/888932402128

unemployment has risen most. Given the large share of low-skilled workers typically employed in this sector, matching problems could be exacerbated by this sectoral concentration of layoffs.[6]

There are no clear indications of geographical mismatch

As regards geographical mismatch, it is difficult to find strong evidence on the basis of indicators of regional unemployment dispersion, even in countries that have been particularly hard hit (*e.g.* Spain, the United Kingdom and the United States). While there are indications of a widening dispersion during the crisis, the rise in dispersion vanishes when the parallel increase in overall unemployment is taken into account (Figure 5.7), suggesting that the decline in the outflow rate bears little relationship with regional differences in unemployment. There have been concerns also that labour mobility may have decreased during the crisis. This could be the case if, for instance, geographical mobility is hampered

6. The percentage of low-skilled workers in construction is 1½ times larger than in the overall economy in the European Union and twice as large in the United States.

Figure 5.7. **Measures of dispersion of regional unemployment rates show no clear indication of mismatch**

Source: Spain, Instituto Nacional de Estadistica; United Kingdom, Office for National Statistics; and US Bureau of Labor Statistics.

StatLink ⌨ http://dx.doi.org/10.1787/888932402090

by housing price developments that lead to negative home equity positions (Andrews *et al.*, 2011). However, recent evidence from the United States indicates, if anything, that homeowners with negative home equity positions have been moving slightly more than other homeowners (Schulhofer-Wohl, 2010).[7]

Unemployment duration dependence could bear on outflow rates

Matching efficiency may also deteriorate if long-term unemployment becomes a trap for the individual. In this regard, a key concern is that as time goes by and unemployment spells lengthen, duration dependence – that the probability of leaving unemployment declines as an unemployment spell becomes longer – may take hold. Empirical evidence on duration dependence is mixed. For instance, one study using aggregate unemployment duration data found evidence of duration dependence in Japan, English-speaking and Nordic countries, but not in Continental European countries (Elsby *et al.*, 2008).[8] Empirical studies based on micro data have also found mixed evidence of pure duration dependence or hysteresis effects.[9] However, more recent estimates based on individual level data point to more conclusive evidence of duration dependence effects in a sample covering a large number of OECD countries. And, these effects appear to be exacerbated by the duration of unemployment benefits (see Box 5.3 and related discussion in next section).

Could persistent unemployment lead to falling participation?

Strong persistence entails risks for labour force participation

Unemployment persistence and high long-term unemployment could in turn lead to labour force withdrawal, at least for some categories of workers, due to loss of human capital and discouragement effects. There is thus a risk that a pick-up in unemployment outflow occurs *via* lower participation rather than higher employment.

7. This result may be specific to the United States. First, the benefit of defaulting in the case of negative home equity position is generally higher than in most other countries, due to specific mortgage bankruptcy rules. Second, the incidence of strongly (as opposed to mildly) negative home equity position has been particularly high in the United States, which further increases the incentives to default.

8. One limitation of the methodology and data used in Elsby *et al.* (2008) is that no control is made for the influence of the composition of the unemployment pool on observed duration dependence. Individuals with different characteristics such as age, gender or education level will generally enter an unemployment spell with different probabilities of exit which is independent from the spell duration. Therefore, it is possible that findings of duration dependence effects reflect a growing share of workers with intrinsically low exit rates in the unemployment pool as average duration increases, rather than a gradual decline over time in the probability of exit faced by individuals due to skill erosion or other hysteresis effects.

9. See in particular Bover *et al.* (2002) and Garcia-Perez *et al.* (2010) in the case of Spain. Earlier studies reviewed in Machin and Manning (1999) generally found little evidence of positive duration dependence in the case of several European countries.

Box 5.3. **Duration dependence and the risk of unemployment hysteresis**

Hysteresis refers to a situation where unemployment shows little tendency to revert to its previous level following an increase, regardless of the source and nature (temporary or permanent) of the shock causing the rise. In such a case, the distinction between the cyclical and trend components of unemployment rates may lose practical relevance. The risk of hysteresis has become a major concern, not least because of the social consequences for the individuals directly affected. Both hysteresis and its corollary – a high incidence of long-term unemployment – have plagued several continental European countries, going as far back as the 1980s. They have also become a concern in the United States since the recent crisis, following the unusually strong increase in the incidence of long-term unemployment (Aaronson *et al.*, 2010).

There are different explanations for hysteresis. According to one, once workers become unemployed, they struggle to get back into employment regardless of the time they have spent in unemployment. In such a case, for a given job-seeker, the exit probability may have fallen at all unemployment durations, *i.e.* even for short-term unemployed. This could reflect an insufficient adjustment of the going wage rate. Another explanation focuses instead on the gradual erosion of skills associated with unemployment spells. The longer a worker remains unemployed, the less attractive he/she appears to employers. As he/she loses attractiveness, the motivation for intensive job search diminishes and the worker becomes more detached from the labour market. Under this explanation, there is a clear negative relationship between the probability of moving from unemployment to employment on the one hand, and the duration of an unemployment spell on the other, a pattern referred to as unemployment duration dependence.

The empirical analysis discussed in the remainder of this box focuses on the latter phenomenon, *i.e.* duration dependence (for details see Dantan and Murtin, 2011). Observations on individual unemployment spells are exploited to assess the influence of unemployment duration on the probability of moving from unemployment into a job. The dataset used is composed of 17 national panels of individuals whose monthly status on the labour market has been observed over the period 2005-07. These data show that in countries where the unemployment outflow rate is relatively high on average, it also tends to exhibit a steeper decline as durations increase. This is the case in general for English-speaking countries, Nordic countries and the Netherlands. In other words, the exit probability is much higher for short-term than long-term unemployed in these countries. Conversely, in countries where the average outflow rate is relatively low (a majority of continental European countries) it is also more stable across unemployment durations.

In principle, this finding could reflect differences in the composition of the unemployment pool at different durations rather than pure duration dependence effects. However, when applying a statistical method to control for composition effects, using observations on individual characteristics, pure duration dependence effects are found to account for about one-third of the decline in the rate of exit from unemployment to employment as unemployment duration increases. This represents an average and the proportion is higher in Germany, Sweden, the United Kingdom and the United States than elsewhere.

The role of policies in mitigating or reinforcing the duration dependence effect can also be assessed in this framework. The influence of two types of policies has been examined more closely, namely the duration of unemployment benefits and spending on active labour market policies (ALMPs). As regards the former, several empirical studies have found a link between benefit duration and the average length of the unemployment spell (for a recent survey, see Krueger and Mueller, 2010). For example, recent estimates have suggested that the combined federal-state extension of benefit in the United States from 26 weeks to 99 weeks (or 90 weeks on a national average) in response to the crisis could, if maintained, raise the average length of the unemployment spell by between 1½ to 3 weeks corresponding to about ½ to 1 percentage point on the unemployment rate (Aaronson *et al.*, 2010). In addition, the unemployment exit rate has been found to increase sharply at the time benefits are exhausted (Katz and Meyer, 1990). The empirical analysis conducted for this study partly corroborates this evidence. Longer benefit duration appears to reinforce duration dependence effects on average across the countries in the sample.

As regards spending on ALMPs, there is fairly robust evidence that it improves the probability of finding a job across all unemployment durations, but that the effect might be stronger for the short-term unemployed than for those who have been unemployed for a longer period.

There is no widespread labour force withdrawal yet but the risk remains

So far, the difficult labour market situation has not led to significant and general labour force withdrawal (Figure 5.8, panel A). Although contraction of the labour force was observed in about half of the countries for which data are available, by mid-2010, a decline of 1 percentage point or more in labour force participation rates had been observed in only six countries (Finland, Iceland, Ireland, Italy, Norway and the United States). In some countries, patterns of labour force participation may also have reflected reverse migration flows in the aftermath of the crisis (e.g. Ireland and Poland). Even so, recent empirical analysis looking at the impact of downturns on labour force participation has shown that severe recessions have in the past led to significant withdrawal that can occur with a significant lag (Duval et al., 2010).

Withdrawal has been significant among youth

The withdrawals observed so far in the current episode have been largely concentrated among youth and the low-skilled (Figure 5.8, panels C and D), who may be harder to redeploy and more prone to discouragement effects than other categories of workers. At the same time, falling labour force participation may to some extent be less of a concern for youth when the alternative is prolonged schooling, especially if this leads to genuine skills acquisition through a completed programme and a diploma (OECD, 2010b, Chapter 1).[10] However, there is no clear indication that the significant decline in youth participation observed in recent years has been associated with youth staying longer in education (OECD, 2010b). This raises the concern that young people become detached from the labour market with a risk of lower labour supply and deep scarring effects.[11] In this context, some form of mandatory vocational training may be the best way to maintain attachment to labour market and improve human capital (OECD, 2010b, Chapter 4).

Earlier reforms may help explain that participation of older workers held up

In the case of older workers, the impact of recessions on participation has in the past been magnified by early retirement incentives, which have been sometimes embedded in pension systems (Duval, 2003). In this regard, the fact that older workers have remained in the labour market during the latest recession (Figure 5.8, panel B) could in part be explained by reforms implemented in many countries and which have led to the closing of many benefit routes to early retirement. And, in contrast to recession episodes of the 1980s and 1990s, governments have not encouraged premature withdrawal of older workers in the vain hope of reducing youth unemployment according to a "lump of labour" view of the market. In some countries, the severe capital losses incurred by many private pension funds or individual early retirement savings schemes may

10. Duval et al., (2010) also find that the sensitivity of youth participation to downturns increases with the ease of access to post-secondary education and can be up to 1½ percentage points higher in countries with generally higher enrolment rates.
11. In this regard, any negative effects on youth attachment to the labour market may have implications for the economy over many years, whereas the long-term damage is lower when a cohort of older workers loses such attachment.

Figure 5.8. **Labour force withdrawal has so far been limited, except for youth and low-skilled**

Percentage points change in labour force participation rates from 2007Q3 to 2010Q3

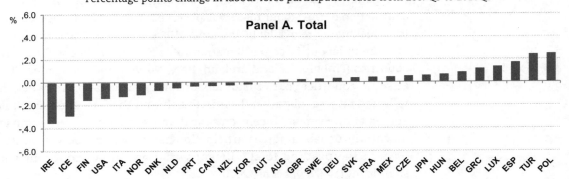

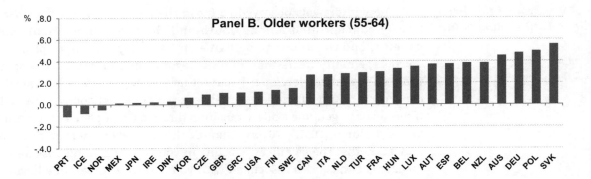

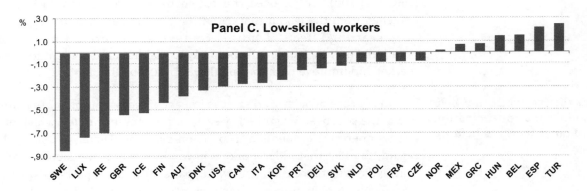

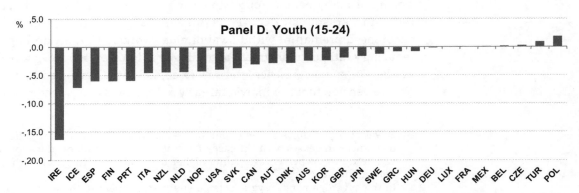

Source: OECD (2011), *Quarterly Labour Market Indicators Database*; Directorate for Employment, Labour and Social Affairs; May, unpublished data.

StatLink ᴬᴵˢᴸ http://dx.doi.org/10.1787/888932402109

have induced older workers to extend their active life in order to sustain prospective incomes (OECD, 2010c, Chapter 5). Relative to past recession episodes, all these factors point to diminished risks of labour force withdrawal among older workers despite the persistence of unemployment.

Disability benefits have in the past provided a route to labour force withdrawal

Besides early retirement programmes, long-term sickness and disability benefit schemes have in the past provided other routes to labour force withdrawal following increases in unemployment rates. Disability rates tend to increase in the wake of recessions, but then do not return to previous levels even after the economy has fully recovered (OECD, 2010d). Indeed, in a number of countries, unemployment peaks associated with recessions have tended to be followed by spikes in disability rates about two years later (Table 5.2). Such a pattern is particularly visible in the United States, but some evidence can also be seen in Denmark, New

Table 5.2. **Episodes of cyclical peaks in unemployment followed by spikes in disability rates**

		Cyclical peak in unemployment rate		Spike in disability rate[1]		
	Episode	Date	Deviation from trend	Date	Deviation from trend	Trend level
Australia	Late 70s	1978	1.1	1980	4.9	2.6
	Mid-80s	1983	2.8	1987	3.2	3.0
	Early 2000s	2001	0.7	2002	1.0	5.5
Denmark	Mid-80s	1983	1.9	1985	0.7	6.5
	Mid-2000s	2004	0.7	2007	0.7	7.5
Finland	Late 70s	1978	4.0	1980	3.1	9.3
	Mid-90s	1993	6.8	1995	1.2	9.9
	Mid-2000s	2003	0.9	2005	0.6	8.4
Ireland	Mid-80s	1984	2.1	1986	2.4	2.6
Netherlands	Mid-70s	1976	0.9	1977	7.1	7.1
New Zealand	Mid-80s	1983	1.2	1985	1.5	1.1
	Early 90s	1991	2.4	1993	1.1	1.7
	Late 90s	1998	1.1	2002	1.3	2.8
Norway	Mid-80s	1983	0.7	1984	1.8	7.1
	Mid-2000s	2005	0.7	2006	0.7	11.0
Sweden	Mid-80s	1983	0.9	1984	0.7	6.5
	Mid-90s	1997	3.8	1998	3.3	8.0
	Mid-2000s	2005	0.5	2005	3.1	10.1
Switzerland	Mid-90s	1993	1.3	1995	0.5	3.6
	Mid-2000s	2004	0.7	2006	2.2	5.4
United Kingdom	Mid-80s	1983	1.8	1985	3.1	3.2
	Mid-90s	1993	1.6	1995	2.8	6.7
United States	Mid-70s	1975	2.4	1977	2.3	3.6
	Early 80s	1982	3.0	1986	2.2	3.3
	Early 90s	1992	1.5	1994	1.7	4.5
	Mid-2000s	2003	0.8	2004	0.3	5.6

1. Disability beneficiaries as a % of working-age population.
Source: OECD Economic Outlook 88 database and OECD (2010d).

StatLink http://dx.doi.org/10.1787/888932402147

Zealand, Norway, Switzerland and, to a lesser extent, the Netherlands and the United Kingdom. The time lapse between high unemployment episodes and the subsequent hike in disability rates varies across countries and episodes but gaps of more than two years have often been seen in the past. Furthermore, in the majority of countries included in Table 5.2, disability rates have been on a trend rise over long periods, with, in some cases, accelerations in years following recessions.[12]

The rising proportion of long-term unemployed raises risks of increases in disability inflows…

There are indications that the impact of recessions on disability rates has been magnified by the tightening of access to other benefit programmes, such as unemployment insurance and social assistance, as well as by the elimination of various financial incentives to early retirement (Autor and Duggan, 2003; Koning and Van Vuuren, 2006), which left fewer options for workers facing the strongest difficulties in returning to work. Many of the countries now facing a significant increase in long-term unemployment have previously experienced high or steadily rising disability rates (*e.g.* Denmark, Ireland, the United States and to a lesser extent, the United Kingdom), which could suggest a risk of higher disability inflow going forward.

… though the risks are mitigated by earlier reforms

However, two factors could help mitigate this risk. One is the fact that older workers have not been as severely affected in the last recession as compared with earlier episodes. Since the probability of people aged between 50 and 64 years experiencing chronic health-related problems or disability is more than twice that of the total working-age population (OECD, 2010d), their relatively good employment performance during the recession should help lower the likelihood of a steep hike in disability enrolment in the near term.[13] Another mitigating factor is that many of the countries facing fast-rising disability rates following past recessions have taken measures to stem the "excess" flow of recipients and also, in some cases, to help existing recipients with work capacity to (re-)join the labour market.

Policy options to accelerate the return to work

Policies should mainly aim at fostering the return to work

This section focuses on the potential contribution of specific policies to boost the unemployment outflow rate in the near term, while at the same time contributing to lower trend unemployment in the medium term. Several combinations of policies can achieve both aims, as illustrated in Table 5.3. However, not all policy options may be equally desirable once other factors or policy objectives are considered. For instance, timing is clearly important in the current context, which would favour policies that can exert a more rapid influence on unemployment

12. The exceptions are Finland, where disability rates have been brought below their early 1980s levels, as well as the Netherlands and the United Kingdom where the trend has been partly reversed during the 2000s.
13. Older workers may be more vulnerable to stress-related factors associated with being unemployed in a period of weak labour market prospects.

Table 5.3. **The impact of policies on unemployment: summary of priors based on available evidence**

More robust findings are reported in bold

	Unemployment:			
	Level	Flow into	Flow out of	Persistence of
Reduction in:				
Unemployment benefit initial replacement rate	**Reduce**	No effect	**Increase**	Reduce
Unemployment benefit duration	No effect	No effect	Increase	Reduce
Higher spending in:				
Active Labour Market Policies	**Reduce**	**Reduce**	**Increase**	No effect
Public Employment Services	**Reduce**	**Reduce**	**Increase**	–
Job creation	Reduce	Reduce	Reduce	–
Training	No effect	Increase	Increase	–
Reduction in:				
Tax wedge	**Reduce**	No effect	**Increase**	**Reduce**
Tax wedge interacted with minimum wage	**Reduce**	No effect	**Increase**	–
Tax wedge interacted with nature of wage bargaining	**Reduce**	No effect	**Increase**	**Reduce**
Share of temporary contracts	No effect / Reduce	Reduce (prime-age women)	Reduce (prime-age women)	Increase
Easing of:				
Employment Protection Legislation (regular contracts)	Reduce (youth)	Increase	Increase (youth)	**Reduce**
Product Market Regulation	Reduce (youth and prime-age women)	Increase	Increase (youth and prime-age women)	Reduce
Increase in:				
Short-time work schemes participation	Reduce[1]	**Reduce**	Reduce	–

1. This favourable assessment relies on the premise that short-time work schemes are implemented on a *temporary* basis, in the context of a downturn.

Source: de Serres, Murtin and de la Maisonneuve (2011).

StatLink ᘳᘴ *http://dx.doi.org/10.1787/888932402166*

outflows. Furthermore, policies that can reduce unemployment persistence may to varying degrees conflict with other objectives such as budgetary consolidation, labour force participation or social protection (in particular ensuring that unemployed workers currently facing bleak jobs prospect do not fall into poverty or lose attachment to the labour market). This raises a number of potential trade-offs, some of which are highlighted in Table 5.4.

Table 5.4. **The impact of policies to reduce unemployment persistence on other economic objectives**

	Timing	Budgetary cost	Social protection / Labour force participation
Reduce initial replacement rate	Rapid	Negative	Reduce
Shorten benefit duration	Rapid	Negative	Reduce
Increase spending on PES	Fairly rapid	High	Improve
Create public sector jobs	Fairly rapid	High	Unclear (risk of strong displacement effect)
Expand training programmes	Fairly rapid	High	Improve
Reduce labour taxation	Rapid	Potentially high	Neutral
Ease EPL on regular contracts	Fairly Slow / Medium term	None unless accompanied by stronger UI benefits	Improve if help reduce duality
Reform wage bargaining	Slow / long-term	None	Improve if reduce insider-outsider divide
Phasing out subsidies to short-term working schemes	Rapid	Negative	Reduce if jobs prospects remain bleak

Source: de Serres, Murtin and de la Maisonneuve (2011).

StatLink http://dx.doi.org/10.1787/888932402185

Policies to provide income support

Poorly designed unemployment benefits may raise persistence

Designing unemployment benefits to minimise their unintentional side effects on unemployment flows is particularly relevant in the current context. Income support to the unemployed serves several purposes, including providing social protection for individuals, promoting continued labour market participation of job losers and, possibly, enabling better matches of job seekers to jobs, especially when benefits are flanked by effective activation measures.[14] However, the design of unemployment benefits can also exert an influence on persistence by raising the wage threshold below which unemployed will turn down job offers (the so-called reservation wage), reducing job-search intensity and making wages less sensitive to unemployment.

Benefit extension was necessary during the crisis...

Measures adopted in many countries in response to the crisis have raised the level, duration and coverage of benefits. While higher unemployment benefits may raise persistence of unemployment by

14. In normal economic conditions, the potential drawbacks of relatively high or durable benefits on unemployment outflows and persistence can, in principle, be partly offset by their potentially positive effects on the quality, and therefore the duration, of job matches (see OECD, 2010a, for a discussion).

lowering the outflow rate, some of the measures should nonetheless stay in place, either temporarily or permanently. For instance, the extension of *coverage* to additional categories of workers was implemented in response to the crisis but should in general be permanently kept for social reasons as well as to enhance the integration of certain groups in the labour market. Still, such extension needs to be coupled with conditionality and activation measures. Increases in benefit *duration* also were a necessary temporary response in a number of countries to ensure adequate social protection and may also have helped to support aggregate demand. The high level of unemployment prevailing in some countries combined with the weak pace of the output recovery suggests that extended duration should be maintained for some time in order to provide added protection and to minimise the risk of labour force withdrawal and dependence on other forms of benefits.

... but should be reconsidered as the recovery gathers momentum

Still, as the recovery gathers momentum in the majority of OECD countries and conditional on a clear pick-up in labour demand, the extension of benefit duration granted as an emergency measure should be reconsidered, as longer benefit duration weighs on the outflow rate and may exacerbate hysteresis effects (see Box 5.3). Indeed, many empirical studies – especially ones using micro data – have found that the average length of unemployment spells is significantly influenced by the duration of unemployment benefits. In any case, benefits should be conditional on job search and acceptance even from the early stages of the unemployment spells. Making the *level* of benefits decline with duration could also be envisaged as a further job search incentive when initial benefit *levels* are relatively high.

Facilitating the return to work of disability benefit recipients remains a challenge

In many countries, there is a risk of disability benefits becoming the *de facto* support of last resort following the tightening of access conditions to unemployment and social assistance benefits as well as the gradual phasing out of early pathways to retirement. This is particularly the case for people with tenuous attachment to the labour market, be they related to health problems, lack of skills or other disadvantages. Most countries where disability rates trended up over time have taken action to stem the inflow into such income support programme, notably through tighter gate-keeping and better control of sickness certificates. However, bringing benefit recipients with considerable work capacity back to the job market has remained a common challenge. A recent review of country experiences (OECD, 2010d) suggests that policies should aim at strengthening financial incentives for beneficiaries to work and for employers to hire them, including through wage subsidies. In this regard, there is a case for better integrating disability benefits with other working-age benefits as part of a broader reform of the tax and benefit system to make work pay. In parallel, public employment services may need to be tailored to better suit the specific needs of those with partial work incapacity.

Active labour market policies

Active labour market policies can reduce persistence

Different kinds of active labour market policies (ALMPs) can reduce persistence by improving matching efficiency, raising the wage sensitivity to unemployment or directly stimulating job creation. The desirability of different ALMP spending programmes can however differ along the business cycle, as the value of job search is higher during upturns (and conversely the costs of not searching for a job while participating in other programmes, such as training, may be lower during downturns).

Job-search assistance and training need adequate resources...

In the context of the recovery, there is a case for ensuring that resources devoted to job-search assistance are commensurate to the increased task. This holds in particular in countries where the average caseload per staff providing public employment services is likely to have risen substantially during the crisis given the sharp increase in registered jobseekers. Between 2007 and 2009, the number of jobseekers has increased by at least 50% in the Czech Republic, Greece, Ireland, Korea, Mexico, New Zealand, Turkey, the United Kingdom and the United States, and the average caseload per staff has increased in most countries (OECD, 2010a).[15] In addition, since reducing the incidence of long-term unemployment is at this juncture crucial, the intensification of training programmes implemented in most countries in response to the crisis should in most cases be maintained, especially where the unemployment outflow rate has remained depressed. Even though the overall effectiveness of such programmes in providing a sustained exit from unemployment remains unclear, they may be worth pursuing in the current context of difficult access to job opportunities so as to help unemployed to preserve work ethics and limit skills erosion.

... in particular for youth which can benefit most from vocational training

Given the high proportion of youth and low-skilled having joined the ranks of unemployment, an allocation of resources towards vocational training would seem particularly desirable. However, it should also be recognised that such programmes involve relatively large fixed costs and capacity constraints. Therefore, their scale cannot be easily and quickly adapted and their budgetary cost can be substantial, clearly a constraint for many countries, not least those confronted with high risk of unemployment persistence. Moreover, they should be carefully designed to limit the public financing of training that firms would have financed anyway (so-called deadweight losses).

Where budget constraints are most severe, resources should be well targeted

Deciding on which groups of unemployed to concentrate ALMP spending is not obvious as there are opposing arguments and trade-offs. For training the obvious candidates would be the low-skilled and long-term unemployed, especially in countries facing severe budget

---

15. Data on public employment service staff are not available for every country. Among those where it is, they indicate that the average caseload has increased by at least 50% in the Czech Republic, New Zealand, Turkey and United Kingdom.

constraints. But there is also a case for involving workers early in unemployment spells if the nature of the economic shock renders job-specific skills obsolete immediately after job loss, for instance because structural adjustment away from a particular sector or activity is needed. For job-search assistance, focusing on cases that stand better chances to find a match would make sense given that the aim is to accelerate the return to work. But it could also generate sizeable waste to the extent that these workers may find a job even without assistance. Indeed, an opposite argument could be made for focusing efforts on the long-term unemployed, but this could also involve waste due to the higher risk of failure. In many countries, the most difficult cases to match are often addressed through jobs subsidies or direct public-sector job creation targeted at specific groups.

Labour taxation

Taxes affect both the level and persistence of unemployment...

There is overwhelming evidence that higher tax wedges boost unemployment, with the size of the effect in individual countries depending, not least, on their wage-bargaining system. In countries where real wages are more rigid, the adverse effect of tax wedge increases are likely to be more substantial than elsewhere.[16] There is also some evidence suggesting that the effects of the tax wedge on unemployment comes primarily through a decline in the outflow rate, which reduces the turnover in the unemployment pool and raises persistence (de Serres, Hijzen and Murtin, 2011).

... and cuts in payroll taxes can be an effective way to boost employment

Hence, in the context of the recovery, cuts in payroll taxation might in principle represent an attractive option to provide a near-term boost to labour demand and reduce the risk of persistence. Several countries have indeed implemented cuts in social security contributions or payroll taxes in response to the crisis. The advantage of such measures is that their impact can be fairly rapid and, in principle, they can be put in place on a temporary basis – though knowledge that they are temporary may reduce their effectiveness. However, the measures that are easier to implement, such as for instance cuts to non-wage costs of all existing jobs below a certain wage level, are also the least cost-effective in the short term (OECD, 2009).

Tax cuts are costly and should therefore be targeted...

By comparison, cuts in payroll taxation targeted at new hires (so-called gross hiring subsidies) are less expensive and involve a smaller deadweight loss (OECD 2010a). For this reason they are to be preferred over across-the-board cuts, not least in a context of fiscal consolidation.

16. This is generally the case with bargaining systems that are neither highly decentralised (*i.e.* at the level of the firm) nor fully centralised (nation-wide), but where negotiations take place at the industry or sector level in an uncoordinated fashion, and where the outcomes of the bargaining are typically extended to all firms in the sector irrespective of whether their workers are represented by unions.

Targeting new hires that involve a net increase in jobs (so-called marginal job subsidies) constitutes in principle an even more effective policy, notably because it avoids "gaming" by firms through a mere increase in labour turnover. Indeed, a number of countries (*e.g.* Finland, France, Hungary, Ireland, Portugal, Spain and Turkey) have reduced social security contributions for new hires, in most cases with measures further targeted at specific groups, regions or firms. However, such marginal subsidies can be complex and lengthy to set up and difficult to monitor and administer. And, in the context of return to work strategies, the choice of instrument should also take into account the speed at which measures to stimulate labour demand can be effectively implemented.

... and could be introduced as part of a broader tax reform

On a longer time frame, in countries where tax wedges remain high, a reduction in social security contributions could be envisaged as part of a revenue-neutral tax reform package that could shift the burden towards tax bases that are less damaging for employment and growth. Based on recent empirical work, prime candidates among potential tax bases would be immovable property (see Arnold *et al.*, 2011) or consumption, but environmental taxation could also be considered since it would help achieve other objectives at the same time. Even if they are reflected to some extent in the tax wedge, shifts towards environmental and consumption taxation would help employment insofar as they are levied on broader bases than taxes on wages.[17]

Employment protection legislation

Stringent employment protection helps smooth the impact of shocks but raises persistence

Earlier empirical analysis (*e.g.* Bassanini and Duval, 2006; OECD, 2011, Chapter 3) reflected in Table 5.3 indicates that if stringent employment protection legislation on regular contracts can play a mitigating role in the event of adverse output shocks, it also raises unemployment persistence. Partly to minimise the impact on persistence, many countries (*e.g.* Belgium, France, Germany, Italy, Netherlands, Portugal, Spain and Sweden) have set up so-called two-tier regimes of employment protection, with different and asymmetric degrees of restrictions on open-ended and fixed-term contracts. In some cases, the use of fixed-term contracts has been facilitated with a view to improve access of the long-term unemployed (outsiders) to a parallel job market where wages may be set more flexibly.[18] However, while two-tier regimes may have contributed to raise the unemployment turnover, they are unlikely to

17. Even though the consumption tax can be seen as part of the labour tax wedge, its broader base would imply that a revenue-neutral shift from income taxes and social contributions towards consumption taxation would still reduce the wedge. However, it should be recognised that this could be difficult to achieve politically as it would involve a redistribution of the tax burden from workers towards pensioners.

18. A recent analysis based on the examination of earnings at the individual level has found that employees on fixed-term contracts earned on average substantially lower wages relative to those on permanent contracts, even in the case of individuals with similar education and experience (IMF, 2010, Chapter 3).

lower the long-term or structural rate unemployment (European Commission, 2010). If anything some evidence suggests that they may even be conducive to higher unemployment in the long run (Cahuc and Postel-Vinay, 2002) and can have the effect of amplifying the short-term response of unemployment to shocks (Bentolila *et al.*, 2010).[19]

Reforms of employment protection legislation may help to boost hiring...

In countries where employment protection legislation for regular contracts is very stringent, and where risks of strong unemployment persistence a concern, there is a case for reducing gaps in protection between regular and temporary contracts so as to facilitate hiring in the short term and eliminate the undesirable longer-run effects of two-tier regimes, such as labour market segmentation. Indeed, significant reforms are already underway in Greece and Spain and, given that most other countries are now into the recovery phase, the risk that such reform leads to an increase in unemployment inflow is diminished. Priority areas for reform would be i) to reduce the uncertainties related to the application of employment protection legislation for regular contracts so as to reduce the legal and other procedural costs, thereby allowing firms to better internalise the cost of the severance payment in their hiring and wage determination decisions; and ii) to better integrate legislation on temporary and regular contracts, for instance by introducing mechanisms for a smooth transition between trial and open-ended phases of a worker's career, with variable degrees of employment protection along this trajectory (*e.g. via* an open-ended contract where severance pay rises gradually with tenure).

... at little or no budgetary cost

An advantage of such reforms is that they entail little or no budgetary cost. However, it should be kept in mind that the favourable impact of such reforms on the outflow rate may take time to materialise and that they can be politically difficult to implement in a context of high unemployment. Furthermore, for many of the countries currently at risk of persistent unemployment, the stance of employment protection legislation is fairly liberal.

Lessons from the crisis

The crisis has brought new insights

Even though it would be premature to draw firm lessons from the crisis, it can be said that labour markets have done comparatively well in view of the magnitude of the recession. This relatively good outcome can in part be attributed to earlier reforms along the lines advocated in the long-standing OECD strategy to boost employment and labour force participation. Even so, the experience over the past few years has clearly put to test many of the policy recommendations conveyed in the OECD strategy and brought a number of insights which could lead to their reassessment.

19. In this regard, the increase in turnover can be viewed as artificial and to some extent counter-productive, especially that workers on fixed-term contracts are less likely to build as much human capital as workers on open-ended contracts given that firms have less incentives to provide training.

Demand conditions and policies are important

- Past experience has shown that recessions accompanied by severe financial and housing market turbulences are usually followed by weak and protracted recoveries, and that more time is needed in such case for the pick-up in activity to translate into lower unemployment. Hence, the role of macro policies and conditions in supporting the on-going recovery remains determinant. While monetary policy is still accommodative, fiscal policy is constrained in many countries by the need to reduce large public-sector deficit and contain rising debt levels. This serves as a reminder of the need for macroeconomic policies during the good times to create room for manoeuvre during bad times.

A flexible benefit system that combines protection and activation helps to cope with a downturn

- Pre-crisis reforms in benefit and activation systems, aimed at broadening coverage, tightening eligibility, increasing conditionality and making work pay, have made a number of countries better prepared to cope with the rapid increase in unemployment, notably by raising the effectiveness of the emergency measures taken in response to the crisis. In this regard, one lesson emerging from the recent episode is that during periods of bleak labour market prospects it may be possible to extend the duration of unemployment benefits without unduly undermining financial incentives to seek work – provided that such extension remains temporary (OECD, 2011, Chapter 1).

The contrasting performance of older workers and youth warrants further analysis

- One of the most striking features of the recent episode has been the good employment performance of older workers, both relative to earlier recessions and in comparison to other age groups. In this regard, the sharp contrast in the performance of older workers and youth may to some extent reflect the large difference in several countries in the degree of employment protection between the two groups. Also, pre-crisis reforms in pension systems, as well as the closing of early routes to retirement, have most likely contributed to the strong labour market participation of older workers during the recent episode. In any case, further analysis is required to better assess the relative contributions of the different possible explanations.

The benefits of partial reforms may be short-lived

- The crisis has exposed the vulnerabilities of partial reform strategies, such as policies that resulted in a high duality of the labour market, in spite of their immediate success in increasing turnover and temporarily bringing down unemployment during the years preceding the recession (Boeri and Garibaldi, 2007).

Work sharing arrangements can play a useful cushioning role

- The relatively benign labour market outcome in countries such as Belgium, Finland, Germany, Japan and Luxembourg has underscored the potential role of work sharing arrangements to cushion the impact of output shocks on employment, an issue which deserves to be further explored (see Box 5.4). Such schemes may work more effectively when implemented in the context of wage bargaining arrangements that provide individual firms more leeway (such as opt-out clauses) in the application of collective agreements.

Box 5.4. **The role of short-time working arrangements during the crisis and beyond**

In many countries, the reduction in average hours worked during the 2008-09 recession has limited the decline in employment given the observed drop in output. In part, hours adjustments rather than headcount adjustment have taken place due to work-sharing arrangements, partly operated *via* public short-time work (STW) schemes. These programmes intend to preserve jobs in firms that experience temporarily low demand by encouraging job sharing, while also providing income support to workers who experience reductions in hours worked. As such, STW schemes are a form of job subsidy. These subsidies can be justified economically insofar as they may avoid losses of specific human capital in the wake of major but temporary economic shocks.

The effectiveness and cost-efficiency of STW schemes have been discussed at length in OECD (2010a) and Hijzen and Venn (2011). Although an empirical assessment of their long-term effects is not yet possible, STW schemes have helped preserve permanent jobs during the economic downturn while promoting reductions in average hours among permanent workers. In Belgium, Finland, Germany, Italy and Japan, STW schemes are estimated to have substantially reduced the impact of the crisis on permanent employment. Hijzen and Venn (2011) estimate that about 234 000 and 416 000 jobs have been saved in Germany and Japan, respectively, thanks to these schemes.[1]

However, their contribution to preserve jobs differed substantially between countries that had already set up those schemes *before* the crisis and those who introduced those schemes *during* the crisis. This may indicate real difficulties in implementing an effective and timely STW scheme after a recession has begun, as the rate of layoffs tends to be higher in early phases of an economic downturn (OECD 2010a, Chapter 5). It also suggests that short-time work programmes could be set up and kept dormant in times of normal activity, and activated if necessary at the onset of future economic downturns.

As with any form of public wage subsidy, STW programmes also entail risks. Firstly, *deadweight losses* may be incurred if subsidies are paid for jobs that employers would have maintained even without public compensations. Secondly, *displacement effects* may occur if STW schemes help preserve jobs that are not viable in the long run, entailing a sub-optimal allocation of capital and workers in the economy. Thirdly, STW could also act to accommodate unwarranted wage increases which might have an adverse influence on wage-setting. To avoid those risks, certain features in the design of STW schemes look desirable:

- *Eligibility conditions,* such as proof of a minimum reduction in production or sales, as well as an explicit agreement between social partners, are likely to reduce deadweight losses. However, too strict eligibility requirements may deter some firms from participating in STW schemes, or might slow down their practical implementation due to excessive administrative costs.

- *Firms co-financing* the cost of STW schemes has two main advantages. First, it is an effective way of reducing deadweight losses. Second, it provides a built-in mechanism for encouraging firms to revert to statutory working hours as the pick-up in demand becomes clear. In practice, firms may either pay some fraction of the wage cost of hours not worked, or pay the full wage during an initial period. Of these two options, the former has an advantage in that it creates better incentives at the margin to withdraw from the scheme. In contrast, when firms pay up-front the full wage for a given period, they have less incentives to withdraw once the period is over. In any case, in several countries, such as Belgium, Canada, Denmark, Finland, Ireland and Spain, firms do not bear any part of the cost.

- Similarly, a *quick phasing out* of short-time work schemes is desirable to minimise the displacement effect. In practice, phasing out can be ensured by a regulatory maximum duration of STW schemes, which was on average equal to 14 months during the crisis (excluding Finland where there is no time limit). This duration limit was substantially increased in Austria, Germany and Switzerland in 2009. It is difficult to determine the optimal timing for scaling down STW programmes, but to avoid hysteresis effects in hours worked, it is important that working-time regulations return to normal within a reasonably short amount of time.

1. In both countries, this represents slightly less than 1% of total permanent employment.

Bibliography

Aaronson, D., B. Mazumder and S. Schechter (2010), "What is Behind the Rise in Long-Term Unemployment?", *Economic Perspectives*, Federal Reserve Bank of Chicago, 2Q/2010.

Abraham, K.G. and R. Shimmer (2002), "Changes in Unemployment and Duration and Labor Force Attachment", in A. Krueger and R. Solow (editors), *The Roaring Nineties: Can Full Employment Be Sustained?*, New York, Russell Sage Foundation and Century Foundation.

Andrews, D., A. Caldera Sanchez and A. Johansson (2011), "Housing Markets and Structural Policies in OECD Countries", *OECD Economics Department Working Paper* No. 836.

Arnold, J., B. Brys, C. Heady, A. Johansson, C. Schwellnus and L. Vartia (2011), "Tax Policy for Economic Recovery and Growth", *Economic Journal*, Vol. 121.

Autor, D. and M. Duggan (2003), "The Rise in the Disability Rolls and the Decline in Unemployment", *Quarterly Journal of Economics*, Vol. 118.

Bassanini, A., and R. Duval (2006), "Employment Patterns in OECD Countries: Reassessing the Role of Policies and Institutions", OECD *Economics Department Working Papers*, No. 486, OECD, Paris.

Bentolila, S., P. Cahuc, J.J. Dolado and T. Le Barbanchon (2010), "Two-Tier Labor Markets in the Great Recession: France vs. Spain", *CEPR Discussion Papers* No. 8152.

Blanchard, O., and P. Diamond (1994), "Ranking, Unemployment Duration and Wages", *Review of Economic Studies* Vol. 61.

Boeri, T. (2010), "Institutional Reforms in European Labour Markets", in O. Ashenfelter and D. Card (eds.), *Handbook of Labour Economics*, Vol. 4, Elsevier.

Boeri, T., and P. Garibaldi (2007), "Two Tier Reforms of Employment Protection: A Honeymoon Effect?", *Economic Journal*, Vol. 117.

Bover, O., M. Arellano and S. Bentolila (2002), "Unemployment Duration, Benefit Duration and the Business Cycle", *Economic Journal*, Vol. 112.

Cahuc, P. and F. Postel-Vinay (2002), "Temporary Jobs, Employment Protection and Labor Market Performance", *Labour Economics* Vol. 9.

Dantan, S. and F. Murtin (2011), "Hysteresis in the Unemployment Exit Rate: A Cross-Country Microeconomic Analysis", *OECD Economics Department Working Papers* (forthcoming), OECD, Paris.

De Serres, A., F. Murtin and C. de la Maisonneuve (2011), "Policies to Facilitate the Return to Work", OECD *Economics Department Working Papers*, forthcoming, OECD, Paris.

De Serres, A., A. Hijzen and F. Murtin (2011), "Labour Market Institutions and the Flow Decomposition of Unemployment", OECD *Economics Department Working Papers*, forthcoming, OECD, Paris.

Duval, R. (2003), "The Retirement Effects of Old-Age Pension and Early Retirement Schemes in OECD Countries", OECD *Economics Department Working Papers* No. 370, OECD, Paris.

Duval, R., M. Eris and D. Furceri (2010), "Labour Force Participation Hysteresis in Industrial Countries: Evidence and Causes", Paper presented at the OECD-Banque de France Seminar on *Structural Reforms, Crisis Exit Strategies and Growth*. Paris, December.

Elsby, M., B. Hobijn and A. Sahin (2008), "Unemployment Dynamics in the OECD", *NBER Working Paper* No. 14617.

Elsby, M., B. Hobijn and A. Sahin (2010), "The Labor Market in the Great Recession", *NBER Working Paper* No. 15979.

European Commission (2010), "Labour Market and Wage Developments 2009", *European Economy*, No. 5.

Garcia Perez, J.I., S. Jimenez-Martin and A. Sanchez-Martin (2010), "Financial Incentives, Individual Heterogeneity and the Transitions to Retirement of Employed and Unemployed Workers", Preliminary Version.

Hijzen, A., and D. Venn (2011), "The Role of Short-Time Work Schemes During the 2008-09 Recession", OECD *Social, Employment and Migration Working Papers*, No. 115, OECD, Paris.

IMF (2010), *World Economic Outlook*, Washington, April.

Katz, L., and B. Meyer (1990), "The Impact of the Potential Duration of Unemployment Benefits on the Duration of Unemployment", *Journal of Public Economics*, Vol. 41.

Koning, P., and D. Van Vuuren (2006), "Disability Insurance and Unemployment Insurance as Substitute Pathways", *CPB Discussion Papers* No. 70, CPB Netherlands Bureau for Economic Policy Analysis.

Krueger, A.B. and A. Mueller (2010), "Job Search and Unemployment Insurance: New Evidence from Time Use Data", *Journal of Public Economics*, Vol. 94.

Lindbeck, A. (1995), "Welfare States Disincentives with Endogenous Habits and Norms", *Scandinavian Journal of Economics*, Vol. 97.

Lockwood, B. (1991), "Information Externalities in the Labour Market and the Duration of Unemployment", *Review of Economic Studies*, No. 58.

Machin, S., and A. Manning (1999), "The Causes and Consequences of Long-Term Unemployment in Europe", in O. Ashenfelter and D. Card (eds.), *Handbook of Labor Economics*, Vol. 3, cpapitre 47.

OECD (2006), OECD *Employment Outlook*, June, OECD Publishing.

OECD (2009), OECD *Employment Outlook*, June, OECD Publishing.

OECD (2010a), OECD *Employment Outlook*, June, OECD Publishing.

OECD (2010b), *Off to a Good Start? Jobs for Youth*, OECD Publishing.

OECD (2010c), OECD *Economic Outlook*, No. 87, Volume 2010/1, OECD Publishing.

OECD (2010d), *Sickness, Disability and Work: Breaking the Barriers – A Synthesis of Findings across OECD Countries*, OECD Publishing.

OECD (2011), OECD *Employment Outlook*, forthcoming.

Pissarides, C. (1992), "Loss of Skill During Unemployment and the Persistence of Employment Shocks", *Quarterly Journal of Economics*, Vol. 107.

Saint-Paul, G. (1996), *Dual Labor Markets, A Macroeconomic Perspective*, MIT Press.

Schulhofer-Wohl (2010), "Negative Equity Does Not Reduce Homeowners' Mobility", *Federal Reserve Bank of Minneapolis, Working Paper* No. 682.

Wilson, D.J. (2010), "Is the Recent Productivity Boom Over?", *FRBSF Economic Letter*, Federal Reserve Bank of San Francisco, September 28.

Yellen, J. (2010), "The Outlook for the Economy and Inflation, and the Case for Federal Reserve Independence", *FRBSF Economic Letter*, Federal Reserve Bank of San Francisco, 29 March.

Chapter 6

GETTING THE MOST OUT OF INTERNATIONAL CAPITAL FLOWS

Introduction and summary

Financial globalisation can be both a blessing and a curse

Increasing international capital flows can support long-term income growth through a better international allocation of saving and investment. However, they can also make macroeconomic management more difficult, as currently being experienced by several emerging economies, because of the faster international transmission of shocks and the increased risks of overheating, credit and asset price boom-and-bust cycles and abrupt reversals in capital inflows.

This chapter assesses how policies could shape financial globalisation

This chapter has two purposes: firstly, to examine the long-term drivers of global financial integration and international capital flows; and secondly to assess the associated vulnerabilities. The focus is on how policies can help to make the most of capital flows both by promoting global financial integration and limiting the associated risks, consistent with the G20 goal to promote strong, sustainable, and balanced global growth. Particular attention is given to the potential role of structural policies – broadly defined to include development of financial markets, general regulatory quality, as well as product market regulation that promotes competition and employment-friendly labour market policies – and how they could complement sound macroeconomic policies and ongoing financial, prudential and macro-prudential reforms which, although not investigated here, have key roles in reducing financial vulnerabilities (see Box 6.1). The main findings of the chapter are as follows:[1]

Structural reforms could help capital flow "downhill" to emerging economies

- Structural policy settings are important long-term drivers of capital flows, having a relatively large impact on gross and net foreign capital positions. Growth-enhancing structural policy reform could help to narrow global imbalances by reducing net capital outflows from countries with large positive net foreign assets positions while also supporting their long-term growth. This is particularly the case in emerging countries where under-developed financial markets limit the ability of economies to absorb domestic and foreign capital, and in both emerging and advanced countries where domestic distortions lower risk-adjusted returns to capital.

A mix of structural and macroeconomic policies can help reduce vulnerabilities

- Large capital inflows are associated with a higher risk of credit booms, financial crises and sudden stops, but macroeconomic and structural policies can complement ongoing necessary financial and prudential

---

1. This chapter draws on empirical analysis which is detailed in three background working papers, Furceri *et al.* (2011a, b and c).

Box 6.1. **How should countries respond to large capital inflows?**

While on average capital has been flowing "uphill" from developing and emerging countries to advanced countries, several emerging countries are now facing large capital inflows. The most recent data (although sometimes only available to the third quarter of 2010) suggest that gross capital inflows seem to be back to, or above, their pre-crisis levels in several countries, including Argentina, Brazil, Colombia, Indonesia, Mexico, South Africa, where they already represent around 5% of GDP, and Chile and Turkey, where they have reached close to 8-9% of GDP. Such large inflows create a real macroeconomic challenge for these economies, given the associated risks of excessive currency appreciation, credit booms and busts and sudden stops.

The analysis in this chapter suggests that structural reforms, in addition to promoting overall cross-borders flows, could help to reduce the associated vulnerabilities mainly *via* a better composition of inflows, with more FDI and less debt. However, structural reforms generally take time to have their full effects and so may be seen as a complement to other policies which have a more immediate effect on large capital inflows and their consequences.

In the short term, macroeconomic policies have a key role to play. Letting the exchange rate appreciate and tightening fiscal policy could help moderate demand and related inflation pressures generated by the inflows, while making the inflows less attractive. Still these general principles have to be adapted to each specific country situation which in practice may mean the room for manoeuvre is limited: exchange rates may already be overvalued; or the fiscal stance may already be tight. The appropriate stance of monetary policy is a more complex issue as higher domestic interest may attract more inflows while a looser stance may fuel inflation pressures and asset prices bubbles. Several factors have therefore to be taken into account in the monetary policy response, including the extent of demand pressures and how they can be contained by exchange rates and fiscal policies, the risk of asset price and credit bubbles and the risks of de-anchoring inflation expectations. Regardless of the scope for using macroeconomic policies, there is likely to be a role for macro and micro-prudential policies, to generally limit excessive risk-taking, but also with the capacity to target particular sectors or asset classes, depending on the precise nature of the inflows and the associated risks.

Reserve accumulation to stabilise the exchange rate is usually costly and not always efficient and should be avoided unless reserves are insufficient from a self-insurance perspective, although the concept of self-insurance needs has been evolving over time (see Box 6.3). Also, reserve accumulation could be justified when the domestic currency is already largely overvalued, putting the export sector at strong risk.

The question of the use of capital controls is being more and more debated (see for instance Ostry *et al.*, 2010; IMF 2010b; IMF, 2011) as controls are being used by several countries, even though their efficiency is still unclear and they create distortions if maintained indefinitely. In any case, such controls are best seen as a last resort and as temporary solution and should preferably be subject to multilateral surveillance as in the framework created by the OECD *Code of Liberalisation of Capital Movements*.

reforms in limiting such vulnerabilities. Appropriate macroeconomic policies, including allowing the exchange rate to appreciate or tightening fiscal policy, can help to reduce the magnitude of the credit cycle during an episode of large capital inflows. Growth-supportive structural policies, while attracting more net inflows, can modify their composition towards sources of financing that are usually seen as more stable and productive. More competition-friendly product market regulation, less stringent job protection, higher institutional quality and greater capital account openness are associated with a larger component of foreign direct investment (FDI) inflows and a smaller share of debt. Such a composition is likely to reduce the likelihood of credit booms as well as banking, currency and balance-of-payments crises.

There may also be a role for capital controls

- There may also be a role for some form of capital controls, if designed in a way that minimises distortions in long-term investments and ordinary business activities, but these should preferably be subject to multilateral surveillance as in the framework created by the OECD *Code of Liberalisation of Capital Movements*.

Large reserve accumulation in some countries needs to be addressed

- International reserves can help countries protect themselves against financial crisis caused by currency outflows. But reserve accumulation in some countries has reached levels far beyond average observed behaviour, related to motives of smooth trade financing and self insurance against outflows, and has become an important driver of capital flows from emerging to high-income countries. To the extent that excess reserve holding indicates mistrust in international financial safety nets, the improvement of these safety nets, which is already part of the G20 agenda, is essential.

The main factors shaping global financial integration

Financial flows have recovered after the crisis

Financial flows collapsed during the crisis

After reaching historical highs in mid-2007, international capital flows collapsed during the financial crisis (Figure 6.1). From mid-2007 to September 2008, the contraction concerned mainly OECD countries' international banking flows (see Milesi-Ferretti and Tille, 2010 for more details). However, the bankruptcy of Lehman Brothers in September 2008 precipitated a broader reversal of international capital flows, demonstrating the complexity and rapidity of the international transmission of financial shocks and the financial vulnerabilities associated with increased international capital flows.

The recovery in financial flows has not been broad based

Capital flows have partially rebounded since spring 2009, but in a very heterogeneous way. They have mainly been driven by a bounce back in portfolio investments from advanced to emerging countries, which have proven quite resilient to the global crisis and have been seen as underweighted in international portfolios (see especially Suttle *et al.*, 2010). As a result, in 2010, although overall cross-border flows remained well below pre-crisis levels, several countries – including Chile, Korea, Mexico and Turkey in the OECD and some large emerging markets – have faced large capital inflows.

International financial integration in the 2000s and its main drivers

Global financial integration accelerated prior to the crisis driven by...

International financial integration accelerated in the decade prior to the financial crisis. The size of annual gross cross-border flows increased considerably from about 5% of world GDP in the mid-1990s to about 20%

Figure 6.1. **Global financial integration**

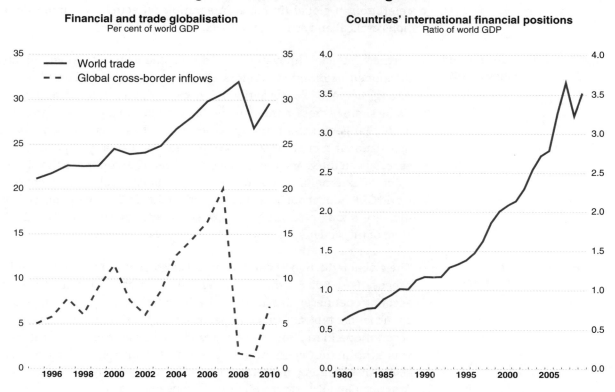

Note: See footnote 2 for more details on the capital flow data. 2010 global cross-border flows are estimated using available quarterly data. Countries' international financial positions are measured as the absolute sum of all countries' gross assets and liabilities positions (taken from Lane and Milesi-Ferretti (2007) and IMF Balance of Payments Statistics after 2004) as a share of world GDP (taken from the IMF World Economic Outlook database).

Source: IMF *Balance of Payments Statistics;* IMF *World Economic Outlook database;* Lane and Milesi-Ferretti (2007); OECD Economic Outlook 89 database; OECD calculations.

StatLink ⟨ꜜ⟩ http://dx.doi.org/10.1787/888932424776

in 2007.[2] As a result, international financial openness (measured by the sum of countries' external assets and liabilities as a share of GDP) more than doubled over that period from 150% of world GDP to 350% in 2007,

2. Cross-border flows series used in this chapter are from the financial account of the *IMF Balance of Payments Statistics* (BOPS). Strictly speaking, according to the *IMF Balance of Payments Manual* what are referred to throughout the chapter as capital flows should instead be referred to as financial flows. Annual cross-border flows are measured by the acquisition of assets abroad (equity and debt securities, cross-border lending and deposits, and foreign direct investment [FDI]) where transactions are recorded in net terms and shown separately for financial assets and liabilities (*i.e.* net transactions in financial assets is acquisitions of assets less reductions of assets, not assets less liabilities). FDI is defined according to the *OECD Benchmark Definition of Foreign Direct Investment*. In this chapter, gross capital inflows or outflows refers to either the credit (gross inflows, *i.e.* net increase in liabilities) or debit (gross outflows, *i.e.* net purchase of assets) while "net" capital flows refers to the difference between gross inflows and gross outflows. Stocks of assets and liabilities used in this paper are from Milesi-Ferretti (2007) before 2004 and the IMF BOPS *International Investment Positions* after 2004. They reflect both the cumulated annual flows in assets and liabilities and valuation effects, including exchange rate movements.

with a substantial acceleration during the 2000s (Figure 6.1). This acceleration in global financial integration reflected a combination of various cyclical and structural factors:

... financial innovation and development...

- Further financial innovation and development in both emerging and developed economies accelerated global financial integration. The strong increase in international banking activity and the associated rising share of cross-border ownership of financial institutions together with changes in the funding structure of these institutions toward international capital markets have played a particularly important role, especially in the years prior to the crisis. Overall, according to the BIS, the value of external assets and liabilities of banks doubled as a share of world GDP from about 30% in 1990 to about 60% in 2007, with most of this increase taking place in the 2000s (see Milesi-Ferretti and Tille, 2010). Most of this activity was concentrated in advanced economies.

... greater capital account openness...

- The global reduction of capital controls also played a major role in this process (see Box 6.2 on issues relating to measurement of capital account openness). Based on available indicators, high-income OECD countries are typically in the upper quartile of the distribution of capital account openness, but the increase in openness over the last decade was similar between high-income OECD and emerging market economies. Among emerging countries it was mainly driven by Latin American and Eastern and Central European countries.

... trade globalisation...

- The rapid growth of world trade also contributed to the global financial integration through the creation of trade credits and export insurance. Still, international capital flows increased about three times more than world trade between 1994 and 2007.

... European financial integration...

- Among advanced countries, the elimination of the intra-euro area exchange risk premium after the creation of the euro contributed to greater European financial integration (see Lane, 2010 and Waysand et al., 2010).

... increased attractiveness of emerging countries...

- Investment opportunities increased in many emerging market economies which also benefited from a substantial reduction in home bias, even though most flows remained between advanced countries.

... and cyclical factors

- The impact of these structural changes was exacerbated in the years to 2007 by cyclical factors including the prolonged period of low interest rates in advanced countries and windfall savings by commodity exporters.

Financial development, capital account and trade openness were the driving forces

The empirical analysis of the long-term drivers of financial openness across countries supports the role of these factors and in particular of financial development, capital account and trade openness as the main long-term forces driving world capital flows (see Furceri et al., 2011a). All

> ### Box 6.2. **Issues in measuring capital account openness**
>
> **Measuring capital account openness across countries is a difficult task**
>
> The measure of capital account openness used in this chapter and background working papers is the Chinn-Ito index computed using principal components extracted from disaggregated capital and current account restriction measures documented in the IMF *Annual Report on Exchange Arrangements and Exchange Restrictions* (AREAER) (see Chinn and Ito, 2008). This is the most commonly-used indicator in the recent empirical literature. It is available for 120 advanced and emerging countries in the 2000s (from around 75 in the 1970s). The index ranges from –2 to +2.5 with higher values implying greater openness. More disaggregated datasets have been constructed recently based on the same source, such as the one by Schindler (2009) which includes more disaggregated information on restrictions on inflows *versus* outflows and on the relative levels of controls across different asset categories.
>
> The shortcomings associated with these measures and other measures based on the AREAER are summarised in Kose *et al.* (2006). First, AREAER focuses on restrictions associated with foreign exchange transactions and does not necessarily fully reflect the degree of openness of the capital account. Second, as a *de jure* measure it does not capture the degree of enforcement of capital controls which may vary over time. Third, some regulations not counted as controls may act as such. This can for instance be the case for prudential regulations limiting the foreign exchange exposure of domestic banks.
>
> **Making use of the OECD *Code of Liberalisation of Capital Movements***
>
> Another potential source of information on capital account openness is the position of countries under the OECD *Code of Liberalisation of Capital Movements* (OECD, 2010). It provides a much more comprehensive coverage of capital account restrictions concerning direct investment, liquidation of direct investment, real estate, securities on capital markets, money markets, negotiable instruments and non-securitised claims, collective investment securities, credits directly linked with international commercial transactions or rendering of international services, financial credits and loans, sureties, guarantees and financial back-up facilities, deposit accounts, foreign exchange, life assurance, personal capital movements, physical movement of capital assets and disposal of non-resident-owned blocked funds. However, due to the so far limited country coverage it has not yet been exploited. With wider country coverage, the Code or a similar international instrument could thus serve as a yardstick to assess the degree of liberalisation achieved by each country in regard to capital movements.
>
> At present, the Code is a binding instrument for the 34 member countries of the OECD and allows countries to pursue liberalisation progressively over time, in line with their level of economic development. An adhering country enjoys the liberalisation measures of other adherents, regardless of its own degree of openness and OECD countries have unilaterally extended their measures to all members of the IMF. The Code provides flexibility to cope with situations of short-term capital volatility, including the introduction of controls on short-term capital operations and the re-imposition of controls on other operations in situations of severe balance-of-payments difficulties or financial disturbance. To avoid a beggar-thy-neighbour approach, or suspicion thereof, which could invite counter-measures, the Code provides an established process of international co-operation, managed and controlled through a forum, in which each country can explain its policies and raise questions about the policies of others.
>
> Adherence to the OECD Codes of Liberalisation is open to non-OECD countries.

together, these three variables explain more than half of the variation of financial integration across countries and over time. Going forward, the same factors that drove increased global financial flows before the crisis are likely to increasingly reassert themselves.

Banking flows within advanced countries dominated the pre-crisis period

The main contribution to the acceleration of world financial integration in the 2000s came more from advanced countries (Figure 6.2) and particularly from banking operations reflecting the rise of cross-border ownership of financial institutions and an increase of their funding on international markets mentioned above. Those countries with large asset and liability positions in which banks played a large role were the most affected by the financial crisis. In the past two years, most countries and jurisdictions have undertaken initiatives to reform financial regulation and tackle the failures that led to the financial crisis. Such reforms are likely to have some impact on capital flows, which may not go back to pre-crisis levels, especially between advanced countries. In particular, higher liquidity requirements, tighter funding rules and regulations to limit leverage of banks and their foreign exchange exposure (resulting notably from Basel III) may constrain the recovery in cross-border bank flows.

Figure 6.2. **Advanced countries drove international cross border flows**
Per cent of world GDP

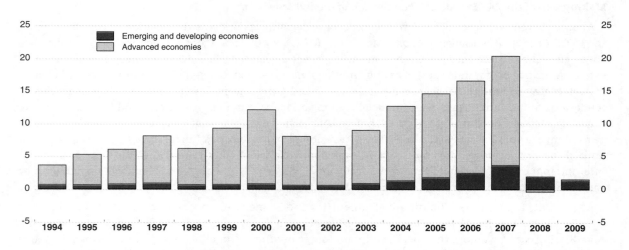

Note: Average of inflows and outflows recorded by each region (both calculated as the sum of flows recorded by individual countries) as a ratio of world GDP; advanced countries are those defined as such by the IMF. See footnote 2 for more details on the capital flow data.
Source: IMF Balance of Payments Statistics; OECD calculations.

StatLink 🔗 http://dx.doi.org/10.1787/888932424795

The contribution of emerging economies to world flows has increased

Emerging markets started to contribute more to global financial integration in the past decade and their share in world capital flows increased from 7% to 17% between 2000 and 2007. Over that period, rising outflows from emerging and developing economies were mainly driven by reserve accumulation and invested in advanced economies' sovereign debt securities or close substitutes, with about one-fifth of the increase corresponding to higher outflows from oil-exporting countries. This increase in reserve accumulation reflects several factors, including exchange rate policies, self-insurance strategies by emerging markets partly due to some mistrust in the current system of financial safety nets (see Box 6.3, and Mateos y Lago *et al.*, 2009). Inflows to emerging and

Box 6.3. **What is driving the demand for international reserves?**

World foreign reserve holdings have risen from around 6% of world GDP in 1999 to almost 15% in 2009, with this increase being overwhelmingly accounted for by Asian and oil-exporting countries. By the end of 2010 the foreign exchange reserves of China alone totalled almost $3 trillion or around half of its annual GDP and accounted for almost one-third of total global foreign exchange reserves. After a temporary slowdown during the global economic downturn, reserve accumulation across the world continued apace through 2009 and 2010.

This rapid increase and high level of reserve holdings in some surplus countries has attracted considerable attention. Firstly, the build-up of reserves is closely associated with global imbalances and indeed, some have argued, contributed to the financial fragility that precipitated the recent global financial crisis. Secondly, the high opportunity cost of holding large stocks of low yielding assets is wasteful from a social welfare standpoint (Rodrik, 2006; Summers, 2006). And thirdly, with the US dollar being the pre-eminent global reserve currency, large holders are constrained in the choices they have regarding divestment, diversification and even the productive use of these assets, as such action could entail significant negative valuation effects (the so-called "dollar trap").

The reasons countries accumulate foreign exchange reserves fall into two broad categories. Firstly, reserves may be amassed as a direct consequence of export-led growth strategies and holding down the real value of the local currency. Reserves may also accumulate as a result of attempts to smooth short-term exchange-rate fluctuations. A second reason to hold foreign reserves is that they may provide a form of self-insurance against balance of payments crises, including sudden stops in access to external funding, or even just a means to smooth high-frequency volatility of flows. Traditionally, the focus was on adequately covering imports. In the late 1990s, following the Asian crisis, the focus shifted to covering a country's stock of short-term debt (the so-called Guidotti-Greenspan rule). Then after the Argentine crisis, the scope of self-insurance broadened to include protecting local financial systems that are exposed to foreign market sentiment, capital flight by domestic agents and exchange rate movements. This evolution has implied a considerable escalation in the global demand for reserves.

There is a considerable literature that tries to explain the levels of foreign exchange reserves held across countries and their changes over time. However, this research is hampered by a number of factors including heterogeneity in reasons for accumulating reserves (for example, the intergenerational considerations of oil and other exporters of finite resources) and also the increasingly large role played by sovereign wealth funds (SWF). This literature falls into two broad categories. The first approach is to use calibrated behavioural models that rely on quantifying risk aversion, discount rates and other fundamental parameters (e.g. Jeanne, 2007 and Jeanne and Rancière, 2008). These models generally conclude that current reserve holdings are well above optimal levels in the large accumulating countries. The second approach is to determine what factors account for reserve accumulation behaviour for a set of countries over time and then to make inferences about the behaviour of individual countries based on this (e.g. Aizenman and Lee, 2007; Obstfeld et al., 2008; Cheung and Ito, 2009). This approach generally concludes that reserve levels in the large accumulating countries are in line with average behaviour given the particular characteristics of, and conditions in, these countries. However, the existing work that takes this second approach is somewhat outdated, and in light of the fact that reserve accumulation has accelerated over the past five years, so might be the conclusions.

Recent OECD work has updated and extended the existing econometrics-approach literature using a panel of over 130 countries between 1980 and 2008 (see Vujanovic, 2011). The long-run determinates of a country's reserve holdings are found to be trade openness and the size of the domestic financial sector (as proxied by M2), both of which may capture the self-insurance motives previously referred to. In addition to these factors, changes in GDP per capita, the exchange rate regime, exchange rate volatility and the degree of financial openness are associated with changes in the level of a country's reserve holdings. This analysis suggests that the current ratio of reserves to GDP in the big accumulating countries is significantly above levels that are consistent with the average behaviour of all countries, even after taking into account developments in trade, financial deepening and other pertinent factors. Specifically, China and Japan record the largest deviations from the levels implied by the long-run cross-country determinants of reserves-to-GDP ratios, followed by South Korea, India and South Africa (see Figure below). Moreover, when expressed in dollar terms the global magnitude of these deviations stands out even more; on average over

295

Box 6.3. **What is driving the demand for international reserves?** *(cont.)*

the three years to 2008, the analysis suggests that China and Japan held reserves in excess of what corresponds to average behaviour of around $600 billion and $450 billion, respectively. Furthermore, back-of-the-envelope calculations suggest that in the case of China, where the accumulation of reserves accelerated after the end of 2008, the deviation from average behaviour eclipsed $1 trillion by 2009. In the case of Japan, large interventions in the foreign exchange market in 2003-04 dramatically pushed up the level of international reserves. So while the long-run level implied by average behaviour also climbed through to 2008 (on the back a surge in trade), a large (but declining) positive gap remains.

To the extent that the level of reserves does indeed exceed adequacy ratios in many countries, a greater proportion of these funds could be invested more diversely (and productively), thereby reducing the opportunity cost of holding reserves. This might include transferring a greater proportion of excess reserves to SWFs which typically invest more aggressively and in assets that are less liquid than do central banks (Jeanne, 2007). Indeed, recent moves in that direction by many countries add credence to the view that the current historically unprecedented levels of reserve holdings in some countries are excessive from the stand point of precaution or self-insurance. Diversification in the currencies in which reserves are held might also be prudent as an excessive concentration in one reserve currency could mean that the benefits of self-insurance might be offset by the risk of large capital losses in the event of a major realignment in exchange rates.

That having been said, there are good reasons that the US dollar is the preferred currency in which to hold foreign reserves. Firstly, reserves need to be in a currency that holds its value in a crisis. Secondly, the market for US dollars is both deep and liquid. Thirdly, to the extent that the stock of reserves serves as insurance against trade and debt shocks, if trade and debt are mostly denominated in US dollars, so therefore should be reserves. Furthermore, if the purpose is to defend a peg to a particular currency, then holding reserves in that counterpart currency would be preferable.

Reserves, deviation from long-run average behaviour
Percentage points of GDP, average over three years to 2008

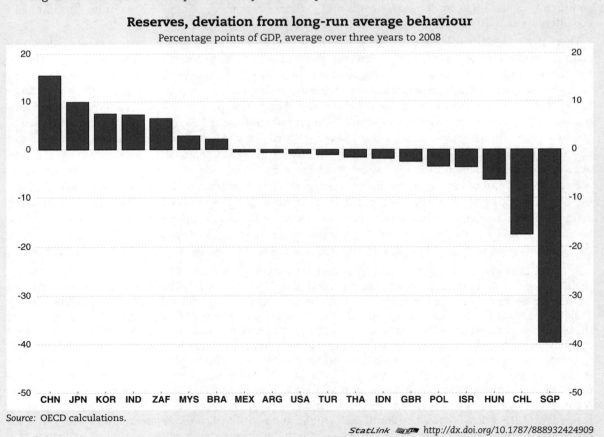

Source: OECD calculations.

StatLink http://dx.doi.org/10.1787/888932424909

developing countries increased less than outflows and FDI remained the main overall source of international financing for these countries until 2007 when debt inflows became more important.

Net international investment positions have widened

While overall financial globalisation has been associated with advanced countries becoming net debtors to the rest of the world, the evolution of net foreign assets has been very heterogeneous across countries. A common feature is, nevertheless, the widening of net international investment positions in the main regions with a strengthening of the creditor positions of Germany, Japan, major oil producers and China and an increase in indebtedness of the United States, France, Italy and the United Kingdom.

Understanding cross-country differences in external positions

Several structural settings tend to be associated with lower net foreign asset positions including...

Cross-country differences in the size and evolution of foreign asset and liability positions can be accounted for by several factors including the level of economic and financial development, capital account restrictions, trade openness and the size of the market, and differences in institutional quality (Lane and Milesi-Ferretti, 2008; Alfaro *et al.*, 2008). Countries with more open financial markets, better institutional quality and more competitive product and labour markets tend to be more able to attract and absorb foreign and domestic capital as well as to export capital, and on balance have lower net foreign assets (Furceri *et al.*, 2011a). More precisely:[3]

... greater financial development and liberalisation and capital account openness...

- More financial development (measured by the size of the domestic credit market and stock market capitalisation) and capital account openness tend to be associated with higher foreign asset and liability positions and overall lower net foreign assets positions. Countries with more liberalised financial systems (as measured by the IMF financial liberalisation indicator) tend to have higher foreign liabilities and lower net foreign asset positions.

... better regulatory quality and product market regulations...

- Better regulatory quality, which likely increases the risk-adjusted return to capital and so increases opportunities for investment in the domestic economy, is associated with lower gross foreign assets and higher foreign liabilities.While the results using a survey-based indicator of regulatory quality have to be interpreted with caution, similar results are obtained, but over a smaller sample of countries,

---

3. The main empirical analysis has focused on the link between stocks of foreign assets and liabilities and structural variables and has a pure cross-section nature, weakening the confidence with which inferences can be drawn about causality. The analysis also suggests that countries with *de facto* more flexible exchange rates (as measured by their monthly volatility) tend to have lower net foreign assets in the medium term.

using OECD product market regulation (PMR) indicators.[4] The finding that better regulation is associated with lower net foreign assets is consistent with results by Kerdrain *et al.* (2010) concerning determinants of current-account balances and suggests that regulatory reform in surplus economies may contribute towards diminishing global imbalances.

... as well as more flexible labour markets

● In general, labour market policies tend to affect returns on investments and could thereby affect foreign asset and liability positions. In particular, labour market reforms that reduce labour costs may affect foreign asset positions *via* two conflicting channels: on the one hand, they will support investment at home at the expense of investment abroad (with a negative effect on net foreign assets), while, on the other hand, labour may be substituted for domestic capital (with a positive effect on net foreign assets). Using a measure of employment protection legislation (EPL) as a proxy measure of the overall stance of labour market policies, the empirical analysis suggests that the first effect dominates so that less stringent EPL is associated with lower gross and net foreign assets.[5] These findings need, however, to be qualified because the set of countries for which the EPL indicator is available is mainly limited to OECD countries over the period under review.

Going forward, growth enhancing reforms could attract more capital inflows...

Overall, these results are consistent with the view that going forward international capital should flow more to emerging markets, given the likely future economic and financial developments and improvements in institutional quality in emerging market economies on the one hand, and the smaller scope for financial development and improvements in institutional quality in advanced economies on the other hand. Hence, while also supporting long-term growth, better regulatory quality, greater financial development and capital account openness and more flexible labour and product markets would contribute to a reduction of net asset positions of emerging economies in the long term. Getting there would involve a reduction in current account imbalances over a long period of time during which net foreign asset positions adjust to their new levels. The magnitude of the effects from structural policy changes is potentially

4.   "Regulatory quality" is measured by the World Bank's survey-based indicator of the perceptions of the governments' ability to formulate and implement sound regulations promoting private sector development. It is widely used in academic research and transparency in the methodology and in the sources used has significantly improved over the years. However, its use could be questioned on a number of grounds including the fact that it is inherently subjective and relies on data collected using a large variety of sources (for more details see Furceri and Mourougane, 2010). The various shortcomings notwithstanding, for the OECD countries the indicator is highly correlated with the OECD's "product market regulation" indicator (with a correlation coefficient of 0.7). OECD product market regulation indicators are available for all OECD countries plus Brazil, China and Russia. The database is currently being expanded to include more non-member countries.

5.   These results, however, contrast with previous OECD empirical evidence on the effect of EPL on current-account balances (Kerdrain *et al.*, 2010).

large. Back-of-the-envelope calculations based on necessarily uncertain regression results suggest that:[6]

... in emerging and transition economies...
- If emerging market and transition economies improved their average level of institutional quality (as proxied either by OECD measures of product market regulation or the World Bank's measure of regulatory quality) to the level of high-income OECD countries, this would eventually and *ceteris paribus* be associated with a long-term reduction in net foreign assets by about 30 percentage points of GDP on average.

... including China
- For China, reducing the gap with the OECD average in respect of regulatory quality by one quarter (as measured either by the World Bank indicator or the OECD's PMR indicator) would eventually be associated with a reduction of the net foreign asset position by about 15 percentage points of GDP. Assuming that half of the effects of such reforms materialise over the first 10 years, China's current-account surplus could be reduced by about ¾ percentage point of GDP on average over a decade.

But individual country situations differ
Individual country situations have to be taken into account. In external surplus countries, reforms would have the double benefit of supporting welfare and long-term growth and reducing imbalances. But in deficit countries, notably emerging ones, growth-enhancing reforms may increase external imbalances. If wider deficits are deemed undesirable they might have to be complemented by other measures to help increase net savings or at least limit their deterioration. In particular, reducing large fiscal deficits would have the double benefit of reducing risks associated with public debt sustainability and shrinking current account deficits.

The role of policies in limiting the risks associated with financial globalisation

Financial globalisation can increase macroeconomic risks

Global financial integration is good for growth but has risks
Global financial integration promotes income growth both directly *via* a better allocation of investment and new insurance possibilities and indirectly *via* incentives for better macroeconomic policies and structural reforms. But it also implies vulnerabilities and risks both at the global and national levels.

The financial transmission of a shock is faster and more complex
First, at the global level, the financial crisis has revealed the complexity of the international transmission of financial shocks and the financial vulnerabilities associated with increased international capital flows and gross positions. The size of bilateral gross positions, the

6. Such illustrative quantifications need to be interpreted with considerable caution given the difficulty to draw causal conclusions based on cross-country variation, the uncertainty around point estimates and the high collinearity between the indicators involved, which further suggests that summing the effect of changes in each indicator may substantially exaggerate the overall impact.

diversity of their composition and the complexity of financing networks make direct and indirect exposure of countries and sectors to a financial shock difficult to assess. The needs for data collection and monitoring of risks have therefore become more important.[7]

Large capital inflows create macroeconomic dilemmas...

At the country level, capital inflows, especially when they are large, create numerous challenges, and can complicate macroeconomic management. Currently, for instance, several emerging market economies are faced with large private capital inflows generating upward pressures on their real exchange rates. This creates the difficult dilemma of either letting the currency appreciate and competitiveness deteriorate or trying to contain the appreciation which may either lead to a risk of over-heating or, if inflows are sterilised, a risk of additional capital flows being attracted.[8]

... risk destabilising the domestic financial system...

In addition, capital inflows are often associated with credit booms and a deterioration of credit quality, as well as with rapid increases in financial asset and real estate prices and associated wealth effects on the economy (Reinhart and Reinhart, 2008). The risk of a misallocation of foreign capital is important, especially when financial markets in host countries are not well developed and not well regulated. But even well-developed and regulated systems are not spared. Countries with strong regulatory standards may also experience misallocation of foreign investment, as for example in Spain in the years before the crisis. Even in the well-developed US financial system, large inflows before the crisis may have been a factor behind a deterioration of lending standards.

... and may end up in a crisis

Overall, large capital inflows make recipient countries more vulnerable to booms and busts and to financial crises and their associated economic and social costs. About 60% of 268 episodes of large foreign capital inflows (identified by large deviations of the net capital inflows-to-GDP ratio from historical trends in Furceri *et al.*, 2011b) ended in a "sudden stop", and about one in ten episodes ended in either a banking crisis or a currency crisis.[9] Considering only OECD countries, about 40% of the 75 large capital inflow episodes ended in a sudden stop and about one in ten episodes in either a banking crisis or a currency crisis. The empirical analysis in Furceri *et al.*

7. Milesi-Ferretti *et al.* (2010) notably highlight some important gaps in data on cross-border asset holdings, mostly related to external claims and liabilities of offshore centres, oil exporters, and other emerging markets. See also Mihaljek (2008) and IMF (2010a).

8. See for instance Ghosh *et al.* (2008) and Roubini (2010) for a review. In some cases, fiscal consolidation may help to ease the trade-off involved in dealing with large capital inflows.

9. Large capital inflow episodes are defined as large inflows (as share of GDP) relative to the trend (and the normal volatility) experienced by each specific country. Banking and currency crises are from Laeven and Valencia (2008) where the starting dates of banking crises are based on a combination of quantitative indicators measuring banking sector distress and currency crisis episodes are identified when a currency has a nominal depreciation of 10% in one year and 30% overall. Sudden stops are defined as a large fall in a country's net capital inflows. See Furceri *et al.* (2011c) for more details.

Figure 6.3. **The annual probability of a banking crisis or a sudden stop**

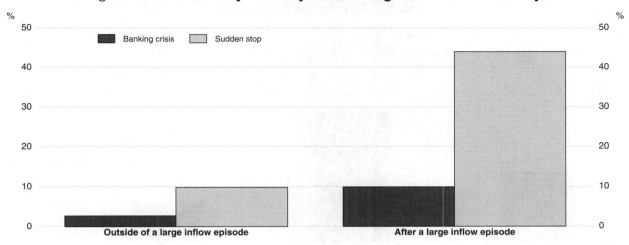

Note: Based on regression results in Table 7 and Table 11 in Furceri *et al.* (2011c). Probabilities are evaluated at sample means for all other variables entering the equation. A large capital inflow episode is defined by a large deviation of the net capital inflow-to-GDP ratio relative to its historical trend.

Source: OECD calculations.

StatLink http://dx.doi.org/10.1787/888932424814

(2011c) shows that the probability of a banking crisis or sudden stop is quadrupled after a large foreign capital inflows episode (Figure 6.3).

Currency and maturity mismatches magnify risks

Currency and maturity mismatches resulting from these flows are an additional potential source of financial instability, and may amplify the impact of a sudden stop or currency crisis (see Park, 2010, for a discussion). Although mismatches are inherent to banking and intermediation activity, large mismatches may make countries extremely vulnerable to financial shocks, for instance, when banks hold local-currency long-term assets funded by short-term borrowing on foreign wholesale funding markets (as was the case in many European countries just before the crisis – a practice that has not totally disappeared). The costs of a financial crisis and exchange rate depreciation are also particularly high in countries with large foreign indebtedness (as depreciation may dramatically increase the cost of debt servicing and external financing dries up), and it may lead to a debt crisis.[10]

The role of structural policies in mitigating vulnerabilities

Structural settings can mitigate vulnerabilities associated with large inflows...

The empirical literature largely finds that capital account liberalisation has a more favourable impact on growth when institutions are strong and of good quality, and when the financial system is deep and developed (see Tirole, 2002; Obstfeld, 2008; Kose

10. A main exception being US legal entities that, thanks to the reserve status of the US dollar, borrow in their own currency, while holding a large share of their foreign assets in foreign currencies so that a depreciation of the dollar reduces US net external debt.

Figure 6.4. **The probability of a banking crisis following a large capital inflow episode under different policy settings**

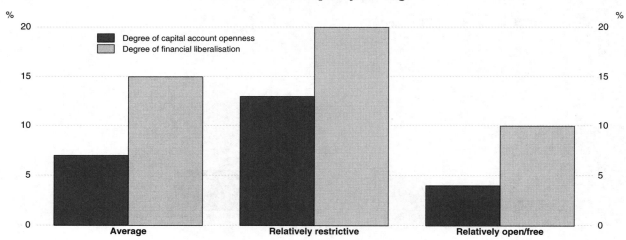

Note: Based on regression results reported in Table 7 in Furceri *et al.* (2011c). Due to differences in data availability the sample varies from one equation to the other and is also different from the sample used for Figure 6.3 resulting in different crisis probability when all variables are at sample mean. Probabilities are evaluated at sample means for all other variables entering the equation. "Relatively restricted" relates to the first quartile of the distribution. "Relatively open/free" relates to the fourth quartile of the distribution. Capital openness is measured using the Chinn-Ito index and financial liberalisation using the IMF index. Most OECD countries are classified in the fourth quartile of the distribution for both indicators (*i.e.* relatively liberalised and open) while no BRICS can be found in that quartile (and most rank in the first quartile).

Source: OECD calculations.

StatLink http://dx.doi.org/10.1787/888932424833

et al., 2009).[11] The analysis by Furceri *et al.* (2011c) also supports the view that structural policies can help to minimise the vulnerabilities generated by large inflows. For instance, capital account openness and greater financial liberalisation are associated with a lower probability of experiencing a banking crisis following large capital inflows (Figure 6.4). However, these relationships have to be interpreted with caution since they may also reflect some form of reverse causality, as countries that are less prone to crises may be more willing to liberalise and open their financial system. In addition, since greater financial liberalisation and capital account openness may also increase the number and scale of episodes of large capital inflows, their total effect on the probability of banking crises remains uncertain.

... notably by improving the composition of inflows

The main channel by which structural policies reduce vulnerabilities associated with capital inflows is indirect *via* the composition of these inflows. Better structural policies – a more liberal financial system, more

11. In particular, there seems to be a non-linear effect of capital account liberalisation on long-term growth that depends on the level of financial development, institutional quality (including strong property rights and accounting standards) and also, but less importantly, trade openness, labour market flexibility and the overall level of development (see Kose *et al.*, 2009, Eichengreen *et al.*, 2009). The composition of inflows is also important in limiting risks and maximising benefits. For instance, the existence of non-linearities between capital account liberalisation and growth seems more important when inflows are mainly debt flows rather than FDI or equity investment (see Kose *et al.*, 2009).

open capital accounts,[12] but also more pro-competition product market regulation and avoidance of overly stringent employment protection – are associated with a higher share of FDI and a lower share of debt (Furceri *et al.* 2011a).[13] Conversely, the probability of facing a crisis or a sudden stop after large inflow episodes is especially high when inflows are driven by debt (Figure 6.5).[14] Moreover, debt-driven episodes of large capital inflows tend to have a stronger impact on domestic credit than when inflows are driven primarily through FDI or equity portfolio investment (Figure 6.6). Also FDI inflows are less volatile than debt and equity inflows

Figure 6.5. **Annual probability of banking crisis and sudden stops depending on the nature of the capital inflows**

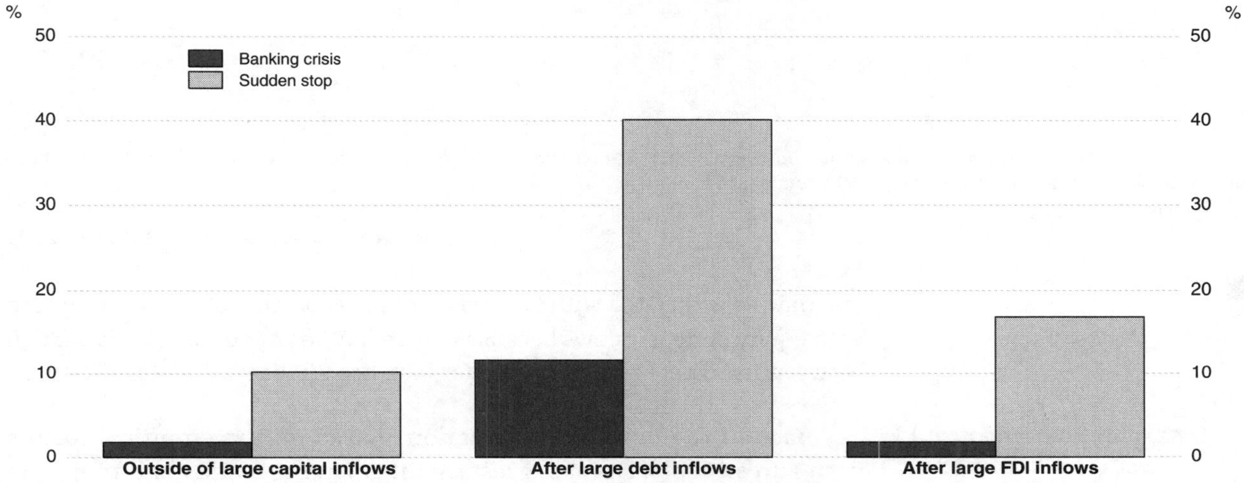

Note: Based on regression results in Tables 10 and 14 in Furceri *et al.* (2011c). Probabilities are evaluated at sample means for all other variables entering the equation.

Source: OECD calculations.

StatLink 🔗 *http://dx.doi.org/10.1787/888932424852*

12. The impact of capital account openness is, however, ambiguous. While it is associated with a higher share of FDI in inflows and a lower probability of banking crises, it is also associated with a higher probability of a sudden stop in capital inflows after a large inflow episode even when controlling for the size of inflows. This may reflect the role played by some forms of capital controls in skewing the composition of inflows towards longer maturity and in limiting subsequent outflows and capital flights. This was the case in Chile in the 1990s and it may have contributed together with structural reforms, some liberalisation of capital outflows and sound macroeconomic policies to the large inflows recorded in the first half of the decade not ending up in a crisis, in sharp contrast with the experience of the late 1970s-early 1980s. In any case, this suggests that more work is needed, notably on the implications of the different types of capital controls.

13. Some of these results are in line with findings in other studies, including previous OECD work. The finding that pro-competition regulations are associated with more FDI and less equity portfolio investment and debt is common to Hajkova *et al.* (2006) and Nicoletti *et al.* (2003). Less stringent EPL in host countries being associated with a higher share of FDI in liabilities is also in line with previous OECD findings and those of Javorcik and Spatareanu (2005).

14. Debt is defined as the sum of bond portfolio investments and other investments.

Figure 6.6. **The response of private credit to capital inflows**
Increase in credit-to-GDP ratio, percentage points of GDP

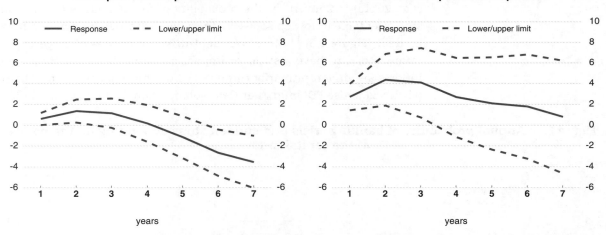

Note: Based on regression results reported in Furceri *et al.* (2011b). Solid lines represent average responses of credit to GDP to a large inflow episode and dotted lines represent 90% confidence bands.

Source: OECD calculations.

StatLink http://dx.doi.org/10.1787/888932424871

and may be associated with lower risks of misallocation of capital compared with equity or debt inflows because they reduce asymmetries of information between foreigners and locals (see for instance Kirabaeva and Razin, 2010).

Emerging countries could attract a higher share of FDI with improved institutions

Back-of-the-envelope calculations based on the empirical results from Furceri *et al.* (2011a) suggest that if emerging market and transition economies increased their level of institutional quality in terms of product market regulation to the average level of OECD countries, this would be associated with an eventual increase in the stock of FDI by about 10 percentage points of the total stock of liabilities, and a corresponding reduction in the stock of portfolio liabilities.[15] Similarly, an increase in their level of capital account openness to the average level of OECD countries would be associated with an increase in the share of FDI in the total stock of liabilities by about 5 percentage points, and a corresponding reduction in the share of debt.[16]

The effect of structural policies on overall macroeconomic risks is ambiguous

The overall effect of better structural policies on macroeconomic risks is, however, ambiguous. On the one hand, improved structural policy settings are likely to increase the overall scale of capital flows which will increase risk. On the other hand, better structural policies (more

15. Since the global composition of liabilities can only change with the global composition of assets, the share of outward FDI in foreign assets should also increase, driven for instance by further financial development and liberalisation in capital exporting countries.
16. These results have to be interpreted with caution, not least because of the complex interactions between FDI and other capital flows. For instance, foreign direct investors may hedge the firm's FDI exposure by borrowing domestically and then taking short-term capital out of the country.

competition-friendly product market regulation, less stringent job protection, higher institutional quality and greater capital account openness) are associated with a composition of capital inflows – principally more FDI and less debt – which is more stable and less prone to risk. The overall net effect on macroeconomic risk will depend on the particular form of structural reforms enacted, but also on how they are buttressed by progress in financial reforms to strengthen the prudential and macro-prudential framework in both emerging and advanced economies.

The role of macroeconomic policies in mitigating vulnerabilities

Macroeconomic policies are an important part of the response to capital inflows

In addition to structural and prudential and macro-prudential policies, macroeconomic policies such as exchange rate and fiscal policies also have a significant role to play to reduce vulnerabilities associated with capital inflows. Exchange rate flexibility appears to reduce some of the effect of large capital inflow episodes on domestic credit (Figure 6.7,

Figure 6.7. **The response of private credit to large capital inflow episodes under different policy stances**

Increase in credit-to-GDP ratio, percentage points of GDP

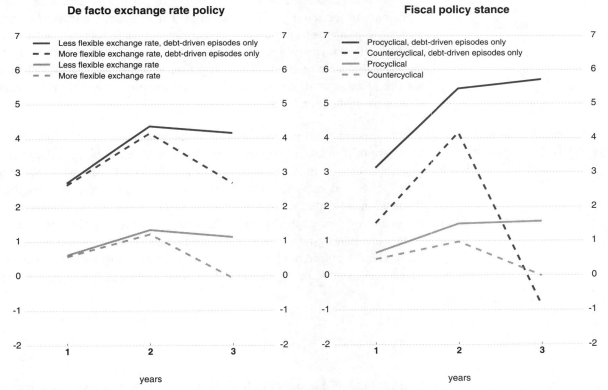

Note: Based on regression results reported in Furceri *et al.* (2011b). The less flexible exchange rates correspond to cases where real exchange rate volatility does not increase in response to an inflow episode and the more flexible exchange rates to cases where it increases. Countries with pro-cyclical (counter-cyclical) fiscal policy are countries where the correlation between the change in government spending and output growth is positive (negative).

Source: OECD calculations.

StatLink http://dx.doi.org/10.1787/888932424890

left hand panel), consistent with the arguments that: *i)* countries which let their exchange rate fluctuate in response to inflows may reduce the duration of a net inflow episode; *ii)* higher exchange rate volatility (and thereby risk) may reduce credit growth by increasing risk premia and reducing foreign currency-denominated credit; *iii)* the alternative of foreign exchange interventions may create credit and asset prices bubbles if not fully sterilised; *iv)* and banks fund themselves less abroad when the exchange rate is more flexible. In addition, countries that typically follow countercyclical fiscal policy have, on average, experienced more moderate credit booms during large inflow episodes, and especially during debt inflow episodes (Figure 6.7, right hand panel). The recommendation for fiscal restraint during episodes of large capital inflows is a common conclusion of the literature (for example Cardarelli *et al.*, 2010).[17] These are, however, general findings and related policy recommendations have to take into account country-specific circumstances and constraints.

Conclusions: the role of policies in making the most of global financial integration

Structural policies have a role to play to reduce vulnerabilities associated with financial globalisation...

Countries' net foreign capital positions are strongly influenced by their structural policy settings.[18] A corollary of the empirical evidence is that growth-enhancing reforms in emerging surplus economies could contribute to reducing global imbalances. The effect of growth enhancing structural policy reforms on macroeconomic risks associated with large capital inflows is ambiguous; better structural policies are likely to increase the scale of capital flows together with the associated risks but also to change their composition away from debt towards FDI which should mitigate such risks.

... but in conjunction with appropriate macroeconomic and financial policies

To ensure that macroeconomic risks associated with large capital flows are minimised, structural policy reforms need to be complemented by an appropriate macroeconomic policy stance, particularly in respect of fiscal policy and exchange rates, as well as financial reforms to strengthen the prudential and macro-prudential framework. There may also be a role for some form of capital controls if designed in a way that minimises distortions in long-term investments and ordinary business activities, but these should preferably be subject to multilateral surveillance as in the framework created by the OECD *Code of Liberalisation of Capital Movements*.

17. An example of a country which has been able to deal with large capital inflows while maintaining capital account openness is Australia in the late 1980s which benefited from high institutional quality, a liberalised and deep financial system and a tight fiscal policy.

18. In this regard, the findings described in this chapter conform with and augment earlier analysis of the link between structural policies and current accounts (OECD, 2011).

Bibliography

Alfaro, L., S. Kalemli-Ozcan and V. Volosovych (2008), "Why Doesn't Capital Flow from Rich to Poor Countries? An Empirical Investigation", *Review of Economics and Statistics* Vol. 90.

Aizenman, J. and J. Lee (2007), "International Reserves: Precautionary *versus* Mercantilist Views, Theory and Evidence", *Open Economies Review* Vol. 18.

Cardarelli, R., S. Elekdag and A. Kose (2010), "Capital inflows: Macroeconomic Implications and Policy Responses", *Economic Systems*, Vol. 34.

Cheung, Y. and H. Ito (2008), "Hoarding of International Reserves: A Comparison of the Asian and Latin American Experiences", *Hong Kong Institute for Monetary Research Working Papers* No. 072008.

Chinn, M. and H. Ito (2008), "A New Measure of Financial Openness", *Journal of Comparative Policy Analysis*, Vol. 10.

Eichengreen, B., R. Gullapalli and U. Panizza (2009), "Capital Account Liberalization, Financial Development and Industry Growth: A Synthetic View", *Department of Public Policy and Public Choice, Working Paper* No. 144, POLIS.

Furceri, D. and A. Mourougane (2010), "Structural Indicators: A Critical Review", *OECD Economic Studies*, Vol. 2010/1.

Furceri, D., S. Guichard and E. Rusticelli (2011a), "Medium-term Determinants of International Investment Positions: the Role of Structural Policies", *OECD Economics Department Working Paper*, No. 863.

Furceri, D., S. Guichard and E. Rusticelli (2011b), "The Effect of Episodes of Large Capital Inflows on Domestic Credit", *OECD Economics Department Working Paper*, No. 864.

Furceri, D., S. Guichard and E. Rusticelli (2011c), "Episodes of Large Capital Inflows and the Likelihood of Banking and Currency Crises and Sudden Stops", *OECD Economics Department Working Paper*, No. 865.

Ghosh, A., M. Goretti, B. Joshi, U. Ramakrishnan, A. Thomas, and J. Zalduendo (2008), "Capital Inflows and Balance of Payments Pressures – Tailoring Policy Responses in Emerging Market Economies", *IMF Policy Discussion Paper* 08/2.

Hajkova, D., G. Nicoletti, L. Vartia and K.-Y. Yoo (2003), "Taxation, Business Environment and FDI Location in OECD Countries", *OECD Economics Department Working Papers*, No. 502.

IMF (2010a), *Understanding Financial Interconnectedness*, Washington DC.

IMF (2010b), *The Fund's Role Regarding Cross-Border Capital Flows*, Washington DC..

IMF (2011), *Recent Experiences in Managing Capital Inflows – Cross-Cutting Themes and Possible Policy Framework*, Washington DC..

Javorcik, B. and M. Spatareanu (2005), "Do Foreign Investors Care About Labour Market Regulations?", *CEPR Discussion Papers* No. 4839.

Jeanne, O. (2007), "International Reserves in Emerging Market Countries: Too Much of a Good Thing?", *Brookings Papers on Economic Activity* Vol. 2007/1.

Jeanne, O. and R. Rancière (2008), "The Optimal Level of International Reserves For Emerging Market Countries: A New Formula and Some Applications", *CEPR Discussion Papers*, No. 6723.

Kerdrain, C., I. Koske, I. Wanner (2010), "The Impact of Structural Policies on Saving, Investment and Current Accounts", *OECD Economics Department Working Papers* No. 815.

Kirabaeva, K. and A. Razin (2010), "Composition of Capital Flows: A Survey", *NBER Working Paper*, No. 16492.

Kose, A., E. Prasad, K. Rogoff, and S.-J. Wei (2006), "Financial Globalization: A Reappraisal", *IMF Working paper* No. 06/189.

Kose, A., E. Prasad and A. Taylor (2009), "Thresholds in the Process of International Financial Integration", *NBER Working Papers* No. 14916.

Lane, P. (2010), "International Financial Integration and the External Positions of the Euro Area Countries", *OECD Economics Department Working Papers*, No. 830.

Lane, P. and G.M. Milesi-Ferretti (2007), "The External Wealth of Nations Mark II: Revised and Extended Estimates of Foreign Assets and Liabilities, 1970-2004", *Journal of International Economics*, No. Vol. 73.

Lane, P. and G. M. Milesi-Ferretti (2008), "The Drivers of Financial Globalization", *American Economic Review: Papers and Proceedings* 2008, Vol. 98.

Leaven, L. and F. Valencia (2008), "Systemic Banking Crises: A New Database", *IMF Working Paper No. 08/224*.

Mateos y Lago, I., R. Duttagupta and R. Goyal (2009), "The Debate on the International Monetary System", *IMF Staff Position Note SPN/09/26*.

Mihaljek, D. (2008), "The Financial Stability Implications of Increased Capital Flows for Emerging Market Economies", *BIS Paper No. 44*.

Milesi-Ferretti, G.-M., F. Strobbe and N. Tamirisa (2010), "Bilateral Financial Linkages and Global Imbalances: A View on the Eve of the Financial Crisis", *IMF Working Papers* No. 10/257.

Milesi-Ferretti, G.-M. and C. Tille (2010), "The Great Retrenchment: International Capital Flows During the Global Financial Crisis", *IHEID Working Papers* No. 18-2010.

Nicoletti, G., S. Golub, D. Hajkova, D. Mirza and K.-Y. Yoo (2003), "Policies and International Integration: Influences on Trade and Foreign Direct Investment", *OECD Economics Department Working Papers*, No. 359.

Obstfeld, M. (2008), "International Finance and Growth in Developing Countries: What have we Learned?", *Commission of Growth and Development Working Paper* No. 34.

Obstfeld, M., J. Shambaugh and A. Taylor (2008), "Financial Stability, the Trilemma and International Reserves", *CEPR Discussion Paper* No. 6693.

OECD (2010), *OECD Code of Liberalisation of Capital Movements*, Paris.

OECD (2011), "Tackling Current Account Imbalances: Is There a Role for Structural Policies?" in *Going for Growth*, Chapter 5, Paris.

Ostry, J., A. Ghosh, K. Habermeier, M. Chamon, M. Qureshi and D. Reinhardt (2010), "Capital Inflows: The Role of Controls", *IMF Staff Position Note 10/04*.

Park, Y.C. (2010), "The Role of Macroprudential Policy for Financial Stability in East Asia's Emerging Economies", based on a paper presented to the conference on "The Banking Regulation and Financial Stability in Asian Emerging Markets" organised by the ADBI, CBRC and IMF, Beijing, 26 May.

Reinhart, C. and V. Reinhart (2008), "Capital Flow Bonanzas: An Encompassing View of the Past and Present", *CEPR Discussion Papers* No. 6996.

Rodrik, D. (2006), "The Social Cost of Foreign Exchange Reserves,"*International Economic Journal* Vol. 20.

Roubini, N. (2010), "How should Emerging Markets Manage Capital Inflows and Currency Appreciation?", mimeo.

Schindler, M. (2009), "Measuring Financial Integration: A New Data Set", *IMF Staff Papers*, Vol. 56.

Summers, L. (2006), "Reflections on Global Account Imbalances and Emerging Markets Reserve Accumulation", L.K. Jha Memorial Lecture, Reserve Bank of India (March).

Suttle, P., R. Koepke and J. Mazzacurati (2010), "Capital Flows to Emerging Market Economies", *IIF Research Note*, 4 October.

Tirole, J. (2002), *Financial Crisis, Liquidity, and the International Monetary System*, Princeton University Press.

Waysand, C., K. Ross and J. de Guzman (2010), "European Financial Linkages: A New Look at Imbalances", *IMF Working Paper* No. WP/09/295.

Vujanovic, P. (2011), "Understanding the Recent Surge in the Accumulation of International Reserves", *OECD Economics Department Working Paper*, forthcoming.

Chapter 7

OECD AT 50

Evolving Paradigms in Economic Policy Making

Introduction

Progress in science is sometimes seen as a continuous increase in the set of accepted facts and theories. But, as shown by Kuhn (1962), periods of continuity are occasionally interrupted by the discovery of anomalies, which lead to a new paradigm, *i.e.* a new way of perceiving and analysing the subject of study. Even though the "dismal science" has never seen universal agreement on a single paradigm, a succession of paradigms can still be distinguished in the history of economic policymaking. Each paradigm defines "not only the goals of economic policy and the kind of instruments that can be used to attain them, but also the very nature of the problems they are meant to be addressing" (Hall, 1993, pp. 279).

A prominent paradigm shift took place in the early 1980s when policies became more oriented towards the medium term and the supply side took centre stage in response to the stagflation of the 1970s. Since then there have been further developments in the paradigm, such as those associated with the rational expectations revolution which called for predictability and transparency of policymaking. The "Great Moderation" of stable growth and prices since the mid-1990s was seen as evidence of the paradigm's success. However, favourable headline statistics masked growing underlying imbalances, and when these erupted with the financial crisis of 2008-09, established certainties again broke down and new approaches to policymaking came to the fore.

This 50th Anniversary Special Chapter takes stock of the paradigm shifts in economic policymaking that have occurred since the Organisation began its work, both prior to the financial crisis and during it, drawing on the OECD's key economic surveillance processes (see Box 7.1). The chapter looks backward and forward. How have political and economic realities shaped the dominant paradigm? How has the financial crisis led the Organisation to reassess the pre-crisis paradigm? What parts of the pre-crisis paradigm appear to have failed and what parts may be worth preserving?

Paradigms of the past[1]

The 1960s and 1970 were dominated by the active use of "demand management" policies to keep unemployment low and prevent unsustainable current account imbalances. While initially successful, they failed to cope with, first, large exchange rate misalignments in the early-1970s and, second, "stagflation" in the wake of the first and second oil price shocks.

In the 1980s the focus of policies shifted to the medium term. Structural policies to liberalise product and labour markets took centre stage, and were embedded in a system of rules-based policymaking in the 1990s. This proved largely successful, although financial crises became more frequent and virulent. In the 2000s emerging market economies gradually – but surely – gained weight in the global economy. Imbalances increased amid regulatory and policy complacency, which eventually led to the recent financial crisis.

---

1. The discussion of the 1960s, 1970s and 1980s in this section draws on the 50th Issue Special Chapter of *OECD Economic Outlook*, No. 50 (OECD, 1991).

Box 7.1. **Key OECD platforms for economic policy assessment and co-ordination**

At its start in 1961, the OECD launched the publication of periodic *OECD Economic Surveys* for each member country, subjecting the OECD's drafts to a full day of discussion before the Economic and Development Review Committee in the first systematic peer review process in any international institution. These pull together expertise not only in the OECD's Economics Department, but increasingly also in specialised Directorates and Committees of the OECD. For several years now there have been periodic *Surveys* covering major non-member countries, such as the "BRICs", Brazil, Russia, India, China, as well as Indonesia and South Africa. For a long time – most of the first three decades of the Organisation's existence – the *Surveys* centred on the shorter-term outlook for a country and the macroeconomic responses to the challenges posed by that outlook. But progressively structural policy issues (and their interaction with macroeconomic developments) gained prominence.

The Economic Policy Committee, a body of senior officials from finance/economics ministries and central banks, provides policy guidance on macroeconomic and structural issues. In this context, the *OECD Economic Outlook* analyses the economic situation and prospects – with an eye to long-run sustainability – and the policy requirements to which they give rise. The *OECD Economic Outlook* first appeared six years after the Organisation started its activities, in 1967. The colophon in the first issue mentions that the *OECD Economic Outlook* "… will appear initially twice a year, in July and December". In fact it has remained a biannual publication, aside from a special issue in March 2009 to cover the exceptional circumstances at the height of the financial crisis in the winter of 2008-09. Since 2005 the annual *Going for Growth* publication has provided an overview of key recommendations for structural reforms in individual countries, along with a checklist on how countries have responded to them. OECD policy analysis and advice also feeds into the G20, the single-most important global platform for the co-ordination of economic and financial policies since the onset of the crisis.

Testing the limits of demand management (1960s and 1970s)

In the 1960s policy was conditioned by the Bretton Woods system of fixed exchange rates. Fiscal and monetary policy instruments were used to restore full employment, low inflation and external balances whenever developments diverged from these objectives. The paradigm appeared to work well. The 1960s were a period of rapid OECD growth (averaging over 5%, see Figure 7.1 and Table 7.1), stable inflation (3¾ per cent) and "full employment" – corresponding to OECD unemployment in the 3-3½ per cent range (Figure 7.3 below).

Still, in this period policy setting became increasingly preoccupied with rising external pressures in several countries and a series of international monetary crises that led to occasional exchange-rate re-adjustment. These pressures arose out of attempts to maintain fixed exchange rates at parities increasingly out of line with fundamentals in view of inflationary policies in the anchor country, the United States.

Events in 1971 marked the end of this period. Pressure from international capital flows led to a series of policy actions, including exchange-rate realignments and periods of floating – most notably of the US dollar from August onwards after its gold convertibility had been abandoned. The so-called Smithsonian realignment in December 1971 brought little relief as exchange rate pressure continued and the Smithsonian parities broke down, with a generalised floating of exchange rates in early 1973. In 1979 the European Community launched the European Monetary System (EMS) of quasi-fixed exchange rates – the frontrunner of the single currency that was established in 1999.

In the 1970s, inflation became a wide-spread problem – even before the oil shocks hit. Overriding importance was attached to avoiding any "unnecessary" cost in terms of marked increases in unemployment in the battle against inflation. This was held to be possible if demand stimulus could be

Figure 7.1. **Economic growth**

In per cent

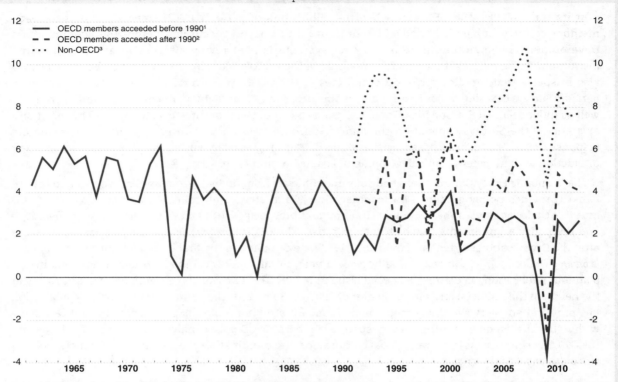

1. Refers to Australia, Austria, Belgium, Canada, Denmark, Finland, France, Germany, Greece, Iceland, Ireland, Italy, Japan, Luxembourg, Netherlands, New Zealand, Norway, Portugal, Spain, Sweden, Switzerland, Turkey, United Kingdom and United States. The weight in world and total OECD GDP equal, respectively, 60 and 89% in 2005 (calculated at purchasing power parity).
2. Refers to Chile, Czech Republic, Estonia, Hungary, Israel, Korea, Mexico, Poland, Slovak Republic, Slovenia. The weight in world and total OECD GDP equal, respectively, 7 and 11% in 2005 (calculated at purchasing power parity).
3. Refers to Enhanced Engagement countries (Brazil, China, India, Indonesia, South Africa and Russia). The weight in world GDP equal 23% in 2005 (calculated at purchasing power parity).

Source: OECD Economic Outlook 89 database.

StatLink http://dx.doi.org/10.1787/888932428880

supported by incomes policies containing wage growth, although views of the effectiveness of incomes policies differed and sometimes fluctuated sharply. But when the first oil shock following the Yom Kippur War in late 1973 sent oil prices to unprecedented heights (Figure 5 below), OECD output sharply fell in 1975 while inflation soared to some 14%.

In the aftermath of the first oil shock policymakers were divided about how best to deal with a situation in which growth failed to recover to the pace desired while inflation remained stubbornly high (dubbed stagflation). One view was that, by careful management and the limiting of short-term growth ambitions it should be possible to achieve both satisfactory expansion and steady disinflation, as advocated by an OECD report prepared by eight leading economists (McCracken *et al.*, 1977). In a similar vein, the *OECD Economic Outlook* No. 22 (OECD, 1977) noted that further expansionary policy action would be necessary while avoiding a very sharp pick-up of activity and an associated acceleration of inflation.

OECD Economic Outlook No. 22 also argued that countries in strong balance-of-payments positions should take up slack faster than countries in a weak position. This view was contested by a number of countries, typically those identified as "best placed" to expand, such as West Germany and Japan. Questions were also raised about whether it was possible to secure durable expansion through fiscal policy; whether there was a stable, long-term trade-off between inflation and unemployment; whether

Table 7.1. **Summary statistics**
Period averages

	1961-1972[1]	1973-1981	1982-1991	1992-1998	1999-2007	2008-2012
Real GDP growth						
United States	4.2	2.9	3.0	3.6	2.8	1.2
Japan	9.5	4.0	4.5	0.8	1.5	-0.5
Euro area	5.1	2.8	2.6	1.8	2.2	0.4
Total OECD	5.0	3.1	3.1	2.7	2.7	1.0
Inflation[2]						
United States	2.7	7.9	4.0	2.1	2.3	1.7
Japan	5.7	8.9	1.7	0.6	-0.8	-0.8
Euro area	4.0	10.3	5.5	2.8	2.0	1.6
Total OECD	3.7	10.9	7.9	5.1	2.7	1.9
Unemployment rate[3]						
United States	4.9	6.7	7.0	5.8	5.0	8.3
Japan	1.2	1.9	2.5	3.1	4.7	4.7
Euro area	2.0	3.8	8.2	9.9	8.4	9.2
Total OECD	3.3	4.8	6.8	7.0	6.4	7.5
Current account balance[4]						
United States	0.4	0.1	-1.9	-1.6	-4.7	-3.6
Japan	1.5	0.1	2.5	2.5	3.3	3.0
Euro area		-0.6	0.2	0.5	0.3	0.1
Total OECD	0.2	-0.5	-0.4	-0.1	-1.1	-0.8
Fiscal balance[4]						
United States	-1.4	-2.2	-4.7	-3.0	-2.2	-9.5
Japan	1.0	-3.3	-0.9	-4.4	-6.0	-7.2
Euro area	-1.4	-3.4	-4.7	-4.7	-1.8	-4.3
Total OECD	-0.9	-3.0	-4.0	-3.8	-2.1	-6.3
Real short-term interest rate[5]						
United States	3.1	2.2	4.8	2.8	1.5	-0.2
Japan	..	-0.5	4.5	1.2	1.0	1.1
Euro area	..	-0.4	4.7	3.9	1.2	0.4
Total OECD	..	-0.7	3.3	1.7	1.1	0.1

Note: OECD is defined as comprising all current members to the extent data are available. The dating of sub-periods corresponds to the following events: 1973: collapse of Bretton Woods; 1982: Reagan and Thatcher administrations in office in the United States and the United Kingdom, respectively; 1992: Maastricht Treaty and Single Market in Europe; 1999: Single Currency in Europe; 2008: onset of the financial crisis.
1. Or earliest period available for current account balance and real interest rates.
2. Private consumption deflator
3. Per cent of the labour force
4. Per cent of GDP
5. Three-month interest rate minus inflation
Source: OECD Economic Outlook 89 database.

StatLink http://dx.doi.org/10.1787/888932428975

disinflation could be achieved without monetary rigour; whether income policies were realistic except in very specific periods and (smaller) countries; and whether the public sector should seek to reduce the share of national resources it absorbed.

An uneasy consensus on a policy package was reached among the major seven (G7) countries at the Bonn Summit in 1978. Specifically, West Germany and Japan agreed to adopt fiscal stimulus measures in exchange for a commitment from the United States to raise its domestic oil price to world levels and the European commitment to reach a successful conclusion of the multilateral trade negotiations within the General Agreement on Tariffs and Trade (GATT).

But within a year of the implementation of the measures agreed at the Bonn Summit, OECD policymaking had to deal urgently with another large external shock: the sharp boost to inflation resulting from soaring oil prices in the wake of the Iranian revolution in 1979. In many countries, in combination with increased economic rigidities, the shock led to sharp rises in rates of structural unemployment, *i.e.* consistent with achieving and maintaining low inflation.[2]

Breaking the back of inflation (1980s)

The second oil shock brought to a head the debate about how to best get out of a situation in which inflation was rising while output was weak – and in which both had been affected adversely by a supply shock. This period saw the launch of structural reforms to make OECD economies more efficient, flexible and competitive – although modestly at first and with the United States and United Kingdom leading the way and Australia, Denmark, Ireland, the Netherlands and New Zealand soon following suit.

Monetary policy was geared to inflation control, for which limiting the growth of money supply initially was seen as crucial. Most OECD countries adopted or reinforced growth targets for monetary aggregates or – in Europe – continued to conduct their monetary policy so as to maintain exchange-rate parity between their currency and that of a country (*i.e.* Germany) that had been – and seemed likely to continue to be – successful in containing inflation. The result was an increase in real interest rates (Figure 7.2). Fiscal policy became medium-term oriented, seeking to reduce or eliminate deficits and to stabilise or bring down debt-to-GDP ratios. The United States was an important exception, at least initially, as the Reagan administration pursued tax cuts while substantially raising expenditures for its Strategic Defence Initiative (commonly known as "Star Wars").

As policy regained a sense of direction in the course of the 1980s, private-sector confidence revived. This, together with the recovery of profits, the effects of financial market liberalisation and, in Europe, the prospect of the 1992 Single Market, underpinned a recovery of OECD economies. Employment increased at a pace not experienced on a durable basis for more than a decade, and the rate of unemployment followed a clear downward path (Figure 7.3).

Inflation did not decline as much as might have been hoped, in part because the monetary expansion to deal with the 1987 stock market crash was not reined in with sufficient firmness (Figure 7.2). As well, in many cases monetary policy was directed for too long towards exchange rate targets that turned out to be unsustainable. As had been predicted by the Mundell-Fleming model, it became more challenging to manage exchange rates as capital accounts were opened.[3] The monetary policy framework also had to be amended towards direct inflation targeting because of the widespread breakdown of the links between monetary aggregates and national income and prices. This was due in part to the deregulation of domestic financial markets and the increase in global capital flows.

In the 1980s international economic co-ordination among OECD countries was initially limited but gained prominence later on. Reluctance to co-ordinate stemmed in part from the perception that the "concerted action" strategy agreed at the Bonn summit had failed. More generally, governments pursued a hands-off approach to the international monetary system on the assumption that the "right" value for an exchange rate was determined in the market.

But massive current account imbalances (Figure 7.4) pointed to an overvalued US dollar exchange rate – in part due to the mix of fiscal expansion and tight monetary policy of the Reagan administration – and were feeding into disquieting protectionist measures. This eventually led to a more active approach to international co-operation, important manifestations being the Plaza (September 1985) and Louvre

---

2. See Blanchard and Wolfers (2000) for a seminal analysis of the interaction effect of adverse supply shocks and economic rigidities on unemployment in Europe.
3. The Mundell-Fleming model, developed in the 1960s (Mundell, 1963, Fleming, 1962), predicted that if capital controls are removed a conflict between pegged exchange rates and monetary policy autonomy would result.

Figure 7.2. **Real short-term interest rates and fiscal positions**

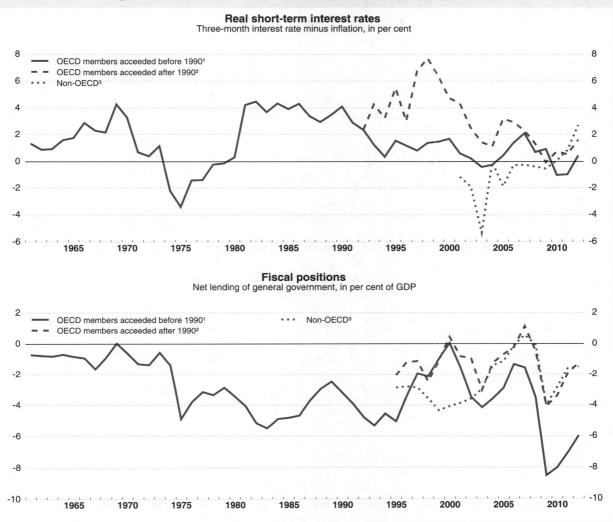

Real short-term interest rates
Three-month interest rate minus inflation, in per cent

— OECD members acceeded before 1990[1]
- - OECD members acceeded after 1990[2]
··· Non-OECD[3]

Fiscal positions
Net lending of general government, in per cent of GDP

— OECD members acceeded before 1990[1]   ··· Non-OECD[3]
- - OECD members acceeded after 1990[2]

1. See footnote 1 of Figure 7.1.
2. See footnote 2 of Figure 7.1.
3. See footnote 3 of Figure 7.1.

Source: OECD Economic Outlook 89 database.

StatLink http://dx.doi.org/10.1787/888932428918

(February 1987) accords to re-align exchange rates through intervention in exchange markets and the co-ordination of monetary policies.[4]

The adjustment burden of global imbalances initially tended to be borne by deficit countries alone. This was appropriate only insofar as a wide deficit reflected excess demand. However, after monetary policy was eased in response to the 1987 stock market crash, a financial and real estate bubble developed in Japan, which popped in the early 1990s. Similar developments were seen in the Nordic countries, as well as in the United States, culminating in the Savings and Loans and LTCM crises. Meanwhile, the analytical

4. Other manifestations were the moves to deal with debt problems of lower-income countries and the decisive action to ensure that the October 1987 stock-market crisis did not provoke a global recession.

Figure 7.3. **Inflation and unemployment rate**

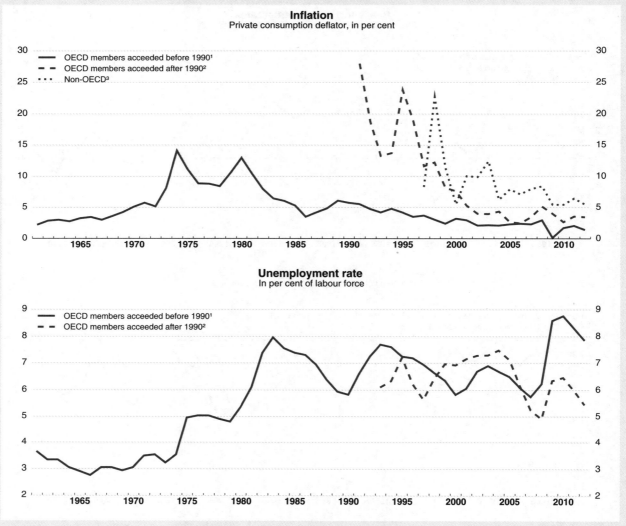

1. See footnote 1 of Figure 7.1.
2. See footnote 2 of Figure 7.1.
3. See footnote 3 of Figure 7.1.

Source: OECD Economic Outlook 89 database.

StatLink ⟨≋⟩ http://dx.doi.org/10.1787/888932428899

focus shifted to evaluating current account positions in the context of the balance between domestic saving and investment in each country.

The recovery ended in 1991 when large private-sector debt positions unwound and policy was tightened in an attempt to limit inflation (Figure 7.3). The recession hit the United States and Japan first, where the Savings and Loan Crisis and the collapse of the "Bubble Economy", respectively, took their toll. Activity in Europe was still buoyed by the boom in Germany associated with its reunification. But tight monetary policy in Germany to stem the boom led to exchange-rate turbulence within the EMS and eventually its breakdown, and pushed Europe into recession in 1993.

Figure 7.4. **Global imbalances**
Current account balance, in per cent of world GDP

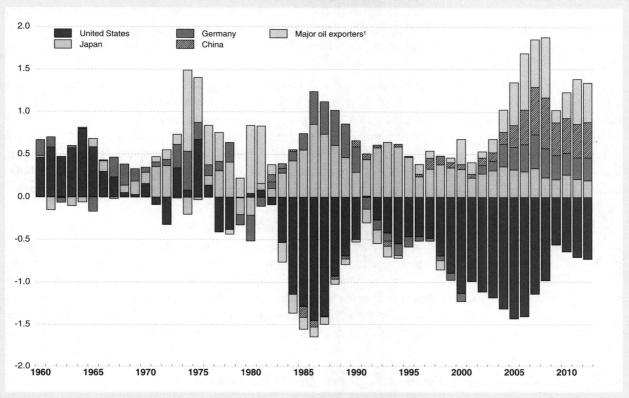

1. Refers to Saudi Arabia before 1992.

Source: OECD Economic Outlook 89 database; OECD Economic Outlook 21 database; and IMF, International Financial Statistics.

StatLink http://dx.doi.org/10.1787/888932428937

Structural reform amid rules-based macroeconomic policies (1990s)

A sobering assessment in the influential 1994 *OECD Jobs Study* (OECD, 1994) concluded that clearly not enough progress had been made on the fiscal front in the 1980s and that this was exposed once economic conditions worsened. The *Jobs Study* also reiterated the evident limits to the degree to which macroeconomic policy can be used to reduce unemployment. This was seen to require more emphasis on structural reforms, in particular greater wage flexibility, reductions in barriers to labour mobility and greater competition in product markets. Structural reform would also ease the speed limits to growth and reduce hysteresis effects.

A stability-oriented, predictable and credible macroeconomic policy was seen to assist microeconomic flexibility because private-sector participants could be more confident about medium-term prospects and thus adjust more easily to changing circumstances. When macroeconomic conditions are sound, moreover, structural reforms may be pursued more actively because the transition costs may be less painful. This approach found inspiration in the rational expectations hypothesis, which predicts that markets will produce optimal outcomes if forward-looking agents can trust policy-makers to be "time consistent", *i.e.* not forced to renege on their commitments other than under exceptional circumstances resulting from major exogenous shocks.

The 1990s started on a weak note as all major OECD economies were in recession. Moreover, Japan entered its "lost decade" in the aftermath of the bubble economy, as balance-sheet repair of financial institutions was not taken on and deflation took root. Other main OECD economies fared better. The US

economy recovered smartly, with growth on average exceeding 3% per annum, led by surging productivity growth attributed to the impact of rapid progress in information and communication technologies. Growth in Europe met headwinds as countries pursued fiscal and monetary austerity to qualify for monetary union, but this also meant that inflation finally came under control and public finances improved. Perhaps even more importantly, product markets were liberalised and labour markets reformed, although at different speeds across countries.

The 1990s saw greater regional economic integration. This included the establishment of the European Monetary Union with the Maastricht Treaty and the Single Market in Europe, both in 1992, and the North American Free Trade Agreement (NAFTA) signed by the governments of Canada, Mexico and the United States, creating a trilateral trading bloc in 1994. With the fall of the "Iron Curtain" in 1989, Eastern European economies entered the scene.[5] This was also the period when the Asian "tigers" emerged, attracting massive capital flows from OECD economies. These economies overheated and saw bubbles inflating, which eventually led to the Asian crisis in 1997, followed by the Russian default in 1998 triggered by a fall in oil prices exacerbating domestic vulnerabilities.

Since the impact of the Asian and Russian crises on OECD economies had been limited, the OECD economy ended the decade on a strong note. It was buoyed by a bubble in stock markets due to the internet (or dotcom) hype. Meanwhile, monetary policy had remained relatively accommodative in response to the Asian and Russian crises and out of fears that the "millennium bug" would corrupt information technologies on which the economy had become more dependent – though it turned out to be a non-issue. Fiscal policy, notably in Europe, was too easy for the circumstances, but this was masked (and partly caused) by windfalls stemming from the sale of UMTS (access to third-generation mobile phone grids) licenses.

Emerging market economies entering the picture (2000s until the crisis)

Since the mid-1990s the world economy has become increasingly integrated, owing to the removal of trade barriers, the liberalisation of capital flows, the spread of new technologies and – last but not least – the fall of the Iron Curtain. World trade soared and cross-border flows grew from around 5% of world GDP in the mid-1990s to about 20% in 2007 – the year preceding the global financial and economic crisis. External assets and liabilities as a share of world GDP more than doubled over this period, from 150% to 350%.

The case of China, now the second-largest economy in the world, deserves a separate mention. China's accession to the World Trade Organisation (WTO) in 2001 represented a milestone in its engagement with the world economy. China has been running large current account surpluses since (Figure 7.4) while also attracting large inflows of foreign direct investment from the OECD area. Coupled with an exchange-rate policy of pegging the currency to the US dollar and strict capital controls on capital outflows, this led to the build-up of over $3 trillion worth of foreign exchange reserves – almost 50% of GDP and one third of the global total. The bulk of China's official reserves have been invested in US Treasury bonds, allowing the United States to finance its large current account deficit at favourable terms and to keep its bond yields low.[6]

In addition, globalisation meant a massive increase in the global supply of low-skilled labour in the world economy which had substantial real-economy effects. Not only were emerging market economies now a major driver of global growth, they also kept inflation in the developed economies low, *via* growth in

---

5. Moreover, OECD membership, which had been stable at 24 since 1973, began to expand to include more countries in Asia, in Latin America and in Eastern Europe.
6. More generally, excess saving in external surplus countries thus was seen to explain the interest rate "conundrum" of persistently low bond yields in deficit countries such as the United States (Bernanke, 2005, Bernanke *et al.*, 2011).

cheap export products, economies of scale associated with integrated supply chains and competition. Gradually this development was offset by the effect of buoyant demand on oil and commodity prices (Figure 7.5), but this was largely discounted as not being part of "core" inflation. In addition, in some OECD countries policy interest rates were systematically lower relative to the guidance offered by simple normative policy rules, such as the Taylor rule.[7] In a context of malfunctioning financial markets (see below), this contributed to excessive risk taking and leveraging.

Figure 7.5. **Real commodity prices**[1]

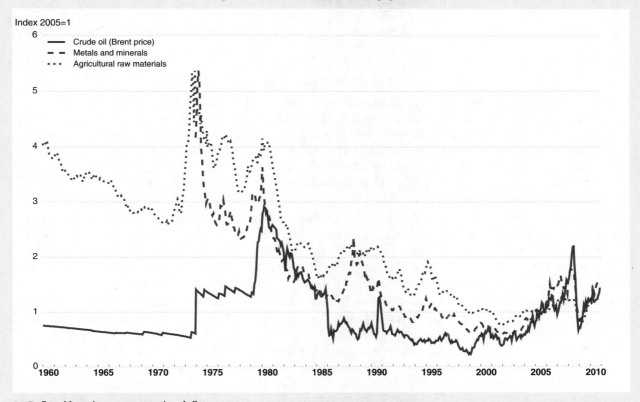

1. Deflated by private consumption deflator.
Source: OECD, Main Economic Indicators database; OECD, Quarterly National Accounts database; and OECD calculations.

StatLink 〰〰〰 http://dx.doi.org/10.1787/888932428956

Indeed, the repetition of bubbles and busts from the late 1980s until the early 2000s, such as the Savings and Loans, LTCM, Asian and dotcom crises, had not only macroeconomic origins, but was also associated with, partly misguided, financial innovation. Technological change allowed the development of new and ever more complex financial products. Weaknesses in supervision and regulation led to a neglect of the associated risks, especially when new products were hard to value properly and banks and corporations removed them from their balance sheet to so-called "special purpose vehicles". Moreover, the mismatch between the generally longer maturity of portfolios and the short maturity of (abundant) money market loans risked leading to acute liquidity shortages if supply increases in money markets stalled.

With hindsight the dotcom bust in 2000-01 should have been taken as a warning signal that systemic risk was unduly increasing. But this shock was again comfortably absorbed by a substantial easing of

7. See Pain *et al.* (2006), Ahrend *et al.* (2008) and Ahrend (2010).

monetary policy, in part also in response to the 11 September terrorist attacks in 2001. Housing and mortgage markets then took over from the stock market as a main attractor of liquidity in search for yield. In this context, real estate prices skyrocketed across a wide range of OECD countries, which produced large wealth effects on consumption and investment. Sustained growth ensued while inflation remained low. As risk appetites recovered and then reached new heights, prices in stock and bond markets also surged.

The prevailing paradigm largely survived the post-dotcom experience. A hallmark of this paradigm was a clear assignment of particular policy instruments to specific tasks (Box 7.2). National macroeconomic policies, especially monetary policy, had become rules-based, forward-looking and stability-oriented, with the intention of becoming more predictable and helping to anchor expectations; structural policies were focused on improving longer-term growth prospects and the resilience to shocks.

Box 7.2. **The pre-crisis paradigm in a nutshell**

- *Monetary policy* was seen to be best conducted by an operationally independent central bank, with price stability as a key objective – in practice typically defined as a low inflation rate of mostly around 2%. The main instrument used was the policy interest rate, accompanied by communication policies designed to ensure that policy actions became more predictable and better understood. Financial markets were viewed as efficient and forward-looking, allocating risks to those who could best bear them, so there would be no role for monetary policy to lean against asset price bubbles, even if these could be detected with any degree of confidence.

- The main objective of *fiscal policy* was seen to attain and maintain sound public finances by stabilising or reducing public debt and deficits, increasingly making use of rules or thresholds for deficits. The role of fiscal policy as a stabilisation tool was mostly limited to the functioning of automatic stabilisers. Discretionary fiscal policy was not regarded as the stabilisation tool of choice, partly because in normal times the costs easily outweigh the benefits.

- The main goal of *structural policies* was seen to foster long-term economic growth and improve labour market outcomes. In the 1990s a wide range of policies had been implemented to improve labour utilisation and labour productivity, including policies to improve human capital and innovation alongside the easing of product and labour market regulations (OECD, 2003 and 2006a). Attention was also paid to enhancing the resilience of economies, so as to allow them to bounce back more quickly from downturns, and the importance of competitive financial markets for promoting growth (OECD, 2006b).

Monetary policy appeared to be generally successful in this period, with low and stable inflation and generally well-anchored inflation expectations. But it was not sufficiently recognised that this outcome was helped by globalisation, a positive aggregate supply shock that kept inflation low – at least until oil and commodity prices surged.

Fiscal consolidation also looked successful, but – as has been a recurrent theme in the OECD's economic history – failure to attain sound underlying public finances was masked by very favourable cyclical developments. Fiscal rules (*e.g.* the European Stability and Growth Pact) failed to provide incentives to encourage the build-up of a sufficient reserve in good times. The implications of rising private-sector imbalances for the sustainability of public finances were ignored and forecasts of underlying public budgets were too optimistic. A possible correction in financial asset and real estate prices was not factored in and implicit fiscal liabilities were not taken into account.

While structural policies had been successful in several countries, there was little international co-ordination on policy choices, contributing to the persistence of cross-country imbalances in savings and

investment and widening global imbalances (Figure 7.4). The excess saving in external surplus countries contributed to the interest rate "conundrum" of persistently low bond yields in deficit countries such as the United States (Bernanke, 2005 and Bernanke *et al.*, 2011). Limited progress was also made in negotiations towards key international reforms, such as the WTO Doha round and climate change accords.

Finally, the potential for systemic financial risks was not effectively monitored, such risks being viewed as low as long as stability-oriented macroeconomic policies were pursued and micro-prudential regulation was conducted effectively. Policy decisions failed to incorporate the implications of the rapid pro-cyclical growth in financial leverage and risk-taking, the concentration of risk, and the increasing potential for the cross-border and cross-market transmission of economic and financial shocks. Efforts by the Bank of International Settlements to set up capital adequacy ratios in Basel I and then revising them in Basel II obscured the risks that were building up in banks' balance sheets.

All this explains how problems in a small corner of US financial markets (subprime mortgages accounted for only 3% of US financial assets) could infect the entire global banking system and set off an explosive spiral of falling asset prices and bank losses in 2008 and 2009. Consumer and investment demand quickly started to fall in the United States. As the US financial crisis intensified, weakness spread globally. With wholesale money markets freezing up, companies started to liquidate inventories and in late 2008 world trade nose-dived. The sharpest contraction since the Great Depression of the 1930s unfolded.

A crisis paradigm: getting around the liquidity trap[8]

The resolve of policymakers around the world, on display in particular at the London G20 summit in April 2009, contributed to prevent a second Great Depression. Massive fiscal and monetary policy stimulus was injected in most OECD and many non-OECD economies. As well, virtually all distressed systemically important financial institutions were rescued following the Lehman Brothers debacle, with central banks and governments providing ample liquidity and balance-sheet support. Many central banks resorted to non-conventional measures (large-scale intervention in capital markets so as to reduce the yields on longer maturities) alongside the provision of unlimited liquidity to the banking system.

While substantial increases in unemployment and public deficits were recorded, dramatic effects at the scale of the Great Depression have thus far been avoided. One lesson to be drawn from this episode is that the Keynesian recipe of active demand management has been appropriate under conditions of extreme financial stress and a threat of the economy heading to a liquidity trap. However, new challenges have emerged for policymaking, chief among which are the complications that arise when the effectiveness of each strand of policy is heavily affected by the stance of other policies and the need to act under extreme uncertainty.

Changing the assignment of policy instruments to targets

While macroeconomic expansion has been instrumental in containing the crisis, the depth of the recession and dysfunctional financial markets overwhelmed the capacity of traditional macroeconomic policy to inject sufficient stimulus. In addition to lowering policy interest rates to close to the zero lower bound and implementing traditional fiscal stimulus measures, many countries opted to use non-conventional policy measures to stimulate aggregate demand and give support to impaired banking systems in a synchronised fashion. Substantial efforts were made to support financial institutions including the provision of credit, funding guarantees and liquidity to the financial system, bank recapitalisation using public funds, deposit guarantee extensions and efforts to move troubled assets from banks' balance sheets to newly created asset management companies.

---

8.   The final two sections of this chapter draw on Pain and Röhn (2011).

Such actions blurred the traditional dividing lines between fiscal, monetary, financial and structural policy, making the effectiveness of separate policy instruments increasingly dependent on others. For example, fiscal support for the financial sector had important ramifications for the transmission of monetary policy. As well, some central banks made large purchases of public debt, often without explicit guarantees against potential losses, while purchases of other assets affected resource allocation, thus blurring the assignments of fiscal and monetary policies. Equally, low policy interest rates and non-standard monetary policies reduced the need for public recapitalisation and for the supervisory authorities to resolve impaired institutions. And structural policies were used to provide support to non-financial enterprises and limit the social and labour-market consequences of the recession even if such settings were not appropriate for the long run.

Policymaking under extreme uncertainty

With time more information about the state of the economy has become available, but extensive uncertainties endure, including:

● *Uncertainty about slack and potential output.* Estimates of economic slack always vary markedly according to the indicator used and are subject to substantial revision over time, reducing the confidence that policy makers can place on any particular output gap measure.[9] The crisis compounds that uncertainty because of the unknown extent to which it may have long-lasting effects on both the level and the rate of growth of potential output. Uncertainty about the output gap has clouded judgements about the extent of deflationary pressures and complicate monetary policy decisions. Uncertainty about the output gap also matters for fiscal policy as a smaller output gap implies that a larger proportion of existing fiscal deficits are structural rather than cyclical. However, with the currently high budget deficits in many OECD countries (Figure 7.2), even a large underestimation of potential output would not change the conclusion that significant consolidation is needed in the coming years.

● *Uncertainty about the impact of monetary policy.* When the crisis was acute uncertainty about the transmission of monetary stimulus was high as financial intermediation had become impaired. With policy rates near the zero bound, many central banks were forced to employ unconventional policy measures in order to support activity in capital markets and work round the impaired banking system, but there is limited knowledge about their effectiveness. With the exit from the crisis, monetary transmission has improved, but balance-sheet repair in the financial sector is far from complete and downside tail risks persist. This complicates the decisions about the timing of the exit from conventional and unconventional measures and their sequencing.[10]

● *Uncertainty about the impact of fiscal policy.* During the acute phase of the crisis fiscal policy was faced with difficult choices about the scale and fiscal cost of the discretionary stimulus and the emergency actions to support the financial system. During the exit phase uncertainty remains, including in estimating the likely effects of consolidation on the economy. Although the short-term effects are likely to be negative, these effects can vary significantly according to the state of the economy as well as the choice of fiscal instrument.[11]

---

9. See Orphanides and van Norden (2002), Beck and Wieland (2008) and Koske and Pain (2008).

10. Uncertainties also arise from difficulties in assessing the likely course of policy actions in other countries and the possible spill-overs from them. In general, stronger cross-border linkages mean that domestic monetary policy may need to react less.

11. In principle, the short-term negative effect from consolidation could be smaller if policy interest rates can be lowered relative to earlier expectations and if the financial sector continues to recover as households are less credit constrained. In addition, households may reduce their savings if they perceive the fiscal consolidation as credible. If credible, the consolidation may also exert a favourable impact on the sovereign risk premium and thereby stimulate demand and ease the fiscal consolidation effort (OECD, 2010a, b).

The policy exit strategy

The exit from the crisis in the OECD economies will take several years. The policy challenges are to eliminate slack in the economy, restore an appropriate inflation level and establish sound public finances and resilient financial markets. This process needs to take place in a large number of countries simultaneously; hence international co-operation, including through the G20, will be essential in the face of cross-country spill-over effects. Moreover, policy in one domain will need to take into account policy setting in others.

The challenge for *monetary policy* will be to exit from exceptional stimulus without exacerbating fragilities in financial markets. In principle, and assuming inflation expectations stay anchored, the aim of monetary authorities should be to bring policy rates to their neutral levels by the time economic slack is eliminated. However, given the uncertainty about the output gap and potential discussed above, central banks may have to give more weight to survey measures of resource utilisation and inflation expectations and only move decisively towards neutral rates once these indicators suggest the economy is robustly on the mend. This strategy would by implication take into account the stance of fiscal policy as well as progress towards financial-sector repair to the extent they affect the outlook for inflation and activity.

During the exit period, monetary policy will also have to keep an eye on macro-prudential risk to the extent new macro-prudential regulatory bodies are not yet fully operational. Abundant liquidity provision at near-zero funding costs allows banks to roll over the debt of non-viable businesses or intensify the search for yield, ultimately producing costly misallocation of resources or a build-up of financial fragilities (BIS, 2010). Thus, barring a relapse into recession or deflation, central banks should move policy interest rates to levels that, while still accommodative, are clearly above zero. Meanwhile, unconventional policy measures may remain in place for some more time and could indeed facilitate the normalisation of conventional policy.

For *fiscal policy*, exiting from crisis measures and restoring sound public finances is likely to continue well into the medium term. The pace of the exit should be commensurate with the state of public finances, the ease of sovereign funding, the strength of the recovery and the scope for monetary policy offsets. It should also take into account that delays in fiscal consolidation might increase interest rates and future growth. A credible fiscal consolidation will likely improve financial market conditions and hence the monetary transmission mechanism.

Furthermore, fiscal consolidations in which expenditure reductions have a high weight are more likely to result in durable retrenchment (Guichard *et al.*, 2007) and more likely to be accommodated by monetary policy once it has departed from the zero-rate bound. Even so, tax increases look unavoidable in view of the size of the consolidation requirements. It is important that consolidation be growth-friendly. For example, raising the retirement age could bring long-term gains while having only limited effects on near-term growth. Priority should be given also to reducing the distortions created by subsidies and tax expenditures, and tax increases should be focused on the least distortive taxes such as on overall consumption and immovable property.

Since the onset of the crisis, attention has been given to identifying structural measures that could offer short-term support to aggregate demand as well as potential long-run benefits for economic growth and public budgets. However, sometimes there are tradeoffs between the two and a balance has to be struck. It is important to consider though that future benefits of growth-enhancing reform can have immediate positive effects as they allow monetary accommodation to continue for longer, bond yields to fall as the prospects of fiscal sustainability improve and private balance sheets to recover sooner. Structural reforms are especially urgent in labour markets to help countries make greater use of their available labour resources more quickly, to ensure that vulnerable groups remain attached to the labour market and to facilitate the reallocation of labour across sectors and regions.

Concerning the emerging market economies, monetary and fiscal stimulus injected during the global crisis should be withdrawn to damp rising inflation pressures and to prevent the development of bubbles in asset and real estate markets. They should not resist currency appreciation where a stronger exchange rate would be in line with the economic fundamentals and necessary to rebalance economic activity towards domestic absorption. Structural policies, including policies to shift activity from the informal to the formal sector of the economy and financial market reforms, should aim to enhance productivity and to achieve more inclusive growth.

A post-crisis paradigm

The repetition of financial crises since the early-1990s should have served as warnings that inadequate regulation and weak financial supervision can be risky in a globalised world economy and financial system. But policymakers took the overall benign economic development as evidence that the dominant paradigm worked and this eventually led to the 2008-09 financial crisis. In a globalised economy and financial system, financial vulnerabilities have increased. Booms and busts tend to be recurrent and so are the associated rescues of financial institutions and sovereigns. This, in turn, gives rise to concerns over moral hazard and the political acceptance – if not the legitimacy – of the policy paradigm.

Parts of the pre-crisis paradigm may remain valid after the crisis, including the orientation towards supply-side "structural" policies to achieve strong sustainable growth, the assignment of monetary policy to achieve price stability and the adoption of rules-based fiscal policy in the pursuit of sustainable public finances. However, in order to preserve and build on the wide-ranging benefits of globalisation, it is essential that the post-crisis paradigm be underpinned by safeguards to maintain financial stability and a strong commitment to sustainable, fair and "green" growth across the globe. All strands of economic policy – prudential, fiscal, structural and monetary – have a role to play, each within their remits and proper assignments. And all of them need to be co-ordinated internationally so as to achieve that policies reinforce, rather than work against, each other.

Stronger micro and macro-prudential policies

Micro-prudential regulation and supervision are needed to ensure that financial institutions have sufficient capital and liquidity buffers, relative to their risk exposure, to withstand adverse shocks. The Basel Committee has defined new required minimum levels of bank capital (and the transition period for achieving these standards).[12] This reform, if fully implemented, along with impending reform of liquidity requirements, should reduce the economic cost of financial crises.[13] It could be usefully complemented by a maximum leverage ratio applicable to all assets so as to avoid regulatory arbitrage in favour of assets with low risk weights leading to over-stretched balance sheets. Moreover, ending the netting of derivatives positions in financial statements or more generally the possibility of keeping risks off-balance would help to better reveal the exposure to counterparty risk. It will also be important to deal with incentives problems embedded in remuneration systems and moral hazard for financial institutions that are too big or interconnected to fail.[14] Finally, to avoid banks shifting risks to non-bank financial institutions, financial reform should encompass pension funds, insurance companies and various types of investment funds.

---

12. See BCBS (2010). Capital adequacy and liquidity are found to be among the most important crisis factors (Barrell *et al.*, 2010).

13. While tighter capital adequacy rules may act as a constraint on lending, their adverse impact on growth is found to be rather limited (Slovik and Cournède, 2011).

14. Such institutions have an incentive to take excessive rise and benefit from a competitive edge in terms of funding costs and the collateral they can accept because of their *de facto* government backstop. This problem can be addressed by breaking up systemically important institutions, although this is challenging politically, or by imposing higher capital requirements.

Improved micro-prudential policies may not suffice. To ensure the stability of the financial system, macro-prudential policy instruments need to be developed to guard against the pro-cyclical build-up of financial imbalances in the economy (OECD, 2010a; Lawson *et al.*, 2009). Specific tools that could be employed include contingent add-ons to the micro-prudential buffers as a function of aggregate borrowers' leverage, and procedures for orderly resolution of cross-border financial institutions. Higher margin requirements, including limits to loan-to-value ratios in mortgage lending, could also be envisaged. In addition, stress tests of banks need to become more systemic, regular and harmonised across jurisdictions, and their results publicly available.[15]

Revisiting the monetary policy framework

The crisis has reopened the longstanding debate about whether monetary policy should lean against asset price bubbles or simply clean up after a bubble has burst. Before the crisis the dominant view was in favour of cleaning but not leaning, pointing to difficulties of indentifying bubbles in real time and concerns that leaning could un-anchor inflation expectations even if it was widely acknowledged that cleaning but not leaning might produce moral hazard and encourage excessive risk taking. However, the severity of the crisis has strengthened the case of those who argue for leaning against asset price bubbles, especially if these are accompanied by rapid credit growth.[16] At the very least, monetary policy should guard against an unnecessarily lax policy stance fuelling asset price misalignments.

This does not mean that credit and asset prices should be included as a formal objective of monetary policy alongside inflation (and resource utilisation). Doing so risks blurring the assignment of policy instruments to targets, thus complicating the communication and accountability of monetary policy. If bubbles can be identified, macro-prudential regulation and supervision (see above) offer better targeted tools to prevent them. Nonetheless, it might be argued that it is necessary for central banks to adopt a sufficiently long horizon over which to achieve price stability – and this would imply a concomitant need to incorporate financial stability considerations in their policy decisions. To date only the European Central Bank has formally incorporated financial variables in its framework, although it is unclear to what extent this has effectively driven its monetary policy decisions.[17]

The crisis has also led to suggestions that inflation targets should be raised above the widely accepted 2% mark. It would provide room for monetary policy to react to large adverse shocks with less risk of hitting the zero-rate bound.[18] It might also enhance wage flexibility and hence facilitate the absorption of large adverse shocks.[19] However, there are also drawbacks attached to such a move, not least that central banks might lose some of their hard-won credibility.[20] A related suggestion is that monetary policy could target the price *level* rather than the inflation rate, notably at times of financial distress. In theory this could provide a stabilising mechanism as inflation expectations automatically increase (and hence real interest rates fall) if

---

15. There are implementation difficulties in adopting such measures, including the choice of indicators to consider when setting these policy instruments. Another issue is whether policy measures should obey a simple rule, or whether more discretion should be allowed for (Yellen, 2010). It will also be important that macro-prudential bodies have a clear mandate and are accountable for it.
16. See Blinder (2010a) and Stark (2010).
17. The monetary pillar of the ECB's policy framework has been discussed extensively in the academic literature, see *inter alia* Svensson (2010a, b), Gerlach and Svensson (2003), Gerlach (2004), Beck and Wieland (2007) and Berger *et al.* (2010). On balance this literature is rather inconclusive as to the role of monetary aggregates in the policy framework.
18. See Williams (2009) and Blanchard *et al.* (2010).
19. See Summers (1991). It would also produce a one-time reduction in the real value of sovereign debt, but this advantage may well be offset by higher risk premiums on sovereign debt yields in the future.
20. See Bean *et al.* (2010). Other drawbacks are that even small increases in trend inflation may compound distortions in the tax system (Feldstein, 1999), and that inflation above 2% could hardly be regarded as price stability as quality adjustments are increasingly incorporated in price estimates.

the price level was below target in a slump. But price-level targeting would be dangerous in the face of one-time hikes in indirect taxes or in commodity prices as the ensuing increase in real interest rates would exacerbate the shock.[21] At any rate, no OECD country pursues a price-level target.

Unconventional monetary policy during the crisis was broadly successful in terms of improving the conditions in financial markets and stabilising the real economy, but it does give rise to a number of as yet unsettled issues.[22] In particular, continued purchases of government debt by the monetary authorities may cast doubt on the independence of the central bank by suggesting that purchases are being made for fiscal reasons. Moreover, central bank interventions in private debt markets could create distortions. Quantitative easing also exposes the central banks balance sheet to market risk, including risks associated with sovereign bonds. The upshot is that in normal times, central banks should not aim to influence the shape of the yield curve other than through communication or conventional sterilised open market purchases of longer-dated securities. As well, impediments in monetary transmission due to distressed banks or solvency concerns about sovereign debt would best be tackled by addressing these problems at source.

Finally, an open question is to what extent macro-prudential and monetary policies need to be co-ordinated since macro-prudential policies will affect the monetary transmission mechanism (especially through the credit channel). Combining both types of policy in a single institution could facilitate such co-ordination, but having separate authorities – each with its area of responsibility and instruments – would offer greater accountability. If the latter set-up were to emerge as the preferred one, an explicit co-ordination mechanism between the two institutions would be needed to indentify the build-up of systemic risks and decide the best response to them.[23] There is a related issue about where responsibility for micro-prudential supervision would lie. Central banks are the lenders of last resort but in normal times should not be involved in the rescue of impaired financial institutions, which is the responsibility of the fiscal authorities. In the event of the failure of cross-border institutions, arrangements will need to be in place between governments for burden sharing.

Reforming fiscal frameworks

Substantial fiscal consolidation is required over the medium term in many countries and in several of them the fiscal challenges are exacerbated in the longer term by spending pressures related to health care, long-term care and pensions (see Chapter 4 in the current issue of the *OECD Economic Outlook*). In addition, future fiscal outcomes may be influenced by the implicit liabilities incurred in rescuing financial institutions. Furthermore, any future fiscal framework will have to take better account of saving-investment imbalances arising in the private sector associated with *e.g.* housing booms, as these have implications for the assessment of structural budget balances and the effectiveness of fiscal policy actions.[24]

A change in the fiscal policy framework, including well-designed fiscal rules, can assist fiscal policy to become more sustainable, transparent, predictable and counter-cyclical. In particular, medium-term

---

21. For the automatic stabilisation argument of price level targeting, see Eggertson and Woodford (2003), Ambler (2009) and Cournède and Moccero (2009). This mechanism would fail though if inflation expectations are adaptive rather forward looking (Murray, 2010). There are also many practical implementation and communication problems (Goodhart, 2005; Edey, 2008; Bean *et al.*, 2010), including the timing of the switch from inflation to price-level targeting (and back).

22. See Borio and Disyatat (2009), Bean *et al.* (2010) and Blinder (2010b).

23. In practice, both types of policy are likely to respond to aggregate demand shocks in a similar manner (easing), but this may not be the case for aggregate supply shocks. Moreover, as noted, if macro-prudential policies are underdeveloped, monetary policy may need to lean against the wind of the asset cycle (White, 2009). As well, if policy interest rates are at the zero bound, macro-prudential policies might have to place greater weight on their macroeconomic effects than would otherwise be the case (Yellen, 2010).

24. Recent work by the OECD shows possible ways to adjust the budget balances for asset-price cycles and to address other sources of uncertainty of the underlying fiscal position. Price and Dang (2011) compare the traditional and a new asset-price adjusted structural balance. In the run-up to the financial crisis the asset-adjusted deficit (as a share of GDP) was between 1½ and 2 percentage points higher than the tradition measure in several OECD countries.

expenditure rules, incorporating expenditure plans or ceilings to complement deficit or debt ceilings, offer a way of limiting boom-bust spending cycles and ensuring that unexpected revenues are saved rather than spent. Expenditure rules can help to build up reserves in cyclical upswings, to create room for the unfettered working of automatic fiscal stabilisers, and possibly discretionary stimulus, in a downturn.[25] Within this framework, decisions on individual spending categories should be made in line with efficiency considerations and other government objectives.

Fiscal rules need to be sufficiently binding in normal times and sufficiently flexible in exceptional times to be credible and effective. Establishing an independent fiscal council can be an important means of strengthening compliance with the fiscal rules, by raising the political cost of deviating from them. To be effective, a council needs to have an important role in the budget process, although government should keep the final fiscal responsibility. A key potential role for an independent council would be to advance independent and authoritative views in the pursuit of transparency of fiscal decision making. It must be supported by fully independent statistical agencies and auditing offices that record outlays and revenues using appropriate accounting principles.

In monetary unions, which share a single currency and monetary policy while maintaining separate national fiscal policies, an instrument to deal with sovereign debt stress needs to be in place. As well, fiscal governance can be strengthened through more intense market discipline by allowing for the possibility of orderly debt restructuring. If markets anticipate that countries with unsustainable fiscal positions would not be bailed out and private-sector losses would have to be incurred, they may price sovereign risk properly. To limit the risk of financial contagion, financial regulations should take into account the possibility of sovereign default in terms of capital requirements, haircuts on collateral for central bank operations and requiring appropriate diversification of risk. This also calls into question whether the zero-risk weighting given to sovereign debt under the Basel II and III frameworks is appropriate.

Pursuing bold structural reform

The risk of a permanent reduction in potential output and persistently high levels of unemployment due to the crisis underlines the central role for structural reforms. As discussed in Chapter 4, structural policies should aim to facilitate a swift return to work so as to minimise this risk. Labour markets have done comparatively well in view of the magnitude of the recession, which can in part be attributed to earlier reforms. But the experience of crisis has yielded a number of new insights, including that temporary extensions of the duration of unemployment benefits and work sharing arrangements at times of distress can be effective, and that partial reform strategies that produce "dual labour markets", leaving some groups particularly vulnerable in bad times, are potentially damaging.

There are several ways in which growth-enhancing structural reforms can also contribute to fiscal consolidation. For example, increasing the retirement age can boost labour utilisation and demand while at the same time mitigating the budget pressures resulting from ageing societies. Furthermore, moving to best practices in the provision of health care and education can create room for consolidation without compromising service levels. Reforms that boost private-sector employment raise tax revenues; reforms can also reduce unemployment benefits and lower the public-sector wage bill relative to GDP.[26]

25. A general problem with fiscal rules, namely that they can encourage "gimmickry" such as one-off measures and creative accounting to circumvent them (Koen and Van den Noord, 2005), might be even more serious with an ambitious expenditure rule since this will bite more often (*i.e.* not only mostly in bad times but even also in good times) than a deficit rule. Part of the solution is to ensure the expenditure rule has a wide ambit to include all outlays (Price, 2010), applies to different levels of government and includes the monitoring of tax expenditures (Anderson and Minarik, 2006). A related risk with strict fiscal rules is that they may induce regulations to attain outcomes previously obtained by fiscal instruments.
26. Calculations in OECD (2010b) suggest that a 1 percentage point improvement in the employment rate improve government balances by between 0.3-0.8% of GDP.

Product-market reforms that enhance productivity also have the potential to raise tax revenues, although they also tend to spill over in higher public-sector wages and transfers, thus offsetting some of this favourable fiscal effect.

Reforms to ease rigidities in labour and product markets remain needed to make economies more resilient to adverse shocks, either by damping their impact or by making their impact less persistent. In particular, reforms that remove gaps in employment protection between groups of workers, ensure sufficient flexibility in wage bargaining and weaken anti-competitive product-market regulations, could all enhance resilience, although potentially at the cost of a deeper initial impact from shocks. The implementation of micro and macro-prudential reforms could also help to improve resilience by securing the transmission of monetary policy and ensuring that financial intermediation continues to function even at times of crisis.

Finally, structural reforms have a key role in addressing the underlying determinants of global imbalances through their impact on consumption, saving and investment (OECD, 2011). Developing social welfare systems in China and other Asian economies would fulfil important social goals, and as a side-effect would reduce the need for precautionary saving, thus curbing the large current account surpluses of some of these countries. Product market reforms in services industries could encourage capital spending and thereby reduce current account surpluses in countries such as Japan and Germany. Removal of policy distortions that encourage consumption, such as tax deductibility of interest payments on mortgages, could help increase household saving and reduce the current account deficit in a number of countries, not least the United States. Financial market reforms could relax borrowing constraints in emerging economies and thereby boost consumption and investment and curb their current account surpluses, but should be accompanied by appropriate prudential controls.

International co-ordination and co-operation

Mechanisms need to be found to allow different policy settings to co-exist across the globe in a way that promotes economic stability and growth. This will require international co-operation, surveillance and communication in setting priorities and in minimising any potential adverse side-effects that can arise from the resulting geographical constellation of policies. One aspect of this is the international effort underway to strengthen prudential frameworks around the world. Beyond this, the role of the G20 *Framework for Strong Sustainable and Balanced Growth* is to identify a combination of macroeconomic, structural and exchange-rate policies that would strengthen growth prospects and helps to achieve more sustainable fiscal positions whilst minimising the risks of renewed widening in global imbalances.

Co-operation is also necessary if the international monetary system is to be strengthened. Eventually, real exchange rates will move in line with policy differences as well as different growth rates, inflation and fiscal positions. Specifically, over time it would be expected that emerging market economies would experience a real appreciation. If the nominal exchange rate is fixed, the required changes have to come through adjustments to wages and prices, which can be costly as it would risk de-anchoring inflation expectations. Persistent currency misalignments in the interim can generate unsustainable external imbalances. Hence reforms are needed to facilitate the movement of exchange rates in line with economic fundamentals so as to ensure that nominal exchange-rate adjustment acts as a safety valve. On the other hand, excessive exchange-rate volatility can also have its costs.

A factor to take into account is that large capital flows to emerging market economies in search for yield risk producing "Dutch disease", reckless risk-taking and sudden stops or reversals. To smoothly channel and absorb capital inflows, emerging market economies should aim to have the appropriate mix of macroeconomic policies in place (move towards sustainable fiscal policy where this is not yet the case and not resist appreciation of their exchange rate) and strengthen macro-prudential frameworks to further

contain the risk of financial instability. Capital restrictions should be a last resort and undertaken in a transparent manner and subject to international discussion. A framework for common principles underlying capital account policies could facilitate and enhance stability while guaranteeing open capital markets. Finally, the OECD has identified a possible role for structural policies to attenuate the financial stability risks associated with capital inflows – by influencing their composition towards more stable and productive forms of financing such as foreign direct investment (see Chapter 6).

References

Ahrend, R. (2010), "Monetary Ease: A Factor Behind Financial Crises? Some Evidence from OECD Countries", *Economics, The Open-Access Open-Assessment E-Journal*, Vol. 4.

Ahrend, R., B. Cournède and R. Price (2008), "Monetary Policy, Market Excesses and Financial Turmoil", *OECD Economics Department Working Papers*, No. 597.

Ambler, S. (2009), "Price-Level Targeting and Stabilisation Policy: A Survey", *Journal of Economic Surveys*, Vol. 23.

Amel, D., C. Barnes, F. Pancetta and C. Salleo (2004), "Consolidation and Efficiency in the Financial Sector: A Review of the International Evidence", *Journal of Banking and Finance*, Vol. 28.

Anderson, B. and J.J. Minarik (2006), "Design Choices for Fiscal Policy Rules", *OECD Journal on Budgeting*, Vol. 5.

Barrell, R., E.P. Davis, D. Karim and I. Liadze (2010), "Bank Regulation, Property Prices and Early Warning Systems for Banking Crises", *Journal of Banking and Finance*, Vol. 34.

BCBS (2010), *The Basel Committee's Response to the Financial Crisis: Report to the G20*, Basel Committee on Banking Supervision, Bank for International Settlements, October.

Bean, C., M. Paustian, A. Penalver and T. Taylor (2010), "Monetary Policy After The Fall", paper presented at Federal Bank of Kansas City Symposium, Jackson Hole, August.

Beck, G. and V. Wieland (2007), "Money in Monetary Policy Design: A Formal Characterization Of ECB-style Cross-checking", *Journal of the European Economic Association*, Vol. 5.

Beck, G. and V. Wieland (2008), "Central Bank Misperceptions and the Role of Money in Interest-Rate Rules", *Journal of Monetary Economics*, Vol. 55.

Berger, H., J. de Haan, J. and J.-E. Sturm, (2011). "Does Money Matter in the ECB Strategy? New Evidence Based on the ECB Communication", *International Journal of Finance and Economics*, Vol. 16.

Bernanke, B. (2005), *The Global Saving Glut and the US Current Account Deficit*, Sandridge Lecture, Virginia Association of Economists, Richmond, Virginia, 10 March 2005.

Bernanke, B., C. Bertaut, L.P. DeMarco and S. Kamin (2011), "International Capital Flows and the Returns to Safe Assets in the United States, 2003-2007", Board of Governors of the Federal Reserve System, *International Finance Discussion Papers* No. 1014.

BIS (2010), *80th Annual Report*, Bank for International Settlements, Basel.

Blanchard, O., G. Dell'Ariccia and P. Mauro (2010), "Rethinking Macroeconomic Policy", *Journal of Money, Credit and Banking*, Vol. 42.

Blanchard, O. and J. Wolfers (2000), "The Role of Shocks and Institutions in the Rise of European Unemployment: the Aggregate Evidence", *Economic Journal*, Vol. 110.

Blinder, A. (2010a), "Commentary: Rethinking Monetary Policy in Light of the Crisis", presentation at Federal Bank of Kansas City Symposium, Jackson Hole, August.

Blinder, A. (2010b), "Quantitative Easing: Entrance and Exit Strategies", *Federal Reserve Bank of St Louis Economic Review*, Vol. 92.

Borio, C. and P. Disyatat (2009), "Unconventional Monetary Policy: An Appraisal", *BIS Working Papers*, No. 292.

Cournède, B. and D. Moccero (2009), "Is There a Case for Price-Level Targeting?", *OECD Economics Department Working Papers*, No. 721.

Edey, M. (2008), "The Future of Inflation Targeting", remarks at Bank of Canada conference on International Experience with the Conduct of Monetary Policy under Inflation Targeting, July.

Eggertsson, G. and M. Woodford (2003), "The Zero Bound on Interest Rates and Optimal Monetary Policy", *Brookings Papers on Economic Activity*, 2003:1.

Feldstein, M.S. (1999), "Capital Income Taxes and the Benefits of Price Stability", in M.S. Feldstein (ed.) *The Costs and Benefits of Price Stability*, University of Chicago Press.

Fleming, J.M. (1962), "Domestic Financial Policies Under Fixed and Floating Exchange Rates", *IMF Staff Papers*, Vol. 9.

Gerlach, S. (2004), "The Two Pillars of the European Central Bank", *Economic Policy*, No. 44.

Gerlach, S. and L.E.O. Svensson (2003). "Money and Inflation in the Euro Area: A Case for Monetary Indicators?", *Journal of Monetary Economics*, Vol. 50.

Goodhart, C.A.E. (2005), "Beyond Current Policy Frameworks", *BIS Working Papers*, No. 189.

Guichard, S., M. Kennedy, E. Wurzel and C. André (2007), "What Promotes Fiscal Consolidation: OECD Country Experiences", *OECD Economics Department Working Papers*, No. 553.

Hall, P. A. (1993), "Policy Paradigms, Social Learning and the State, the Case of Policy Making in Britain", *Comparative Politics*, Vol. 25.

Koen, V. and P. van den Noord (2005), "Fiscal Gimmickry in Europe: One-off Measures and Creative Accounting", *OECD Economics Department Working Papers*, No. 417.

Koske, I. and N. Pain (2008), "The Usefulness of Output Gaps for Policy Analysis", *OECD Economics Department Working Papers*, No. 621.

Kuhn, T.S. (1962), *The Structure of Scientific Revolutions*, Chicago, University of Chicago Press.

Lawson, J., S. Barnes and M. Sollie (2009), "Financial Market Stability in the European Union: Enhancing Regulation and Supervision", *OECD Economics Department Working Papers*, No. 670.

McCracken, P. et al. (1977), *Towards Full Employment and Price Stability – A Report to the OECD by a Group of Independent Experts*, OECD, Paris.

Mundell, R.A. (1963), "Capital Mobility and Stabilization Policy Under Fixed and Flexible Exchange Rates". *Canadian Journal of Economic and Political Science*, Vol. 29.

Murray, J. (2010), "Re-examining Canada's Monetary Policy Framework – Recent Research and Outstanding Issues", speech to the Canadian Association for Business Economics, Kingston, August.

OECD (1977), *OECD Economic Outlook*, No. 22, Paris.

OECD (1991), *OECD Economic Outlook*, No. 50, Paris.

OECD (1994), *The OECD Jobs Study – Facts, Analysis, Strategies*, Paris.

OECD (2003), *Sources of Economic Growth*, Paris.

OECD (2006a), *OECD Employment Outlook 2006 – Boosting Jobs and Incomes: Policy Lessons from Reassessing the OECD Job Strategy*, Paris.

OECD (2006b), "Regulation of Financial Systems and Economic Growth", *Going For Growth* 2006 edition, Paris.

OECD (2010a), "Counter-Cyclical Economic Policy", *OECD Economic Outlook*, No. 87.

OECD (2010b), "Fiscal Consolidation: Requirements, Timing, Instruments and Institutional Arrangements", *OECD Economic Outlook*, No. 88.

OECD (2011), *Economic Policy Reforms 2011: Going for Growth*, Paris.

Orphanides, A. and S. van Norden (2002), "The Unreliability of Output Gap Estimates in Real Time", *Review of Economics and Statistics*, Vol. 84.

Pain, N., I. Koske and M. Sollie (2006), "Globalisation and Inflation in OECD Economies", *OECD Economics Department Working Papers*, No. 524.

Pain, N. and O. Röhn (2011), "Policy Frameworks in the Post-crisis Environment", *OECD Economics Department Working Papers*, No. 857.

Price, R. and T.-T. Dang (2011), "Adjusting Fiscal Balances for Asset Price Cycles: Proposals for a New Set of Indicators", *OECD Economics Department Working Paper*, forthcoming.

Price, R. (2010), "Political Economy of Fiscal Consolidation", *OECD Economics Department Working Papers*, No. 776.

Slovik, P. and B. Cournède (2011), "Estimating the Impact of Basle III", *OECD Economics Department Working Paper, OECD Economics Department Working Papers*, No. 844.

Stark, J. (2010), "In Search of a Robust Monetary Policy Framework", presented at the 6th ECB Central Banking Conference, Frankfurt am Main, November.

Summers, L. (1991), "Panel Discussion: How Should Long-Term Monetary Policy Be Determined?", *Journal of Money, Credit and Banking*, Vol. 23.

Svensson, L.E.O. (2010a), "Monetary Policy After the Financial Crisis", speech at the Second International Journal of Central Banking Fall Conference, Tokyo, September.

Svensson, L.E.O. (2010b), "Inflation Targeting", in B.M. Friedman and M. Woodford (eds.), *Handbook of Monetary Economics: Volume 3*, Elsevier.

White, W. (2009), "Should Monetary Policy 'Lean or Clean'?", *Federal Reserve Bank of Dallas Globalization and Monetary Policy Institute Working Paper*, No. 34.

Williams, J.C. (2009), "Heeding Daedalus: Optimal Inflation and the Zero Lower Bound", *Brookings Papers on Economic Activity*, Fall 2009.

Yellen, J. (2010), "Macroprudential Supervision and Monetary Policy in the Post-Crisis World", speech at the Annual Meeting of the National Association for Business Economics, Denver, November.

Special chapters in recent issues of OECD Economic Outlook

No. 88, November 2010

Fiscal Consolidation: Requirements, Timing, Instruments and Institutional Arrangements

No. 87, June 2010

Prospects for growth and imbalances beyond the short term

Return to work after the crisis

Counter-cyclical economic policy

No. 86, November 2009

The automobile industry in and beyond the crisis

No. 85, June 2009

Beyond the crisis: medium-term challenges relating to potential output unemployment and fiscal positions

No. 84, December 2008

Responses to inflation shocks: Do G7 counties behave differently?

No. 83, June 2008

The implication of supply-side uncertainties for economic policy

No. 82, December 2007

Corporate saving and investment: recent trends and prospects

No. 81, June 2007

Making the most of globalisation

Fiscal consolidation: lessons from pas experiences

No. 80, December 2006

Has the rise in debt made households more vulnerable?

No. 79, June 2006

Future budget pressures arising from spending on health and long-term care

No. 78, December 2006

Recent house price developments: the role of fundamentals

No. 77, June 2005

Measuring and assessing underlying inflation

STATISTICAL ANNEX

This annex contains data on key economic series which provide a background to the recent economic developments in the OECD area described in the main body of this report. Data for 2010 to 2012 are OECD estimates and projections. The data in some of the tables have been adjusted to conform to internationally agreed concepts and definitions in order to make them more comparable across countries, as well as consistent with historical data shown in other OECD publications. Regional aggregates are based on weights that change each period, with the weights depending on the series considered. For details on aggregation, see *OECD Economic Outlook* Sources and Methods.

The OECD projection methods and underlying statistical concepts and sources are described in detail in *OECD Economic Outlook* Sources and Methods (*www.oecd.org/eco/sources-and-methods*).

Corrigenda for the current and earlier issues, as applicable, can be found at *www.oecd.org/publishing/corrigenda*.

The statistical data for Israel are supplied by and under the responsibility of the relevant Israeli authorities. The use of such data by the OECD is without prejudice to the status of the Golan Heights, East Jerusalem and Israeli settlements in the West Bank under the terms of international law.

NOTE ON FORECASTING FREQUENCIES

OECD quarterly projections are on a seasonal and working-day-adjusted basis for selected key variables. This implies that differences between adjusted and unadjusted annual data may occur, though these in general are quite small. In some countries, official forecasts of annual figures do not include working-day adjustments. Even when official forecasts do adjust for working days, the size of the adjustment may in some cases differ from that used by the OECD. The cut-off date for information used in the compilation of the projections is 19 May 2011.

Additional information

2010 weights used for real GDP regional aggregates

	OECD Euro area[1]	OECD	World		OECD Euro area[1]	OECD	World
Australia		2.1	1.2	Slovenia	0.5	0.1	0.1
Austria	2.9	0.8	0.5	Spain	13.1	3.6	2.1
Belgium	3.5	1.0	0.6	Sweden		0.9	0.5
Canada		3.2	1.9	Switzerland		0.9	0.5
Chile		0.6	0.4	Turkey		2.7	1.6
Czech Republic		0.7	0.4	United Kingdom		5.3	3.1
Denmark		0.5	0.3	United States		34.8	20.5
Estonia	0.2	0.1	0.0	Euro area	100.0	27.3	16.1
Finland	1.7	0.5	0.3	OECD total		100.0	59.0
France	19.5	5.3	3.1				
Germany	27.0	7.4	4.3			Non OECD	World
Greece	2.8	0.8	0.4				
Hungary		0.5	0.3	Argentina		2.4	1.0
Iceland		0.0	0.0	Brazil		7.6	3.1
Ireland	1.5	0.4	0.2	China		35.2	14.4
Israel		0.5	0.3	Indonesia		3.6	1.5
Italy	17.3	4.7	2.8	India		14.6	6.0
Japan		10.2	6.0	Russian Federation		9.6	4.0
Korea		3.4	2.0	Saudi Arabia		2.1	0.9
Luxembourg	0.4	0.1	0.1	South Africa		1.8	0.7
Mexico		3.9	2.3	Dynamic Asian Economies		5.9	2.4
Netherlands	6.0	1.6	1.0	Other major oil producers		8.1	3.3
New Zealand		0.3	0.2	Rest of non OECD		9.1	3.7
Norway		0.7	0.4				
Poland		1.8	1.1	Non-OECD countries		100.0	41.0
Portugal	2.4	0.6	0.4				
Slovak Republic	1.1	0.3	0.2	World			100.0

Note Weights are calculated using nominal GDP at PPP rates in 2010. Regional aggregates are calculated using moving nominal GDP weights evaluated at PPP rates. Thus, the country weights differ from year to year. Also weights may vary for different components of GDP, as the weights are based on countries' share in the total of the particular component.

1. Countries that are members of both the euro area and the OECD.

Irrevocable euro conversion rates

National currency unit per euro

Austria	13.7603	Italy	1936.27
Belgium	40.3399	Luxembourg	40.3399
Estonia	15.6466	Netherlands	2.20371
Finland	5.94573	Portugal	200.482
France	6.55957	Spain	166.386
Germany	1.95583	Slovak Republic	30.126
Greece	340.75	Slovenia	239.64
Ireland	0.78756		

Source: European Central Bank.

Non-OECD trade regions

Other industrialised Asia: Dynamic Asia (Chinese Taipei; Hong Kong, China; Malaysia; Philippines; Singapore; Thailand and Vietnam) plus Indonesia and India.

Other oil producers: Azerbaijan, Kazakhstan, Turkmenistan, Brunei, Timor-Leste, Bahrain, Iran, Iraq, Kuwait, Libya, Oman, Qatar, Saudi Arabia, United Arab Emirates, Yemen, Ecuador, Trinidad and Tobago, Venezuela, Algeria, Angola, Chad, Republic of Congo, Equatorial Guinea, Gabon, Nigeria, Sudan.

National accounts reporting systems, base years and latest data updates

In the present edition of the OECD Economic Outlook, *the status of national accounts in the OECD countries is as follows :*

	Expenditure accounts	Household accounts	Government accounts	Benchmark/ base year
Australia	SNA08 (1959q3-2010q4)	SNA08 (1959q3-2010q4)	SNA08 (1959q3-2010q4)	2008/2009
Austria	ESA95 (1988q1-2010q4)	ESA95 (1995-2010)	ESA95 (1976-2010)	2005
Belgium	ESA95 (1995q1-2010q4)	ESA95 (1995-2009)	ESA95 (1985-2010)	2008
Canada	SNA93 (1961q1-2010q4)	SNA93 (1961q1-2010q4)	SNA93 (1961q1-2010q4)	2002
Chile	SNA93 (1995q1-2010q4)	..	..	2003
Czech Republic	ESA95 (1995q1-2010q4)	ESA95 (1995-2009)	ESA95 (1995-2010)	2000
Denmark	ESA95 (1990q1-2010q4)	ESA95 (1990-2009)	ESA95 (1990-2010)	2000
Estonia	ESA95 (1995q1-2010q4)	ESA95 (1995-2009)	ESA95 (1995-2010)	2000
Finland	ESA95 (1990q1-2010q4)	ESA95 (1975-2010)	ESA95 (1975-2010)	2000
France	ESA95 (1949q1-2010q4)	ESA95 (1978q1-2010q4)	ESA95 (1978-2010)	2000
Germany	ESA95 (1991q1-2010q4)	ESA95 (1991-2010)	ESA95 (1991-2010)	2000
Greece	ESA95 (2000-2010)	..	ESA95 (2000-2010)	2000
Hungary	ESA95 (1995q1-2010q4)	ESA95 (1995-2009)	ESA95 (1995-2010)	2000
Iceland	SNA93 (1997q1-2010q4)	..	SNA93 (1995-2010)	2000
Ireland	ESA95 (1997q1-2010q4)	ESA95 (2002-2010)	ESA95 (1990-2010)	2008
Israel	ESA95 (1995q1-2010q4)	..	ESA95 (1990-2010)	2005
Italy	ESA95 (1980q1-2010q4)	ESA95 (1990-2009)	ESA95 (1980-2010)	2000
Japan	SNA93 (1980q1-2011q1)	SNA93 (1980-2009)	SNA93 (1980-2009)	2000
Korea	SNA93 (1970q1-2011q1)	SNA93 (1975-2010)	SNA93 (1975-2010)	2005
Luxembourg	ESA95 (1995q1-2010q4)	..	ESA95 (1990-2010)	2000
Mexico	SNA93 (2000q1-2010q4)	..	..	2003
Netherlands	ESA95 (1987q1-2010q4)	ESA95 (1990-2009)	ESA95 (1969-2010)	2000
New Zealand	SNA93 (1987q2-2010q4)	..	SNA93 (1986-2009)	1995/1996
Norway	SNA93 (1978q1-2010q4)	SNA93 (1978-2010)	SNA93 (1995-2010)	2007
Poland	ESA95 (1995q1-2010q4)	ESA95 (1995-2009)	ESA95 (1995-2009)	2000
Portugal	ESA95 (1995q1-2010q4)	ESA95 (1999-2010)	ESA95 (1995-2010)	2006
Slovak Republic	ESA95 (1997q1-2010q4)	ESA95 (1995q1-2010q4)	ESA95 (1995-2010)	2000
Slovenia	ESA95 (1995q1-2010q4)	ESA95 (2000-2009)	ESA95 (1995-2009)	2000
Spain	ESA95 (1995q1-2010q4)	ESA95 (2000-2010)	ESA95 (1995-2010)	2000
Sweden	ESA95 (1993q1-2010q4)	ESA95 (1993q1-2010q4)	ESA95 (1993-2010)	2009
Switzerland	SNA93 (1980q1-2010q4)	SNA93 (1990-2008)	SNA93 (1990-2009)	2000
Turkey	SNA93 (1998q1-2010q4)	..	..	1998
United Kingdom	ESA95 (1955q1-2010q4)	ESA95 (1987q1-2010q4)	ESA95 (1987q1-2010q4)	2006
United States	NIPA (SNA93) (1947q1-2011q1)	NIPA (SNA93) (1947q1-2011q1)	NIPA (SNA93) (1947q1-2011q1)	2005

Note: SNA: System of National Accounts. ESA: European Standardised Accounts. NIPA: National Income and Product Accounts. GFS: Government Financial Statistics. The numbers in brackets indicate the starting year for the time series and the latest available historical data included in this Outlook database.

1. Data prior to 1991 refer to the new SNA93/ESA95 accounts for western Germany data.

Annex Tables

Interest Rates and Exchange Rates

External Trade and Payments

Other background Data

Annex Table 1. Real GDP
Percentage change from previous year

	Average 1986-96	1997	1998	1999	2000	2001	2002	2003	2004	2005	2006	2007	2008	2009	2010	2011	2012	Fourth quarter 2010	2011	2012
Australia	3.4	4.1	5.2	4.3	3.4	2.7	3.9	3.6	3.3	3.4	2.5	4.7	2.4	1.4	2.6	2.9	4.5	2.5	3.7	4.5
Austria	2.4	2.2	3.8	3.7	3.3	0.5	1.6	0.7	2.6	2.8	3.5	3.7	2.2	-3.9	2.1	2.9	2.1	3.1	2.2	2.3
Belgium	2.3	3.9	1.9	3.5	3.8	0.7	1.4	0.8	3.1	2.0	2.7	2.8	0.8	-2.7	2.1	2.4	2.0	2.1	2.2	2.3
Canada	2.2	4.2	4.1	5.5	5.2	1.8	2.9	1.9	3.1	3.0	2.8	2.2	0.5	-2.5	3.1	3.0	2.8	3.2	3.0	3.0
Chile	..	6.7	3.3	-0.8	4.6	3.4	2.1	3.7	5.9	5.6	4.9	4.9	3.2	-1.5	5.1	6.5	5.1	5.8	5.7	4.5
Czech Republic	..	-0.7	-0.7	1.2	3.9	2.4	1.8	3.6	4.3	6.4	7.0	6.1	2.3	-4.0	2.2	2.4	3.5	2.6	2.1	5.0
Denmark	1.7	3.2	2.2	2.6	3.5	0.7	0.5	0.4	2.3	2.4	3.4	1.6	-1.1	-5.2	2.1	1.9	2.1	2.9	2.0	2.2
Estonia	..	11.7	6.7	-0.3	10.0	7.5	7.9	7.6	7.2	9.4	10.6	6.9	-5.1	-13.9	3.1	5.9	4.7	6.8	4.3	5.8
Finland	1.4	6.1	5.1	4.0	5.3	2.2	1.7	2.1	4.1	3.0	4.4	5.3	1.0	-8.3	3.1	3.8	2.8	5.0	2.0	4.0
France	2.1	2.2	3.5	3.2	4.1	1.8	1.1	1.1	2.3	2.0	2.4	2.3	0.1	-2.7	1.4	2.2	2.1	1.6	2.4	2.3
Germany	2.6	1.8	1.8	1.9	3.5	1.4	0.0	-0.2	0.7	0.9	3.6	2.8	0.7	-4.7	3.5	3.4	2.5	4.0	3.1	2.7
Greece	1.4	3.6	3.4	3.4	4.5	4.2	3.4	5.9	4.4	2.3	5.2	4.3	1.0	-2.0	-4.5	-2.9	0.6	-7.5	0.3	1.4
Hungary	..	4.1	4.7	4.1	4.9	4.0	4.1	3.9	4.3	3.4	3.7	0.8	0.6	-6.5	1.0	2.7	3.1	2.5	3.0	3.2
Iceland	1.6	4.9	6.3	4.1	4.3	3.9	0.1	2.4	7.7	7.5	4.6	6.0	1.4	-6.9	-3.5	2.2	2.9	0.1	3.8	2.4
Ireland	5.5	11.5	8.5	10.9	9.7	5.7	6.6	4.4	4.6	6.0	5.3	5.6	-3.6	-7.6	-1.0	0.0	2.3	-0.5	2.1	2.5
Israel	..	3.5	4.1	3.3	9.2	0.0	-0.4	1.5	5.0	4.9	5.7	5.4	4.2	0.8	4.7	5.4	4.7	5.4	4.9	4.6
Italy	2.0	1.9	1.3	1.4	3.9	1.7	0.5	0.1	1.4	0.8	2.1	1.4	-1.3	-5.2	1.2	1.1	1.6	1.5	1.3	1.6
Japan	3.2	1.6	-2.0	-0.1	2.9	0.2	0.3	1.4	2.7	1.9	2.0	2.4	-1.2	-6.3	4.0	-0.9	2.2	2.4	0.3	1.5
Korea	8.6	5.8	-5.7	10.7	8.8	4.0	7.2	2.8	4.6	4.0	5.2	5.1	2.3	0.3	6.2	4.6	4.5	4.7	5.5	4.1
Luxembourg	4.9	5.9	6.5	8.4	8.4	2.5	4.1	1.5	4.4	5.4	5.0	6.6	1.4	-3.6	3.5	3.2	3.9	4.6	1.1	6.9
Mexico	2.5	7.2	5.0	3.6	6.0	-0.9	0.1	1.4	4.0	3.2	5.2	3.2	1.5	-6.1	5.5	4.4	3.8	4.4	3.9	3.8
Netherlands	2.8	4.3	3.9	4.7	3.9	1.9	0.1	0.3	2.2	2.0	3.4	3.9	1.9	-3.9	1.8	2.3	1.9	2.2	2.1	2.1
New Zealand	2.2	2.9	0.6	4.7	3.7	2.5	4.6	4.4	4.1	3.2	2.0	3.4	-0.7	0.0	2.5	0.8	4.1	1.6	1.8	4.4
Norway	2.8	5.4	2.7	2.0	3.3	2.0	1.5	1.0	3.9	2.7	2.3	2.7	0.8	-1.4	0.4	2.5	3.0	1.6	2.3	3.3
Poland	..	7.0	4.9	4.4	4.5	1.3	1.5	3.9	5.2	3.6	6.2	6.8	5.0	1.7	3.8	3.9	3.8	3.9	3.9	3.6
Portugal	3.6	4.4	5.0	4.1	3.9	2.0	0.7	-0.9	1.6	0.8	1.4	2.4	0.0	-2.5	1.3	-2.1	-1.5	1.0	-2.9	-0.7
Slovak Republic	..	5.7	4.4	0.0	1.4	3.5	4.6	4.8	5.1	6.7	8.5	10.5	5.8	-4.8	4.0	3.6	4.4	3.4	3.6	5.1
Slovenia	..	4.9	3.6	5.4	4.4	2.8	4.0	2.8	4.3	4.5	5.9	6.9	3.7	-8.1	1.2	1.8	2.6	2.0	1.7	3.2
Spain	2.9	3.9	4.5	4.7	5.0	3.6	2.7	3.1	3.3	3.6	4.0	3.6	0.9	-3.7	-0.1	0.9	1.6	0.6	1.0	1.9
Sweden	1.5	2.9	4.1	4.4	4.6	1.4	2.5	2.5	3.7	3.1	4.6	3.4	-0.8	-5.3	5.3	4.5	3.1	7.2	3.1	3.2
Switzerland	1.4	2.1	2.6	1.3	3.6	1.2	0.4	-0.2	2.5	2.6	3.6	3.6	1.9	-1.9	2.6	2.7	2.5	3.2	2.5	2.4
Turkey	4.4	7.5	3.1	-3.4	6.8	-5.7	6.2	5.3	9.4	8.4	6.9	4.7	0.7	-4.8	8.9	6.5	5.3	..	..	..
United Kingdom	2.4	3.3	3.6	3.5	3.9	2.5	2.1	2.8	3.0	2.2	2.8	2.7	-0.1	-4.9	1.3	1.4	1.8	1.5	1.7	2.2
United States	2.9	4.5	4.4	4.8	4.1	1.1	1.8	2.5	3.6	3.1	2.7	1.9	0.0	-2.6	2.9	2.6	3.1	2.8	2.7	3.3
Euro area	2.4	2.6	2.8	2.9	4.0	1.9	1.0	0.8	1.9	1.8	3.2	2.8	0.3	-4.1	1.7	2.0	2.0	2.0	2.1	2.2
Total OECD	2.9	3.7	2.7	3.4	4.2	1.3	1.7	2.0	3.2	2.7	3.2	2.7	0.3	-3.5	2.9	2.3	2.8	2.8	2.4	3.0

StatLink 🖴 http://dx.doi.org/10.1787/888932442940

Note: The adoption of national accounts systems SNA93 or ESA95 has been proceeding at an uneven pace among OECD member countries, both with respect to variables and the time period covered. As a consequence, there are breaks in many national series. Moreover, most countries have shifted to chain-weighted price indices to calculate real GDP and expenditures components. For further information, see table "National Accounts Reporting Systems, base years and latest data updates" at the beginning of the Statistical Annex and *OECD Economic Outlook Sources and Methods* *(http://www.oecd.org/eco/sources-and-methods).* These numbers are working-day adjusted and hence may differ from the basis used for official projections.

Source: OECD Economic Outlook 89 database.

Annex Table 2. Nominal GDP
Percentage change from previous year

	Average 1986-96	1997	1998	1999	2000	2001	2002	2003	2004	2005	2006	2007	2008	2009	2010	2011	2012	Fourth quarter 2010	2011	2012
Australia	7.2	5.3	5.3	5.4	7.8	6.5	7.1	5.9	7.6	7.9	7.9	9.1	9.0	0.5	7.8	7.7	7.4	9.0	7.9	7.4
Austria	5.2	2.0	3.9	3.8	4.7	2.5	3.2	1.9	4.0	4.6	5.7	5.7	3.7	-2.9	3.8	4.7	3.7	5.0	3.8	4.0
Belgium	4.9	4.8	3.8	3.8	5.8	2.8	3.4	2.8	5.3	4.4	5.0	5.2	2.8	-1.6	4.0	4.6	4.1	4.5	4.1	4.4
Canada	5.0	5.5	3.7	7.4	9.6	2.9	4.0	5.2	6.4	6.4	5.6	5.5	4.6	-4.5	6.2	5.4	4.5	5.9	5.2	4.6
Chile	..	11.2	5.3	1.7	9.3	7.3	6.5	10.0	14.0	13.5	17.6	10.3	3.9	1.1	15.1	12.0	9.9	14.8	10.5	9.1
Czech Republic	..	7.6	10.2	4.1	5.5	7.4	4.7	4.6	9.1	6.1	8.2	9.7	4.2	-1.6	1.1	2.5	5.1	1.3	2.8	6.8
Denmark	4.3	5.3	3.4	4.3	6.6	3.2	2.8	2.0	4.7	5.4	5.6	3.9	2.7	-4.9	5.4	4.0	3.9	5.5	4.0	3.9
Estonia	..	23.3	12.3	6.5	15.0	13.2	11.6	12.1	11.1	15.5	19.8	18.2	1.8	-13.9	4.6	8.8	7.0	9.7	6.3	8.3
Finland	4.9	8.0	8.8	4.9	7.9	5.4	3.0	1.4	4.7	3.4	5.5	8.3	2.8	-7.2	5.2	5.5	4.8	7.9	3.9	5.3
France	4.3	3.2	4.5	3.2	5.6	3.8	3.5	3.0	3.9	4.0	4.9	4.9	2.7	-2.0	2.2	3.7	3.4	2.8	4.1	3.5
Germany	5.2	2.1	2.4	2.2	2.8	2.6	1.4	0.9	1.7	1.6	4.0	4.7	1.7	-3.3	4.1	4.2	3.8	4.3	4.1	4.1
Greece	16.0	10.7	8.7	6.6	8.0	7.4	7.0	10.1	7.4	5.2	8.5	7.5	4.3	-0.8	-2.1	-2.6	1.3	-5.6	1.1	1.5
Hungary	..	24.5	18.5	11.2	14.5	15.3	12.6	9.2	9.7	6.1	8.3	6.8	4.9	-2.1	3.9	6.7	6.4	4.8	6.8	6.3
Iceland	11.7	8.0	11.8	7.5	8.1	12.9	5.8	3.0	10.4	10.5	13.8	12.0	13.3	0.8	3.0	4.2	5.8	0.4	7.4	5.1
Ireland	8.4	15.7	15.5	15.2	16.2	11.6	11.4	7.3	6.7	8.6	9.3	6.8	-4.9	-11.3	-3.6	-1.3	3.5	-4.6	5.3	3.3
Israel	..	11.5	11.5	9.8	10.9	1.7	3.5	1.0	5.2	6.0	8.1	5.9	5.2	5.9	5.8	6.9	7.3	7.7	6.7	7.0
Italy	7.7	4.6	3.9	3.2	5.9	4.8	3.7	3.2	4.0	2.9	4.0	4.0	1.4	-3.1	1.9	2.4	3.3	2.2	3.4	2.9
Japan	4.0	2.1	-2.1	-1.4	1.1	-1.0	-1.3	-0.2	1.6	0.7	1.1	1.6	-2.2	-6.6	1.8	-2.2	1.7	0.7	-0.7	1.2
Korea	16.5	9.8	-1.0	9.6	9.9	8.0	10.6	6.5	7.8	4.6	5.0	7.3	5.3	3.8	10.1	5.6	7.3	9.5	4.9	8.1
Luxembourg	8.0	4.0	6.1	14.2	10.6	2.6	6.3	7.7	6.3	10.3	12.0	10.5	5.7	-4.0	9.3	5.9	5.6	12.9	1.7	8.1
Mexico	40.1	26.0	20.2	21.5	17.4	4.4	2.7	10.9	13.5	7.9	12.2	9.1	7.8	-2.2	10.1	8.7	8.1	9.4	8.1	8.0
Netherlands	4.5	7.0	5.9	6.5	8.2	7.1	3.9	2.5	3.0	4.5	5.2	5.8	4.3	-4.1	3.4	2.2	3.5	4.4	1.9	3.9
New Zealand	6.2	3.6	1.6	5.1	6.4	6.8	5.9	6.1	8.1	5.4	4.7	7.6	3.3	0.7	4.8	5.2	7.4	6.9	4.7	9.2
Norway	6.1	8.3	1.9	8.8	19.4	3.8	-0.3	4.0	9.4	11.6	11.0	5.2	10.8	-5.4	5.2	11.3	5.9	7.9	10.8	4.9
Poland	..	21.9	16.5	10.7	12.1	5.1	3.7	4.3	9.3	6.6	7.8	11.1	8.3	5.3	5.4	6.9	6.8	6.1	6.9	6.7
Portugal	12.6	8.5	9.0	7.5	7.3	5.6	4.5	2.0	4.1	3.3	4.3	5.6	1.6	-2.0	2.3	-1.1	-0.5	1.7	-2.2	0.2
Slovak Republic	..	10.9	9.7	7.4	10.9	8.7	8.6	10.3	11.2	9.2	11.7	11.8	8.9	-5.9	4.5	5.6	7.2	4.4	5.7	8.6
Slovenia	..	13.8	10.8	12.3	10.0	11.8	12.0	8.6	7.8	6.2	8.0	11.3	7.9	-5.1	1.9	2.8	4.8	2.3	3.4	5.6
Spain	8.7	6.3	7.1	7.5	8.7	8.0	7.1	7.4	7.4	8.1	8.3	7.0	3.3	-3.1	0.8	2.1	2.4	2.0	2.0	2.8
Sweden	6.3	4.3	4.8	5.6	5.9	3.7	4.1	4.1	4.6	4.1	6.3	6.2	2.5	-3.6	6.8	5.8	4.7	9.2	4.1	5.0
Switzerland	3.9	1.9	2.9	1.9	4.8	2.0	0.9	0.8	3.1	2.8	5.8	6.2	4.4	-1.6	2.0	3.1	3.3	2.6	3.1	3.2
Turkey	76.2	95.2	81.1	49.0	59.3	44.1	45.9	29.8	22.9	16.1	16.9	11.2	12.7	0.2	16.0	13.2	11.7	..	..	..
United Kingdom	7.2	6.2	5.9	5.6	5.1	4.6	5.3	6.0	5.5	4.2	5.9	5.8	2.9	-3.5	4.2	4.8	4.0	4.2	5.0	4.3
United States	5.8	6.3	5.5	6.4	6.4	3.4	3.5	4.7	6.5	6.5	6.0	4.9	2.2	-1.7	3.8	4.0	4.5	4.2	4.2	4.7
Euro area	6.1	4.1	4.4	3.9	5.5	4.4	3.6	3.0	3.9	3.8	5.2	5.3	2.3	-3.2	2.6	3.1	3.4	3.1	3.4	3.6
Total OECD	9.2	8.0	6.4	6.3	7.4	4.4	4.2	4.6	5.9	5.2	5.9	5.4	2.8	-2.5	4.3	3.9	4.5	4.5	4.1	4.8

StatLink http://dx.doi.org/10.1787/888932442959

Note: The adoption of national accounts systems SNA93 or ESA95 has been proceeding at an uneven pace among OECD member countries, both with respect to variables and the time period covered. As a consequence, there are breaks in many national series. For further information, see table "National Accounts Reporting Systems, base years and latest data updates" at the beginning of the Statistical Annex and *OECD Economic Outlook* Sources and Methods (*http://www.oecd.org/eco/sources-and-methods*). Working-day adjusted -- see note to Annex Table 1.

Source: OECD Economic Outlook 89 database.

Annex Table 3. Real private consumption expenditure
Percentage change from previous year

	Average 1986-96	1997	1998	1999	2000	2001	2002	2003	2004	2005	2006	2007	2008	2009	2010	2011	2012	Fourth quarter 2010	2011	2012
Australia	3.2	3.7	4.4	5.3	3.7	3.2	3.8	3.8	5.5	3.3	3.4	5.4	2.0	1.0	2.7	2.7	3.6	2.8	2.9	3.7
Austria	2.5	1.1	1.7	2.2	2.3	1.3	1.1	1.4	1.8	2.1	1.8	0.9	0.7	1.2	1.0	0.9	1.2	0.9	0.9	1.4
Belgium	2.0	2.1	2.6	2.0	2.8	1.3	0.5	0.7	1.4	1.3	1.8	1.7	1.4	-0.2	1.6	2.0	1.9	1.7	1.7	2.2
Canada	2.2	4.6	2.8	3.8	4.0	2.3	3.6	3.0	3.3	3.7	4.2	4.6	2.9	0.4	3.4	2.6	2.7	3.4	2.1	3.0
Chile	..	6.6	4.7	-1.0	3.7	2.9	2.4	4.2	7.2	7.4	7.1	7.0	4.5	0.9	10.4	7.7	5.7	10.8	6.2	5.2
Czech Republic	..	2.2	-0.8	2.6	1.5	2.2	2.1	5.9	2.9	2.5	5.3	5.0	3.5	-0.1	0.4	0.5	2.6	-0.3	2.6	2.6
Denmark	1.1	3.0	2.3	-0.4	0.2	0.1	1.5	1.0	4.7	3.8	3.6	3.0	-0.6	-4.5	2.2	1.9	2.0	2.5	1.9	2.2
Estonia	..	11.9	5.1	0.8	7.9	7.1	10.3	8.7	9.5	9.8	13.7	8.6	-5.4	-18.4	-1.9	2.3	4.5	2.8	3.3	5.0
Finland	1.4	3.3	4.6	2.8	2.2	2.8	2.5	4.8	3.5	3.1	4.3	3.5	1.6	-2.1	2.7	2.4	2.1	2.9	1.6	2.4
France	1.8	0.4	3.9	3.5	3.7	2.5	2.3	2.1	2.4	2.5	2.6	2.5	0.5	0.6	1.3	1.5	1.9	1.1	1.5	2.2
Germany	2.7	0.9	1.4	2.9	2.5	1.9	-0.8	0.1	-0.2	0.4	1.5	-0.2	0.6	-0.1	0.4	1.3	1.4	1.4	1.2	1.6
Greece	2.9	2.7	3.5	2.5	2.0	5.0	4.7	3.3	3.8	4.5	5.2	2.8	3.2	-2.2	-4.5	-5.4	-0.2	..	..	..
Hungary	..	1.6	4.1	6.3	4.3	6.5	10.8	8.6	3.1	3.3	1.9	0.2	0.4	-7.9	-2.1	1.6	2.1	-0.3	2.6	1.9
Iceland	0.9	6.3	10.2	7.9	4.2	-2.8	-1.5	6.1	7.0	12.7	3.6	5.6	-7.9	-15.6	-0.2	2.9	2.7	2.4	1.0	3.4
Ireland	3.8	7.7	7.6	9.1	10.3	4.7	3.9	2.9	3.5	6.7	6.5	6.3	-1.8	-7.2	-1.2	-2.1	0.3	-1.5	-1.8	1.2
Israel	..	3.1	5.6	3.9	8.7	3.5	0.8	-0.1	5.3	3.0	4.3	6.4	3.0	1.7	5.1	4.9	4.5	4.3	4.6	4.2
Italy	1.9	3.2	3.5	2.6	2.3	0.7	0.2	1.0	0.8	1.2	1.3	1.1	-0.8	-1.8	1.0	0.9	1.2	1.0	0.9	1.3
Japan	3.1	0.7	-0.9	1.0	0.7	1.6	1.1	0.4	1.6	1.3	1.5	1.6	-0.7	-1.9	1.8	-1.3	1.6	0.6	-0.5	1.8
Korea	8.5	4.0	-12.5	11.9	9.2	5.7	8.9	-0.4	0.3	4.6	4.7	5.1	1.3	0.0	4.1	3.5	3.6	2.9	4.0	3.1
Luxembourg	3.4	3.8	5.7	3.6	5.0	3.4	5.8	-5.3	2.2	2.6	3.2	3.3	4.7	0.2	2.0	1.8	2.8	2.9	1.9	3.2
Mexico	2.2	6.5	5.5	4.3	8.2	2.5	1.6	2.3	5.6	4.8	5.7	4.0	1.8	-7.1	5.0	4.7	4.1	4.5	4.1	4.1
Netherlands	2.3	3.5	5.1	5.3	3.7	1.8	0.9	-0.2	1.0	1.0	-0.3	1.8	1.1	-2.5	0.4	0.7	1.3	1.3	0.6	1.5
New Zealand	2.2	2.4	2.5	3.5	1.9	2.0	4.3	5.7	5.3	4.6	2.2	4.1	-0.3	-0.7	2.0	0.9	2.2	1.2	1.3	2.2
Norway	1.7	3.1	2.8	3.7	4.2	2.1	3.1	2.8	5.6	4.0	4.8	5.4	1.6	0.2	3.6	3.9	4.1	3.2	3.9	4.2
Poland	..	7.4	4.9	5.6	2.9	2.5	3.1	2.4	4.2	2.5	5.1	4.9	5.2	2.4	3.0	3.0	3.3	3.5	3.0	3.3
Portugal	3.6	3.7	5.1	5.5	3.8	1.3	1.3	-0.2	2.7	1.7	1.8	2.5	1.3	-1.1	2.2	-4.1	-3.7	1.0	-6.1	-2.7
Slovak Republic	..	7.3	6.6	0.4	2.2	5.5	5.7	1.7	4.6	6.5	5.9	6.8	6.2	0.3	-0.3	0.4	3.0	0.8	0.8	4.2
Slovenia	..	2.8	2.8	6.8	1.2	2.5	2.5	3.3	2.7	2.6	2.9	6.7	2.9	-0.8	0.5	0.9	2.0	0.8	0.9	2.6
Spain	2.8	3.2	4.8	5.3	5.0	3.4	2.8	2.9	4.2	4.2	3.8	3.7	-0.6	-4.2	1.2	0.4	1.6	1.6	0.8	1.9
Sweden	1.0	2.9	3.2	3.9	5.4	0.8	2.6	2.3	2.6	2.8	2.8	3.8	-0.1	-0.5	3.5	3.4	2.8	4.4	3.0	2.7
Switzerland	1.3	1.4	2.2	2.3	2.4	2.3	0.1	0.9	1.6	1.7	1.6	2.3	1.3	1.0	1.7	1.7	2.3	1.5	2.1	2.3
Turkey	3.4	8.4	0.6	0.1	5.9	-6.6	4.7	10.2	11.0	7.9	4.6	5.5	-0.3	-2.3	6.6	6.6	5.3	..	..	..
United Kingdom	2.8	3.8	4.3	5.2	4.7	3.1	3.5	3.0	3.1	2.2	1.7	2.2	0.4	-3.2	0.6	0.2	1.1	-0.1	0.6	1.6
United States	2.9	3.7	5.2	5.5	5.1	2.7	2.7	2.8	3.5	3.4	2.9	2.4	-0.3	-1.2	1.7	2.9	2.9	2.6	2.8	3.0
Euro area	2.3	1.8	3.1	3.4	3.1	2.1	0.9	1.2	1.5	1.9	2.2	1.7	0.4	-1.1	0.7	0.8	1.4	0.9	0.8	1.7
Total OECD	2.8	3.1	3.2	4.2	4.2	2.3	2.4	2.3	3.0	2.9	2.8	2.6	0.3	-1.5	1.9	2.0	2.5	2.1	2.0	2.7

StatLink http://dx.doi.org/10.1787/888932442978

Note: The adoption of national accounts systems SNA93 or ESA95 has been proceeding at an uneven pace among OECD member countries, both with respect to variables and the time period covered. As a consequence, there are breaks in many national series. Moreover, most countries have shifted to chain-weighted price indices to calculate real GDP and expenditure components. For further information, see table "National Accounts Reporting Systems, base years and latest data updates" at the beginning of the Statistical Annex and *OECD Economic Outlook Sources and Methods* (*http://www.oecd.org/eco/sources-and-methods*). Working-day adjusted -- see note to Annex Table 1.

Source: OECD Economic Outlook 89 database.

Annex Table 4. Real public consumption expenditure
Percentage change from previous year

	Average 1986-96	1997	1998	1999	2000	2001	2002	2003	2004	2005	2006	2007	2008	2009	2010	2011	2012	Fourth quarter 2010	2011	2012
Australia	2.9	2.8	3.5	3.1	3.8	2.3	2.6	3.9	3.8	2.3	3.5	3.3	3.2	1.5	3.5	2.6	1.7	4.2	1.8	1.7
Austria	2.1	3.7	2.7	3.8	0.0	-0.3	0.7	1.0	1.1	1.6	2.7	2.2	3.9	0.4	-2.4	0.3	0.4	-2.5	0.0	0.6
Belgium	1.2	1.1	1.6	2.7	3.1	1.6	3.2	1.4	1.8	1.2	0.6	2.1	2.5	0.4	1.1	1.4	0.5	1.3	1.4	0.0
Canada	1.3	-1.0	3.2	2.1	3.1	3.9	2.5	3.1	2.0	1.4	3.0	2.7	3.9	3.5	3.4	1.6	-0.4	2.1	0.6	-0.5
Chile	..	5.8	2.2	2.7	3.0	2.9	3.1	2.4	6.1	5.9	6.4	7.1	0.5	7.5	3.3	5.3	2.0	7.1	2.0	2.0
Czech Republic	..	3.0	-1.6	3.7	0.7	3.6	6.7	7.1	-3.5	2.9	1.2	0.5	1.1	2.6	0.3	-1.2	1.3	-1.6	-0.9	1.7
Denmark	1.5	0.7	3.5	2.4	2.3	2.2	2.1	0.7	1.8	1.3	2.8	1.3	1.6	3.1	1.0	-0.3	0.3	-0.2	0.0	0.5
Estonia	..	-1.7	2.2	-0.2	-2.2	2.6	2.6	0.8	2.0	-0.2	3.9	3.9	3.8	0.0	-2.1	0.3	1.1	-1.6	0.8	1.2
Finland	1.2	4.0	1.8	1.2	0.5	1.5	2.7	1.6	1.7	2.2	0.3	1.0	2.5	0.9	0.4	0.9	0.6	0.7	0.8	0.5
France	2.3	1.2	-0.6	1.4	2.0	1.1	1.9	2.0	2.2	1.3	1.3	1.5	1.6	2.8	1.2	0.5	0.1	0.4	0.3	0.2
Germany	1.7	0.5	1.8	1.2	1.4	0.5	1.5	0.4	-0.7	0.4	1.0	1.6	2.3	2.9	2.3	1.5	1.0	2.9	1.0	1.0
Greece	0.4	3.0	1.7	2.1	14.8	0.7	7.2	-0.9	3.5	1.1	8.8	8.2	1.5	10.3	-6.5	-7.1	-4.3	..	..	..
Hungary	..	0.0	-0.5	1.5	0.7	3.1	5.6	5.0	1.5	2.2	3.7	-7.3	1.0	-0.1	-1.7	-2.6	-0.2	-3.6	-1.5	0.0
Iceland	3.0	2.6	4.2	4.4	3.8	4.7	5.3	1.8	2.2	3.5	4.0	4.1	4.6	-1.7	-3.2	-4.0	-1.8	-2.0	-4.6	-0.6
Ireland	1.1	5.5	5.6	5.9	9.5	10.4	7.2	1.9	2.4	4.6	5.9	7.3	2.8	-4.2	-2.1	-1.9	-2.0	-0.8	-2.0	-2.0
Israel	..	2.7	1.5	2.7	1.7	3.6	5.0	-2.8	-1.7	2.0	3.1	3.1	2.4	1.9	2.1	3.3	1.5	4.4	1.5	1.5
Italy	0.8	0.5	1.8	1.4	2.2	3.9	2.4	1.9	2.2	1.9	0.5	0.9	0.5	1.0	-0.6	-0.1	-0.1	-1.1	0.6	-0.5
Japan	3.4	0.8	1.8	4.2	4.3	3.0	2.4	2.3	1.9	1.6	0.4	1.5	0.5	3.0	2.3	2.6	-0.4	1.5	2.2	-1.0
Korea	6.6	2.7	2.2	3.0	1.8	5.0	4.9	4.4	3.8	4.3	6.6	5.4	4.3	5.6	3.0	4.0	4.0	3.4	5.8	3.6
Luxembourg	5.3	3.2	1.6	8.3	4.7	6.1	4.6	4.1	4.5	3.3	1.7	2.8	2.7	4.6	2.9	0.4	3.1	0.3	0.2	5.3
Mexico	1.3	2.6	2.5	4.5	2.6	-2.4	-0.2	1.0	-2.8	2.5	1.9	3.1	1.1	3.5	2.8	0.6	1.5	2.1	1.2	1.5
Netherlands	2.1	2.5	2.5	2.8	2.0	4.6	3.3	2.9	-0.1	0.5	9.5	3.5	2.5	3.7	1.5	-0.2	-0.4	0.9	-0.9	-0.4
New Zealand	1.6	6.3	-0.3	6.9	-2.4	4.3	1.5	3.4	6.0	4.1	4.5	4.4	5.0	0.6	2.3	1.5	-0.6	2.6	1.0	-1.2
Norway	3.0	3.3	3.4	3.1	1.9	4.6	3.1	1.7	1.5	0.7	1.9	3.0	4.1	4.7	2.2	2.1	1.9	3.1	0.9	2.5
Poland	..	3.6	1.8	2.0	1.4	2.9	1.7	4.5	3.2	5.6	5.9	3.5	6.6	2.6	3.8	3.2	0.8	5.5	1.3	0.6
Portugal	3.9	2.6	6.2	3.8	4.2	3.8	1.6	0.4	2.4	3.3	-0.7	0.5	0.4	3.7	1.8	-7.2	-5.6	2.6	-10.3	-5.6
Slovak Republic	..	0.2	5.6	-7.3	4.6	5.4	3.0	4.3	-2.9	3.9	9.7	0.1	6.1	5.6	0.1	-3.6	0.3	-3.0	-2.9	1.1
Slovenia	..	3.3	4.8	3.3	3.1	3.8	3.3	2.2	3.4	3.4	4.0	0.7	6.2	3.0	0.8	0.6	0.8	3.2	-2.2	2.1
Spain	4.3	2.5	3.5	4.0	5.3	3.9	4.5	4.8	6.3	5.5	4.6	5.5	5.8	3.2	-0.7	-1.7	-1.3	-0.9	-1.6	-1.3
Sweden	1.3	-0.5	3.6	1.5	-1.1	0.9	2.1	1.1	-0.9	0.2	2.0	0.8	0.7	1.8	2.3	1.7	0.8	2.9	0.9	0.8
Switzerland	2.5	0.4	-1.1	0.5	2.3	4.5	1.2	1.9	0.8	1.2	0.3	0.3	1.7	1.6	-1.6	1.1	0.5	-1.4	0.2	0.7
Turkey	4.2	4.1	7.8	4.0	5.7	-1.1	5.8	-2.6	6.0	2.5	8.4	6.5	1.7	7.8	2.0	5.3	4.4			
United Kingdom	0.9	-0.5	1.1	3.6	3.1	2.4	3.5	3.4	3.0	2.0	1.4	1.3	1.6	1.0	0.8	0.2	-0.7	0.6	0.0	-1.0
United States	1.1	1.7	1.8	2.8	1.8	3.7	4.5	2.2	1.4	0.6	1.0	1.3	2.5	1.9	0.9	-0.6	0.2	0.7	-0.7	0.5
Euro area	1.9	1.3	1.3	1.8	2.4	2.0	2.4	1.7	1.6	1.6	2.2	2.2	2.3	2.5	0.6	0.0	-0.1	0.4	-0.6	-0.1
Total OECD	1.8	1.3	1.8	2.7	2.5	2.8	3.2	2.2	1.7	1.5	1.9	2.0	2.3	2.5	1.3	0.5	0.3	1.1	0.0	0.5

Note: The adoption of national accounts systems SNA93 or ESA95 has been proceeding at an uneven pace among OECD member countries, both with respect to variables and the time period covered. As a consequence, there are breaks in many national series. Moreover, most countries have shifted to chain-weighted price indices to calculate real GDP and expenditure components. For further information, see table "National Accounts Reporting Systems, base years and latest data updates" at the beginning of the Statistical Annex and OECD Economic Outlook Sources and Methods (http://www.oecd.org/eco/sources-and-methods). Working-day adjusted -- see note to Annex Table 1.

Source: OECD Economic Outlook 89 database.

StatLink ꞋꞋꞋ http://dx.doi.org/10.1787/888932442997

Annex Table 5. Real total gross fixed capital formation
Percentage change from previous year

	Average 1986-96	1997	1998	1999	2000	2001	2002	2003	2004	2005	2006	2007	2008	2009	2010	2011	2012	Fourth quarter 2010	2011	2012
Australia	3.5	9.5	6.2	4.7	2.0	-3.6	16.1	9.6	6.3	9.4	4.2	10.3	7.2	-2.4	4.9	4.3	9.5	0.8	8.0	9.7
Austria	3.8	0.2	3.0	1.7	4.8	-1.5	-4.0	3.3	1.6	2.4	0.9	3.5	2.8	-7.9	-1.2	3.0	2.5	1.5	2.2	2.8
Belgium	3.9	6.2	3.4	2.6	5.1	1.1	-4.5	0.1	7.5	7.0	2.8	6.0	2.2	-5.0	-1.5	2.2	3.2	0.0	2.3	4.1
Canada	2.0	15.2	2.4	7.3	4.7	4.0	1.6	6.2	7.8	9.3	7.1	3.5	1.4	-11.7	8.3	6.8	5.4	9.6	6.5	4.4
Chile	..	10.5	1.9	-18.2	8.9	4.3	1.5	5.7	10.0	23.9	2.3	11.2	19.4	-15.9	18.8	13.4	12.3	20.4	15.9	9.9
Czech Republic	..	-5.7	-0.9	-3.3	5.1	6.6	5.1	0.4	3.9	1.8	6.0	10.8	-1.5	-7.9	-4.6	3.9	4.8	-2.3	2.5	6.5
Denmark	1.4	10.3	8.1	-0.1	7.6	-1.4	0.1	-0.2	3.9	4.7	14.3	0.4	-3.3	-14.3	-4.0	3.6	5.1	2.5	4.8	4.9
Estonia	..	23.6	21.4	-15.5	16.7	9.9	24.0	18.6	5.2	15.3	23.2	6.0	-15.0	-32.9	-9.2	14.8	10.3	11.7	6.6	12.7
Finland	-0.7	10.5	11.4	3.8	6.0	3.0	-4.0	2.9	4.9	3.6	2.2	10.1	0.0	-14.5	0.1	5.7	5.8	5.8	5.3	5.8
France	2.0	0.4	7.2	8.1	7.5	2.3	-1.6	2.2	3.3	4.5	4.5	5.9	0.3	-6.9	-1.1	4.0	4.6	1.9	4.3	4.8
Germany	3.1	0.8	3.6	4.4	3.7	-3.4	-6.1	-0.3	-1.3	1.1	8.7	4.9	1.8	-10.0	5.7	6.3	4.0	7.5	6.2	4.6
Greece	1.3	6.8	10.6	11.0	8.0	4.8	9.5	11.8	0.4	-6.3	10.6	5.5	-7.5	-11.2	-16.5	-10.4	0.3	:	:	:
Hungary	..	6.5	11.5	6.0	7.2	4.7	10.5	2.1	7.9	5.7	-3.2	1.7	2.9	-8.0	-5.6	0.6	2.9	-6.5	4.5	3.7
Iceland	1.4	9.3	34.4	-4.1	11.8	-4.3	-14.0	11.1	28.1	35.7	22.4	-11.1	-19.7	-50.9	-8.1	14.7	12.4	-8.8	6.6	13.3
Ireland	5.6	16.4	14.7	13.8	5.9	0.1	2.9	6.5	9.5	15.0	4.4	2.6	-14.4	-30.9	-27.7	-11.0	0.8	-26.6	-1.0	1.3
Israel	..	-0.9	-4.0	-0.3	3.2	-3.7	-6.5	-4.1	0.5	3.4	13.6	14.6	4.1	-6.5	12.6	13.3	7.2	21.2	9.2	6.9
Italy	1.7	1.9	3.6	3.7	7.1	2.4	3.7	-0.9	1.5	1.4	3.2	1.4	-3.8	-12.0	2.3	1.2	2.5	2.7	1.9	2.6
Japan	3.9	-0.3	-7.2	-0.8	1.2	-0.9	-4.9	-0.5	1.4	3.1	0.5	-1.2	-3.6	-11.7	-0.2	0.0	6.5	1.3	3.2	4.0
Korea	12.9	-1.5	-22.0	8.7	12.3	0.3	7.1	4.4	2.1	1.9	3.4	4.2	-1.9	-1.0	7.0	-0.4	5.9	3.4	1.9	5.2
Luxembourg	5.9	10.4	6.1	22.0	-4.7	8.8	5.5	6.3	2.7	2.5	3.8	17.9	1.4	-19.2	2.6	8.0	4.0	2.7	13.1	-1.2
Mexico	3.1	21.1	10.5	7.7	11.4	-5.6	-0.7	0.4	8.0	7.4	9.9	6.9	5.9	-11.2	2.3	8.6	8.3	6.3	8.4	8.2
Netherlands	3.0	8.5	6.8	8.7	0.6	0.2	-4.5	-1.5	-1.6	3.7	7.5	5.5	5.1	-12.7	-4.8	5.4	5.0	0.8	7.3	5.5
New Zealand	3.0	1.3	-4.0	7.0	8.1	-1.2	10.8	10.9	12.7	5.4	-1.4	6.0	-4.4	-10.6	2.4	6.0	17.5	7.4	6.5	20.0
Norway	0.1	15.8	13.6	-5.4	-3.5	-1.1	-1.1	0.2	10.2	13.3	11.7	12.5	2.0	-7.4	-8.9	6.4	7.1	-6.6	4.0	7.8
Poland	..	21.0	14.1	6.7	2.8	-9.7	-6.3	-0.1	6.4	6.5	14.9	17.2	9.6	-0.8	-2.2	9.7	9.7	0.9	10.8	8.3
Portugal	5.9	14.2	11.8	6.0	3.9	0.6	-3.2	-7.1	0.0	-0.5	-1.3	2.6	-0.3	-11.2	-5.0	-10.0	-6.7	-4.5	-10.2	-4.4
Slovak Republic	..	14.0	9.4	-15.7	-9.6	12.9	0.2	-2.7	4.8	17.5	9.3	9.1	1.0	-19.9	3.6	6.7	7.1	10.9	5.3	7.9
Slovenia	..	13.3	8.9	14.6	2.2	0.7	0.7	8.1	5.6	3.7	10.1	12.8	8.5	-21.6	-6.7	0.4	4.3	-6.3	3.9	4.6
Spain	4.3	5.0	11.3	10.4	6.6	4.8	3.4	5.9	5.1	7.0	7.2	4.5	-4.8	-16.0	-7.6	-3.4	2.0	-6.1	-0.7	3.2
Sweden	1.2	0.9	8.6	8.3	6.0	0.7	-1.3	1.8	4.9	8.0	9.7	9.1	1.0	-16.2	5.9	7.8	6.1	10.8	6.6	6.0
Switzerland	1.7	2.1	6.4	1.5	4.2	-3.5	-0.5	-1.2	4.5	3.8	4.7	5.1	0.5	-4.9	4.6	6.5	3.5	6.2	4.1	2.8
Turkey	9.2	14.8	-3.9	-16.2	17.5	-30.0	14.7	14.2	28.4	17.4	13.3	3.1	-6.2	-19.0	29.9	16.4	9.2	:	:	:
United Kingdom	3.0	6.8	13.7	3.0	2.7	2.6	3.6	1.1	5.1	2.4	6.4	7.8	-5.0	-15.4	3.0	1.7	4.2	5.8	2.4	5.2
United States	3.3	8.1	9.7	9.0	6.8	-1.0	-2.7	3.1	6.2	5.3	2.5	-1.2	-4.5	-14.8	3.3	4.2	8.0	6.5	4.7	8.0
Euro area	2.7	2.7	5.8	5.9	5.3	0.6	-1.5	1.3	1.9	3.4	5.7	4.6	-1.0	-11.3	-0.8	2.5	3.4	1.5	3.1	3.9
Total OECD	3.6	5.4	3.8	5.1	5.6	-1.0	-0.8	2.3	4.6	4.9	4.4	2.6	-1.9	-11.9	2.5	3.7	6.2	4.8	4.2	6.4

Note: The adoption of national accounts systems SNA93 or ESA95 has been proceeding at an uneven pace among OECD member countries, both with respect to variables and the time period covered. As a consequence, there are breaks in many national series. Moreover, most countries have shifted to chain-weighted price indices to calculate real GDP and expenditure components. For further information, see table "National Accounts Reporting Systems, base years and latest data updates" at the beginning of the Statistical Annex and *OECD Economic Outlook Sources and Methods* (*http://www.oecd.org/eco/sources-and-methods*). Working-day adjusted -- see note to Annex Table 1.

Source: OECD Economic Outlook 89 database.

StatLink ᵇᵖ http://dx.doi.org/10.1787/888932443016

Annex Table 6. Real gross private non-residential fixed capital formation

Percentage change from previous year

	Average 1986-96	1997	1998	1999	2000	2001	2002	2003	2004	2005	2006	2007	2008	2009	2010	2011	2012	Fourth quarter 2010	2011	2012
Australia	4.5	7.8	3.4	4.5	0.4	-1.4	13.5	14.5	7.7	14.9	7.8	13.1	7.0	-2.7	-0.8	7.3	14.0	-2.9	12.6	13.9
Austria	4.4	6.9	6.3	3.8	10.3	2.1	-4.8	6.2	2.6	2.5	0.6	4.6	3.9	-9.3	-0.7	4.6	3.1	2.9	3.2	3.3
Belgium	4.3	6.1	7.3	0.4	7.7	4.2	-4.7	-1.2	8.3	5.2	2.0	7.9	3.4	-7.5	-0.9	2.4	4.0	1.1	2.1	5.6
Canada	3.1	22.6	5.3	7.2	4.7	0.2	-4.1	6.9	8.2	12.4	9.9	3.3	3.4	-19.9	5.2	12.7	10.7	14.2	12.5	8.7
Denmark	2.6	12.1	11.9	-1.5	6.7	-0.3	0.7	-3.0	-0.3	-0.2	16.3	4.1	-0.4	-15.9	-3.8	2.4	8.3	0.8	6.9	8.5
Finland	-0.8	6.0	15.0	2.7	8.8	9.5	-8.5	-2.2	1.6	6.5	2.6	17.3	5.8	-19.1	-11.1	5.4	10.0	-4.0	9.3	10.0
France	2.4	2.0	10.4	9.1	8.7	3.3	-3.0	1.2	3.6	3.2	5.6	6.9	2.6	-7.4	2.0	6.1	6.6	4.5	6.3	7.0
Germany	2.5	2.8	6.0	5.8	7.9	-2.6	-7.0	0.7	0.7	4.3	10.3	8.5	3.0	-16.1	7.6	9.3	6.3	12.7	8.4	6.7
Greece	11.7	5.1	13.0	20.7	13.3	5.8	9.4	12.2	-0.8	-6.4	-2.6	19.2	5.5	-9.8	-16.2	-8.7	1.9	..	..	..
Iceland	0.8	17.6	46.2	-7.4	11.1	-11.3	-20.2	20.9	33.9	60.2	24.2	-22.1	-23.3	-54.7	0.9	26.0	18.1	-16.9	15.9	16.4
Ireland	7.0	18.2	20.6	13.2	2.2	-8.6	1.7	5.9	14.1	17.2	4.6	9.7	-20.8	-26.4	-34.6	-7.1	6.3	-40.8	18.7	2.1
Italy	2.6	3.4	4.0	4.1	8.4	2.0	4.5	-3.4	1.1	-0.3	3.4	2.0	-6.2	-17.3	6.3	3.2	6.6	7.0	3.7	8.0
Japan	3.1	8.4	-6.5	-4.3	7.5	1.3	-5.2	4.4	5.6	9.2	2.3	2.6	-1.4	-16.7	2.1	0.7	8.5	5.1	3.1	6.9
Korea	13.2	-2.5	-28.1	13.8	18.8	-3.3	8.1	2.3	1.9	2.0	7.6	6.9	-0.4	-6.2	15.3	-0.8	6.7	10.7	0.3	6.6
Netherlands	3.0	13.5	8.3	11.3	-2.0	-3.0	-7.6	-1.0	-2.7	2.2	9.7	6.4	7.1	-18.2	-1.6	10.3	8.0	4.7	12.2	8.6
New Zealand	5.3	-5.9	-1.9	7.4	18.9	-3.1	-0.4	13.1	14.3	7.9	-0.9	10.1	1.6	-17.4	9.3	11.7	13.5	21.8	6.3	16.1
Norway	0.1	16.1	16.0	-8.3	-3.9	-4.3	-1.9	-2.9	10.3	17.3	14.5	16.3	5.7	-7.5	-10.8	7.0	7.7	-5.7	6.9	8.2
Spain	5.4	6.5	11.4	11.7	7.9	3.2	1.2	5.3	6.8	7.7	7.8	3.9	-3.1	-18.5	-2.1	0.8	5.2	-2.0	5.1	5.2
Sweden	2.9	5.4	9.7	8.4	7.9	-0.9	-5.7	2.4	3.9	8.3	9.0	10.6	4.5	-19.0	3.9	7.6	7.3	9.1	8.0	7.1
Switzerland	1.8	2.5	8.2	4.4	5.4	-2.3	-0.5	-4.4	4.7	6.4	7.6	8.1	1.5	-7.7	3.7	7.1	3.5	6.1	4.2	2.5
United Kingdom	4.5	10.0	19.3	4.1	4.4	1.5	1.2	-1.0	1.2	17.9	-7.1	12.5	-1.1	-18.9	2.6	6.7	8.0	12.2	7.2	8.8
United States	4.6	12.1	12.0	10.4	9.8	-2.8	-7.9	0.9	6.0	6.7	7.9	6.7	0.3	-17.1	5.7	8.3	11.4	10.6	8.9	11.1
Euro area	2.9	4.3	7.6	7.0	7.6	0.8	-2.5	0.9	2.6	3.5	6.3	6.3	0.2	-14.4	2.0	5.2	6.1	5.1	5.8	6.7
Total OECD	4.1	8.3	5.2	6.5	8.4	-0.8	-3.6	1.9	4.6	7.0	5.9	6.5	0.3	-15.2	4.0	5.6	8.9	7.5	6.6	8.7

Note: The adoption of national account systems SNA93 or ESA95 has been proceeding at an uneven pace among OECD member countries, both with respect to variables and the time period covered. As a consequence, there are breaks in many national series. Moreover, most countries have shifted to chain-weighted price indices to calculate real GDP and expenditure components. For further information, see table "National Accounts Reporting Systems, base years and latest data updates" at the beginning of the Statistical Annex. Some countries (e.g. United States, Canada and France) use hedonic price indices to deflate current-price values of investment in certain information and communication technology products such as computers. National account data do not always have a sectoral breakdown of investment expenditures, and for some countries data are estimated by the OECD. See also *OECD Economic Outlook* Sources and Methods *(http://www.oecd.org/eco/sources-and-methods)*. Working-day adjusted -- see note to Annex Table 1.

Source: OECD Economic Outlook 89 database.

StatLink http://dx.doi.org/10.1787/888932443035

Annex Table 7. **Real gross residential fixed capital formation**
Percentage change from previous year

	Average 1986-96	1997	1998	1999	2000	2001	2002	2003	2004	2005	2006	2007	2008	2009	2010	2011	2012	Fourth quarter 2010	2011	2012
Australia	2.2	16.3	12.0	5.7	1.3	-10.9	25.9	4.6	2.9	-3.5	-2.8	3.1	1.9	-4.1	4.9	2.1	4.3	2.2	3.1	4.5
Austria	4.3	-1.2	-3.0	-1.7	-5.0	-6.4	-5.0	-4.2	-0.5	1.5	2.6	1.8	-1.7	-4.2	-2.9	-1.8	0.6	-2.6	-1.2	1.5
Belgium	5.6	7.5	-4.4	3.1	-1.1	-2.7	-5.5	3.4	8.1	10.9	6.4	3.4	-0.6	-3.0	-2.5	1.5	1.6	0.1	1.2	2.0
Canada	-0.7	8.2	-3.6	3.6	5.2	10.5	14.1	5.4	7.5	3.3	2.2	2.9	-3.7	-8.1	10.3	-0.9	1.3	3.5	-0.3	2.2
Denmark	-2.1	9.7	1.9	4.3	10.3	-9.3	0.8	11.8	11.9	17.3	9.6	-6.0	-10.9	-16.9	-9.4	2.4	2.5	1.8	0.9	3.2
Finland	-0.9	16.5	10.9	8.8	5.8	-9.4	-0.2	11.3	11.8	5.6	4.6	0.0	-9.7	-13.6	21.3	9.4	2.1	27.9	2.2	2.0
France	0.7	1.0	3.7	7.1	2.5	1.4	1.3	2.1	3.2	5.8	6.2	4.8	-2.3	-8.0	-1.4	2.2	2.0	2.3	1.4	2.0
Germany	6.0	0.2	0.2	1.6	-1.8	-5.9	-6.0	-0.9	-3.6	-3.7	6.2	-1.7	-1.8	-1.0	4.0	2.3	2.2	2.8	4.3	2.6
Greece	-4.1	6.6	8.8	3.8	-4.3	4.3	15.2	12.1	-1.0	-0.5	29.8	-8.6	-29.1	-21.7	-18.6	-13.8	-3.5	..	..	..
Iceland	1.8	-9.3	1.0	0.6	12.7	12.3	12.4	3.7	14.2	11.9	16.5	13.2	-21.9	-55.5	-17.0	14.1	12.6	47.8	12.6	12.6
Ireland	6.1	15.8	6.5	13.0	7.7	1.9	3.9	18.3	11.2	16.0	2.8	-10.7	-23.5	-42.2	-36.4	-7.2	0.5	-26.0	-1.3	0.8
Italy	0.8	-2.4	-1.2	1.3	5.1	1.5	2.5	3.5	2.4	5.3	4.1	0.5	-1.4	-9.0	-2.4	0.6	1.8	0.3	1.1	1.9
Japan	3.8	-12.1	-14.3	0.2	0.9	-5.3	-4.0	-1.0	1.9	-1.5	0.5	-9.6	-8.0	-14.0	-6.3	6.8	10.2	6.5	7.4	9.0
Korea	13.4	-4.8	-13.4	-5.5	-9.6	12.5	11.2	8.6	3.6	2.4	-2.4	-3.0	-7.8	-2.0	-10.2	-10.4	2.0	-12.4	-5.5	2.1
Netherlands	2.6	5.6	3.0	2.8	1.6	3.2	-6.5	-3.7	4.1	5.0	5.8	4.7	0.9	-13.6	-10.9	1.1	3.7	-5.6	4.6	4.4
New Zealand	4.1	6.8	-12.8	7.5	0.5	-11.7	21.3	19.8	4.6	-4.4	-2.5	5.0	-19.2	-18.9	5.1	-11.9	40.1	-5.1	1.0	49.7
Norway	-2.9	12.1	7.7	3.0	5.6	8.1	-0.7	1.9	16.3	10.8	4.1	2.9	-12.1	-18.9	-3.5	5.4	4.9	5.4	4.9	4.9
Spain	3.4	2.2	10.9	11.4	10.3	7.5	7.0	9.3	5.9	6.1	6.2	2.5	-10.7	-24.5	-16.8	-6.6	-0.4	-11.4	-3.5	0.3
Sweden	-8.3	-8.1	5.4	13.3	14.8	7.4	11.3	4.3	12.4	11.9	15.5	8.0	-13.1	-23.3	16.0	10.4	6.8	19.0	7.2	6.8
Switzerland	1.2	-0.1	2.8	-5.5	-2.7	-4.1	-3.7	14.4	7.0	1.1	-1.6	-3.0	-4.2	2.2	9.5	7.4	5.3	..	..	..
United Kingdom	1.2	7.4	5.6	2.1	1.1	0.4	6.0	0.5	11.5	-3.6	9.0	0.2	-23.4	-26.9	5.5	1.0	4.2	3.3	2.2	4.6
United States	1.3	1.9	7.7	6.3	1.0	0.6	5.3	8.2	9.8	6.2	-7.3	-18.7	-24.0	-22.9	-3.0	-1.9	3.3	-4.6	1.2	3.6
Euro area	2.8	1.2	1.8	3.7	1.4	-1.1	-1.0	2.7	1.9	3.4	6.3	0.8	-5.0	-10.6	-3.2	0.6	1.8	-0.5	1.7	2.1
Total OECD	2.3	0.0	1.3	4.0	1.2	-0.3	3.3	4.9	6.1	3.7	-0.5	-7.7	-13.0	-14.8	-2.2	0.2	3.4	-0.8	1.9	3.7

Note: The adoption of national account systems SNA93 or ESA95 has been proceeding at an uneven pace among OECD member countries, both with respect to variables and the time period covered. As a consequence, there are breaks in many national series. Moreover, most countries have shifted to chain-weighted price indices to calculate real GDP and expenditure components. For further information, see table "National Accounts Reporting Systems, base years and latest data updates" at the beginning of the *Statistical Annex* and *OECD Economic Outlook Sources and Methods* (*http://www.oecd.org/eco/sources-and-methods*). Working-day adjusted -- see note to Annex Table 1.

Source: OECD Economic Outlook 89 database.

StatLink 🔗 http://dx.doi.org/10.1787/888932443054

Annex Table 8. Real total domestic demand
Percentage change from previous year

	Average 1986-96	1997	1998	1999	2000	2001	2002	2003	2004	2005	2006	2007	2008	2009	2010	2011	2012	Fourth quarter 2010	2011	2012
Australia	3.3	3.2	6.4	4.8	2.4	1.5	5.7	6.3	5.0	4.8	3.0	7.2	3.4	-0.4	3.7	3.4	5.0	2.7	4.1	5.1
Austria	2.5	0.9	2.5	3.0	2.0	0.0	-0.1	1.7	2.1	2.3	2.1	2.3	1.1	-1.5	0.7	1.6	1.3	1.8	1.0	1.5
Belgium	2.8	2.9	2.2	2.2	3.9	-0.1	0.1	0.6	2.8	2.5	1.8	2.8	1.8	-1.3	0.9	1.9	1.8	1.3	1.8	2.1
Canada	2.0	6.1	2.5	4.2	4.7	1.3	3.2	4.5	4.1	4.9	4.4	3.9	2.5	-2.6	5.2	2.6	2.6	4.2	2.9	2.6
Chile	..	7.2	3.7	-6.2	6.1	2.3	2.3	4.6	7.3	10.4	7.1	7.8	7.3	-5.8	16.4	9.0	6.9	15.0	7.9	6.0
Czech Republic	..	-1.0	-1.3	1.0	4.0	3.7	3.7	4.2	2.9	1.8	5.6	5.2	1.1	-3.6	1.2	0.3	2.8	1.9	2.1	3.3
Denmark	1.2	4.7	3.7	-0.6	3.2	0.0	1.7	0.2	4.3	3.4	5.2	2.3	-1.2	-6.5	1.7	1.3	2.0	2.0	1.8	2.1
Estonia	..	13.5	6.8	-4.0	10.1	7.2	12.1	9.7	7.4	9.4	16.2	9.6	-10.5	-22.1	1.1	3.4	4.9	4.5	3.4	5.7
Finland	0.9	5.5	5.8	1.6	3.8	2.0	1.4	3.6	3.6	4.2	2.4	4.6	0.6	-5.9	2.4	2.3	2.5	3.2	2.2	2.6
France	1.9	0.9	4.1	3.7	4.5	1.7	1.1	1.7	3.0	2.7	2.7	3.2	0.4	-2.3	1.2	2.6	2.0	1.4	2.6	2.3
Germany	2.6	0.9	2.2	2.6	2.4	-0.4	-2.0	0.6	-0.5	0.1	2.5	1.3	1.0	-1.9	2.4	2.1	1.8	3.6	2.4	2.1
Greece	2.0	3.4	4.4	3.7	5.4	4.1	4.4	5.7	2.4	1.0	6.4	5.7	1.2	-4.0	-6.1	-6.9	-0.9	..	..	..
Hungary	..	4.4	8.1	4.9	4.1	2.0	6.2	6.0	4.4	1.0	1.1	-1.3	0.8	-10.8	-1.1	0.8	1.7	0.3	1.1	1.8
Iceland	1.6	5.5	13.8	4.2	5.9	-2.1	-2.3	5.7	9.9	15.7	9.5	-0.1	-8.5	-20.7	-2.5	2.7	3.0	0.4	1.4	3.9
Ireland	4.8	10.5	9.1	8.9	9.3	3.8	4.3	4.2	4.2	8.9	6.4	5.3	-5.5	-13.8	-5.4	-4.0	-0.2	-4.8	-1.8	0.5
Israel	..	2.2	2.6	4.1	5.6	2.1	-0.1	-1.7	2.8	4.4	4.6	6.4	2.6	-0.4	4.5	5.4	4.5	6.7	5.1	4.2
Italy	1.7	2.6	2.8	2.7	3.2	1.5	1.3	0.8	1.3	1.0	2.0	1.2	-1.3	-4.0	1.6	1.3	1.2	2.3	0.6	1.2
Japan	3.4	0.5	-2.4	0.0	2.4	1.0	-0.4	0.8	1.9	1.7	1.2	1.3	-1.4	-4.8	2.2	-0.6	2.2	2.0	0.4	1.7
Korea	9.6	1.4	-16.9	14.6	9.5	3.7	7.9	1.5	1.5	3.8	4.9	4.7	1.4	-3.3	7.0	2.9	4.3	3.7	4.7	3.7
Luxembourg	4.3	6.0	6.3	8.0	4.5	4.5	2.6	0.5	3.3	5.2	1.9	5.9	3.1	-5.9	3.0	2.8	3.4	-1.1	5.2	2.4
Mexico	2.6	9.2	5.8	3.9	7.2	-0.4	0.1	0.9	3.9	3.7	5.8	3.7	2.3	-8.0	5.2	4.7	4.7	4.6	4.7	4.7
Netherlands	2.4	4.5	5.1	4.9	2.7	2.3	-0.4	0.4	0.5	1.3	4.1	3.2	2.2	-4.0	0.9	1.4	1.5	1.2	2.2	1.7
New Zealand	2.4	2.5	0.3	5.9	1.9	1.7	5.6	6.1	7.2	4.6	1.0	4.8	0.4	-5.0	4.2	2.6	4.7	4.6	1.9	5.3
Norway	1.3	6.8	5.8	0.4	2.9	0.6	2.3	1.7	6.7	5.5	5.6	5.0	1.9	-3.7	4.2	4.3	4.2	6.6	3.1	4.6
Poland	..	9.5	6.4	5.1	2.7	-1.1	0.8	3.0	6.0	2.8	7.2	8.7	5.2	-0.7	4.2	4.7	4.1	5.0	4.5	3.8
Portugal	4.3	5.4	7.1	5.7	3.3	1.7	-0.2	-1.9	2.9	1.4	0.8	2.0	0.9	-2.9	0.7	-5.6	-4.6	0.2	-7.7	-3.5
Slovak Republic	..	6.1	4.7	-6.2	1.2	8.2	4.0	-0.7	5.8	8.5	6.6	6.3	5.8	-7.3	2.4	1.2	3.3	2.6	2.4	4.3
Slovenia	..	5.1	4.7	8.4	1.9	1.1	3.0	4.8	4.8	2.3	5.6	8.9	4.2	-9.8	0.4	1.1	2.3	2.3	1.1	2.9
Spain	3.4	3.4	6.2	6.4	5.3	3.8	3.2	3.8	4.8	5.1	5.2	4.1	-0.6	-6.0	-1.1	-0.9	1.0	-0.6	-0.1	1.4
Sweden	1.1	1.6	4.6	3.5	4.0	0.4	1.5	2.1	1.8	3.0	4.1	4.7	-0.1	-4.9	5.9	3.8	2.8	6.6	3.1	2.8
Switzerland	1.5	0.6	3.7	0.2	2.2	2.0	0.1	0.5	1.9	1.8	1.4	1.4	0.2	0.6	0.5	3.6	2.4	4.1	2.3	2.2
Turkey	5.3	8.9	0.9	-1.9	7.8	-11.5	8.7	8.6	11.5	9.2	6.7	5.7	-1.0	-6.5	12.0	8.3	5.8	..	..	..
United Kingdom	2.4	3.5	5.1	4.6	3.9	2.9	3.2	3.0	3.5	2.1	2.4	3.1	-0.7	-5.5	2.4	0.4	1.2	2.8	0.1	1.5
United States	2.7	4.7	5.5	5.7	4.8	1.2	2.4	2.8	4.0	3.2	2.6	1.3	-1.1	-3.6	3.2	2.4	3.3	3.2	2.8	3.3
Euro area	2.3	2.0	3.5	3.4	3.5	1.3	0.4	1.4	1.7	2.0	3.0	2.6	0.3	-3.5	1.0	1.2	1.4	1.5	1.3	1.7
Total OECD	2.8	3.5	3.1	4.0	4.3	1.1	1.9	2.3	3.3	2.9	3.0	2.5	-0.1	-3.9	3.0	2.0	2.8	3.1	2.2	3.0

StatLink ⟐ http://dx.doi.org/10.1787/888932443073

Note: The adoption of national accounts systems SNA93 or ESA95 has been proceeding at an uneven pace among OECD member countries, both with respect to variables and the time period covered. As a consequence, there are breaks in many national series. Moreover, most countries have shifted to chain-weighted price indices to calculate real GDP and expenditure components. For further information, see table "National Accounts Reporting Systems, base years and latest data updates" at the beginning of the Statistical Annex and OECD Economic Outlook Sources and Methods (http://www.oecd.org/eco/sources-and-methods). Working-day adjusted -- see note to Annex Table 1.

Source: OECD Economic Outlook 89 database.

Annex Table 9. Foreign balance contributions to changes in real GDP

Percentage points

	Average 1986-96	1997	1998	1999	2000	2001	2002	2003	2004	2005	2006	2007	2008	2009	2010	2011	2012	Fourth quarter[1] 2010	2011	2012
Australia	0.5	1.4	-0.9	-0.2	1.4	1.4	-1.4	-2.1	-1.6	-1.0	-0.9	-2.0	-1.4	2.8	-1.7	-0.5	-0.5	-0.1	-0.4	-0.7
Austria	-0.1	1.5	1.2	0.5	1.4	0.6	1.7	-1.0	0.6	0.5	1.4	1.5	1.2	-2.6	1.9	1.5	0.8	1.1	0.8	0.9
Belgium	-0.1	1.0	-0.4	1.3	0.3	0.8	1.4	0.0	0.3	-0.7	0.5	0.1	-1.0	-0.5	1.8	0.3	0.2	-4.6	0.1	0.3
Canada	0.2	-1.7	1.7	1.4	0.6	0.7	-0.1	-2.5	-0.9	-1.7	-1.5	-1.5	-2.0	-0.3	-2.2	0.3	0.2	4.5	0.1	0.4
Chile	0.2	-0.8	-0.5	4.7	-1.2	1.1	-0.2	-0.9	-1.1	-3.7	-1.4	-1.0	-2.7	3.2	-8.5	-1.1	-0.4	-4.2	-0.7	-0.1
Czech Republic	-3.5	0.4	0.6	0.2	-0.1	-1.4	-2.0	-0.6	1.4	4.6	1.5	1.1	1.3	-0.6	1.0	2.0	0.8	14.0	-1.2	2.2
Denmark	0.6	-1.3	-1.4	3.2	0.5	0.7	-1.1	0.2	-1.8	-0.8	-1.5	-0.7	0.1	1.1	0.5	0.6	0.2	-0.5	0.3	0.2
Estonia	-6.2	-4.6	-0.7	5.3	-1.2	-2.7	-5.9	-2.6	-0.9	-0.5	-6.0	-5.4	5.7	11.3	1.7	4.7	0.1	7.7	-0.4	0.6
Finland	0.4	1.6	0.9	2.9	1.8	0.3	0.3	-1.8	0.8	-1.0	2.1	0.9	0.3	-2.0	0.9	1.5	0.4	17.5	-1.0	1.5
France	0.2	1.3	-0.5	-0.4	-0.3	0.0	0.0	-0.6	-0.7	-0.7	-0.3	-0.9	-0.3	-0.3	0.1	-0.5	0.0	1.1	0.0	-0.1
Germany	0.1	0.9	-0.3	-0.6	1.1	1.8	2.0	-0.8	1.2	0.8	1.2	1.5	-0.2	-2.9	1.2	1.5	0.8	3.0	0.9	0.7
Greece	-0.8	-0.4	-1.7	-1.1	-2.0	-0.4	-1.5	-0.4	1.6	1.1	-2.0	-2.1	-0.5	2.2	2.3	4.8	1.5	:	:	:
Hungary	2.3	-0.5	-3.2	-0.9	0.6	1.7	-2.1	-2.1	-0.1	2.4	2.2	2.0	0.0	4.0	2.2	1.6	1.5	3.1	1.4	1.5
Iceland	-0.2	-0.8	-7.5	-0.3	-1.9	6.2	2.5	-3.2	-2.5	-9.1	-6.0	6.1	10.8	14.4	-1.2	-0.2	0.2	-12.1	0.7	-1.1
Ireland	2.2	2.7	0.0	4.2	1.7	2.5	3.0	1.7	0.5	-1.7	-0.5	1.0	1.4	3.8	3.6	2.2	2.5	-5.3	2.6	2.1
Israel	-1.0	1.1	1.4	-0.8	3.5	-2.0	-0.3	3.3	2.1	0.4	1.1	-1.1	1.5	1.1	0.6	-0.2	0.2	-1.4	0.2	0.5
Italy	0.3	-0.6	-1.4	-1.2	0.8	0.2	-0.8	-0.8	0.1	-0.2	0.1	0.1	0.0	-1.2	-0.4	-0.2	0.4	-3.5	0.4	0.3
Japan	-0.2	1.0	0.4	-0.1	0.5	-0.8	0.7	0.7	0.8	0.3	0.8	1.1	0.2	-1.5	1.8	-0.2	-0.1	-0.3	0.0	-0.1
Korea	-0.7	4.2	11.2	-2.1	-0.2	0.4	-0.5	1.3	3.1	0.4	0.3	0.5	1.0	3.7	-0.6	1.9	0.3	4.5	0.4	0.4
Luxembourg	1.3	1.2	1.3	1.7	4.8	-1.1	2.0	1.1	1.9	1.5	3.6	2.6	-0.6	0.3	1.5	1.3	1.8	18.0	-1.6	7.7
Mexico	-0.1	-1.7	-0.8	-0.3	-1.3	-0.5	0.0	0.5	0.0	-0.6	-0.7	-0.6	-0.9	2.2	0.2	-0.3	-1.0	-0.2	-0.9	-1.1
Netherlands	0.5	0.0	-0.9	0.1	1.3	-0.2	0.5	-0.1	1.7	0.8	-0.3	1.0	-0.2	-0.2	1.0	1.5	0.5	4.0	0.4	0.5
New Zealand	-0.3	0.5	0.1	-1.2	2.2	0.5	-0.8	-1.9	-2.7	-1.7	1.2	-1.6	-1.1	5.3	-1.9	-1.4	-0.6	-4.8	-1.0	-0.7
Norway	1.7	-0.8	-2.6	1.6	0.6	1.5	-0.4	-0.5	-2.0	-2.0	-2.4	-1.4	-0.8	1.4	-2.9	-1.0	-0.5	-2.4	-0.4	-0.4
Poland	-0.8	-2.5	-1.7	-1.0	1.3	2.3	0.5	0.9	-0.8	0.5	-1.5	-2.1	-0.3	3.4	-0.5	-1.0	-0.4	-1.0	-0.6	-0.2
Portugal	-0.8	-1.4	-2.5	-2.1	0.2	0.1	0.9	1.1	-1.5	-0.8	0.6	0.2	-1.0	0.7	0.6	3.9	3.2	-3.6	3.5	2.8
Slovak Republic	-1.0	-1.2	-0.8	6.9	0.1	-4.9	0.3	5.5	-0.9	-2.1	1.6	3.9	0.0	2.6	1.0	2.4	1.1	11.6	1.3	0.5
Slovenia	-3.0	-0.2	-1.1	-3.3	2.5	1.7	1.0	-1.9	-0.5	2.2	0.2	-2.0	-0.4	2.0	0.8	0.2	0.4	-2.8	0.4	0.2
Spain	-0.7	0.5	-1.7	-1.7	-0.4	-0.2	-0.6	-0.8	-1.7	-1.7	-1.4	-0.8	1.5	2.7	1.0	1.8	0.6	2.3	0.5	0.4
Sweden	0.5	1.3	-0.1	1.2	0.7	1.0	1.1	0.5	2.3	0.4	0.7	-1.0	-0.6	-0.9	0.0	0.4	0.5	-0.4	0.4	0.7
Switzerland	-0.1	1.6	-0.8	1.1	1.5	-0.7	0.4	-0.7	0.8	1.0	2.3	2.4	1.7	-2.5	2.1	-0.4	0.4	0.9	0.4	0.4
Turkey	-0.1	-0.9	2.1	-1.5	-1.1	6.5	-3.0	-3.8	-2.4	-1.3	-0.3	-1.3	1.7	2.8	-4.3	-2.8	-1.0	:	:	
United Kingdom	0.0	-0.2	-1.4	-1.0	-0.1	-0.5	-1.1	-0.1	-0.7	0.0	0.2	-0.5	0.7	0.9	-1.0	0.9	0.6	-2.0	0.6	0.6
United States	0.1	-0.3	-1.2	-1.0	-0.8	-0.2	-0.7	-0.4	-0.6	-0.3	-0.1	0.6	1.1	1.2	-0.4	0.1	-0.3	3.2	-0.3	-0.2
Euro area	0.1	0.5	-0.6	-0.5	0.5	0.6	0.5	-0.6	0.2	-0.1	0.2	0.3	0.1	-0.8	0.8	0.9	0.7	1.6	0.6	0.6
Total OECD	0.0	0.2	-0.4	-0.6	-0.1	0.2	-0.2	-0.4	-0.1	-0.2	0.0	0.2	0.4	0.6	-0.1	0.3	0.0	1.6	0.1	0.0

StatLink ⟶ http://dx.doi.org/10.1787/888932443092

Note: The adoption of national accounts systems SNA93 or ESA95 has been proceeding at an uneven pace among OECD member countries, both with respect to variables and the time period covered. As a consequence, there are breaks in many national series. Moreover, most countries have shifted to chain-weighted price indices to calculate real GDP and expenditure components. For further information, see table "National Accounts Reporting Systems, base years and latest data updates" at the beginning of the Statistical Annex and OECD Economic Outlook Sources and Methods (http://www.oecd.org/eco/sources-and-methods). Working-day adjusted -- see note to Annex Table 1.

1. Contributions to per cent change from the previous period, seasonally adjusted at annual rates.

Source: OECD Economic Outlook 89 database.

Annex Table 10. Output gaps

Deviations of actual GDP from potential GDP as a per cent of potential GDP

	1993	1994	1995	1996	1997	1998	1999	2000	2001	2002	2003	2004	2005	2006	2007	2008	2009	2010	2011	2012
Australia	-2.3	-0.8	-0.8	-0.9	-0.6	0.7	1.1	0.5	-0.4	0.3	0.4	0.6	1.0	0.2	1.4	0.3	-1.9	-2.7	-3.0	-1.8
Austria	-1.1	-1.6	-1.2	-0.9	-0.9	0.6	1.8	2.5	0.3	-0.6	-2.3	-1.9	-1.1	0.4	2.1	2.3	-3.3	-3.0	-2.0	-1.6
Belgium	-2.5	-1.3	-1.0	-1.9	-0.3	-0.7	0.4	1.7	0.1	-0.5	-1.4	0.1	0.1	0.6	1.1	0.0	-4.0	-3.3	-2.1	-1.4
Canada	-4.2	-1.8	-1.5	-2.7	-1.7	-1.1	0.9	2.4	0.8	0.9	0.2	0.6	0.9	1.0	0.7	-1.1	-5.2	-3.9	-2.8	-2.2
Chile	..	..	..	-0.9	2.1	2.0	-2.1	-1.0	-1.0	-2.4	-2.5	-0.6	0.8	1.6	2.4	1.5	-3.8	-1.8	0.2	0.7
Czech Republic		-1.4	1.8	3.9	1.3	-1.2	-1.9	-0.5	-0.6	-1.8	-2.1	-2.1	-0.4	1.9	3.3	3.0	-2.8	-2.3	-2.3	-1.7
Denmark	-3.8	-0.7	-0.2	0.2	0.9	0.5	0.8	2.1	1.0	-0.3	-1.3	-0.4	0.2	1.8	2.2	-0.4	-6.6	-5.6	-4.8	-4.0
Estonia	..	..	..	..	..	..	..	0.0	-0.7	-0.4	0.1	1.1	5.0	11.6	15.9	7.2	-9.3	-7.5	-3.8	-2.3
Finland	-8.8	-6.3	-4.5	-3.7	-1.0	0.2	0.3	1.8	0.2	-1.3	-2.4	-1.2	-1.1	0.5	2.9	1.2	-8.9	-7.3	-5.1	-3.9
France	-1.7	-1.1	-0.7	-1.4	-1.1	0.1	0.8	2.0	1.1	0.0	-0.8	-0.4	-0.2	0.4	0.8	-0.6	-4.3	-4.1	-3.3	-2.9
Germany	-1.4	-0.5	-0.3	-1.0	-0.7	-0.6	-0.6	1.0	0.7	-0.7	-2.0	-2.2	-2.1	0.4	1.9	1.1	-4.7	-2.5	-0.6	0.3
Greece	-3.1	-2.9	-2.7	-2.6	-1.8	-1.4	-1.8	-1.5	-1.6	-2.1	-0.4	-0.2	-1.6	0.5	1.9	0.5	-3.1	-8.2	-11.1	-11.2
Hungary	..	..	-0.5	-2.4	-1.4	-0.4	-0.3	0.5	0.6	1.0	1.5	2.5	2.7	3.6	1.9	0.7	-6.5	-6.3	-4.6	-2.7
Iceland	-4.7	-2.6	-4.3	-2.0	-0.5	1.5	1.5	1.4	1.3	-1.8	-2.6	1.0	4.7	3.5	4.9	1.9	-5.1	-8.0	-6.0	-4.6
Ireland	-4.3	-4.6	-2.2	-1.6	1.5	1.1	3.3	4.6	2.9	3.1	2.3	2.1	3.1	3.6	4.8	-1.8	-9.6	-10.2	-9.9	-8.2
Israel	..	..	..	..	..	..	0.2	5.1	1.3	-2.4	-3.9	-2.5	-1.3	0.4	1.7	1.8	-1.5	-1.0	0.0	0.3
Italy	-3.3	-2.3	-0.8	-1.3	-0.9	-1.1	-1.3	0.8	1.1	0.2	-0.7	-0.1	0.2	1.6	2.2	0.4	-4.9	-3.6	-2.8	-1.5
Japan	0.1	-0.7	-0.3	1.0	1.3	-1.8	-2.9	-1.1	-2.1	-2.8	-2.6	-1.1	-0.3	0.9	2.5	0.6	-6.4	-3.6	-5.6	-4.4
Luxembourg	2.1	1.2	-2.1	-5.1	-4.0	-2.6	0.5	3.8	1.7	1.7	-0.7	-0.4	0.9	1.8	4.5	1.9	-5.5	-5.2	-4.8	-3.9
Mexico	0.6	2.7	-6.3	-3.9	-0.1	1.7	2.0	4.9	1.1	-1.5	-2.7	-1.3	-0.7	1.8	2.6	1.8	-6.5	-3.8	-2.3	-1.7
Netherlands	-1.6	-1.3	-0.9	-0.4	0.5	1.1	2.2	2.8	1.7	-0.7	-2.3	-1.8	-1.4	0.3	2.3	2.2	-3.2	-2.6	-1.5	-0.8
New Zealand	-1.9	0.7	1.3	1.8	0.7	-2.1	-0.6	0.1	-0.3	1.3	1.8	2.7	2.7	0.7	1.2	-1.1	-4.1	-3.6	-3.8	-1.3
Norway[1]	-1.6	-0.7	-0.3	0.8	2.1	2.1	0.9	0.9	0.1	-0.9	-2.1	-0.4	0.6	1.2	2.3	0.6	-2.5	-2.1	-1.1	-0.3
Poland	..	..	-3.2	-2.2	0.0	0.4	1.3	2.0	-0.5	-2.4	-2.1	-0.8	-1.7	-0.6	0.8	1.0	-1.1	-0.4	0.5	1.3
Portugal	-1.2	-3.0	-1.7	-1.1	0.0	1.6	2.2	2.9	2.3	1.0	-1.4	-1.3	-1.7	-1.3	0.1	-0.9	-3.7	-2.9	-5.5	-7.5
Slovak Republic	..	-2.0	-0.8	1.7	3.3	3.9	0.2	-2.1	-2.1	-2.0	-2.2	-2.7	-2.1	0.3	4.7	6.0	-2.8	-2.7	-3.0	-2.2
Spain	-3.5	-3.4	-3.2	-3.5	-2.4	-0.9	0.5	1.9	1.8	0.7	0.1	-0.2	-0.1	0.2	0.2	-1.6	-6.8	-7.5	-7.4	-7.0
Sweden	-5.7	-3.8	-1.8	-2.4	-1.9	-0.6	0.6	1.7	-0.1	-0.3	-0.2	1.3	1.9	3.7	4.3	0.6	-6.9	-3.9	-1.6	-0.8
Switzerland	-1.1	-0.9	-1.6	-2.0	-1.0	0.3	-0.1	1.6	0.7	-0.8	-2.8	-2.0	-1.2	0.5	2.0	1.5	-2.4	-1.8	-0.9	-0.3
United Kingdom	-2.9	-0.9	-0.4	-0.3	0.1	0.5	0.5	1.1	0.5	0.0	0.5	1.2	1.3	2.0	2.7	1.1	-4.6	-3.6	-3.1	-2.7
United States	-1.8	-0.7	-1.2	-0.7	0.1	0.8	1.8	2.1	0.0	-0.8	-0.6	0.7	1.4	1.6	1.2	-0.8	-5.0	-3.8	-3.2	-2.4
Euro area	-2.2	-1.5	-1.0	-1.4	-0.9	-0.4	0.1	1.5	1.0	-0.2	-1.2	-0.9	-0.8	0.6	1.6	0.3	-4.8	-4.0	-3.1	-2.4
Total OECD	-1.8	-0.9	-1.2	-0.9	-0.1	0.0	0.5	1.5	0.1	-0.8	-1.0	-0.1	0.4	1.2	1.7	0.5	-4.9	-3.7	-3.2	-2.4

Note: Potential output for countries where data availability permits follows the methodology outlined in Beffy, P.O., P. Olivaud, P Richardson and F. Sedillot (2006), "New OECD Methods for Supply-Side and Medium-Term Assessments: A Capital Services Approach", *OECD Economics Department Working Papers,* No. 482. Revisions to this method are discussed in Chapter 4 of *OECD Economic Outlook no. 85* "Beyond the crisis: medium-term challenges relating to potential output, employment and fiscal positions". In countries where extensive data are not available, more simplified methodologies are used.

1. Mainland Norway.

Source: OECD Economic Outlook 89 database.

StatLink ⟐ http://dx.doi.org/10.1787/888932443111

Annex Table 11. **Compensation per employee in the private sector**

Percentage change from previous period

	Average 1983-1993	1994	1995	1996	1997	1998	1999	2000	2001	2002	2003	2004	2005	2006	2007	2008	2009	2010	2011	2012
Australia	5.8	3.1	3.4	5.6	4.6	2.8	3.7	3.4	4.9	3.3	4.1	6.4	4.9	6.4	7.1	3.4	-0.5	3.3	4.3	5.0
Austria	4.9	3.5	1.6	1.2	1.1	2.7	1.7	2.4	1.9	2.1	2.3	0.6	2.2	3.0	3.1	3.5	1.2	1.7	2.4	2.4
Belgium	5.2	3.9	0.0	1.4	2.9	1.1	3.6	1.9	3.8	3.4	1.5	2.0	1.3	3.5	3.5	3.2	1.7	0.8	3.2	3.7
Canada	4.5	0.3	1.8	2.8	5.9	2.9	3.2	5.2	2.2	0.9	1.8	5.3	5.1	4.7	3.7	2.9	1.6	2.5	3.2	3.7
Czech Republic	..	..	..	16.3	9.2	9.8	7.6	6.8	7.3	6.9	8.1	6.2	4.5	6.7	6.3	6.3	-0.5	3.4	3.1	3.6
Denmark	5.1	1.7	2.2	4.0	3.8	4.0	3.7	3.1	4.1	3.7	3.5	3.2	4.5	3.4	4.1	2.6	0.6	2.7	1.8	2.8
Finland	7.2	4.4	5.2	2.3	2.0	4.6	2.6	4.3	4.8	1.2	2.5	3.7	3.3	3.1	3.4	4.6	1.5	1.5	2.3	2.4
France	4.7	1.1	1.4	1.4	1.4	1.4	1.9	2.3	2.4	3.4	3.0	3.9	3.0	3.7	2.6	2.4	1.1	2.4	2.7	2.7
Germany	4.1	2.9	3.4	1.0	0.6	0.8	1.0	2.0	1.6	1.3	1.6	0.1	-0.1	1.3	1.1	2.1	-0.3	2.2	2.6	2.9
Greece	..	..	..	..	..	5.5	6.4	6.3	3.0	12.0	6.7	2.4	5.2	3.9	9.1	5.6	0.0	-0.5	-1.1	-0.3
Hungary	..	..	..	22.4	21.7	12.7	4.0	15.1	14.3	10.8	7.5	13.1	7.1	5.2	7.3	6.4	-0.8	1.3	2.0	3.6
Iceland	20.6	3.7	4.9	5.1	3.8	9.4	8.5	9.8	5.8	7.6	0.7	12.2	10.0	13.2	9.7	2.5	-7.7	4.3	4.5	4.6
Ireland	5.6	1.5	3.4	4.3	4.2	5.0	3.8	8.4	6.4	3.5	5.3	4.6	4.7	4.6	5.0	2.6	-0.1	-0.3	-0.3	0.0
Israel	..	..	..	..	..	7.8	7.0	7.0	2.5	0.8	-1.6	-0.2	2.4	7.7	1.8	2.5	0.8	3.8	5.5	5.3
Italy	7.8	4.4	5.5	4.2	3.5	-1.1	1.8	1.8	2.4	1.7	1.5	3.1	2.5	1.7	2.9	2.7	-0.8	2.0	2.2	2.2
Japan	3.0	1.4	1.0	-0.1	1.2	-1.2	-1.6	0.1	-1.2	-2.1	-1.2	-0.9	0.0	0.4	-1.8	-0.4	-3.3	0.9	0.4	1.5
Korea	11.9	12.0	14.8	12.2	4.4	4.2	3.2	4.2	7.5	6.1	7.2	4.9	5.3	3.5	4.3	4.1	2.1	3.4	6.1	6.2
Luxembourg	5.1	4.1	0.5	1.0	2.0	1.4	4.7	6.0	3.4	2.4	0.5	3.1	4.6	2.5	3.8	2.1	1.3	1.1	3.1	3.9
Mexico	..	9.4	8.3	20.7	22.1	20.3	19.3	14.9	9.8	3.4	4.7	3.4	6.0	3.6	5.7	4.4	2.0	3.4	4.9	4.9
Netherlands	1.1	1.9	0.3	1.9	2.5	4.2	3.5	4.8	4.8	4.4	3.2	3.4	0.9	2.6	3.1	3.4	1.9	0.9	1.9	2.2
Norway	6.2	3.7	3.4	4.4	5.0	6.8	5.6	4.5	5.5	4.1	2.7	4.2	4.3	5.5	5.8	5.1	3.7	4.5	3.9	4.4
Poland	..	..	..	29.0	20.4	14.7	12.4	10.3	9.7	0.5	0.3	1.5	0.9	1.0	4.3	8.2	5.1	6.3	6.0	6.6
Portugal	..	..	..	5.1	4.6	3.6	3.6	5.1	3.4	2.4	5.7	2.4	4.5	3.0	5.0	3.3	2.8	2.0	1.3	0.5
Slovak Republic	..	..	..	11.7	17.7	9.5	6.6	17.1	5.7	6.9	7.4	10.0	8.0	7.4	9.6	5.7	4.3	2.0	4.0	4.7
Slovenia	..	..	..	13.4	13.2	8.8	8.2	10.5	11.0	8.9	7.9	8.5	6.4	5.7	7.1	6.0	0.9	4.6	2.3	3.6
Spain	9.0	4.0	3.5	5.2	3.6	1.3	1.9	2.9	4.1	3.5	2.7	1.8	2.8	2.4	3.9	5.6	3.4	1.5	1.7	1.7
Sweden	7.8	6.9	2.3	7.1	5.5	2.7	1.3	6.8	4.0	2.6	2.5	4.6	3.2	2.0	5.2	0.5	1.1	1.7	2.5	2.4
Switzerland	4.4	1.5	2.3	1.1	2.7	0.6	1.5	2.6	3.8	1.4	-0.5	-0.9	3.5	2.5	3.5	2.1	1.6	0.7	1.0	1.2
United Kingdom	6.9	3.4	2.6	2.2	4.0	7.2	4.4	5.8	4.8	2.8	4.6	3.2	3.0	4.1	5.4	0.8	2.8	3.1	2.8	3.0
United States	4.2	1.9	2.3	3.0	4.0	5.4	4.2	7.0	3.2	3.0	4.0	4.1	3.3	4.0	4.0	2.9	0.6	3.1	3.0	3.5
Euro area	5.1	2.9	3.0	2.6	2.3	1.4	2.1	3.0	2.8	2.8	2.6	2.3	2.1	2.5	2.9	3.2	0.9	1.8	2.3	2.4
Total OECD	5.1	3.3	3.4	5.3	5.3	4.8	4.2	5.4	3.6	2.4	3.0	2.9	2.9	3.1	3.3	2.8	0.7	2.6	2.9	3.3

Note: The private sector in the OECD terminology is defined as total economy less the public sector. Hence private sector employees are defined as total employees less public sector employees. For further information, see also *OECD Economic Outlook* Sources and Methods *(http://www.oecd.org/eco/sources-and-methods)*.

Source: OECD Economic Outlook 89 database.

StatLink ⇄ http://dx.doi.org/10.1787/888932443130

Annex Table 12. Labour productivity in the total economy

Percentage change from previous period

	Average 1983-1993	1994	1995	1996	1997	1998	1999	2000	2001	2002	2003	2004	2005	2006	2007	2008	2009	2010	2011	2012
Australia	1.5	1.6	-0.3	2.6	2.9	3.1	2.6	0.8	1.6	1.8	1.2	1.4	0.0	-0.1	1.6	-0.4	0.7	-0.1	0.7	2.4
Austria	1.7	1.8	2.5	1.9	1.5	2.8	2.2	2.3	-0.2	1.7	0.7	1.2	1.3	2.0	1.8	0.5	-3.0	1.2	1.7	1.3
Belgium	1.6	3.7	1.7	0.8	3.2	0.2	2.1	1.7	-0.7	1.5	0.8	2.1	0.6	1.5	1.2	-0.9	-2.3	1.4	1.6	1.1
Canada	1.1	2.7	1.0	0.7	2.1	1.6	2.9	2.7	0.6	0.5	-0.5	1.4	1.7	1.0	-0.2	-1.1	-0.9	1.7	1.3	1.3
Chile	..	..	..	..	4.7	1.1	0.7	2.7	2.4	0.2	-0.2	3.1	1.7	3.2	2.0	0.2	-1.5	-2.1	3.0	3.1
Czech Republic	..	1.3	5.2	3.2	-0.9	0.8	4.8	4.1	2.0	1.3	5.0	4.0	5.3	5.0	3.4	1.0	-2.9	3.0	1.6	2.7
Denmark	1.6	3.8	2.3	1.9	1.8	0.7	1.7	3.0	-0.2	0.4	1.5	2.9	1.4	1.3	-1.2	-2.9	-2.2	4.3	1.8	1.0
Estonia	..	..	..	8.2	11.8	8.8	4.3	11.7	6.6	6.6	6.0	6.9	7.5	5.0	6.2	-5.3	-4.5	8.3	3.7	3.0
Finland	2.9	5.1	2.2	2.1	2.6	3.2	1.4	3.2	0.9	0.8	2.0	3.7	1.6	2.5	3.0	-0.6	-5.7	3.5	3.0	2.3
France	1.9	2.0	1.4	0.7	1.8	2.0	1.1	1.4	0.0	0.4	0.9	2.1	1.4	1.4	0.9	-0.5	-1.5	1.2	1.4	1.1
Germany	1.8	2.8	1.7	1.3	1.9	0.6	0.5	1.6	0.9	0.6	0.7	0.3	1.0	2.9	1.1	-0.7	-4.7	3.0	2.4	1.9
Greece	0.8	0.1	1.2	1.1	4.0	-1.0	3.1	3.0	4.1	1.2	4.7	1.9	1.5	1.8	2.5	0.8	-1.3	-2.4	0.8	0.9
Hungary	1.2	..	..	0.4	4.2	2.9	1.3	3.8	4.4	4.3	3.8	5.8	3.6	3.1	1.1	1.9	-3.8	0.8	2.6	2.2
Iceland	..	2.8	-2.9	4.8	4.9	2.1	0.4	2.3	2.2	1.6	2.3	8.2	4.1	-0.5	1.4	0.6	-0.9	-3.2	2.1	1.2
Ireland	3.4	2.4	4.5	4.4	5.6	0.0	4.2	5.0	2.5	4.9	2.5	1.2	1.0	1.0	1.9	-2.5	0.1	3.2	2.5	3.0
Israel	..	..	..	..	..	..	..	5.5	-1.5	-0.8	0.7	2.7	1.1	2.4	0.5	0.1	0.1	1.2	1.6	1.5
Italy	1.9	4.0	3.1	0.4	1.6	0.3	0.3	1.9	-0.3	-1.2	-1.4	0.9	0.2	0.1	0.1	-1.6	-3.6	2.0	0.4	0.8
Japan	2.8	0.8	1.8	2.2	0.5	-1.4	0.7	3.1	0.7	1.5	1.6	2.5	1.5	1.6	1.9	-0.7	-4.8	4.4	-0.9	2.4
Korea	6.1	5.4	5.9	4.9	4.0	0.3	8.8	4.4	1.9	4.3	3.0	2.7	2.6	3.8	3.8	1.7	0.6	4.7	3.6	3.6
Luxembourg	3.4	1.2	-1.5	-1.0	2.8	1.9	3.3	2.7	-2.9	0.8	-0.3	2.1	2.5	1.3	2.1	-3.2	-4.6	1.9	1.4	1.8
Mexico	0.1	..	..	1.4	1.4	2.3	2.4	3.9	-1.0	-2.2	0.6	0.6	2.6	1.6	1.5	-0.7	-5.0	3.7	2.3	1.3
Netherlands	1.8	2.3	0.8	1.1	1.1	1.3	2.1	1.7	-0.1	-0.4	0.8	3.1	1.5	1.7	1.3	0.4	-2.8	2.3	1.7	1.2
New Zealand	2.5	0.6	0.6	0.7	2.1	-2.4	1.3	4.1	0.0	1.8	1.4	1.2	-1.0	-1.2	1.8	-2.5	-1.0	0.4	-0.4	1.9
Norway	2.1	3.6	2.0	3.0	2.4	0.0	1.1	2.7	1.6	1.1	2.1	3.4	1.5	-1.3	-1.3	-2.4	-1.0	0.6	1.5	1.6
Poland	..	..	..	5.2	5.2	3.7	8.0	6.9	3.6	4.7	5.1	4.0	1.4	2.5	2.5	1.2	1.3	3.4	3.2	2.5
Portugal	2.1	1.1	4.9	2.0	1.7	2.2	2.7	1.8	0.1	0.1	-0.3	1.6	1.1	0.9	2.4	-0.5	0.1	2.9	-0.5	-0.2
Slovak Republic	..	..	4.0	4.8	6.8	4.9	2.6	3.4	2.9	4.5	3.7	5.3	5.0	6.3	8.3	2.8	-2.3	5.5	2.6	3.4
Slovenia	..	..	..	..	..	..	..	3.1	2.4	2.4	3.2	4.0	4.7	4.3	3.8	0.9	-6.4	3.4	3.1	2.5
Spain	1.8	2.9	0.9	0.7	0.3	0.0	0.2	0.0	0.5	0.3	0.0	-0.3	-0.5	0.1	0.5	1.3	3.1	2.2	1.7	0.6
Sweden	1.9	4.9	2.5	2.5	4.3	2.4	2.3	2.1	-0.7	2.4	3.1	4.5	2.9	2.8	1.1	-1.7	-3.3	4.1	2.3	1.9
Switzerland	0.3	1.8	0.4	0.7	2.2	1.3	0.5	2.6	-0.5	-0.3	0.1	2.2	2.0	1.4	1.0	-0.2	-2.6	2.1	0.9	0.9
Turkey	4.0	-12.4	4.2	4.0	7.5	0.4	-4.5	9.0	-5.7	6.5	6.1	7.3	6.1	5.1	3.1	-1.5	-5.2	2.7	3.2	3.3
United Kingdom	1.7	3.5	1.8	1.9	1.5	2.6	2.1	2.7	1.6	1.3	1.8	1.9	1.1	1.9	2.0	-0.8	-3.4	1.0	0.9	1.7
United States	1.4	1.0	0.2	1.8	2.1	2.1	2.8	2.4	2.4	3.0	2.5	2.5	1.4	0.9	1.1	0.7	3.1	3.6	1.5	1.1
Euro area	1.7	2.7	2.0	1.1	1.9	1.0	1.0	1.6	0.5	0.4	0.5	1.2	0.9	1.6	1.1	-0.4	-2.3	2.2	1.6	1.3
Total OECD	2.0	1.4	1.6	2.0	2.2	1.2	2.0	1.6	0.6	1.7	1.8	2.2	1.7	1.7	1.5	-0.1	-1.6	2.9	1.5	1.7

Note: Labour productivity measured as GDP per person employed. For further information, see OECD Economic Outlook Sources and Methods (http://www.oecd.org/eco/sources-and-methods).
Source: OECD Economic Outlook 89 database.

Annex Table 13. Unemployment rates: commonly used definitions
Per cent of labour force

	2007 Unemployment thousands	1997	1998	1999	2000	2001	2002	2003	2004	2005	2006	2007	2008	2009	2010	2011	2012	Fourth quarter 2010	2011	2012
Australia	484	8.4	7.7	6.9	6.2	6.7	6.3	5.9	5.4	5.0	4.8	4.4	4.2	5.6	5.2	5.0	4.9	5.2	5.0	4.9
Austria	185	4.3	4.3	3.7	3.5	3.6	3.9	4.3	4.9	5.2	4.7	4.4	3.8	4.8	4.4	4.2	4.0	4.2	4.0	4.0
Belgium	359	9.2	9.3	8.5	6.9	6.6	7.5	8.2	8.4	8.5	8.3	7.5	7.0	7.9	8.3	7.6	7.3	8.0	7.6	7.1
Canada	1 082	9.1	8.3	7.6	6.8	7.3	7.7	7.6	7.2	6.7	6.3	6.0	6.1	8.3	8.0	7.5	7.0	7.7	7.2	6.8
Chile	497	6.1	6.4	10.1	9.7	9.9	9.8	9.5	10.0	9.2	7.8	7.2	7.8	10.8	8.1	7.3	7.2	7.7	7.2	7.2
Czech Republic	276	4.8	6.5	8.8	8.9	8.2	7.3	7.8	8.3	8.0	7.2	5.3	4.4	6.7	7.3	6.6	6.3	7.1	6.3	6.2
Denmark	110	5.2	4.8	5.0	4.3	4.4	4.5	5.3	5.5	4.8	3.9	3.6	3.2	5.9	7.2	7.2	6.4	7.5	7.0	6.1
Estonia	32	..	..	..	13.6	12.6	10.3	10.0	9.7	7.9	5.9	4.7	5.6	13.9	16.8	14.2	13.0	14.5	13.8	12.5
Finland	183	12.8	11.4	10.3	9.8	9.1	9.1	9.0	8.8	8.4	7.7	6.9	6.4	8.3	8.4	7.9	7.1	8.1	7.5	6.9
France	2 222	10.8	10.3	10.0	8.6	7.8	7.9	8.5	8.8	8.9	8.8	8.0	7.4	9.1	9.3	9.0	8.7	9.2	8.9	8.7
Germany	3 608	9.3	8.9	8.2	7.4	7.5	8.3	9.2	9.7	10.5	9.8	8.3	7.3	7.4	6.8	6.0	5.4	6.6	5.8	5.2
Greece	407	10.6	11.2	12.1	11.4	10.8	10.3	9.7	10.5	9.9	8.9	8.3	7.7	9.5	12.5	16.0	16.4	..	..	..
Hungary	312	8.9	7.9	7.1	6.5	5.8	5.9	5.9	6.2	7.3	7.5	7.4	7.9	10.1	11.2	11.5	11.0	11.3	11.6	10.5
Iceland	4	3.9	2.7	2.0	2.3	2.3	3.3	3.4	3.0	2.6	2.9	2.3	3.0	7.2	7.5	7.0	5.8	7.9	6.6	5.3
Ireland	101	10.7	7.6	5.6	4.3	3.9	4.4	4.7	4.5	4.3	4.4	4.6	6.0	11.7	13.5	14.7	14.6	14.3	14.8	14.4
Israel	212	..	..	8.8	8.7	9.3	10.3	10.7	10.3	9.0	8.4	7.3	6.1	7.6	6.6	6.2	5.7	6.6	5.9	5.7
Italy	1 520	11.3	11.4	11.0	10.1	9.1	8.7	8.4	8.0	7.7	6.8	6.1	6.8	7.8	8.4	8.4	8.1	8.5	8.3	8.0
Japan	2 566	3.4	4.1	4.7	4.7	5.0	5.4	5.3	4.7	4.4	4.1	3.8	4.0	5.1	5.1	4.8	4.6	5.0	4.7	4.5
Korea	783	2.6	7.0	6.6	4.4	4.0	3.3	3.6	3.7	3.7	3.5	3.2	3.2	3.6	3.6	3.5	3.4	3.5	3.3	3.4
Luxembourg	10	3.6	3.1	2.9	2.6	2.5	2.9	3.7	4.2	4.7	4.4	4.4	4.4	5.7	6.0	5.4	4.8	6.2	5.1	4.7
Mexico[1]	1 643	4.1	3.6	2.6	2.6	2.6	2.9	3.0	3.7	3.6	3.6	3.7	4.0	5.5	5.3	4.6	3.9	5.2	4.3	3.7
Netherlands	306	5.2	4.1	3.4	2.9	2.4	3.0	4.0	4.9	5.1	4.2	3.4	3.0	3.7	4.3	4.2	4.0	4.3	4.2	3.8
New Zealand	83	6.9	7.7	7.0	6.1	5.5	5.3	4.8	4.0	3.8	3.8	3.7	4.2	6.1	6.5	6.9	6.0	6.7	6.9	5.6
Norway	63	4.0	3.2	3.2	3.4	3.5	3.9	4.5	4.5	4.6	3.4	2.5	2.6	3.2	3.6	3.4	3.2	3.7	3.3	3.1
Poland	1 619	11.2	10.6	14.0	16.1	18.2	19.9	19.6	19.0	17.7	13.8	9.6	7.1	8.2	9.6	9.4	8.5	9.5	9.1	8.0
Portugal	449	6.7	5.0	4.4	4.0	4.0	5.0	6.3	6.7	7.7	7.7	8.0	7.6	9.5	10.8	11.7	12.7	11.2	12.1	13.0
Slovak Republic	296	11.9	12.6	16.4	18.8	19.3	18.7	17.5	18.2	16.2	13.4	11.1	9.5	12.1	14.4	13.8	12.8	14.2	13.6	12.3
Slovenia	50	..	..	7.4	6.7	6.2	6.3	6.7	6.3	6.5	6.0	4.8	4.4	5.8	7.2	7.7	7.5	7.7	7.7	7.4
Spain	1 834	16.3	14.6	12.2	10.8	10.1	11.0	11.0	10.5	9.2	8.5	8.3	11.3	18.0	20.1	20.3	19.3	20.5	20.0	18.8
Sweden	297	11.7	9.7	8.2	6.7	5.8	6.0	6.6	7.4	7.7	7.1	6.1	6.2	8.3	8.4	7.5	7.0	7.9	7.2	6.9
Switzerland	157	4.1	3.4	2.9	2.6	2.3	3.0	4.0	4.3	4.3	3.9	3.6	3.4	4.3	4.5	4.1	3.9	4.2	4.1	3.9
Turkey	2 376	7.3	7.3	8.1	6.9	8.7	10.7	10.8	10.6	10.4	10.0	10.1	10.7	13.7	11.7	10.6	10.4	..	..	8.2
United Kingdom	1 653	7.0	6.3	6.0	5.5	5.1	5.2	5.0	4.8	4.8	5.4	5.4	5.7	7.6	7.9	8.1	8.3	7.9	8.3	8.2
United States	7 077	4.9	4.5	4.2	4.0	4.8	5.8	6.0	5.5	5.1	4.6	4.6	5.8	9.3	9.6	8.8	7.9	9.6	8.5	7.5
Euro area	11 561	10.4	9.9	9.2	8.3	7.9	8.3	8.7	8.9	8.9	8.3	7.4	7.4	9.4	9.9	9.7	9.3	9.9	9.6	9.1
Total OECD	32 855	6.7	6.6	6.5	6.0	6.3	6.8	7.0	6.8	6.6	6.1	5.7	6.0	8.2	8.3	7.9	7.4	8.2	7.7	7.1

StatLink http://dx.doi.org/10.1787/888932443168

Note: Labour market data are subject to differences in definitions across countries and to many breaks in series, though the latter are often of a minor nature. For information about definitions, sources, data coverage, breaks in series and rebasings, see *OECD Economic Outlook* Sources and Methods (http://www.oecd.org/eco/sources-and-methods).
1. Based on National Employment Survey.
Source: OECD Economic Outlook 89 database.

Annex Table 14. Harmonised unemployment rates
Per cent of civilian labour force

	1992	1993	1994	1995	1996	1997	1998	1999	2000	2001	2002	2003	2004	2005	2006	2007	2008	2009	2010
Australia	10.8	10.9	9.7	8.5	8.5	8.5	7.7	6.9	6.3	6.8	6.4	5.9	5.4	5.0	4.8	4.4	4.2	5.6	5.2
Austria	..	4.0	3.8	3.9	4.3	4.4	4.5	3.9	3.6	3.6	4.2	4.3	4.9	5.2	4.7	4.4	3.8	4.8	4.4
Belgium	7.1	8.6	9.8	9.7	9.6	9.2	9.3	8.5	6.9	6.6	7.5	8.2	8.4	8.5	8.3	7.5	7.0	7.9	8.3
Canada	11.2	11.4	10.4	9.5	9.6	9.1	8.3	7.6	6.8	7.2	7.7	7.6	7.2	6.8	6.3	6.0	6.1	8.3	8.0
Chile	6.7	6.5	7.8	7.3	6.3	6.1	6.4	10.1	9.7	9.9	9.8	9.5	10.0	9.2	7.8	7.1	7.8	10.8	8.2
Czech Republic	2.8	4.4	4.3	4.1	3.9	4.8	6.4	8.6	8.7	8.0	7.3	7.8	8.3	7.9	7.2	5.3	4.4	6.7	7.3
Denmark	8.6	9.5	7.7	6.8	6.3	5.2	4.9	5.1	4.3	4.5	4.6	5.4	5.5	4.8	3.9	3.8	3.3	6.0	7.4
Estonia	..	..	..	..	..	9.7	9.2	11.4	13.7	12.6	10.2	10.0	9.7	7.8	5.9	4.6	5.6	13.8	16.8
Finland	11.6	16.2	16.7	15.1	14.9	12.7	11.4	10.3	9.6	9.1	9.1	9.0	8.9	8.3	7.7	6.9	6.4	8.2	8.4
France	9.8	11.0	11.6	11.0	11.5	11.4	11.0	10.4	9.0	8.3	8.6	9.0	9.2	9.3	9.2	8.3	7.8	9.5	9.8
Germany	6.6	7.8	8.4	8.3	9.0	9.7	9.4	8.6	8.0	7.9	8.7	9.8	10.5	11.2	10.2	8.8	7.6	7.7	7.1
Greece	7.8	8.6	8.9	9.1	9.7	9.6	11.0	12.0	11.2	10.7	10.3	9.7	10.5	9.9	8.9	8.3	7.7	9.5	12.6
Hungary	9.9	12.1	11.0	10.4	9.6	9.0	8.4	6.9	6.4	5.7	5.8	5.9	6.1	7.2	7.5	7.4	7.8	10.0	11.2
Iceland	4.3	5.3	5.3	4.9	3.7	3.9	2.7	2.0	2.3	2.3	3.3	3.4	3.1	2.6	2.9	2.3	3.0	7.2	7.5
Ireland	15.4	15.6	14.4	12.3	11.7	9.9	7.6	5.7	4.2	4.0	4.5	4.6	4.5	4.4	4.5	4.6	6.3	11.9	13.7
Israel	8.8	..	..	..	..	..	11.3	10.9	10.1	9.3	10.3	10.7	10.4	9.0	8.4	7.3	6.1	7.5	6.7
Italy	8.8	9.8	10.6	11.2	11.2	11.2	11.3	10.9	10.1	9.1	8.6	8.5	8.0	7.7	6.8	6.1	6.8	7.8	8.4
Japan	2.2	2.5	2.9	3.1	3.4	3.4	4.1	4.7	4.7	5.0	5.4	5.3	4.7	4.4	4.1	3.9	4.0	5.1	5.1
Korea	2.5	2.9	2.5	2.1	2.0	2.6	7.0	6.6	4.4	4.0	3.3	3.6	3.7	3.7	3.5	3.2	3.2	3.6	3.7
Luxembourg	2.1	2.6	3.2	2.9	2.9	2.7	2.7	2.4	2.3	1.9	2.6	3.8	4.9	4.6	4.6	4.2	4.9	5.1	4.5
Mexico	2.8	3.4	3.7	6.2	5.5	3.7	3.2	2.5	2.5	2.8	3.0	3.4	3.9	3.6	3.6	3.7	4.0	5.5	5.4
Netherlands	4.9	5.6	6.2	7.0	6.4	5.4	4.3	3.6	3.0	2.6	3.1	4.1	5.1	5.3	4.3	3.6	3.1	3.7	4.5
New Zealand	10.7	9.8	8.4	6.5	6.3	6.8	7.7	7.1	6.2	5.5	5.3	4.8	4.1	3.8	3.9	3.7	4.2	6.1	6.5
Norway	6.5	6.6	6.0	5.5	4.8	3.9	3.1	3.0	3.2	3.4	3.7	4.2	4.3	4.5	3.4	2.5	2.5	3.1	3.5
Poland	..	14.0	14.4	13.3	12.4	10.9	10.2	13.4	16.2	18.3	20.0	19.7	19.0	17.8	13.9	9.6	7.2	8.2	9.7
Portugal	4.1	5.5	6.8	7.2	7.2	6.7	5.0	4.5	4.0	4.0	5.1	6.4	6.8	7.7	7.8	8.1	7.7	9.6	11.0
Slovak Republic	..	..	13.7	13.1	11.3	11.8	12.6	16.3	18.8	19.3	18.7	17.6	18.2	16.2	13.4	11.1	9.5	12.0	14.4
Slovenia	..	..	..	..	6.9	6.9	7.4	7.4	6.7	6.2	6.3	6.7	6.3	6.5	6.0	4.9	4.4	5.9	7.3
Spain	14.7	18.4	19.5	18.4	17.8	16.7	15.0	12.5	11.1	10.4	11.1	11.1	10.6	9.2	8.5	8.3	11.4	18.0	20.1
Sweden	5.6	9.0	9.3	8.8	9.5	9.9	8.2	6.7	5.6	5.9	6.0	6.6	7.4	7.7	7.1	6.1	6.2	8.3	8.4
Switzerland	2.7	3.6	3.6	3.2	3.5	3.9	3.3	2.8	2.5	2.2	2.9	3.9	4.1	4.2	3.8	3.4	3.2	4.1	4.2
Turkey														9.2	8.7	8.8	9.7	12.5	10.7
United Kingdom	9.8	10.2	9.3	8.5	7.9	6.8	6.1	5.9	5.4	5.0	5.1	5.0	4.7	4.8	5.4	5.3	5.6	7.6	7.8
United States	7.5	6.9	6.1	5.6	5.4	4.9	4.5	4.2	4.0	4.7	5.8	6.0	5.5	5.1	4.6	4.6	5.8	9.3	9.6
Euro area	8.5	10.0	10.7	10.5	10.7	10.7	10.2	9.5	8.6	8.1	8.5	9.0	9.2	9.1	8.4	7.6	7.7	9.5	10.1
Total OECD	7.4	7.8	7.7	7.3	7.2	6.9	6.8	6.8	6.3	6.6	7.1	7.3	7.1	6.8	6.2	5.7	6.1	8.3	8.6

Note: In so far as possible, the data have been adjusted to ensure comparability over time and to conform to the guidelines of the International Labour Office. Annual figures are calculated by averaging the monthly and/or quarterly estimates (for both unemployed and the labour force). Further information is available from OECD.stat (*http://stats.oecd.org/index.aspx*), see the metadata relating to the harmonised unemployment rate.

Source: OCDE, Main Economic Indicators.

StatLink http://dx.doi.org/10.1787/888932443187

Annex Table 15. Labour force, employment and unemployment

Millions

	1994	1995	1996	1997	1998	1999	2000	2001	2002	2003	2004	2005	2006	2007	2008	2009	2010	2011	2012
Labour force																			
Major seven countries	329.3	331.2	334.1	337.9	340.3	343.1	347.5	349.6	351.3	353.7	355.5	358.6	361.7	364.4	366.8	366.9	366.6	367.0	368.9
Total of smaller countries	177.2	179.9	182.3	185.3	187.7	192.9	195.9	198.1	201.4	203.1	207.1	210.1	213.4	216.7	220.2	223.2	226.5	228.6	230.6
Euro area	135.7	136.4	137.5	138.4	140.1	142.4	145.1	146.7	148.3	149.8	151.4	153.2	154.6	156.0	157.6	158.0	158.1	158.4	158.7
Total OECD	506.6	511.0	516.4	523.2	528.0	536.0	543.4	547.7	552.7	556.8	562.6	568.7	575.2	581.1	586.9	590.1	593.1	595.7	599.5
Employment																			
Major seven countries	306.8	309.5	312.1	316.3	319.3	322.5	328.2	329.2	328.8	330.4	333.1	336.6	340.9	344.7	345.3	337.5	336.8	339.2	342.7
Total of smaller countries	162.4	164.6	168.1	171.8	173.9	178.8	182.4	184.2	186.3	187.6	191.1	194.6	199.2	203.5	206.5	204.4	207.0	209.7	212.5
Euro area	121.4	122.4	123.2	124.0	126.2	129.3	133.1	135.1	136.1	136.7	137.9	139.5	141.8	144.4	145.8	143.2	142.5	142.9	143.9
Total OECD	469.1	474.0	480.1	488.0	493.2	501.3	510.6	513.4	515.1	518.0	524.1	531.1	540.1	548.3	551.8	541.9	543.8	548.8	555.2
Unemployment																			
Major seven countries	22.6	21.7	22.0	21.6	21.1	20.6	19.3	20.3	22.5	23.3	22.5	22.0	20.9	19.7	21.4	29.3	29.8	27.9	26.2
Total of smaller countries	14.9	15.4	14.3	13.6	13.8	14.1	13.4	14.0	15.1	15.5	16.0	15.6	14.2	13.1	13.7	18.8	19.5	19.0	18.1
Euro area	14.2	14.1	14.4	14.5	13.9	13.1	12.1	11.6	12.3	13.0	13.5	13.6	12.8	11.6	11.7	14.8	15.7	15.4	14.8
Total OECD	37.4	37.1	36.3	35.2	34.9	34.7	32.8	34.3	37.6	38.8	38.5	37.6	35.1	32.9	35.1	48.1	49.3	46.8	44.2

Source: OECD Economic Outlook 89 database.

StatLink ⬛⬛⬛ http://dx.doi.org/10.1787/888932443206

Annex Table 16. GDP deflators
Percentage change from previous year

	Average 1986-96	1997	1998	1999	2000	2001	2002	2003	2004	2005	2006	2007	2008	2009	2010	2011	2012	Fourth quarter 2010	2011	2012
Australia	3.7	1.2	0.1	1.1	4.3	3.6	3.1	2.3	4.2	4.4	5.3	4.2	6.4	-0.9	5.1	4.7	2.8	6.3	4.1	2.8
Austria	2.7	-0.2	0.1	0.1	1.3	2.0	1.5	1.2	1.4	1.8	2.1	2.0	1.5	1.0	1.6	1.7	1.6	1.9	1.6	1.6
Belgium	2.5	0.8	1.9	0.3	1.9	2.1	2.0	2.0	2.2	2.4	2.3	2.3	1.9	1.1	1.9	2.1	2.0	2.4	1.9	2.0
Canada	2.7	1.2	-0.4	1.7	4.1	1.1	1.1	3.3	3.2	3.3	2.7	3.2	4.0	-2.1	3.0	2.4	1.6	2.6	2.1	1.6
Chile	..	4.3	2.0	2.6	4.5	3.8	4.3	6.1	7.7	7.5	12.1	5.2	0.7	2.7	9.5	5.1	4.5	8.4	4.6	4.3
Czech Republic	..	8.4	11.1	2.9	1.5	4.9	2.8	0.9	4.5	-0.3	1.1	3.4	1.8	2.5	-1.1	0.1	1.5	-1.3	0.7	1.7
Denmark	2.6	2.0	1.2	1.7	3.0	2.5	2.3	1.6	2.3	2.9	2.1	2.3	3.9	0.4	3.3	2.1	1.7	2.5	2.0	1.7
Estonia	..	10.3	5.2	6.8	4.5	5.3	3.3	4.2	3.6	5.5	8.3	10.5	7.2	-0.1	1.5	2.7	2.2	2.8	1.9	2.4
Finland	3.4	1.8	3.6	0.9	2.5	3.1	1.2	-0.6	0.5	0.4	1.1	2.9	1.8	1.1	2.0	1.7	2.0	2.7	1.9	1.3
France	2.2	1.0	0.9	0.1	1.4	2.0	2.4	1.9	1.6	2.0	2.4	2.5	2.6	0.7	0.8	1.5	1.3	1.2	1.7	1.2
Germany	2.6	0.3	0.6	0.3	-0.7	1.2	1.4	1.2	1.0	0.7	0.4	1.8	1.0	1.4	0.6	0.7	1.2	0.3	1.0	1.4
Greece	14.4	6.8	5.2	3.0	3.4	3.1	3.4	3.9	2.9	2.8	3.1	3.1	3.3	1.3	2.5	0.3	0.7	2.1	0.8	0.1
Hungary	..	19.7	13.1	6.8	9.2	10.9	8.1	5.0	5.2	2.7	4.4	5.9	4.3	4.7	2.8	3.9	3.2	2.2	3.7	3.0
Iceland	10.0	2.9	5.1	3.3	3.6	8.6	5.6	0.6	2.5	2.8	8.8	5.7	11.8	8.3	6.7	1.9	2.8	0.2	3.5	2.6
Ireland	2.7	3.8	6.5	3.8	5.9	5.5	4.5	2.8	2.0	2.5	3.7	1.1	-1.4	-4.0	-2.5	-1.3	1.1	-4.0	3.1	0.7
Israel	..	7.8	7.1	6.3	1.6	1.7	4.0	-0.5	0.2	1.1	2.3	0.5	0.9	5.0	1.1	1.4	2.5	2.2	1.7	2.3
Italy	5.6	2.6	2.6	1.8	1.9	3.0	3.3	3.1	2.6	2.1	1.8	2.6	2.8	2.3	0.6	1.3	1.6	0.7	2.0	1.3
Japan	0.8	0.5	0.0	-1.3	-1.7	-1.2	-1.5	-1.6	-1.1	-1.2	-0.9	-0.7	-1.0	-0.4	-2.1	-1.3	-0.5	-1.6	-0.9	-0.3
Korea	7.2	3.9	5.0	-1.0	1.0	3.9	3.2	3.6	3.0	0.7	-0.1	2.1	2.9	3.4	3.7	1.0	2.6	4.5	-0.6	3.8
Luxembourg	3.0	-1.9	-0.4	5.3	2.0	0.1	2.1	6.0	1.8	4.6	6.7	3.6	4.2	-0.3	5.5	2.6	1.6	7.9	0.6	1.2
Mexico	36.6	17.5	14.5	17.4	10.8	5.4	2.6	9.4	9.1	4.5	6.7	5.6	6.2	4.1	4.4	4.0	4.1	4.7	4.0	4.1
Netherlands	1.6	2.6	1.9	1.8	4.1	5.1	3.8	2.2	0.7	2.4	1.8	1.8	2.4	-0.2	1.6	-0.1	1.6	2.1	-0.2	1.8
New Zealand	4.0	0.7	1.0	0.3	2.6	4.2	1.2	1.6	3.8	2.2	2.6	4.0	4.0	0.7	2.2	4.3	3.2	5.2	2.8	4.6
Norway	3.2	2.8	-0.8	6.6	15.7	1.7	-1.8	3.0	5.3	8.7	8.5	2.4	10.0	-4.0	4.7	8.6	2.8	6.2	8.3	1.5
Poland	..	14.0	11.0	6.0	7.3	3.8	2.2	0.4	3.8	2.9	1.5	4.0	3.1	3.5	1.5	2.9	2.9	2.2	2.9	3.0
Portugal	8.6	3.9	3.8	3.3	3.2	3.6	3.7	3.0	2.5	2.5	2.8	3.2	1.6	0.5	1.0	1.0	1.0	0.7	0.7	0.9
Slovak Republic	..	4.9	5.1	7.4	9.4	5.0	3.9	5.3	5.8	2.4	2.9	1.1	2.9	-1.2	0.5	1.9	2.6	0.9	2.1	3.4
Slovenia	..	8.5	7.0	6.6	5.3	8.7	7.7	5.6	3.4	1.6	2.0	4.2	4.0	3.2	0.7	1.0	2.1	0.4	1.6	2.4
Spain	5.6	2.4	2.5	2.6	3.5	4.2	4.3	4.1	4.0	4.3	4.1	3.3	2.4	0.6	1.0	1.2	0.9	1.4	0.9	0.8
Sweden	4.8	1.3	0.6	1.2	1.3	2.2	1.5	1.6	0.8	0.9	1.7	2.6	3.3	1.8	1.5	1.3	1.5	1.8	1.0	1.7
Switzerland	2.5	-0.1	0.3	0.6	1.1	0.8	0.5	1.0	0.6	0.1	2.1	2.5	2.5	0.3	-0.5	0.4	0.7	-0.6	0.6	0.8
Turkey	68.9	81.5	75.7	54.2	49.2	52.9	37.4	23.3	12.4	7.1	9.3	6.2	12.0	5.3	6.5	6.3	6.1	..	..	..
United Kingdom	4.7	2.8	2.2	2.1	3.2	2.9	3.1	3.1	2.5	2.0	3.0	3.0	3.0	1.4	2.9	3.4	2.1	2.7	3.3	2.0
United States	2.8	1.8	1.1	1.5	2.2	2.3	1.6	2.2	2.8	3.3	3.3	2.9	2.2	0.9	1.0	1.4	1.4	1.3	1.5	1.4
Euro area	3.6	1.4	1.6	1.0	1.4	2.5	2.6	2.2	1.9	1.9	1.9	2.4	2.0	1.0	0.9	1.1	1.3	1.0	1.3	1.3
Total OECD	6.2	4.1	3.6	2.9	3.0	3.2	2.5	2.5	2.6	2.4	2.6	2.6	2.5	1.1	1.3	1.6	1.6	1.6	1.6	1.7

StatLink http://dx.doi.org/10.1787/888932443225

Note: The adoption of national accounts systems SNA93 or ESA95 has been proceeding at an uneven pace among OECD member countries, both with respect to variables and the time period covered. As a consequence, there are breaks in many national series. For further information, see table "National Accounts Reporting Systems, base years and latest data updates" at the beginning of the Statistical Annex and *OECD Economic Outlook* Sources and Methods (*http://www.oecd.org/eco/sources-and-methods*).

Source: OECD Economic Outlook 89 database.

Annex Table 17. Private consumption deflators
Percentage change from previous year

	Average 1986-96	1997	1998	1999	2000	2001	2002	2003	2004	2005	2006	2007	2008	2009	2010	2011	2012	Fourth quarter 2010	2011	2012
Australia	4.1	1.5	1.2	0.9	3.1	3.6	3.2	1.9	1.3	1.9	3.0	2.9	2.7	1.6	1.9	2.8	2.6	1.8	3.2	2.6
Austria	2.4	1.5	0.5	0.5	2.5	1.8	0.7	1.6	2.0	2.6	2.1	2.7	2.5	-0.7	1.5	2.8	1.9	2.0	2.7	1.8
Belgium	2.5	1.6	1.0	0.4	3.4	1.9	1.2	1.5	2.4	2.7	3.0	2.9	3.2	-0.5	2.4	3.4	2.3	3.1	3.7	2.0
Canada	2.9	1.6	1.2	1.7	2.2	1.8	2.0	1.6	1.5	1.7	1.4	1.6	1.6	0.5	1.3	1.7	1.4	1.2	1.6	1.4
Chile	..	4.5	3.4	2.3	4.7	4.6	3.2	3.2	0.5	3.7	2.5	3.6	7.9	0.9	0.2	2.9	3.9	1.5	4.6	3.7
Czech Republic	..	9.0	8.9	1.9	3.1	3.9	1.2	-0.4	3.3	0.8	1.4	2.9	4.9	0.3	1.3	2.9	3.0	1.9	2.7	3.3
Denmark	2.6	2.0	1.4	1.9	2.7	2.3	1.7	1.3	1.3	1.5	1.9	1.2	3.1	1.3	2.6	2.5	1.7	2.8	2.4	1.6
Estonia	..	9.8	7.2	4.2	3.6	6.2	2.7	2.0	2.0	3.6	5.0	7.5	8.7	-0.9	2.1	5.6	3.0	3.4	3.8	2.8
Finland	3.4	1.9	2.1	1.4	4.4	2.4	2.2	-0.5	0.4	0.8	1.4	2.2	3.5	0.6	1.0	3.7	2.1	1.6	3.9	1.6
France	2.4	0.9	0.2	-0.5	2.3	1.7	1.0	1.9	1.9	1.8	2.1	2.1	2.9	-0.4	1.2	2.1	1.4	1.5	2.1	1.2
Germany	2.4	1.4	0.5	0.3	0.9	1.8	1.2	1.5	1.3	1.4	1.1	1.8	1.7	0.0	2.0	2.2	1.6	1.9	2.1	1.6
Greece	14.3	5.6	4.5	2.3	3.3	2.7	2.6	3.4	2.9	3.4	3.4	3.3	4.0	1.1	4.7	2.6	0.7	..	..	..
Hungary	..	18.4	14.7	9.5	9.8	7.9	3.6	3.8	4.5	3.8	3.6	6.3	5.4	4.1	5.0	4.6	3.2	4.5	4.2	3.1
Iceland	10.3	0.8	1.5	2.8	5.0	7.8	4.8	1.3	3.0	1.9	7.7	4.6	14.0	13.8	3.5	1.2	2.4	-0.4	3.2	2.4
Ireland	2.8	2.7	4.0	2.8	5.1	4.4	5.4	4.1	1.8	1.8	2.4	3.3	4.8	-4.3	-2.2	0.8	0.5	-1.2	1.6	0.2
Israel	..	5.6	6.3	5.9	2.1	1.0	4.3	0.3	0.5	1.9	2.7	1.8	4.8	2.4	2.9	3.6	3.4	2.8	3.6	3.0
Italy	5.7	2.2	1.8	1.8	3.4	2.6	2.9	2.8	2.6	2.3	2.7	2.3	3.2	0.0	1.5	2.6	1.7	1.9	2.6	1.6
Japan	1.1	1.2	0.1	-0.5	-1.1	-1.1	-1.4	-0.9	-0.7	-0.8	-0.2	-0.6	0.4	-2.1	-1.5	-0.5	-0.2	-1.1	-0.2	-0.1
Korea	7.3	6.2	6.2	2.8	4.4	4.3	3.1	3.2	3.2	2.3	1.5	2.0	4.5	2.6	2.6	4.3	3.6	3.3	4.2	3.7
Luxembourg	2.7	1.4	1.7	2.5	4.0	2.0	0.5	2.2	2.4	2.8	2.4	2.2	2.0	0.8	1.8	2.8	2.1	3.0	1.6	2.3
Mexico	37.1	16.6	20.4	14.0	10.3	7.1	5.3	7.1	6.5	3.3	3.5	4.8	5.5	7.2	3.0	3.0	3.7	3.3	3.8	3.7
Netherlands	2.0	2.3	2.0	1.9	3.8	4.5	3.0	2.4	1.0	2.1	2.2	1.8	1.4	-0.6	1.7	2.0	1.9	1.8	2.0	1.8
New Zealand	4.1	1.9	2.0	0.7	2.2	2.3	2.0	0.8	1.5	2.2	3.0	1.6	3.6	2.3	1.4	3.6	2.6	3.0	3.1	2.3
Norway	3.6	2.4	2.5	2.0	2.9	2.2	1.4	3.0	0.7	1.1	1.9	1.2	3.6	2.5	1.9	1.4	2.0	2.4	1.7	2.0
Poland	..	14.4	10.6	6.3	10.1	3.6	3.4	0.2	3.4	1.8	1.2	2.5	4.6	2.1	2.9	3.8	2.9	3.5	3.4	2.9
Portugal	8.6	3.0	2.4	2.3	3.5	3.5	2.8	3.0	2.5	2.7	3.0	3.0	2.6	-2.5	1.6	3.3	1.3	2.4	2.8	1.1
Slovak Republic	..	4.8	5.7	9.9	8.3	5.6	2.9	6.5	7.3	2.6	4.9	2.6	4.5	0.1	0.9	3.9	2.9	1.3	4.0	3.1
Slovenia	..	8.6	6.9	6.4	7.2	7.6	7.8	5.3	3.0	2.1	2.2	4.1	5.4	0.0	2.9	2.9	2.0	3.3	2.4	1.8
Spain	5.5	2.7	1.9	2.3	3.7	3.4	2.8	3.1	3.6	3.4	3.6	3.3	3.5	0.1	2.8	3.0	0.9	3.6	2.1	0.7
Sweden	5.3	1.3	0.5	1.6	0.8	2.1	1.5	1.6	1.0	1.1	1.1	1.3	3.2	1.9	1.3	1.3	1.6	1.0	1.3	1.8
Switzerland	2.6	0.8	-0.1	0.4	0.8	0.7	0.9	0.4	0.8	0.5	1.3	1.3	2.6	-0.4	0.2	0.3	0.8	0.0	0.7	0.8
Turkey	70.4	82.1	83.0	53.4	54.9	49.7	38.5	23.4	10.8	8.3	9.8	6.6	10.8	4.9	8.3	5.7	6.2	..	..	..
United Kingdom	4.7	2.5	2.4	1.2	1.1	2.0	1.5	1.9	1.8	2.4	2.8	2.9	3.1	1.3	4.3	4.5	2.2	4.6	4.0	1.9
United States	3.2	1.9	0.9	1.6	2.5	1.9	1.4	2.0	2.6	3.0	2.7	2.7	3.3	0.2	1.7	1.9	1.3	1.1	2.0	1.3
Euro area	3.7	1.8	1.1	0.9	3.6	2.4	1.9	2.1	2.0	2.1	2.2	2.3	2.7	-0.2	1.8	2.4	1.5	2.1	2.3	1.4
Total OECD	6.5	4.4	4.0	3.0	3.6	3.2	2.3	2.4	2.4	2.3	2.4	2.4	3.2	0.5	1.8	2.3	1.7	1.8	2.3	1.7

StatLink http://dx.doi.org/10.1787/888932443244

Note: The adoption of national accounts systems SNA93 or ESA95 has been proceeding at an uneven pace among OECD member countries, both with respect to variables and the time period covered. As a consequence, there are breaks in many national series. For further information, see table "National Accounts Reporting Systems, base years and latest data updates" at the beginning of the Statistical Annex and *OECD Economic Outlook* Sources and Methods (*http://www.oecd.org/eco/sources-and-methods*).

Source: OECD Economic Outlook 89 database.

Annex Table 18. Consumer price indices
Percentage change from previous year

	Average 1986-96	1997	1998	1999	2000	2001	2002	2003	2004	2005	2006	2007	2008	2009	2010	2011	2012	Fourth quarter 2010	Fourth quarter 2011	Fourth quarter 2012
Australia	4.5	0.3	0.9	1.5	4.5	4.4	3.0	2.8	2.3	2.7	3.5	2.3	4.4	1.8	2.8	3.4	2.5	2.7	3.4	2.6
Austria	..	1.2	0.8	0.5	2.0	2.3	1.7	1.3	2.0	2.1	1.7	2.2	3.2	0.4	1.7	3.1	1.8	2.0	3.0	1.8
Belgium	..	1.5	0.9	1.1	2.7	2.4	1.6	1.5	1.9	2.5	2.3	1.8	4.5	0.0	2.3	3.6	2.4	3.2	3.4	2.1
Canada	..	1.6	1.0	1.7	2.7	2.5	2.3	2.7	1.8	2.2	2.0	2.1	2.4	0.3	1.8	2.9	1.6	2.2	2.5	1.5
Chile	15.3	6.1	5.1	3.3	3.8	3.6	2.5	2.8	1.1	3.1	3.4	4.4	8.7	0.4	1.4	3.9	3.9	2.5	4.6	3.7
Czech Republic	..	8.5	10.7	2.1	3.9	4.7	1.8	0.1	2.8	1.9	2.6	3.0	6.3	1.0	1.5	2.2	3.1	2.1	2.9	3.3
Denmark	2.8	2.2	1.8	2.5	2.9	2.3	2.4	2.1	1.2	1.8	1.9	1.7	3.4	1.3	2.3	2.6	1.7	2.6	2.7	1.6
Estonia	..	9.3	8.8	3.1	3.9	5.6	3.6	1.4	3.0	4.1	4.4	6.7	10.6	0.2	2.7	4.6	3.0	4.9	3.8	2.8
Finland	..	1.2	1.3	1.3	2.9	2.7	2.0	1.3	0.1	0.8	1.3	1.6	3.9	1.6	1.7	3.2	1.6	2.5	2.4	1.6
France	..	1.3	0.7	0.6	1.8	1.8	1.9	2.2	2.3	1.9	1.9	1.6	3.2	0.1	1.7	2.4	1.6	1.9	2.5	1.5
Germany	..	1.5	0.6	0.6	1.4	1.9	1.4	1.0	1.8	1.9	1.8	2.3	2.8	0.2	1.2	2.6	1.7	1.6	2.6	1.6
Greece	..	5.4	4.5	2.1	2.9	3.7	3.9	3.4	3.0	3.5	3.3	3.0	4.2	1.3	4.7	2.9	0.7	5.1	1.9	0.1
Hungary	..	18.3	14.2	10.0	9.8	9.1	5.3	4.7	6.7	3.6	3.9	8.0	6.0	4.2	4.9	4.0	3.3	4.3	4.4	3.2
Iceland[1]	9.7	1.8	1.7	3.2	5.1	6.4	5.2	2.1	3.2	4.0	6.7	5.1	12.7	12.0	5.4	2.7	2.6	2.8	3.1	2.4
Ireland	..	1.3	2.1	2.5	5.3	4.0	4.7	4.0	2.3	2.2	2.7	2.9	3.1	-1.7	-1.6	1.3	0.4	-0.6	1.6	0.2
Israel	14.8	9.0	5.4	5.2	1.1	1.1	5.7	0.7	-0.4	1.3	2.1	0.5	4.6	3.3	2.7	3.7	3.4	2.5	3.6	3.0
Italy	..	1.9	2.0	1.7	2.6	2.3	2.6	2.8	2.3	2.2	2.2	2.0	3.5	0.8	1.6	2.4	1.7	2.0	2.3	1.6
Japan	1.3	1.7	0.7	-0.3	-0.5	-0.8	-0.9	-0.3	0.0	-0.6	0.3	0.1	1.4	-1.3	-0.7	0.3	-0.2	0.1	0.1	-0.2
Korea	6.0	4.4	7.5	0.8	2.3	4.1	2.7	3.6	3.6	2.8	2.2	2.5	4.7	2.8	3.0	4.2	3.5	3.6	3.8	3.6
Luxembourg	..	1.4	1.0	1.0	3.8	2.4	2.1	2.5	3.2	3.8	3.0	2.7	4.1	0.0	2.8	4.2	2.3	2.9	3.9	2.2
Mexico	36.7	20.6	15.9	16.6	9.5	6.4	5.0	4.5	4.7	4.0	3.6	4.0	5.1	5.3	4.2	4.3	3.7	4.2	4.2	3.7
Netherlands	..	1.9	1.8	2.0	2.3	5.1	3.9	2.2	1.4	1.5	1.7	1.6	2.2	1.0	0.9	2.2	1.9	1.5	2.1	1.8
New Zealand	4.6	1.2	1.3	-0.1	2.6	2.6	2.7	1.8	2.3	3.0	3.4	2.4	4.0	2.1	2.3	4.6	2.8	4.0	3.4	2.6
Norway	3.7	2.6	2.3	2.3	3.1	3.0	1.3	2.5	0.5	1.5	2.3	0.7	3.8	2.2	2.4	1.7	2.0	2.2	2.0	2.0
Poland	..	14.9	11.6	7.2	9.9	5.4	1.9	0.7	3.4	2.2	1.3	2.4	4.2	3.8	2.6	4.2	3.1	2.9	3.9	3.1
Portugal	..	1.9	2.2	2.2	2.8	4.4	3.7	3.3	2.5	2.1	3.0	2.4	2.7	-0.9	1.4	3.3	1.3	2.3	2.8	1.1
Slovak Republic	..	6.0	6.7	10.4	12.2	7.2	3.5	8.4	7.5	2.8	4.3	1.9	3.9	0.9	0.7	3.9	2.9	1.0	4.5	3.1
Slovenia	..	8.3	7.9	6.1	8.9	8.6	7.5	5.7	3.7	2.5	2.5	3.8	5.5	0.9	2.1	2.5	2.2	2.0	2.8	2.0
Spain	..	1.9	1.8	2.2	3.5	2.8	3.6	3.1	3.1	3.4	3.6	2.8	4.1	-0.2	2.0	2.9	0.9	2.5	2.2	0.7
Sweden[2]	4.8	0.7	-0.3	0.5	0.9	2.4	2.2	1.9	0.4	0.5	1.4	2.2	3.4	-0.5	1.2	2.9	2.4	1.9	2.8	2.6
Switzerland	2.8	0.5	0.0	0.8	1.6	1.0	0.6	0.6	0.8	1.2	1.1	0.7	2.4	-0.5	0.7	0.7	1.1	0.3	0.8	1.2
Turkey	70.0	85.7	84.6	64.9	54.9	54.4	45.0	21.6	8.6	8.2	9.6	8.8	10.4	6.3	8.6	5.7	6.1	..	..	..
United Kingdom[3]	..	1.8	1.6	1.3	0.8	1.2	1.3	1.4	1.3	2.0	2.3	2.3	3.6	2.2	3.3	4.2	2.1	3.4	3.9	1.7
United States	3.6	2.3	1.5	2.2	3.4	2.8	1.6	2.3	2.7	3.4	3.2	2.9	3.8	-0.3	1.6	2.6	1.5	1.2	2.5	1.6
Euro area	..	1.7	1.2	1.2	2.2	2.4	2.3	2.1	2.2	2.2	2.2	2.1	3.3	0.3	1.6	2.6	1.6	2.0	2.5	1.4

Note: For the euro area countries, the euro area aggregate and the United Kingdom: harmonised index of consumer prices (HICP).
1. Excluding rent, but including imputed rent.
2. The consumer price index includes mortgage interest costs.
3. Known as the CPI in the United Kingdom.
Source: OECD Economic Outlook 89 database.

StatLink ⬛ http://dx.doi.org/10.1787/888932443263

Annex Table 19. Oil and other primary commodity markets

	1995	1996	1997	1998	1999	2000	2001	2002	2003	2004	2005	2006	2007	2008	2009	2010	2011	2012
Oil market conditions[1]																		
Demand								*Million barrels per day*										
OECD	44.9	46.0	46.8	47.0	47.9	48.0	48.1	48.0	48.7	49.5	49.9	49.6	49.3	47.6	45.6	46.1	45.9	..
of which: North America	21.6	22.2	22.7	23.1	23.8	24.1	24.1	24.2	24.6	25.5	25.6	25.4	25.5	24.2	23.3	23.9	23.7	..
Europe	14.7	15.0	15.1	15.4	15.4	15.2	15.4	15.3	15.5	15.5	15.7	15.7	15.5	15.4	14.6	14.4	14.3	..
Pacific	8.6	8.8	8.9	8.4	8.7	8.7	8.6	8.5	8.6	8.5	8.6	8.5	8.4	8.0	7.7	7.8	7.9	..
Non-OECD	25.2	26.0	27.2	27.5	28.3	29.0	29.6	30.3	31.1	33.4	34.2	35.6	37.2	38.4	39.5	41.7	43.3	..
Total	70.1	72.1	73.9	74.5	76.2	77.0	77.6	78.3	79.9	82.9	84.1	85.1	86.5	86.0	85.1	87.9	89.2	..
Supply																		
OECD	21.0	21.7	22.0	21.8	21.4	21.9	21.7	21.8	21.5	21.0	20.1	19.8	19.5	18.7	18.8	18.9	18.9	..
OPEC total	27.4	28.1	29.7	30.6	29.2	30.8	30.3	28.9	30.8	33.3	34.7	35.0	34.6	35.6	33.5	34.5	..	..
Former USSR	7.1	7.1	7.2	7.3	7.4	8.0	8.6	9.5	10.5	11.4	11.8	12.3	12.8	12.8	13.3	13.6	13.7	..
Other non-OECD	15.1	15.7	16.0	16.3	16.6	16.8	16.9	17.2	17.4	17.7	18.0	18.4	18.6	19.4	19.7	20.4	..	..
Total	70.7	72.6	74.9	76.0	74.6	77.4	77.6	77.4	80.2	83.5	84.7	85.5	85.5	86.6	85.3	87.4	..	..
Trade																		
OECD net imports	23.6	24.4	25.1	25.5	25.8	26.3	26.6	26.0	27.5	28.7	30.0	30.0	29.7	29.2	26.8	27.3	26.9	..
Former USSR net exports	2.8	3.2	3.4	3.5	3.7	4.2	4.8	5.7	6.6	7.6	7.9	8.3	8.7	8.6	9.3	9.2	9.3	..
Other non-OECD net exports	20.7	21.2	21.7	22.0	22.1	22.1	21.8	20.3	20.9	21.1	22.1	21.8	21.0	20.6	17.5	18.0	17.6	..
Prices[2]								*cif, $ per bl*										
Brent crude oil price	17.0	20.7	19.1	12.7	17.9	28.4	24.5	25.0	28.8	38.2	54.4	65.1	72.5	97.0	61.5	79.5	116.2	120.0
Prices of other primary commodities[2]								*$ indices*										
Food and tropical beverages	120	126	128	106	86	81	75	83	90	102	100	111	140	187	161	179	243	243
Agricultural raw materials	116	99	96	83	82	88	76	73	88	98	100	111	132	126	105	140	163	163
Minerals, ores and metals	75	66	68	57	56	63	57	56	63	84	100	143	160	167	116	164	202	204
Total[3]	95	89	90	75	69	73	66	67	75	92	100	128	149	164	125	163	205	206

1. Based on data published in various issues of International Energy Agency, *Oil Market Report.*
2. Indices through 2010 are based on data compiled by the International Energy Agency for oil and by the Hamburg Institute of International Economics for the prices of other primary commodities; OECD estimates and projections for 2011 and 2012.
3. OECD calculations. The total price index for non-energy primary commodities is a weighted average of the individual HWWI non-oil commodities price indices with the weights based on the commodities' share in total non-energy commodities world trade.

Source: OECD Economic Outlook 89 database.

StatLink http://dx.doi.org/10.1787/888932443282

Annex Table 20. **Employment rates, participation rates and labour force**

| | Employment rates | | | | | | Labour force participation rates | | | | | | Labour force | | | | | |
| | Per cent | | | | | | Per cent | | | | | | Percentage change | | | | | |
	Average 1989-98	Average 1999-08	2009	2010	2011	2012	Average 1989-98	Average 1999-08	2009	2010	2011	2012	Average 1989-98	Average 1999-08	2009	2010	2011	2012
Australia	68.1	72.2	74.1	74.9	75.3	75.9	74.5	76.4	78.5	79.0	79.3	79.9	1.4	2.1	2.2	2.3	2.0	1.9
Austria	67.7	69.3	72.2	72.2	72.9	73.2	70.4	72.3	75.8	75.6	76.1	76.2	1.2	1.2	0.7	0.1	1.2	0.5
Belgium	58.9	62.7	63.4	63.3	63.3	63.5	64.3	67.9	68.9	69.0	68.6	68.6	0.6	1.0	0.6	1.1	0.1	0.6
Canada	69.2	73.3	73.4	73.7	74.3	74.9	76.5	78.8	80.0	80.1	80.3	80.5	1.0	1.7	0.7	1.1	1.2	1.0
Chile	54.6	55.4	57.3	60.7	62.0	62.5	58.8	60.9	64.2	66.1	66.9	67.3	2.2	2.2	3.4	4.2	2.5	1.9
Czech Republic	69.0	65.7	66.2	65.9	66.5	67.5	72.4	71.0	71.0	71.0	71.3	72.1	..	0.1	1.1	-0.4	0.0	0.4
Denmark	75.2	78.3	79.0	77.4	77.4	78.2	81.0	81.9	84.0	83.4	83.4	83.6	0.0	0.6	-0.4	-0.6	0.1	0.3
Estonia	100.0	70.0	65.5	63.0	65.5	67.0	100.0	75.8	76.0	75.7	76.4	77.0	..	..	-0.5	-0.8	0.1	0.1
Finland	64.8	68.4	69.0	68.7	69.3	69.9	73.7	74.8	75.3	75.0	75.2	75.2	-0.3	0.6	-0.9	-0.3	0.1	-0.3
France	61.2	63.1	63.2	63.1	63.3	63.6	67.6	68.9	69.5	69.6	69.5	69.7	0.4	0.7	1.0	0.4	0.3	0.7
Germany	68.0	70.8	74.6	75.3	76.2	76.8	73.3	77.5	80.5	80.8	81.0	81.2	0.7	0.4	0.2	-0.1	0.1	0.0
Greece	55.1	60.1	62.4	60.7	58.4	58.2	60.9	66.7	69.0	69.4	69.5	69.6	1.4	0.8	0.9	0.8	0.3	0.2
Hungary	51.9	55.4	54.5	54.7	54.7	55.4	57.8	59.4	60.6	61.6	61.9	62.2	..	0.4	0.0	1.3	0.2	0.4
Iceland	82.1	83.6	78.0	78.6	79.5	81.0	85.3	85.9	84.1	85.0	85.5	86.0	0.9	1.8	-1.7	0.0	-0.4	0.4
Ireland	56.0	67.9	63.3	61.4	60.5	60.2	64.4	71.3	71.7	71.0	70.9	70.5	2.3	3.0	-2.8	-1.9	-1.0	-0.7
Israel	100.0	58.2	61.6	62.5	63.5	64.0	100.0	63.9	66.6	67.0	67.7	67.9	..	2.6	3.6	2.5	2.9	2.2
Italy	53.4	57.3	58.5	57.8	57.9	58.4	59.4	62.4	63.4	63.2	63.2	63.6	0.0	0.8	-0.4	0.0	0.4	0.5
Japan	73.9	75.2	77.1	77.4	77.7	78.4	76.0	78.8	81.2	81.5	81.6	82.1	0.9	-0.2	-0.5	-0.4	-0.3	-0.4
Korea	62.4	64.9	66.4	66.9	67.2	67.5	64.2	67.6	69.0	69.5	69.6	69.8	1.9	1.3	0.2	1.5	1.0	0.7
Luxembourg	60.7	64.2	64.8	65.1	65.9	66.6	62.2	66.7	68.7	69.3	69.6	70.0	1.2	2.4	2.6	2.2	1.4	1.4
Mexico	69.0	62.3	61.6	61.7	..	..	71.1	64.4	65.1	65.2	..	..	..	1.9	2.0	1.6	1.4	1.4
Netherlands	67.3	75.9	77.6	77.0	77.3	77.7	71.5	78.7	80.6	80.5	80.7	80.9	1.7	1.0	-0.5	0.2	0.4	0.5
New Zealand	68.6	74.3	75.4	75.1	..	..	74.7	78.0	80.3	80.3	..	..	1.5	2.1	1.0	1.2	1.4	1.2
Norway	74.3	77.4	78.4	77.5	77.4	77.6	78.2	80.3	80.9	80.4	80.2	80.1	0.8	1.2	-0.1	0.5	1.0	1.1
Poland	58.3	54.3	58.4	58.6	59.0	59.9	66.8	64.3	63.5	64.8	65.2	65.5	..	-0.1	1.6	2.2	0.4	0.2
Portugal	68.8	72.1	70.5	69.5	68.4	67.5	73.0	76.8	77.9	78.0	77.5	77.3	0.9	1.0	-0.7	0.0	-0.4	-0.2
Slovak Republic	67.1	58.0	60.3	59.0	59.5	60.2	74.3	69.0	68.6	68.9	69.0	69.0	0.9	0.6	0.1	0.6	0.2	-0.1
Slovenia	..	66.5	69.4	67.9	67.3	67.5	..	70.9	73.7	73.2	73.0	73.0	..	1.0	0.0	0.0	-0.2	0.1
Spain	50.3	62.1	61.1	59.9	59.6	60.4	59.4	69.3	74.5	74.9	74.8	74.8	1.3	3.4	0.8	0.2	-0.4	-0.4
Sweden	75.8	74.8	73.9	74.4	..	..	82.3	80.2	80.6	81.2	..	..	-0.3	0.8	0.2	1.1	1.3	0.8
Switzerland	81.7	81.8	82.5	81.8	82.3	82.8	84.1	84.7	86.1	85.6	85.8	86.1	1.0	1.1	1.6	0.5	1.1	1.2
Turkey	51.4	46.8	45.3	47.2	47.9	48.0	56.0	51.8	52.5	53.4	53.5	53.5	1.8	1.0	3.9	3.5	2.0	1.7
United Kingdom	69.7	72.0	70.9	71.3	71.6	71.3	76.0	76.0	76.7	77.4	77.9	77.7	-0.1	0.9	0.5	0.5	0.7	0.4
United States	71.6	71.9	68.1	..	..	..	76.1	75.7	75.0	..	..	..	1.2	1.1	-0.1	-0.2	-0.1	0.9
Euro area	60.6	65.0	66.2	65.8	66.0	66.4	66.7	70.9	73.0	73.1	73.1	73.2	0.8	1.1	0.2	0.1	0.1	0.2
Total OECD	64.4	67.0	66.5	66.2	66.9	67.3	69.1	71.5	72.4	71.8	72.7	72.8	1.1	1.0	0.5	0.5	0.4	0.6

Note: Employment rates are calculated as the ratio of total employment to the population of working age. The working age population concept used here and for the labour force participation rate is defined as all persons of the age 15 to 64 years (16 to 64 years for Spain). This definition does not correspond to the commonly-used working age population concepts for Mexico (15 years and above), the United States and New Zealand (16 years and above) and Sweden (15-74). Hence for these countries no projections are available. For information about sources and definitions, see *OECD Economic Outlook Sources and Methods (http://www.oecd.org/eco/sources-and-methods).*

Source: OECD Economic Outlook 89 database.

StatLink http://dx.doi.org/10.1787/888932443301

Annex Table 21. Potential GDP, employment and capital stock

Percentage change from previous period

	Potential GDP						Employment						Capital stock[1]					
	Average 1989-98	Average 1999-08	2009	2010	2011	2012	Average 1989-98	Average 1999-08	2009	2010	2011	2012	Average 1989-98	Average 1999-08	2009	2010	2011	2012
Australia	3.3	3.4	3.7	3.4	3.3	3.2	1.2	2.4	0.7	2.7	2.2	2.0	3.0	5.2	6.9	6.7	6.5	6.9
Austria	2.4	2.2	1.7	1.8	1.9	1.7	1.1	1.1	-0.3	0.5	1.4	0.7	2.9	2.4	0.9	0.8	1.0	1.1
Belgium	2.2	2.0	1.4	1.3	1.2	1.2	0.4	1.1	-0.3	0.7	0.8	0.9	3.3	2.3	1.6	1.4	1.6	1.8
Canada	2.6	2.8	1.8	1.7	1.9	2.1	0.9	1.9	-1.6	1.4	1.7	1.6	4.5	4.8	2.7	2.3	3.2	3.5
Chile	..	3.8	3.9	2.9	4.4	4.7	2.4	2.5	0.0	7.4	3.4	2.0	..	..	..	..	..	..
Czech Republic	..	3.6	1.7	1.7	2.3	2.8	..	0.6	-1.3	-1.0	0.7	0.7	..	..	..	..	..	..
Denmark	2.2	1.6	1.1	1.0	1.0	1.2	0.3	0.8	-3.1	-2.1	0.0	1.1	3.6	4.0	3.6	3.3	3.3	3.5
Estonia	..	..	1.8	1.1	1.8	3.0	..	..	-9.2	-4.2	3.2	1.6	..	..	..	..	..	..
Finland	2.0	3.1	1.8	1.4	1.3	1.5	-1.2	1.1	-2.9	-0.5	0.7	0.5	1.6	2.2	1.0	0.0	0.1	0.5
France	1.9	2.0	1.1	1.2	1.4	1.6	0.1	1.1	-0.9	0.2	0.6	1.0	2.8	3.4	2.3	1.7	1.9	2.1
Germany	2.2	1.3	1.1	1.1	1.5	1.6	0.5	0.5	0.0	0.5	1.0	0.6	3.0	1.7	1.0	1.0	1.4	1.6
Greece	2.1	3.6	1.6	0.8	0.4	0.7	1.0	1.4	-1.1	-2.7	-3.7	-0.3	2.9	5.0	3.1	2.0	1.5	1.5
Hungary	..	3.2	0.7	0.7	0.8	1.2	..	0.3	-2.3	0.0	-0.2	1.0	4.0	5.3	1.4	1.4	0.9	1.1
Iceland	2.0	4.1	0.0	-0.4	0.1	1.4	0.9	1.7	-6.0	-0.3	0.1	1.7	..	..	..	..	..	..
Ireland	6.5	5.5	0.3	-0.3	-0.3	0.4	3.3	3.0	-8.8	-3.8	-2.4	-0.6	3.5	6.5	1.9	0.5	-0.1	-0.1
Israel	..	3.7	4.1	4.2	4.3	4.3	..	2.9	2.0	3.5	3.4	2.7	..	..	..	..	..	..
Italy	1.8	1.0	0.0	-0.1	0.2	0.3	-0.1	1.3	-1.5	-0.7	0.4	0.8	3.0	3.0	0.9	0.9	0.9	1.0
Japan	2.1	1.0	0.7	0.9	1.2	0.9	0.7	-0.1	-1.6	-0.4	0.0	-0.2	4.2	1.6	0.1	0.1	-0.4	0.4
Korea	..	..	..	..	..	..	1.4	1.7	-0.3	1.4	1.2	0.8	..	..	..	..	..	..
Luxembourg	5.1	4.2	3.9	3.2	2.7	2.9	1.0	2.2	1.2	1.8	2.2	2.0	..	..	..	..	..	..
Mexico	..	2.6	2.3	2.6	2.9	3.2	..	1.7	0.5	1.8	2.1	2.2	..	..	..	..	..	..
Netherlands	3.0	2.2	1.5	1.2	1.1	1.2	2.0	1.1	-1.1	-0.5	0.6	0.7	3.4	2.9	2.1	1.6	2.1	2.7
New Zealand	2.5	3.1	1.0	1.0	0.8	1.5	1.5	2.4	-1.1	0.7	1.0	2.2	3.1	5.2	-0.1	2.3	-1.6	5.1
Norway	2.5	3.2	1.8	1.7	2.4	3.2	1.0	1.2	-0.6	0.0	1.1	1.4	1.4	2.1	-1.9	-2.1	0.4	2.2
Poland	..	4.2	3.8	3.1	2.9	3.0	..	0.8	0.4	0.6	0.7	1.2	..	..	..	..	..	..
Portugal	3.2	1.6	0.4	0.5	0.5	0.6	0.9	0.6	-2.7	-1.4	-1.5	-1.3	4.4	2.9	-0.1	-0.6	-1.5	-1.9
Slovak Republic	..	5.0	3.9	3.9	3.9	3.5	..	1.5	-2.7	-2.1	-0.9	1.0	..	..	..	..	..	..
Slovenia	..	3.6	1.2	2.2	1.6	1.5	..	1.3	-1.5	-1.5	-0.8	0.3	..	..	..	..	..	..
Spain	2.8	3.6	1.6	0.7	0.8	1.1	1.1	3.6	-6.8	-2.3	-0.7	0.9	5.0	6.0	4.2	3.1	2.7	2.8
Sweden	2.0	2.8	2.3	2.0	2.1	2.3	-1.2	1.1	-2.1	1.0	2.3	1.2	3.6	4.1	0.9	1.1	1.8	2.0
Switzerland	1.4	2.0	2.0	1.8	1.8	1.9	0.7	1.0	0.6	0.2	1.4	1.4	3.4	2.9	2.3	2.4	2.6	2.6
Turkey	..	..	..	..	..	..	2.0	0.7	0.4	6.0	3.2	1.9	..	..	..	..	..	..
United Kingdom	2.4	2.4	0.8	0.2	0.9	1.4	0.0	0.9	-1.6	0.2	0.5	0.2	4.5	4.3	1.2	1.3	1.4	1.5
United States	3.1	2.6	1.7	1.6	1.9	2.3	1.3	1.0	-3.8	-0.6	0.9	1.9	4.6	4.4	2.3	2.3	2.5	2.9
Euro area	2.2	1.9	1.1	0.9	1.1	1.3	0.5	1.3	-1.8	-0.5	0.3	0.7	3.2	3.1	1.8	1.4	1.5	1.7
Total OECD	2.6	2.3	1.4	1.3	1.6	1.8	1.0	1.1	-1.8	0.3	0.9	1.2	4.0	3.7	1.9	1.8	1.9	2.3

Note: Estimates of potential output are based on a production function approach outlined in Beffy *et al.* (2006), "New OECD methods for supply-side and medium-term assessments: a new capital services approach", *OECD Economics Department Working Papers*, No. 482. Revisions to this method are discussed in Chapter 4 of *OECD Economic Outlook* No. 85, "Beyond the crisis: medium-term challenges relating to potential output, employment and fiscal positions".

1. Total economy less housing.

Source: OECD Economic Outlook 89 database.

StatLink http://dx.doi.org/10.1787/888932443320

Annex Table 22. **Structural unemployment and unit labor costs**

| | Structural unemployment rate | | | | | | | | | Unit labour costs[1] | | | | | | | | |
| | *Per cent* | | | | | | | | | *Percentage change* | | | | | | | | |
	Average 1986-95	Average 1996-05	2006	2007	2008	2009	2010	2011	2012	Average 1986-95	Average 1996-05	2006	2007	2008	2009	2010	2011	2012
Australia	7.7	6.4	5.2	5.1	5.1	5.1	5.2	5.2	5.2	3.4	2.2	6.0	5.4	4.1	-0.9	3.4	3.8	2.5
Austria	3.6	4.0	4.3	4.3	4.3	4.3	4.3	4.3	4.3	3.1	0.3	1.2	1.4	3.1	4.9	0.2	0.6	0.9
Belgium	8.0	8.1	8.0	8.0	8.0	8.2	8.2	8.3	8.4	2.5	1.5	2.0	2.3	4.6	4.2	-0.4	1.4	2.1
Canada	8.6	7.5	6.6	6.5	6.5	6.5	6.6	6.6	6.6	2.5	1.9	4.0	3.3	3.8	2.6	0.9	1.7	2.0
Czech Republic	4.2	7.3	6.8	6.1	5.8	5.9	6.1	6.3	6.3	11.7	3.8	0.9	3.1	5.3	2.5	-1.0	1.1	0.5
Denmark	6.6	5.2	4.5	4.4	4.4	4.8	4.8	4.9	5.0	2.6	2.4	2.3	5.0	6.9	4.5	-1.6	0.3	1.4
Estonia	:	10.1	9.6	10.1	10.4	11.0	11.9	12.2	12.1	:	4.0	8.7	16.1	17.9	0.7	-8.0	0.1	1.0
Finland	8.0	9.6	7.8	7.5	7.4	7.6	7.8	7.8	7.8	2.9	1.3	0.3	0.7	5.4	7.3	-1.4	-0.9	-0.1
France	8.9	9.1	8.5	8.3	8.3	8.6	8.7	8.8	8.8	2.1	1.5	1.8	1.6	3.0	2.8	0.9	1.0	1.4
Germany	6.7	7.9	8.2	8.0	7.8	7.8	7.6	7.5	7.3	2.4	0.0	-1.8	-0.1	2.8	5.2	-0.7	-0.1	0.6
Greece	7.2	9.4	9.1	8.9	8.9	9.1	9.9	10.8	11.2	15.0	5.1	2.3	4.4	6.3	4.8	-1.3	-4.2	-2.2
Hungary	10.3	7.4	6.6	6.6	6.8	7.6	7.8	8.1	8.2	:	9.4	2.8	6.2	5.3	2.2	-0.7	1.1	2.0
Iceland	2.5	3.2	2.8	2.8	2.8	3.0	3.2	3.4	3.4	11.6	5.2	12.1	8.8	4.7	-1.8	7.0	1.0	2.8
Ireland	14.3	7.0	4.7	4.7	5.1	6.8	8.0	8.8	9.2	1.4	3.1	4.5	2.5	5.2	-0.9	-4.2	-3.0	-2.9
Israel	:	9.3	8.3	7.9	7.5	7.1	6.8	6.5	6.3	:	1.4	3.3	1.6	2.5	0.1	2.3	2.6	2.5
Italy	9.1	8.6	6.6	6.3	6.4	6.8	7.1	7.2	7.2	4.7	2.3	2.5	2.5	5.3	4.3	-0.5	1.2	0.6
Japan	2.8	4.0	4.1	4.1	4.1	4.1	4.1	4.1	4.2	1.3	-1.5	0.0	-2.9	1.4	2.2	-3.1	1.5	-1.0
Korea	3.0	3.9	3.6	3.5	3.5	3.5	3.5	3.5	3.5	9.4	2.1	0.7	1.7	3.3	3.5	0.5	2.6	2.6
Luxembourg	:	3.4	3.2	3.2	3.2	3.2	3.2	:	:	3.0	1.9	1.5	1.8	5.6	6.7	-0.3	1.2	0.3
Mexico	4.0	3.4	3.2	3.2	3.2	3.2	3.2	3.2	3.2	37.1	11.1	3.0	4.0	5.8	8.7	-2.4	1.4	2.1
Netherlands	6.6	4.3	3.8	3.8	3.7	3.7	3.7	3.7	3.7	1.2	2.5	0.7	1.8	3.2	5.3	-1.2	-0.1	0.6
New Zealand	7.0	5.7	4.1	4.0	4.0	4.1	4.2	4.3	4.4	1.5	2.3	4.8	4.8	5.8	3.3	-4.1	2.3	1.2
Norway	4.2	4.0	3.6	3.3	3.3	3.3	3.4	3.4	3.4	2.4	3.2	6.7	7.8	8.5	4.6	3.5	2.0	2.8
Poland	11.8	14.5	13.6	11.4	9.8	9.4	9.5	9.5	9.5	28.8	4.0	0.9	3.9	8.3	4.6	1.9	2.6	3.1
Portugal	6.4	6.1	6.8	6.9	7.0	7.7	8.1	8.5	8.7	9.4	3.7	1.5	1.6	3.4	4.1	0.0	0.9	0.8
Slovak Republic	12.4	15.9	14.4	13.4	12.5	11.9	11.4	11.3	11.3	:	4.2	1.5	-0.1	3.3	5.4	-2.7	-0.3	0.9
Slovenia	:	6.5	6.2	6.3	6.3	6.3	6.5	6.8	7.0	:	5.3	1.1	2.7	6.0	8.4	-0.3	-0.6	0.8
Spain	14.1	12.0	9.1	8.9	9.5	11.1	12.7	13.5	13.8	6.6	3.2	3.7	4.4	4.9	1.0	-1.4	-0.9	0.3
Sweden	5.7	7.6	7.2	7.2	7.1	7.0	7.0	7.0	6.9	4.3	1.2	-0.8	4.1	3.6	4.6	-1.4	0.4	0.5
Switzerland	2.0	3.4	3.7	3.7	3.7	3.7	3.8	3.9	3.9	3.2	0.6	0.6	1.6	3.5	5.0	-1.5	-0.8	0.0
United Kingdom	9.0	6.2	5.3	5.3	5.4	5.6	5.8	5.9	6.0	4.5	2.8	2.3	2.8	2.3	5.9	1.6	1.4	0.9
United States	6.1	5.3	5.0	4.9	5.0	5.2	5.3	5.4	5.5	2.7	2.1	3.1	3.2	2.6	-0.6	-0.5	1.5	2.2
Euro area	8.8	8.6	7.8	7.6	7.6	8.0	8.4	8.5	8.5	3.8	1.7	1.1	1.8	3.9	3.9	-0.6	0.1	0.6
Total OECD	6.5	6.4	5.9	5.7	5.7	5.9	6.0	6.1	6.1	4.1	2.4	2.0	2.2	3.6	2.9	-0.6	1.2	1.3

Note: The structural unemployment rate corresponds to "NAIRU" and is estimated on the basis of the methods outlined in Richardson *et al.* (2000). "The concept, policy use and measurement of structural unemployment", *OECD Economics Department Working Papers*, No 250. The most recent updates of the OECD's estimates are described in Gianella *et al.* (2008) "What drives the NAIRU? Evidence from a panel of OECD countries", *OECD Economics Department Working Papers*, No. 649. Details on the methods used to project the NAIRUs can be found in the technical note "Adjustments to the OECD method of projecting the NAIRU" (*http://www.oecd.org/dataoecd/56/9/43098869.pdf*). For more information about sources and definitions, see *OECD Economic Outlook Sources and Methods* (*http://www.oecd.org/eco/sources-and-methods*).

1. Total economy.

Source: OECD Economic Outlook 89 database.

StatLink ⬛⬛⬛ http://dx.doi.org/10.1787/888932443339

Annex Table 23. Household saving rates
Per cent of disposable household income

	1993	1994	1995	1996	1997	1998	1999	2000	2001	2002	2003	2004	2005	2006	2007	2008	2009	2010	2011	2012
Net saving																				
Australia	6.0	7.3	6.6	7.3	6.2	3.3	2.5	2.6	3.1	-0.3	-0.6	-0.6	-0.2	1.9	3.1	5.4	9.7	9.3	9.5	9.2
Austria	11.3	11.5	11.8	9.3	7.7	8.5	9.8	9.2	8.0	8.0	9.1	9.3	9.7	10.4	11.6	11.8	11.1	9.1	9.0	8.9
Belgium	15.1	14.8	16.3	14.3	13.2	12.7	13.1	12.3	13.7	12.9	12.2	10.7	10.2	11.0	11.3	11.9	13.4	12.2	11.2	11.0
Canada	11.9	9.5	9.2	7.0	4.9	4.9	4.0	4.7	5.2	3.5	2.6	3.2	2.1	3.5	2.8	3.6	4.6	4.4	4.3	4.2
Czech Republic	6.4	1.2	10.0	6.1	6.0	4.1	3.4	3.3	2.2	3.0	2.4	0.5	3.2	4.8	6.3	5.7	4.5	1.6	1.8	1.8
Denmark	1.3	-2.7	0.2	-0.2	-2.8	-1.2	-5.6	-4.0	2.1	2.1	2.4	-1.3	-4.2	-2.3	-4.0	-3.3	-0.5	-1.2	-1.4	-1.4
Estonia	..	..	4.2	2.0	-0.1	-2.8	-5.4	-3.0	-4.0	-6.4	-7.1	-12.8	-11.1	-13.1	-8.1	-2.5	7.6	6.4	6.3	5.4
Finland	7.2	1.4	4.2	0.7	2.5	0.6	2.4	0.5	0.4	0.5	1.4	2.7	0.9	-1.1	-0.9	-0.2	3.9	4.3	2.3	2.1
Germany	12.1	11.4	11.0	10.5	10.1	10.1	9.5	9.2	9.4	9.9	10.3	10.4	10.5	10.6	10.8	11.7	11.1	11.4	10.9	10.9
Hungary	..	..	14.3	15.5	14.2	13.4	9.9	8.9	8.5	6.4	4.3	6.8	7.0	7.7	5.4	3.2	5.6	8.9	9.6	8.6
Ireland	..	..	..	..	..	..	..	..	..	2.4	2.4	5.5	3.6	2.2	0.0	3.8	12.1	19.3	16.1	14.4
Italy	19.5	18.1	17.0	17.9	15.1	11.4	10.2	8.4	10.5	11.2	10.3	10.2	9.9	9.1	8.4	8.2	7.1	6.1	6.0	5.7
Japan	14.2	13.3	12.6	10.5	10.3	11.4	10.0	8.7	5.1	5.0	3.9	3.6	3.9	3.8	2.4	2.2	5.0	6.5	7.9	7.5
Korea	23.1	21.8	18.5	18.1	16.1	23.2	16.1	9.3	5.2	0.4	5.2	9.2	7.2	5.2	2.9	2.9	4.6	4.3	3.5	3.5
Netherlands	14.1	14.4	14.3	12.7	13.3	12.2	9.0	6.9	9.7	8.7	7.6	7.4	6.4	6.1	6.9	5.7	6.8	6.6	6.0	5.7
Norway	6.4	5.4	4.8	2.6	3.0	5.7	4.7	4.3	3.1	8.2	8.9	7.2	10.1	0.1	1.5	3.7	7.3	7.2	7.1	6.7
Poland	..	..	14.6	11.7	11.7	12.1	10.5	10.0	11.9	8.3	7.7	7.0	7.3	7.5	6.1	0.8	7.8	6.5	4.6	3.8
Slovak Republic	..	..	5.3	8.3	8.7	7.4	6.6	6.5	4.0	3.6	1.3	0.2	1.3	0.9	3.1	2.3	4.0	3.8	3.6	2.7
Sweden	9.4	8.1	8.3	6.3	3.4	2.8	2.8	4.3	8.4	8.2	7.2	6.1	5.5	6.6	8.8	11.2	12.9	10.8	10.0	8.9
Switzerland	13.0	12.4	12.7	10.9	10.7	10.7	10.8	11.7	11.9	10.7	9.4	9.0	10.1	11.4	12.6	11.8	11.1	10.1	9.9	9.0
United States	5.8	5.2	5.2	4.9	4.6	5.3	3.1	2.9	2.7	3.5	3.5	3.4	1.4	2.4	2.1	4.1	5.9	5.8	5.5	5.0
Gross saving																				
France	15.5	14.8	15.9	15.0	16.0	15.5	15.2	15.0	15.7	16.9	15.7	15.8	15.0	15.0	15.5	15.4	16.2	16.0	15.4	15.3
Portugal	..	..	12.6	11.7	10.9	10.3	10.7	10.6	10.6	10.3	10.7	10.0	10.0	8.0	7.0	7.1	10.9	9.8	9.9	12.5
Spain	15.5	13.1	17.5	17.4	16.0	14.4	12.7	11.1	11.1	11.4	12.0	11.3	11.3	11.1	10.7	13.4	18.0	13.1	11.1	11.0
United Kingdom	10.8	9.3	10.3	9.4	9.6	7.4	5.2	4.7	6.0	4.8	5.1	3.7	3.9	3.4	2.6	2.0	6.0	5.4	4.6	4.6

Note: The adoption of new national account systems SNA93 or ESA95 has been proceeding at an uneven pace among OECD member countries, both with respect to variables and the time period covered. As a consequence, there are breaks in many national series. See table "National Accounts Reporting Systems and Base-years and latest data updates" at the beginning of the Statistical Annex and *OECD Economic Outlook* Sources and Methods *(http://www.oecd.org/eco/sources-and-methods).* Countries differ in the way household disposable income is reported (in particular whether private pension benefits less pension contributions are included in disposable income or not), but the calculation of household saving is adjusted for this difference. Most countries report household saving on a net basis (i.e. excluding consumption of fixed capital by households and unincorporated businesses). In most countries household saving includes saving by non-profit institutions (in some cases referred to as personal saving). Other countries (Czech Republic, Finland, France and Japan) report saving of households only.

Source: OECD Economic Outlook 89 database.

StatLink http://dx.doi.org/10.1787/888932443358

Annex Table 24. Gross national saving
Per cent of nominal GDP

	1991	1992	1993	1994	1995	1996	1997	1998	1999	2000	2001	2002	2003	2004	2005	2006	2007	2008	2009	2010
Australia	17.5	19.4	21.2	20.3	20.3	21.2	21.3	20.6	21.3	20.7	21.5	21.0	21.6	21.0	22.5	22.8	23.3	23.7	..	..
Austria	23.5	22.7	21.9	21.8	22.2	22.1	22.7	23.3	23.1	23.6	23.0	24.8	24.5	25.0	24.7	25.6	27.2	26.9	23.8	25.2
Belgium	22.8	23.2	24.3	25.5	25.4	24.4	25.7	25.6	26.3	26.7	25.4	25.0	24.9	25.3	25.1	25.8	26.7	25.1	22.2	22.8
Canada	14.7	13.4	14.0	16.2	18.3	18.8	19.6	19.1	20.7	23.6	22.2	21.2	21.4	23.0	23.9	24.5	23.7	23.5	17.7	..
Chile	..	..	..	..	..	22.3	22.2	21.1	20.4	20.0	19.9	20.0	20.0	22.2	23.4	24.9	25.1	22.8	20.5	..
Czech Republic	..	..	..	..	29.0	27.0	24.4	26.3	24.6	24.8	24.2	22.4	20.7	22.0	23.9	24.7	24.4	24.5	20.5	..
Denmark	19.5	20.0	19.1	19.3	20.4	20.5	21.4	20.7	21.7	22.6	23.5	22.9	23.1	23.4	25.2	25.7	24.7	24.5	20.7	21.6
Estonia	..	..	..	..	21.4	20.7	20.3	21.7	20.7	23.1	22.9	21.9	21.8	21.7	23.6	23.0	22.0	20.6	24.5	25.9
Finland	16.3	13.7	14.8	18.1	21.7	20.7	23.8	24.8	26.4	28.5	28.9	27.7	24.5	26.3	25.3	25.9	27.1	25.2	20.6	21.8
France	20.2	19.6	18.3	18.7	19.1	18.7	19.9	21.0	21.8	21.6	21.3	19.8	19.1	19.0	18.5	19.3	20.0	19.3	16.1	..
Germany	22.6	22.3	21.2	20.9	21.0	20.5	20.7	20.9	20.3	20.2	19.5	19.4	19.5	22.0	22.1	24.2	26.0	25.2	21.5	22.6
Greece	10.7	10.9	10.9	11.0	11.3	11.4	11.2	11.3	11.3	11.3	11.8	9.6	12.2	12.0	9.0	7.7	6.3	4.2	2.1	2.8
Hungary	..	..	..	19.1	19.1	22.3	22.9	23.1	20.5	21.7	21.3	18.8	16.3	17.2	15.9	16.3	16.4	16.8	18.8	..
Iceland	16.0	15.7	17.6	17.9	17.1	17.2	17.9	17.4	15.0	13.1	17.0	19.7	15.0	13.6	12.3	11.4	12.6	0.2	3.8	4.9
Ireland	17.4	15.4	17.5	17.8	20.4	21.7	23.4	24.8	23.7	23.7	21.7	20.5	22.9	23.3	23.6	24.8	21.7	16.4	11.5	..
Israel	23.2	24.4	21.8	19.9	19.9	19.6	20.3	20.7	20.0	18.6	18.3	17.0	17.8	19.7	22.0	24.0	22.9	19.5	20.3	..
Italy	20.0	19.1	19.7	19.9	22.0	22.2	22.2	21.6	21.1	20.6	20.9	20.8	19.8	20.3	19.5	19.6	20.1	18.0	15.9	16.0
Japan	34.3	33.6	32.2	30.5	29.5	29.7	29.7	28.8	27.2	27.5	25.8	25.2	25.4	25.8	26.8	26.9	27.3	25.0	..	..
Korea	37.9	37.0	37.0	36.4	36.1	34.6	34.4	36.4	34.3	32.9	31.0	30.4	31.8	34.0	32.0	30.8	30.8	30.7	30.1	..
Luxembourg	13.6	14.3	13.6	13.4	13.5	13.6	13.7	13.7	13.0	13.2	13.6	12.1	11.3	11.7	11.1	10.9	10.7	11.4	12.3	..
Mexico	21.7	18.8	16.7	16.2	21.3	26.0	28.5	23.5	23.8	24.1	20.3	21.1	21.9	24.1	23.5	25.4	25.5	25.5	23.0	..
Netherlands	25.6	24.8	25.0	26.1	27.2	26.7	28.1	25.2	27.1	28.4	26.7	25.8	25.4	27.6	26.5	29.0	28.8	25.7	21.8	24.9
New Zealand	13.6	14.4	17.0	17.8	17.7	16.6	16.3	16.0	15.6	17.6	19.4	18.8	18.9	18.2	16.0	15.2	16.2	14.8	16.8	..
Norway	24.0	23.1	23.3	24.2	25.9	27.9	29.6	26.3	28.5	35.4	35.1	31.5	30.5	32.7	37.4	39.2	37.7	39.9	33.3	34.2
Poland	40.5	36.2	29.1	23.2	20.1	19.8	20.1	21.2	20.2	19.5	18.4	16.5	17.0	15.9	18.1	18.0	19.4	11.6	11.0	..
Portugal	22.9	21.8	19.3	18.5	20.6	19.8	20.1	20.6	19.9	17.8	17.2	17.3	16.9	15.8	13.3	12.4	12.7	10.6	9.2	9.2
Slovak Republic	..	..	23.7	26.3	26.7	24.5	25.1	24.1	23.7	23.4	22.4	21.6	18.2	19.7	20.3	19.7	22.1	20.7	16.4	20.2
Slovenia	..	..	..	..	23.0	23.2	24.2	24.6	24.1	24.1	24.4	24.7	24.3	24.8	25.5	26.5	27.2	25.2	21.7	22.2
Spain	21.6	20.0	20.0	19.5	21.7	21.5	22.2	22.4	22.4	22.3	22.0	22.9	23.4	22.4	22.0	22.0	21.0	19.4	18.9	..
Sweden	20.7	16.9	14.4	18.0	21.0	20.6	21.0	21.8	22.3	23.3	23.2	22.5	24.0	23.7	24.8	26.6	28.9	29.1	23.0	24.6
Switzerland	31.1	28.6	29.7	29.3	29.6	28.8	30.8	32.0	32.9	34.7	31.4	29.0	33.1	32.9	36.0	35.5	31.0	23.6	17.9	..
United Kingdom	15.4	14.3	14.0	15.7	15.9	16.1	17.1	18.0	15.7	15.0	15.4	15.3	15.1	15.0	14.4	14.1	15.6	15.0	11.7	12.1
United States	15.0	13.9	13.7	14.9	16.0	16.7	18.0	18.5	17.9	17.8	16.2	14.3	13.5	14.1	14.6	15.8	13.9	11.9	10.3	..

Note: Based on SNA93 or ESA95.
Source: National accounts of OECD countries database.

StatLink http://dx.doi.org/10.1787/888932443377

Annex Table 25. General government total outlays
Per cent of nominal GDP

	1993	1994	1995	1996	1997	1998	1999	2000	2001	2002	2003	2004	2005	2006	2007	2008	2009	2010	2011	2012
Australia	37.4	37.5	37.3	36.5	35.4	34.6	34.5	34.8	35.3	34.7	34.1	34.6	34.0	33.5	33.4	34.2	33.1	36.3	35.6	34.8
Austria	56.4	56.2	56.6	56.1	53.7	54.1	53.8	52.2	51.7	50.9	51.7	54.3	50.4	49.6	49.0	49.5	53.1	53.0	52.1	51.7
Belgium	54.9	52.6	52.1	52.6	51.2	50.4	50.2	49.1	49.2	49.9	51.1	49.5	52.1	48.6	48.4	50.2	54.1	53.1	52.2	51.6
Canada	52.2	49.7	48.5	46.6	44.3	44.8	42.7	41.1	42.0	41.2	41.2	39.9	39.3	39.4	39.4	39.8	44.1	43.8	43.1	42.0
Czech Republic	..	..	54.5	42.6	43.2	43.2	42.3	41.8	44.3	46.3	47.3	45.2	45.0	43.7	42.4	42.9	45.9	45.2	45.1	44.5
Denmark	60.2	60.2	59.3	58.9	56.7	56.3	55.5	53.7	54.2	54.6	55.1	54.6	52.8	51.6	50.8	51.9	58.4	58.2	58.1	57.5
Estonia	..	..	41.3	39.5	37.4	39.2	40.1	36.1	34.8	35.8	34.8	34.0	33.6	33.6	34.4	39.9	45.2	40.0	37.6	38.0
Finland	64.8	63.7	61.4	60.0	56.6	52.9	51.7	48.3	47.8	48.9	50.2	50.0	50.2	49.0	47.3	49.3	56.2	55.1	54.1	53.4
France	55.0	54.2	54.4	54.5	54.1	52.7	52.6	51.6	51.6	52.6	53.2	53.3	53.4	52.7	52.4	52.9	56.2	56.2	55.3	54.6
Germany	48.3	47.9	54.8	49.3	48.3	48.1	48.2	45.1	47.5	48.0	48.4	47.2	46.9	45.3	43.5	43.8	47.5	46.7	45.3	44.4
Greece	46.5	44.7	45.7	44.1	44.9	44.3	44.4	46.7	45.3	45.1	44.7	45.5	44.0	45.2	46.6	49.7	52.9	49.5	49.4	48.9
Hungary	..	..	54.9	50.2	49.0	50.1	48.4	46.7	46.8	50.7	49.0	48.7	49.9	51.6	49.5	48.8	50.2	48.6	49.2	45.4
Iceland	40.4	39.9	42.7	42.2	40.7	41.3	42.0	41.9	42.6	44.3	45.6	44.1	42.2	41.6	42.3	57.6	51.0	50.0	45.3	43.8
Ireland	44.6	43.9	41.1	39.1	36.7	34.5	34.1	31.3	33.1	33.4	33.2	33.6	34.0	34.5	36.7	42.8	48.2	67.0	45.5	43.2
Israel	..	..	..	..	..	55.0	53.7	51.5	53.7	55.7	54.3	50.9	49.3	47.6	46.2	46.0	45.6	45.5	45.1	44.4
Italy	56.4	53.5	52.5	52.5	50.2	49.3	48.2	46.1	48.0	47.4	48.3	47.8	48.1	48.7	47.9	48.8	51.8	50.6	50.5	49.4
Japan	34.5	35.0	36.0	36.7	35.7	42.5	38.6	39.0	38.6	38.8	38.4	37.0	38.4	36.2	35.9	37.2	42.0	40.7	42.1	41.2
Korea	21.2	20.6	20.4	21.2	21.8	24.1	23.2	22.4	23.9	23.6	28.9	26.1	26.6	27.7	28.7	30.4	33.1	30.9	31.2	31.0
Luxembourg	39.8	38.9	39.7	41.1	40.7	41.1	39.2	37.6	38.1	41.5	41.8	42.6	41.5	38.6	36.2	36.9	42.2	41.2	40.5	40.6
Netherlands	55.7	53.5	56.4	49.4	47.5	46.7	46.0	44.2	45.4	46.2	47.1	46.1	44.8	45.5	45.3	46.0	51.4	51.2	49.9	48.8
New Zealand	45.2	42.8	41.9	40.8	41.6	40.6	40.2	38.3	37.8	36.9	37.5	37.1	38.2	39.6	39.6	41.9	42.8	43.0	46.2	43.0
Norway	54.7	53.6	50.9	48.5	46.9	49.2	47.7	42.3	44.2	47.1	48.3	45.6	42.3	40.6	41.2	40.6	46.4	46.0	43.5	43.3
Poland	..	..	47.7	51.1	46.6	44.5	42.9	41.2	43.7	44.2	44.6	42.7	43.5	43.9	42.2	43.2	44.6	45.8	45.8	45.1
Portugal	43.9	42.4	41.5	42.1	41.1	40.8	41.0	41.1	42.5	42.3	43.8	44.7	45.8	44.5	44.4	44.7	49.8	50.7	47.5	46.7
Slovak Republic	..	..	48.6	53.7	48.9	45.8	48.1	52.1	44.5	45.1	40.1	37.7	38.0	36.6	34.3	35.0	41.5	41.0	38.7	37.3
Slovenia	..	..	52.6	44.5	44.8	45.7	46.5	46.7	47.6	46.3	46.4	45.9	45.3	44.6	42.5	44.1	49.0	49.0	49.3	47.7
Spain	49.0	46.7	44.4	43.2	41.6	41.1	39.9	39.1	38.6	38.9	38.4	38.9	38.4	38.4	39.2	41.3	45.8	45.0	42.4	40.6
Sweden	71.7	69.6	64.9	62.9	60.7	58.8	58.1	55.1	54.5	55.6	55.7	54.2	53.9	52.7	51.0	51.7	55.2	53.1	51.9	50.8
Switzerland	35.1	35.2	35.0	35.3	35.5	35.8	34.3	35.1	34.8	36.2	36.4	35.9	35.3	33.5	32.3	32.2	33.7	33.7	33.0	32.1
Turkey	..	..	..	..	..	..	..	..	..	..	..	..	..	33.2	34.5	34.2	39.4	37.1	35.9	35.3
United Kingdom	45.3	44.6	44.1	42.2	40.6	39.5	38.8	36.6	39.9	40.9	42.4	43.1	44.0	44.3	44.1	47.4	51.2	51.0	50.1	48.8
United States[1]	38.1	37.1	37.1	36.6	35.4	34.6	34.2	33.9	35.0	35.9	36.3	36.0	36.2	36.0	36.8	39.0	42.2	42.3	41.3	40.4
Euro area	52.2	50.9	53.1	50.6	49.3	48.5	48.1	46.2	47.2	47.5	48.0	47.6	47.4	46.6	46.0	47.0	50.9	50.5	49.0	48.0
Total OECD	42.9	42.0	42.8	41.7	40.5	40.8	39.8	38.9	39.9	40.4	40.9	40.2	40.4	39.7	39.8	41.4	44.9	44.5	43.7	42.7

Note: Data refer to the general government sector, which is a consolidation of accounts for the central, state and local governments plus social security. Total outlays are defined as current outlays plus capital outlays. For more details, see *OECD Economic Outlook* Sources and Methods (*http://www.oecd.org/eco/sources-and-methods*).

1. These data include outlays net of operating surpluses of public enterprises.

Source: OECD Economic Outlook 89 database.

StatLink ⟐ http://dx.doi.org/10.1787/888932443396

Annex Table 26. General government total tax and non-tax receipts
Per cent of nominal GDP

	1993	1994	1995	1996	1997	1998	1999	2000	2001	2002	2003	2004	2005	2006	2007	2008	2009	2010	2011	2012
Australia	32.5	32.8	33.4	33.9	34.3	35.4	35.6	35.2	34.8	35.4	35.4	35.5	35.2	34.8	34.8	34.0	28.2	30.4	32.7	33.4
Austria	52.0	51.3	50.7	52.0	51.8	51.6	51.3	50.4	51.5	50.0	50.0	49.7	48.6	47.9	48.0	48.5	49.0	48.3	48.4	48.5
Belgium	47.4	47.4	47.6	48.5	49.0	49.5	49.6	49.0	49.5	49.7	51.0	49.1	49.3	48.7	48.1	48.9	48.2	48.9	48.5	48.8
Canada	43.5	43.0	43.2	43.8	44.5	44.9	44.3	44.1	42.6	41.1	41.1	40.7	40.8	41.1	40.8	39.8	38.5	38.3	38.3	38.5
Czech Republic	..	..	41.0	39.3	39.4	38.2	38.6	38.1	38.7	39.5	40.7	42.2	41.4	41.1	41.8	40.2	40.1	40.6	41.3	41.8
Denmark	56.3	56.8	56.4	56.9	56.1	56.2	56.8	55.8	55.4	54.8	55.0	56.4	57.8	56.6	55.6	55.2	55.6	55.3	54.4	54.5
Estonia	..	..	42.4	39.1	39.6	38.5	36.7	35.9	34.7	36.0	36.5	35.6	35.2	36.0	36.9	37.0	43.4	40.1	37.1	36.3
Finland	56.5	57.0	55.3	56.5	55.2	54.4	53.2	55.2	52.8	52.9	52.5	52.1	52.7	52.8	52.4	53.5	53.3	52.4	52.7	52.8
France	48.5	48.8	48.9	50.4	50.8	50.0	50.1	50.1	50.0	49.4	49.1	49.6	50.5	50.3	49.6	49.6	48.7	49.1	49.7	50.0
Germany	45.3	45.6	45.1	45.9	45.7	45.9	46.7	46.4	44.7	44.4	44.4	43.5	43.6	43.7	43.8	43.9	44.5	43.4	43.2	43.2
Greece	34.6	36.5	36.7	37.4	39.0	40.5	41.3	43.0	40.9	40.3	39.0	38.1	38.6	39.2	40.0	39.9	37.3	39.1	41.8	42.3
Hungary	..	..	46.3	45.7	43.0	42.2	43.0	43.7	42.7	41.9	41.9	42.3	42.0	42.3	44.6	45.1	45.8	44.4	51.7	42.2
Iceland	35.9	35.3	39.8	40.6	40.7	40.9	43.2	43.6	41.9	41.7	42.8	44.1	47.1	48.0	47.7	44.1	41.1	42.3	42.6	42.5
Ireland	41.9	41.9	39.1	39.0	38.1	36.8	36.7	36.1	34.1	33.1	33.6	35.0	35.6	37.4	36.8	35.5	33.9	34.6	35.4	35.1
Israel	..	..	..	..	..	47.0	47.4	47.5	47.4	47.6	46.0	44.8	44.4	45.1	44.7	42.2	39.2	40.5	41.4	41.5
Italy	46.3	44.4	45.1	45.5	47.6	46.2	46.5	45.3	44.9	44.4	44.7	44.2	43.8	45.3	46.4	46.1	46.5	46.1	46.6	46.8
Japan	32.0	31.2	31.2	31.6	31.7	31.3	31.2	31.4	32.2	30.8	30.5	30.9	31.7	34.5	33.5	35.1	33.3	32.5	33.2	33.0
Korea	23.0	22.9	23.9	24.4	24.8	25.5	25.5	27.9	28.3	28.7	29.4	28.8	30.0	31.7	33.3	33.4	31.9	30.9	31.7	32.2
Luxembourg	41.2	41.4	42.1	42.3	44.3	44.4	42.6	43.6	44.2	43.6	42.2	41.5	41.5	39.9	39.8	39.8	41.3	39.5	39.6	40.6
Netherlands	52.9	50.0	47.2	47.5	46.3	45.8	46.4	46.1	45.1	44.1	43.9	44.3	44.5	46.1	45.4	46.6	45.9	45.9	46.2	46.8
New Zealand	44.8	45.5	44.4	43.3	42.6	40.6	40.0	40.0	39.3	40.6	41.3	41.2	42.9	44.9	44.1	42.3	40.2	38.4	37.7	37.2
Norway	53.3	53.8	54.2	54.8	54.5	52.5	53.7	57.7	57.5	56.3	55.5	56.7	57.3	59.0	58.7	59.7	56.9	56.5	56.0	55.1
Poland	..	..	43.3	46.3	41.9	40.2	40.6	38.1	38.5	39.2	38.4	37.3	39.4	40.3	40.3	39.6	37.2	37.9	40.1	41.4
Portugal	36.4	35.3	36.5	37.5	37.8	37.3	38.3	38.2	38.2	39.4	40.7	41.3	39.9	40.5	41.1	41.1	39.7	41.5	41.6	42.2
Slovak Republic	..	..	45.2	43.8	42.6	40.5	40.7	39.9	38.0	36.8	37.4	35.3	35.2	33.4	32.5	32.9	33.6	33.1	33.5	33.3
Slovenia	..	..	44.3	43.3	42.5	43.3	43.4	43.0	43.6	43.9	43.7	43.6	43.8	43.2	42.4	42.3	43.1	43.4	43.7	43.6
Spain	41.7	40.0	38.0	38.4	38.2	37.8	38.4	38.1	38.0	38.4	38.2	38.5	39.4	40.4	41.1	37.1	34.7	35.7	36.2	36.2
Sweden	60.5	60.5	57.6	59.6	59.0	59.7	58.9	58.7	56.1	54.1	54.4	54.6	55.8	54.9	54.5	53.9	54.2	52.7	52.2	52.2
Switzerland	31.6	32.4	33.0	33.5	32.7	33.8	33.8	35.2	34.7	35.0	34.6	34.2	34.6	34.3	34.0	34.5	34.9	34.2	33.6	33.0
Turkey	..	..	..	..	..	..	..	..	..	..	..	..	..	34.0	33.4	32.0	32.7	32.5	32.6	32.2
United Kingdom	37.3	37.8	38.2	38.0	38.4	39.4	39.8	40.3	40.6	39.0	38.7	39.6	40.8	41.5	41.2	42.6	40.3	40.7	41.4	41.7
United States[1]	33.0	33.4	33.8	34.3	34.6	34.9	34.9	35.4	34.4	31.9	31.3	31.6	33.0	33.8	33.9	32.6	30.9	31.6	31.2	31.3
Euro area	46.4	45.9	45.6	46.4	46.6	46.2	46.7	46.2	45.4	44.9	44.9	44.6	44.8	45.3	45.3	45.0	44.5	44.5	44.8	45.0
Total OECD	37.8	37.6	37.9	38.4	38.6	38.7	38.8	38.9	38.4	37.1	36.8	36.8	37.6	38.5	38.5	38.1	36.7	36.7	37.0	37.1

Note: Data refer to the general government sector, which is a consolidation of accounts for central, state and local governments plus social security. Non-tax receipts consist of property income (including dividends and other transfers from public enterprises), fees, charges, sales, fines, capital tranfers received by the general government, etc. For more details, see OECD Economic Outlook Sources and Methods (http://www.oecd.org/eco/sources-and-methods).
1. Excludes the operating surpluses of public enterprises.
Source: OECD Economic Outlook 89 database.

StatLink 🔗 http://dx.doi.org/10.1787/888932443415

Annex Table 27. General government financial balances

Surplus (+) or deficit (-) as a per cent of nominal GDP

	1993	1994	1995	1996	1997	1998	1999	2000	2001	2002	2003	2004	2005	2006	2007	2008	2009	2010	2011	2012
Australia	-4.9	-4.7	-3.9	-2.6	-1.0	0.8	1.2	0.4	-0.5	0.7	1.3	1.0	1.2	1.3	1.4	-0.2	-4.9	-5.9	-2.8	-1.4
Austria	-4.4	-4.9	-5.9	-4.2	-2.0	-2.5	-2.4	-1.9	-0.2	-0.9	-1.7	-4.6	-1.8	-1.7	-1.0	-1.0	-4.2	-4.6	-3.7	-3.2
Belgium	-7.5	-5.2	-4.5	-4.0	-2.3	-1.0	-0.7	-0.1	0.4	-0.2	-0.2	-0.4	-2.8	0.1	-0.4	-1.3	-6.0	-4.2	-3.6	-2.8
Canada	-8.7	-6.7	-5.3	-2.8	0.2	0.1	1.6	2.9	0.7	-0.1	-0.1	0.9	1.5	1.6	1.4	0.0	-5.5	-5.5	-4.9	-3.5
Czech Republic	..	..	-13.4	-3.3	-3.8	-5.0	-3.7	-3.7	-5.6	-6.8	-6.6	-2.9	-3.6	-2.6	-0.7	-2.7	-5.8	-4.7	-3.8	-2.8
Denmark	-3.9	-3.4	-2.9	-2.0	-0.6	-0.1	1.3	2.2	1.2	0.3	-0.1	1.9	5.0	5.0	4.8	3.3	-2.8	-2.9	-3.8	-3.0
Estonia	..	..	1.1	-0.3	2.2	-0.7	-3.5	-0.2	-0.1	0.3	1.7	1.6	1.6	2.4	2.5	-2.9	-1.8	0.1	-0.5	-1.7
Finland	-8.3	-6.7	-6.2	-3.5	-1.4	1.5	1.6	6.8	5.0	4.0	2.3	2.1	2.5	3.9	5.2	4.2	-2.9	-2.8	-1.4	-0.6
France	-6.4	-5.5	-5.5	-4.0	-3.3	-2.6	-1.8	-1.5	-1.6	-3.2	-4.1	-3.6	-3.0	-2.3	-2.7	-3.3	-7.5	-7.0	-5.6	-4.6
Germany	-3.0	-2.3	-9.7	-3.3	-2.6	-2.2	-1.5	1.3	-2.8	-3.6	-4.0	-3.8	-3.3	-1.6	0.3	0.1	-3.0	-3.3	-2.1	-1.2
Greece	-11.9	-8.3	-9.1	-6.6	-5.9	-3.8	-3.1	-3.7	-4.4	-4.8	-5.7	-7.4	-5.3	-6.0	-6.7	-9.8	-15.6	-10.4	-7.5	-6.5
Hungary	..	..	-8.7	-4.6	-6.0	-7.9	-5.4	-3.0	-4.0	-8.9	-7.2	-6.4	-7.9	-9.3	-5.0	-3.6	-4.4	-4.2	2.6	-3.3
Iceland	-4.5	-4.7	-3.0	-1.6	0.0	-0.4	1.1	1.7	-0.7	-2.6	-2.8	0.0	4.9	6.3	5.4	-13.5	-10.0	-7.8	-2.7	-1.4
Ireland	-2.7	-2.0	-2.1	-0.1	1.4	2.3	2.6	4.8	1.0	-0.3	0.4	1.4	1.6	2.9	0.1	-7.3	-14.3	-32.4	-10.1	-8.2
Israel	..	..	..	..	..	-8.0	-6.3	-4.0	-6.4	-8.2	-8.3	-6.1	-4.9	-2.5	-1.5	-3.7	-6.4	-5.0	-3.7	-2.9
Italy	-10.1	-9.1	-7.4	-7.0	-2.7	-3.1	-1.8	-0.9	-3.1	-3.0	-3.5	-3.6	-4.4	-3.3	-1.5	-2.7	-5.3	-4.5	-3.9	-2.6
Japan	-2.5	-3.8	-4.7	-5.1	-4.0	-11.2	-7.4	-7.6	-6.3	-8.0	-7.9	-6.2	-6.7	-1.6	-2.4	-2.2	-8.7	-8.1	-8.9	-8.2
Korea	1.7	2.3	3.5	3.2	3.0	1.3	2.4	5.4	4.3	5.1	0.5	2.7	3.4	3.9	4.7	3.0	-1.1	0.0	0.5	1.3
Luxembourg	1.5	2.5	2.4	1.2	3.7	3.4	3.4	6.0	6.1	2.1	0.5	-1.1	0.0	1.4	3.7	3.0	-0.9	-1.7	-0.9	0.0
Netherlands	-2.8	-3.5	-9.2	-1.9	-1.2	-0.9	0.4	2.0	-0.3	-2.1	-3.2	-1.8	-0.3	0.5	0.2	0.5	-5.5	-5.3	-3.7	-2.1
New Zealand	-0.4	2.7	2.5	2.5	0.9	0.0	-0.2	1.8	1.5	3.6	3.8	4.1	4.7	5.3	4.5	0.4	-2.6	-4.6	-8.5	-5.8
Norway	-1.4	0.3	3.2	6.3	7.6	3.3	6.0	15.4	13.3	9.2	7.3	11.1	15.1	18.4	17.5	19.1	10.5	10.5	12.5	11.9
Poland	..	..	-4.4	-4.9	-4.6	-4.3	-2.3	-3.0	-5.3	-5.0	-6.2	-5.4	-4.1	-3.6	-1.9	-3.7	-7.4	-7.9	-5.8	-3.7
Portugal	-7.5	-7.1	-5.0	-4.5	-3.4	-3.5	-2.7	-2.9	-4.3	-2.9	-3.1	-3.4	-5.9	-4.1	-3.2	-3.6	-10.1	-9.2	-5.9	-4.5
Slovak Republic	..	..	-3.4	-9.9	-6.3	-5.3	-7.4	-12.3	-6.5	-8.2	-2.8	-2.4	-2.8	-3.2	-1.8	-2.1	-8.0	-7.9	-5.1	-4.0
Slovenia	..	..	-8.4	-1.1	-2.4	-2.4	-3.0	-3.7	-4.0	-2.5	-2.7	-2.3	-1.5	-1.4	-0.1	-1.8	-6.0	-5.6	-5.6	-4.1
Spain	-7.3	-6.8	-6.5	-4.9	-3.4	-3.2	-1.4	-1.0	-0.7	-0.5	-0.2	-0.4	1.0	2.0	1.9	-4.2	-11.1	-9.2	-6.3	-4.4
Sweden	-11.2	-9.1	-7.3	-3.3	-1.6	0.9	0.8	3.6	1.6	-1.5	-1.3	0.4	1.9	2.2	3.6	2.2	-0.9	-0.3	0.3	1.4
Switzerland	-3.5	-2.8	-2.0	-1.8	-2.8	-1.9	-0.5	0.1	-0.1	-1.2	-1.7	-1.8	-0.7	0.8	1.7	2.3	1.2	0.5	0.6	0.9
Turkey														0.8	-1.2	-2.2	-6.7	-4.6	-3.3	-3.0
United Kingdom	-8.0	-6.8	-5.8	-4.2	-2.2	-0.1	0.9	3.7	0.6	-2.0	-3.7	-3.6	-3.3	-2.7	-2.8	-4.8	-10.8	-10.3	-8.7	-7.1
United States	-5.1	-3.7	-3.3	-2.3	-0.9	0.3	0.7	1.5	-0.6	-4.0	-5.0	-4.4	-3.3	-2.2	-2.9	-6.3	-11.3	-10.6	-10.1	-9.1
Euro area	-5.8	-5.0	-7.5	-4.3	-2.7	-2.3	-1.4	-0.1	-1.9	-2.6	-3.1	-3.0	-2.6	-1.4	-0.7	-2.1	-6.3	-6.0	-4.2	-3.0
Total OECD	-5.1	-4.3	-4.8	-3.3	-1.9	-2.2	-1.0	0.1	-1.4	-3.3	-4.1	-3.4	-2.8	-1.3	-1.3	-3.3	-8.2	-7.7	-6.7	-5.6

Memorandum items

General government financial balances excluding social security

	1993	1994	1995	1996	1997	1998	1999	2000	2001	2002	2003	2004	2005	2006	2007	2008	2009	2010	2011	2012
United States	-5.8	-4.5	-4.1	-3.2	-1.9	-0.9	-0.7	-0.1	-2.2	-5.5	-6.3	-5.8	-4.6	-3.6	-4.3	-7.6	-12.1	-11.1	-10.8	-9.9
Japan	-4.8	-5.8	-6.7	-6.9	-5.8	-12.5	-8.5	-8.2	-6.5	-7.9	-8.0	-6.6	-7.0	-1.7	-2.2	-1.6	-7.5	-7.3	-8.0	-7.1

Note: Financial balances include one-off factors, such as those resulting from the sale of the mobile telephone licenses, but exclude most financial transactions. As data are on a national accounts basis (SNA93/ESA95), the government financial balances may differ from the numbers reported to the European Commission under the Excessive Deficit Procedure for some EU countries. For more details, see footnotes to Annex Tables 25 and 26 and OECD Economic Outlook Sources and Methods (*http://www.oecd.org/eco/sources-and-methods*).

Source: OECD Economic Outlook 89 database.

StatLink ⟶ http://dx.doi.org/10.1787/888932443434

Annex Table 28. General government cyclically-adjusted balances

Surplus (+) or deficit (-) as a per cent of potential GDP

	1993	1994	1995	1996	1997	1998	1999	2000	2001	2002	2003	2004	2005	2006	2007	2008	2009	2010	2011	2012
Australia	-3.8	-4.2	-3.6	-2.2	-0.7	0.7	0.9	0.0	-0.5	0.7	1.2	0.8	0.8	1.1	0.9	-0.6	-4.3	-5.0	-1.9	-0.8
Austria	-4.0	-4.2	-5.3	-3.6	-1.4	-2.5	-3.1	-3.4	-0.8	-0.8	-0.9	-3.5	-1.0	-1.5	-1.6	-2.1	-3.2	-3.2	-2.7	-2.5
Belgium	-6.1	-4.2	-3.8	-2.8	-1.9	-0.4	-0.8	-1.2	-0.2	0.0	0.5	-0.4	-2.8	-0.2	-1.0	-1.6	-4.0	-2.6	-2.8	-2.5
Canada	-6.5	-5.6	-4.6	-1.7	1.0	0.6	1.4	2.2	0.3	-0.4	-0.2	0.7	1.3	1.3	1.1	0.2	-3.6	-3.8	-3.6	-2.7
Czech Republic	..	..	..	..	..	..	-3.0	-3.5	-5.4	-6.0	-5.7	-2.1	-3.4	-3.4	-1.9	-3.9	-4.7	-3.7	-2.9	-2.1
Denmark	-1.7	-2.3	-2.7	-2.0	-1.1	-0.6	0.9	1.1	0.1	0.1	0.5	2.4	5.1	4.3	3.6	2.6	0.0	0.8	-0.5	-0.4
Estonia	..	..	..	..	..	..	..	..	0.2	0.4	1.6	1.4	0.2	-0.7	-2.0	-5.4	1.5	2.6	0.7	-1.0
Finland	-3.4	-3.1	-3.5	-1.4	-0.8	1.5	1.4	6.2	4.9	4.5	3.3	2.7	3.0	3.7	4.2	3.5	0.6	0.3	0.7	0.8
France	-5.7	-4.7	-5.1	-3.4	-2.6	-2.4	-2.0	-2.3	-2.5	-3.5	-3.9	-3.4	-2.8	-2.3	-3.1	-3.4	-5.7	-4.8	-3.8	-3.2
Germany	-2.4	-1.8	-9.4	-2.7	-2.0	-1.7	-1.1	-1.6	-3.2	-3.4	-3.0	-2.6	-2.1	-1.4	-0.3	-0.5	-1.3	-2.5	-2.1	-1.7
Greece	-10.6	-7.0	-7.9	-5.6	-5.1	-3.2	-2.3	-3.0	-4.2	-3.9	-5.5	-7.3	-4.7	-6.2	-7.6	-10.1	-14.0	-6.5	-2.3	-1.3
Hungary	..	..	..	-3.6	-5.3	-7.6	-5.2	-3.2	-4.4	-9.4	-7.9	-7.5	-9.1	-10.9	-5.9	-4.0	-2.0	-1.5	4.2	-2.1
Iceland	-2.6	-3.5	-1.5	-0.7	0.3	-0.8	0.5	1.1	-1.2	-2.1	-1.8	0.0	3.6	4.9	3.8	-14.8	-8.3	-4.5	0.0	0.6
Ireland	-0.9	0.1	-0.9	0.6	1.2	1.8	1.4	3.2	-0.4	-1.6	-0.4	0.6	0.6	1.7	-1.6	-6.8	-9.8	-25.3	-5.3	-4.1
Israel	..	..	..	..	..	..	..	-6.0	-7.0	-7.1	-6.5	-4.9	-4.3	-2.6	-2.2	-4.5	-5.8	-4.6	-3.7	-3.1
Italy	-8.3	-7.6	-6.7	-6.2	-2.0	-2.4	-1.0	-2.1	-3.6	-3.2	-3.2	-3.4	-4.4	-4.0	-2.6	-3.1	-3.1	-2.2	-2.1	-1.5
Japan	-2.7	-3.7	-4.6	-5.4	-4.5	-10.6	-6.4	-7.1	-5.6	-7.0	-6.9	-5.7	-6.5	-1.8	-3.1	-2.4	-6.7	-6.7	-7.0	-6.5
Korea	1.8	2.2	3.1	2.5	2.4	2.4	3.1	5.5	4.4	4.9	0.4	2.7	3.3	3.7	4.2	2.7	-0.5	0.3	0.6	1.2
Luxembourg	0.5	1.9	2.9	3.1	5.6	4.7	3.5	4.8	5.1	1.3	0.5	-0.8	-0.2	0.8	2.3	2.0	0.8	0.7	1.3	1.8
Netherlands	-2.4	-2.6	-8.5	-1.5	-1.3	-1.4	-0.6	-0.1	-1.7	-2.5	-2.4	-0.7	0.7	0.9	-0.5	-0.6	-5.1	-3.8	-2.6	-1.5
New Zealand	0.4	2.5	2.0	1.8	0.7	0.8	0.1	1.7	1.6	3.2	3.1	3.2	3.7	5.0	4.0	0.9	-0.7	-2.9	-6.6	-5.0
Norway[1]	-6.8	-5.5	-2.2	-1.9	-1.2	-2.1	-0.5	1.6	0.7	-1.7	-3.7	-1.9	-0.8	1.4	3.4	2.3	-0.3	-0.8	-1.6	-2.2
Poland	..	..	..	-3.9	-4.6	-4.4	-2.7	-3.7	-5.1	-4.1	-5.4	-5.1	-3.5	-3.4	-2.2	-4.1	-7.0	-7.8	-6.0	-4.2
Portugal	-7.1	-5.9	-4.3	-4.0	-3.3	-4.2	-3.7	-4.6	-5.5	-3.4	-2.5	-2.9	-5.1	-3.4	-3.1	-3.2	-8.3	-7.6	-3.3	-1.0
Spain	-5.9	-4.8	-4.6	-3.1	-2.0	-2.5	-1.6	-2.1	-1.6	-0.9	-0.3	-0.3	0.9	1.9	1.7	-3.4	-7.8	-5.2	-2.4	-1.0
Sweden	-7.5	-6.6	-6.1	-1.8	-0.4	1.4	0.6	2.7	1.4	-1.6	-1.3	-0.1	1.1	0.6	1.6	1.9	2.4	1.6	1.1	1.7
Switzerland	-2.9	-2.3	-1.4	-1.1	-2.3	-1.9	-0.5	-0.5	-0.6	-1.1	-0.8	-1.0	-0.2	0.8	1.1	1.8	1.9	1.2	0.9	1.0
United Kingdom	-6.6	-6.2	-5.6	-4.0	-2.3	-0.3	0.7	1.0	0.3	-2.0	-3.9	-4.1	-3.9	-3.6	-3.9	-5.5	-9.0	-8.3	-7.0	-5.6
United States	-4.4	-3.4	-2.9	-2.0	-0.9	0.0	0.1	0.7	-0.8	-3.7	-4.7	-4.5	-3.7	-2.7	-3.4	-6.1	-9.3	-8.8	-8.6	-7.9
Euro area	-4.8	-4.0	-6.9	-3.4	-2.1	-2.0	-1.3	-1.7	-2.5	-2.7	-2.6	-2.4	-2.1	-1.5	-1.3	-2.4	-4.3	-3.9	-2.6	-1.9
Total OECD	-4.5	-4.0	-4.7	-3.1	-1.9	-2.2	-1.2	-1.1	-1.9	-3.5	-3.9	-3.6	-3.1	-2.0	-2.3	-3.8	-6.7	-6.3	-5.7	-5.0

Note: Cyclically-adjusted balances exclude one-off revenues from the sale of mobile telephone licenses. For more details on the methodology used for estimating the cyclical component of government balances, see *OECD Economic Outlook* Sources and Methods (*http://www.oecd.org/eco/sources-and-methods*).

1. As a percentage of mainland potential GDP. The financial balances shown are adjusted to exclude net revenues from petroleum activities.

Source: OECD Economic Outlook 89 database.

StatLink http://dx.doi.org/10.1787/888932443453

Annex Table 29. General government underlying balances
Surplus (+) or deficit (-) as a per cent of potential GDP

	1993	1994	1995	1996	1997	1998	1999	2000	2001	2002	2003	2004	2005	2006	2007	2008	2009	2010	2011	2012
Australia	-4.8	-4.9	-3.8	-2.3	-0.7	0.7	0.9	0.2	0.2	1.2	1.3	1.1	1.2	1.3	1.1	-0.5	-4.0	-4.1	-2.2	-1.2
Austria	-4.0	-4.3	-5.6	-3.7	-1.6	-2.2	-3.3	-3.5	-0.8	-1.3	-1.4	-0.5	-1.4	-2.0	-1.6	-2.3	-3.4	-3.0	-2.6	-2.4
Belgium	-5.9	-4.1	-3.8	-2.8	-1.7	-0.1	-0.6	-1.0	-0.3	-0.2	-0.9	-0.8	-0.6	-0.4	-1.0	-1.6	-3.6	-2.6	-2.9	-2.6
Canada	-6.7	-5.7	-4.6	-1.8	0.7	0.4	1.1	2.1	0.2	-0.4	-0.2	0.8	1.4	1.5	1.2	0.2	-3.5	-3.7	-3.7	-2.7
Czech Republic	..	..	..	..	..	..	-5.1	-6.0	-4.9	-4.8	-5.3	-2.4	-3.1	-3.4	-2.0	-3.4	-4.9	-3.5	-2.3	-0.7
Denmark	-1.5	-2.0	-2.5	-1.8	-0.9	-0.3	1.0	1.3	0.3	0.0	0.5	2.1	4.8	3.9	3.4	2.9	0.0	0.8	-0.3	-0.2
Estonia	..	..	..	..	..	..	..	..	0.1	0.4	1.6	1.2	0.2	-0.6	-1.4	-3.8	-1.2	-0.4	-0.9	-0.1
Finland	-2.8	-2.2	-1.6	-0.8	-1.4	1.0	1.4	5.9	4.7	4.3	3.0	2.5	2.9	3.5	4.1	3.4	0.8	0.5	0.8	1.0
France	-5.3	-4.5	-4.5	-3.4	-3.0	-2.3	-1.8	-2.4	-2.4	-3.5	-4.1	-3.5	-3.4	-2.4	-3.0	-3.2	-5.5	-4.7	-3.7	-3.2
Germany	-3.0	-2.7	-3.6	-3.5	-2.7	-2.1	-1.5	-1.7	-3.0	-3.2	-2.8	-2.5	-1.9	-1.4	-0.4	-0.4	-1.3	-2.2	-2.0	-1.6
Greece	-8.9	-7.9	-8.5	-7.0	-5.1	-3.2	-1.4	-3.8	-3.6	-3.6	-5.4	-6.5	-4.5	-7.1	-8.0	-10.5	-13.8	-6.5	-2.4	-1.4
Hungary	..	..	..	-4.8	-5.9	-6.4	-6.2	-3.6	-4.5	-8.0	-8.1	-8.2	-9.6	-11.0	-5.6	-3.8	-2.3	-2.6	-3.2	-2.3
Iceland	-3.0	-3.2	-1.8	-0.8	0.1	-1.4	-0.1	0.5	-1.7	-3.0	-2.6	-0.8	2.5	3.6	2.3	-3.1	-9.7	-4.4	-1.5	-1.0
Ireland	-1.1	0.7	-0.6	0.7	1.0	1.6	2.9	3.0	-0.2	-1.4	-0.5	0.6	0.6	1.4	-2.1	-6.1	-7.6	-7.4	-4.9	-4.0
Israel	..	..	..	..	..	..	..	-6.0	-7.1	-7.2	-6.9	-4.9	-4.3	-2.5	-2.1	-4.3	-5.5	-4.6	-3.8	-3.2
Italy	-8.6	-7.6	-6.1	-6.0	-2.7	-2.6	-0.9	-2.1	-3.3	-2.7	-4.1	-3.8	-4.2	-2.8	-2.3	-3.1	-3.6	-2.6	-2.0	-1.3
Japan	-2.9	-4.1	-4.9	-5.5	-4.9	-5.4	-6.7	-6.8	-6.1	-7.1	-6.7	-6.8	-5.3	-3.7	-3.6	-3.5	-7.2	-6.9	-6.4	-5.9
Korea	1.6	2.0	2.9	2.6	2.6	2.9	3.1	5.0	4.1	4.6	3.8	2.4	2.8	3.3	3.7	2.5	-0.4	0.3	0.6	1.2
Luxembourg	0.5	2.1	3.0	3.1	5.6	4.5	3.4	4.8	3.5	1.4	0.7	-0.4	0.1	1.3	2.3	1.9	0.9	0.7	1.3	1.8
Netherlands	-3.1	-3.3	-3.9	-2.5	-1.8	-1.9	-0.9	-0.3	-1.4	-2.5	-2.3	-0.8	0.4	0.4	-0.7	-0.6	-4.2	-3.2	-2.6	-1.7
New Zealand	-0.3	1.9	1.8	1.9	0.9	0.9	0.3	2.0	1.8	3.4	3.2	3.2	3.6	5.0	3.8	0.9	-0.9	-3.1	-5.2	-5.4
Norway[1]	-6.8	-5.5	-2.3	-2.3	-1.5	-2.4	-0.6	2.2	0.6	-1.7	-3.7	-2.1	-0.9	1.3	3.4	2.4	-0.4	-0.6	-1.5	-2.0
Poland	..	..	..	-3.4	-4.6	-4.2	-3.1	-3.9	-5.2	-4.3	-5.1	-5.2	-3.6	-3.5	-2.4	-4.0	-6.9	-7.6	-5.9	-4.1
Portugal	-7.1	-6.0	-4.4	-4.0	-3.4	-3.4	-3.2	-4.0	-5.1	-4.7	-4.8	-4.4	-4.6	-3.0	-2.8	-3.3	-7.6	-7.8	-3.4	-0.9
Spain	-4.8	-4.5	-4.8	-3.6	-2.3	-2.4	-1.6	-1.7	-1.5	-0.9	-0.5	-0.1	0.7	1.7	1.7	-2.6	-7.3	-4.9	-2.4	-1.2
Sweden	-5.8	-6.3	-6.1	-2.2	-0.3	0.3	0.4	2.4	1.2	-1.6	-1.3	-0.2	1.3	0.7	1.7	1.9	2.6	1.9	0.9	1.6
Switzerland	-3.0	-2.5	-1.7	-1.5	-2.8	-1.8	-1.0	0.8	-0.2	-0.5	-0.9	-1.1	-0.4	0.6	1.1	2.1	1.8	1.1	0.8	0.9
United Kingdom	-6.3	-6.1	-5.2	-3.9	-2.2	-0.4	0.5	0.7	0.3	-2.1	-3.8	-4.2	-4.1	-3.5	-4.1	-5.2	-8.4	-8.3	-6.9	-5.7
United States	-4.3	-3.3	-3.0	-2.1	-1.1	-0.1	0.0	0.6	-1.0	-3.8	-4.7	-4.6	-3.6	-3.0	-3.5	-5.9	-8.7	-8.6	-8.7	-8.2
Euro area	-4.9	-4.3	-4.4	-3.8	-2.6	-2.1	-1.3	-1.7	-2.3	-2.6	-2.8	-2.4	-3.0	-1.4	-1.3	-2.2	-4.2	-3.5	-2.5	-1.9
Total OECD	-4.6	-4.1	-4.0	-3.3	-2.6	-1.6	-1.3	-1.1	-2.0	-3.5	-3.9	-3.7	-3.0	-2.3	-2.4	-3.8	-6.4	-6.1	-5.7	-5.0

Note: The underlying balances are adjusted for the cycle and for one-offs. For more details, see OECD Economic Outlook Sources and Methods (http://www.oecd.org/eco/sources-and-methods).
1. As a percentage of mainland potential GDP. The financial balances shown are adjusted to exclude net revenues from petroleum activities.
Source: OECD Economic Outlook 89 database.

StatLink http://dx.doi.org/10.1787/888932443472

Annex Table 30. General government underlying primary balances
Surplus (+) or deficit (-) as a per cent of potential GDP

	1993	1994	1995	1996	1997	1998	1999	2000	2001	2002	2003	2004	2005	2006	2007	2008	2009	2010	2011	2012
Australia	-2.0	-1.4	-0.3	0.7	1.9	2.8	2.8	1.8	1.6	2.6	2.5	2.2	2.2	2.1	1.7	0.0	-3.1	-2.9	-0.7	0.6
Austria	-1.0	-1.4	-2.3	-0.3	1.6	1.0	-0.4	-0.6	1.9	1.3	0.9	1.7	0.8	0.2	0.5	-0.2	-1.3	-1.0	-0.4	0.1
Belgium	4.1	4.5	4.5	5.1	5.7	6.8	5.9	5.4	5.8	5.2	4.1	3.8	3.5	3.4	2.7	1.9	-0.3	0.5	0.3	0.9
Canada	-1.5	-0.6	1.0	3.4	5.4	5.1	5.4	5.2	3.1	2.2	1.7	2.4	2.5	2.1	1.8	0.2	-2.7	-3.1	-3.0	-1.8
Czech Republic	..	..	..	..	..	..	-4.6	-5.8	-4.5	-4.5	-4.9	-1.8	-2.4	-2.7	-1.3	-2.7	-3.9	-2.4	-1.2	0.3
Denmark	2.2	1.6	1.0	1.4	2.1	2.4	3.5	3.4	2.1	1.7	2.0	3.3	5.8	4.6	3.8	3.0	0.3	1.3	0.5	0.8
Estonia	..	..	..	..	..	..	..	..	0.0	0.3	1.3	0.9	0.0	-0.9	-1.8	-4.3	-1.3	-0.7	-1.2	-0.3
Finland	-3.2	-1.2	-0.8	0.6	0.4	2.6	2.8	6.8	5.2	4.3	2.9	2.4	2.7	3.2	3.4	2.5	0.2	0.1	0.5	0.8
France	-2.6	-1.6	-1.5	-0.2	0.1	0.7	1.0	0.3	0.4	-0.8	-1.5	-0.9	-0.9	0.0	-0.5	-0.5	-3.4	-2.5	-1.4	-0.6
Germany	-0.5	-0.1	-0.7	-0.6	0.2	0.9	1.2	1.0	-0.4	-0.7	-0.3	-0.1	0.4	1.1	2.1	2.0	0.9	-0.2	0.0	0.6
Greece	1.4	3.5	1.8	2.7	2.5	3.9	4.8	2.6	2.2	1.5	-0.8	-1.9	-0.2	-2.7	-3.5	-5.8	-8.9	-1.7	2.6	3.5
Hungary	..	..	..	2.5	1.2	-0.3	-0.2	1.1	-0.5	-4.4	-4.3	-4.1	-5.7	-7.2	-1.8	-0.1	1.4	0.7	0.2	1.1
Iceland	-1.7	-1.8	-0.4	0.6	1.2	-0.3	0.8	1.2	-1.2	-2.6	-2.0	-0.5	2.2	2.9	1.3	-3.6	-6.8	-1.2	1.8	2.6
Ireland	4.7	6.0	4.2	4.7	4.5	4.7	5.1	4.8	0.9	-0.3	0.7	1.7	1.5	2.3	-1.2	-5.3	-6.4	-5.3	-2.2	-0.4
Israel	..	..	..	..	..	..	..	-1.2	-2.5	-3.2	-2.1	-0.1	-0.1	1.4	1.9	-1.2	-2.4	-1.5	-0.6	0.0
Italy	3.1	2.8	4.5	4.6	6.0	5.1	5.4	4.1	2.8	2.7	0.9	0.9	0.3	1.7	2.5	1.9	0.5	1.4	2.3	3.3
Japan	-1.7	-2.9	-3.6	-4.1	-3.6	-3.9	-5.2	-5.3	-4.7	-5.8	-5.4	-5.6	-4.5	-3.1	-3.0	-2.6	-6.1	-5.5	-4.9	-4.2
Korea	1.1	1.5	2.3	1.9	1.7	1.8	2.2	3.8	3.1	3.6	3.0	1.5	1.8	2.0	2.2	1.2	-1.4	-0.4	-0.1	0.5
Luxembourg	-1.5	0.5	1.6	2.0	4.6	3.5	2.5	3.5	2.1	0.3	-0.2	-1.2	-0.6	0.5	1.3	0.7	0.5	0.8	1.4	2.0
Netherlands	1.2	0.8	0.5	1.9	2.4	2.1	2.7	2.7	1.0	-0.3	-0.3	1.0	2.2	2.0	1.0	1.0	-2.8	-2.0	-1.3	0.0
New Zealand	2.9	5.5	4.6	4.3	2.7	2.5	1.7	3.4	2.9	4.4	4.0	3.9	4.2	5.4	3.9	0.9	-0.7	-2.5	-4.3	-4.0
Norway[1]	-9.7	-7.7	-4.2	-4.2	-3.3	-3.7	-2.3	-0.1	-2.0	-4.4	-6.0	-4.6	-3.6	-1.8	-0.6	-1.9	-3.5	-3.3	-4.6	-5.1
Poland	..	..	1.1	0.7	-0.8	-0.5	-0.7	-1.3	-2.5	-2.2	-2.7	-2.8	-1.5	-1.4	-0.7	-2.4	-4.9	-5.5	-3.5	-1.5
Portugal	-0.3	-0.3	-0.3	0.7	0.3	-0.3	-0.2	-1.0	-2.2	-1.9	-2.2	-1.9	-2.2	-0.4	0.2	-0.2	-4.8	-4.9	0.6	3.5
Spain	-0.5	-0.3	-0.3	1.0	1.8	1.3	1.6	1.3	1.2	1.5	1.6	1.7	2.2	3.0	2.9	-1.5	-6.0	-3.5	-0.9	0.5
Sweden	-3.7	-3.4	-3.7	0.5	2.7	2.9	2.9	4.6	3.0	0.5	0.0	0.7	2.3	1.5	2.4	2.4	2.8	2.0	1.8	2.6
Switzerland	-2.3	-1.7	-0.8	-0.7	-1.9	-0.8	0.1	1.8	0.6	0.5	0.1	-0.1	0.6	1.3	1.6	2.6	2.1	1.3	1.1	1.2
United Kingdom	-4.0	-3.5	-2.2	-0.8	1.0	2.7	3.0	3.1	2.3	-0.4	-2.1	-2.5	-2.3	-1.7	-2.2	-3.4	-6.8	-5.7	-4.4	-3.0
United States	-1.0	0.0	0.5	1.3	2.2	3.0	2.8	3.1	1.2	-1.8	-2.9	-2.8	-1.8	-1.1	-1.5	-4.2	-7.3	-7.0	-6.8	-5.8
Euro area	0.0	0.3	0.3	1.0	1.8	2.1	2.3	1.8	1.0	0.5	0.1	0.4	0.6	1.2	1.4	0.5	-1.8	-1.1	0.0	0.9
Total OECD	-1.0	-0.6	-0.4	0.3	1.2	1.6	1.6	1.5	0.4	-1.2	-1.9	-1.8	-1.1	-0.4	-0.5	-2.0	-4.8	-4.4	-3.7	-2.8

Note: Adjusted for the cycle and for one-offs, and excludes the impact of net interest payments. For more details, see OECD Economic Outlook Sources and Methods (http://www.oecd.org/eco/sources-and-methods).

1. As a percentage of mainland potential GDP. The financial balances shown are adjusted to exclude net revenues from petroleum activities.

Source: OECD Economic Outlook 89 database.

StatLink http://dx.doi.org/10.1787/888932443491

Annex Table 31. General government net debt interest payments

Per cent of nominal GDP

	1993	1994	1995	1996	1997	1998	1999	2000	2001	2002	2003	2004	2005	2006	2007	2008	2009	2010	2011	2012
Australia	2.8	3.6	3.5	3.0	2.6	2.1	1.8	1.6	1.4	1.4	1.2	1.2	1.0	0.8	0.6	0.5	0.9	1.3	1.5	1.8
Austria	3.1	2.9	3.4	3.4	3.2	3.1	2.9	2.8	2.7	2.6	2.4	2.3	2.2	2.2	2.1	2.1	2.2	2.1	2.3	2.6
Belgium	10.3	8.8	8.4	8.0	7.3	7.0	6.5	6.3	6.1	5.4	5.0	4.6	4.1	3.8	3.7	3.6	3.4	3.3	3.3	3.5
Canada	5.3	5.2	5.7	5.3	4.8	4.8	4.3	3.1	2.9	2.6	1.8	1.6	1.0	0.7	0.6	0.0	0.9	0.6	0.7	0.9
Czech Republic	..	..	0.3	0.5	0.4	0.5	0.5	0.2	0.4	0.3	0.5	0.7	0.7	0.7	0.7	0.8	1.1	1.1	1.1	1.0
Denmark	3.9	3.6	3.5	3.2	2.9	2.7	2.5	2.1	1.8	1.7	1.5	1.3	0.9	0.6	0.4	0.0	0.4	0.5	0.8	1.1
Estonia	..	..	0.2	0.1	-0.1	0.1	-0.1	0.0	-0.1	-0.1	-0.3	-0.3	-0.2	-0.2	-0.3	-0.5	-0.2	-0.3	-0.3	-0.2
Finland	-0.5	1.0	0.8	1.4	1.8	1.6	1.4	0.9	0.5	0.0	-0.1	-0.1	-0.2	-0.4	-0.6	-0.9	-0.6	-0.4	-0.3	-0.2
France	2.8	2.9	3.0	3.2	3.1	3.0	2.8	2.7	2.7	2.7	2.6	2.6	2.5	2.4	2.5	2.7	2.2	2.3	2.5	2.7
Germany	2.6	2.6	2.9	2.9	2.9	3.0	2.7	2.7	2.6	2.5	2.6	2.5	2.4	2.4	2.4	2.3	2.3	2.0	2.1	2.2
Greece	10.7	11.7	10.5	9.9	7.7	7.2	6.4	6.5	5.8	5.2	4.7	4.6	4.4	4.4	4.4	4.6	5.1	5.3	5.6	5.6
Hungary	..	..	8.1	7.5	7.1	6.1	6.1	4.7	4.0	3.6	3.7	4.0	3.8	3.7	3.8	3.7	4.0	3.6	3.5	3.5
Iceland	1.4	1.5	1.5	1.4	1.1	1.0	0.9	0.7	0.5	0.3	0.6	0.3	-0.4	-0.7	-0.9	-0.5	3.0	3.5	3.5	3.8
Ireland	6.1	5.6	4.9	4.1	3.4	3.1	2.1	1.7	1.1	1.0	1.1	1.0	0.9	0.8	0.9	0.8	1.4	2.4	3.0	3.9
Israel	..	..	..	..	..	5.1	4.6	4.6	4.5	4.1	5.0	4.9	4.2	4.0	4.0	3.1	3.1	3.2	3.2	3.2
Italy	12.1	10.6	10.7	10.8	8.8	7.8	6.4	6.1	6.0	5.4	5.0	4.7	4.5	4.4	4.7	4.9	4.3	4.2	4.4	4.7
Japan	1.2	1.2	1.3	1.3	1.3	1.5	1.5	1.5	1.4	1.4	1.3	1.2	0.8	0.6	0.6	0.9	1.1	1.4	1.6	1.8
Korea	-0.5	-0.4	-0.6	-0.7	-0.9	-1.2	-1.0	-1.2	-0.9	-0.9	-0.8	-1.0	-1.0	-1.2	-1.5	-1.3	-1.0	-0.7	-0.7	-0.7
Luxembourg	-1.9	-1.6	-1.4	-1.1	-1.0	-1.0	-0.9	-1.2	-1.4	-1.1	-0.9	-0.8	-0.7	-0.7	-1.0	-1.2	-0.5	0.1	0.1	0.2
Netherlands	4.4	4.2	4.4	4.4	4.2	4.0	3.6	2.9	2.4	2.2	2.0	1.9	1.8	1.6	1.6	1.6	1.5	1.2	1.4	1.7
New Zealand	3.2	3.5	2.8	2.3	1.8	1.6	1.4	1.4	1.2	1.0	0.7	0.7	0.6	0.4	0.1	0.0	0.2	0.7	1.0	1.4
Norway	-2.5	-1.9	-1.6	-1.6	-1.4	-1.1	-1.5	-1.7	-1.9	-2.1	-1.9	-2.0	-2.0	-2.2	-3.0	-3.1	-2.5	-2.2	-2.4	-2.4
Poland	..	..	5.1	4.2	3.8	3.7	2.4	2.5	2.7	2.1	2.4	2.5	2.2	2.1	1.7	1.6	2.1	2.1	2.4	2.6
Portugal	6.9	5.9	5.6	4.8	3.7	3.1	2.9	2.9	2.9	2.8	2.7	2.6	2.4	2.7	3.0	3.1	2.9	3.0	4.2	4.8
Slovak Republic	..	..	1.3	1.6	1.8	2.1	2.9	3.1	3.1	3.0	1.7	1.4	1.1	0.5	0.7	0.6	1.0	0.9	1.0	1.1
Slovenia	..	..	1.6	1.7	2.0	1.8	1.9	1.8	1.8	1.8	1.5	1.4	1.3	1.2	1.1	0.7	1.1	1.3	1.4	1.6
Spain	4.5	4.4	4.7	4.7	4.2	3.8	3.3	2.9	2.6	2.4	2.1	1.8	1.6	1.3	1.1	1.1	1.4	1.5	1.7	1.9
Sweden	2.3	3.0	2.4	2.8	3.0	2.6	2.5	2.1	1.7	2.1	1.3	0.9	1.0	0.8	0.7	0.5	0.2	0.2	1.0	1.0
Switzerland	0.7	0.8	0.8	0.8	0.9	0.9	1.1	1.0	0.9	1.0	1.0	1.0	0.9	0.7	0.6	0.5	0.4	0.3	0.3	0.2
United Kingdom	2.4	2.6	3.1	3.1	3.2	3.0	2.5	2.4	2.0	1.7	1.7	1.7	1.8	1.7	1.8	1.8	1.6	2.6	2.6	2.9
United States	3.4	3.4	3.5	3.4	3.2	3.1	2.7	2.5	2.2	2.0	1.8	1.8	1.8	1.8	1.9	1.8	1.4	1.6	1.9	2.4
Euro area	5.0	4.7	4.8	4.9	4.4	4.2	3.7	3.5	3.3	3.1	2.9	2.8	2.7	2.6	2.6	2.6	2.5	2.4	2.6	2.8
Total OECD	3.5	3.4	3.6	3.5	3.2	3.1	2.7	2.5	2.3	2.1	2.0	1.9	1.8	1.7	1.7	1.7	1.6	1.7	1.9	2.2

Note: In the case of New Zealand where data on net interest payments are not available, net property income paid is used as a proxy. For Denmark, net interest payments include dividends received. For further information, see *OECD Economic Outlook Sources and Methods* (*http://www.oecd.org/eco/sources-and-methods*).

Source: OECD Economic Outlook 89 database.

StatLink ᐧ http://dx.doi.org/10.1787/888932443510

Annex Table 32. General government gross financial liabilities
Per cent of nominal GDP

	1993	1994	1995	1996	1997	1998	1999	2000	2001	2002	2003	2004	2005	2006	2007	2008	2009	2010	2011	2012
Australia	30.3	39.6	41.3	38.6	37.0	32.0	27.6	24.6	21.8	19.8	18.3	16.5	16.1	15.3	14.2	13.6	19.4	25.3	29.3	30.9
Austria	62.1	65.4	69.7	70.2	66.7	68.4	71.2	71.1	72.1	73.0	71.2	70.8	70.9	66.6	63.1	67.3	72.6	78.6	80.0	81.6
Belgium[1]	140.7	137.8	135.4	133.4	128.0	123.2	119.7	113.7	112.0	108.4	103.5	98.5	95.9	91.7	88.1	93.3	100.5	100.7	100.7	100.4
Canada	96.3	98.0	101.6	101.7	96.3	95.2	91.4	82.1	82.7	80.6	76.6	72.6	71.6	70.3	66.5	71.3	83.4	84.2	85.9	88.0
Czech Republic	..	..	..	..	..	..	..	..	..	32.8	34.7	34.5	34.3	33.9	33.7	36.3	42.4	46.6	49.3	50.8
Denmark	92.4	85.8	81.7	79.1	74.8	72.4	67.1	60.4	58.4	58.2	56.6	54.0	45.9	41.2	34.3	42.6	52.4	55.5	57.1	60.0
Estonia	..	..	13.3	12.3	11.3	10.0	10.9	9.4	8.9	10.2	10.8	8.5	8.2	8.0	7.3	8.3	12.4	12.1	15.2	19.2
Finland	57.8	60.9	65.3	66.2	64.8	61.2	54.9	52.5	50.0	49.6	51.5	51.5	48.4	45.5	41.4	40.6	52.1	57.4	62.7	66.1
France	51.0	60.2	62.7	66	68.8	70.3	66.8	65.6	64.3	67.3	71.4	73.9	75.7	70.9	72.3	77.8	89.2	94.1	97.3	100.0
Germany[2]	46.2	46.5	55.7	58.8	60.3	62.2	61.5	60.4	59.8	62.2	65.4	68.8	71.2	69.3	65.3	69.3	76.4	87.0	87.3	86.9
Greece	..	..	101.1	103.1	100.0	97.7	101.5	115.3	118.1	117.6	112.3	114.8	121.2	115.6	112.9	116.1	131.6	147.3	157.1	159.3
Hungary	91.6	91.4	88.1	75.6	66.0	64.0	66.3	60.8	59.1	60.2	61.3	65.0	68.5	71.7	71.8	76.3	84.7	85.6	79.8	80.8
Iceland	..	..	..	..	..	77.3	73.6	72.9	75.0	72.0	71.0	64.5	52.6	57.4	53.3	102.0	120.0	102.2	121.0	120.2
Ireland	..	..	..	..	..	62.1	51.2	39.4	36.9	35.2	34.1	32.8	32.6	28.8	28.8	49.6	71.6	102.4	120.4	125.6
Israel	..	..	..	..	..	100.9	94.9	84.5	89.0	96.6	99.2	97.4	93.5	84.3	77.7	76.7	79.2	76.1	73.5	70.1
Italy	116.3	120.9	122.5	128.9	130.3	132.6	126.4	121.6	120.8	119.4	116.8	117.3	120.0	117.4	112.8	115.2	127.8	126.8	129.0	128.4
Japan[3]	73.9	79.0	86.2	93.8	100.5	113.2	127.0	135.4	143.7	152.3	158.0	165.5	175.3	172.1	167.0	174.1	194.1	199.7	212.7	218.7
Korea[4]									19.2	19.3	22.6	24.6	27.7	27.9	29.6	32.5	33.9	33.3	33.4	
Luxembourg	..	..	9.5	10.1	10.2	11.2	10.0	9.2	8.2	8.4	7.9	8.6	7.6	12.1	11.7	16.4	14.7	19.7	20.5	23.9
Netherlands	96.5	86.7	89.6	88.1	82.2	80.8	71.6	63.9	59.4	60.3	61.4	61.9	60.7	54.5	51.5	64.5	67.6	71.4	74.3	75.2
New Zealand	..	56.8	50.7	44.3	41.7	41.6	39.0	36.9	34.9	33.0	30.9	28.2	26.9	26.6	25.7	28.9	34.5	38.7	45.8	52.0
Norway	37.8	34.6	37.9	33.6	29.7	28.0	29.1	32.7	31.6	38.8	48.2	51.0	47.9	59.4	57.4	54.9	48.0	49.5	56.1	51.2
Poland	..	..	51.6	51.5	48.4	44.0	46.8	45.4	43.7	55.0	55.3	54.8	54.7	55.2	51.7	54.5	58.4	62.4	65.6	66.3
Portugal	..	..	66.8	66.5	65.3	63.3	60.5	60.2	61.7	65.0	66.8	69.3	72.8	77.6	75.4	80.6	93.1	103.1	110.8	115.8
Slovak Republic	..	..	38.2	37.6	39.0	41.2	53.5	57.6	57.1	50.2	48.2	47.6	39.1	34.1	32.8	31.8	39.9	44.5	48.7	51.2
Slovenia	..	..	..	..	..	..	..	..	33.7	34.8	34.2	35.0	33.9	33.8	30.0	29.7	44.2	47.5	52.9	56.5
Spain	65.5	64.3	69.3	76.0	75.0	75.3	69.4	66.5	61.9	60.3	55.3	53.4	50.4	45.9	42.1	47.4	62.3	66.1	73.6	74.8
Sweden	78.2	82.5	81.1	84.4	83.0	82.0	73.2	64.3	62.7	60.2	59.3	60.0	60.8	53.9	49.3	49.6	52.0	49.1	45.4	41.1
Switzerland	42.9	45.5	47.7	50.1	52.1	54.8	51.9	52.4	51.2	57.2	57.0	57.9	56.4	50.2	46.8	43.7	41.5	40.2	38.7	37.0
United Kingdom	48.7	46.8	51.6	51.2	52.0	52.5	47.4	45.1	40.4	40.8	41.5	43.8	46.4	46.1	47.2	57.0	72.4	82.4	88.5	93.3
United States	71.9	71.1	70.7	69.9	67.4	64.2	60.5	54.5	54.4	56.8	60.2	61.2	61.4	60.8	62.0	71.0	84.3	93.6	101.1	107.0
Euro area	69.0	71.3	75.4	73.9	80.8	81.5	78.1	75.8	74.3	75.2	75.9	77.1	78.1	74.5	73.1	76.5	86.9	92.7	95.6	96.5
Total OECD	68.8	69.9	72.4	73.9	73.5	74.2	72.5	69.8	69.6	71.6	73.4	74.9	76.3	74.5	73.1	79.3	90.9	97.6	102.4	105.4

StatLink ▓▓▓ http://dx.doi.org/10.1787/888932443529

Note: Gross debt data are not always comparable across countries due to different definitions or treatment of debt components. Notably, they include the funded portion of government employee pension liabilities for some OECD countries, including Australia and the United States. The debt position of these countries is thus overstated relative to countries that have large unfunded liabilities for such pensions which according to ESA95/SNA93 are not counted in the debt figures, but rather as a memorandum item to the debt. Maastricht debt for European Union countries is shown in Annex Table 62. For more details, see OECD Economic Outlook Sources and Methods (http://www.oecd.org/eco/sources-and-methods).

For euro area countries with unsustainable fiscal positions that have asked for assistance from the European Union and the IMF (Greece, Ireland and Portugal) the change in 2010 in government financial liabilities has been approximated by the change in government liabilities recorded for the Maastricht definition of general government debt (see Box 1.3 on policy and other assumptions in chapter 1).

1. Includes the debt of the Belgium National Railways Company (SNCB) from 2005 onwards.
2. Includes the debt of the Inherited Debt Fund from 1995 onwards.
3. Includes the debt of the Japan Railway Settlement Corporation and the National Forest Special Account from 1998 onwards.
4. Data are on a non-consolidated basis (SNA93).
Source: OECD Economic Outlook 89 database.

Annex Table 33. General government net financial liabilities
Per cent of nominal GDP

	1993	1994	1995	1996	1997	1998	1999	2000	2001	2002	2003	2004	2005	2006	2007	2008	2009	2010	2011	2012
Australia	20.8	25.1	25.6	20.4	20.6	15.7	14.5	8.6	6.2	4.4	2.3	0.2	-1.4	-4.7	-7.3	-7.6	-3.8	1.8	6.1	7.6
Austria	33.3	35.2	38.8	40.3	36.5	36.7	35.8	34.8	35.6	37.0	36.1	38.0	38.0	33.9	30.8	33.6	38.6	44.0	45.7	47.2
Belgium[1]	115.1	114.5	114.6	115.5	110.9	107.8	103.1	97.5	95.0	93.3	90.3	83.9	82.0	77.2	73.3	73.9	80.1	80.8	80.8	80.5
Canada	64.2	67.9	70.7	70.0	64.7	60.8	55.8	46.2	44.3	42.6	38.7	35.2	31.0	26.3	22.9	22.4	28.4	30.4	33.7	35.8
Czech Republic	..	..	..	..	..	..	..	..	..	-16.2	-7.5	-9.7	-11.4	-11.7	-14.2	-6.0	3.7	-1.1	7.4	9.8
Denmark	32.5	32.9	33.4	33.3	32.3	35.1	28.4	22.5	20.1	19.1	18.0	14.8	10.5	1.9	-3.8	-6.6	-4.6	-1.1	2.7	5.7
Estonia	..	..	-39.2	-28.6	-23.5	-40.4	-39.8	-30.4	-28.5	-28.6	-29.1	-32.1	-31.9	-31.4	-29.6	-26.2	-29.1	-35.2	-31.9	-28.1
Finland[2]	-16.0	-16.3	-7.3	-6.7	-7.5	-14.5	-50.3	-31.1	-31.7	-31.4	-38.5	-46.7	-58.7	-69.4	-72.6	-52.4	-63.2	-63.9	-59.2	-55.9
France	26.8	29.7	37.5	41.8	42.3	40.5	33.5	35.1	36.7	41.8	44.2	45.3	43.2	37.2	34.8	42.7	49.3	56.6	60.2	62.8
Germany[3]	18.3	19.1	29.7	32.7	32.4	36.2	34.7	33.9	36.2	40.3	43.1	47.2	49.3	47.4	42.2	43.9	47.9	50.1	50.2	49.6
Greece	..	..	81.0	81.4	76.8	72.6	70.6	89.0	93.2	95.1	87.6	87.7	91.8	86.1	80.4	88.9	100.5	114.2	124.8	129.7
Hungary	-19.3	3.3	24.3	25.1	24.7	31.4	33.7	32.3	31.7	36.4	37.3	41.5	46.0	51.2	52.3	51.4	58.5	60.6	54.2	54.3
Iceland	..	..	..	..	..	42.6	35.9	37.5	29.2	28.5	30.7	27.7	13.6	7.9	-1.0	26.0	39.9	43.1	44.1	43.0
Ireland	..	..	..	..	..	42.3	27.3	15.7	12.3	13.8	11.5	8.3	6.1	1.5	-0.2	12.5	26.8	59.1	70.0	75.8
Italy	100.5	104.5	99.0	104.5	104.6	107.0	101.1	95.6	96.3	95.7	92.7	92.5	93.8	90.7	87.1	89.9	100.5	99.1	100.6	100.0
Japan[4]	17.1	19.6	23.8	29.2	34.8	46.2	53.8	60.4	66.3	72.6	76.5	82.7	84.6	84.3	81.5	96.5	110.0	116.3	127.8	133.9
Korea[5]	..	..	..	..	..	..	..	..	..	-32.3	-30.9	-31.4	-35.6	-37.0	-40.4	-37.9	-38.4	-37.3	-38.1	-39.0
Luxembourg	..	..	-37.7	-41.0	-41.6	-46.8	-47.8	-50.7	-58.2	-55.5	-56.7	-52.2	-48.6	-44.7	-44.1	-44.7	-45.6	-40.0	-36.9	-35.0
Netherlands	45.5	44.6	54.1	52.8	49.7	48.2	36.7	34.9	33.0	34.9	36.2	37.6	35.0	31.6	27.9	26.8	29.9	34.6	37.6	38.4
New Zealand	..	43.9	37.6	32.4	29.8	27.8	25.4	23.4	21.1	16.8	11.0	4.8	-1.5	-8.1	-13.1	-12.6	-8.9	-4.5	4.2	9.7
Norway	-32.0	-30.6	-36.1	-41.0	-48.5	-51.9	-57.3	-67.2	-84.4	-80.7	-95.1	-104.2	-121.5	-135.2	-141.6	-126.4	-156.0	-165.9	-161.5	-164.4
Poland	..	..	-15.0	-5.7	0.3	6.4	13.5	15.5	18.5	22.1	22.7	20.8	23.5	14.9	17.0	17.3	22.5	28.7	32.6	34.2
Portugal	..	..	24.3	26.5	31.2	32.5	30.4	28.0	29.8	34.0	36.2	41.1	44.1	50.1	49.6	54.0	64.3	68.8	75.5	80.4
Slovak Republic	..	..	-30.7	-18.2	-12.1	-3.7	1.2	12.5	10.9	1.7	1.8	7.6	4.9	6.4	7.3	8.9	17.2	20.4	24.5	26.8
Slovenia	..	..	..	..	..	..	..	..	-15.7	-14.2	-9.5	-9.7	-8.5	-9.9	-17.6	-5.7	0.1	7.2	12.6	16.2
Spain	43.5	46.4	51.6	55.5	54.2	53.7	47.7	44.2	41.5	40.3	36.8	34.6	29.5	23.2	18.7	23.3	34.8	40.2	45.7	49.0
Sweden	10.5	20.7	25.6	26.6	24.6	22.0	12.4	5.5	-2.5	3.9	0.0	-2.7	-7.9	-18.9	-22.5	-16.6	-24.4	-26.1	-25.0	-25.2
Switzerland	..	..	..	..	..	..	6.0	3.3	2.8	7.3	7.4	9.3	8.4	5.5	1.0	2.8	1.7	1.2	0.5	-0.4
United Kingdom	17.4	19.7	26.3	27.9	30.6	32.6	29.0	26.8	23.2	23.7	23.9	25.9	27.1	27.5	28.5	33.0	44.0	56.3	62.4	67.1
United States	54.9	54.4	53.8	51.9	48.8	44.9	40.2	35.3	34.6	37.2	40.5	42.1	42.5	41.7	42.6	48.2	59.8	67.3	74.8	80.7
Euro area	42.8	44.3	49.0	53.4	53.3	53.9	48.5	47.5	48.1	50.4	50.5	51.4	50.7	46.6	42.5	46.6	53.6	57.5	60.0	61.0
Total OECD	40.5	41.8	43.3	44.2	43.5	44.0	40.5	38.2	37.8	40.0	41.4	42.5	42.2	40.0	38.2	43.5	52.1	57.7	62.6	65.8

Note: Net debt measures are not always comparable across countries due to different definitions or treatment of debt (and asset) components. First, the treatment of government liabilities with respect to their employee pension plans may be different (see note to Annex Table 32). Second, the range of items included as general government assets differs across countries. For example, equity holdings are excluded from government assets in some countries whereas foreign exchange, gold and SDR holdings are considered as assets in the United States and the United Kingdom. For details, see OECD Economic Outlook Sources and Methods (http://www.oecd.org/eco/sources-and-methods).
For euro area countries with unsustainable fiscal positions that have asked for assistance from the European Union and the IMF (Greece, Ireland and Portugal) the change in 2010 in government financial liabilities has been approximated by the change in government liabilities recorded for the Maastricht definition of general government debt (see Box 1.3 on policy and other assumptions in chapter 1).

1. Includes the debt of the Belgium National Railways Company (SNCB) from 2005 onwards.
2. From 1995 onwards housing corporation shares are no longer classified as financial assets.
3. Includes the debt of the Inherited Debt Fund from 1995 onwards.
4. Includes the debt of the Japan Railway Settlement Corporation and the National Forest Special Account from 1998 onwards.
5. Data are on a non-consolidated basis (SNA93).
Source: OECD Economic Outlook 89 database.

StatLink ═╗ http://dx.doi.org/10.1787/888932443548

Annex Table 34. Short-term interest rates
Per cent, per annum

	1996	1997	1998	1999	2000	2001	2002	2003	2004	2005	2006	2007	2008	2009	2010	2011	2012	Fourth quarter 2010	Fourth quarter 2011	Fourth quarter 2012
Australia	7.2	5.4	5.0	5.0	6.2	4.9	4.7	4.9	5.5	5.6	6.0	6.7	7.0	3.4	4.7	5.1	5.6	5.0	5.4	5.6
Austria	3.4	3.5	3.6	3.0																
Belgium	3.2	3.4	3.6	3.0																
Canada	4.5	3.6	5.1	4.9	5.7	4.0	2.6	3.0	2.4	2.8	4.1	4.6	3.5	0.8	0.8	1.6	3.1	1.2	2.2	3.4
Chile	..	..	16.4	11.0	10.8	7.2	3.9	2.8	1.8	3.5	4.8	5.2	7.3	1.7	1.9	4.9	6.5	3.3	6.2	6.5
Czech Republic	12.0	15.9	14.3	6.9	5.4	5.2	3.5	2.3	2.4	2.0	2.3	3.1	4.0	2.2	1.3	1.5	2.3	1.2	1.7	2.7
Denmark	3.9	3.7	4.1	3.3	4.9	4.6	3.5	2.4	2.1	2.2	3.1	4.3	4.9	1.8	0.7	1.2	2.0	0.8	1.5	2.3
Estonia	8.0	8.6	13.9	7.8	5.7	5.3	3.9	2.9	2.5	2.4	3.2	4.9	6.7	5.9	1.6			1.1	1.5	2.3
Finland	3.6	3.2	3.6	3.0																
France	3.9	3.5	3.6	3.0																
Germany	3.3	3.3	3.5	3.0																
Greece	12.8	10.4	11.6	8.9	6.1															
Hungary	24.0	20.1	18.0	14.7	11.0	10.8	8.9	8.2	11.3	7.0	6.9	7.6	8.9	8.5	5.4	5.9	5.8	5.4	5.9	5.7
Iceland	7.0	7.1	7.5	9.3	11.2	12.0	9.0	5.3	6.3	9.4	12.4	14.3	15.8	11.3	6.8	4.2	4.4	4.8	4.2	4.5
Ireland	5.4	6.1	5.4	3.0																
Israel	15.7	13.8	11.9	12.0	9.0	6.5	7.2	6.6	4.3	3.9	5.5	4.3	3.6	0.6	1.6	3.6	5.3	2.0	4.7	5.5
Italy	8.8	6.9	5.0	3.0																
Japan	0.6	0.6	0.7	0.2	0.2	0.1	0.1	0.0	0.0	0.0	0.2	0.7	0.7	0.3	0.2	0.3	0.2	0.1	0.2	0.2
Korea	12.6	13.4	15.2	6.8	7.1	5.3	4.8	4.3	3.8	3.6	4.5	5.2	5.5	2.6	2.7	3.6	4.7	2.7	4.2	4.8
Luxembourg	3.2	3.4	3.6	3.0																
Mexico	32.9	21.3	26.2	22.4	16.2	12.2	7.4	6.5	7.1	9.3	7.3	7.4	7.9	5.5	4.6	4.6	5.6	4.4	4.9	6.0
Netherlands	3.0	3.3	3.5	3.0																
New Zealand	9.3	7.7	7.3	4.8	6.5	5.7	5.7	5.4	6.1	7.1	7.5	8.3	8.0	3.0	3.0	2.8	4.1	3.2	2.8	4.8
Norway	4.9	3.7	5.8	6.5	6.7	7.2	6.9	4.1	2.0	2.2	3.1	5.0	6.2	2.5	2.5	2.9	4.0	2.6	3.3	4.5
Poland	21.3	23.1	19.9	14.7	18.9	15.7	8.8	5.7	6.2	5.2	4.2	4.8	6.3	4.3	3.9	4.9	5.6	3.9	5.6	5.6
Portugal	7.4	5.7	4.3	3.0																
Slovak Republic	12.0	22.4	21.1	15.7	8.6	7.8	7.8	6.2	4.7	2.9	4.3	4.3	4.2							
Slovenia	..	..	..	..	..	..	8.0	6.8	4.7	4.0	3.6									
Spain	7.5	5.4	4.2	3.0																
Sweden	5.8	4.1	4.2	3.1	4.0	4.1	4.1	3.0	2.1	1.7	2.3	3.6	3.9	0.4	0.5	1.9	3.0	1.1	2.3	3.4
Switzerland	2.0	1.6	1.5	1.4	3.2	2.9	1.1	0.3	0.5	0.8	1.6	2.6	2.5	0.4	0.2	0.4	1.2	0.2	0.6	1.6
Turkey	..	..	..	..	38.4	92.4	59.5	38.5	23.8	15.9	17.9	18.2	18.8	11.0	7.8	8.8	10.1	7.5	9.3	10.5
United Kingdom	6.0	6.8	7.3	5.4	6.1	5.0	4.0	3.7	4.6	4.7	4.8	6.0	5.5	1.2	0.7	0.9	1.6	0.8	1.1	2.3
United States	5.4	5.7	5.5	5.4	6.5	3.7	1.8	1.2	1.6	3.5	5.2	5.3	3.2	0.9	0.5	0.8	1.9	0.4	1.3	2.5
Euro area	5.0	4.5	4.1	3.1	4.4	4.3	3.4	2.4	2.1	2.2	3.1	4.3	4.6	1.2	0.8	1.3	2.0	1.0	1.5	2.3

Note: Three-month money market rates where available, or rates on similar financial instruments. For further information, see OECD Economic Outlook Sources and Methods (http://www.oecd.org/eco/sources-and-methods). Individual euro area countries are not shown after 1998 (2000 for Greece, 2007 for Slovenia, 2008 for the Slovak Republic and 2011 for Estonia) since their short-term interest rates are equal to the euro area rate.

Source: OECD Economic Outlook 89 database.

StatLink http://dx.doi.org/10.1787/88932443567

Annex Table 35. Long-term interest rates
Per cent, per annum

	1996	1997	1998	1999	2000	2001	2002	2003	2004	2005	2006	2007	2008	2009	2010	2011	2012	Fourth quarter 2010	Fourth quarter 2011	Fourth quarter 2012
Australia	8.2	7.0	5.5	6.0	6.3	5.6	5.8	5.4	5.6	5.3	5.6	6.0	5.8	5.0	5.4	5.7	5.9	5.3	5.9	5.9
Austria	6.3	5.7	4.7	4.7	5.6	5.1	5.0	4.2	4.2	3.4	3.8	4.3	4.4	3.9	3.2	3.7	4.3	3.1	3.9	4.5
Belgium	6.3	5.6	4.7	4.7	5.6	5.1	4.9	4.1	4.1	3.4	3.8	4.3	4.4	3.8	3.3	4.2	4.8	3.5	4.3	5.0
Canada	7.2	6.1	5.3	5.5	5.9	5.5	5.3	4.8	4.6	4.1	4.2	4.3	3.6	3.2	3.2	3.4	4.2	3.0	3.6	4.5
Chile	..	..	..	..	..	..	..	..	..	6.0	6.1	6.1	7.0	5.7	6.3	7.0	7.7	6.1	7.2	7.7
Czech Republic	..	..	..	..	..	6.3	4.9	4.1	4.8	3.5	3.8	4.3	4.6	4.8	3.9	4.2	5.0	3.6	4.5	5.3
Denmark	7.2	6.3	5.0	4.9	5.7	5.1	5.1	4.3	4.3	3.4	3.8	4.3	4.3	3.6	2.9	3.6	4.3	2.7	3.9	4.5
Finland	7.1	6.0	4.8	4.7	5.5	5.0	5.0	4.1	4.1	3.4	3.8	4.3	4.3	3.7	3.0	3.6	4.3	2.9	3.9	4.5
France	6.3	5.6	4.6	4.6	5.4	4.9	4.9	4.1	4.1	3.4	3.8	4.3	4.2	3.6	3.1	3.7	4.4	3.0	3.9	4.6
Germany	6.2	5.7	4.6	4.5	5.3	4.8	4.8	4.1	4.0	3.4	3.8	4.2	4.0	3.2	2.7	3.3	4.0	2.6	3.6	4.2
Greece	..	9.9	8.5	6.3	6.1	5.3	5.1	4.3	4.3	3.6	4.1	4.5	4.8	5.2	9.1	13.5	11.3	11.0	14.2	9.5
Hungary	..	..	..	..	8.6	7.9	7.1	6.8	8.3	6.6	7.1	6.7	8.2	9.1	7.3	7.3	6.5	7.4	7.2	6.5
Iceland	9.2	8.7	7.7	8.5	11.2	10.4	8.0	6.7	7.5	7.7	9.3	9.8	11.1	8.0	5.0	3.4	4.5	3.8	3.7	5.0
Ireland	7.2	6.3	4.7	4.8	5.5	5.0	5.0	4.1	4.1	3.3	3.8	4.3	4.6	5.2	6.0	9.6	8.3	8.4	9.8	7.3
Israel	..	4.1	4.9	5.2	5.5	4.8	5.3	4.7	7.6	6.4	6.3	5.6	5.9	5.1	4.7	5.4	6.0	4.5	5.8	6.1
Italy	9.4	6.9	4.9	4.7	5.6	5.2	5.0	4.3	4.3	3.6	4.0	4.5	4.7	4.3	4.0	4.8	5.4	4.2	5.0	5.6
Japan	3.1	2.4	1.5	1.7	1.7	1.3	1.3	1.0	1.5	1.4	1.7	1.7	1.5	1.3	1.1	1.3	1.8	1.1	1.5	2.0
Korea	10.9	11.7	12.8	8.7	8.5	6.9	6.6	5.0	4.7	5.0	5.2	5.4	5.6	5.2	4.8	5.2	5.4	4.4	5.4	5.4
Luxembourg	6.3	5.6	4.7	4.7	5.5	4.9	4.7	3.3	2.8	2.4	3.3	4.5	4.6	4.2	3.2	3.7	4.4	3.0	4.0	4.7
Mexico	34.4	22.4	24.8	24.1	16.9	13.8	8.5	7.4	7.7	9.3	7.5	7.6	8.1	5.8	4.9	5.0	5.8	4.7	5.3	6.2
Netherlands	6.2	5.6	4.6	4.6	5.4	5.0	4.9	4.1	4.1	3.4	3.8	4.3	4.2	3.7	3.0	3.6	4.2	2.8	3.8	4.5
New Zealand	7.9	7.2	6.3	6.4	6.9	6.4	6.5	5.9	6.1	5.9	5.8	6.3	6.1	5.5	5.6	5.5	5.8	5.5	5.6	6.0
Norway	6.8	5.9	5.4	5.5	6.2	6.2	6.4	5.0	4.4	3.7	4.1	4.8	4.5	4.0	3.5	4.0	4.6	3.4	4.2	4.8
Portugal	8.6	6.4	4.9	4.8	5.6	5.2	5.0	4.2	4.1	3.4	3.9	4.4	4.5	4.2	5.4	8.7	7.9	6.5	9.4	7.1
Slovak Republic	9.7	9.4	21.7	16.2	9.8	8.0	6.9	5.0	5.0	3.5	4.4	4.5	4.7	4.7	3.9	4.4	5.1	3.8	4.7	5.3
Slovenia	..	..	..	..	..	..	..	6.4	4.7	3.8	3.9	4.5	4.6	4.4	3.8	4.5	5.1	3.8	4.7	5.5
Spain	8.7	6.4	4.8	4.7	5.5	5.1	5.0	4.1	4.1	3.4	3.8	4.3	4.4	4.0	4.2	5.3	5.6	4.7	5.5	5.6
Sweden	8.1	6.7	5.0	5.0	5.4	5.1	5.3	4.6	4.4	3.4	3.7	4.2	3.9	3.2	2.9	3.5	4.1	2.9	3.7	4.3
Switzerland	4.0	3.4	3.0	3.0	3.9	3.4	3.2	2.7	2.7	2.1	2.5	2.9	2.9	2.2	1.6	2.2	3.0	1.6	2.5	3.3
Turkey	..	..	..	..	36.9	95.2	65.0	46.5	25.2	16.5	17.9	18.3	19.2	11.6	8.4	8.8	10.1	7.6	9.3	10.6
United Kingdom	7.8	7.1	5.6	5.1	5.3	4.9	4.9	4.5	4.9	4.4	4.5	5.0	4.6	3.6	3.6	3.8	4.5	3.3	4.0	4.9
United States	6.4	6.4	5.3	5.6	6.0	5.0	4.6	4.0	4.3	4.3	4.8	4.6	3.7	3.3	3.2	3.5	4.6	2.9	3.8	5.1
Euro area	7.2	6.0	4.8	4.7	5.4	5.0	4.9	4.2	4.1	3.4	3.8	4.3	4.3	3.8	3.6	4.4	4.9	3.7	4.6	5.0

Note: 10-year benchmark government bond yields where available or yield on similar financial instruments (for Korea a 5-year bond is used). For further information, see also *OECD Economic Outlook Sources and Methods* (http://www.oecd.org/eco/sources-and-methods).

Source: OECD Economic Outlook 89 database.

StatLink http://dx.doi.org/10.1787/888932443586

Annex Table 36. Nominal exchange rates (*vis-à-vis* the US dollar)
Average of daily rates

	Monetary unit	1999	2000	2001	2002	2003	2004	2005	2006	2007	2008	2009	Estimates and assumptions[1] 2010	2011	2012
Australia	Dollar	1.550	1.727	1.935	1.841	1.542	1.359	1.313	1.328	1.195	1.198	1.282	1.090	0.949	0.933
Austria	Schilling	12.91													
Belgium	Franc	37.86													
Canada	Dollar	1.486	1.485	1.548	1.570	1.400	1.301	1.212	1.134	1.074	1.068	1.141	1.030	0.970	0.966
Chile	Peso	508.8	539.5	634.9	688.9	691.4	609.5	559.8	530.3	522.5	523.5	558.9	510.0	471.5	468.0
Czech Republic	Koruny	34.59	38.64	38.02	32.73	28.13	25.69	23.95	22.59	20.29	17.08	19.05	19.08	17.01	16.749
Denmark	Krone	6.980	8.088	8.321	7.884	6.577	5.988	5.996	5.943	5.443	5.099	5.359	5.622	5.244	5.180
Estonia	Krone	0.938	1.084	1.117	1.062	0.885	0.804	0.804	0.797	0.731	0.684	0.720	0.755	0.731	0.731
Finland	Markka	5.580													
France	Franc	6.157													
Germany	Deutschemark	1.836													
Greece	Drachma	305.7													
Hungary	Forint	237.1	282.3	286.5	257.9	224.3	202.6	199.5	210.4	183.6	172.5	202.1	207.8	187.5	183.8
Iceland	Krona	72.43	78.84	97.67	91.59	76.69	70.19	62.88	69.90	64.07	88.00	123.66	122.24	113.75	112.98
Ireland	Pound	0.739													
Israel	Sheqel	4.14	4.08	4.21	4.74	4.55	4.48	4.49	4.46	4.11	3.58	3.93	3.73	3.49	3.46
Italy	Lira	1 817													
Japan	Yen	113.9	107.8	121.5	125.3	115.9	108.1	110.1	116.4	117.8	103.4	93.6	87.8	81.0	80.3
Korea	Won	1 186.7	1 130.6	1 290.4	1 251.0	1 191.0	1 145.2	1 024.2	954.7	929.5	1 100.9	1 274.9	1 155.4	1 093.1	1 085.1
Luxembourg	Franc	37.86													
Mexico	Peso	9.553	9.453	9.344	9.660	10.790	11.281	10.890	10.903	10.929	11.153	13.504	12.632	11.734	11.615
Netherlands	Guilder	2.068													
New Zealand	Dollar	1.892	2.205	2.382	2.163	1.724	1.509	1.421	1.542	1.361	1.425	1.600	1.388	1.274	1.256
Norway	Krone	7.797	8.797	8.993	7.986	7.078	6.739	6.441	6.415	5.858	5.648	6.290	6.044	5.541	5.494
Poland	Zloty	3.964	4.346	4.097	4.082	3.888	3.651	3.234	3.103	2.765	2.410	3.119	3.015	2.774	2.740
Portugal	Escudo	188.2													
Slovak Republic	Koruna	41.36	46.23	48.35	45.30	36.76	32.23	31.04	29.65	24.68					
Slovenia	Tolar	181.7	222.7	242.8	240.3	207.1	192.3	192.8	191.0						
Spain	Peseta	156.2													
Sweden	Krona	8.262	9.161	10.338	9.721	8.078	7.346	7.472	7.373	6.758	6.597	7.653	7.202	6.302	6.252
Switzerland	Franc	1.503	1.688	1.687	1.557	1.345	1.243	1.246	1.253	1.200	1.084	1.086	1.043	0.894	0.876
Turkey	Lira	0.419	0.624	1.228	1.512	1.503	1.426	1.341	1.430	1.300	1.299	1.547	1.499	1.543	1.536
United Kingdom	Pound	0.618	0.661	0.694	0.667	0.612	0.546	0.550	0.543	0.500	0.546	0.641	0.647	0.614	0.610
United States	Dollar	1.000	1.000	1.000	1.000	1.000	1.000	1.000	1.000	1.000	1.000	1.000	1.000	1.000	1.000
Euro area	Euro	0.938	1.084	1.118	1.060	0.885	0.806	0.805	0.797	0.730	0.681	0.718	0.754	0.703	0.695

1. On the technical assumption that exchange rates remain at their levels of 6 May 2011.

Source: OECD Economic Outlook 89 database.

StatLink http://dx.doi.org/10.1787/888932443605

Annex Table 37. Effective exchange rates
Indices 2005 = 100, average of daily rates

	1997	1998	1999	2000	2001	2002	2003	2004	2005	2006	2007	2008	2009	Estimates and assumptions[1] 2010	2011	2012
Australia	96.0	89.0	89.4	83.0	77.7	80.8	90.3	97.5	100.0	98.6	104.8	102.6	98.0	111.3	121.0	122.3
Austria	95.0	96.9	97.2	95.0	95.4	96.2	99.6	100.7	100.0	100.1	100.8	101.3	102.3	99.8	99.7	99.8
Belgium	92.4	94.7	94.4	90.6	91.7	93.6	98.6	100.4	100.0	100.2	101.6	103.7	104.6	101.4	102.1	102.3
Canada	87.1	82.9	82.7	83.5	81.0	79.7	88.1	93.5	100.0	106.6	111.3	110.7	104.8	115.1	119.9	120.1
Chile	119.5	115.6	107.8	105.0	94.0	92.0	86.8	94.5	100.0	103.6	100.6	98.2	95.3	102.8	106.1	106.3
Czech Republic	78.5	79.7	79.2	80.1	84.2	93.9	93.8	94.1	100.0	105.0	107.4	119.7	114.9	117.3	122.7	123.2
Denmark	94.1	96.5	95.8	91.8	93.4	94.9	99.5	100.9	100.0	99.9	101.2	103.2	105.7	101.6	101.2	101.5
Estonia	80.7	85.7	93.7	91.4	92.8	94.8	99.3	100.8	100.0	99.8	100.9	102.4	106.1	101.8	101.3	101.4
Finland	88.6	91.4	93.9	89.6	91.5	93.5	98.9	100.8	100.0	99.9	101.6	103.7	106.0	100.9	100.9	101.2
France	93.7	96.1	95.4	91.8	92.7	94.3	99.0	100.5	100.0	100.1	101.5	103.2	103.9	101.0	101.5	101.7
Germany	91.2	94.5	94.4	90.2	91.3	93.2	99.0	101.1	100.0	100.1	101.6	103.0	104.6	100.6	100.9	101.1
Greece	101.4	98.1	98.3	91.6	92.5	94.4	99.2	100.9	100.0	100.0	101.3	103.2	104.2	101.1	101.7	101.9
Hungary	108.8	98.4	94.7	89.7	91.4	97.8	97.4	99.5	100.0	93.7	99.2	99.6	90.6	89.5	92.6	93.5
Iceland	91.8	94.2	95.5	96.3	82.1	84.8	89.0	89.9	100.0	89.7	90.7	65.8	47.7	48.9	49.1	48.9
Ireland	98.6	96.0	93.3	86.8	87.9	90.1	97.9	100.2	100.0	100.2	102.6	107.9	110.1	105.9	107.3	107.8
Israel	126.3	120.3	113.3	122.9	124.3	109.1	104.9	101.1	100.0	100.3	103.7	115.6	109.9	115.2	118.0	118.3
Italy	92.9	94.9	94.6	91.0	92.3	94.3	99.1	100.8	100.0	100.1	101.4	102.9	104.1	100.7	101.1	101.3
Japan	83.9	86.4	99.4	108.0	99.5	95.6	98.9	103.1	100.0	92.6	87.5	97.5	111.2	115.9	119.6	120.0
Korea	106.6	76.7	88.3	94.5	87.3	90.3	89.8	89.8	100.0	107.4	106.8	86.0	73.4	78.8	78.9	78.9
Luxembourg	97.0	97.7	97.5	94.7	95.1	96.2	99.5	100.6	100.0	100.2	101.6	102.8	102.4	100.6	101.2	101.4
Mexico	136.9	121.6	116.1	118.6	122.0	118.5	103.4	97.2	100.0	99.3	97.3	94.6	78.7	83.3	87.6	88.3
Netherlands	90.4	93.6	93.3	88.3	89.6	91.8	98.2	100.7	100.0	100.1	102.0	104.0	104.6	100.5	101.2	101.5
New Zealand	93.8	83.8	81.1	73.4	72.3	78.4	89.3	95.5	100.0	92.4	98.8	92.4	84.8	91.5	92.6	93.0
Norway	95.5	92.6	92.3	90.2	93.2	101.2	99.1	95.8	100.0	99.5	101.0	100.9	97.8	101.9	102.9	102.8
Poland	102.3	100.3	93.4	96.1	105.9	101.5	91.4	89.5	100.0	103.1	106.8	116.3	95.5	100.9	102.1	102.3
Portugal	98.1	98.0	97.5	95.1	96.0	97.1	99.8	100.5	100.0	100.0	100.8	101.9	102.5	100.3	100.7	100.8
Slovak Republic	97.0	96.3	89.2	90.6	88.5	88.9	94.0	98.1	100.0	103.1	113.6	122.6	131.3	127.1	126.6	126.6
Slovenia	117.0	118.5	117.4	107.6	102.3	100.1	101.7	101.3	100.0	99.8	101.0	102.2	104.5	101.1	101.4	101.6
Spain	94.6	96.1	95.6	92.5	93.6	95.4	99.3	100.5	100.0	100.2	101.3	102.9	104.0	101.3	101.7	101.9
Sweden	101.1	101.0	100.7	100.9	92.7	95.1	100.7	102.5	100.0	100.4	101.6	99.6	91.4	98.7	105.5	105.2
Switzerland	86.9	91.2	91.9	90.1	93.8	98.7	100.4	100.8	100.0	98.6	96.1	101.6	107.2	113.7	124.7	126.0
Turkey	910.1	548.7	361.9	263.0	148.1	110.3	97.4	95.0	100.0	93.2	95.3	91.4	81.4	84.7	77.1	76.7
United Kingdom	91.3	97.2	97.7	100.0	99.1	100.6	96.9	101.5	100.0	100.6	102.4	89.5	79.5	79.3	78.7	78.5
United States	95.9	105.5	105.2	107.7	113.3	113.9	107.3	102.6	100.0	98.3	94.0	90.6	95.7	92.2	86.7	86.0
Euro area	85.7	90.6	89.7	81.5	83.5	87.0	97.7	101.6	100.0	100.2	103.4	107.1	109.6	102.0	102.8	103.3

StatLink http://dx.doi.org/10.1787/888932443624

Note: For details on the method of calculation, see the section on exchange rates and competitiveness indicators in *OECD Economic Outlook Sources and Methods* (http://www.oecd.org/eco/sources-and-methods).
1. On the technical assumption that exchange rates remain at their levels of 6 May 2011.
Source: OECD Economic Outlook 89 database.

Annex Table 38. Export volumes of goods and services
National accounts basis, percentage changes from previous year

	1993	1994	1995	1996	1997	1998	1999	2000	2001	2002	2003	2004	2005	2006	2007	2008	2009	2010	2011	2012
Australia	8.3	8.8	5.0	10.4	12.6	0.4	4.5	11.0	2.9	0.7	-2.0	4.2	2.8	2.3	2.5	4.7	2.8	5.2	6.1	7.5
Austria	-2.0	5.8	7.0	4.3	12.3	8.3	6.3	13.3	6.3	3.8	1.6	10.0	7.6	7.7	8.6	0.5	-15.6	10.6	9.6	6.8
Belgium	-0.4	8.3	5.0	3.3	10.3	4.8	4.3	12.0	1.0	2.7	0.8	6.3	5.0	5.0	4.3	1.4	-11.4	10.6	6.9	6.2
Canada	10.8	12.7	8.5	5.6	8.3	9.1	10.7	8.9	-3.0	1.2	-2.3	5.0	1.9	0.6	1.2	-4.6	-14.2	6.4	8.4	7.9
Chile	..	..	..	11.8	11.2	5.2	7.3	5.1	7.2	1.6	6.5	13.3	4.3	5.1	7.6	3.2	-6.4	1.9	7.8	7.3
Czech Republic	..	0.2	16.7	5.7	8.4	10.4	5.0	17.3	11.2	2.0	7.2	20.3	11.8	16.2	15.0	5.7	-10.5	17.6	9.4	9.5
Denmark	1.0	8.4	3.1	4.2	4.9	4.1	11.6	12.7	3.1	4.1	-1.0	2.8	8.0	9.0	2.8	2.8	-9.7	3.6	5.2	4.9
Estonia	..	..	..	0.3	26.4	13.4	0.4	27.4	0.4	-1.0	7.4	14.6	18.6	6.7	1.5	0.4	-18.7	21.7	20.0	8.6
Finland	16.4	13.4	8.7	5.8	14.0	9.4	10.9	17.3	1.7	3.3	-1.8	8.1	7.0	12.2	8.2	6.5	-20.3	5.0	8.2	6.0
France[1]	0.5	8.2	8.5	3.3	13.1	8.4	4.2	13.0	2.5	1.4	-1.2	3.5	3.5	5.0	2.5	-0.8	-12.6	9.5	6.6	7.7
Germany	-4.8	8.1	6.7	6.2	11.8	7.4	5.6	14.2	6.8	4.3	2.4	9.2	8.0	13.5	7.9	2.0	-14.3	13.8	10.4	7.7
Greece	-2.6	7.4	3.0	3.5	20.0	5.3	18.1	14.1	0.0	-8.4	2.9	17.3	2.5	5.3	5.8	4.0	-20.1	3.8	9.4	9.4
Hungary	..	..	..	11.1	21.0	16.5	11.1	19.7	8.0	3.8	6.2	15.0	11.3	18.6	16.2	5.7	-9.6	14.1	9.1	10.5
Iceland	6.5	9.3	-2.3	9.9	5.6	2.5	4.0	4.2	7.4	3.8	1.6	8.4	7.5	-4.6	17.7	7.0	7.0	1.1	2.7	3.3
Ireland	9.7	15.1	20.0	12.5	17.6	23.1	15.5	20.2	8.7	5.2	0.5	7.5	4.7	4.9	8.2	-0.8	-4.2	9.4	5.3	6.6
Israel	..	..	..	5.9	9.1	6.8	14.2	22.9	-10.5	-2.0	8.1	17.6	4.2	5.9	9.3	5.9	-11.7	13.6	7.1	8.7
Italy	8.7	10.6	12.7	0.6	5.7	1.7	-0.6	13.0	2.2	-2.8	-1.5	3.6	2.0	6.6	4.0	-4.4	-18.4	8.9	6.9	6.9
Japan	0.4	3.9	4.2	5.9	11.1	-2.7	1.9	12.7	-6.9	7.5	9.2	13.9	7.0	9.7	8.4	1.6	-23.9	23.9	3.2	8.2
Korea	7.9	16.4	24.7	11.6	19.8	12.9	14.4	18.1	-3.4	12.1	14.5	19.7	7.8	11.4	12.6	6.6	-1.2	14.5	11.7	11.2
Luxembourg	4.8	7.7	4.6	2.3	11.4	11.2	14.2	12.6	4.5	2.1	6.8	11.1	4.5	13.0	9.1	6.6	-8.2	6.3	6.3	6.1
Mexico	8.1	17.7	30.2	18.2	10.6	12.3	12.3	16.3	-3.5	1.4	2.7	11.5	6.7	11.0	5.7	0.7	-14.0	24.5	4.9	8.6
Netherlands	4.0	8.7	9.2	4.4	10.9	6.8	8.7	13.5	1.9	0.9	1.5	7.9	6.0	7.3	6.4	2.8	-7.9	10.9	6.7	6.7
New Zealand	4.8	9.9	3.8	3.8	3.9	1.5	7.9	7.0	3.3	6.4	2.3	6.2	-0.5	1.7	3.9	-1.7	1.7	3.0	3.1	5.8
Norway	3.1	8.4	5.0	10.0	7.8	0.7	2.8	3.2	4.3	-0.3	-0.2	1.1	1.1	0.0	2.3	1.0	-4.0	-1.3	0.7	3.1
Poland	..	13.1	22.9	10.9	13.3	14.3	-2.6	22.2	4.2	4.8	14.0	12.8	9.2	14.8	9.1	5.9	-6.0	10.1	5.4	6.7
Portugal	-3.3	8.4	8.8	7.2	7.1	8.3	3.8	8.8	1.8	2.8	3.6	4.1	0.2	11.6	7.6	-0.1	-11.6	8.8	6.4	7.4
Slovak Republic	..	14.8	4.5	-1.4	10.0	21.0	12.2	8.9	6.9	5.2	15.9	7.4	10.0	21.0	14.3	3.1	-15.9	16.4	10.4	7.8
Slovenia	..	..	..	..	11.1	7.5	1.6	13.1	6.4	6.8	3.1	12.4	10.6	12.5	13.7	3.3	-17.7	7.8	5.6	6.8
Spain	7.8	16.7	9.4	10.3	15.0	8.0	7.5	10.2	4.2	2.0	3.7	4.2	2.5	6.7	6.7	-1.1	-11.6	10.3	9.9	8.7
Sweden	8.3	13.3	11.7	4.5	14.1	8.8	6.7	11.9	0.8	1.3	4.4	10.0	6.6	9.4	5.9	1.3	-13.3	10.4	7.9	6.5
Switzerland	1.4	1.9	0.6	3.7	11.2	4.3	6.5	12.5	0.5	-0.1	-0.5	7.9	7.8	10.3	9.6	3.3	-8.7	9.3	3.3	5.7
Turkey	7.7	15.2	8.0	22.0	19.1	12.0	-10.7	16.0	3.9	6.9	6.9	11.2	7.9	6.6	7.3	2.7	-5.0	3.4	9.1	9.8
United Kingdom	4.5	9.2	9.4	8.8	8.1	3.1	3.7	9.1	3.0	1.0	1.8	5.0	7.9	11.1	-2.6	1.0	-10.1	5.3	8.0	6.1
United States[1]	3.3	8.7	10.1	8.3	11.9	2.3	4.4	8.6	-5.6	-2.0	1.6	9.5	6.7	9.0	9.3	6.0	-9.5	11.7	7.5	8.9
Total OECD	2.7	8.9	9.0	6.6	11.3	5.4	5.5	12.1	0.0	1.9	2.5	8.5	6.0	8.7	6.4	2.0	-11.7	11.3	7.5	7.7

Note: Regional aggregates are calculated inclusive of intra-regional trade as the sum of volumes expressed in 2005 $.
1. Volume data use hedonic price deflators for certain components.
Source: OECD Economic Outlook 89 database.

StatLink http://dx.doi.org/10.1787/888932443643

Annex Table 39. Import volumes of goods and services
National accounts basis, percentage changes from previous year

	1993	1994	1995	1996	1997	1998	1999	2000	2001	2002	2003	2004	2005	2006	2007	2008	2009	2010	2011	2012
Australia	4.7	14.1	8.3	8.0	10.4	6.7	8.4	7.4	-4.6	11.2	10.6	15.1	8.6	7.1	12.5	11.3	-9.1	13.4	8.4	9.2
Austria	-3.6	8.7	6.5	4.1	7.8	5.1	5.1	10.2	5.3	0.3	4.0	9.4	7.1	5.5	6.5	-1.7	-12.5	7.5	7.7	6.0
Belgium	-0.4	7.3	4.7	3.8	9.1	5.6	2.6	12.4	0.0	0.9	0.8	6.3	6.4	4.6	4.4	2.8	-10.9	8.4	6.9	6.1
Canada	7.4	8.1	5.7	5.1	14.2	5.1	7.8	8.1	-5.1	1.7	4.1	8.0	7.1	4.9	5.9	1.2	-13.9	13.4	6.8	7.1
Chile	..	..	..	11.8	13.2	6.7	-9.5	10.1	4.1	2.3	9.7	18.4	17.2	10.6	14.5	12.6	-14.6	29.5	12.7	10.1
Czech Republic	..	7.8	21.2	12.2	6.9	8.4	4.6	17.1	12.7	4.9	8.0	17.5	5.2	14.7	14.2	4.3	-10.4	17.6	7.2	9.2
Denmark	-1.1	12.8	7.2	3.3	9.5	8.5	3.5	13.0	1.9	7.5	-1.6	7.7	11.1	13.4	4.3	2.7	-12.5	2.9	4.6	5.1
Estonia	..	..	..	8.5	28.6	12.5	-5.9	27.2	3.5	6.2	10.1	14.4	17.5	13.3	7.8	-7.0	-32.6	21.0	15.2	9.2
Finland	1.3	13.0	8.2	7.2	11.9	8.7	4.2	16.7	1.3	3.2	3.2	7.4	11.4	7.9	7.0	6.5	-17.6	2.6	4.7	5.5
France[1]	-3.2	8.8	7.3	2.0	8.1	11.6	6.4	15.4	2.4	1.6	1.2	6.4	6.3	5.9	5.7	0.3	-10.6	8.2	7.7	6.8
Germany	-4.6	8.3	6.8	3.7	8.3	9.0	8.2	10.7	1.5	-1.4	5.3	6.5	6.9	12.3	5.2	2.9	-9.4	12.4	8.0	6.7
Greece	0.6	1.5	8.9	7.0	14.2	9.2	15.0	15.1	1.2	-1.3	3.0	5.7	-1.5	9.7	9.9	4.0	-18.6	-4.9	-8.7	2.7
Hungary	..	..	..	9.0	22.2	22.9	12.3	18.0	5.4	6.7	9.3	14.3	7.1	14.8	13.3	5.8	-14.6	12.0	8.0	9.8
Iceland	-7.5	3.8	3.6	16.5	8.0	23.4	4.4	8.6	-9.1	-2.6	10.7	14.5	29.3	10.4	-0.7	-18.4	-24.0	3.9	3.8	3.5
Ireland	7.5	15.5	16.4	12.9	16.6	27.5	12.4	21.7	7.1	2.7	-1.6	8.5	8.3	6.5	7.9	-2.9	-9.8	6.5	4.0	5.3
Israel	..	..	..	7.3	4.0	1.8	15.6	11.8	-5.1	-1.1	-1.3	11.7	3.3	3.2	11.9	2.3	-14.1	12.6	8.1	8.1
Italy	-11.6	8.7	9.7	-1.2	9.8	8.6	4.7	10.7	1.4	0.2	1.6	3.3	2.7	6.2	3.3	-4.4	-13.8	10.3	7.2	4.9
Japan	-1.3	8.2	14.2	13.4	0.5	-6.8	3.6	9.2	0.6	0.9	3.9	8.1	5.8	4.2	1.6	0.4	-15.3	9.7	5.2	8.7
Korea	4.9	22.8	22.5	14.7	4.2	-22.0	26.4	22.6	-4.9	14.4	11.1	11.7	7.6	11.3	11.7	4.4	-8.0	16.9	8.5	10.9
Luxembourg	5.2	6.7	4.2	5.4	12.6	11.8	14.8	10.5	6.0	0.8	6.9	11.8	4.2	12.8	9.3	8.5	-10.2	6.7	6.9	6.5
Mexico	1.9	21.2	-15.1	22.7	22.7	16.8	13.9	21.6	-1.5	1.4	0.7	10.7	8.4	12.7	7.0	3.2	-19.0	22.3	5.6	11.1
Netherlands	0.4	9.0	10.2	5.3	11.9	9.0	9.3	12.2	2.5	0.3	1.8	5.7	5.4	8.8	5.6	3.4	-8.5	10.5	5.4	6.7
New Zealand	5.4	13.1	8.7	7.6	2.1	1.3	12.0	-0.4	2.0	9.6	8.4	15.9	5.4	-2.5	8.9	2.1	-14.6	10.2	8.5	8.0
Norway	4.8	5.8	5.8	8.8	12.5	8.8	-1.6	2.0	1.7	1.0	1.4	8.8	8.7	8.4	8.6	4.3	-11.4	8.7	4.5	6.8
Poland	..	11.3	24.2	26.2	23.1	18.6	1.2	13.6	-3.6	2.6	9.6	14.2	7.6	18.8	13.7	6.2	-13.2	11.4	7.7	7.2
Portugal	-3.3	8.8	7.4	5.8	10.5	14.7	9.0	5.6	1.0	-0.5	-0.5	7.6	2.3	7.2	5.5	2.3	-10.6	5.2	-4.8	-1.8
Slovak Republic	..	-4.7	11.6	17.3	10.2	19.1	0.4	8.1	13.4	4.4	7.4	8.3	12.3	17.8	9.2	3.1	-18.6	14.9	7.4	6.5
Slovenia	..	..	..	..	11.3	9.6	7.8	7.1	3.1	4.9	6.7	13.3	6.7	12.2	16.7	3.8	-19.7	6.6	5.3	6.3
Spain	-5.2	11.4	11.1	8.8	13.3	14.8	13.7	10.8	4.5	3.7	6.2	9.6	7.7	10.2	8.0	-5.3	-17.8	5.4	2.9	6.6
Sweden	-2.1	12.6	7.6	3.5	12.9	11.1	4.6	12.0	-1.5	-1.2	4.0	5.6	6.9	9.6	9.3	3.0	-13.4	12.0	8.0	6.3
Switzerland	-0.1	7.7	4.0	4.0	8.1	7.4	4.1	10.3	2.3	-1.1	1.3	7.3	6.6	6.5	6.1	0.3	-5.4	6.7	5.3	6.3
Turkey	35.8	-21.9	29.6	20.5	22.4	2.3	-3.7	21.8	-24.8	20.9	23.5	20.8	12.2	6.9	10.7	-4.1	-14.3	20.7	17.9	10.6
United Kingdom	3.3	5.9	5.5	9.7	9.7	9.3	7.9	8.9	4.8	4.9	2.2	6.9	7.1	9.1	-0.8	-1.2	-11.9	8.5	4.0	3.7
United States[1]	8.6	11.9	8.0	8.7	13.5	11.7	11.5	13.0	-2.8	3.4	4.4	11.0	6.1	6.1	2.7	-2.6	-13.8	12.6	5.4	3.7
Total OECD	0.9	9.6	8.3	7.3	10.2	7.6	8.4	12.2	-0.1	2.5	4.0	8.7	6.6	8.0	5.2	0.5	-12.5	11.1	6.3	7.3

Note: Regional aggregates are calculated inclusive of intra-regional trade as the sum of volumes expressed in 2005 $.
1. Volume data use hedonic price deflators for certain components.
Source: OECD Economic Outlook 89 database.

StatLink http://dx.doi.org/10.1787/888932443662

Annex Table 40. **Export prices of goods and services**

National accounts basis, percentage changes from previous year, national currency terms

	1993	1994	1995	1996	1997	1998	1999	2000	2001	2002	2003	2004	2005	2006	2007	2008	2009	2010	2011	2012
Australia	1.0	-3.7	6.0	-2.2	-0.9	1.8	-4.6	12.6	6.0	-2.3	-5.2	4.2	11.9	13.1	1.5	21.7	-12.2	8.1	5.4	0.7
Austria	0.2	1.3	1.6	0.5	0.9	0.1	0.6	1.4	0.6	0.3	-0.4	1.1	1.7	2.6	1.8	2.8	-1.1	2.2	2.3	1.3
Belgium	-1.3	1.3	1.6	-1.5	1.2	-1.0	-0.1	5.5	1.4	-0.7	-1.3	2.0	4.1	2.7	2.2	4.1	-5.3	5.0	2.2	2.0
Canada	4.4	5.9	6.4	0.6	0.2	-0.3	1.1	6.2	1.3	-1.9	-1.3	2.2	2.8	0.3	0.8	10.5	-9.4	2.1	4.7	2.0
Chile	..	..	..	-8.1	-0.7	-2.9	6.6	11.0	5.5	7.1	11.2	12.3	10.3	23.9	5.9	-4.8	-5.8	17.4	4.3	3.1
Czech Republic	..	5.2	6.4	4.7	5.6	3.9	1.1	3.2	-0.3	-5.5	0.1	2.7	-2.2	-1.3	-0.1	-5.2	-1.2	-1.7	-0.6	0.5
Denmark	-1.7	-0.3	1.0	1.5	2.7	-2.1	-0.5	8.2	1.6	-1.3	-1.1	1.9	5.4	3.0	1.4	5.4	-8.4	7.2	1.2	1.6
Estonia	..	..	..	19.1	13.0	2.9	0.2	8.3	6.3	0.2	1.8	2.3	3.6	5.0	8.3	7.3	-4.3	4.1	2.6	0.8
Finland	6.6	1.5	4.8	-0.5	-1.0	-1.0	-5.1	3.5	-1.3	-2.6	-1.4	-0.4	1.2	2.2	0.9	-0.9	-7.4	4.1	4.3	2.5
France[1]	-2.2	-0.4	-0.5	0.9	1.3	-1.5	-1.6	2.4	-0.3	-1.7	-1.8	0.6	2.1	2.5	1.5	3.9	-3.5	1.8	3.6	1.1
Germany	0.1	0.8	1.2	-0.5	0.9	-0.9	-0.9	2.5	0.4	-0.2	-1.7	0.0	0.7	1.3	0.4	0.6	-3.0	2.6	3.8	0.9
Greece	9.1	8.6	8.7	5.6	3.6	4.1	1.9	8.0	3.9	2.4	1.6	2.3	2.9	3.3	2.3	3.8	-0.2	4.9	0.3	0.8
Hungary	..	18.5	45.5	19.3	15.8	13.2	4.8	10.3	3.0	-4.1	0.1	-1.1	-0.4	6.5	-4.0	1.0	2.2	1.7	4.4	3.2
Iceland	4.8	6.2	4.8	-0.2	2.1	4.5	0.0	3.8	21.5	-1.7	-7.1	1.3	-4.5	21.3	2.2	35.5	12.5	8.6	6.7	3.4
Ireland	6.8	0.2	1.9	-0.3	1.2	2.7	2.3	6.1	4.6	-0.4	-5.0	-0.6	1.0	1.3	0.1	-0.7	0.6	0.0	0.5	1.0
Israel	..	..	..	7.8	6.3	6.7	9.7	-1.9	0.9	11.9	-2.0	0.8	5.0	2.2	-3.7	-6.3	3.7	-0.7	-0.9	1.8
Italy	10.4	3.4	8.2	0.3	1.3	1.4	0.7	4.4	2.3	1.4	0.4	2.6	4.0	4.6	4.1	5.0	-1.4	4.9	4.1	2.2
Japan	-7.1	-3.4	-1.9	3.5	1.8	0.9	-8.8	-4.1	2.2	-1.2	-3.4	-1.2	1.4	3.7	2.5	-4.1	-11.6	-1.2	-0.8	-0.7
Korea	1.5	1.8	1.8	-2.0	5.0	22.7	-19.6	-3.6	3.6	-8.5	-0.7	4.1	-6.7	-4.7	0.7	24.9	-1.5	1.3	1.6	-2.4
Luxembourg	5.7	3.1	1.5	6.8	1.6	0.6	5.3	9.8	-4.0	-0.1	-1.8	6.4	8.0	8.1	4.9	0.6	-1.8	8.4	4.1	1.9
Mexico	3.3	5.9	79.5	23.0	7.2	9.3	6.6	3.4	-2.3	3.3	11.2	6.7	3.0	4.3	3.0	7.4	12.1	-3.9	5.9	3.3
Netherlands	-2.5	0.6	0.7	0.8	2.5	-2.0	-1.2	6.0	0.9	-1.8	-0.8	0.6	3.4	2.6	1.3	4.7	-5.8	5.6	3.3	1.4
New Zealand	2.1	-2.6	-0.5	-2.5	-2.4	4.9	-0.1	14.3	7.2	-7.2	-7.3	-0.1	1.2	6.9	1.2	15.9	-8.5	3.4	5.9	2.5
Norway	2.1	-2.8	1.8	6.9	2.0	-7.9	10.7	36.7	-2.2	-10.2	2.1	12.9	17.3	15.4	1.4	16.6	-14.1	5.5	17.4	3.4
Poland	..	31.7	19.6	7.8	12.8	13.0	6.7	1.2	1.2	4.9	7.2	8.3	-2.8	1.8	3.1	-0.5	11.3	0.5	4.8	3.3
Portugal	4.9	6.4	5.6	-0.8	3.3	1.4	0.4	5.4	0.7	0.0	-1.4	1.5	1.7	4.4	1.9	2.5	-4.4	4.3	4.0	1.3
Slovak Republic	..	10.7	8.4	4.3	6.5	-4.8	-1.1	17.3	4.9	1.0	1.5	1.8	1.6	2.2	0.5	1.4	-5.1	2.9	3.9	1.4
Slovenia	30.4	17.3	9.6	13.0	5.4	2.6	2.1	10.3	8.1	4.4	2.9	3.0	2.9	2.8	2.3	1.2	-0.5	3.2	2.5	2.1
Spain	5.0	4.6	5.9	1.4	3.0	0.5	0.0	7.3	1.8	0.7	-0.2	1.6	4.3	4.1	2.5	2.8	-3.3	2.7	3.0	2.2
Sweden	8.7	3.8	6.2	-4.7	-0.3	-1.4	-1.0	2.2	2.3	-1.6	-2.1	0.4	2.9	2.5	1.7	4.4	0.6	-0.1	0.5	1.1
Switzerland	2.0	-0.4	-0.3	-1.1	0.7	-0.3	-0.8	2.9	0.3	-2.4	0.5	0.5	0.8	2.7	3.8	1.6	-1.5	-2.1	-0.7	0.6
Turkey	59.9	164.8	73.0	69.0	87.0	60.1	52.0	42.0	89.4	25.4	10.7	13.3	-0.2	13.7	2.1	17.5	2.9	1.5	5.9	2.2
United Kingdom	9.1	1.2	3.3	1.6	-4.1	-4.7	0.3	1.9	-0.4	0.3	1.7	-0.5	0.9	2.9	1.5	11.9	2.8	4.1	3.7	1.6
United States[1]	0.0	1.1	2.3	-1.3	-1.7	-2.3	-0.6	1.8	-0.4	-0.4	2.2	3.5	3.6	3.4	3.3	4.7	-5.4	4.2	5.6	1.5
Total OECD	2.7	4.3	6.8	2.7	2.8	2.1	-0.1	4.1	2.5	-0.2	0.3	2.2	2.1	3.1	1.9	5.0	-2.9	2.7	3.6	1.3

Note: Regional aggregates are calculated inclusive of intra-regional trade. They are calculated as the geometric averages of prices weighted by 2005 GDP volumes expressed in $.
1. Certain components are estimated on a hedonic basis.
Source: OECD Economic Outlook 89 database.

StatLink ⬛ http://dx.doi.org/10.1787/88893243681

Annex Table 41. Import prices of goods and services

National accounts basis, percentage changes from previous year, national currency terms

	1993	1994	1995	1996	1997	1998	1999	2000	2001	2002	2003	2004	2005	2006	2007	2008	2009	2010	2011	2012
Australia	5.6	-4.4	3.2	-6.5	-1.5	6.5	-4.3	7.4	5.9	-4.2	-8.5	-4.8	0.6	4.2	-4.0	7.5	-2.2	-7.1	-3.8	0.8
Austria	0.8	1.2	1.4	2.2	1.8	0.3	0.5	2.9	0.5	-1.1	-0.6	1.3	2.6	3.1	2.3	4.5	-2.0	4.0	4.0	1.3
Belgium	-2.8	1.8	1.7	-0.6	1.5	-1.8	1.1	7.7	1.3	-1.8	-1.2	3.0	4.2	3.6	2.0	6.6	-8.5	6.9	3.3	2.1
Canada	6.4	6.6	3.4	-1.1	0.8	3.7	-0.2	2.1	3.0	0.6	-6.5	-2.2	-0.7	-0.7	-2.2	5.5	0.2	-3.7	2.6	1.8
Chile	..	..	..	5.4	-1.0	-0.2	3.9	8.0	10.2	3.6	2.9	-6.2	0.7	-0.5	4.3	14.0	-10.0	-5.2	-0.9	3.4
Czech Republic	..	2.6	5.8	1.7	5.2	-1.7	1.6	6.1	-2.6	-8.4	-0.4	1.3	-0.5	-0.1	-1.2	-3.7	-3.6	0.5	1.3	1.8
Denmark	-1.3	0.5	0.5	-0.1	2.4	-2.1	-0.5	7.2	1.5	-2.5	-2.0	0.7	3.3	3.3	1.8	4.0	-7.7	4.4	1.9	1.4
Estonia	..	..	..	16.7	8.6	2.2	0.8	5.8	2.0	-0.1	-0.2	1.5	3.3	4.1	3.3	5.9	-1.1	5.7	6.6	1.3
Finland	8.2	-0.5	0.1	0.3	0.4	-2.8	-2.1	7.4	-3.0	-2.7	0.0	1.9	4.8	5.7	1.2	1.8	-8.0	5.6	5.1	2.5
France[1]	-2.2	-0.5	-0.5	0.8	0.6	-2.8	-1.7	5.4	-0.9	-4.2	-1.6	1.3	3.2	3.2	0.7	3.9	-5.2	4.0	5.8	1.1
Germany	-1.8	-0.1	-0.3	0.2	3.1	-2.4	-1.4	7.7	0.5	-2.2	-2.6	0.2	2.2	2.7	0.0	1.8	-6.8	4.9	6.7	1.2
Greece	7.4	5.6	7.5	5.0	2.8	3.8	1.7	9.3	3.0	0.8	-0.3	2.1	3.7	3.8	2.4	5.2	-0.7	2.4	2.9	0.9
Hungary	..	15.6	41.1	20.8	13.7	12.0	5.6	12.7	2.4	-5.3	0.4	-1.0	1.3	8.0	-4.3	1.7	1.5	1.7	4.7	3.3
Iceland	8.7	5.9	3.7	3.1	0.0	-0.7	0.6	6.3	21.1	-2.3	-3.1	2.6	-5.4	17.3	2.1	44.3	24.8	2.7	6.4	3.4
Ireland	4.5	2.4	3.8	-0.5	0.8	2.5	2.6	7.1	3.9	-1.4	-4.0	0.1	1.8	2.3	1.6	1.9	-0.3	0.8	1.0	0.4
Israel	..	..	..	5.0	3.0	4.4	7.4	0.6	1.5	12.2	0.8	3.8	6.8	3.0	-1.9	-2.4	-4.4	1.8	2.9	2.9
Italy	15.4	4.8	11.4	-2.6	1.7	-1.6	0.7	11.2	1.4	-0.3	-1.3	2.7	6.3	7.7	2.6	6.8	-7.4	8.6	7.1	2.4
Japan	-8.4	-4.7	-2.5	8.4	6.5	-2.7	-8.5	1.5	2.4	-0.9	-0.8	2.9	8.3	11.4	7.3	6.4	-21.8	5.8	4.8	0.4
Korea	0.2	1.0	4.3	3.0	11.4	26.8	-17.0	4.0	6.4	-8.6	0.2	7.0	-3.2	-1.2	1.4	35.2	-4.2	1.5	7.2	-1.6
Luxembourg	3.2	2.1	1.3	5.9	5.2	1.7	3.0	12.3	-3.2	-1.0	-5.8	7.6	7.7	6.0	4.5	-1.0	-1.3	7.6	1.8	2.0
Mexico	3.7	5.1	95.1	21.4	3.6	12.0	3.7	0.1	-2.8	2.0	12.5	8.4	0.3	1.9	3.0	7.0	15.9	-2.0	4.7	3.2
Netherlands	-2.4	0.3	0.3	0.7	1.5	-2.4	-0.9	5.8	-0.4	-2.9	-0.9	1.4	2.7	3.0	1.5	4.5	-5.0	6.2	6.7	1.6
New Zealand	-1.6	-3.8	-1.8	-3.7	-0.4	5.7	0.7	15.4	2.2	-5.9	-11.4	-4.3	1.0	10.0	-4.7	13.3	-1.8	-3.7	4.5	1.5
Norway	1.6	0.7	0.6	0.8	0.3	1.2	-1.1	7.5	-0.1	-5.0	1.1	4.8	1.5	3.1	3.9	3.0	-0.2	-0.7	2.5	1.7
Poland	..	27.0	18.0	11.6	14.2	10.9	6.9	9.3	0.0	5.4	6.6	5.3	-5.9	2.2	1.1	2.3	9.4	1.9	5.7	3.3
Portugal	4.4	4.3	3.9	1.7	2.6	-1.4	-0.8	8.5	0.4	-1.6	-1.7	2.2	3.0	3.9	1.3	5.0	-8.5	4.7	6.7	1.5
Slovak Republic	..	12.3	7.3	9.6	3.6	-2.4	0.3	14.1	6.0	1.0	1.9	2.1	1.7	3.6	1.6	3.0	-4.1	4.9	5.6	1.4
Slovenia	23.1	14.4	6.9	11.6	5.0	1.9	1.9	13.9	6.3	2.5	2.1	4.1	5.0	3.3	1.4	2.7	-4.6	5.8	4.2	1.6
Spain	6.1	5.8	4.4	0.4	3.4	-1.5	0.3	10.6	-0.2	-2.0	-1.5	2.2	3.7	3.8	1.9	4.5	-6.7	6.5	4.5	1.0
Sweden	14.0	3.3	4.2	-3.9	0.0	-0.8	1.6	3.8	3.7	0.1	-2.3	1.9	4.6	2.8	0.3	4.9	-0.3	0.3	0.8	1.9
Switzerland	-1.4	-4.5	-2.6	-0.4	3.8	-1.6	-0.1	5.8	0.5	-5.9	-1.4	1.2	3.3	3.9	4.1	2.2	-6.1	-1.1	-0.5	0.4
Turkey	48.9	163.3	85.0	80.4	74.1	62.5	47.9	56.7	93.4	22.1	7.1	10.8	0.2	19.0	0.1	21.3	0.8	4.7	6.7	2.3
United Kingdom	8.6	3.0	5.9	0.1	-7.0	-5.7	-1.1	3.1	-0.2	-2.2	0.4	-0.7	3.8	2.9	0.2	11.9	3.7	4.4	4.9	1.8
United States[1]	-0.8	0.9	2.7	-1.7	-3.5	-5.4	0.6	4.3	-2.4	-1.1	3.5	4.8	6.2	4.1	3.3	10.4	-10.7	6.4	8.1	1.1
Total OECD	2.5	4.6	7.9	2.8	2.6	1.3	0.2	6.5	2.2	-1.3	0.2	2.6	3.2	4.0	1.7	7.8	-5.3	3.8	5.5	1.4

Note: Regional aggregates are calculated inclusive of intra-regional trade. They are calculated as the geometric averages of prices weighted by 2005 GDP volumes expressed in $.
1. Certain components are estimated on a hedonic basis.
Source: OECD Economic Outlook 89 database.

StatLink http://dx.doi.org/10.1787/888932443700

Annex Table 42. Competitive positions: relative consumer prices
Indices, 2005 = 100

	1993	1994	1995	1996	1997	1998	1999	2000	2001	2002	2003	2004	2005	2006	2007	2008	2009	2010
Australia	79.3	83.2	81.9	89.6	88.5	80.8	81.5	77.7	74.7	79.1	89.5	97.0	100.0	99.9	105.9	103.8	100.6	115.0
Austria	102.4	102.6	105.5	103.1	99.3	99.6	98.4	95.9	96.1	96.6	99.5	100.5	100.0	99.4	99.8	100.0	100.6	98.2
Belgium	98.0	99.6	103.0	100.5	95.3	96.1	94.8	91.1	92.0	93.5	98.0	99.8	100.0	99.7	100.5	103.3	103.4	100.4
Canada	99.4	91.3	89.3	89.4	88.7	83.7	83.1	83.6	81.1	80.4	89.4	94.2	100.0	105.6	109.6	107.3	101.9	111.8
Chile	..	..	..	..	113.1	111.8	105.5	104.1	95.7	94.7	88.6	94.7	100.0	104.0	102.1	103.6	100.0	106.5
Czech Republic	62.2	65.3	67.6	72.0	73.1	80.1	78.9	80.4	85.9	95.5	93.5	94.3	100.0	105.5	108.3	123.9	118.9	120.9
Denmark	94.2	94.0	97.3	95.9	93.4	95.5	95.6	92.2	95.4	100.3	101.0	99.7	100.0	99.7	100.2	101.8	104.9	101.2
Estonia	..	..	..	..	82.2	86.1	90.7	88.5	91.2	93.7	97.0	99.3	100.0	101.7	106.4	113.9	116.3	112.4
Finland	97.8	101.5	109.1	102.7	98.9	100.6	100.3	96.0	97.3	98.5	102.7	102.6	100.0	99.0	100.3	102.1	103.0	97.1
France	102.0	101.9	104.1	103.4	99.0	99.8	97.8	93.3	94.7	99.4	99.4	101.0	100.0	99.6	99.9	100.7	100.8	97.5
Germany	107.4	108.1	112.2	107.7	102.2	103.3	100.9	94.8	95.8	100.5	100.5	101.9	100.0	99.4	100.5	100.4	101.2	96.2
Greece	88.5	89.2	92.1	94.7	95.3	93.9	94.2	88.1	91.7	97.3	97.3	99.6	100.0	100.9	102.6	104.8	106.1	105.5
Hungary	72.1	70.4	66.9	67.5	71.7	72.1	74.2	75.1	81.3	89.7	91.9	98.0	100.0	95.4	106.3	109.0	102.4	104.1
Iceland	83.9	78.6	77.5	77.0	78.6	80.6	82.7	85.9	76.3	81.6	85.8	88.1	100.0	93.7	97.5	76.4	62.0	66.0
Ireland	86.9	86.8	87.8	89.3	88.4	86.4	83.7	80.6	83.7	88.4	97.6	100.0	100.0	101.8	106.9	112.7	108.8	101.4
Israel	..	..	..	..	128.7	125.5	120.9	128.6	127.6	115.6	109.4	102.5	100.0	99.7	100.6	112.5	109.5	114.9
Italy	93.7	91.1	84.6	93.6	93.8	95.2	94.3	90.6	91.9	94.0	99.4	101.0	100.0	100.0	100.5	101.3	102.4	98.4
Japan	118.9	128.3	130.6	109.1	102.6	102.9	115.8	122.4	109.6	103.0	104.4	106.0	100.0	90.5	82.9	89.3	99.9	100.8
Korea	93.1	94.2	95.3	98.7	92.6	70.2	80.2	86.4	81.7	86.1	87.5	89.0	100.0	107.8	107.1	86.7	76.0	82.4
Luxembourg	98.7	99.9	102.3	99.9	96.2	96.2	95.5	93.5	94.1	95.4	98.9	100.2	100.0	100.9	102.3	103.1	102.9	101.4
Mexico	104.6	100.0	67.8	75.7	87.5	88.3	96.7	105.1	112.1	112.5	100.4	96.4	100.0	100.0	99.1	97.4	85.4	92.4
Netherlands	94.2	94.3	97.9	95.2	89.9	92.5	91.9	86.9	89.5	93.1	99.7	101.3	100.0	99.0	99.8	100.2	101.2	96.4
New Zealand	76.4	80.5	86.3	91.5	92.9	82.7	78.9	71.6	70.7	77.5	88.3	94.6	100.0	93.2	93.1	89.0	86.7	93.7
Norway	94.3	91.9	94.1	93.0	94.0	91.6	92.1	91.0	94.5	102.0	100.5	96.0	100.0	99.9	99.7	99.7	98.1	102.7
Poland	69.0	69.7	74.5	79.9	82.6	88.0	85.4	94.0	106.2	101.5	90.2	89.4	100.0	102.2	105.7	115.4	97.6	103.7
Portugal	92.2	90.8	94.1	94.0	92.7	93.5	93.6	91.7	94.0	96.2	99.9	100.7	100.0	100.6	101.2	101.1	100.3	103.7
Slovak Republic	66.0	65.3	66.7	66.6	70.2	70.7	69.7	76.9	77.9	78.9	89.1	97.6	100.0	105.4	116.1	125.8	135.2	129.5
Slovenia	..	..	..	..	91.4	96.5	97.3	94.1	93.9	96.3	100.9	101.4	100.0	99.8	101.6	104.2	106.0	102.1
Spain	94.9	90.7	92.0	93.5	89.2	90.2	90.1	88.1	90.1	92.5	97.2	99.3	100.0	101.5	103.0	105.1	105.1	102.2
Sweden	110.8	109.2	108.4	116.7	110.8	107.8	105.7	104.2	95.6	98.2	104.0	104.2	100.0	99.6	100.5	98.1	88.8	95.0
Switzerland	99.6	104.1	110.4	106.4	106.4	100.2	99.1	96.2	102.3	102.3	102.7	101.8	100.0	97.4	93.2	97.1	101.1	105.8
Turkey	83.3	61.2	66.4	67.1	71.5	78.8	82.8	92.4	75.4	82.3	86.9	89.9	100.0	99.6	108.1	109.6	102.5	113.4
United Kingdom	88.2	88.1	84.3	85.7	98.6	104.1	103.8	104.4	101.8	102.3	97.9	101.6	100.0	100.6	102.1	89.0	80.3	81.3
United States	89.8	90.0	88.7	91.5	95.9	103.3	102.3	105.6	111.6	112.0	105.7	101.4	100.0	99.3	95.1	91.4	95.3	91.1
Euro area	100.2	99.8	103.4	102.0	92.8	95.2	91.9	82.7	84.3	87.8	98.5	102.0	100.0	99.7	101.9	103.9	105.1	96.5

StatLink http://dx.doi.org/10.1787/888932443719

Note. Competitiveness-weighted relative consumer prices in dollar terms. Competitiveness weights take into account the structure of competition in both export and import markets of the manufacturing sector of 42 countries. An increase in the index indicates a real effective appreciation and a corresponding deterioration of the competitive position. For details on the method of calculation, see Durand, M., C. Madaschi and F. Terrible (1998), "Trends in OECD Countries' International Competitiveness: The Influence of Emerging Market Economies", OECD Economics Department Working Papers, No. 195. See also OECD Economic Outlook Sources and Methods (http://www.oecd.org/eco/sources-and-methods).

Source: OECD Economic Outlook 89 database.

Annex Table 43. Competitive positions: relative unit labour costs

Indices, 2005 = 100

	1993	1994	1995	1996	1997	1998	1999	2000	2001	2002	2003	2004	2005	2006	2007	2008	2009	2010
Australia	64.5	68.1	71.2	79.3	80.5	73.4	77.5	73.2	67.0	71.5	81.7	92.1	100.0	100.3	109.5	106.7	105.7	117.3
Austria	111.2	111.4	109.1	103.6	100.4	101.7	100.4	94.8	93.9	95.1	98.8	100.4	100.0	98.2	96.7	94.0	95.1	93.4
Belgium	99.9	103.2	105.1	100.8	93.2	93.9	95.2	90.2	92.2	94.3	99.6	100.3	100.0	102.5	104.0	104.7	105.9	101.1
Canada	72.0	67.2	69.0	71.8	71.5	68.1	68.5	65.7	66.0	69.1	79.7	92.1	100.0	109.4	118.0	116.0	109.6	117.7
Czech Republic	65.5	63.7	63.4	69.0	69.5	78.7	75.0	75.1	85.7	97.0	102.4	99.2	100.0	100.4	102.1	109.4	101.1	99.3
Denmark	82.5	80.2	84.0	85.2	82.5	85.8	86.6	83.7	85.5	89.5	95.8	98.7	100.0	100.9	103.2	101.0	101.2	97.6
Estonia	..	..	..	..	78.6	85.0	90.7	87.9	85.3	90.3	95.7	99.6	100.0	104.0	117.4	125.5	132.2	109.3
Finland	104.1	109.3	126.8	119.8	112.7	112.5	112.8	101.7	100.2	98.0	100.7	101.7	100.0	93.7	88.1	87.2	89.7	86.8
France	110.4	111.1	112.9	112.5	105.3	102.8	100.0	95.1	93.9	96.1	98.6	101.5	100.0	101.3	103.6	104.7	107.1	103.3
Germany	105.0	105.1	114.7	112.7	103.7	106.3	106.0	99.4	98.1	100.4	104.8	104.8	100.0	95.9	95.3	97.6	101.1	98.4
Hungary	103.6	92.5	83.9	78.2	79.0	76.5	75.9	81.6	86.4	93.3	91.0	97.4	100.0	92.5	98.3	100.1	92.5	85.1
Iceland	62.0	60.4	61.1	60.8	64.1	69.9	77.6	84.2	73.5	78.2	82.6	85.6	100.0	97.4	104.5	77.4	53.2	60.0
Ireland	127.7	125.7	117.9	117.0	111.3	101.9	94.6	87.8	86.0	80.8	90.0	93.6	100.0	99.6	96.1	96.3	83.9	70.4
Israel	..	..	..	..	110.4	111.6	111.8	122.1	125.3	111.5	103.4	100.1	100.0	102.6	107.5	117.9	108.8	118.6
Italy	80.8	76.6	69.7	79.1	81.8	82.4	83.4	79.1	80.6	84.7	94.2	98.7	100.0	100.9	104.0	108.2	110.8	106.1
Japan	132.9	151.7	151.2	123.0	116.9	120.5	138.1	141.4	129.0	121.3	113.5	111.2	100.0	88.0	77.7	82.1	95.0	96.8
Korea	103.0	106.8	117.9	127.4	112.8	77.9	80.5	85.0	79.3	84.2	84.3	87.4	100.0	103.9	101.7	77.7	62.7	67.3
Luxembourg	90.8	91.1	98.0	96.2	91.6	88.3	84.8	82.9	88.2	89.4	92.0	95.4	100.0	106.7	99.7	108.5	113.6	102.0
Mexico	88.6	85.7	53.3	56.0	66.7	88.3	78.9	91.4	100.8	105.4	96.0	95.8	100.0	100.7	101.2	95.1	78.3	85.1
Netherlands	97.6	95.1	97.7	94.5	91.6	95.1	94.7	87.9	89.5	93.5	101.5	103.4	100.0	98.1	97.8	100.5	99.8	94.3
New Zealand	64.6	69.8	73.9	80.3	83.4	74.8	72.1	64.5	64.5	70.9	83.0	92.6	100.0	95.5	103.6	96.2	86.9	96.4
Norway	69.2	71.8	76.2	75.9	80.3	83.1	87.3	88.5	90.9	101.5	96.9	93.9	100.0	108.4	115.2	115.4	111.0	118.7
Poland	100.2	106.2	111.6	118.0	121.7	129.0	122.7	125.7	129.5	114.3	93.8	88.5	100.0	97.9	98.8	107.8	82.7	82.7
Portugal	92.8	92.7	95.2	91.8	90.3	93.3	94.9	92.9	93.3	94.7	96.5	98.2	100.0	101.2	99.9	100.2	98.6	99.1
Slovak Republic	75.5	91.0	96.4	100.3	121.2	110.0	100.3	116.4	103.6	104.3	105.2	101.1	100.0	104.5	109.1	111.1	111.0	104.9
Slovenia	..	..	..	..	81.8	85.8	87.9	87.2	88.3	89.8	95.4	99.6	100.0	100.9	103.8	105.4	112.2	110.4
Spain	90.9	86.7	87.1	89.0	87.0	87.4	85.7	84.8	85.8	88.3	94.0	97.6	100.0	102.5	107.3	111.1	110.1	107.1
Sweden	144.7	135.0	129.5	145.9	135.4	126.9	118.0	118.1	113.0	108.7	110.7	106.2	100.0	95.2	99.3	100.3	98.0	96.4
Turkey	118.2	82.3	70.1	68.4	77.1	84.0	108.4	116.3	87.9	89.7	87.6	90.4	100.0	96.4	104.5	106.5	99.7	111.1
United Kingdom	69.5	71.1	68.6	69.6	83.5	93.6	95.9	98.4	95.7	98.8	95.8	101.1	100.0	102.1	104.7	90.1	84.0	91.7
United States	127.0	125.0	118.5	120.0	124.1	131.7	128.7	135.1	138.0	129.0	119.8	105.3	100.0	96.8	88.9	85.7	90.0	84.9
Euro area	99.4	98.2	103.8	104.4	93.7	95.0	93.4	82.8	82.3	87.2	98.4	103.0	100.0	99.0	101.4	106.0	109.3	101.7

Note: Competitiveness-weighted relative unit labour costs in the manufacturing sector in dollar terms. Competitiveness weights take into account the structure of competition in both export and import markets of the manufacturing sector of 42 countries. An increase in the index indicates a real effective appreciation and a corresponding deterioration of the competitive position. For details on the method of calculation, see Durand, M., C. Madaschi and F. Terrible (1998), "Trends in OECD Countries' International Competitiveness: The Influence of Emerging Market Economies", *OECD Economics Department Working Papers*, No. 195. See also *OECD Economic Outlook Sources and Methods* (*http://www.oecd.org/eco/sources-and-methods*).

Source: OECD Economic Outlook 89 database.

StatLink ᴬˢᴾ http://dx.doi.org/10.1787/888932443738

Annex Table 44. **Export performance for total goods and services**

Percentage changes from previous year

	1995	1996	1997	1998	1999	2000	2001	2002	2003	2004	2005	2006	2007	2008	2009	2010	2011	2012
Australia	-7.0	0.6	5.3	1.7	-0.2	-1.5	2.8	-4.9	-9.5	-8.1	-6.2	-6.0	-4.9	-0.2	13.3	-7.3	-2.6	-2.0
Austria	-1.4	-1.0	2.3	0.1	0.1	1.7	4.0	2.1	-3.4	1.2	0.1	-2.6	1.0	-2.3	-4.7	-0.8	1.4	-0.4
Belgium	-3.1	-2.1	0.2	-3.5	-2.0	-0.1	-0.8	1.0	-3.0	-1.9	-1.9	-3.7	-1.9	-0.5	-0.3	0.0	-0.5	-0.9
Canada	0.4	-3.0	-3.8	-0.9	0.2	-3.6	-1.0	-2.3	-6.7	-5.5	-4.5	-5.8	-2.4	-3.4	-1.3	-5.6	2.2	-0.6
Chile	..	1.7	1.0	2.2	1.7	-6.5	6.8	-1.2	-0.4	1.6	-3.8	4.4	-0.9	-0.5	4.3	-11.3	-1.1	-2.1
Czech Republic	7.4	-0.6	-1.5	0.8	-0.6	5.6	8.1	0.6	2.0	11.0	3.7	4.4	7.1	2.8	2.1	5.7	1.3	2.5
Denmark	-4.9	-2.1	-5.1	-3.8	5.4	1.3	2.0	2.3	-5.3	-5.4	0.3	-0.4	-4.0	0.3	2.4	-6.7	-2.0	-2.1
Estonia	..	-5.2	14.1	5.3	-3.3	13.6	-1.6	-3.8	2.7	5.1	8.5	-3.1	-7.1	-4.5	-4.7	11.1	10.5	1.7
Finland	-0.5	-0.2	3.6	3.5	7.0	4.1	-0.7	-0.2	-7.6	-2.3	-2.3	1.2	-1.9	1.6	-7.7	-6.9	-1.7	-2.1
France	0.0	-2.7	2.5	1.0	-1.7	1.7	0.7	-1.2	-5.7	-5.1	-4.0	-3.6	-4.4	-3.1	-1.3	-0.6	-1.0	0.3
Germany	-2.2	-0.4	1.2	-0.1	0.0	1.6	4.8	1.2	-2.2	-0.5	0.3	4.2	0.3	-0.1	-2.6	2.7	2.5	0.1
Greece	-5.3	-2.2	8.8	-1.9	12.8	3.8	-1.7	-11.3	-2.4	6.9	-5.6	-3.2	-2.7	0.2	-9.4	-5.6	-0.1	2.2
Hungary	24.7	5.1	10.4	7.7	5.1	7.9	5.3	2.1	1.1	5.8	3.4	7.6	7.8	2.8	2.7	3.0	0.8	3.4
Iceland	-9.6	3.3	-4.0	-5.8	-3.0	-6.1	5.0	1.3	-2.0	0.2	0.2	-12.8	11.4	5.4	21.3	-7.4	-3.3	-3.1
Ireland	11.3	5.6	7.0	14.3	7.7	7.7	7.4	2.5	-3.2	-0.8	-2.0	-3.1	3.4	-1.7	8.2	-1.0	-1.1	-0.2
Israel	..	-1.6	-1.8	0.6	7.7	8.8	-9.7	-5.3	2.5	5.8	-3.0	-1.9	3.1	4.6	0.2	0.3	-0.6	0.3
Italy	4.0	-5.6	-4.1	-5.5	-6.1	1.2	0.2	-5.4	-6.3	-5.6	-5.7	-2.5	-4.0	-7.3	-7.7	-1.2	-1.1	-0.7
Japan	-6.9	-2.8	1.2	-3.9	-6.3	-1.8	-5.9	0.2	-0.3	-0.1	-2.1	-0.2	0.1	-2.3	-17.0	7.7	-5.1	-1.4
Korea	11.6	1.5	9.6	10.5	7.3	3.7	-4.1	4.7	3.6	4.7	-2.1	1.0	3.3	2.0	7.0	-0.2	2.4	0.9
Luxembourg	-2.8	-2.3	1.8	2.7	7.6	0.8	2.7	0.8	3.3	3.5	-2.2	4.1	3.3	5.3	3.6	-3.4	-0.8	-0.5
Mexico	20.5	8.9	-2.2	1.4	1.8	3.4	-1.3	-1.7	-1.9	0.5	0.1	4.2	1.9	2.2	-0.8	10.6	-1.1	0.2
Netherlands	1.2	-1.0	1.1	-1.1	2.5	1.5	0.2	-1.0	-2.5	-0.5	-1.3	-1.8	-0.1	0.5	4.1	0.4	-0.8	-0.2
New Zealand	-5.9	-4.4	-4.5	-1.4	1.0	-4.0	4.3	0.4	-4.8	-5.5	-8.7	-6.3	-4.0	-7.0	12.8	-8.5	-4.9	-2.9
Norway	-2.7	3.5	-2.3	-7.1	-3.8	-7.6	2.8	-2.8	-3.6	-6.5	-5.8	-8.3	-2.6	-0.5	9.0	-10.7	-5.6	-3.2
Poland	13.0	5.7	3.5	5.9	-7.5	9.7	1.2	2.9	8.5	3.6	1.4	3.7	0.9	2.4	7.4	-1.3	-3.0	-0.4
Portugal	0.5	1.0	-3.2	-1.1	-3.4	-2.4	-0.8	0.2	-0.7	-4.2	-7.0	2.5	0.5	-0.8	0.9	-0.1	-0.4	0.2
Slovak Republic	-5.4	-7.3	-0.1	10.9	5.9	-3.0	3.4	3.2	9.8	-2.5	2.9	8.7	5.1	0.2	-4.7	3.9	2.3	0.4
Slovenia	-7.8	-1.6	1.5	-0.4	-3.0	2.1	2.9	4.8	-1.7	3.5	2.9	2.2	4.7	0.0	-5.9	-2.6	-3.2	0.1
Spain	1.7	4.5	4.4	-0.9	1.5	-0.8	2.3	0.2	0.3	-3.7	-4.2	-1.8	0.3	-3.4	-0.4	0.3	2.8	2.0
Sweden	3.3	-2.2	3.2	1.1	2.0	0.7	-0.7	-1.6	0.3	0.5	-1.9	0.1	-1.1	-1.8	-1.6	0.3	0.5	-0.8
Switzerland	-7.4	-2.1	1.3	-2.8	0.1	0.7	-1.0	-2.2	-5.2	-1.1	0.2	1.1	2.5	1.0	2.8	-1.7	-4.3	-1.7
Turkey	-0.1	15.9	8.4	4.4	-14.9	5.1	0.4	3.7	2.0	1.8	-1.1	-2.1	-2.3	-2.0	6.8	-4.5	0.3	1.9
United Kingdom	0.2	2.1	-2.2	-4.4	-2.4	-3.0	1.9	-1.7	-2.5	-4.4	-0.1	2.7	-9.5	-1.3	1.2	-4.6	0.3	-1.7
United States	3.0	-0.5	0.9	-1.7	-1.9	-3.4	-5.1	-4.9	-3.4	-1.1	-1.7	0.2	1.2	2.1	2.4	-1.9	-0.6	0.2
Total OECD	0.3	-0.5	0.9	-1.1	-0.9	-0.2	-0.8	-1.3	-2.7	-1.6	-1.9	-0.2	-0.8	-0.7	-0.6	-0.5	-0.3	-0.3
Memorandum items																		
China	-3.0	9.3	13.0	3.2	6.0	13.6	6.5	21.4	19.5	11.5	14.5	14.7	12.2	5.1	2.2	14.3	2.3	2.3
Other industrialised Asia[1]	1.0	-1.8	-0.7	-0.9	-0.9	3.1	-2.8	1.9	0.7	2.0	1.4	1.4	0.0	0.1	-1.0	2.5	0.7	0.0
Russia	..	-2.9	-10.3	-5.1	5.9	-1.6	2.3	6.6	6.2	1.7	-1.7	-2.0	-2.4	-2.8	6.3	-3.1	-4.2	-1.8
Brazil	..	..	-1.7	-1.3	2.5	2.3	10.3	8.8	2.2	1.8	-0.9	-4.2	-3.7	-4.6	1.6	-2.5	2.3	1.7
Other oil producers	-3.6	-4.5	-0.2	0.1	-8.4	-6.1	1.0	-4.3	3.9	-2.4	1.1	-6.4	-2.8	0.6	5.7	-9.1	-1.1	-1.0
Rest of the world	1.0	-1.5	-3.2	-1.9	0.4	-3.6	3.4	0.1	0.0	-0.2	-2.4	-2.8	-2.1	0.2	4.4	-3.8	0.4	0.1

Note: Regional aggregates are calculated inclusive of intra-regional trade. Export performance is the ratio between export volumes and export markets for total goods and services. The calculation of export markets is based on a weighted average of import volumes in each exporting country's markets, with weights based on trade flows in 2005.

1. Chinese Taipei; Hong Kong, China; Malaysia; Philippines; Singapore; Vietnam; Thailand; India and Indonesia.

Source: OECD Economic Outlook 89 database.

StatLink ᴪᴪ http://dx.doi.org/10.1787/888932443757

Annex Table 45. Shares in world exports and imports
Percentage, values for goods and services, national accounts basis

	1996	1997	1998	1999	2000	2001	2002	2003	2004	2005	2006	2007	2008	2009	2010	2011	2012
A. Exports																	
Canada	3.5	3.6	3.7	4.0	4.2	4.1	3.8	3.5	3.4	3.3	3.1	2.9	2.7	2.4	2.5	2.5	2.4
France	5.4	5.3	5.7	5.4	4.8	4.9	4.9	5.0	4.7	4.3	4.1	4.0	3.9	3.9	3.5	3.4	3.4
Germany	9.1	8.6	9.2	8.8	8.0	8.7	9.0	9.4	9.3	8.9	9.0	9.1	8.7	8.6	8.1	8.2	8.1
Italy	4.7	4.4	4.5	4.1	3.8	4.0	3.9	4.0	3.9	3.6	3.5	3.6	3.3	3.2	2.9	2.9	2.9
Japan	6.8	6.7	6.2	6.4	6.5	5.7	5.6	5.5	5.4	5.1	4.7	4.5	4.3	4.0	4.5	4.1	4.0
United Kingdom	5.3	5.6	5.7	5.5	5.2	5.2	5.2	5.1	4.9	4.7	4.7	4.3	4.0	3.9	3.5	3.4	3.4
United States	13.0	13.7	14.0	14.0	13.9	13.5	12.5	11.2	10.5	10.1	9.9	9.6	9.3	10.0	9.8	9.2	9.2
Other OECD countries	26.5	26.1	27.2	27.3	26.6	27.2	27.5	28.0	28.1	27.4	27.1	27.5	27.4	27.8	26.7	26.5	26.3
Total OECD	74.3	73.9	76.0	75.5	72.9	73.2	72.5	71.6	70.1	67.5	66.1	65.5	63.6	63.9	61.5	60.1	59.6
China	2.6	3.0	3.0	3.1	3.5	3.9	4.5	5.2	5.8	6.5	7.2	7.8	8.0	8.5	9.4	9.4	9.8
Other industrialised Asia	12.4	12.4	11.4	11.6	12.4	11.8	11.9	11.5	11.5	11.6	11.7	11.5	11.2	11.9	12.9	12.6	12.8
Brazil	0.8	0.9	0.9	0.8	0.8	0.9	0.9	0.9	1.0	1.0	1.1	1.1	1.1	1.1	1.2	1.3	1.4
Russia	1.5	1.4	1.3	1.2	1.5	1.5	1.5	1.6	1.8	2.1	2.3	2.3	2.6	2.2	2.4	2.7	2.7
Other oil producers	3.9	3.8	2.9	3.5	4.7	4.3	4.3	4.6	5.1	6.5	7.0	7.0	8.1	6.9	7.2	8.2	8.1
Rest of the world	4.4	4.5	4.5	4.3	4.2	4.4	4.4	4.5	4.6	4.7	4.8	4.9	5.2	5.4	5.4	5.7	5.6
Total of non-OECD countries	25.7	26.1	24.0	24.5	27.1	26.8	27.5	28.4	29.9	32.5	33.9	34.5	36.4	36.1	38.5	39.9	40.4
B. Imports																	
Canada	3.2	3.5	3.6	3.7	3.7	3.5	3.4	3.2	3.0	3.0	3.0	2.8	2.6	2.7	2.7	2.6	2.6
France	5.2	4.8	5.2	5.0	4.7	4.7	4.7	4.8	4.7	4.5	4.4	4.4	4.3	4.3	3.9	3.9	3.9
Germany	8.9	8.4	8.8	8.7	8.0	8.1	7.9	8.4	8.1	7.8	8.0	7.9	7.7	7.8	7.3	7.5	7.4
Italy	3.9	3.8	4.0	3.8	3.7	3.8	3.8	3.9	3.8	3.6	3.7	3.7	3.5	3.3	3.2	3.3	3.2
Japan	6.6	6.1	5.2	5.4	5.6	5.3	4.9	4.7	4.7	4.6	4.5	4.1	4.4	4.0	4.2	4.1	4.1
United Kingdom	5.4	5.6	5.9	5.9	5.5	5.7	5.8	5.6	5.5	5.3	5.3	4.9	4.4	4.3	4.0	3.8	3.7
United States	14.7	15.6	16.6	17.8	18.7	18.3	17.9	16.7	16.1	15.9	15.4	14.1	13.2	12.8	12.9	12.1	12.0
Other OECD countries	26.2	25.7	26.5	26.5	25.9	26.0	26.4	27.0	27.2	26.8	26.8	27.5	27.5	26.8	25.8	25.5	25.4
Total OECD	74.2	73.6	75.8	76.9	75.8	75.4	74.9	74.3	73.0	71.7	70.9	69.4	67.5	65.9	64.0	62.9	62.1
China	2.4	2.4	2.4	2.7	3.2	3.5	4.1	4.8	5.4	5.6	5.9	6.1	6.4	7.2	8.3	8.7	9.1
Other industrialised Asia	12.7	12.8	10.7	10.8	11.5	10.9	10.9	10.5	10.9	11.1	11.0	10.9	11.1	11.6	12.5	12.4	12.5
Brazil	1.1	1.2	1.1	0.9	1.0	1.0	0.8	0.7	0.7	0.8	0.9	1.0	1.2	1.2	1.4	1.4	1.5
Russia	1.3	1.3	1.1	0.7	0.8	1.0	1.1	1.1	1.2	1.3	1.4	1.7	1.9	1.6	1.8	1.9	2.0
Other oil producers	3.1	3.2	3.1	2.9	2.9	3.2	3.4	3.4	3.6	4.1	4.2	4.8	5.3	5.9	5.6	5.8	6.0
Rest of the world	5.3	5.5	5.7	5.1	4.9	5.1	4.9	5.0	5.2	5.5	5.7	6.1	6.7	6.6	6.4	6.9	6.7
Total of non-OECD countries	25.8	26.4	24.2	23.1	24.2	24.6	25.1	25.7	27.0	28.3	29.1	30.6	32.5	34.1	36.0	37.1	37.9

Note: Regional aggregates are calculated inclusive of intra-regional trade.
Source: OECD Economic Outlook 89 database.

StatLink http://dx.doi.org/10.1787/888932443776

Annex Table 46. Geographical structure of world trade growth
Average of export and import volumes

A. Trade growth

Percentage changes from previous year

	1996	1997	1998	1999	2000	2001	2002	2003	2004	2005	2006	2007	2008	2009	2010	2011	2012
OECD America[1]	8.8	12.7	7.8	8.8	11.3	-3.7	1.2	2.7	9.8	6.2	6.9	5.2	0.8	-12.8	13.1	6.5	8.6
OECD Europe	5.5	10.7	8.2	5.9	12.3	2.9	1.7	2.5	7.2	6.3	9.2	5.6	1.0	-11.8	9.7	7.1	6.6
OECD Asia & Pacific[2]	10.3	7.2	-4.0	7.1	12.7	-2.9	6.6	7.7	12.1	6.6	7.8	7.7	3.3	-12.7	15.3	6.7	9.3
Total OECD	7.0	10.7	6.5	6.9	12.1	0.4	2.1	3.2	8.5	6.3	8.4	5.8	1.2	-12.2	11.3	6.9	7.5
China	23.1	17.5	1.7	17.5	25.4	6.8	25.7	28.2	23.8	18.9	20.2	17.1	6.5	-4.0	24.8	10.4	12.2
Other industrialised Asia	6.5	7.6	-2.4	2.4	17.4	-4.0	7.8	10.0	16.9	11.2	10.8	7.6	6.7	-9.7	16.6	9.6	9.4
Brazil	..	13.3	2.0	-6.7	11.6	5.7	-2.6	4.8	14.5	9.0	10.8	12.5	7.8	-10.9	24.4	15.6	12.7
Russia	2.8	-0.2	-5.0	2.4	15.3	8.4	11.7	14.2	15.7	10.1	12.6	14.4	7.0	-17.2	14.6	11.8	8.2
Other oil producers	4.5	9.4	2.0	-2.4	6.2	4.2	3.5	9.6	10.2	13.7	2.9	11.7	8.7	-3.6	1.5	9.8	10.1
Rest of the world	5.3	8.5	5.1	0.9	5.1	5.0	1.7	6.6	11.1	8.7	8.9	11.0	7.3	-10.6	8.5	11.8	7.0
Total Non-OECD	7.0	8.8	0.5	2.2	13.2	1.7	7.9	12.2	15.7	12.5	11.1	11.4	7.1	-8.0	14.8	10.4	9.9
World	7.0	10.2	4.9	5.7	12.4	0.7	3.6	5.5	10.5	8.1	9.2	7.5	3.1	-10.8	12.5	8.1	8.4

B. Contribution to World Trade growth

Percentage points

	1996	1997	1998	1999	2000	2001	2002	2003	2004	2005	2006	2007	2008	2009	2010	2011	2012
OECD America[1]	1.7	2.5	1.6	1.8	2.4	-0.8	0.2	0.5	1.9	1.2	1.3	0.9	0.1	-2.2	2.2	1.1	1.4
OECD Europe	2.4	4.6	3.6	2.7	5.6	1.3	0.8	1.1	3.2	2.7	3.9	2.4	0.4	-4.8	3.9	2.8	2.6
OECD Asia & Pacific[2]	1.0	0.7	-0.4	0.6	1.1	-0.2	0.6	0.7	1.1	0.6	0.7	0.7	0.3	-1.1	1.3	0.6	0.8
Total OECD	5.1	7.8	4.8	5.1	9.1	0.3	1.6	2.3	6.2	4.4	5.8	4.0	0.8	-8.1	7.4	4.5	4.8
China	0.5	0.4	0.0	0.4	0.7	0.2	0.9	1.1	1.2	1.0	1.2	1.1	0.5	-0.3	2.0	0.9	1.1
Other industrialised Asia	0.7	0.8	-0.3	0.2	1.7	-0.4	0.7	1.0	1.8	1.2	1.2	0.9	0.8	-1.2	2.0	1.2	1.2
Brazil	..	0.1	0.0	-0.1	0.1	0.1	0.0	0.0	0.1	0.1	0.1	0.1	0.1	-0.1	0.2	0.2	0.2
Russia	0.0	0.0	-0.1	0.0	0.2	0.1	0.2	0.2	0.2	0.2	0.2	0.3	0.1	-0.3	0.3	0.2	0.2
Other oil producers	0.3	0.5	0.1	-0.1	0.3	0.2	0.2	0.5	0.5	0.7	0.2	0.6	0.5	-0.2	0.1	0.5	0.6
Rest of the world	0.3	0.5	0.3	0.0	0.3	0.2	0.1	0.3	0.6	0.4	0.4	0.6	0.4	-0.6	0.5	0.6	0.4
Total Non-OECD	1.9	2.4	0.1	0.6	3.3	0.4	2.0	3.2	4.4	3.7	3.4	3.5	2.3	-2.7	5.1	3.7	3.5
World	7.0	10.2	4.9	5.7	12.4	0.7	3.6	5.5	10.5	8.1	9.2	7.5	3.1	-10.8	12.5	8.1	8.4

Note: Regional aggregates are calculated inclusive of intra-regional trade as the sum of volumes expressed in 2005 $.
1. Canada, Chile, Mexico and United States.
2. Australia, Japan, Korea and New Zealand.
Source: OECD Economic Outlook 89 database.

StatLink http://dx.doi.org/10.1787/888932443795

Annex Table 47. Trade balances for goods and services
$ billion, national accounts basis

	1993	1994	1995	1996	1997	1998	1999	2000	2001	2002	2003	2004	2005	2006	2007	2008	2009	2010	2011	2012
Australia	-1.7	-4.6	-5.4	-0.6	1.7	-6.7	-10.2	-4.2	2.3	-4.4	-13.8	-18.0	-13.5	-9.2	-18.4	-9.1	-4.4	15.4	40.8	39.4
Austria	-0.6	-2.5	-2.5	-3.8	-1.1	1.3	2.4	3.5	4.5	9.5	9.1	11.5	12.0	16.0	22.4	26.3	16.0	19.3	23.6	27.5
Belgium	7.2	8.9	11.1	8.7	9.4	9.8	10.6	6.7	8.5	14.4	17.0	17.8	15.4	15.3	17.6	4.6	13.2	14.9	12.9	14.1
Canada	0.0	6.7	18.9	24.7	12.6	12.3	24.2	41.6	41.2	32.4	32.5	42.7	42.5	32.0	27.1	24.8	-23.1	-29.9	-15.6	-11.5
Chile	..	..	1.5	-1.3	-1.7	-2.6	1.6	1.4	1.0	1.6	3.1	8.8	10.2	22.1	22.9	7.0	12.7	14.8	18.3	17.8
Czech Republic	0.0	-1.0	-2.4	-3.6	-3.1	-0.7	-0.7	-1.7	-1.6	-1.6	-2.1	0.1	4.0	4.9	8.8	10.1	10.8	9.2	11.3	10.9
Denmark	9.4	8.1	7.4	9.1	6.3	3.7	8.8	9.6	10.7	10.2	13.3	11.9	12.7	8.7	7.2	10.9	11.8	17.4	19.7	21.3
Estonia	..	..	-0.3	-0.5	-0.5	-0.6	-0.3	-0.2	-0.2	-0.5	-0.7	-0.8	-0.9	-1.7	-2.3	-1.0	1.2	1.3	1.7	1.7
Finland	3.9	5.6	9.7	8.9	9.1	10.5	11.8	11.1	11.6	12.5	11.2	12.3	8.0	9.8	12.5	11.2	5.5	6.3	10.2	11.7
France	12.3	12.2	18.1	23.2	40.9	38.0	30.7	12.8	15.0	25.1	17.7	2.3	-18.2	-29.5	-50.3	-64.5	-54.4	-64.1	-102.8	-105.3
Germany	-0.9	2.7	11.8	22.1	27.0	29.6	18.0	7.0	38.4	93.4	98.2	137.8	147.0	168.1	239.4	234.4	165.4	169.8	197.6	228.0
Greece	-10.7	-9.3	-12.4	-14.1	-13.1	-14.7	-15.7	-17.2	-17.2	-20.1	-23.9	-23.1	-21.9	-28.0	-37.2	-44.7	-34.9	-25.9	-15.2	-10.9
Hungary	..	..	0.0	0.3	0.6	-0.6	-1.2	-1.6	-0.5	-1.3	-3.2	-3.7	-2.4	-1.2	1.6	0.8	6.9	9.6	13.1	16.1
Iceland	0.2	0.3	0.3	0.0	0.0	-0.4	-0.4	-0.6	-0.1	0.1	-0.3	-0.7	-2.0	-3.0	-2.2	-0.7	1.0	1.3	1.5	1.6
Ireland	5.4	5.6	7.8	8.7	10.4	10.2	13.3	12.9	16.3	21.3	25.5	27.8	23.9	21.7	23.5	23.8	34.1	38.7	45.5	53.3
Israel	..	..	-7.8	-7.9	-5.4	-3.0	-3.1	-0.4	-3.0	-3.4	-0.9	0.1	-0.3	0.7	-2.2	-3.0	4.8	4.4	0.9	0.3
Italy	31.4	36.1	43.2	58.5	46.3	37.1	22.1	10.5	15.3	11.6	9.0	11.4	-0.9	-14.9	-5.2	-15.9	-8.6	-36.7	-66.7	-60.6
Japan	96.9	96.5	74.8	23.4	47.4	72.4	69.4	68.0	26.1	51.2	69.3	89.0	63.3	54.5	73.3	6.1	15.7	62.4	4.2	-10.6
Korea	3.1	-1.5	-2.8	-15.8	-3.6	43.2	29.8	15.3	11.4	8.4	14.7	29.9	22.9	13.2	15.8	-11.8	31.2	28.3	19.3	16.8
Luxembourg	2.8	3.6	4.4	4.2	3.2	3.2	4.1	4.3	3.6	4.4	7.0	8.3	9.6	13.1	16.6	18.9	17.5	19.4	24.6	26.4
Mexico	-15.8	-20.1	7.8	7.2	0.0	-8.5	-7.5	-11.3	-13.6	-11.4	-10.1	-13.2	-12.2	-11.6	-16.2	-23.8	-12.3	-16.7	-18.3	-30.6
Netherlands	17.7	19.8	23.8	22.1	21.9	18.9	17.4	21.3	23.2	28.8	33.9	45.1	54.5	52.5	64.5	71.5	57.7	62.9	60.9	65.5
New Zealand	1.2	1.1	0.7	0.3	0.3	0.2	-0.6	0.4	1.5	0.8	0.7	-0.4	-2.2	-1.7	-1.5	-2.4	1.6	2.0	0.7	0.2
Norway	7.6	7.6	9.2	14.3	13.0	2.8	11.6	28.7	28.9	25.8	29.2	35.1	49.6	60.8	59.9	87.0	56.3	56.7	87.4	91.0
Poland	0.9	2.2	3.2	-2.2	-6.2	-8.5	-9.8	-11.3	-7.1	-6.8	-5.2	-5.0	-0.6	-6.2	-11.7	-21.3	0.7	-4.4	-12.6	-15.6
Portugal	-6.9	-7.2	-7.9	-8.7	-9.4	-11.4	-13.0	-13.0	-12.3	-11.0	-11.0	-15.5	-18.1	-17.5	-18.6	-25.5	-17.6	-16.4	-10.9	-3.3
Slovak Republic	-0.6	0.8	0.4	-2.3	-2.1	-2.4	-0.9	-0.5	-1.7	-1.8	-0.6	-1.2	-2.2	-2.2	-0.8	-2.3	-0.3	-0.9	0.0	1.1
Slovenia	..	..	-0.4	-0.2	-0.2	-0.3	-0.9	-0.7	-0.2	0.3	-0.1	-0.4	-0.1	-0.2	-0.8	-1.7	0.6	0.3	-0.2	0.2
Spain	-3.2	0.1	0.0	3.3	5.0	-1.4	-11.3	-18.2	-15.4	-14.7	-21.1	-41.8	-59.5	-79.0	-97.3	-92.9	-31.1	-30.3	-12.6	1.5
Sweden	7.5	9.7	17.3	18.3	18.9	17.0	16.8	15.7	15.2	17.0	21.6	29.6	29.0	32.4	34.6	33.1	26.4	27.0	32.3	33.5
Switzerland	14.4	14.6	16.1	14.7	14.1	13.1	14.9	14.6	12.6	18.4	21.4	25.1	25.0	32.4	44.6	57.4	54.3	63.1	70.0	75.1
Turkey	-4.8	6.1	-0.1	-3.1	-1.1	2.7	0.8	-8.0	7.7	3.7	-3.1	-10.4	-16.9	-26.1	-33.8	-33.6	-7.1	-40.9	-65.2	-75.5
United Kingdom	-7.4	-4.5	-1.4	1.0	7.3	-11.3	-21.9	-27.2	-34.6	-42.2	-42.7	-59.5	-77.7	-76.7	-86.1	-71.3	-46.4	-75.0	-65.7	-52.4
United States	-64.4	-92.7	-90.7	-96.3	-101.4	-161.8	-262.1	-382.1	-371.0	-427.2	-504.1	-618.7	-722.7	-769.3	-714.0	-710.5	-386.4	-516.4	-598.6	-637.3
Euro area	57.8	76.4	106.9	129.9	146.6	127.8	88.0	40.1	89.4	173.0	171.0	191.4	148.4	123.3	183.8	142.1	164.4	158.6	168.6	250.9
Total OECD	105.0	104.9	153.5	112.5	146.2	91.0	-51.4	-213.0	-183.3	-155.6	-208.6	-265.8	-443.0	-520.0	-406.6	-508.1	-81.0	-213.1	-287.9	-258.6

Source: OECD Economic Outlook 89 database.

StatLink ⟶ http://dx.doi.org/10.1787/888932443814

Annex Table 48. Investment income, net
$ billion

	1993	1994	1995	1996	1997	1998	1999	2000	2001	2002	2003	2004	2005	2006	2007	2008	2009	2010	2011	2012
Australia	-7.9	-11.4	-13.4	-14.2	-13.8	-11.3	-11.9	-11.0	-10.2	-11.5	-15.0	-21.9	-27.6	-31.8	-40.9	-39.6	-38.0	-45.8	-56.1	-60.2
Austria	-1.5	-0.4	-2.1	-0.6	-1.3	-1.7	-2.8	-2.3	-3.0	-1.5	-1.1	-1.3	-2.0	-1.9	-2.4	2.4	-1.1	-0.4	-0.3	-0.3
Belgium[1]	7.1	7.6	7.5	6.9	6.4	7.0	6.7	6.5	4.8	4.6	6.6	5.9	5.2	5.5	7.7	12.6	6.6	7.3	5.8	6.2
Canada	-20.8	-18.9	-22.7	-21.5	-20.9	-20.0	-22.6	-22.3	-25.4	-19.3	-21.3	-18.6	-18.9	-11.9	-12.6	-15.2	-12.6	-15.2	-26.3	-26.6
Chile	..	..	..	-2.5	-2.6	-1.9	-2.2	-2.9	-2.5	-2.8	-4.5	-7.8	-10.5	-18.4	-18.6	-13.8	-11.7	-15.4	-20.7	-22.1
Czech Republic	-0.1	0.0	-0.1	-0.7	-0.8	-1.1	-1.4	-1.4	-2.2	-3.5	-4.3	-6.1	-6.0	-7.4	-12.7	-10.4	-13.2	-13.5	-15.1	-19.1
Denmark	-3.8	-3.8	-3.8	-3.7	-3.4	-2.8	-2.6	-3.6	-3.6	-2.7	-2.6	-2.2	1.6	2.8	1.8	3.5	3.9	4.2	5.2	4.4
Estonia	0.0	0.0	0.0	0.0	-0.1	-0.1	-0.1	-0.2	-0.3	-0.3	-0.5	-0.6	-0.6	-0.9	-1.4	-1.3	-0.5	-1.0	-3.1	-3.7
Finland	-4.9	-4.2	-4.6	-3.7	-2.5	-3.0	-2.0	-1.7	-1.0	-0.6	-2.6	0.2	-0.3	0.8	-0.7	-1.4	2.3	2.6	3.0	3.1
France	-7.0	-6.2	-8.4	-1.9	7.1	8.7	22.8	19.5	19.5	8.7	14.9	22.5	29.5	37.1	42.8	42.6	32.2	39.0	55.3	55.7
Germany	11.5	1.4	-2.9	0.8	-2.7	-10.8	-12.4	-8.9	-10.0	-17.4	-17.4	24.7	29.9	55.6	59.8	53.6	71.7	59.4	65.4	68.4
Greece	-1.8	-1.5	-1.9	-2.4	-1.7	-1.6	-0.7	-0.9	-1.8	-2.0	-4.5	-5.4	-7.0	-9.1	-12.7	-15.6	-12.5	-12.2	-12.5	-12.9
Hungary	..	..	-1.7	-2.0	-2.7	-3.0	-2.9	-2.6	-2.9	-3.6	-4.2	-5.4	-6.2	-6.6	-10.1	-11.1	-6.6	-7.2	-10.0	-14.1
Iceland	-0.1	-0.2	-0.2	-0.2	-0.2	-0.2	-0.2	-0.2	-0.3	0.0	-0.2	-0.6	-0.6	-1.0	-1.2	-3.6	-2.4	-2.3	-2.1	-1.9
Ireland	-5.2	-5.4	-7.3	-8.2	-9.7	-10.5	-13.5	-13.8	-16.4	-22.4	-24.8	-28.0	-31.0	-30.2	-38.1	-37.1	-38.8	-41.1	-46.0	-50.9
Israel	..	..	-2.6	-3.4	-4.0	-4.0	-5.1	-8.3	-5.5	-4.6	-4.7	-4.0	-1.4	-0.8	-0.8	-4.1	-5.1	-6.3	-6.5	-7.0
Italy	-17.3	-16.8	-15.8	-15.1	-10.2	-11.0	-10.9	-11.8	-10.4	-14.4	-20.2	-18.4	-17.1	-17.1	-26.8	-28.2	-13.8	-10.7	-11.1	-11.3
Japan	40.7	40.6	44.2	53.3	58.1	54.8	58.0	60.6	69.3	66.0	71.8	86.2	103.4	118.2	139.0	153.4	131.8	133.3	154.1	167.8
Korea	-0.4	-0.5	-1.4	-1.9	-2.5	-5.6	-5.1	-2.4	-1.2	0.4	0.3	1.0	-1.8	0.1	0.1	4.4	2.3	0.8	0.9	1.2
Luxembourg	..	..	1.6	1.3	0.5	0.2	-0.5	-1.3	-1.6	-3.4	-4.0	-4.3	-6.5	-11.0	-15.3	-17.2	-15.8	-19.6	-23.5	-25.7
Mexico	-11.4	-13.0	-13.3	-13.9	-12.8	-13.3	-12.9	-15.1	-13.9	-12.7	-12.4	-10.6	-14.9	-18.9	-19.1	-17.1	-14.9	-14.5	-16.0	-16.5
Netherlands	0.9	3.6	7.3	3.5	7.0	-2.7	3.5	-2.3	-0.2	0.1	1.3	11.3	3.8	16.7	-0.7	-18.6	-9.5	6.8	9.5	9.2
New Zealand	-2.9	-3.4	-4.0	-4.7	-4.9	-2.6	-3.1	-3.2	-2.9	-3.1	-4.0	-5.4	-6.9	-7.6	-9.5	-10.1	-5.1	-7.8	-9.8	-11.2
Norway	-3.3	-2.2	-1.9	-1.9	-1.7	-1.2	-1.3	-2.3	0.2	0.6	1.4	0.5	2.1	0.4	-1.2	-2.4	-2.1	1.5	-2.9	-4.6
Poland	..	-2.6	-2.0	-1.1	-1.1	-1.2	-1.0	-0.7	-0.6	-1.1	-2.5	-8.2	-6.7	-9.7	-16.4	-12.8	-16.6	-17.4	-20.2	-21.8
Portugal	0.2	-0.1	0.0	-1.0	-1.5	-1.6	-1.6	-2.4	-3.5	-3.0	-2.6	-3.7	-4.8	-7.9	-9.6	-11.4	-10.9	-10.3	-14.6	-16.8
Slovak Republic	0.0	-0.1	0.0	0.0	-0.1	-0.2	-0.3	-0.4	-0.3	-0.5	-1.8	-2.2	-2.0	-2.5	-3.2	-3.3	-1.8	-2.2	-2.6	-3.1
Slovenia	..	..	0.0	0.2	0.1	0.1	0.1	0.0	0.0	-0.2	-0.3	-0.4	-0.4	-0.6	-1.1	-1.5	-1.1	-0.8	-1.2	-1.4
Spain	-3.6	-7.8	-5.4	-7.5	-7.4	-8.6	-9.5	-6.9	-11.3	-11.6	-11.7	-15.1	-21.3	-26.2	-41.4	-52.0	-41.0	-28.7	-33.5	-39.8
Sweden	-8.7	-5.9	-5.5	-6.3	-4.9	-3.2	-2.0	-1.4	-1.4	-1.8	3.9	0.0	2.7	7.5	14.2	17.1	6.6	7.8	4.6	5.3
Switzerland	7.4	6.0	9.8	10.7	14.2	15.2	17.8	19.2	11.8	9.4	24.3	25.2	33.8	32.0	2.7	-36.3	14.4	25.9	28.4	32.4
Turkey	-2.7	-3.3	-3.2	-2.9	-3.0	-3.0	-3.5	-4.0	-5.0	-4.6	-5.6	-5.6	-5.8	-6.7	-7.1	-8.4	-8.2	-7.8	-8.0	-8.0
United Kingdom	-3.8	2.0	-1.4	-3.8	0.5	19.6	-1.7	3.0	13.6	27.6	28.7	32.8	40.0	15.5	40.5	54.6	32.3	49.3	68.7	70.2
United States	25.3	17.1	20.9	22.3	12.6	4.3	13.9	21.1	31.7	27.4	45.3	67.2	72.4	48.1	99.6	152.0	121.4	163.0	141.9	121.9
Euro area	-21.8	-29.9	-32.1	-27.9	-16.2	-35.9	-21.2	-26.7	-35.3	-63.7	-68.7	-14.9	-24.6	8.4	-43.2	-76.3	-34.0	-12.1	-9.5	-23.1
Total OECD	-14.5	-29.3	-34.3	-26.2	-10.1	-16.4	-11.0	-4.2	13.6	-3.8	25.8	101.8	124.0	112.0	105.0	123.8	142.3	220.4	200.6	167.0

Note: The classification of non-factor services and investment income is affected by the change in reporting system to the International Monetary Fund, Fifth Balance of Payments Manual.
1. Including Luxembourg until 1994.
Source: OECD Economic Outlook 89 database.

StatLink ⟲ http://dx.doi.org/10.1787/888932443833

Annex Table 49. Total transfers, net
$ billion

	1993	1994	1995	1996	1997	1998	1999	2000	2001	2002	2003	2004	2005	2006	2007	2008	2009	2010	2011	2012
Australia	0.3	0.2	0.3	0.5	0.4	0.2	0.4	0.1	0.3	0.4	0.3	0.1	-0.3	-0.5	-0.1	-0.3	-1.1	-1.4	-1.6	-1.6
Austria	-0.8	-0.7	-1.9	-2.1	-2.0	-1.9	-2.1	-1.8	-1.8	-1.6	-1.8	-1.7	-1.9	-1.8	-1.6	-2.1	-2.5	-2.9	-3.1	-3.3
Belgium[1]	-2.0	-2.6	-3.4	-3.4	-2.9	-3.6	-3.9	-3.4	-3.8	-3.8	-5.8	-6.0	-6.0	-6.4	-6.4	-9.5	-8.4	-7.4	-6.4	-6.5
Canada	-0.6	-0.3	-0.1	0.5	0.5	0.6	0.5	0.8	1.0	0.0	-0.2	-0.5	-1.2	-1.3	-1.8	-0.6	-1.9	-2.4	-2.5	-2.7
Chile	:	:	:	0.5	0.5	0.5	0.6	0.6	0.4	0.6	0.6	1.1	1.8	3.4	3.1	2.9	1.6	5.1	3.6	3.4
Czech Republic	0.1	0.1	0.6	0.4	0.4	0.5	0.6	0.4	0.5	0.9	0.6	0.2	0.3	-0.9	-1.4	-1.0	-0.6	-0.1	-1.1	-0.5
Denmark	-1.7	-2.0	-2.4	-2.6	-1.8	-2.3	-2.9	-3.0	-2.6	-2.6	-3.7	-4.6	-4.2	-4.8	-5.3	-5.5	-5.2	-5.4	-4.9	-5.3
Estonia	0.1	0.1	0.1	0.1	0.1	0.1	0.1	0.1	0.1	0.1	0.1	0.1	0.1	0.1	0.2	0.2	0.3	0.3	1.3	1.3
Finland	-0.4	-0.4	-0.6	-1.0	-0.9	-1.1	-1.0	-0.7	-0.7	-0.7	-1.1	-1.5	-1.5	-1.7	-2.0	-2.3	-2.4	-2.1	-2.6	-2.9
France	-8.1	-10.6	-5.9	-7.4	-13.2	-12.3	-13.2	-14.0	-14.8	-14.2	-19.2	-21.8	-27.3	-27.5	-32.1	-35.4	-37.4	-34.6	-37.1	-37.5
Germany	-33.0	-36.2	-38.8	-34.0	-30.5	-30.2	-26.6	-25.9	-24.1	-25.9	-32.0	-34.7	-36.0	-36.1	-45.1	-48.7	-46.1	-50.6	-54.0	-57.6
Greece[2]	8.3	8.3	9.0	8.9	8.3	7.9	4.1	3.3	3.5	3.6	4.3	4.5	3.8	4.3	2.2	4.1	1.7	0.1	0.2	0.2
Hungary	0.8	0.9	0.2	0.0	0.2	0.2	0.4	0.4	0.4	0.5	0.6	-0.2	-0.4	-0.4	-0.7	-0.9	0.5	0.5	0.7	0.7
Iceland	0.0	0.0	0.0	0.0	0.0	0.0	0.0	0.0	0.0	0.0	0.0	0.0	0.0	0.0	-0.1	0.0	-0.1	-0.1	-0.1	-0.1
Ireland	1.9	1.7	1.8	2.2	2.0	1.5	1.3	0.9	0.3	0.7	0.5	0.5	0.3	-0.6	-1.4	-1.7	-1.2	-1.5	-1.2	-0.4
Israel	:	:	5.5	6.0	6.1	6.1	6.2	6.6	6.7	6.9	6.5	6.3	6.1	7.5	7.3	8.3	7.4	8.4	8.6	9.3
Italy	-7.7	-7.6	-4.9	-7.5	-5.0	-8.1	-5.8	-4.4	-6.0	-5.6	-8.0	-10.3	-12.5	-16.6	-19.6	-22.5	-17.1	-24.5	-23.5	-23.8
Japan	-5.3	-6.1	-7.8	-9.1	-8.8	-8.8	-10.8	-9.8	-8.1	-5.6	-7.7	-8.0	-7.3	-10.6	-11.6	-13.2	-12.2	-12.7	-12.3	-13.1
Korea	1.2	1.3	0.0	0.0	0.6	3.3	1.9	0.6	-0.4	-1.6	-2.9	-2.4	-2.5	-4.1	-3.5	-0.7	-0.7	-3.2	-5.0	-5.0
Luxembourg	:	:	-0.6	-0.6	-0.5	-0.4	-0.6	-0.5	-0.5	-0.3	-0.6	-1.1	-1.1	-1.2	-2.0	-2.6	-1.4	-0.9	-1.3	-1.3
Mexico	3.6	3.8	4.0	4.5	5.2	6.0	6.3	7.0	9.3	10.3	15.6	18.8	22.1	25.9	26.4	25.5	21.5	21.5	24.0	25.0
Netherlands	-4.5	-5.2	-6.4	-6.8	-6.1	-7.2	-6.4	-6.2	-6.7	-6.5	-6.8	-9.6	-10.8	-10.4	-16.2	-17.2	-10.3	-13.7	-8.3	-8.4
New Zealand	0.2	0.3	0.3	0.6	0.3	0.3	0.2	0.2	0.2	0.1	0.2	0.1	0.2	0.4	0.4	0.7	0.3	2.5	6.9	0.6
Norway	-1.3	-1.7	-2.0	-1.5	-1.4	-1.5	-1.5	-1.2	-1.6	-2.2	-2.9	-2.6	-2.6	-2.8	-3.5	-3.5	-4.2	-4.7	-5.9	-6.3
Poland	:	1.3	1.0	1.7	2.0	2.9	2.2	1.3	1.5	2.0	2.5	3.7	5.0	6.6	8.5	8.3	6.5	6.0	6.9	7.5
Portugal[2]	7.2	5.5	7.3	4.4	3.8	4.1	3.8	3.3	3.4	2.8	3.3	3.5	2.8	3.2	3.6	3.6	3.0	2.9	3.1	3.2
Slovak Republic	0.1	0.1	0.1	0.2	0.2	0.4	0.2	0.1	0.2	0.2	0.2	0.2	0.0	-0.1	-0.4	-1.3	-1.0	-0.1	0.2	0.4
Slovenia	:	:	:	0.1	0.2	0.2	0.2	0.1	0.1	0.1	0.0	-0.1	-0.1	-0.2	-0.3	-0.4	-0.2	0.1	0.6	0.4
Spain	1.3	1.2	4.8	3.2	3.0	3.2	3.0	1.6	1.3	2.4	-0.6	-0.1	-4.2	-8.2	-9.8	-13.7	-11.2	-9.4	-4.7	-4.9
Sweden	-1.2	-1.2	-2.6	-1.9	-2.4	-2.5	-2.7	-2.5	-2.5	-2.9	-2.2	-4.7	-4.6	-5.0	-4.9	-6.3	-5.2	-6.3	-9.3	-9.3
Switzerland	-3.0	-3.5	-4.4	-4.3	-4.0	-4.6	-5.3	-4.5	-5.5	-5.9	-5.6	-6.5	-11.0	-9.3	-9.5	-12.8	-12.3	-12.1	-13.2	-16.3
Turkey	3.7	3.0	4.4	4.1	4.5	5.5	4.9	4.8	3.0	2.4	1.0	1.1	1.5	1.9	2.2	2.1	2.3	1.4	2.4	2.9
United Kingdom	-7.6	-7.9	-11.6	-7.1	-9.4	-13.6	-11.8	-14.7	-9.4	-13.3	-16.1	-18.8	-21.5	-21.9	-27.2	-26.3	-22.9	-30.4	-39.7	-39.9
United States	-39.8	-40.3	-38.1	-43.0	-45.1	-53.2	-50.4	-58.6	-51.3	-64.9	-71.8	-88.4	-105.8	-91.5	-115.6	-122.0	-124.9	-137.5	-140.1	-144.1
Euro area	-37.6	-46.5	-39.2	-43.7	-43.7	-47.4	-46.8	-47.4	-49.7	-48.9	-67.4	-78.0	-94.4	-103.3	-131.1	-149.7	-134.2	-144.3	-136.8	-140.9
Total OECD	-88.3	-98.7	-92.1	-94.5	-95.9	-107.8	-108.0	-119.2	-107.6	-124.0	-152.6	-183.5	-218.8	-210.6	-268.2	-294.9	-285.5	-315.1	-319.3	-335.8

1. Including Luxembourg until 1994.
2. Breaks between 1998 and 1999 for Greece and between 1995 and 1996 for Portugal, reflecting change in methodology to the International Monetary Fund, Fifth Balance of Payments Manual (capital transfers from European Union are excluded from the current account).

Source: OECD Economic Outlook 89 database.

StatLink http://dx.doi.org/10.1787/888932443852

Annex Table 50. **Current account balances**
$ billion

	1993	1994	1995	1996	1997	1998	1999	2000	2001	2002	2003	2004	2005	2006	2007	2008	2009	2010	2011	2012
Australia	-9.3	-15.8	-18.4	-14.3	-11.7	-17.7	-21.7	-15.2	-7.6	-15.5	-28.5	-39.7	-41.4	-41.5	-59.4	-48.9	-43.7	-31.8	-16.9	-22.4
Austria	-1.4	-1.5	-6.9	-7.2	-5.3	-3.5	-3.6	-1.0	-1.5	5.5	4.2	5.3	6.7	9.5	13.3	19.3	10.9	9.7	13.2	16.8
Belgium[1]	13.8	15.1	16.3	14.7	14.7	14.1	13.7	10.0	8.4	12.4	13.7	13.3	10.1	8.9	7.8	-8.6	1.5	6.2	5.5	6.8
Canada	-21.7	-13.0	-4.4	3.4	-8.2	-7.7	1.7	19.7	16.3	12.6	10.6	22.9	21.6	18.0	11.8	8.0	-38.6	-48.5	-45.4	-42.0
Chile	0.5	-0.8	..	-3.1	-3.7	-3.9	0.1	-0.9	-1.1	-0.6	-0.8	2.1	1.4	7.2	7.5	-3.3	2.6	5.0	1.8	-0.3
Czech Republic	..	..	-1.4	-4.1	-3.6	-1.3	-1.5	-2.7	-3.3	-4.2	-5.8	-5.7	-1.7	-3.4	-5.6	-1.3	-5.9	-7.2	-6.8	-8.1
Denmark	3.9	2.3	1.2	2.7	0.7	-1.5	3.4	2.5	4.2	5.0	7.3	5.7	11.1	8.2	4.4	9.0	11.1	17.1	20.1	20.4
Estonia	0.0	-0.2	-0.2	-0.4	-0.6	-0.5	-0.2	-0.3	-0.3	-0.8	-1.1	-1.4	-1.4	-2.6	-3.7	-2.4	0.9	0.7	0.7	0.2
Finland	-1.1	1.2	5.4	5.1	6.7	7.3	8.1	9.9	10.7	12.0	8.5	12.1	7.1	9.5	10.5	7.9	6.7	7.1	8.2	9.1
France	9.4	8.2	11.0	20.8	37.2	38.9	45.8	19.4	23.5	17.4	13.7	10.6	-10.1	-12.3	-26.0	-55.7	-54.4	-58.1	-76.1	-78.5
Germany	-19.4	-30.4	-29.4	-13.6	-10.1	-17.0	-28.2	-34.1	0.1	40.9	47.6	125.5	138.7	181.2	250.9	229.2	189.6	185.1	203.5	233.2
Greece[2]	-0.9	-0.2	-3.2	-5.1	-5.3	-3.8	-7.7	-9.9	-9.5	-9.7	-12.8	-13.3	-18.3	-29.8	-44.8	-51.2	-36.0	-32.1	-27.5	-23.6
Hungary	..	..	-1.6	-1.7	-2.0	-3.4	-3.7	-4.2	-3.3	-4.7	-6.7	-8.5	-8.4	-8.6	-9.6	-11.3	0.9	2.8	4.2	3.1
Iceland	0.0	0.1	0.1	-0.1	-0.1	-0.6	-0.6	-0.9	-0.4	0.1	-0.5	-1.3	-2.6	-4.0	-3.3	-4.3	-1.3	-1.0	-0.9	-0.5
Ireland	1.8	1.5	1.7	2.0	1.9	0.7	0.6	0.1	-0.7	-1.2	0.0	-1.1	-7.0	-7.9	-13.9	-15.2	-6.6	-1.4	8.1	12.0
Israel	..	..	-5.0	-5.3	-3.4	-1.0	-1.7	-4.0	-1.8	-1.2	0.9	2.1	4.4	7.5	4.2	1.9	7.1	6.8	3.0	2.7
Italy	7.4	12.5	24.4	39.1	32.8	22.4	7.9	-5.8	-0.8	-9.7	-19.6	-16.4	-29.5	-48.1	-51.8	-66.4	-43.6	-71.5	-91.4	-85.7
Japan	130.0	130.6	114.3	65.4	96.8	119.1	115.5	120.2	87.9	112.0	136.4	172.3	166.8	171.2	210.4	158.2	142.7	195.3	152.5	150.6
Korea	3.0	-3.5	-8.0	-23.0	-8.2	42.6	24.5	14.8	8.4	7.5	15.6	32.3	18.6	14.1	21.8	3.2	32.8	28.2	22.0	19.7
Luxembourg	..	..	2.5	2.3	1.9	1.8	1.8	2.7	1.8	2.3	2.4	4.1	4.4	4.4	5.2	3.1	3.6	4.3	3.4	3.1
Mexico	-23.4	-29.7	-1.6	-2.5	-7.7	-16.0	-14.0	-18.7	-17.7	-14.2	-7.2	-5.2	-5.0	-4.8	-9.1	-16.3	-6.4	-5.7	-15.6	-27.4
Netherlands	13.2	17.3	25.8	21.5	25.0	13.0	15.7	7.3	9.8	11.1	30.3	46.8	47.3	63.3	52.7	39.0	39.2	60.2	62.1	66.3
New Zealand	-1.7	-2.0	-3.0	-3.9	-4.3	-2.1	-3.5	-2.5	-1.2	-2.2	-3.1	-5.7	-8.8	-8.9	-10.6	-11.5	-3.4	-3.2	-2.8	-11.1
Norway	2.2	3.8	5.3	11.0	10.0	0.0	8.8	25.1	27.5	24.2	27.7	32.9	49.2	58.3	55.2	80.9	49.9	53.5	78.7	80.2
Poland	..	1.0	0.9	-3.3	-5.7	-6.9	-12.5	-10.3	-5.9	-5.5	-5.5	-10.1	-3.7	-9.4	-20.3	-25.6	-9.6	-15.9	-24.3	-28.2
Portugal[2]	0.2	-1.6	-0.2	-5.0	-6.7	-8.5	-10.3	-12.2	-12.4	-10.9	-10.5	-15.5	-19.8	-21.5	-23.5	-31.9	-23.9	-22.2	-19.0	-13.5
Slovak Republic	-0.5	0.8	0.5	-2.0	-1.8	-2.0	-1.0	-0.7	-1.7	-1.9	-1.9	-3.3	-4.0	-4.4	-4.0	-6.3	-2.8	-3.0	-2.3	-1.4
Slovenia	..	..	..	0.1	0.1	-0.2	-0.9	-0.6	0.0	0.2	-0.2	-0.9	-0.6	-1.0	-2.3	-3.7	-0.7	-0.5	-0.7	-0.7
Spain	-5.6	-6.5	-1.7	-1.5	-0.6	-7.2	-17.9	-23.0	-24.0	-22.5	-31.1	-54.9	-83.1	-111.1	-144.6	-154.6	-75.5	-63.3	-45.2	-37.4
Sweden	-2.6	2.5	8.4	9.8	10.3	9.7	10.7	9.4	8.5	9.8	22.1	23.8	25.0	33.7	42.7	43.2	28.2	29.0	30.5	32.4
Switzerland	18.8	16.9	20.8	21.1	24.6	25.2	29.0	30.1	21.0	24.8	43.4	48.6	52.2	58.4	39.2	9.5	57.2	77.1	86.1	92.1
Turkey	-6.4	2.6	-2.3	-2.4	-2.7	2.0	-0.9	-9.9	3.8	-0.6	-7.5	-14.4	-22.3	-32.3	-38.4	-42.0	-14.0	-48.6	-70.7	-80.5
United Kingdom	-18.7	-10.4	-14.3	-9.8	-1.6	-5.3	-35.4	-38.9	-30.4	-27.9	-30.0	-45.6	-59.2	-83.1	-72.8	-43.1	-37.1	-56.1	-36.7	-22.2
United States	-84.8	-121.6	-113.6	-124.8	-140.7	-215.1	-301.6	-417.4	-384.7	-458.1	-520.7	-630.5	-747.6	-802.6	-718.1	-668.9	-378.4	-470.2	-567.9	-630.5
Euro area	16.9	16.1	46.1	70.7	90.0	55.7	23.6	-38.4	3.4	45.2	43.2	111.0	40.4	38.1	25.7	-97.3	8.9	21.2	42.5	106.7
Total OECD	6.7	-20.8	23.3	-14.3	28.8	-28.1	-179.8	-342.1	-276.3	-293.2	-309.0	-313.1	-510.1	-584.0	-524.3	-659.8	-197.2	-252.2	-346.7	-365.5

StatLink 🔗 http://dx.doi.org/10.1787/888932443871

Note: Balance-of-payments data in this table are based on the concepts and definition of the International Monetary Fund, Fifth Balance of Payments Manual.
1. Including Luxembourg until 1994.
2. Breaks between 1998 and 1999 for Greece and between 1995 and 1996 for Portugal, reflecting change in methodology to the International Monetary Fund, Fifth Balance of Payments Manual (capital transfers from European Union are excluded from the current account).
Source: OECD Economic Outlook 89 database.

Annex Table 51. **Current account balances as a percentage of GDP**

	1993	1994	1995	1996	1997	1998	1999	2000	2001	2002	2003	2004	2005	2006	2007	2008	2009	2010	2011	2012
Australia	-3.0	-4.4	-4.8	-3.3	-2.8	-4.7	-5.3	-3.7	-2.0	-3.6	-5.2	-6.0	-5.6	-5.3	-6.2	-4.5	-4.3	-2.6	-1.1	-1.3
Austria	-0.7	-0.8	-2.9	-3.1	-2.5	-1.7	-1.7	-0.5	-0.8	2.6	1.6	1.8	2.2	2.9	3.5	4.6	2.9	2.6	3.1	3.8
Belgium[1]	6.2	6.2	5.7	5.3	5.9	5.5	5.4	4.3	3.6	4.9	4.4	3.7	2.8	2.0	1.7	-1.8	0.3	1.3	1.0	1.2
Canada	-3.9	-2.3	-0.8	0.5	-1.3	-1.2	0.3	2.7	2.3	1.7	1.2	2.3	1.9	1.4	0.8	0.4	-2.8	-3.1	-2.6	-2.3
Chile	..	..	..	-4.1	-4.4	-4.9	0.2	-1.2	-1.5	-0.9	-1.1	2.2	1.2	4.9	4.6	-2.2	1.5	2.4	0.7	-0.1
Czech Republic	1.2	-1.8	-2.5	-6.6	-6.2	-2.0	-2.4	-4.8	-5.3	-5.5	-6.2	-5.2	-1.3	-2.4	-3.2	-0.6	-3.2	-3.8	-3.0	-3.4
Denmark	2.8	1.5	0.7	1.4	0.4	-0.9	1.9	1.6	2.6	2.9	3.4	2.3	4.3	3.0	1.4	2.7	3.6	5.5	5.8	5.6
Estonia	..	..	-4.2	-8.4	-11.1	-8.6	-4.3	-5.4	-5.2	-10.6	-11.3	-11.3	-10.0	-15.3	-17.2	-9.7	4.5	3.6	3.2	0.7
Finland	-1.3	1.2	4.1	4.0	5.5	5.6	6.2	8.2	8.6	8.9	5.1	6.4	3.6	4.6	4.2	2.9	2.7	2.9	3.0	3.2
France	0.7	0.6	0.7	1.3	2.6	2.6	3.1	1.4	1.8	1.2	0.8	0.5	-0.5	-0.5	-1.0	-1.9	-2.1	-2.2	-2.6	-2.6
Germany	-1.0	-1.4	-1.2	-0.6	-0.4	-0.8	-1.3	-1.8	0.0	2.0	1.9	4.6	5.0	6.2	7.5	6.3	5.6	5.6	5.5	6.0
Greece[2]	-0.9	-0.2	-2.4	-3.7	-3.9	-2.8	-5.6	-7.8	-7.2	-6.5	-6.5	-5.8	-7.6	-11.2	-14.4	-14.7	-11.0	-10.4	-8.6	-7.2
Hungary	..	..	-3.3	-3.8	-4.3	-6.9	-7.5	-8.8	-6.1	-6.8	-7.9	-8.3	-7.6	-7.6	-6.9	-7.2	0.5	2.1	2.7	1.8
Iceland	0.7	1.9	0.7	-1.8	-1.8	-6.8	-6.8	-10.2	-4.3	1.5	-4.8	-9.8	-16.1	-23.8	-16.3	-24.8	-10.7	-8.0	-6.2	-3.6
Ireland	3.6	2.7	2.6	2.7	2.4	0.8	0.6	0.0	-0.6	-1.0	0.0	-0.6	-3.5	-3.6	-5.3	-5.6	-3.0	-0.7	3.7	5.3
Israel	..	..	-5.2	-5.0	-3.1	-0.9	-1.5	-3.2	-1.5	-1.1	0.8	1.6	3.3	5.2	2.5	0.9	3.6	3.1	1.2	1.0
Italy	0.8	1.2	2.2	3.1	2.7	1.9	0.6	-0.6	-0.1	-0.8	-1.3	-0.9	-1.7	-2.6	-2.4	-2.9	-2.1	-3.5	-4.1	-3.6
Japan	3.0	2.7	2.2	1.4	2.3	3.1	2.6	2.6	2.1	2.9	3.2	3.7	3.7	3.9	4.8	3.3	2.8	3.6	2.6	2.5
Korea	0.8	-0.8	-1.5	-4.0	-1.3	12.0	5.3	2.8	1.7	1.3	2.4	4.5	2.2	1.5	2.1	0.5	3.9	2.8	1.9	1.6
Luxembourg	..	..	12.1	11.2	10.4	9.2	8.4	13.2	8.8	10.5	8.1	11.9	11.5	10.4	10.1	5.3	6.9	7.8	5.5	4.7
Mexico	-4.8	-5.8	-0.4	-0.7	-1.6	-3.3	-2.5	-2.8	-2.5	-2.0	-1.0	-0.7	-0.6	-0.5	-0.9	-1.5	-0.7	-0.5	-1.3	-2.1
Netherlands	4.0	4.9	6.2	5.1	6.5	3.2	3.8	1.9	2.4	2.5	5.6	7.6	7.4	9.3	6.7	4.4	4.9	7.7	7.2	7.4
New Zealand	-3.9	-3.8	-5.0	-5.7	-6.3	-3.7	-6.1	-4.6	-2.2	-3.6	-3.9	-5.7	-7.9	-8.2	-8.0	-8.7	-2.9	-2.2	-1.6	-6.3
Norway	1.8	3.0	3.5	6.8	6.3	0.0	5.6	15.0	16.1	12.6	12.3	12.7	16.3	17.3	14.1	17.9	13.1	12.9	15.6	14.9
Poland	..	0.9	0.6	-2.1	-3.7	-4.0	-7.5	-6.0	-3.1	-2.8	-2.5	-4.0	-1.2	-2.7	-4.7	-4.8	-2.2	-3.4	-4.5	-4.8
Portugal[2]	0.3	-1.6	-0.1	-4.2	-5.8	-6.9	-8.2	-10.4	-10.3	-8.3	-6.5	-8.4	-10.4	-10.7	-10.1	-12.6	-10.2	-9.7	-7.8	-5.5
Slovak Republic	-3.9	4.9	2.6	-9.3	-8.5	-8.9	-4.8	-3.5	-8.3	-7.9	-5.9	-7.8	-8.5	-7.8	-5.3	-6.6	-3.2	-3.5	-2.4	-1.3
Slovenia	..	-1.2	-0.3	0.3	0.3	-0.7	-4.0	-3.2	0.2	1.1	-0.8	-2.7	-1.7	-2.5	-4.8	-6.7	-1.5	-1.1	-1.3	-1.3
Spain	-1.1	-1.2	-0.3	-0.2	-0.1	-1.2	-2.9	-4.0	-3.9	-3.3	-3.5	-5.3	-7.4	-9.0	-10.0	-9.6	-5.2	-4.5	-2.9	-2.3
Sweden	-1.3	1.1	3.3	3.5	4.1	3.8	4.1	3.8	3.7	4.0	7.0	6.6	6.7	8.4	9.2	8.8	7.0	6.3	5.5	5.5
Switzerland	7.7	6.2	6.6	6.9	9.3	9.3	10.8	12.0	8.2	8.8	13.3	13.4	14.0	14.9	9.0	1.9	11.5	14.7	13.6	13.9
Turkey	-2.6	2.0	-1.2	-1.0	-1.0	0.9	-0.6	-3.7	2.0	-0.3	-2.5	-3.7	-4.6	-6.1	-5.9	-5.6	-2.2	-6.6	-8.7	-8.9
United Kingdom	-1.9	-1.0	-1.2	-0.8	-0.1	-0.4	-2.4	-2.6	-2.1	-1.7	-1.6	-2.1	-2.6	-3.4	-2.6	-1.6	-1.7	-2.5	-1.5	-0.9
United States	-1.3	-1.7	-1.5	-1.6	-1.7	-2.4	-3.2	-4.2	-3.7	-4.3	-4.7	-5.3	-5.9	-6.0	-5.1	-4.7	-2.7	-3.2	-3.7	-4.0
#N/A	0.3	0.3	0.6	1.0	1.3	0.8	0.3	-0.6	0.1	0.6	0.5	1.1	0.4	0.3	0.2	-0.7	0.0	0.2	0.3	0.8
Total OECD	0.0	-0.1	0.1	-0.1	0.1	-0.1	-0.7	-1.3	-1.1	-1.1	-1.0	-0.9	-1.4	-1.5	-1.3	-1.5	-0.5	-0.6	-0.7	-0.7

1. Including Luxembourg until 1994.
2. Breaks between 1998 and 1999 for Greece and between 1995 and 1996 for Portugal, reflecting change in methodology to the International Monetary Fund, Fifth Balance of Payments Manual (capital transfers from European Union are excluded from the current account).
Source: OECD Economic Outlook 89 database.

StatLink http://dx.doi.org/10.1787/888932443890

Annex Table 52. **Structure of current account balances of major world regions**

$ billion

	1995	1996	1997	1998	1999	2000	2001	2002	2003	2004	2005	2006	2007	2008	2009	2010	2011
Goods and services trade balance[1]																	
OECD	154	113	146	91	-51	-213	-183	-156	-209	-266	-443	-520	-407	-508	-81	-213	-288
China	12	18	43	44	31	29	28	37	36	49	125	209	308	349	220	232	205
Other industrialised Asia[2]	-19	-4	-3	54	65	68	67	84	97	84	89	119	143	61	91	111	129
Russia	10	16	9	12	33	52	39	37	49	72	105	126	113	155	94	124	190
Brazil	-12	-15	-19	-17	-8	-11	-8	6	16	26	32	32	20	3	-2	-21	-17
Other oil producers	28	59	50	-12	46	143	87	76	116	180	322	419	408	567	179	335	575
Rest of the world	-47	-49	-61	-75	-55	-48	-48	-37	-44	-62	-90	-121	-184	-260	-153	-164	-236
World[3]	126	138	164	97	60	19	-18	49	62	83	138	263	401	368	348	404	559
Investment income, net																	
OECD	-34	-26	-10	-16	-11	-4	14	-4	26	102	124	112	105	124	142	220	201
China	-12	-12	-11	-17	-14	-15	-19	-15	-8	-4	-16	-5	8	18	7	30	59
Other industrialised Asia[2]	-6	-9	-8	-9	-15	-18	-13	-17	-13	-23	-33	-27	-26	-27	-24	-45	-54
Russia	-3	-5	-9	-12	-8	-7	-4	-7	-13	-13	-19	-29	-31	-49	-40	-48	-52
Brazil	-11	-12	-15	-18	-19	-18	-20	-18	-19	-21	-26	-27	-29	-41	-34	-40	-47
Other oil producers	0	-2	2	1	-2	-9	-11	-20	-26	-34	-44	-30	-36	-53	-43	-69	-92
Rest of the world	-20	-24	-25	-23	-25	-28	-29	-30	-37	-42	-43	-46	-60	-67	-60	-76	-92
World[3]	-86	-91	-76	-93	-94	-98	-82	-111	-89	-34	-58	-54	-70	-96	-51	-27	-78
Net transfers, net																	
OECD	-92	-95	-96	-108	-108	-119	-108	-124	-153	-183	-219	-211	-268	-295	-286	-315	-319
China	1	2	5	4	5	6	8	13	18	23	25	29	39	46	34	43	53
Other industrialised Asia[2]	6	10	11	7	15	16	17	20	27	24	34	42	53	66	66	69	72
Russia	0	0	0	1	0	0	-1	-1	0	-1	-1	-2	4	-3	-3	-4	-5
Brazil	4	2	2	1	2	2	2	2	3	3	4	4	4	4	3	3	3
Other oil producers	-22	-19	-18	-18	-18	-19	-20	-20	-19	-19	-13	-8	-21	-30	-36	-37	-51
Rest of the world	32	33	35	39	40	46	52	58	68	79	90	105	121	139	134	140	150
World[3]	-70	-66	-62	-74	-64	-69	-49	-52	-57	-74	-80	-40	-76	-72	-88	-101	-98
Current balance																	
OECD	23	-14	29	-28	-180	-342	-276	-293	-309	-313	-510	-584	-524	-660	-197	-252	-347
China	2	7	37	31	21	21	17	35	46	69	134	233	354	412	261	305	318
Other industrialised Asia[2]	-28	-18	-8	46	59	46	60	77	104	77	70	119	157	89	137	109	120
Russia	7	11	0	0	25	47	34	29	35	60	85	95	78	104	49	71	133
Brazil	-18	-24	-30	-33	-25	-24	-23	-8	4	12	14	14	2	-28	-24	-48	-47
Other oil producers	1	31	24	-35	19	109	52	31	68	125	264	381	352	484	99	226	429
Rest of the world	-37	-43	-55	-62	-42	-33	-26	-8	-13	-28	-47	-68	-129	-194	-86	-106	-186
World[3]	-51	-50	-4	-80	-123	-177	-162	-137	-64	1	10	190	289	207	237	306	419

Note: Historical data for the OECD area are aggregates of reported balance-of-payments data of each individual country. Because of various statistical problems as well as a large number of non-reporters among non-OECD countries, trade and current account balances estimated on the basis of these countries' own balance-of-payments records may differ from corresponding estimates shown in this table.
1. National-accounts basis for OECD countries and balance-of-payments basis for the non-OECD regions.
2. Dynamic Asian Economies (Chinese Taipei; Hong Kong, China; Malaysia; Philippines; Singapore; Vietnam and Thailand), India and Indonesia.
3. Reflects statistical errors and asymmetries. Given the very large gross flows of world balance-of-payments transactions, statistical errors and asymmetries easily give rise to world totals (balances) that are significantly different from zero.
Source: OECD Economic Outlook 89 database.

StatLink http://dx.doi.org/10.1787/888932443909

Annex Table 53. Export market growth in goods and services

Percentage changes from previous year

	1993	1994	1995	1996	1997	1998	1999	2000	2001	2002	2003	2004	2005	2006	2007	2008	2009	2010	2011	2012
Australia	4.3	10.2	13.0	9.7	6.9	-1.3	4.8	12.7	0.1	6.0	8.4	13.4	9.6	8.8	7.7	4.9	-9.2	13.5	8.9	9.7
Austria	-1.1	7.2	8.6	5.3	9.7	8.2	6.2	11.4	2.2	1.7	5.2	8.8	7.4	10.6	7.5	2.9	-11.5	11.5	8.1	7.3
Belgium	-0.5	7.9	8.4	5.5	10.0	8.6	6.5	12.1	1.8	1.7	3.9	8.4	7.1	9.1	6.3	2.0	-11.2	10.5	7.4	7.1
Canada	7.2	11.2	8.0	8.9	12.6	10.1	10.5	13.0	-2.0	3.6	4.7	11.0	6.7	6.8	3.7	-1.2	-13.1	12.7	6.1	8.6
Chile	3.3	8.8	9.0	9.9	10.1	3.0	5.6	12.4	0.4	2.8	6.8	11.6	8.5	9.5	8.5	3.7	-10.2	14.8	9.0	9.6
Czech Republic	..	6.7	8.6	6.3	10.1	9.6	5.7	11.1	2.8	1.4	5.1	8.4	7.8	11.2	7.4	2.8	-12.3	11.3	8.0	6.9
Denmark	0.4	8.4	8.4	6.5	10.5	8.2	5.8	11.3	1.1	1.8	4.6	8.7	7.7	9.4	7.1	2.5	-11.8	11.1	7.4	7.2
Estonia	2.5	8.3	8.8	5.8	10.8	7.7	3.8	12.2	2.0	2.9	4.6	9.0	9.3	10.1	9.2	5.1	-14.6	9.5	8.5	6.8
Finland	0.6	6.1	9.2	6.0	10.0	5.6	3.6	12.7	2.5	3.5	6.2	10.6	9.5	10.9	10.2	4.8	-13.6	12.8	10.0	8.3
France	0.0	6.7	8.5	6.2	10.3	7.4	6.0	11.1	1.8	2.6	4.8	9.1	7.7	9.0	7.2	2.4	-11.4	10.2	7.6	7.3
Germany	0.8	7.4	9.1	6.6	10.4	7.5	5.6	12.3	1.9	3.1	4.7	9.7	7.7	8.9	7.6	2.1	-12.0	10.8	7.7	7.6
Greece	3.7	4.4	8.8	5.8	10.4	7.3	4.7	9.9	1.7	3.3	5.4	9.8	8.6	8.8	8.7	3.9	-11.8	10.0	9.5	7.1
Hungary	..	6.4	8.6	5.7	9.6	8.2	5.7	10.9	2.7	1.7	5.0	8.7	7.7	10.3	7.8	2.8	-12.0	10.7	8.2	6.9
Iceland	-0.1	8.0	8.1	6.4	10.0	8.8	7.2	11.0	2.3	2.5	3.6	8.2	7.3	9.4	5.7	1.6	-11.8	9.2	6.2	6.6
Ireland	0.6	8.3	7.7	6.5	9.9	7.7	7.2	11.6	1.2	2.6	3.8	8.5	6.9	8.3	4.7	0.9	-11.5	10.6	6.5	6.8
Israel	4.8	9.4	9.4	7.7	11.1	6.1	6.0	13.0	-0.9	3.5	5.4	11.2	7.5	7.9	6.0	1.3	-11.9	13.2	7.8	8.3
Italy	1.3	6.2	8.4	6.5	10.2	7.7	5.9	11.7	2.0	2.7	5.1	9.8	8.2	9.3	8.3	3.2	-11.6	10.2	8.1	7.6
Japan	6.0	11.0	11.9	8.9	9.8	1.3	8.8	14.8	-1.1	7.3	9.6	14.1	9.3	9.8	8.3	4.0	-8.4	15.1	8.8	9.7
Korea	5.5	8.7	11.7	10.0	9.3	2.1	6.6	13.8	0.7	7.1	10.5	14.4	10.1	10.3	9.0	4.5	-7.6	14.7	9.1	10.2
Luxembourg	-2.3	7.9	7.6	4.7	9.4	8.3	6.2	11.0	1.7	1.3	3.4	7.3	6.8	8.5	5.6	1.3	-11.3	10.1	7.2	6.7
Mexico	7.8	10.9	8.0	8.5	13.1	10.7	10.3	12.5	-2.2	3.1	4.7	11.0	6.6	6.5	3.8	-1.4	-13.4	12.5	6.1	8.4
Netherlands	-0.9	7.4	7.9	5.4	9.7	7.9	6.1	11.8	1.7	2.0	4.2	8.4	7.4	9.2	6.5	2.3	-11.5	10.5	7.6	7.0
New Zealand	3.9	9.5	10.3	8.6	8.8	3.0	6.8	11.5	-0.9	6.0	7.5	12.4	9.0	8.5	8.2	5.7	-9.8	12.7	8.4	9.0
Norway	0.8	8.5	7.9	6.4	10.3	8.3	6.9	11.6	1.5	2.6	3.5	8.1	7.3	9.0	5.0	1.5	-11.9	10.6	6.7	6.5
Poland	..	6.7	8.7	5.0	9.4	8.0	5.3	11.4	3.0	1.8	5.0	8.8	7.8	10.7	8.1	3.4	-12.5	11.6	8.7	7.1
Portugal	-1.4	7.5	8.3	6.1	10.7	9.5	7.5	11.5	2.6	2.6	4.4	8.7	7.8	8.9	7.1	0.7	-12.4	8.9	6.8	7.2
Slovak Republic	..	7.6	10.5	6.4	10.1	9.1	6.0	12.3	3.4	2.0	5.6	10.1	6.8	11.2	8.8	2.9	-11.8	12.1	7.9	7.4
Slovenia	-1.0	6.3	9.0	4.3	9.5	7.9	4.7	10.8	3.3	1.8	4.9	8.6	7.5	10.1	8.6	3.3	-12.5	10.6	9.1	6.7
Spain	-0.5	7.0	7.5	5.5	10.1	9.0	5.9	11.2	1.9	1.8	3.4	8.2	7.1	8.6	6.4	2.3	-11.2	10.0	7.0	6.5
Sweden	1.5	7.5	8.2	6.9	10.6	7.6	4.7	11.1	1.5	3.0	4.1	9.5	8.6	9.3	7.1	3.2	-11.9	10.0	7.4	7.4
Switzerland	-0.5	7.5	8.6	5.9	9.8	7.3	6.4	11.7	1.5	2.2	5.0	9.1	7.5	9.2	7.0	2.3	-11.1	11.2	8.0	7.6
Turkey	-0.4	3.5	8.1	5.3	9.9	7.3	5.0	10.4	3.5	3.1	4.7	9.2	9.1	8.9	9.8	4.8	-11.0	8.3	8.9	7.8
United Kingdom	1.2	7.8	9.3	6.6	10.6	7.9	6.3	12.6	1.1	2.8	4.4	9.8	8.0	8.2	7.6	2.4	-11.1	10.4	7.6	7.9
United States	3.1	8.6	6.9	8.9	10.9	4.0	6.4	12.4	-0.5	3.1	5.2	10.7	8.5	8.7	8.0	3.8	-11.6	13.9	8.2	8.7
Total OECD	1.8	8.1	8.7	7.2	10.3	6.5	6.6	12.3	0.8	3.2	5.3	10.2	8.0	9.0	7.3	2.7	-11.2	11.9	7.8	8.1
Memorandum items																				
China	3.6	9.1	10.7	8.1	9.1	2.8	6.5	12.5	-0.9	3.9	5.8	11.3	8.1	8.0	6.8	3.3	-12.1	12.3	8.1	8.6
Other industrialised Asia	5.2	10.8	12.8	9.1	8.5	0.8	6.7	14.1	-0.6	6.7	9.5	14.1	9.9	10.0	8.0	5.1	-8.2	14.2	8.7	9.8
Russia	2.7	5.2	10.1	6.8	10.9	7.4	5.0	11.3	1.9	3.5	6.1	9.9	8.3	9.5	8.9	3.5	-10.4	10.5	8.7	7.7
Brazil	4.7	8.2	6.2	9.0	12.8	6.2	3.1	10.4	-0.3	-1.2	8.1	13.4	10.3	9.6	10.2	5.4	-11.7	14.4	10.0	9.4
Other oil producers	2.9	8.3	11.6	8.6	8.6	1.7	6.4	12.6	0.0	4.7	6.9	11.5	8.4	8.5	7.8	3.3	-10.4	12.5	8.3	9.0
Rest of the world	2.4	5.1	9.1	9.1	10.5	5.7	3.5	11.5	2.0	3.5	5.9	11.0	9.2	9.3	9.8	4.7	-11.9	12.0	9.7	8.5

Note: Regional aggregates are calculated inclusive of intra-regional trade. The calculation of export markets is based on a weighted average of import volumes in each exporting country's market, with weights based on goods and services trade flows in 2005.

1. Chinese Taipei; Hong Kong, China; Malaysia; Philippines; Singapore; Vietnam; Thailand; India and Indonesia.

Source: OECD Economic Outlook 89 database.

StatLink ⟨ms⟩ http://dx.doi.org/10.1787/888932443928

Annex Table 54. Import penetration
Goods and services import volume as a percentage of total final expenditure, constant prices

	1993	1994	1995	1996	1997	1998	1999	2000	2001	2002	2003	2004	2005	2006	2007	2008	2009	2010	2011	2012
Australia	10.4	11.2	11.6	11.9	12.5	12.7	13.2	13.6	12.7	13.5	14.3	15.7	16.3	17.0	18.0	19.3	17.5	19.1	19.9	20.6
Austria	24.5	25.8	26.4	26.8	27.7	28.0	28.4	29.8	30.7	30.4	31.0	32.5	33.5	33.9	34.5	33.6	31.7	32.7	33.6	34.4
Belgium	37.5	38.3	38.5	39.1	40.3	41.2	41.0	43.0	42.8	42.6	42.7	43.5	44.7	45.2	45.7	46.2	43.8	45.2	46.3	47.3
Canada	24.0	24.6	25.1	25.8	27.6	27.8	28.2	28.8	27.3	27.1	27.5	28.5	29.4	29.8	30.6	30.8	28.1	30.2	31.0	32.0
Chile	..	..	..	22.4	23.5	24.1	22.4	23.3	23.5	23.5	24.5	26.6	28.7	29.8	31.7	33.6	30.5	35.1	36.4	37.5
Czech Republic	27.5	28.6	31.3	32.8	34.4	36.3	37.1	39.9	42.3	43.0	44.1	47.3	47.0	48.9	51.0	51.6	49.6	53.9	55.4	57.0
Denmark	22.6	23.8	24.5	24.6	25.7	26.9	27.0	28.8	29.1	30.5	30.1	31.2	33.0	35.2	35.8	36.7	34.8	35.0	35.6	36.3
Estonia	..	..	39.3	40.1	43.6	44.8	43.1	46.9	46.6	46.5	47.1	48.8	50.7	51.3	52.0	51.6	43.9	48.5	50.4	51.6
Finland	20.1	21.4	21.8	22.5	23.3	23.7	23.7	25.6	25.5	25.8	26.1	26.7	28.4	29.0	29.4	30.5	28.1	28.0	28.2	28.7
France	15.9	16.7	17.4	17.5	18.3	19.5	19.9	21.7	21.8	21.8	21.9	22.6	23.3	24.0	24.6	24.6	23.0	24.2	25.2	26.1
Germany	18.3	19.1	19.9	20.3	21.3	22.5	23.6	24.8	24.9	24.6	25.6	26.7	27.9	29.6	30.1	30.5	29.4	31.2	32.2	33.1
Greece	19.3	19.2	20.2	21.0	22.7	23.7	25.8	27.7	27.1	26.2	25.7	25.9	25.2	26.0	27.0	27.6	24.1	24.1	22.9	23.3
Hungary	25.7	26.8	29.7	31.4	34.9	38.6	40.4	43.3	43.7	44.3	45.7	48.2	49.3	52.3	55.8	57.3	54.5	57.8	59.3	61.3
Iceland	22.3	22.3	22.9	24.8	25.3	28.1	28.2	29.0	26.3	25.8	27.3	28.6	32.5	33.7	32.3	27.7	24.0	25.3	25.5	25.6
Ireland	31.6	33.4	34.4	35.2	36.1	39.8	39.9	42.2	42.5	41.6	40.1	41.1	41.6	42.0	42.4	42.6	42.4	44.1	45.3	46.0
Israel	..	..	28.1	28.4	28.5	28.0	30.4	31.0	29.7	29.6	29.0	30.4	30.0	29.5	30.8	30.4	27.1	28.6	29.2	29.9
Italy	15.6	16.5	17.4	17.1	18.1	19.2	19.7	20.8	20.7	20.7	20.9	21.2	21.6	22.2	22.6	22.0	20.4	21.9	22.9	23.5
Japan	6.5	6.9	7.7	8.4	8.3	8.0	8.2	8.7	8.7	8.8	9.0	9.4	9.7	9.9	9.8	10.0	9.2	9.6	10.1	10.6
Korea	18.3	20.1	22.0	23.1	22.9	19.8	21.8	23.9	22.4	23.5	24.9	26.1	26.8	27.9	29.1	29.6	27.9	29.8	30.5	31.7
Luxembourg	..	..	50.4	51.5	53.1	54.4	55.8	56.3	57.2	56.3	57.7	59.5	59.2	61.0	61.6	63.3	61.5	62.3	63.2	63.9
Mexico	12.1	13.7	12.5	14.3	16.0	17.5	18.9	21.1	21.0	21.2	21.1	22.2	23.0	24.3	25.0	25.3	22.6	25.3	25.5	26.8
Netherlands	30.8	32.0	33.4	33.8	35.3	36.4	37.4	39.2	39.3	39.4	39.8	40.6	41.4	42.8	43.6	43.6	42.3	44.5	45.1	46.3
New Zealand	20.0	21.1	21.7	22.4	22.2	22.4	23.6	22.9	22.9	23.7	24.3	26.4	26.9	25.9	27.0	27.7	24.4	26.0	27.3	28.1
Norway	17.9	18.0	18.2	18.7	19.6	20.5	20.0	19.8	19.7	19.7	19.7	20.4	21.4	22.4	23.3	24.0	22.0	23.4	23.7	24.4
Poland	14.2	15.0	16.9	19.4	21.7	23.9	23.3	24.9	24.0	24.3	25.3	26.8	27.6	30.0	31.3	31.6	28.0	29.4	30.2	30.9
Portugal	20.3	21.6	22.1	22.4	23.4	25.1	25.9	26.2	26.0	25.8	25.9	27.0	27.3	28.4	29.1	29.5	27.8	28.5	27.9	27.9
Slovak Republic	35.4	33.1	34.3	36.5	37.5	40.5	40.6	42.2	44.5	44.4	45.0	45.8	47.2	49.3	49.0	48.3	44.3	47.0	48.0	48.5
Slovenia	..	..	..	32.8	34.1	35.3	35.9	36.5	36.5	36.7	37.6	39.7	40.2	41.6	43.8	43.9	40.4	41.8	42.6	43.5
Spain	15.7	16.9	18.0	19.0	20.3	21.9	23.3	24.3	24.5	24.7	25.3	26.4	27.2	28.5	29.4	28.0	24.8	25.9	26.3	27.3
Sweden	21.7	23.1	23.7	24.0	25.8	27.0	27.1	28.5	27.9	27.2	27.5	27.8	28.5	29.5	30.6	31.4	29.6	30.8	31.7	32.3
Switzerland	22.7	23.8	24.5	25.1	26.2	27.1	27.6	28.9	29.1	28.8	29.1	30.1	30.9	31.5	32.1	31.7	30.9	31.8	32.4	33.2
Turkey	13.8	11.8	13.9	15.2	16.9	16.8	16.7	18.7	15.4	17.2	19.7	21.3	21.9	22.0	23.0	22.1	20.2	22.1	24.0	24.9
United Kingdom	16.1	16.3	16.7	17.6	18.5	19.3	20.0	20.8	21.1	21.6	21.4	22.1	22.9	24.0	23.4	23.2	21.8	23.0	23.4	23.8
United States	8.4	9.0	9.4	9.8	10.6	11.2	11.9	12.7	12.3	12.5	12.7	13.5	13.8	14.2	14.3	14.0	12.6	13.6	14.0	14.6
Total OECD	13.4	14.1	14.8	15.3	16.2	16.8	17.5	18.6	18.4	18.5	18.8	19.7	20.3	21.0	21.5	21.5	19.9	21.2	21.9	22.6

Note: The OECD aggregate is calculated inclusive of intra-regional trade as the sum of import volumes expressed in 2005 $ divided by the sum of total final expenditure expressed in 2005 $.
Source: OECD Economic Outlook 89 database.

StatLink http://dx.doi.org/10.1787/888932443947

Annex Table 55. **Quarterly demand and output projections**
Percentage changes from previous period, seasonally adjusted at annual rates, volume

	2010	2011	2012	2010 Q4	2011 Q1	Q2	Q3	Q4	2012 Q1	Q2	Q3	Q4	2010	2011	2012
													Q4 / Q4		
Private consumption															
Canada	3.4	2.6	2.7	4.9	1.4	2.3	2.3	2.3	2.8	2.9	3.0	3.2	3.4	2.1	3.0
France	1.3	1.5	1.9	1.4	2.3	0.8	1.2	1.6	2.1	2.1	2.3	2.3	1.1	1.5	2.2
Germany	0.4	1.3	1.4	0.9	1.8	0.8	0.8	1.3	1.6	1.6	1.7	1.7	1.4	1.2	1.6
Italy	1.0	0.9	1.2	1.0	0.6	0.9	0.9	1.0	1.3	1.4	1.4	1.3	1.0	0.9	1.3
Japan	1.8	-1.3	1.6	-3.9	-2.2	-4.8	3.3	2.0	1.3	2.3	1.8	1.8	0.6	-0.5	1.8
United Kingdom	0.6	0.2	1.1	-1.3	0.7	0.2	0.6	0.7	1.1	1.3	1.7	2.2	-0.1	0.6	1.6
United States	1.7	2.9	2.9	4.0	2.7	2.8	2.8	2.9	2.9	3.0	3.0	3.0	2.6	2.8	3.0
Euro area	0.7	0.8	1.4	0.7	0.9	0.5	0.8	1.2	1.5	1.6	1.7	1.7	0.9	0.8	1.7
Total OECD	1.9	2.0	2.5	2.2	1.8	1.5	2.3	2.3	2.5	2.8	2.8	2.8	2.1	2.0	2.7
Public consumption															
Canada	3.4	1.6	-0.4	3.2	3.0	-0.1	-0.3	-0.3	-0.4	-0.4	-0.5	-0.5	2.1	0.6	-0.5
France	1.2	0.5	0.1	0.4	1.0	0.0	0.0	0.0	0.2	0.2	0.2	0.2	0.4	0.3	0.2
Germany	2.3	1.5	1.0	2.2	1.0	1.0	1.0	1.0	1.0	1.0	1.0	1.0	2.9	1.0	1.0
Italy	-0.6	-0.1	-0.1	-2.3	0.2	1.1	0.9	0.3	-0.4	-0.7	-0.6	-0.3	-1.1	0.6	-0.5
Japan	2.3	2.6	-0.4	1.5	3.9	3.9	0.5	0.6	0.1	-4.4	0.3	0.1	1.5	2.2	-1.0
United Kingdom	0.8	0.2	-0.7	1.5	0.6	0.2	-0.2	-0.6	-0.8	-1.0	-1.2	-1.2	0.6	0.0	-1.0
United States	0.9	-0.6	0.2	-2.2	-2.5	0.1	-0.1	-0.2	0.2	0.4	0.6	0.7	0.7	-0.7	0.5
Euro area	0.6	0.0	-0.1	2.4	-2.4	0.0	0.1	0.0	-0.1	-0.1	-0.1	0.0	0.4	-0.6	-0.1
Total OECD	1.3	0.5	0.3	1.4	-0.8	0.8	0.1	-0.1	0.3	0.0	0.8	1.0	1.1	0.0	0.5
Business investment															
Canada	5.2	12.7	10.7	10.4	11.0	12.5	12.5	14.0	11.0	8.0	8.0	8.0	14.2	12.5	8.7
France	2.0	6.1	6.6	3.6	7.8	5.3	5.7	6.6	7.0	7.0	7.0	7.0	4.5	6.3	7.0
Germany	7.6	9.3	6.3	1.0	21.1	0.9	6.0	6.7	7.3	6.5	6.5	6.5	12.7	8.4	6.7
Italy	6.3	3.2	6.6	-1.7	2.5	4.2	4.3	3.8	7.8	9.0	8.3	6.8	7.0	3.7	8.0
Japan	2.1	0.7	8.5	0.4	-3.5	-11.6	15.4	14.6	10.2	6.6	5.8	5.0	5.1	3.1	6.9
United Kingdom	2.6	6.7	8.0	-0.1	8.7	6.3	6.5	7.4	8.2	8.7	9.1	9.1	12.2	7.2	8.8
United States	5.7	8.3	11.4	7.7	1.8	10.5	11.4	12.2	11.6	10.9	11.0	11.1	10.6	8.9	11.1
Euro area	2.0	5.2	6.1	2.2	8.7	3.6	5.3	5.6	6.7	6.8	6.7	6.5	5.1	5.8	6.7
Total OECD	4.0	5.6	8.9	3.8	2.3	5.2	9.4	9.7	9.3	8.6	8.5	8.3	7.5	6.6	8.7
Total investment															
Canada	8.3	6.8	5.4	5.9	5.7	6.7	6.7	6.9	5.1	4.1	4.1	4.3	9.6	6.5	4.4
France	-1.1	4.0	4.6	2.2	4.7	3.9	4.0	4.5	4.8	4.8	4.8	4.8	1.9	4.3	4.8
Germany	5.7	6.3	4.0	-4.1	17.2	1.2	3.5	3.7	4.0	4.4	4.9	5.0	7.5	6.2	4.6
Italy	2.3	1.2	2.5	-2.9	0.7	1.9	2.5	2.5	2.6	2.6	2.7	2.7	2.7	1.9	2.6
Japan	-0.2	0.0	6.5	-2.9	-3.0	-6.6	13.3	10.7	8.4	5.4	1.3	0.9	1.3	3.2	4.0
United Kingdom	3.0	1.7	4.2	-7.2	1.7	2.1	2.5	3.4	4.4	5.0	5.6	5.9	5.8	2.4	5.2
United States	3.3	4.2	8.0	5.5	-3.7	6.3	8.4	8.4	8.1	7.8	7.9	8.1	6.5	4.7	8.0
Euro area	-0.8	2.5	3.4	-0.8	5.3	1.3	2.8	3.2	3.6	3.8	4.1	4.2	1.5	3.1	3.9
Total OECD	2.5	3.7	6.2	3.5	0.4	3.6	6.6	6.4	6.4	6.3	6.2	6.5	4.8	4.2	6.4

Note: The adoption of national accounts systems SNA93 or ESA95 has been proceeding at an uneven pace among OECD member countries, both with respect to variables and the time period covered. As a consequence, there are breaks in many national series. Moreover, most countries have shifted to chain-weighted price indices to calculate real GDP and expenditures components. For further information, see table "National Account Reporting Systems, base years and latest data updates" at the beginning of the Statistical Annex and *OECD Economic Outlook* Sources and Methods *(http://www.oecd.org/eco/sources-and-methods)*.

Source: OECD Economic Outlook 89 database.

StatLink http://dx.doi.org/10.1787/888932443966

Annex Table 55. **Quarterly demand and output projections** *(cont'd)*
Percentage changes from previous period, seasonally adjusted at annual rates, volume

	2010	2011	2012	2010 Q4	2011 Q1	Q2	Q3	2012 Q4	Q1	Q2	Q3	Q4	2010 Q4/Q4	2011 Q4/Q4	2012 Q4/Q4
Total domestic demand															
Canada	5.2	2.6	2.6	-1.2	3.6	2.6	2.7	2.8	2.7	2.5	2.5	2.7	4.2	2.9	2.6
France	1.2	2.6	2.0	0.2	5.4	1.9	1.4	1.8	2.2	2.2	2.3	2.3	1.4	2.6	2.3
Germany	2.4	2.1	1.8	-1.6	6.1	0.4	1.4	1.7	2.0	2.1	2.2	2.2	3.6	2.4	2.1
Italy	1.6	1.3	1.2	3.7	-1.0	1.1	1.2	1.1	1.2	1.2	1.2	1.2	2.3	0.6	1.2
Japan	2.2	-0.6	2.2	-2.7	-3.0	-3.5	4.7	3.5	2.6	1.6	1.4	1.3	2.0	0.4	1.7
United Kingdom	2.4	0.4	1.2	0.1	-2.5	1.5	0.7	0.8	1.2	1.4	1.6	2.0	2.8	0.1	1.5
United States	3.2	2.4	3.3	-0.2	1.8	3.2	3.1	3.2	3.2	3.3	3.4	3.4	3.2	2.8	3.3
Euro area	1.0	1.2	1.4	-0.1	2.5	0.6	1.0	1.3	1.6	1.7	1.8	1.8	1.5	1.3	1.7
Total OECD	3.0	2.0	2.8	0.7	1.7	1.9	2.6	2.6	2.8	2.9	3.1	3.2	3.1	2.2	3.0
Export of goods and services															
Canada	6.4	8.4	7.9	17.1	11.0	3.5	9.0	8.5	8.0	8.0	8.0	7.2	7.2	8.0	7.8
France	9.5	6.6	7.7	1.2	5.9	6.1	7.8	7.8	7.8	7.8	7.8	7.8	11.5	6.9	7.8
Germany	13.8	10.4	7.7	10.2	9.1	7.8	7.7	7.8	7.6	7.6	7.6	7.6	15.7	8.1	7.6
Italy	8.9	6.9	6.9	1.9	9.1	6.0	6.1	6.3	7.0	7.2	7.6	7.6	10.1	6.9	7.3
Japan	23.9	3.2	8.2	-3.3	2.8	-11.3	23.1	11.3	7.0	7.0	6.0	6.0	12.9	5.7	6.5
United Kingdom	5.3	8.0	6.1	7.1	14.3	2.3	5.8	5.9	6.3	6.7	6.7	6.7	5.4	7.0	6.6
United States	11.7	7.5	8.9	8.6	5.0	8.5	8.7	9.0	9.0	9.0	9.0	9.0	8.9	7.8	9.0
Total OECD[1]	11.6	7.7	7.9	7.4	7.5	5.6	8.6	8.1	7.9	8.0	8.1	8.1	10.6	7.4	8.0
Import of goods and services															
Canada	13.4	6.8	7.1	0.5	9.0	3.8	9.0	8.0	8.0	6.0	6.0	6.0	10.1	7.4	6.5
France	8.2	7.7	6.8	-2.8	11.1	6.1	5.7	6.8	7.1	7.1	7.2	7.3	9.8	7.4	7.2
Germany	12.4	8.0	6.7	3.8	9.5	5.7	6.5	6.6	6.9	6.9	7.1	7.0	16.5	7.1	7.0
Italy	10.3	7.2	4.9	14.5	2.0	4.1	4.1	4.5	4.9	5.3	5.7	6.1	13.3	3.6	5.5
Japan	9.7	5.2	8.7	-1.3	8.2	-10.6	20.2	11.4	9.0	7.0	7.5	6.3	9.8	6.7	7.4
United Kingdom	8.5	4.0	3.7	13.5	-2.7	1.0	3.1	3.5	3.9	4.3	4.3	4.3	9.4	1.2	4.2
United States	12.6	5.4	8.4	-12.6	4.4	8.0	9.0	9.0	8.5	8.0	8.0	8.0	10.9	7.6	8.1
Total OECD[1]	11.8	6.4	7.5	1.4	5.7	5.4	7.8	7.5	7.5	7.5	7.8	8.0	11.7	6.6	7.7
GDP															
Canada	3.1	3.0	2.8	3.3	4.1	2.5	2.7	2.9	2.6	3.1	3.2	3.1	3.2	3.0	3.0
France	1.4	2.2	2.1	1.3	3.9	1.8	1.8	1.9	2.2	2.2	2.3	2.3	1.6	2.4	2.3
Germany	3.5	3.4	2.5	1.5	6.1	1.6	2.3	2.6	2.6	2.7	2.7	2.8	4.0	3.1	2.7
Italy	1.2	1.1	1.6	0.5	0.5	1.6	1.7	1.6	1.6	1.6	1.6	1.5	1.5	1.3	1.6
Japan	4.0	-0.9	2.2	-3.1	-3.7	-3.7	5.3	3.5	2.3	1.6	1.2	1.2	2.4	0.3	1.5
United Kingdom	1.3	1.4	1.8	-1.9	2.0	1.8	1.4	1.4	1.8	2.0	2.3	2.7	1.5	1.7	2.2
United States	2.9	2.6	3.1	3.1	1.7	3.1	2.9	3.0	3.1	3.3	3.3	3.4	2.8	2.7	3.3
Euro area	1.7	2.0	2.0	1.0	3.4	1.3	1.7	1.9	2.1	2.2	2.3	2.4	2.0	2.1	2.2
Total OECD	2.9	2.3	2.8	2.0	2.2	2.0	2.8	2.7	2.9	3.0	3.1	3.2	2.8	2.4	3.0

Note: The adoption of national accounts systems SNA93 or ESA95 has been proceeding at an uneven pace among OECD member countries, both with respect to variables and the time period covered. As a consequence, there are breaks in many national series. Moreover, most countries have shifted to chain-weighted price indices to calculate real GDP and expenditures components. For further information, see table "National Account Reporting Systems, base years and latest data updates" at the beginning of the Statistical Annex and *OECD Economic Outlook* Sources and Methods *(http://www.oecd.org/eco/sources-and-methods).*

1. Includes intra-regional trade.
Source: OECD Economic Outlook 89 database.

StatLink http://dx.doi.org/10.1787/888932443966

Annex Table 56. **Quarterly price, cost and unemployment projections**

Percentage changes from previous period, seasonally adjusted at annual rates, volume

	2010	2011	2012	2010 Q4	2011 Q1	Q2	Q3	Q4	2012 Q1	Q2	Q3	Q4	2010	2011	2012
													Q4 / Q4		
Consumer price index[1]															
Canada	1.8	2.9	1.6	4.4	3.6	3.1	1.8	1.5	1.5	1.5	1.5	1.5	2.2	2.5	1.5
France	1.7	2.4	1.6	2.6	3.1	3.6	1.8	1.4	1.4	1.4	1.4	1.5	1.9	2.5	1.5
Germany	1.2	2.6	1.7	2.8	3.6	3.6	1.7	1.5	1.5	1.5	1.6	1.8	1.6	2.6	1.6
Italy	1.6	2.4	1.7	2.9	2.8	2.8	2.0	1.6	1.6	1.6	1.6	1.6	2.0	2.3	1.6
Japan	-0.7	0.3	-0.2	2.3	0.4	0.4	0.0	-0.3	-0.3	-0.2	-0.1	-0.1	0.1	0.1	-0.2
United Kingdom	3.3	4.2	2.1	4.6	7.6	3.1	2.6	2.4	2.2	1.8	1.4	1.2	3.4	3.9	1.7
United States	1.6	2.6	1.5	2.6	5.2	2.3	1.3	1.3	1.4	1.5	1.6	1.6	1.2	2.5	1.6
Euro area	1.6	2.6	1.6	3.0	3.6	3.0	1.8	1.5	1.4	1.4	1.4	1.5	2.0	2.5	1.4
GDP deflator															
Canada	3.0	2.4	1.6	3.7	2.8	2.3	1.7	1.5	1.5	1.6	1.6	1.6	2.6	2.1	1.6
France	0.8	1.5	1.3	0.3	2.0	1.9	1.5	1.2	1.2	1.2	1.1	1.2	1.2	1.7	1.2
Germany	0.6	0.7	1.2	0.0	1.4	0.8	0.6	1.0	1.5	1.4	1.4	1.4	0.3	1.0	1.4
Italy	0.6	1.3	1.6	-1.9	1.5	2.2	2.5	2.0	1.8	0.8	0.9	1.6	0.7	2.0	1.3
Japan	-2.1	-1.3	-0.5	-1.1	-1.6	-0.9	-0.7	-0.5	-0.5	-0.4	-0.3	-0.2	-1.6	-0.9	-0.3
United Kingdom	2.9	3.4	2.1	4.1	6.8	2.4	2.1	2.0	2.2	2.0	2.0	1.9	2.7	3.3	2.0
United States	1.0	1.4	1.4	0.3	1.9	1.4	1.3	1.3	1.4	1.4	1.4	1.5	1.3	1.5	1.4
Euro area	0.9	1.1	1.3	-0.1	1.1	1.4	1.4	1.4	1.4	1.2	1.2	1.3	1.0	1.3	1.3
Total OECD	1.3	1.6	1.6	1.5	2.0	1.2	1.4	1.9	1.8	1.3	1.6	2.1	1.6	1.6	1.7
Unit labour cost (total economy)															
Canada	0.9	1.7	2.0	2.4	0.6	1.9	1.7	1.8	2.3	2.0	1.8	2.0	1.6	1.5	2.0
France	0.9	1.0	1.4	1.6	-0.2	1.9	1.7	1.8	1.4	1.1	0.9	1.0	1.1	1.3	1.1
Germany	-0.7	-0.1	0.6	1.3	-2.8	2.1	1.4	1.3	1.0	-0.3	-0.4	-0.8	-0.3	0.5	-0.1
Italy	-0.5	1.2	0.6	3.9	3.3	1.0	0.3	0.0	0.7	0.8	0.8	0.9	-0.2	1.2	0.8
Japan	-3.1	1.5	-1.0	2.0	3.4	7.9	-3.6	-2.7	-1.5	-0.8	-0.1	0.1	-1.2	1.1	-0.6
United Kingdom	1.6	1.4	0.9	3.1	2.8	2.2	1.1	0.9	1.0	0.8	0.5	0.1	0.6	1.8	0.6
United States	-0.5	1.5	2.2	0.1	2.1	1.2	2.0	2.1	2.3	2.4	2.4	2.7	0.6	1.9	2.4
Euro area	-0.6	0.1	0.6	1.2	-0.9	1.0	0.8	0.9	0.8	0.4	0.3	0.2	-0.3	0.5	0.4
Total OECD	-0.6	1.2	1.3	1.5	1.5	2.0	0.8	1.0	1.3	1.3	1.5	1.5	0.3	1.3	1.4
Unemployment				Per cent of labour force											
Canada	8.0	7.5	7.0	7.7	7.7	7.6	7.4	7.2	7.1	7.0	6.9	6.8			
France	9.3	9.0	8.7	9.2	9.1	9.1	9.0	8.9	8.8	8.7	8.7	8.7			
Germany	6.8	6.0	5.4	6.6	6.3	6.1	5.9	5.8	5.6	5.5	5.4	5.2			
Italy	8.4	8.4	8.1	8.5	8.5	8.4	8.4	8.3	8.2	8.2	8.1	8.0			
Japan	5.1	4.8	4.6	5.0	4.7	4.8	4.8	4.7	4.7	4.7	4.6	4.5			
United Kingdom	7.9	8.1	8.3	7.9	7.8	7.9	8.2	8.3	8.3	8.3	8.3	8.2			
United States	9.6	8.8	7.9	9.6	8.9	8.9	8.7	8.5	8.3	8.1	7.8	7.5			
Euro area	9.9	9.7	9.3	9.9	9.9	9.8	9.7	9.6	9.5	9.4	9.2	9.1			
Total OECD	8.3	7.9	7.4	8.2	8.0	7.9	7.8	7.7	7.6	7.5	7.3	7.1			

Note: The adoption of national accounts systems SNA93 or ESA95 has been proceeding at an uneven pace among OECD member countries, both with respect to variables and the time period covered. As a consequence, there are breaks in many national series. Moreover, most countries have shifted to chain-weighted price indices to calculate real GDP and expenditures components. For further information, see table "National Account Reporting Systems, base years and latest data updates" at the beginning of the Statistical Annex and *OECD Economic Outlook* Sources and Methods *(http://www.oecd.org/eco/sources-and-methods)*.

1. For the United Kingdom, the euro area countries and the euro area aggregate, the Harmonised Index of Consumer Prices (HICP) is used.
Source: OECD Economic Outlook 89 database.

StatLink http://dx.doi.org/10.1787/888932443985

Annex Table 57. **Contributions to changes in real GDP in OECD countries**

	2009	2010	2011	2012		2009	2010	2011	2012
Australia					**France**				
Final domestic demand	0.1	3.4	3.1	5.0	Final domestic demand	-0.5	0.8	1.8	2.1
Stockbuilding	-0.5	0.2	0.3	0.0	Stockbuilding	-1.8	0.4	0.9	0.0
Net exports	2.8	-1.7	-0.5	-0.5	Net exports	-0.3	0.1	-0.5	0.0
GDP	1.4	2.6	2.9	4.5	GDP	-2.7	1.4	2.2	2.1
Austria					**Germany**				
Final domestic demand	-1.0	-0.2	1.1	1.2	Final domestic demand	-1.4	1.7	2.2	1.7
Stockbuilding	-0.8	0.9	0.6	0.0	Stockbuilding	-0.3	0.6	-0.2	0.0
Net exports	-2.6	1.9	1.5	0.8	Net exports	-2.9	1.2	1.5	0.8
GDP	-3.9	2.1	2.9	2.1	GDP	-4.7	3.5	3.4	2.5
Belgium					**Greece**				
Final domestic demand	-1.1	0.8	1.9	1.8	Final domestic demand	-2.1	-7.7	-7.1	-0.9
Stockbuilding	-0.2	0.1	0.0	0.0	Stockbuilding	-2.5	0.9	-0.4	0.0
Net exports	-0.5	1.8	0.3	0.2	Net exports	2.2	2.3	4.8	1.5
GDP	-2.7	2.1	2.4	2.0	GDP	-2.0	-4.5	-2.9	0.6
Canada					**Hungary**				
Final domestic demand	-1.9	4.7	3.5	2.8	Final domestic demand	-6.3	-2.8	0.4	1.7
Stockbuilding	-0.7	0.8	-0.7	0.0	Stockbuilding	-4.7	1.6	1.0	0.0
Net exports	-0.3	-2.2	0.3	0.2	Net exports	4.0	2.2	1.6	1.5
GDP	-2.5	3.1	3.0	2.8	GDP	-6.5	1.0	2.7	3.1
Chile					**Iceland**				
Final domestic demand	-3.2	12.5	10.1	8.2	Final domestic demand	-20.6	-1.9	2.2	2.6
Stockbuilding	-3.2	4.9	0.4	0.0	Stockbuilding	0.0	-0.2	-0.1	0.0
Net exports	3.2	-8.5	-1.1	-0.4	Net exports	14.4	-1.2	-0.2	0.2
GDP	-1.5	5.1	6.5	5.1	GDP	-6.9	-3.5	2.2	2.9
Czech Republic					**Ireland**				
Final domestic demand	-1.4	-0.8	0.8	2.7	Final domestic demand	-11.2	-5.3	-2.7	-0.1
Stockbuilding	-2.0	1.9	-0.5	0.0	Stockbuilding	-1.3	0.7	-0.5	0.0
Net exports	-0.6	1.0	2.0	0.8	Net exports	3.8	3.6	2.2	2.5
GDP	-4.0	2.2	2.4	3.5	GDP	-7.6	-1.0	0.0	2.3
Denmark					**Israel**				
Final domestic demand	-4.4	0.7	1.5	2.0	Final domestic demand	0.3	5.5	5.9	4.3
Stockbuilding	-2.0	0.9	-0.1	0.0	Stockbuilding	-0.6	-1.1	-0.7	0.0
Net exports	1.1	0.5	0.6	0.2	Net exports	1.1	0.6	-0.2	0.2
GDP	-5.2	2.1	1.9	2.1	GDP	0.8	4.7	5.4	4.7
Estonia					**Italy**				
Final domestic demand	-20.7	-3.7	4.3	4.8	Final domestic demand	-3.3	0.9	0.8	1.2
Stockbuilding	-3.4	4.5	-0.8	0.0	Stockbuilding	-0.7	0.7	0.6	0.0
Net exports	11.3	1.7	4.7	0.1	Net exports	-1.2	-0.4	-0.2	0.4
GDP	-13.9	3.1	5.9	4.7	GDP	-5.2	1.2	1.1	1.6
Finland					**Japan**				
Final domestic demand	-3.7	1.5	2.4	2.2	Final domestic demand	-3.1	1.5	-0.3	2.1
Stockbuilding	-1.7	0.8	-0.3	0.0	Stockbuilding	-1.5	0.7	-0.4	0.0
Net exports	-2.0	0.9	1.5	0.4	Net exports	-1.5	1.8	-0.2	-0.1
GDP	-8.3	3.1	3.8	2.8	GDP	-6.3	4.0	-0.9	2.2

Note: The adoption of national accounts systems SNA93 or ESA95 has been proceeding at an uneven pace among OECD member countries, both with respect to variables and the time period covered. As a consequence, there are breaks in many national series. Moreover, most countries have shifted to chain-weighted price indices to calculate real GDP and expenditures components. For further information, see table "National Account Reporting Systems, base years and latest data updates" at the beginning of the Statistical Annex and *OECD Economic Outlook* Sources and Methods *(http://www.oecd.org/eco/sources-and-methods).*

Source: OECD Economic Outlook 89 database.

StatLink ⇗ http://dx.doi.org/10.1787/888932444004

Annex Table 57. **Contributions to changes in real GDP in OECD countries** *(cont'd)*

	2009	2010	2011	2012		2009	2010	2011	2012
Korea					**Slovenia**				
Final domestic demand	0.5	4.5	2.2	3.9	Final domestic demand	-6.1	-1.2	0.7	2.3
Stockbuilding	-3.9	2.0	0.5	0.0	Stockbuilding	-4.0	1.6	0.9	0.0
Net exports	3.7	-0.6	1.9	0.3	Net exports	2.0	0.8	0.2	0.4
GDP	0.3	6.2	4.6	4.5	GDP	-8.1	1.2	1.8	2.6
Luxembourg					**Spain**				
Final domestic demand	-3.5	1.8	2.2	2.3	Final domestic demand	-6.5	-1.3	-0.9	1.1
Stockbuilding	-0.8	0.4	-0.1	0.0	Stockbuilding	0.0	0.1	-0.1	-0.1
Net exports	0.3	1.5	1.3	1.8	Net exports	2.7	1.0	1.8	0.6
GDP	-3.6	3.5	3.2	3.9	GDP	-3.7	-0.1	0.9	1.6
Mexico					**Sweden**				
Final domestic demand	-7.2	4.3	5.1	4.8	Final domestic demand	-3.0	3.4	3.5	2.6
Stockbuilding	-1.1	1.0	-0.4	0.0	Stockbuilding	-1.6	2.1	0.1	0.0
Net exports	2.2	0.2	-0.3	-1.0	Net exports	-0.9	0.0	0.4	0.5
GDP	-6.1	5.5	4.4	3.8	GDP	-5.3	5.3	4.5	3.1
Netherlands					**Switzerland**				
Final domestic demand	-2.8	-0.3	1.2	1.4	Final domestic demand	-0.3	1.8	2.5	2.2
Stockbuilding	-0.9	1.1	0.1	0.0	Stockbuilding	0.9	-1.3	0.7	0.0
Net exports	-0.2	1.0	1.5	0.5	Net exports	-2.5	2.1	-0.4	0.4
GDP	-3.9	1.8	2.3	1.9	GDP	-1.9	2.6	2.7	2.5
New Zealand					**Turkey**				
Final domestic demand	-2.8	2.2	2.1	4.9	Final domestic demand	-4.4	10.0	8.5	6.2
Stockbuilding	-1.9	1.4	1.1	0.0	Stockbuilding	-2.5	2.0	0.2	0.0
Net exports	5.3	-1.9	-1.4	-0.6	Net exports	2.8	-4.3	-2.8	-1.0
GDP	0.0	2.5	0.8	4.1	GDP	-4.8	8.9	6.5	5.3
Norway					**United Kingdom**				
Final domestic demand	-0.6	0.1	3.4	3.6	Final domestic demand	-4.4	1.0	0.4	1.2
Stockbuilding	-2.4	3.5	0.2	0.0	Stockbuilding	-1.2	1.4	0.0	0.1
Net exports	1.4	-2.9	-1.0	-0.5	Net exports	0.9	-1.0	0.9	0.6
GDP	-1.4	0.4	2.5	3.0	GDP	-4.9	1.3	1.4	1.8
Poland					**United States**				
Final domestic demand	1.8	2.2	4.4	4.2	Final domestic demand	-3.2	1.9	2.6	3.3
Stockbuilding	-2.5	2.1	0.4	0.0	Stockbuilding	-0.6	1.4	-0.1	0.0
Net exports	3.4	-0.5	-1.0	-0.4	Net exports	1.2	-0.4	0.1	-0.3
GDP	1.7	3.8	3.9	3.8	GDP	-2.6	2.9	2.6	3.1
Portugal					**Euro area**				
Final domestic demand	-2.5	0.8	-6.2	-4.8	Final domestic demand	-2.5	0.4	0.9	1.4
Stockbuilding	-0.6	-0.1	0.2	0.0	Stockbuilding	-0.8	0.6	0.2	0.0
Net exports	0.7	0.6	3.9	3.2	Net exports	-0.8	0.8	0.9	0.7
GDP	-2.5	1.3	-2.1	-1.5	GDP	-4.1	1.7	2.0	2.0
Slovak Republic					**Total OECD**				
Final domestic demand	-3.6	0.6	0.9	3.1	Final domestic demand	-2.9	1.9	2.1	2.8
Stockbuilding	-3.6	1.8	0.3	0.0	Stockbuilding	-1.1	1.1	0.0	0.0
Net exports	2.6	1.0	2.4	1.1	Net exports	0.6	-0.1	0.3	0.0
GDP	-4.8	4.0	3.6	4.4	GDP	-3.5	2.9	2.3	2.8

Note: The adoption of national accounts systems SNA93 or ESA95 has been proceeding at an uneven pace among OECD member countries, both with respect to variables and the time period covered. As a consequence, there are breaks in many national series. Moreover, most countries have shifted to chain-weighted price indices to calculate real GDP and expenditures components. For further information, see table "National Account Reporting Systems, base years and latest data updates" at the beginning of the Statistical Annex and *OECD Economic Outlook* Sources and Methods *(http://www.oecd.org/eco/sources-and-methods)*.

Source: OECD Economic Outlook 89 database.

StatLink http://dx.doi.org/10.1787/888932444004

Annex Table 58. **Household wealth and indebtedness**

	1998	1999	2000	2001	2002	2003	2004	2005	2006	2007	2008	2009
Canada												
Net wealth	498.4	507.0	502.2	503.2	512.7	516.1	518.1	534.5	545.5	548.5	547.4	549.2
Net financial wealth	233.7	239.1	240.1	235.5	231.4	224.0	214.6	216.5	217.9	210.6	211.7	211.0
Non-financial assets	264.7	267.9	262.0	267.7	281.3	292.1	303.5	318.0	327.7	337.9	335.6	338.2
Financial assets	345.6	353.2	352.7	349.6	348.5	344.7	338.9	345.9	349.6	347.9	353.4	359.4
of which: Equities	79.5	81.1	84.3	84.2	83.6	81.0	79.4	79.4	85.2	85.2	96.3	92.3
Liabilities	112.0	114.1	112.6	114.1	117.1	120.6	124.3	129.4	131.8	137.3	141.7	148.4
of which: Mortgages	71.8	71.8	69.6	69.6	71.2	73.2	75.9	79.1	80.7	84.7	87.9	92.3
France												
Net wealth	494.9	545.8	552.5	552.3	571.3	621.2	682.1	748.2	792.6	806.3	753.2	746.3
Net financial wealth	185.5	211.8	205.7	188.4	183.1	189.6	194.9	200.5	210.4	213.6	185.8	201.7
Non-financial assets	309.4	334.1	346.8	363.9	388.2	431.6	487.3	547.7	582.2	592.7	567.4	544.6
Financial assets	258.1	287.2	282.5	266.4	258.7	269.2	278.6	291.5	306.9	313.8	288.1	308.3
of which: Equities	67.3	86.6	83.5	69.8	63.1	69.7	72.4	77.5	87.1	92.2	66.2	73.6
Liabilities	72.5	75.4	76.8	78.0	75.6	79.7	83.7	91.0	96.5	100.3	102.3	106.6
of which: Long-term loans	51.5	53.8	53.4	53.6	54.6	57.1	60.2	65.3	69.5	73.2	76.6	..
Germany												
Net wealth	527.6	539.1	536.5	531.2	533.6	547.8	561.2	581.4	605.7	627.6	614.6	..
Net financial wealth	143.4	153.8	151.4	150.7	145.9	158.2	167.2	180.2	189.4	198.2	184.9	202.0
Non-financial assets	384.1	385.3	385.2	380.5	387.8	389.6	394.0	401.2	416.3	429.4	429.7	..
Financial assets	252.8	267.9	265.9	262.4	257.9	269.1	276.8	287.3	294.2	299.9	282.4	300.6
of which: Equities	61.1	74.5	75.2	71.3	57.4	63.3	63.9	71.3	72.0	72.7	54.2	59.2
Liabilities	109.4	114.2	114.5	111.8	112.1	110.9	109.6	107.1	104.8	101.7	97.5	98.6
of which: Mortgages	67.1	71.0	71.7	71.2	72.3	72.2	71.8	71.0	70.8	68.9	66.1	67.1
Italy												
Net wealth	728.4	742.8	756.2	738.6	747.5	768.9	793.8	825.5	846.7	857.0	841.8	877.4
Net financial wealth	294.5	314.2	319.1	298.8	284.7	279.3	286.6	295.3	292.3	281.6	261.1	276.4
Non-financial assets	433.9	428.6	437.1	439.7	462.8	489.6	507.1	530.3	554.4	575.3	580.6	601.1
Financial assets	339.9	363.0	371.9	351.1	344.9	344.0	355.9	370.2	371.3	364.5	345.0	364.2
of which: Equities	66.9	87.1	91.2	77.1	70.9	65.1	68.7	77.8	78.8	72.8	57.9	65.0
Liabilities	45.5	48.8	52.8	52.3	60.2	64.7	69.3	74.9	79.0	82.9	83.9	87.9
of which: Medium and long-term loans	24.6	27.2	28.4	28.2	35.3	38.4	42.3	46.4	49.0	51.5	51.7	54.5
Japan												
Net wealth	722.5	746.2	743.9	740.5	719.4	728.1	720.1	739.2	744.7	735.3	700.5	703.6
Net financial wealth	296.3	327.3	335.6	341.6	340.7	361.1	369.4	397.1	401.4	386.3	359.5	375.7
Non-financial assets	426.2	418.9	408.3	398.9	378.7	367.0	350.7	342.1	343.3	349.0	341.1	327.8
Financial assets	428.8	460.7	470.2	477.5	474.4	494.7	500.8	529.0	531.8	513.7	485.6	501.3
of which: Equities	27.0	45.6	41.5	31.8	29.8	42.1	48.9	75.5	75.8	50.3	31.8	35.8
Liabilities	132.5	133.4	134.5	135.9	133.6	133.6	131.4	131.8	130.4	127.4	126.2	125.6
of which: Mortgages[1]	56.0	58.9	61.0	63.1	62.8	63.9	63.4	64.1	65.2	64.9	64.8	65.3
United Kingdom												
Net wealth	686.4	769.1	768.1	714.3	715.6	748.0	797.2	827.0	866.7	900.8	752.7	800.8
Net financial wealth	359.6	410.3	380.3	323.5	260.8	265.9	270.0	304.3	310.7	307.6	243.3	286.5
Non-financial assets	326.8	358.8	387.8	390.8	454.9	482.2	527.2	522.7	556.0	593.2	509.3	514.4
Financial assets	469.0	524.0	497.4	445.0	394.7	410.9	430.0	466.6	486.7	491.3	420.9	457.2
of which: Equities	97.1	121.4	113.6	85.9	61.4	67.3	71.4	76.0	77.2	72.9	46.6	63.0
Liabilities	109.4	113.7	117.1	121.4	134.0	145.0	160.0	162.3	176.0	183.6	177.6	170.7
of which: Mortgages	79.4	82.7	85.4	88.5	97.1	106.8	119.0	121.2	130.1	138.2	135.6	132.6
United States												
Net wealth	576.8	625.3	582.4	555.1	514.3	562.2	592.7	639.9	645.9	615.7	468.5	486.3
Net financial wealth	366.0	406.4	353.6	315.6	266.7	303.2	316.2	334.5	348.2	347.2	246.1	272.7
Non-financial assets	210.8	219.0	228.8	239.4	247.6	259.0	276.5	305.4	297.6	268.5	222.4	213.6
Financial assets	461.4	505.9	454.2	420.3	376.6	420.9	440.3	465.8	483.8	485.1	375.9	399.9
of which: Equities	151.8	186.2	148.1	123.5	92.2	115.8	122.7	126.8	139.5	136.5	83.1	104.2
Liabilities	95.4	99.6	100.7	104.7	109.9	117.8	124.1	131.3	135.6	137.8	129.9	127.2
of which: Mortgages	63.8	66.6	67.2	71.3	77.2	84.2	90.2	97.7	101.7	103.4	97.8	95.5

Note: Assets and liabilities are amounts outstanding at the end of the period, in per cent of nominal disposable income.

Households include non-profit institutions serving households, except for Italy. Net wealth is defined as non-financial and financial assets minus liabilities; net financial wealth is financial assets minus liabilities. Non-financial assets consist mainly of dwellings and land. For a more detailed description of the variables, see *OECD Economic Outlook* Sources and Methods (*http://www.oecd.org/eco/sources-and-methods*).

1. Fiscal year data.

Sources: Canada: Statistics Canada; France: INSEE; Germany: Deutsche Bundesbank, Federal Statistical Office (Destatis); Italy: Banca d'Italia; Japan: Economic Planning Agency; United Kingdom: Office for National Statistics; United States: Federal Reserve.

StatLink 🖼️ http://dx.doi.org/10.1787/888932444023

Annex Table 59. **House prices**
Percentage change from previous year

	1994	1995	1996	1997	1998	1999	2000	2001	2002	2003	2004	2005	2006	2007	2008	2009	2010
Nominal																	
United States	2.3	3.0	3.6	3.6	5.1	4.8	6.5	7.7	6.5	6.3	9.4	11.3	7.1	1.6	-3.4	-4.1	-3.3
Japan	-2.4	-1.6	-1.9	-1.4	-1.6	-3.2	-3.8	-4.2	-4.6	-5.4	-6.1	-4.8	-3.0	-1.0	-1.6	-3.8	..
Germany		1.3	-1.3	-1.8	-1.0	0.2	0.4	0.0	-0.7	-1.3	-1.4	-0.9	0.1	0.9	0.6	0.6	2.3
France			-1.7	0.1	1.9	7.1	8.8	7.9	8.3	11.7	15.2	15.3	12.1	6.6	1.2	-7.1	6.3
Italy	-2.8	0.8	-3.3	-4.6	2.1	5.6	8.3	8.2	9.6	10.3	9.9	7.5	6.4	5.2	1.7	-3.7	..
United Kingdom	2.6	0.7	3.7	8.8	11.5	10.9	14.9	8.1	16.1	15.7	11.9	5.5	6.3	10.9	-0.9	-7.8	7.3
Canada	3.3	-4.6	0.1	2.9	-1.4	3.8	3.7	4.6	9.8	9.5	9.4	9.9	11.4	10.8	-1.3	4.6	6.8
Australia	3.6	1.2	0.8	4.0	7.3	7.2	8.3	11.2	18.8	18.2	6.5	1.5	7.8	11.3	4.4	3.4	12.2
Belgium	6.4	4.5	2.2	2.4	6.4	7.1	5.4	4.8	6.4	6.9	8.7	12.7	11.8	9.3	4.9	-0.3	5.4
Denmark	12.2	7.6	10.7	11.5	9.0	6.7	6.5	5.8	3.6	3.2	8.9	17.6	21.6	4.6	-4.5	-12.0	2.4
Finland							3.9	-1.4	6.0	6.3	8.2	8.1	6.4	5.5	0.6	-0.3	8.7
Grece	..	..	..	..	14.4	8.9	10.6	14.4	13.9	5.4	2.3	10.9	13.0	6.2	1.5	-4.3	-3.9
Ireland	4.7	6.3	8.6	14.7	24.1	21.5	20.6	12.4	7.0	14.2	11.2	7.4	13.5	-0.5	-9.1	-13.7	-15.5
Korea	-1.6	-0.1	1.0	2.7	-9.2	-1.3	1.8	4.0	16.6	9.1	1.1	0.8	6.1	9.0	4.0	0.2	2.4
Netherlands	12.3	6.9	10.8	12.0	10.9	16.3	18.2	11.1	6.5	3.6	4.3	3.8	4.6	4.2	2.9	-3.3	-2.0
Norway	13.2	7.2	9.2	11.8	11.1	11.2	15.7	7.0	4.9	1.7	10.1	8.2	13.7	12.6	-1.1	2.0	8.2
New Zealand	13.7	9.3	10.3	6.1	-1.7	2.1	-0.4	1.8	9.5	19.4	17.8	14.5	10.5	10.9	-4.4	-1.6	1.9
Spain	1.5	3.5	2.6	4.2	4.9	7.0	7.5	9.5	16.9	20.0	18.3	14.6	10.0	5.5	0.2	-7.6	-3.6
Sweden	4.6	0.3	0.8	6.6	9.5	9.4	11.2	7.9	6.3	6.6	9.3	9.0	12.2	10.4	3.3	1.6	7.8
Switzerland	-0.1	-3.9	-5.3	-3.5	-0.9	-0.1	0.9	1.9	4.6	3.0	2.4	1.1	2.5	2.1	2.6	5.0	4.7
Real[1]																	
United States	0.3	0.7	1.5	1.7	4.1	3.2	3.9	5.7	5.0	4.2	6.6	8.1	4.3	-1.1	-6.5	-4.3	-5.0
Japan	-2.9	-1.3	-1.8	-2.6	-1.7	-2.6	-2.7	-3.1	-3.2	-4.6	-5.5	-4.1	-2.8	-0.4	-2.0	-1.7	..
Germany		0.0	-2.2	-3.1	-1.4	-0.1	-0.5	-1.7	-1.8	-2.8	-2.7	-2.2	-1.0	-0.9	-1.1	0.5	0.4
France			-3.3	-0.8	1.7	7.7	6.4	6.0	7.3	9.7	13.1	13.3	9.8	4.4	-1.6	-6.7	5.0
Italy	-7.6	-5.0	-7.1	-6.7	0.3	3.7	4.7	5.4	6.5	7.3	7.2	5.2	3.7	2.8	-1.4	-3.7	..
United Kingdom	0.6	-2.5	0.2	6.2	8.9	9.5	13.7	6.1	14.4	13.6	9.9	3.0	3.4	7.8	-3.9	-9.1	3.0
Canada	2.2	-5.8	-1.5	1.3	-2.6	2.1	1.5	2.7	7.7	7.8	7.8	8.1	9.8	9.1	-2.8	4.0	5.4
Australia	2.0	-1.4	-1.3	2.5	6.1	6.3	5.1	7.3	15.1	16.0	5.1	-0.4	4.6	8.1	1.7	1.7	10.1
Belgium	3.6	2.4	1.5	0.8	5.4	6.7	1.9	2.9	5.1	5.3	6.2	9.7	8.6	6.2	1.6	0.1	2.9
Denmark	9.3	5.6	9.0	9.4	7.5	4.8	3.7	3.4	1.9	1.9	7.6	15.8	19.3	3.3	-7.3	-13.2	-0.2
Finland							-0.4	-3.7	3.7	6.9	7.8	7.2	4.9	3.3	-2.8	-0.9	7.6
Greece	..	..	..	..	9.5	6.4	7.0	11.4	11.0	2.0	-0.6	7.2	9.2	2.8	-2.4	-5.3	-8.2
Ireland	2.1	3.8	5.7	11.7	19.3	18.2	14.7	7.8	1.5	9.7	9.2	5.5	10.9	-3.6	-11.8	-9.8	-13.6
Korea	-10.3	-6.2	-5.5	-3.3	-14.6	-3.9	-2.5	-0.4	13.2	5.7	-2.0	-1.4	4.5	6.9	-0.5	-2.3	-0.2
Netherlands	9.5	4.7	8.6	9.4	8.7	14.1	13.8	6.4	3.4	1.2	3.3	1.7	2.3	2.3	1.5	-2.7	-3.6
Norway	12.1	4.7	7.9	9.2	8.4	9.0	12.4	4.8	3.5	-1.2	9.3	7.1	11.6	11.3	-4.5	-0.6	6.2
New Zealand	12.1	6.8	7.5	4.2	-3.7	1.5	-2.6	-0.4	7.3	18.4	16.1	12.1	7.3	9.2	-7.7	-3.9	0.5
Spain	-3.2	-1.3	-0.6	1.5	2.9	4.6	3.6	5.8	13.7	16.3	14.2	10.8	6.2	2.1	-3.2	-7.7	-6.2
Sweden	1.8	-2.5	-0.1	5.2	9.0	7.7	10.3	5.7	4.7	5.0	8.2	7.9	11.0	9.0	0.1	-0.4	6.5
Switzerland	-0.4	-5.2	-6.5	-4.3	-0.8	-0.5	0.1	1.3	3.7	2.6	1.5	0.6	1.1	0.7	0.0	5.5	4.5

1. Nominal house prices deflated by the private consumption deflator.
Source: Various national sources and Nomisma, see table A.1 in Girouard, N., M. Kennedy, P. van den Noord and C. André, "Recent house price developments: the role of fundamentals", *OECD Economics Department Working Papers*, No. 475, 2006.

StatLink http://dx.doi.org/10.1787/888932444042

Annex Table 60. House price ratios
Long-term average = 100

Price-to-rent ratio

	1994	1995	1996	1997	1998	1999	2000	2001	2002	2003	2004	2005	2006	2007	2008	2009	2010
United States	89.7	89.5	89.9	90.3	91.8	93.6	96.6	100.2	102.8	106.8	113.8	123.5	127.8	125.3	118.1	112.0	108.7
Japan	113.7	109.8	106.2	103.2	100.9	97.8	93.9	89.8	85.8	81.2	76.4	72.8	70.6	70.0	68.8	66.3	64.3
Germany		100.1	95.8	92.0	90.1	89.4	88.7	87.8	86.1	84.0	82.2	80.7	79.8	79.4	78.8	78.2	79.2
France			75.6	74.6	74.5	78.5	85.4	91.8	97.0	105.4	118.1	131.4	142.4	147.2	145.8	132.7	138.8
Italy	103.0	97.8	88.0	78.7	76.3	78.0	82.4	87.2	93.4	100.2	107.2	112.8	117.1	120.4	119.5	111.4	107.4
United Kingdom	73.1	70.1	69.5	72.7	78.3	84.4	94.0	98.4	111.3	126.6	138.5	141.8	146.7	157.2	150.1	134.9	141.7
Canada	96.2	90.5	90.7	93.6	91.9	94.4	95.8	97.9	105.6	112.7	120.6	129.3	139.2	148.2	141.0	145.7	154.4
Australia	85.2	84.8	83.0	83.9	87.3	91.2	95.9	103.3	119.9	139.0	144.5	143.4	149.7	158.0	153.2	148.3	159.5
Belgium	86.5	87.9	87.7	88.3	92.8	98.0	101.9	104.8	108.8	113.8	121.4	134.2	145.0	155.6	160.2	156.5	163.1
Denmark	71.8	75.6	82.6	89.7	95.9	99.7	103.4	106.6	107.6	108.2	114.6	131.5	156.7	160.5	149.6	127.9	127.3
Finland							103.6	98.6	105.0	112.3	120.3	126.5	128.9	128.2	123.7	127.9	138.1
Greece	..	..	..	73.6	79.1	82.4	87.7	96.5	104.7	104.9	101.9	108.3	117.3	119.1	116.4	107.5	100.8
Ireland	66.3	66.2	72.6	78.3	94.0	137.6	148.4	137.9	151.0	183.1	198.1	196.0	181.8	137.7	111.2	144.2	118.9
Korea	97.1	92.9	90.4	89.9	79.9	81.8	83.4	83.5	92.6	97.4	96.3	96.9	102.0	109.0	110.2	108.5	109.1
Netherlands	76.8	78.2	83.2	89.8	96.2	108.5	124.9	134.8	139.5	140.2	141.8	143.6	146.6	149.5	151.1	143.2	137.5
Norway	69.4	73.2	78.6	85.8	93.2	100.8	112.2	115.6	116.2	113.6	122.7	130.2	144.7	159.8	153.5	151.2	159.2
New Zealand	74.6	76.6	80.6	82.9	79.6	82.2	81.7	91.8	98.7	114.2	130.5	145.8	157.6	169.9	157.6	152.8	153.5
Spain	93.5	91.7	87.5	86.0	85.9	88.8	92.0	96.6	108.2	124.5	141.5	155.6	164.0	165.8	159.4	142.9	136.2
Sweden	67.0	65.2	63.4	65.5	71.2	77.8	86.1	91.4	95.1	98.8	104.8	111.6	124.1	134.8	135.9	133.7	141.9
Switzerland	96.4	91.7	85.7	82.3	81.6	80.9	80.4	79.7	82.5	84.8	85.7	85.5	85.9	85.7	85.9	88.0	91.1

Price-to-income ratio

	1994	1995	1996	1997	1998	1999	2000	2001	2002	2003	2004	2005	2006	2007	2008	2009	2010
United States	92.8	91.8	91.2	90.7	90.1	91.3	91.3	95.2	97.7	100.1	104.2	112.2	113.6	110.9	102.9	98.8	93.5
Japan	105.4	103.5	101.7	98.7	97.2	95.2	93.4	92.8	88.7	85.3	79.5	75.1	72.0	71.4	70.4	68.5	65.0
Germany		104.7	101.6	98.3	95.7	93.5	91.4	88.1	87.0	84.1	81.7	79.4	77.7	77.0	74.9	76.5	76.3
France			80.9	79.4	78.4	82.3	85.2	88.0	91.6	100.5	111.7	125.6	135.5	138.1	136.5	126.1	131.5
Italy	98.3	93.4	85.3	79.8	81.0	83.2	87.1	89.4	94.3	101.1	107.9	114.0	118.0	121.1	121.4	121.5	118.5
United Kingdom	78.0	74.3	72.4	74.1	79.2	84.9	93.1	95.0	107.1	118.5	130.3	132.2	136.1	147.3	139.7	124.1	129.4
Canada	104.7	97.5	97.1	97.5	93.1	92.9	90.7	91.7	98.1	104.4	109.3	116.1	121.6	128.9	122.3	127.3	131.4
Australia	91.2	87.6	84.5	85.5	90.5	93.2	95.6	100.1	116.3	131.9	133.1	129.4	130.1	134.2	133.5	130.8	143.4
Belgium	90.2	87.8	89.8	90.2	93.3	97.5	97.8	97.9	103.8	110.0	117.5	129.2	137.3	144.1	144.7	143.5	148.0
Denmark	76.8	76.3	82.5	90.7	95.3	104.1	107.7	107.8	108.0	107.8	113.1	128.6	151.2	156.6	146.0	128.8	127.2
Finland							96.8	90.5	92.1	93.1	96.0	102.1	104.8	104.8	100.2	97.7	102.9
Greece	..	..	..	76.8	82.0	87.7	94.3	101.3	109.9	107.5	104.0	109.8	114.4	108.0	107.7	99.8	96.8
Ireland	76.0	73.6	73.9	78.0	87.4	101.0	110.9	111.1	122.7	133.7	138.9	143.6	156.0	148.3	130.1	116.0	99.3
Korea	97.9	88.0	78.9	75.7	67.9	63.8	62.6	62.2	68.5	69.3	65.1	62.9	64.3	67.2	66.1	63.8	61.5
Netherlands	80.6	82.7	87.8	92.8	98.1	110.4	123.9	125.8	131.6	137.3	141.4	144.6	147.4	147.3	150.3	146.7	141.5
Norway	75.8	77.5	81.0	85.8	88.5	94.7	103.3	108.7	104.7	99.7	105.8	106.1	127.6	134.8	126.0	121.3	125.8
New Zealand	91.1	93.1	97.7	99.9	94.1	89.5	91.0	87.7	95.8	106.6	119.4	133.1	141.7	144.9	136.4	130.4	125.4
Spain	95.2	88.1	86.0	86.4	86.8	88.8	90.0	93.5	104.6	119.9	135.0	146.0	152.6	154.7	148.5	135.5	133.6
Sweden	78.6	76.7	77.2	81.7	87.6	91.7	96.3	95.8	97.5	101.7	109.3	116.0	124.5	129.6	126.9	125.6	133.0
Switzerland	100.4	94.1	89.6	84.9	82.2	80.0	77.6	77.0	81.5	84.8	84.9	83.8	82.9	81.3	82.6	86.9	91.3

Source: Various national sources and Nomisma, see table A.1 in Girouard, N., M. Kennedy, P. van den Noord and C. André, "Recent house price developments: the role of fundamentals", *OECD Economics Department Working Papers,* No. 475, 2006 and OECD estimates.

StatLink http://dx.doi.org/10.1787/888932444061

Annex Table 61. **Central government financial balances**
Surplus (+) or deficit (-) as a percentage of nominal GDP

	1996	1997	1998	1999	2000	2001	2002	2003	2004	2005	2006	2007	2008	2009	2010
Canada	-2.0	0.7	0.8	0.9	1.9	1.1	0.8	0.3	0.8	0.1	0.9	1.0	-0.1	-2.6	-2.5
France	-3.6	-3.1	-2.8	-2.4	-2.1	-2.1	-3.1	-3.6	-2.6	-2.6	-2.1	-2.6	-3.5	-6.4	-5.8
Germany[1]	-1.9	-1.6	-1.8	-1.5	1.4	-1.3	-1.7	-1.8	-2.4	-2.1	-1.5	-0.8	-0.6	-1.6	-2.3
Italy	-6.8	-2.6	-2.5	-1.5	-1.2	-3.1	-3.1	-3.0	-3.0	-4.0	-2.8	-2.0	-2.6	-4.7	-4.4
Japan[2]	-4.1	-3.5	-10.6	-7.3	-6.4	-5.9	-6.7	-6.7	-5.2	-6.2	-1.0	-2.6	-2.6	-7.9	-7.9
United Kingdom[3]	-4.1	-2.0	0.2	1.1	3.9	0.8	-1.9	-3.4	-3.1	-3.0	-2.7	-2.6	-4.6	-10.9	-10.0
United States	-2.0	-0.6	0.5	1.0	1.9	0.3	-2.6	-3.8	-3.6	-2.8	-1.8	-2.2	-5.3	-10.5	-10.3
less social security	-2.9	-1.7	-0.7	-0.4	0.3	-1.3	-4.2	-5.2	-4.9	-4.1	-3.3	-3.6	-6.5	-11.3	-10.8
Total of above countries	-2.9	-1.6	-2.0	-1.0	0.2	-1.2	-3.0	-3.8	-3.4	-3.2	-1.7	-2.0	-3.8	-8.2	-8.0

Note: Central government financial balances include one-off revenues from the sale of mobile telephone licenses.
1. In 1995, this includes the central government's assumption of the debt of the Inherited Debt Fund.
2. Data for central government financial balances are only available for fiscal years beginning April 1 of the year shown. The 1998 deficit includes the central government's assumption of the debt of the Japan Railway Settlement Corporation and the National Forest Special Account which represent some 5.3 percentage points of GDP.
3. The data for 2000 and onwards reflect Eurostat's decision concerning the recording of one-off revenues from the sale of the mobile telephone licenses.
Source: OECD Economic Outlook 89 database.

StatLink http://dx.doi.org/10.1787/888932444080

Annex Table 62. **Maastricht definition of general government gross public debt**
As a percentage of nominal GDP

	1998	1999	2000	2001	2002	2003	2004	2005	2006	2007	2008	2009	2010	2011	2012
Austria	64.8	67.1	66.6	67.1	66.3	65.5	64.9	64.1	62.1	60.8	64.1	69.8	72.3	73.7	75.3
Belgium[1]	117.4	113.8	107.9	106.6	103.5	98.5	94.3	92.0	88.0	84.2	89.8	96.3	96.7	96.7	96.4
Czech Republic	15.0	16.4	18.5	24.8	28.2	29.8	30.2	29.7	29.4	28.9	30.0	35.3	38.5	41.3	42.7
Denmark	61.4	58.1	52.4	49.6	49.5	47.2	45.1	37.8	32.1	27.5	34.5	41.8	43.6	45.2	48.1
Estonia	5.5	6.0	5.1	4.8	5.7	5.6	5.0	4.6	4.4	3.7	4.6	7.2	6.6	9.7	13.8
Finland	48.4	45.7	43.9	42.5	41.6	44.6	44.4	41.7	39.6	35.2	34.1	43.8	48.4	53.7	57.2
France	59.4	58.9	57.3	56.9	58.8	62.9	65.0	66.4	63.6	63.9	67.7	78.2	81.6	84.8	87.5
Germany	60.4	61.0	59.7	58.7	60.3	63.9	66.0	68.1	67.5	64.8	66.4	73.5	83.4	83.7	83.3
Greece	94.5	94.0	103.4	103.7	101.7	97.4	98.9	100.3	106.1	105.4	110.7	127.1	142.8	152.5	154.7
Hungary	59.5	59.5	54.8	51.5	55.1	57.9	59.1	61.5	65.2	65.5	72.2	77.9	79.8	74.0	75.1
Ireland	53.6	48.5	37.8	35.5	32.1	30.9	29.6	27.4	24.8	25.0	44.4	65.6	96.2	114.1	119.3
Italy	115.0	113.8	109.1	108.8	105.7	104.4	104.0	105.9	106.5	103.6	106.3	116.1	119.1	121.3	120.8
Luxembourg	7.1	6.4	6.2	6.3	6.3	6.1	6.3	6.1	6.7	6.7	13.6	14.6	18.4	19.2	22.5
Netherlands	65.7	61.1	53.8	50.7	50.5	52.0	52.4	51.8	47.4	45.3	58.2	60.8	62.7	65.6	66.5
Poland	39.0	39.7	36.9	37.5	42.1	47.0	45.8	47.1	47.8	45.0	47.2	51.0	55.1	57.3	57.3
Portugal	50.4	49.6	48.5	51.2	53.8	55.9	57.6	62.8	63.9	68.3	71.6	83.0	93.0	100.7	105.7
Slovak Republic	34.5	47.8	50.3	48.9	43.4	42.4	41.5	34.2	30.5	29.6	27.8	35.4	41.0	45.2	47.6
Slovenia	..	..	..	26.8	28.0	27.5	27.2	27.0	26.7	23.1	21.9	35.2	38.0	43.4	47.0
Spain	64.1	62.3	59.3	55.5	52.5	48.7	46.2	43.0	39.6	36.1	39.8	53.3	60.1	67.6	68.8
Sweden	69.9	64.3	53.9	54.7	52.5	51.7	50.3	50.4	45.0	40.2	38.8	42.8	39.8	36.0	31.8
United Kingdom	46.7	43.7	41.0	37.7	37.5	39.0	40.9	42.5	43.4	44.5	54.4	69.6	80.0	86.1	90.9
Euro area	72.7	71.9	69.3	68.1	67.9	69.0	69.5	70.1	68.4	66.2	70.0	79.4	85.5	88.4	89.3

Note: For the period before 2010, gross debt figures are provided by Eurostat, the Statistical Office of the European Communities, unless more recent data are available, while GDP figures are provided by national authorities. This explains why these ratios can differ significantly from the ones published by Eurostat. For the projections period, debt ratios are in line with the OECD projections for general government gross financial liabilities and GDP. For further information, see *OECD Economic Outlook* Sources and Methods *(http://www.oecd.org/eco/sources-and-methods)*.
1. Includes the debt of the Belgium National Railways Company (SNCB) from 2005 onwards.
Source: OECD Economic Outlook 89 database.

StatLink http://dx.doi.org/10.1787/888932444099

Annex Table 63. **Monetary and credit aggregates: recent trends**
Annualised percentage change, seasonally adjusted

		Annual change (to 4th quarter)					Latest twelve months	
		2006	2007	2008	2009	2010		
Canada	M2	8.9	6.4	12.5	10.9	5.2	5.1	(Mar 2011)
	BL[1]	7.6	9.9	7.3	3.8	4.6	5.7	(Mar 2011)
Japan	M2	0.6	2.0	1.8	3.2	2.6	2.7	(Mar 2011)
	BL[1]	-0.2	-0.9	3.4	3.5	3.6	3.2	(Feb 2011)
United Kingdom	M2	8.1	7.5	5.1	5.7	3.9	2.9	(Mar 2011)
	M4	13.2	12.4	15.8	6.5	6.6	-2.9	(Mar 2011)
	BL[1]	12.6	12.5	14.3	11.5	2.6	-4.2	(Mar 2011)
United States	M2	5.7	6.3	8.6	5.0	3.2	4.6	(Mar 2011)
	BL[1]	12.1	11.3	8.1	-7.8	1.3	-3.1	(Apr 2011)
Euro area	M2	8.8	11.3	9.7	2.1	2.5	2.6	(Mar 2011)
	M3	9.0	12.2	9.0	-0.3	1.7	2.3	(Mar 2011)
	BL[1]	7.9	11.5	9.1	3.1	4.5	3.7	(Mar 2011)

1. Commercial bank credit.

Source: OECD Main Economic Indicators; US Federal Reserve Board; Bank of Japan; European Central Bank; Bank of England; Statistics Canada.

StatLink http://dx.doi.org/10.1787/888932444118

Annex Table 64. Macroeconomic indicators for selected non-member economies
Calendar year basis

	1998	1998	1999	2000	2001	2002	2003	2004	2005	2006	2007	2008	2009	2010	2011	2012
Real GDP growth																
China	9.3	7.8	7.6	8.4	8.3	9.1	10.0	10.1	11.3	12.7	14.2	9.6	9.2	10.3	9.0	9.2
Brazil	3.4	0.1	0.2	4.3	1.3	2.6	1.2	5.7	3.2	4.0	6.1	5.2	-0.7	7.5	4.1	4.5
India	4.4	5.9	6.9	5.5	4.0	4.6	7.0	8.3	9.1	9.4	9.9	6.2	7.2	10.4	8.5	8.6
Indonesia	4.7	-13.1	0.8	4.9	3.6	4.5	4.8	5.0	5.7	5.5	6.3	6.0	4.6	6.1	6.6	6.4
Russian Federation	1.4	-5.3	6.4	10.0	5.1	4.7	7.3	7.2	6.4	8.2	8.5	5.2	-7.8	4.0	4.9	4.5
South Africa	2.6	0.5	2.4	4.2	2.7	3.7	2.9	4.6	5.3	5.6	5.6	3.6	-1.7	2.8	3.9	4.2
Inflation[1]																
China	1.8	-1.7	-2.2	-0.8	0.3	-0.7	1.1	3.8	1.8	1.7	4.8	5.9	-0.7	3.2	4.6	3.4
Brazil	5.2	1.7	8.9	6.0	7.7	12.5	9.3	7.6	5.7	3.1	4.5	5.9	4.3	5.9	6.6	5.1
India	7.4	13.2	4.7	3.9	3.7	4.5	3.7	3.9	4.0	6.3	6.4	8.3	10.9	12.0	9.2	6.8
Indonesia	6.2	58.4	20.5	3.7	11.5	11.9	6.8	6.1	10.5	13.1	6.4	10.2	4.4	5.1	6.8	5.5
Russian Federation	14.7	27.8	85.7	20.8	21.5	15.8	13.7	10.9	12.7	9.7	9.0	14.1	11.7	6.9	9.4	6.4
South Africa	..	..	..	..	5.7	9.2	5.9	1.4	3.4	4.6	7.1	11.0	7.1	4.3	4.8	5.4
Fiscal balance[2]																
China	-0.4	-0.9	-1.6	-1.9	-1.6	-1.6	-1.2	-0.4	-0.2	0.5	1.9	0.9	-1.2	-0.7	0.4	0.4
Brazil	..	..	-5.3	-3.4	-3.3	-4.4	-5.2	-2.9	-3.6	-3.6	-2.8	-2.0	-3.3	-2.5	-2.6	-2.6
India	-6.7	-8.3	-9.2	-9.2	-9.6	-9.4	-8.5	-7.4	-6.7	-5.7	-4.1	-7.3	-9.7	-7.7	-6.8	-6.4
Indonesia	..	..	..	..	..	..	..	..	..	-1.0	-1.2	-0.1	-1.6	-0.6	-1.4	-1.6
Russian Federation	..	..	..	..	..	-0.7	1.7	6.0	6.0	8.3	5.6	7.2	-6.8	-4.3	0.2	0.3
South Africa	-5.1	-3.5	-2.0	-1.4	-0.4	-1.6	-2.1	-2.7	0.0	0.6	1.0	-0.6	-5.3	-4.5	-4.0	-3.4
Current account balance[2]																
China	3.9	3.1	1.9	1.7	1.3	2.4	2.8	3.6	5.9	8.6	10.1	9.1	5.2	5.2	4.5	4.4
Brazil	-3.5	-4.0	-4.3	-3.8	-4.1	-1.2	0.7	1.8	1.6	1.3	0.1	-1.7	-1.4	-2.3	-1.8	-2.0
India	-0.7	-1.6	-0.6	-0.9	0.4	1.4	1.8	0.3	-1.2	-1.1	-0.7	-2.5	-2.1	-3.1	-2.8	-3.0
Indonesia	-1.9	4.1	3.8	4.9	4.3	4.0	3.5	0.7	0.1	3.0	2.4	0.0	1.9	0.8	0.1	0.1
Russian Federation	0.0	2.4	12.8	18.1	11.1	8.5	8.2	10.1	11.1	9.6	6.0	6.1	3.9	4.8	6.8	5.8
South Africa	-1.5	-1.8	-0.5	-0.1	0.3	0.8	-1.0	-3.0	-3.5	-5.3	-7.0	-7.1	-4.1	-2.8	-3.2	-4.2

1. Percentage change from previous period in Consumer Price Index (CPI).
2. Percentage of GDP. Fiscal balances are not comparable across countries due to different definitions.
Source: OECD Economic Outlook 89 database.

StatLink http://dx.doi.org/10.1787/888932444137

OECD ECONOMICS DEPARTMENT

A wide range of news and information about recent Economics Department studies and publications on a variety of topics is now regularly available via Internet on the OECD website at the following address: **www.oecd.org/eco**. This includes links to the *Economics Department Working Papers* series (**www.oecd.org/eco/Working_Papers**), which can be downloaded free of charge, as well as summaries of recent editions in the *OECD Economic Surveys* **(www.oecd.org/eco/surveys)** series, the Department's *Economic Policy Reforms: Going for Growth* (**www.oecd.org/growth/GoingForGrowth2007**) and the *OECD Economic Outlook* (**www.oecd.org/OECDEconomicOutlook**).

OECD ECONOMIC OUTLOOK

The *OECD Economic Outlook* Flashfile, containing a summary of the *Economic Outlook* forecasts is available on Internet at the time of its preliminary publication (a month to six weeks before the final publication date) at **www.oecd.org/OECDEconomicOutlook** under extracts. This includes key macroeconomic variables for all OECD countries and regions in Excel format, which can be input directly into most statistical and analytical software. The *Economic Outlook* Flashfile is available free of charge.

Subscribers to the *OECD Economic Outlook,* in addition to the two print editions, also have access to an online (PDF) edition, published on internet six to eight weeks prior to the release of the print edition :

www.SourceOECD.org/periodical/OECDEconomicOutlook

The full set of historical time series data and projections underlying the *OECD Economic Outlook* is available online as a **statistical database** via SourceOECD and on CD-ROM. It contains approximately 4 000 macroeconomic time series for OECD countries and non-OECD zones, beginning in 1960 and extending to the end of the published forecast horizon. Subscriptions to the database editions can be combined in sets with the subscriptions to the Print and PDF editions and can be made at any time of the year.

For more information, visit the OECD bookshop at **www.OECDbookshop.org,** or contact your nearest OECD supplier : **www.oecd.org/publishing/distributors** .

ORGANISATION FOR ECONOMIC CO-OPERATION AND DEVELOPMENT

The OECD is a unique forum where governments work together to address the economic, social and environmental challenges of globalisation. The OECD is also at the forefront of efforts to understand and to help governments respond to new developments and concerns, such as corporate governance, the information economy and the challenges of an ageing population. The Organisation provides a setting where governments can compare policy experiences, seek answers to common problems, identify good practice and work to co-ordinate domestic and international policies.

The OECD member countries are: Australia, Austria, Belgium, Canada, Chile, the Czech Republic, Denmark, Estonia, Finland, France, Germany, Greece, Hungary, Iceland, Ireland, Israel, Italy, Japan, Korea, Luxembourg, Mexico, the Netherlands, New Zealand, Norway, Poland, Portugal, the Slovak Republic, Slovenia, Spain, Sweden, Switzerland, Turkey, the United Kingdom and the United States. The European Commission takes part in the work of the OECD.

OECD Publishing disseminates widely the results of the Organisation's statistics gathering and research on economic, social and environmental issues, as well as the conventions, guidelines and standards agreed by its members.

OECD PUBLISHING, 2, rue André-Pascal, 75775 PARIS CEDEX 16
(12 2011 01 1 P) ISBN 978-92-64-06347-1 – No. 58083 2011-02